MW01094935

Anthology of
Modern Palestinian Literature

Anthology of

MODERN
PALESTINIAN
LITERATURE

Edited and introduced by
Salma Khadra Jayyusi

Columbia University Press
New York

This anthology was prepared under the auspices of PROTA, Project of Translation from Arabic, founded and directed by Salma Khadra Jayyusi.

Columbia University Press
New York   Oxford

Library of Congress Cataloging-in-Publication Data

Anthology of Modern Palestinian Literature / edited and introduced
by Salma Khadra Jayyusi.
    p. cm.
    Translations from the Arabic.
    Includes bibliographical references (p.   ).
    ISBN 0–231–07508–1
    1. Arabic literature—Palestine—Translations into English.
    2. Arabic literature—20th century—Translations into English.
    I. Jayyusi, Salma Khadra.
    PJ8190.55.E5A58   1992
    892'.708089274—dc20   92–5189
                                                     CIP

"A Land of Rock and Thyme" by Liyana Badr appeared in *A Balcony over the Fakihani*, published in 1992 by Interlink Publishing Group, Inc. Translation copyright © 1992 by Salma Khadra Jayyusi. Reprinted by permission.

Columbia University Press wishes to express its appreciation of assistance given by the Pushkin Fund in the publication of this translation.

∞

Casebound editions of
Columbia University Press books
are Smyth-sewn and printed on
permanent and durable acid-free paper.

Book design: Teresa Bonner
Printed in the United States of America

c 10 9 8 7 6 5 4 3 2 1

This book is dedicated to
the new generations of Palestinians everywhere,
who epitomize the
Undying Spirit of Our People
with special mention
of Yasser Abu Ghosh (1972–1989)
a heroic spirit of the Intifada

Contents

PROSE 367

Short Stories 369

Selections from Novels 587

Extracts from Personal Accounts 607

Acknowledgments

The production of this anthology has been even more difficult than such projects normally are. Since Palestinian poets and writers are scattered over so many countries the task of collecting material and contacting authors for permission and curricula vitae has, therefore, been an arduous one. In these circumstances I am all the more grateful to the many Palestinians and others who have helped bring this work to fruition.

First of all, I must express my heartfelt appreciation and profound joy at the contribution made by my brother, Faisal al-Khadra, who in 1986 took upon himself the task of raising the main, initial funds for the translations from patriotic Palestinian colleagues of his, mostly in Kuwait. He then, as these funds fell short of the sum necessary for an anthology that grew into something far more substantial than I had originally envisaged, shouldered the further burden with such generosity that his personal contribution finally grew to represent one third of the total funds initially contributed by himself and his colleagues. The benefits from this gesture will be felt by readers everywhere, but the sense of fulfillment will be his.

As for all those colleagues of his, whose names are noted under the "List of Contributors," the unified front they have presented in bringing the treasures of Palestinian culture to the attention of the world should serve as a shining example to Palestinian communities in other countries. How could I ever have conceived a work on such a scale as this had I not been sure that so many proud and patriotic Palestinians exist, resolved never to allow their cultural identity and the genius of their people to be lost? I thank them from the depths of my heart.

The time that it took us to revise an already large anthology also gave me the opportunity to discover some new, very gifted Palestinian poets and writers, who, I felt, had to be included. By then I had also realized that another genre, that of personal account literature, had grown to such dimensions among Palestinian poets and writers—in terms both of sheer quantity and of fine literary quality—that its inclusion in this anthology became an absolute imperative. It was at this point that two Palestinian benefactors came to the aid of the anthology: Dr. Ramzi Dalloul and my son, Usama Jayyusi. Their contribution was so generous and given with such warmth and joy that it imbued me with all the greater zest and endurance for this additional work, and I should like to thank them both very much for their care and generosity.

When all the translations were completed, we were confronted with the task of making the final preparations for a publishers' ready copy. There was new typing to be done and other new overheads to be met, but the available funds had already been exhausted. Since the amount needed did not require the support of members of the business community, I sought the help of members of the Palestinian/American medical community in the United States who, with great enthusiasm and cheerful kindness, quickly sent us the necessary funds to set the last touches to the work. This Project has indeed proved the inner pride and basic generosity of our people and the deep respect for culture that they are traditionally known to have. It has also shown that, wherever the diaspora lands the Palestinian, a part of Palestine is forever lodged in his or her heart.

On the academic level my deep gratitude goes to a distinguished scholar, Dr. Walid Khalidi, the epitome of the Palestinian expatriate, who has pursued his greatest goal, to serve the cause of his country, with clear-sighted dedication and evident success. With characteristic generosity he found time to furnish me with expert advice on the political history of our people, and authorized us to use part of the chronology of his book, *Before Their Diaspora, A Photographic History of the Palestinians 1876–1948.*

To another distinguished Palestinian, Dr. Edward Said, I owe the warmest thanks for his decisive help in solving some of the difficult problems which such a work is inevitably bound to engender. This is only one of the many services to his culture for which he is so widely and justly renowned. No one is more proudly aware than myself of Dr. Said's outstanding intellectual contribution to world literature and culture, and of his brilliant and devoted services to the Palestinian and Arab cause.

I owe profound thanks to Dr. Naseer Aruri, an outstanding Palestinian spokesman for his country's cause in both the United States and the Arab world. His tireless services toward a better understanding of the Palestine issue have included much help to me in the form of advice on the political aspects of Palestine's recent history. His dedication is an inspiration and a cause of pride for all Palestinians who believe that their cause is best served through intellectual address and the rapport of intelligent minds.

I would also like here to acknowledge the enthusiastic help of Dr. Hanan Mikha'il 'Ashrawi, another outstanding Palestinian whose steadfast dedication to the culture and human rights of her people has not only led to clearer international understanding and wide sympathy for their cause, but has also greatly enhanced the reputation of Palestinian women in the world. Despite her major patriotic duties, she has, as an expert on Palestinian literature inside Israel and the Occupied Territories, taken time to secure material and provide me with critical literary information. I take the opportunity here to applaud her efforts in her manifold spheres of expertise.

I also warmly thank Dr. 'Abd al-Latif al-Barghouthy for taking time to supply me with books needed for my work, Dr. Nasir Tahboub for his supportive spirit and great kindness, and Mr. Amin 'Abd al-Hafeez for his constant generosity in volunteering to help out with the checking of translated material.

As with all other PROTA projects, Dr. Roger Allen has stood by this work from the very beginning. His constant collegial support has not only been a source of intellectual illumination, but has also reinforced my resolution. I cannot thank him enough for his unwavering support of PROTA's goals.

I owe special mention to the Palestinian poets and writers. They all rallied to my call and either sent me or, when I visited the various countries where they now live, kindly came to see me and provided me with their books and other necessary information. They have demonstrated the utmost seriousness concerning both literature itself and the specific goal of this anthology, which is the dissemination of Palestinian creative writings abroad. As poets and writers, they not only endeavor to excel in their art, often with conspicuous success, but also earnestly aspire to reach out to the world. I am truly proud of their openness and good will and their undying optimism and faith in humanity.

The translators who, after all, are the ones who make the work possible, deserve my deepest acknowledgment for the competence and dedication they brought to their task, with particular thanks due to special friends and members of my family for occasionally volunteering unpaid work to ensure the completion of the anthology. In this regard, I would like to thank PROTA's main editor, Mr. Christopher Tingley, and also the poet Naomi Shihab Nye, Dr. Aida Bamia, and Dr. Sharif Elmusa, four of PROTA's staunchest friends.

To members of my own family I owe perpetual gratitude. My son Usama's contribution, mentioned above, is only part of the constant intellectual and financial support he has lent not only to this particular project so dear to his heart, but to all other PROTA work over the years. My daughter-in-law, Salwa Jabsheh, has never failed to do her utmost to supply all possible help. My son-in-law, Tawfiq Abu Rahmeh, deserves heartfelt mention here for his great assistance to this particular project. He has sent me, from Jerusalem, many books by Palestinian writers in Israel and the Occupied Territories, some of which came from his private collection and has obtained addresses and necessary material from them, thus accomplishing a task that would have been impossible for a Palestinian expatriate like myself to achieve. Finally, with joy and satisfaction I would like to acknowledge the help I have received from my daughters, Lena and May. They have been a constant source of stimulating intellectual challenge and encouragement, and have lent much critical acumen to this and other PROTA endeavors, volunteering much of their time and energy to help accomplish this book—particularly in 1989, which was a time of great personal difficulty for myself.

Thanks are due, too, to Kate Kline and Erna Hoffmann for the meticulous secretarial help they gave during the course of the project.

Last but by no means least, I must mention the great debt I owe to my parents, whose spirit constantly guides and inspires me. When I opened my eyes, it was to see my father, Subhi al-Khadra, working night and day for Palestinian rights; I watched him being sent from exile to prison to concentration camp, only to come out and resume the fight. As for my mother, Anisah Sleem, her endurance at my father's side was exemplary in its faith and pride. Poetic, sensitive, and full of humor and idealism, she was Lebanese by origin, but adopted Palestine as her own country with her heart and mind and soul. Apart from all other services she contributed during the great Palestinian revolution of the mid-thirties, her poetic nature inspired her to rewrite many current songs as well as the major traditional folk songs of Palestine, which she filled with patriotic words, and which were sung for many years in the Galilee where she lived. This book should have been dedicated to my parents, but I know that, were they alive, they would endorse the work's dedication to the "Undying Spirit of Our People."

Salma Khadra Jayyusi
Boston, September 25, 1991

List of Donors

The translation and preparation of this Anthology for publication has been subsidized by the following professionals and businessmen who, regardless of the nationality they carry now, are Palestinians by origin and culture and are all committed to the confirmation, continuity and dissemination of Palestinian culture at its best:

The following individuals were donors in 1986:
Amir Abou Ghazaleh, Farouk Abou Ghazaleh, Mahmoud Abou Ghazaleh, Akram Alkadi, Haydar Ataya, Nazmi M. Badawi, Ibrahim Dabdoub, Nasrat Faddah, Dr. Subhi Ghosheh, Nabeel Kamhawi, Faisal Subhi Khadra, Omar Faisal Khadra, Subhi Faisal Khadra, Hamzah Mughrabi, Nemeh Sabbagh, Abdul Karim Sayegh, Hisham Shibl, Ghazi Shihabi, Muhammad Tahboub, Farouq Zuaiter.

The following individuals were donors in 1990:
Ramzi Dalloul, Usama Burhan Jayyusi.

The following professionals were contributors in 1990 in the United States:
Dr. Saadi Abou Srour; Dr. Subhi Ali; Dr. Abdulla Attum; Dr. Shukri M. F. Elkhairi; Dr. and Mrs. George Hawwa; Dr. Mazin H. Ibrahim; Dr. Akram Khalaf; Dr. Zahi H. Masri.

Chronology of Modern Palestinian History

1858 Ottoman land reform creates a powerful, landowning, urban leadership that supplants tribal leadership and ushers in the modern era in Palestine. This leadership will play an important role in later conflict with Zionist movement.

1867 A new Ottoman law permits foreigners to own land.

1878 The first Zionist colony is founded near Jaffa. Thirty Zionist colonies would be founded, mostly near the coast, by 1914. At that time the Jewish population reached about 80,000, a little more than 10 percent, in the region. Two thirds of the land Zionists will buy will be sold by Arabs living outside Palestine, particularly in Beirut.

1882 First Aliyah (wave of Zionist immigration); Baron Edmond de Rothschild, French Jewish banker, begins to support Jewish settlement in Palestine.

1890s Boom in exports of Jaffa oranges as agriculture is commercialized and Palestinians convert to a market economy. Zionists begin to grow oranges but will not dominate their cultivation until World War II.

1897 The mufti (top Muslim leader) of Jerusalem heads a commission to analyze Jewish land acquisition.

August: The first Zionist congress is held at Basel, where it founds the World Zionist Organization.

1903 Second Aliyah: Russian and Eastern European Jews flee pogroms.

1908 The Palestinian journal *Al-Karmil* is founded in Haifa to oppose Zionist colonization.

July: The Young Turk Revolution deposes Sultan Abdul Hamid. A new constitution and parliament bring crowds to the streets in the Arab provinces.

1908–1914 Friction grows between Istanbul and Arab Provinces as the government espouses Turkish nationalism. Arabs, including many Palestinians, form the Arab Nationalist movement to seek autonomy.

1911 The first book in Arabic on Zionism, *Zionism: Its History, Objective, and Importance*, is published by Palestinian journalist Najib Nasser. The Palestinian newspaper *Filastin* begins publication.

1914 August: World War I begins. The Ottoman Empire allies with Germany against Britain.

1916 May: The British, French, and Russians agree secretly on a postwar plan to divide the Arab world under separate spheres of influence in the Sykes-Picot Agreement.

June: Sharif Hussein of Mecca leads Arab Nationalists in the Arab revolt. Allied with Britain, Arab armies sweep north from the Saudi peninsula against the Ottomans. The Sharif understands from Sir Henry McMahon, the British High Commissioner in Egypt, that Britain will permit the Arabs to form an independent, unified state after the war.

1917 November: Arthur James Balfour, British secretary of state for foreign affairs, sends a secret letter to Baron Lionel Walter de Rothschild, a British Zionist, seeking Jewish support in the war. The Balfour Declaration promises a national home for Jews in Palestine and protection of the civil and religious rights of "non-Jewish" inhabitants.

1918 September: British General Sir Edmund Allenby occupies all of Palestine.

November: World War I ends.

1919 January: The First Palestinian National Congress in Jerusalem rejects the Balfour Declaration and demands Arab independence under King Faisal in Damascus.

June: The Treaty of Versailles and the Covenant of the League of Nations are signed, allowing for the establishment of mandates in the Middle East.

1920 April: The mandate for Palestine is awarded to Britain at the San Remo conference. Riots in Palestine kill 5 Jews, wound 200 others.

May: The British block the convening of the second Palestinian Congress.

August: The first quota on Jewish immigration is set at 16,500 per year in an attempt to balance conflicting aims of Balfour Declaration.

December: In response to the fall in July of King Faisal's Arab nationalist regime in Damascus, the Third Palestinian Congress in Haifa breaks with Arab nationalists and focuses policy on securing the independence of Palestine only. It appoints an executive committee to head the movement for a representative Palestinian national government and a rejection of the Jewish national home.

1924 Third Aliyah: mostly traders and artisans from Poland.

1929 Several weeks of riots in Jerusalem, Hebron, and Safed kill 133 Jews and wound 339; 116 Palestinians are killed, 232 wounded, mostly by British soldiers. The riots are sparked by the founding of the Jewish Agency in August and by a right-wing Jewish protest of customs regarding use of the Wailing Wall.

1931–1936 Fourth Aliyah: 64 more Zionist colonies are founded as refugees arrive particularly from Nazi Germany. Jewish population rises to nearly 30 percent of the total in Palestine.

1932–1935 The Palestinian movement reorganizes, as five new political parties are established. After the failure of Palestinian delegations to London to change British policy, the idea of armed rebellion is born with the formation of a commando group by Shaikh 'Izz al-Din al-Qassam.

1936 April: The Great Rebellion begins and will last for three years. The rebellion is sparked partly by unemployment and by the British Parliament's refusal in March of Arab demands for elections. On April 15, Palestinian commandos kill three Jews, followed by the killing of two Arabs. On April 21, the five Palestinian parties initiate a six month general strike. On April 25, the five parties unite under the Arab Higher Committee, headed by the mufti of Jerusalem, al-Hajj Amin al-Husseini.

1937 July: The Royal Peel Commission recommends partition of Palestine into three states: Arab, Jewish and a British-controlled central region including Jerusalem. This plan for the first time formally recognizes the incompatibility of the Balfour declaration's twin aims. The plan draws a divided response: A majority of Zionists accepts the partition while Palestinian leaders reject it.

Autumn: Renewal of the Arab rebellion, as commando groups capture control of many areas of the countryside. British repression includes detention camps and blowing up homes of suspects.

1938 George Antonius publishes *The Arab Awakening* in English.

1939 British crackdown on the rebellion succeeds. More than 1,000

Palestinians are killed during the three years and most of their leaders are exiled.

May: A British White Paper formally drops the partition plan and offers a ten year plan to reunite Arabs and Jews under a single, independent state. It includes a policy of limiting Jewish land acquisition and immigration in an attempt to foster Arab good will. Both Zionist and Palestinian groups reject the plan.

1944–1947 Zionist forces begin guerilla warfare against British, undertaking terrorist raids and assassinations which are followed by British reprisals. In 1946, the militant right wing Zionist group Irgun, headed by Menachem Begin, blows up British headquarters in the King David Hotel.

1947 February: Britain announces that it will withdraw from Palestine and cedes responsibility for the country's future to the United Nations.

November 29: Partition Day. The United Nations General Assembly votes for the partition of Palestine into Jewish and Palestinian states. With less than one-third of the population in mandated Palestine, the Zionists receive 55 percent of its total land area. Zionists welcome the plan, while Palestinians are dismayed.

1948 January: Fighting between Palestinians and Zionists escalates into war, with 1,974 killed on both sides by January 10. The Palestinians are ill-organized and poorly armed. Between 5,000 and 7,000 Arab volunteers enter Palestine to join the fighting. The Zionist Haganah's operation had been organized since at least 1946 when it numbered 62,000 troops armed with weapons smuggled from Europe and stolen from the British.

April: On April 9, 254 villagers are massacred by Irgun and the Stern Gang at Dair Yasin. By the end of April, more than 10,000 Palestinians have fled as Zionist military groups conquer Tiberias, Haifa, Jaffa, eastern Galilee, and areas near Jerusalem.

May: Fighting continues with more Palestinian losses. On May 14, the British high commissioner leaves and an independent Jewish state is proclaimed at Tel Aviv. The British mandate ends May 15, as troops from Syria, Jordan, Lebanon, Egypt, and Iraq cross the border, and as United States President Harry Truman recognizes the state of Israel. By then, about 200 Palestinian villages have been attacked and conquered by Zionists, and 200,000 Palestinians have fled their homes.

Fighting continues throughout the year and Israeli victories in the summer extend the size of Israel well beyond the 1947 United Nations partition plan. Many villages are razed and replaced by Israeli settlements, as absentee Arab lands are transferred to the Israeli government. By December, there are nearly 1,000,000 Palestinian refugees. Palestinians and other Arabs refer to the events of 1948 as "The Catastrophe."

1949   February–July: Israel signs armistice agreements with individual Arab countries.

December: 430,000 Palestinians are living in Red Cross and United Nations refugee camps, while an additional 250,000 are receiving free food rations.

1950   April: Jordan annexes central Palestine, absorbing more than 600,000 Palestinian refugees and residents of what comes to be called the West Bank.

May: The United Nations Relief and Works Agency (UNRWA) is set up to aid Palestinian refugees.

October 29, 1956: The Suez War. Israel, Britain, and France attack and occupy Egypt's Sinai Peninsula after President Jamal Abd al-Nasser nationalizes the Suez Canal.

The eve of October 29: The eve of the attack on the Suez Canal Israeli forces entered the village of Kufr Qasim, a border village in the "Little Triangle" prohibited to Israeli forces by the United Nations Document S/1302/Rev. 1 of June 20, 1949, Article VI, para. 6, imposed a curfew while the villagers were still in their fields. Unaware of the curfew, the Israelis opened fire at them. Fifty-one were killed (among them twelve women and seventeen children), and thirteen others were wounded.

The three allies are later forced to withdraw from Egypt under American pressure. As a result of the war, Nasser becomes the preeminent Arab nationalist leader, popular among most Arabs, especially the Palestinians, who see in him their best hope for regaining their homeland.

1957–58   Yasir Arafat and others found the Palestine Liberation Movement, Fatah, a commando group, in Kuwait. Other commando groups also form, including the Arab Nationalist Movement (later the Popular Front for the Liberation of Palestine), which the famous Palestinian writer Ghassan Kanafani joins.

1964   The Arab League establishes the Palestine Liberation Organization (PLO) as the political directorate of a projected Palestinian entity. It is virtually under the political control of the United Arab Republic (Egypt).

1965   January: The first Palestinian commando raids cross into Israel from Lebanon, Syria, and Jordan. Israeli retaliatory raids lead to escalation in tensions, culminating in the June War.

1967 The June War begins on June 5, when the Israel Air Force attacks and destroys the Egyptian Air Force. By June 11, Israel occupies the Sinai Peninsula, the Gaza Strip, the West Bank, and the Golan Heights. More than 350,000 refugees flee from the West Bank and Golan Heights. On June 28, Israel annexes the Old City of Jerusalem.

November: The United Nations General Assembly passes Resolution 242 calling for withdrawal of Israeli armed forces from all areas of recent conflict, end of war claims, and the right of every state to live peacefully within secure boundaries.

1968 March: Palestinian commandos battle an Israeli column at Karameh in Jordan. Their stiff defense increases the popularity of the Palestinian resistance movement. Various Palestinian groups join the PLO. Palestinian National Covenant, stating the basic aims of the Palestinian movement, is adopted.

Gush Emunim—bloc of the faithful—establishes the first Israeli settlement in Hebron in the West Bank.

1969 Fatah takes over command of the PLO, freeing it from Egyptian control, and increases the frequency and scope of guerilla activity. In Lebanon, clashes between Palestinians and Christian militias become frequent. In Jordan, King Hussein struggles to maintain sovereignty over Palestinians who come to resemble a state within a state.

1970 Black September civil war: Fierce fighting breaks out between the Jordanian army and Palestinian commandos. The Palestinians are defeated, and after being expelled from Jordan in the summer of 1971, they set up headquarters in Lebanon.

1973 August 1: The Palestine National Front (PNF) was set up in the occupied West Bank as a union of varied, indigenous and progressive underground groups engaged in civil disobedience under the leadership of the PLO.

The October War: On October 6, Syria and Egypt attacked Israeli positions in occupied Sinai and Golan Heights. After initial gains Israel counterattacks, and crosses the Suez Canal into Egypt. The Organization of Petroleum Exporting Countries (OPEC) declares an oil embargo against the United States, the Netherlands and other supporters of Israel.

November 28: The Algiers Arab Summit Conference recognizes the PLO as sole legitimate representatives of the Palestinian people.

1974 June 8: The Palestine National Council endorses the concept of a "Palestian National Authority" to be established in any area vacated by Israel.

October 14: The United Nations General Assembly adopts resolution 3210 recognizing the PLO as representative of the Palestinian people and conferring upon it the status of "observer".

October 29: Rabat Arab Summit Conference declares the PLO sole legitimate representative of the Palestinian people.

November: PLO leader Yasser Arafat addresses the United Nations General Assembly. In his call for settlement of the Palestine question, he declares: "Today I have come bearing an olive branch and a freedom fighter's gun. Do not let the olive branch fall from my hand."

November 22: United Nations General Assembly passes resolution 3236 reaffirming the right of the Palestinians to "self-determination, national independence and sovereignty," and requests the Secretary-General to establish contacts with the PLO on all matters concerning the question of Palestine.

1975 April: Civil war breaks out in Lebanon. Palestinians are drawn into the hostilities.

1976 April 12: First municipal elections held in Palestinian occupied territories produce an overwhelming victory of nationalists affiliated with the PLO.

June: At the request of Lebanese President Franjieh, Syria invades Lebanon in support of Christian Phalangist militias against the Palestinian/Lebanese leftist alliance.

August: Tel al-Zaatar and Karantina Palestinian refugee camps in Beruit are overrun by the Lebanese Christian Phalangist militias with the help of Syrian forces and their inhabitants massacred. Christian inhabitants of Damour in southern Lebanon are massacred.

1977 June: The "Iron Fist" policy is announced in the occupied territories almost as soon as Menachem Begin becomes Prime Minister of Israel for the first time.

November: Egyptain president Anwar Sadat addresses the Israeli Knesset in Jerusalem.

1978 September: Egypt and Israel sign the Camp David accords. Israel agrees to a staged withdrawal from Sinai. The agreement calls for "self-rule" of Palestinians in occupied territories.

The Israeli army invades Lebanon, engaging the Palestinian forces and occupying South Lebanon for two months.

President Carter threatens Israel with the application of the Export Control Act because they used United States weapons "offensively" not defensively.

1979 March: The National Guidance Committee is set up in the occupied territories to coordinate the non-violent resistance to the Israeli occupation.

The Israeli–Egyptain peace treaty is signed.

1980 May: The mayors of Hebron and Halhul are expelled by Israeli occupation authorities.

June: The mayors of Nablus, Ramallah and Bireh are maimed in a terrorist attack by an Israeli underground organization.

1982 June: The Israeli ambassador to the United Kingdom is attacked in London. Israel invades Lebanon with the goal of expelling the PLO from Lebanon. Israelis battle PLO fighters and the Syrian army. Israel lays siege to Beirut and directs a massive artillery and air assault against the city in an effort to force a PLO evacuation. Several Palestinian refugee camps are destroyed, more than 1,500 Palestinians are killed or wounded, and over 300,000 left homeless.

August: PLO fighters leave Beirut under protection of multinational forces.

September: Israeli forces look on as Christian militias massacre over 1700 Palestinians in Sabra and Shatila refugee camps in Beirut.

1987 December 8: The Intifada, the most comprehensive revolt since 1936, breaks out in the West Bank and Gaza Strip. A local leadership structure, the Unified National Command, is established and directs the mass uprising against Israeli occupation. The Israelis respond with administrative detentions, curfews, expulsion of Palestinian activists, closing of Palestinian schools and universities, and destruction of Palestinian homes. In the first three years of the Intifada, about 700 Palestinians are killed by the Israeli military, and an estimated 200–300 accused of collaboration with the Israelis are killed by fellow Palestinians. Almost 12,000 Palestinians are wounded, and about 10,000 Palestinians are placed under administrative detention. Israeli casualties through July of 1990 are 18 killed and 3,300 wounded.

1988 July: King Hussein of Jordan officially severs Jordanian administrative and judicial ties in the West Bank.

November 15: The Palestine National Council declares Palestinian independence and launches a peace initiative based on the United

Nations resolution 181 of November 29, 1947, known as the Partition Plan.

December: Arafat officially recognizes Israel and rejects use of terror, thereby removing obstacles to talks between the United States and the PLO.

1990 June: The United States/PLO dialogue is suspended following aborted commando attack on Tel Aviv. The PLO denies any connection with this attack.

Introduction: Palestinian Literature in Modern Times

Although I have, in my study of modern Arabic poetry, given attention to social (and political) factors as "important [external] forces behind the changes in the mind and consciousness of the creative Arab talent,"[1] *primary* importance has been given to the internal evolution of the poetic art, an evolution determined first and foremost by elements intrinsic to the poetic art itself. This approach is based on the notion that art has its own internal laws of growth and development, and that, although these laws are influenced by external forces, social, political, and psychological, the ultimate determinant in the development of art will be the demands, needs, and possibilities of art itself at a certain moment of its history.

The development of literature depends on many factors that combine to influence change. Critical opinion, however, differs in the importance it accords to these varied influences. In the first place, there are those who emphasize social determinism as the basis of artistic change, regarding art as dependent on social (and political) factors that decide its attitudes, themes, and techniques. The writings of the French critic Hippolyte Taine are extremely well known in this respect, as are the writings of socially oriented followers of Marx and Engels.[2] Other literary historians such as Charles Augustin Sainte-Beuve (and, later on, followers of Freud) regard psychological factors in the personality of the author as the prime determinant of literary development. Still others, however, recognize that literature as an art form is affected not only by external determinants but by a dynamism within art itself that promotes or impedes change.[3] Because of their immediacy, political factors often tend to interfere in the artistic process, sometimes diverting it from its natural course in favor of a certain commitment or ideology. However, the history of modern Arabic literature, particularly poetry, and especially in the decades since the Palestine disaster of 1948, shows that art has its own way of reasserting its natural course of development and growth.

This is notably the case, as will be seen, with Palestinian literature, particularly poetry, which is the Arabs' most rooted art form. There remains, however, a noticeable difference between the way the Palestinian creative writer has treated and interacted with external factors and the way other writers in the Arab world have done so. The primary object of this introduction is to show not simply the historical development of modern Palestinian literary genres—this forms part of the development of Arab literary genres in general and is treated by me in a general "Arab" context in other writings[4]—but rather the way Palestinian literature has achieved a particularity of its own, or at least differed in certain instances from other contemporary literature in the Arab world.

For although Palestinian literature is an integral part of modern Arabic literature, and has participated fully in all the vigorous revolutionary experiments undertaken in Arabic letters during this century, particularly since the fifties, it has shown marked differences in certain respects, especially in the treatment of place and time, of tone and attitude, and in its particular involvement with the pervasive political issue. While one can say that all Arabic literature nowadays is involved in the social and political struggle of the Arab people, politics nevertheless imposes a greater strain on the Palestinian writer. It usually determines where and how this writer lives, and prefigures a degree of personal struggle greater than that which other Arab writers—although often dissidents and politically involved themselves—tend to experience. There are problems of identity, even problems over the simple acquisition of a passport; Palestinian writers have to spend their lives either as exiles in other people's countries, or, if they have in fact remained in their own ancestral homeland, either as second-class citizens in Israel proper or lacking any citizenship at all under Israeli military rule in the West Bank and Gaza. Because of the repressive conditions in many Arab states, there are, of course, many *Arab* writers who now live as voluntary exiles in the world at large, but many more such writers live, unlike the Palestinians, in their own sovereign states.

Modern Palestinian experience is harsh, unrelenting, and all-penetrating; no Palestinian is free from its grip and no writer can evade it. It cannot be forgotten and its anguish cannot be transcended. Whether in Israel, or in the West Bank and the Gaza Strip, or in the diaspora, Palestinians are committed by their very identity to a life determined by events and circumstances arising out of their own rejection of captivity and national loss, as well as by other people's intentions, suspicions, fears, and aggressions. There is no escape. For the writer to contemplate an orientation completely divorced from political life is to belie reality, to deny experience; for to engross oneself for too long in "normal" everyday experiences is to betray one's own life and one's own people. This means that Palestinian writers have little scope for indulging in escapism; they are compromised by the events of contemporary history even before they are born. The luxury of choosing one's past, of selecting memories, of re-arranging relations that transcend events and external circumstances, is not theirs; they have become permanent exiles, the prototype of the strangers of all times, struggling against obstacles of every kind and magnitude. But the greatest struggle and the greatest triumph of Palestinian writers lies in their refusal to become humanity's cringing victims during the second half of the twentieth century. While never ceasing to be aware of the particular predicament of their people, they exhibit a resilience that transcends tragedy and overcomes necessity. This has colored contemporary Palestinian literature and directed its intention and tone.

Without studying this literature, critics and literary historians might tend to expect monotony and mere imitativeness; for what scope is there, one might think, for creative writers irretrievably bound to the Palestinian situation, when this situation dictates the whole fundamental direction of their lives and binds it to its necessity? It is, therefore, a pleasurable surprise to discover that within these restricted boundaries Palestinian poets and writers of fiction and literary prose[5] have been creative in great measure, and have actually risen to the forefront of contemporary Arabic letters. They have not only participated in the various robust avant-garde experiments that are continuously taking place, they have often led the way in inventiveness and change.

Even within these thematic limitations it must be remembered, moreover, that there is actually rich material for literature in the present Palestinian dilemma. Inherent in the Palestine catastrophe are still many situations conducive on the one hand to a tragic and, on the other, to a heroic vision of resistance, hope, and faith in the ultimate triumph

of justice. Many such situations lend themselves well to literary interpretation: the gratuitous death of innocent victims; the premature but
willed death of heroes; the constant foiled endeavors, the endless uprooting, the continual degradation of Palestinian expatriates in the rest
of the Arab world; and their highly diminished status as a people without a country. In the Israeli controlled West Bank and the Gaza Strip
there are the large-scale taking of prisoners by Israel; the deportations;
the blowing up of houses; the closing of educational institutions; the
confiscation both of water resources and of Arab land where militant
Zionist settlers are encouraged by the Israeli authorities to build towns
and settlements in defiance of UN resolutions; the emotional conflict
of workers from the West Bank and Gaza, taken as cheap labor to build
Israel itself;[6] and the deep alienation, both physical and spiritual, that
has taken hold of the Palestinian spirit everywhere.

Yet this spirit has rebelled against its own plight through the *intifada*,
the unarmed revolution of thousands of Palestine's children and young
people who have taken up the fight for liberation, continuing almost
a century of struggle and resistance by the Palestinians against all the
odds of organized colonialism. The Stone Revolution, which began in
December 1987 and continues still, changed the tragic into the heroic
and reached out to assert its dignity in the world, altering the way
others looked at the Palestinian issue. For the first time a new language
was spoken, against which negative rhetoric was completely impotent.
It became clear, to the millions of spectators around the world, that
here was a people who would not accept injustice and indignity; for,
although quickly embraced by Palestinians in exile inside and outside
the PLO, the *intifada* was a spontaneous, indigenous uprising—timely,
heart-rending, self-sacrificing, deeply appealing, and almost poetic.

This introduction will not elaborate further on the recent political
history of Palestine . There is a chronology of the major political events
that have crucially directed the development of Palestinian literature
during this century at the beginning of this book, but for more details the reader is referred to specialized books about the history and
scope of the Palestine problem. Where relevant, certain specific events
reflected in the pieces offered in this anthology are explained in footnotes.

When we speak of "contemporary" Palestinian literature, we are, in
fact, immediately faced with two literatures: that of writers still living
on the soil of the historical land of Palestine,[7] and that of writers living
in the diaspora. In 1948, a unified, well-rooted culture was split, and

for almost twenty years there were virtually no direct relations between Arab authors writing in Israel and those writing in exile. Life under direct foreign occupation in Israel differed in certain major ways from either that in Jordan (which now included the West Bank and had a majority of Palestinian citizens) or in the diaspora into other Arab states where a great number of Palestinian exiles were living as "refugees." Most Arab states, while feeling a political and emotional involvement with the Palestine question, were often coercive in their stance toward the refugees, a situation that created many and unprecedented problems for the Palestinians. However, when, after the June War of 1967, the borders between Israel and the West Bank and Gaza Strip were opened, the two wings of Palestinian culture on the soil of Palestine itself were reunited, and each side then fully understood and identified with the experience of the other.

Some cultural differences have indeed remained. Young Arab talents in Israel, growing up learning Hebrew as a second language and interacting with a culture intrinsically foreign to their own, have inevitably developed a somewhat different perspective, which may perhaps have influenced their writings.[8] It should also be noted that, despite the coercive political measures that Israel often imposes on Palestinian writers—committing many to house arrest and imprisonment and sometimes suppressing their work—a good many creative works in Arabic, particularly fiction, have been translated into Hebrew. There has been no actual boycott of literary interaction between the two cultures: one, the Arab, rooted in language and conventions inherited from time immemorial; the other groping with a newly renovated idiom and a new experience (an experience of self-realization that Jews for centuries have craved) and trying to find meaning (and often rationalization) for its new experience of a sovereignty based on forcible appropriation, and unprecedented in its history also since time immemorial. On the other hand, Palestinian authors in the diaspora came into direct contact with the radical literary experiments that have dominated Arabic letters since the fifties and were able to participate directly and fully in one of the richest periods of Arab literary history. Once out in the world they began to excel and to discover their full literary potential. Exiled Palestinian poets are now among the foremost avant-garde poets of the Arab world.

Historically, Palestinian literature has displayed none of these avant-garde qualities. A recent writer describes its state early in the twentieth century thus:"Until the advent of the twentieth century, Palestinian poetry was bent on niceties, affected eulogies, and special social occasions. Meanings were conventional and repetitive, and metaphors were hackneyed. The poetry lacked any representation of real human preoccupations, but stemmed, rather, from a spiritual and intellectual void."[9]

This description applies indeed to much of Arabic poetry before the modern Arab literary renaissance, which began in the nineteenth century but matured in some regions of the Arab world earlier than in others.[10] However, there is another observation to make here: although Palestinians were highly appreciative of culture and had quickly developed a modern educational system in the twentieth century, Palestine had, prior to the 1948 disaster, remained less affected by the *literary* currents blowing across the Arab world and had never been a center for the more innovative trends that other Arab countries in the vicinity of Palestine—Egypt, Syria, Lebanon, and Iraq—had exhibited. Several writers on the literary history of Palestine have commented on this phenomenon. In the words of Muhammad Salim Rashdan, "If we go deep into the history of Palestine, we will find that it had not produced along the centuries any but a few talents that appeared every now and then . . . and it was rare that any two of them lived contemporaneously."[11] However, the reasons Rashdan advances for such aridity— that Palestine is a holy place and that it lacks scenes of natural beauty— are invalid. There is no reason why the "holiness" of a place should be an impediment to creativity—the unceasing creativity of the Iraqi city of Najaf, the holiest Shi'a center in the world, is a proof of this. As for natural beauty, the statement is also untenable, for Palestine contains the scenic beauty of sea, mountain, and lake. Even if the writer's claim was true, it is a fact that some of the greatest poetry in Arabic was born and matured in an exclusively desert environment. Perhaps the reason lies "in the fact that Palestine seems to have . . . remained cut off from the main cultural currents that flowed between Egypt and Lebanon, Lebanon and Iraq. . . . Unlike other Arab capitals, Jerusalem has never been the home of any central political authority, and had no princes and patrons of art to help and encourage poets and writers."[12] The development of modern Palestinian literature in the past has demonstrated, however, an interesting and rather consistent phenomenon, namely, that many of the Palestinian talents that flourished before 1948 had lived and usually studied outside Palestine; all it needed, apparently, for Palestinian creativity to bloom was direct contact with a flourishing literary life, which could only be found at that time outside its borders.[13]

This also, perhaps, underlies the present discrepancy between Palestinian literature written by authors still living in their own country and Palestinian literature written in exile. Arabic writing inside Israel and in the Occupied West Bank and Gaza Strip is robust and clearly innovative: several gifted authors have risen to fame, with some notable figures, such as Emile Habiby, deservedly winning international fame for the originality and high esthetic value of their work.[14] However, the balance still tilts decidedly in favor of Palestinian literature written in exile, this being true both of poetry and of prose,[15] even if the many innovative experiments in drama within Palestine do redress the balance to some extent.

Palestinian Literature Before 1948

Poetry

Though authors rising to fame in Palestine before 1948 were mainly poets, there were also a number of distinguished prose writers, including important essayists such as Is'af al-Nashashibi (1880–1947) and some early writers of fiction. Al-Nashashibi was a stylist, classicist, and connoisseur of literature whose preferred Arab author among his contemporaries was the Egyptian poet Ahmad Shauqi (1889–1932). His own attempts at poetry were rather weak, but he wielded considerable literary influence on his compatriots in Palestine by virtue of his passionate interest in Arabic literature, including poetry; he also won local and pan-Arab fame as a speaker and writer of fine literary prose. The early writers of fiction will be discussed in a separate section.

After 1948, Palestinian poets found themselves heirs not only to a long Arab poetic tradition, but also to a new and intricately involved political situation to which they felt committed. Before the fifties, Palestinian poetry had tended to react spontaneously to events, drifting along with the semantic intention of the poem, and satisfying itself with the expression of a specific message that seemed crucial and held absolute priority.

Foremost among the early poets was Ibrahim Tuqan (1905–1941), whose fiery, terse poetry, poignantly expressing the innermost feelings of Palestinians everywhere, won him great fame in the twenties and thirties. It was during his studies at the American University of Beirut, where he met other poets and participated in the active literary life of the university, that his talent began to sparkle. He came back to Palestine fully confident of his role as poet and strongly armed with the spirit of one who felt responsible for awakening his countrymen to their predicament. Tuqan's political commitment, however, could not completely strangle his other tendencies as a poet, notably his predisposition to humor and the comic representation of experience. He wrote some delightful, light-hearted personal verse in this mode which is still as much memorized by his countrymen as is his political verse; in some of the latter he would, when opportunity lent itself, mix political invective with bitter sarcasm. This rare gift, where the tragic merges with the comic and the ironic mode underlies the most serious thematic involvement, has not been repeated in Palestinian literature on any important scale except in the fiction of Emile Habiby, who is also a master of the tragi-comic. Other, later Palestinian poets—some of them greater perhaps than Tuqan—have failed to show any real interest in the comic or ironic; they write in a somber, tragic, or heroic mode. Even among the younger Palestinian poets of the eighties and nineties, who have, as will shortly be seen, arrived at a genuine modernist delineation of experience, there is no parallel to Ibrahim Tuqan's versatile tone. For all his rare gifts as a poet, Mahmoud Darwish (b. 1942) has become trapped in his own kind of commitment: to the cause of his people, and, equally firmly, to the image he holds of himself as their confirmed poet-spokesman, obliged constantly to reiterate their grievances, to the exclusion of almost all other experience.[16] However, modern Arab poets (and modern Arab fiction writers) from every Arabic country, even those who have never had to face the tragedies and upheavals of the recent Palestinian experience on a personal level, have also tended, almost invariably, toward a markedly serious tone, whether writing in the romantic, realistic, symbolist, or surrealistic mode.

> The comic apprehension of experience, burlesque and parody, double meaning, the picaresque, the ironic and sarcastic, were not easily adopted [in modern Arabic literature], and the richness of both Classical Arabic and Western literatures in these modes was rarely utilized . . . [It is possible that there has] been some impediment that prevented most writers from finding a way to apprehend the comic spirit in literature as they sought to depict human experience at a time of great political and social upheaval.[17]

Several other poets rose to fame before the Catastrophe of 1948.[18] With the exception of Mutlaq 'Abd al-Khaliq (1910–1937), and Fadwa Tuqan (b. 1917) in her early phase, they were all first and foremost committed to political verse and to acting as resounding spokespersons for their country and its plight.

'Abd al-Khaliq is unique for his time, being, until the rise of Fadwa Tuqan, the only fully Romantic poet in Palestine. Deeply influenced by the work of the Arab émigré poets in North America, he differed sharply from his compatriots in his pessimistic and "private" outlook on life and wrote a poetry full of spleen and bent on self-annihilation.

> I love death, immeasurably; to me
> life is a baneful sickness

In another poem he describes death as his "tender maiden." His pessimism reaches its climax with the words, "Man, your world is a moldering corpse!" In his poetry, collected posthumously in a volume entitled *The Departure* (1938), he displays "spiritual and philosophical depths hitherto unattained in poetry in Palestine . . . showing a sensitive perception and a deep insight into the enigma of existence."[19] Consider, for example, the following:

> In a moment we love and hate
> in a second we rejoice and mourn.
> We doubt till a thing becomes certain,
> and we believe in the utterly doubtful.
> Our eyes see not in light,
> but in pitch blackness.

'Abd Khaliq was certainly a talented poet who, had he lived, could perhaps have added flair and originality to poetry in Palestine. However, the preponderance of the political theme in Palestinian poetry, and his own limited output, means that his poetry had no real effect on other poets, who continued to write within the convention of realism established by Ibrahim Tuqan, but without Tuqan's particular talent. Long before the call for politically committed literature began to resound through the Arab world in the fifties,[20] Palestinian poets were writing some of the most authentic politically committed poetry in Arabic.

Two of these poets merit special mention here, namely, 'Abd al-Raheem Mahmoud (1913–1948) and Abu Salma ('Abd al-Karim al-Karmi, 1911–1984). Political involvement lies at the root of 'Abd al-Raheem Mahmoud's fame. As early as the late thirties, his terse, emotionally charged poems prophetically anticipated the doom that would befall the Palestinians; the courage and noble self-denial in defense of honor and country, which this poet also revealed in his verse, were abiding qualities that found their ultimate expression in the poet's death in action in 1948.[21] In these succinct, fiery pronouncements of faith and devotion, 'Abd al-Raheem Mahmoud lives on as a poet-martyr.

This political involvement also largely underlies Abu Salma's fame. He began writing in the thirties, commemorating Palestinian valor and resistance, and emphasizing the unity of Palestinian Arabs, where "the

Cross embraces the Crescent," as Christians and Muslims come to adopt a shared stance. After 1948 he lived as an exile in Damascus, voicing the grievances and aspirations of Palestinians throughout the world, and gaining greater popularity with the years.

Neither Abu Salma nor 'Abd al-Raheem Mahmoud was a great poet, but the political theme so prominent in their writing ensured the survival of their special status. In their work, politics takes the form of an overriding preoccupation, but it is a preoccupation with the discovered, the accepted, the craved; their work never shows any tendency to go firmly against the grain, as does 'Abd al-Khaliq's. This was to be a major problem for Palestinian literature, even for that produced by superior talents: with rare exceptions, such as the poetry of Tawfiq Sayigh (1924–1971), it seldom, before the end of the seventies, ventured beyond the expectations of readers and listeners to violate established continuities in theme, tone, and outlook. It was only later that highly gifted Palestinian poets, while continuing to embrace a positive political stance, would find ways of writing a sophisticated and avant-garde poetry that still for the most part satisfied the spiritual needs of readers and listeners.[22] The problem seems to have been largely confined to poetry; for although Palestinian fiction, when it began to flourish in the sixties and after, was also very politically committed, it had greater freedom and greater maneuverability. Being a rather new medium, fiction was less entrenched in the literary tradition, and the audience felt less possessive toward it. Poetry, on the other hand, was a medium with which the audience interacted spontaneously and with great immediacy. Right from the beginning its audience was large, bringing together the educated elite and the common people. Poetry craved high pronouncements of bitter denunciation and assured aspiration.

With the exception of Ibrahim Tuqan, no political poet before the fifties could offer anything sufficiently novel to establish a new approach. Even Abu Salma, who continued to write well into the late seventies, and who retained his popularity, contributed little to the technique and real esthetic value of Palestinian poetry after the fifties.[23]

When Fadwa Tuqan came upon the scene in the forties, she shocked the contemporary poetic sensibility in Palestine by what seemed an introverted stance. She was, in fact, fighting a fierce personal war against tradition, first through feminine lament, then, as her consciousness sharpened with the years, through protest, and finally through the self-assertion that was her greatest triumph.[24] It was only after she had won her war against her diminished status as a woman that she was able to participate freely in the nation's political struggle against the external enemy. She herself addresses this question in her autobiography, when, reacting retrospectively to her father's demand in the forties that she write *political* poetry, she says, "How and with what right or logic does father ask me to compose political poetry, when I am shut up inside these walls? I don't sit with men, I don't listen to their heated discussions, nor do I participate in the turmoil of life outside. I'm still not even acquainted with the face of my own country as I was not allowed to travel."[25]

It was only her achievement of personal freedom that provided the scope for a more communal involvement with political life, at a time when her country was plunging from one disaster into another.

Fiction

Before moving on to discuss Fadwa Tuqan's later poetry, and the rest of Palestinian poetry after 1948, we should perhaps consider Palestinian fiction before this date. In the first half of the twentieth century, this fiction, in its modern forms of the short story and the novel, was still in its experimental stages. Literature is a cumulative process; it is also a matter of would-be authors reacting to influences, and, often, of the will to develop. Arabic fiction needed the cumulative experience, and the courage and dedication to experiment with a new form that was still unsure of itself—and such a situation becomes even more intractable when writers are faced with immediate political necessity; in such circumstances they will normally tend to shy away from experimentation in a still unexplored field. During this early period, fiction in Palestine remained a struggling genre whose status reflected the weakness of fiction in most Arab countries, where writers had not yet succeeded in establishing the norms and forms of the new art form and where aspiring writers were still unable to translate the realities of contemporary Arab life into a narrative of real esthetic value. There is, it is true, a long tradition of fiction in Arabic (both oral and written) that has been handed down over the centuries. When we consider the tales of love and romance that abounded especially in the Umayyad period,[26] the allegorical stories of *Kalila wa Dimna*,[27] the *Arabian Nights*, the Abbasid *maqamat* ("assemblies"),[28] the philosophic allegory as exemplified by *Hay ibn Yaqdhan*,[29] the art of the anecdote, the many heroic folk romances and thousands of other folk stories memorized by ordinary people—especially women—we can see that Arabic literature is in fact very rich in this area. However, these various narrative arts are not the same as the art of the modern short story and the modern novel, which are the products of a bourgeois society and a tradition established since the crucial invention of the printing press. The way they translate material from life into fictional art involves a different process of narration.

In its early stages twentieth-century Palestinian fiction seems to have been inspired primarily by Western fiction that had been translated into Arabic; this was indeed to be the story of Arabic fiction everywhere, with the earliest guidelines taken directly from the modern prototype of the novel and the short story in modern Western literature. It was only later on, around the midcentury, that writers began to look for inspiration and example in the variety of fictional genres in which Arabic literature itself is so immensely rich.

The first concentrated effort to draw the attention of aspiring Palestinian writers to the art of fiction and to its suitability to the needs of a fast-growing reading public was made by such writers as Khalil Baydas (1875–1949), Ahmad Shakir al-Karmi (1894–1927) and Jamil al-Bahri (d. prematurely in 1930). They were influential in several ways. First, they all founded and edited their own literary reviews, which became early platforms for the publication of fiction, mostly translated from European languages.[30] Second, all three were involved in the important task of literary translation: Baydas, who had studied at the Russian Orthodox school in Nazareth, translated either directly from Russian literature or from Russian translations of other European writers such as Marie Corelli and Victor Hugo; al-Karmi was proficient in English and translated from Oscar Wilde and Mark Twain, and from English translations of such European writers as Guy de Maupassant, Bernardin de Saint-Pierre, Tolstoy, and Chekhov; while al-Bahri dramatized many fictional texts,[31] and was particularly fond of translating detective stories. Third, these writers wrote on theory, emphasizing the importance of fiction for their contemporary Palestinian society. Baydas believed that fiction was "one of the greatest foundations of civilization, the most easily disseminated, and the most capable of affecting the heart and soul [of people], and of influencing their morals and customs."[32] The writer of fiction, in his opinion, should write for the majority, not for the elite, and should therefore mix with ordinary people and learn about their lives and problems. He is a prophet who sees what others cannot see. "The authentic writer of fiction is he who lives for art, and writes for art."[33] The perfect work of fiction is the one that aspires to lofty goals, glorifying virtue and condemning vice, with a view to refining the reader's character and enlightening his or her mind. "There is no doubt," he adds, "that the value of fiction lies in the benefit it contains and the moral it seeks."[34] Ahmad Shakir al-Karmi also felt that fiction should aspire to be a moral benefit and to offer constructive criticism against obsolete aspects of the Palestinian society of his day.[35] The same moralistic stance is exhibited by Jamil al-Bahri, who did not hesitate to tamper with the original text he dramatized, expunging what he regarded as unnecessary love scenes, unfit in his view for the eyes and ears of young people.[36]

Khalil Baydas is credited with the first known Palestinian novel, *The Heir*, which appeared in Jerusalem in 1920; he also wrote short stories, publishing his first collection, *Vistas of the Mind*, in Cairo in 1924 (with the preface quoted above).[37] Because of his many-sided involvement in its promotion, he is rightly regarded as the father of Palestinian fiction. *The Heir* depicts the life of the son of a Syrian mercantile family that has emigrated to Egypt. There the young man falls in love with a Jewish dancer, who is portrayed as a blood sucker and helped in her attempts to extract money from the young man by some of her compatriots. He falls into their trap and incurs heavy debts, only to be saved from illness and bankruptcy by a return to his work, to the family fold, and to a "normal" life. The novel's schema does not, however, revolve around the real dangers facing Palestinian society at the end of the second decade of the twentieth century—immediately after the Balfour Declaration became known and organized Jewish immigration into Palestine began—but merely offers a pejorative, Shylock-like view of Jews, depicting them as insatiably greedy for money and ready to commit any act of cruelty to obtain it. If the author did indeed mean to warn his Palestinian compatriots against Jewish plans to appropriate parts of their country, he tackled the problem in an indirect, and hence ineffective manner, making the characters Syrian and the locality Egypt, and emphasizing inherited morals and a traditional outlook rather than grasping the real dimensions of the Zionist movement and its implications for Palestinians.[38]

The next important novel[39] by a Palestinian writer is *A Chicken's Memoirs* (1943), by Ishaq Musa al-Husaini (d. 1990).[40] With its preface by Taha Husain, one of the major figures of Arabic literature at the time, *Memoirs* gained immediate fame in the Arab world, and ran through several printings. It is probably the first work of contemporary fiction to benefit directly from the Arab traditional literary heritage, being an allegorical story in the vein of Ibn al-Muqaffaʿ's *Kalila wa Dimna*, where the story is told by animals. In *Memoirs*, the animal is a hen that demonstrates great wisdom and benevolence, and a capacity for sound judgment on moral and existential issues.

The story begins with the hen moving to a new home where new relationships have to be made. However, the hen's contentment is shaken when enemies, in the form of giants, attack the place where the chickens live and drive away most of the inhabitants. A new generation of birds, which is resolved to avenge the aggression, is dissuaded from fighting by the hen, and persuaded to try to solve the problem by dispersing throughout the world and preaching justice, thus convincing the aggressor that his actions will militate against him. "Disperse through the world," the hen says, "and . . . spread noble ideals and lofty principles among people, and I am sure that we will eventually meet again in this home of ours after we have purified the [whole] world—not just our small dwelling place—from these evils."[41] With its call for caution, for appeasement, and peace at all costs, the novel's ideal of spiritual aspiration is out of touch with the realities of the political life around the author; he clearly cherishes the illusion that this kind of self-sacrificing attitude, even in the face of a ruthless enemy, will guarantee peace and final success.[42]

There were several other attempts at fiction in Arab Palestine, but the works in question never became central to the Palestinian literature of the time. This is, first, because poetry still dominated the literary field, and, second, because such attempts were still in their experimental phase and were not producing works of art capable of attracting widespread interest.[43] However, a number of points merit critical attention. In the first place, a didactic and moralistic attitude is present in almost all the works in question, reflecting a society still markedly traditional and strongly resistant to the onslaught of a foreign culture diametrically opposed to its basic principles—which the European culture of immigrant Jews represented at that time.

The didacticism was focused mainly on social problems. Indeed, Palestinian literature in this period presents an interesting case of the predominance of social over political problems (even though the political problems were so threatening) in a society newly awakened to modern life; political consciousness had clearly not yet become part of the artistic involvement of the writer of fiction. The general outlook toward political struggle was an idealistic one, embodying the particular values of courage, self-sacrifice, heroism, resistance, endurance, and redemption, etc., that were spontaneously linked with political strife in a traditional society still unconversant with modern political diplomacy and intrigue. Such lofty ideals are the stuff of poetry, and Palestinian poetry was brimming with them; but the political themes suitable to fiction—more analytical, more mundane, more worldly-wise, and embracing far wider aspects of experience—were not easily appropriated by writers still unable to visualize the nonideal situations of modern fictional characters and to internalize a political awareness and translate it into the daily experience of ordinary individuals. The struggle of the fiction writer was two-fold, it should be emphasized: he or she not only had to learn to manage the tools of this new art form, it was also necessary to come to intellectual terms with the political dilemma imposed upon the writer's people by the dangerous global Zionist strategy. The kind of inner knowledge necessary for the latter was not acquired before the 1948 upheaval which brought not only tragedy, but also a deeper insight into the general, particularly Western, global conspiracy that has surrounded Palestinian life through most of the twentieth century.

Seen in this light, the preponderance of social over political problems in the fiction of this pre–1948 era becomes understandable. Moreover, since writers were now being influenced by a Western fiction that had very little tradition of political involvement (being associated with quieter and more confident periods), Palestinian experimentalists could not find ready-made models on which to base their own work.

In the second place, attitudes towards inherited values were simultaneously affirmative and defensive. As I have said before, it was the immediate impact of a Jewish presence in the country that first preoccupied the Arabs, feeling as they did that the social and personal freedom demonstrated by European Jews now living in almost all the major cities of Palestine posed a threat to inherited Palestinian values and to their strict traditional code of moral behavior. These given values, both of Palestinian society and of Arab society in general, were tenaciously upheld in Palestine during this period. They were only to become a target for attack later on in the century, first after the failure of the 1948 attempt to reclaim the country with the help of the Arab world's armies, then, even more loudly, after the 1967 June War, which proclaimed the bankruptcy of many inherited Arab norms and values.

In the third place, there was an interest on the part of authors and translators of fiction not only to teach, but to entertain. When translating from Western fiction, writers went straight to the type of fiction appropriate to the spirit of the age, a case in point being the Victorian novelist Marie Corelli, whose books were moralistic yet written in a flamboyant style, and were widely popular in their time. It was in any case customary to expect amusement and entertainment from fiction, since the traditional Arab genres of folk tale and folk romance had largely tended in this direction.[44]

Palestinian Literature After 1948

The Palestine disaster of 1948, with the great psychological and physical upheaval it produced, is perhaps the first event that may be accurately regarded as a turning point for modern Arabic literature *on a pan-Arab scale*. It represents a fundamental division between a time of relative calm and false confidence and hope, and a time of brutal self-realization, despair, deep loss of faith, anxiety, and general restlessness.

However, the disaster also proved to be an eye-opener. With the bankruptcy of the old Arab order suddenly recognized, a new strength appeared born out of affliction, the kind of will to be and to transcend known only to people who have experienced tragedy and loss. In the fifties Palestinians as well as the whole Arab nation sprang suddenly to life with a robust challenge to the self and to many of the inherited cultural, social, and political institutions in a way that would have been unimaginable in the forties. On the political front, the region was shaken by periodic revolutions and coups d'état that changed the political demography of the area. Several coups took place in Syria, while the great Egyptian revolution of 1952 put an end to the government of King Farouq and the cruel and obsolete economic system that existed in the country at the time. In Iraq, the 1958 revolution terminated the rule of the Hashemite royal family and introduced a republic. In Algeria, the ten-year revolution against a deeply rooted French colonialism, which ended in triumph in 1962, was a source of faith and pride to an Arab world in great need of renewed self-confidence. In the late sixties Yemen (South Yemen in 1967 and North Yemen in 1969) succeeded in ending the unenlightened rule of the Imams, which had dragged the country down to abject poverty and backwardness. Everywhere, on external and internal fronts alike, the aspiration toward liberation and freedom could be felt.

On the social level a new courage was born, one that questioned the inherited system, challenged repressive attitudes toward love, sexuality, and, above all, the status of women and their role in society. The great yearning, so movingly expressed all over the Arab world in the romantic poetry of the twenties, thirties, and forties, for the attainment of love and individual happiness no longer seemed to represent a focal point in poetry. Not only was there a relaxation of the rigid code of sexual behavior—at least among intellectuals and creative writers (and also among painters and sculptors, whose numbers were constantly growing)—but there also arose a much more urgent involvement in questions of political and national destiny, which directly affected literature.

The 1948 tragedy also posed a challenge to the literary heritage, making it possible for intellectuals and thinkers to subject that heritage to critical examination. This would have been a basically healthy situation, if it had not in practice driven some writers to a completely rejectionist stance that denied, even at the expense of scholarly integrity and rigor, any worth in this immensely rich and varied classical achievement.

The art of poetry was markedly influenced by the new stance; for the first time in Arab poetic history the challenge to inherited, almost sanctified forms of poetry became a major issue, wide open not only to theoretical discussion, but also to emotionally based viewpoints. Free verse had been attempted as a purely esthetic experiment even before the Palestine tragedy when, in 1947, the Iraqis Badr Shakir al-Sayyab and Nazik al-Mala'ika, probably experimenting together in Baghdad, simultaneously published several examples of free verse, improving on earlier and little-known experiments in this form.[45] However, the Sayyab-Mala'ika experiment won popularity in the fifties not only because it was artistically successful, but also because the psychological climate had, after 1948, become receptive to the idea of dismantling the traditionally venerated form of the monorhyme and two-hemistich verse, thus dislocating the symmetrical, balanced arrangements that had dominated Arabic poetic forms since pre-Islamic times. This was a revolution unprecedented in the history of Arabic poetry. The old veneration evaporated among the young poets coming of age in the fifties, and the following decades saw adventurous and highly successful experiments in form, ranging from free verse to the *poème en prose*.[46] On the semantic level, the 1948 tragedy imposed new thematic and attitudinal dimensions on the poem, and the great call for social and (especially) political commitment that resounded through the Arab world in the mid-fifties emphasized that poetry should be socially and politically committed also.[47]

What must be stressed here, however, is that the political upheaval of the late forties coincided with a literary period vibrant with experimentation and adventurism. The urge to experiment had in fact been growing steadily since the beginning of the century as authors eagerly sought to master new literary tools, and this had gone hand in hand with a conscious acquisition of literary theory and a growing direct acquaintance with modern developments in world literature. Now, in the fifties, the remarkable resurgence of poetic creativity, together with the introduction of major innovations in the art of poetry, the serious attention to esthetics, the steady development of fictional and dramatic genres, and the vibrant controversy in the theoretical field, were all to lead to a high level of esthetic creativity in the second half of the twentieth century.

It was in poetry, for reasons that I have already discussed, that the 1948 tragedy particularly accelerated this process—whereas the new "modern" fictional and dramatic genres have developed, one feels, at the same rate as they would have done in any case. Still based primarily on Western patterns, they had no dependence on strict and revered traditions to serve as a focus of rebellion for this new mood of rejection and challenge.

The short story had been developing steadily, growing in sophistication as more and more educated writers emerged, armed with greater courage and with an ever enriched knowledge both of the new forms of world fiction and of the new theories about it. Although the stories written by Palestinians (and by many other Arab authors) often reflected the new situation in their subject matter, there is no indication that their artistic development in the fifties took on an added pace because of the tragedy. As for the Arabic novel, which had been the subject of experiments throughout the thirties and forties, its resurgence in the late fifties and sixties was mainly due to the rise of Najib Mahfouz and the success and growing sophistication of his experiments.[48]

Poetry 1948–1967

On the esthetic level, the development of Palestinian literature mirrors a general development in the main literary centers of the Arab world. The mass exodus of 1948 exposed poets and writers in the diaspora to new influences, and eventually led to a quicker development of their art than was the case with most of their compatriots who remained on the soil of Palestine, in what had now become "Israel." Whether inside or outside Israel, however, Palestinian authors underwent a period of stunned bewilderment following the 1948 disaster, and took some time to find themselves again and embark on the arduous task of creative writing. But by the mid-fifties Palestinian writers, particularly in the diaspora (despite their constrained situation), seemed to have overcome the initial shock and to have surged back with determined energy. Several poets and writers of fiction rose to fame, some of them actually taking the lead in poetic creativity and fictional innovation.

Because of the complex development of Palestinian poetry after 1948 and the dramatic impact of subsequent political events on all Arabic poetry, particularly after 1967, I will deal with recent Palestinian poetry in two stages: that written between 1948 and 1967, and that written since 1967. The same division cannot be applied to the development of Palestinian fiction which, although influenced by political events, did not exhibit similar dramatic changes of direction on their account; the crucial factor here was the artistic maturation of fictional creativity. Kanafani's best works, *Men in the Sun* and *All That's Left to You*, were both written before 1967 (in 1963 and 1966 respectively), while Jabra's *The Ship* (1970) shows very little reaction to 1967, concentrating more on the events of 1948. Habiby's fictional works, discussed below, are more thematically influenced by the aftermath of 1967, but the great esthetic sophistication of his novel *The Secret Life of Saeed, the Ill-Fated Pessoptimist* (1974) cannot be seen as springing from those events. It shows an artistic maturation hitherto unknown in Arabic, and markedly reflects the author's own style and attitudes.

Of the poets already known in mandatory Palestine, the leading figures were Fadwa Tuqan, now living in the West Bank under Jordanian rule, and Abu Salma, who had settled in Damascus. Abu Salma's nostalgic poetry about his lost homeland, his constant deep yearning for its fauna and flora, and his faith in an inevitable reunion with it endeared him to thousands of Palestinians, and he was eventually given the name "The Olive Tree of Palestine" as a symbol of permanent rootedness and unswerving love and faith. However, his diaspora poetry displays a lack of coherence and an affected tone not present in the fiery, compact, spontaneous verse he wrote in Palestine before 1948; it is as if his vision had become shaky and unsure. This is seen particularly in his profuse use of abstract imagery, his employment of a vocabulary that, if elegant, was often redundant and repetitive, and his use of rather flimsy and unconvincing themes. However, his poems continued to charm his audience, particularly his listeners—he often declaimed his verse, in the "high" fashion of Arabic platform poetry,[49] to large audiences in the Arab world. His popularity with the latter perhaps stems from the fact that his poems are studded with the names of Palestinian villages, rivers, mountains, and shores, and also have a touch of erotic romanticism as he mixes love of country with the love of the woman he will meet:

> . . . . . . in the breezes that wander
> homeless from Mount Jarmaq, from Jerusalem's hills
> . . . . . . meet, on the soil of the fatherland
> On Mount Carmel, sad since our parting,
> On the sands of the blue shores.[50]

The woman he addresses in his verse is always a nameless, abstract being, a nostalgic figure remote from any concrete experience, united to the poet by the shared fate of exile. Yet, despite the poet's frequent allusion to this exile, his poetry fails to express the true dimensions of his country's tragedy, or to reflect the real aspirations of Palestinians.

Fadwa Tuqan developed in a quite different way. As with Abu Salma, her fame continued to grow, particularly after the 1967 June War, but between 1948 and 1967 she was mainly bent on developing her own personal mode of expression, enriching modern Arabic poetry with the most eloquent, but also unpretentious poetry of feminine self-discovery and self-realization.[51] She also served poetry by her liberation of the erotic and, more than most poets of her generation, by paving the way toward emotional veracity. Unlike most other women authors who began writing in the aftermath of 1948 when the psychological climate was dominated by a mood of deep rejection of outmoded concepts and mores, Tuqan showed a superb capacity to express elation at the liberation of body and soul, while keeping her inner decorum and never falling prey to the then fashionable outbursts of bravado and unrestrained audacity. Her poem "In the Flux," written just before the 1967 June War, reflects this great inner liberation and instinctive control over her poetic tools, whereby "love, desire, spiritual buoyancy, and physical freedom are merged together."[52]

However, it was after the June War of 1967 that Fadwa Tuqan rose to greater poetic eminence when she joined the powerful group of resistance poets who had for some time been writing in Israel proper, protesting against Israeli domination. Seeing her country fall prey to occupation yet again, and watching the new mass exodus of Palestinians forced to leave their homes, she was transformed into one of the most powerful voices raised in defense of her people and their rights, often appearing at large gatherings in the campaign to maintain people's confidence in the outcome of struggle and resistance.[53]

For many years Palestinian poets and writers inside Israel remained physically isolated from their expatriate countrymen. It was only in the midsixties that the first connection between the two groups was made, as the diaspora writers discovered, with apparently unexpected joy, the presence of an already powerful poetic activity behind the iron walls that divided the Palestinian people. It was then that the names of Tawfiq Zayyad, Mahmoud Darwish (then still living in Israel) and Samih al-Qasim came to be known for the first time as their poetry provided Arab readers with a potent verbal weapon against the tragic circumstances of their people. Exultantly received, they were destined, with the years, to become household names.

It was clear, however, that their physical isolation from colleagues in the Arab world did not entail a total lack of familiarity with currents of poetic change and innovation; they had in fact kept in carefully close touch with the revolutionary poetic movement of the fifties and after in the main Arab literary centers, which had established free verse and revolutionized the other elements of the poem. If diaspora poets like Abu Salma, Kamal Nasir, and Hasan al-Buhairi remained faithful to the old poetic forms dominant before 1948, these new poets coming of age in the sixties within Palestine had kept abreast of the momentous poetic events taking place. One of them, Darwish, was to leave Israel in the early seventies and become one of the foremost Arab poets of the modern age.

It is impossible, in this short introduction, to follow all the twists and turns of literary history, but it is important, nevertheless, to try and single out experiments where poets and writers have shown an innovative streak and a robust creative vigor. Among the diaspora poets participating in the poetic revolution of the fifties were Tawfiq Sayigh, Jabra Ibrahim Jabra, and Salma Khadra Jayyusi. Jabra, who (along with his robust literary criticism) also showed an early interest in fiction, later became one of the foremost novelists in the Arab world. As a poet he was among the few early authors to introduce prose poetry, and to incorporate the fertility myths that became very fashionable in Arabic poetry in the late fifties; he had, in fact, helped introduce Arab poets to the latter by his skillful translation, in 1957, of that part of Frazer's *The Golden Bough* dealing with the myths of Adonis or Tammuz. (Several Western poets were also influential in this respect, notably T. S. Eliot.) The use of such myths, where the god rises from death and the world is again filled with fertility and life, reflected a profound hope in the resurgence of the Arab spirit after the catastrophe of 1948, a renewed faith in the possibility of resurrection after symbolic death.

Tawfiq Sayigh, however, was the first Palestinian poet of the fifties to contribute to the modernist trend in Arabic, then still in its infancy. He published his first volume of avant-garde prose poetry, *Thirty Poems*, in 1953, without, however, attracting much attention to its modernist qualities. This was a time when poets and audience expected completely different poetics, when poetry aspired to be *modern*[54] not *modernist*, and the concept of modernity in literature as such had not yet been discovered, let alone discussed.[55]

It was only later, in the early seventies, that the concept was brought to light and the 'doctrine' of modernity, *Hadatha*, became the subject of numerous discussions and writings. Yet, despite the profuse literature surrounding it in book form or in essays—many of the latter submitted at conferences—it still to this day remains a vague issue in Arabic. There are many reasons for this, but two appear to be dominant: first, it could not be affiliated to the movement of European modernism during the first three decades of this century, which sprang from a particular kind of impetus absent in the Arab experiment; and second, some of the major writers on Arab modernity were trying, impossibly, to accommodate the concepts they were evolving to the kind of poetry they wrote. Despite the marked modernist elements in Adunis'* poetry (the revolution in diction and metaphor, the will to destroy, the rejection of given institutions, etc.), there were many residual elements in his verse (his vision of himself as hero and sage, and his tone of the potent, all-knowing prophet) that could not be reconciled with a genuine modernist vision. Along with the rhetorical tone that lingered on in much poetry, it was this heroic concept of the master and hero who rises above circumstances and is endowed with the power to teach and illuminate (probably a fit vision for the times, but decidedly not modernist) that stood as a wedge between several highly gifted poets of the fifties (later called "the generation of the pioneers") and a true modernism.

The fifties were dominated, it must be remembered, by a wish for redemption following the failure of 1948, and this often expressed itself through ostentatious heroics or at least through the affirmation of strength and defiance, of anger and loud rejection, that preserved the

---

*Pseudonym for 'Ali Ahmad Sa'id, a Syrian poet b. 1929, one of the foremost poets of the post–1948 Arab world.

rhetorical eloquence and self-assertive tones of the traditional poetic language. As such, the low tone and nonheroic demeanor of Tawfiq Sayigh's poetry attracted only very limited attention among his contemporaries. Even today, when a genuine modernist voice has quietly asserted itself in poetry, neither this trend nor Sayigh's much earlier experiment have become central for critics attempting to write on modernity, and Sayigh's work itself has not yet been given its rightful place in the history of modern Arabic poetry.

Saddened but undaunted, Sayigh continued to write in the same manner, his work growing in sophistication with the years. In 1960, his collection, *The Poem Kaf,* appeared, and in 1963 his *Ode of Tawfiq Sayigh*. His modernist attributes are manifold. Always using the prose-poetry medium, his treatment of form in poetry was very revolutionary for the early fifties; he proved the absolute validity of prose-poetry for Arabic, despite the voices raised against it during the fifties and sixties as a hybrid form that could never equal the splendor of rich traditional metrics. His treatment of diction was also revolutionary. He discarded hackneyed and poetic diction and wrote in a language closer to that of modern Arabs, often using a rare and witty vocabulary. His metaphors, moreover, were new and fresh, taken mostly from his city environment, with no pastoral references. The split with the romantic poetry of his immediate predecessors was complete.

Most important of all, he employed a tone removed from rhetoric, often speaking in an ironic mode that was full of wit and meaningful allusions. Shy of self-aggrandizement, he discarded personal heroism and the status of the poet-seer and poet-prophet. In an era of general crisis, of world conspiracies, and tragic global duplicity, when life was full of turmoil and suffering, Sayigh recognized his status as the *victim* not the hero of his times, revealing the alienation and suffering imposed by contemporary evil, internal and external, on the life of the individual. Sayigh's early experiment is of considerable importance for the development of Arabic poetry in the direction of modernity, a major aspect of this being his relation to new experiences. He wrote a poetry that was universal in an era of nationalist verse, personal in an age of communal orientations, and individual in a period dominated by fashions and styles. Loner, victim, and wanderer, his poetry is a supreme example of an early modernity achieved because of the poet's particular qualities of vision and technique.[56] In a period still struggling with the inherited, often stubborn relics of previous periods of poetry—the classical of medieval times and the neo-classical of the modern Arab poetic renaissance, which still imposed their sublime rhetoric and self-assertive tone on poets and audience; the Romantic with its misty language, its sentimental tone, its hazy outlook, its dilution and its self-centeredness; the symbolist with its ivory-tower attitudes and its rarefied use of language and image—Sayigh's appearance at this very early stage must be addressed as an artistic phenomenon of great poignancy.

Fiction After 1948

The Short Story

The early experiments in Palestinian fiction, discussed in the previous section, did not produce any major examples to build on, and a critic might well conclude that Palestinian fiction after 1948 was largely influenced by the good examples of fiction produced in a number of Arab countries during the same period; this conclusion would be confirmed by the fact that Palestinian fiction in the fifties, like Arabic fiction in general, concentrated more on the short story than on the novel—a reversal of the early fictional situation in Palestine. Four writers of fiction, all now living outside Palestine, rose to fame during this period: Mahmoud Sayf al-Din al-Irani, Jabra Ibrahim Jabra, Samira 'Azzam, and Ghassan Kanafani.

Al-Irani (1914–1974) had in fact been writing and publishing since the forties, and his factual, often moralistic and rather simple plots were far more mature than those found in earlier experiments in the short story in Palestine. In 1942 he moved to Jordan, where he worked as a teacher and inspector of schools, and later held important cultural positions within the Jordanian establishment. His literary output demonstrates the basic unity of Palestinian and Jordanian cultures, and he has been perhaps the most important pioneer of the short story in East Jordan (which merged with the West Bank to become "Jordan" in 1949)—indeed, in the whole area of Palestine and Jordan during the forties and early fifties. His collection, *With the People*, which appeared in 1956, established his influence and confirmed his versatility.

The fictional work of Jabra Ibrahim Jabra (b. 1917) immediately heralded a different order, a new and more modern direction. Destined to become one of Palestine's most prominent novelists, his first fictional experiment was a volume of short stories entitled *'Araq and Other Stories* (1956). He had spent the Second World War years in Cambridge, England, working on a higher degree in literature and absorbing Western culture, literary knowledge, and critical erudition in a way that later benefited the modern movement in Arabic literature.

'Araq contains nine short stories. Five stories are about the Palestinian experience before the diaspora, three revolve around his experiences in Iraq (where he had emigrated after the 1948 debacle and taken up citizenship), and the last, three-part story is about his life in England. Right from the beginning Jabra showed a genuine fascination with Western culture and deep affinities with it, which was quite untypical of the attitudes and cultural outlook of the time. Throughout his work he was to display an elitist stance, with a marked bias toward intellectualism and the elucidation of ideas and arguments, some of which had plagued Arab intellectuals throughout the post-1948 period, but others of which were superimposed from a highly complex technological Western culture onto the preindustrial contemporary Arab culture. Readers of fiction in the fifties and early sixties were, however, understandably impressed by the new attitudes and concepts expounded in this early collection.

Tawfiq Sayigh, who wrote the introduction to *'Araq*, expressed complete acceptance and evident admiration of Jabra's treatment of the themes of "love" and "the city" in some of the stories—it apparently did not dawn on him that Jabra's description of malfunction and decadence belonged much more to the Western industrial city than to the Arab city of the time. It is true that the Arab metropolis had begun, in the mid-century, to attract increasing numbers of rural people seeking work, a better life, and, in some cases, education. However, the many existential problems facing these immigrants had little relation, surely, to the complex and highly westernized interpretations that Jabra gave them. Take for example the question of love in the Arab city, a theme celebrated with great flair during the same period by the Syrian Nizar Qabbani, one of the most urbane of modern Arab poets, who had been born and brought up in the ancient city of Damascus. Qabbani's poetry, perhaps the most popular modern poetry among Arabs, reflects city life, habits, mannerisms, attitudes, and norms without ever confusing the experience of Arab men and women in love with any of the notions of estrangement, and even sterility, with which Jabra's work is filled. Love in Qabbani's poetry is a multicolored, multilayered experience, one that is never impotent or stale; and if it can at times be unhealthy, this has nothing to do with the alienation and solitude that the European city engenders.[57] Qabbani's city, ever present in the background, and sometimes, as in his Beirut poems, firmly in the foreground, is a robust Arab city that allows many situations of love, including prostitution and lesbianism, but it is neither sterile nor dead; it is, rather, gregarious, often fun-loving, with opportunities for erotic adventurism and secret liaisons. Jabra's is a city that has turned men into impotent males and compelled city women to seek sexual satisfaction by becoming either promiscuous or lesbians.

But even though Jabra used the short story medium to expound new ideas taken directly from the West, without effectually proving their real relevance to the Arab life of the time, his work was still an inspiration for the select audience of the period and gained him substantial recognition. Neither critics nor readers in the fifties and early sixties had yet grown critical of or impatient with "borrowed" stances and concepts introduced into literature before the social and cultural moment could naturally accommodate them.[58] Most of Jabra's stories in this collection, particularly those about Baghdadi life, display an assumed stance; a few of his ideas—such as the argument he introduces about literary commitment in "Voices at Night"—are relevant, mirroring as they do an ongoing argument about the subject in Arab literary circles; but other ideas in the same story, such as those about love and the sterility and impurity of the city as compared with the freedom and potency of the desert, simply do not ring true. Although Jabra's own outlook on the city was to change drastically, his preoccupation with intellectualism remained obsessive and overwhelming in one work of fiction after another.

Samira 'Azzam (1924–1967) was the third Palestinian writer of fiction to rise to fame in the fifties. She came from the coastal town of Acre, having been forced to leave her country in the exodus of 1948. Before her untimely death in 1967 she lived first in Cyprus, working as an employee at the British-administered Near East Broadcasting Service, then in Baghdad, and finally in Beirut, where she was active in the literary movement of that literature-loving city. Her experiment was based on a realistic view of experience, but one restrained within well-ordered artistic limits. She excelled in her presentation of various domains of human experience, including the varied experience of women in Arabic culture, and wrote in a style that was precise, economic, lucid, and free of sentimentalism, exhibitionism, or vulgarity. Her stories stem from a shrewd observation of human behavior, mainly in its universal aspects, but sometimes, though more rarely, in its particularly Palestinian aspects;[59] she could always account in telling terms for the inevitable change befalling her protagonists—the mark of a good short story. Her story "Tears for Sale,"[60] for example, is a superb treatment of a universal theme considered within a Middle Eastern setting; in it she describes the antithetical reaction of a woman whose profession as a hired mourner requires her to weep at wakes and jerk other people's tears, but who defies all expectations by being unable to shed a single tear when her only daughter dies. The story included in this anthology, "Bread of Sacrifice," is one of those she wrote about the Palestinian experience; and, like several of her other stories, it shows the irony implicit in intricate human predicaments at times of violent upheaval.

'Azzam began writing before 1948, and both her work and Jabra's early fictional works clearly reflect the limited awareness possessed by Palestinian writers of that period of the momentous events about to take over their own lives and those of so many others. A comparison of their work during that early period before and immediately after the 1948 catastrophe with the work of other Palestinian writers (including Jabra himself, 'Azzam having died in 1967) after the 1967 June War, demonstrates how political consciousness progressively took hold of Palestinian writers everywhere and how, correspondingly, the political expectations of their audience became heightened.

Unlike Arabic poetry, the short story in Arabic developed as a conscious creation of the imagination, artistically free of the gripping hold of well-entrenched traditions; but, as political consciousness deepened, the Palestinian short story found itself bound to the existential situation of the Palestinians. It quickly created thematic traditions based on the reality of this experience and thus lost part of the freedom enjoyed by the short story not only in the West, but also in the rest of the Arab world, where fiction remained freer in its choice of the experiences it delineated.

When 'Azzam and Jabra first began writing, they still enjoyed such freedom, though with all her universal outlook on human experience 'Azzam remained more representative of the particular possibilities of a wider Arabic culture. If we compare 'Azzam's work with Jabra's more sophisticated and complex experiment, we may say that Jabra, in several stories in *'Araq*, translated reality into another, often unrelated reality, while 'Azzam remained faithful to the possibilities of the reality she knew existed in the Arab world and that she elevated into art. Moreover, on the technical level, some of Jabra's stories in *'Araq* do not attempt to capture a moment of resolved tension, to "see the world in a grain of sand" as it were, but rather endeavor, as in "Voices at Night," to offer a whole system of thought and ideas in a single story. 'Azzam, on the other hand, exercises the successful, self-imposed discipline that a new art form—here the short story—demands, a discipline that must find its own rules and principles. Her work reflects a deep respect for her artistic tools and a commitment to the principles of the short story as an art form that seeks to capture a *moment of reality,* delineating one phase of action and keeping to what Elizabeth Bowen calls "objective demonstration rather than personal narration."[61] 'Azzam's work does not possess Jabra's eloquence and flamboyance of style or the depth of his intellectual argument. Her best work delineates universal social (particularly feminine) experiences; yet, when she writes about the Palestinian experience, her short stories are perhaps the most representative Palestinian short fiction written during the fifties and sixties, except for those of Ghassan Kanafani.

Ghassan Kanafani formally entered the literary field in the early sixties, with the publication of *The Death of Bed No.* 12 (1961), which is a collection of seventeen short stories. If it took some time for the genius of this writer to be fully recognized, this can only reflect the shortcomings of a contemporary criticism that did not detect the depth and variety of which Kanafani was capable. Although (like his three later collections) this volume is artistically uneven, it contains some of the most potent short fiction in modern Arabic, including such stories as "The Death of Bed No. 12," "Pearls in the Street," "Eight Minutes," "The Slaves' Fortress," "Six Eagles and a Child," "The Crucified Lambs," and what I believe to be an autobiographical story, "In my Funeral." His second collection, *Land of Sad Oranges* (1963), which contains ten short stories, concentrates more on the varied but ever tragic experience of the Palestinians; the trilogy "Three Papers from Palestine" became famous as a fictional representation of possible occurrences on the tortuous road of Palestinian exile. His third collection, *A World Not for Us* (1965), contains fifteen stories and reveals his sensitivity as an observer of human behavior in its universal aspect in such superior stories as "The Hawk," "Kufr al-Manjam," "The Shore," "The Serpent's Thirst," "Had I been a Horse," and "Skidrow." His fourth collection, *On Men and Guns* (1968), is dedicated to the Palestinian experience.

The Novel

Kanafani had begun writing while working as a teacher in Kuwait. In 1959 he returned to Damascus where his family had lived since the 1948 diaspora, then moved to Beirut, where he became the spokesman for the Popular Front of Palestine. Although suffering from diabetes, Kanafani had boundless energy as a writer; apart from editing the Front's journal, he continued his experiments in fiction, attaining great heights of creativity in his three novellas, *Men in the Sun* (1963), *All That's Left to You* (1966) and *Return to Haifa* (1969).

It was *Men in the Sun*[62] that first earned him serious recognition among the arbiters of Arabic literature. The story deals with the problem of survival. Three men of varied age and social background seek entry into Kuwait (then the land of milk and honey promising sustenance to many homeless, destitute Palestinians). There were rumors in the Arab world that Palestinians without passports were often smuggled into Kuwait in one of the large tanks bringing water to the tiny desert state from Basra (those were the early days of Kuwait, before the huge distilling plants had been installed). In this story, such a tank is owned by a middleman, Abu al-Khayzaran, a Palestinian and a veteran of the 1948 war in which he had sustained wounds that made him impotent. Having charged the three unfortunate protagonists a huge fee, Abu al-Khayzaran hides the men in his empty water tank before they arrive at the frontier, with the intention of releasing them when they are clear of the border police. This time, however, the customs official chooses to dally at his job, and spends precious time joking with Abu al-Khayzaran about the latter's supposed escapades with women in Iraq. Crouched for too long in the burning hot tank, the three men suffocate, and the story ends poignantly with Abu al-Khayzaran hurling the three corpses onto a garbage dump (after stripping them of all their valuables), shouting, "Why didn't you bang on the wall of the tank?" The story ironically emphasizes the miserable experience of Palestinians immediately after 1948: the desperate quest for survival, the unified tragedy of men from all walks of life, and, above all, the stifled spirit of Palestinians who have already experienced such devastating rejection and such exacting conditions within the wider Arab world that, numbed by fear and desperately eager to fulfill their dream in Kuwait, they let precious time slip through their hands. This crucially important symbolic story, with its economical but vivid depiction of the physical and psychological world of the four Palestinians, immediately put Kanafani in the forefront of fictional writing in Arabic and, more particularly, in Palestinian literature.

His second novella, *All That's Left To You*,[63] is one of the most sophisticated works of Palestinian fiction, a genuine early attempt, probably very much unconscious, at modernizing Arabic literature. It is most unfortunate that Kanafani died too young for these sporadic modernist thrusts that we see in his work to become a steady, even flow. It is a critical delight, however, to watch the attempts, to see the way

Kanafani (and other early modernist or semimodernist authors such as Tawfiq Sayigh and the Syrian Muhammad al-Maghut [b. 1934])[64] audaciously experimented with modernist tools many years before the discussion of modernism had even started in Arabic; and it is perhaps even more interesting to note that, when this discussion became a central issue in Arabic in the seventies and after, the experiments of these three authors and that of the Egyptian Salah ʿAbd al-Sabur (1931–1981), another early modernist, did not become a focus in the discussion. A study of these early authors reveals that modernism started impulsively in the Arab world, without the aid of theories and manifestos—a telling testimony to the way art works naturally in the subconscious of creative writers, pushing the more sensitive among them toward change in a specific direction.

In Kanafani's case, we can see how his genius, which responded so sensitively to the artistic possibilities of the time, had to struggle with the heavy weight of commitment that, as a dedicated writer, he felt he owed to his people; this accounts, probably, for the unevenness in his writing that I have already discussed. *All That's Left To You* never gained the same wide applause as *Men in the Sun*, with its clear-cut definition of the philosophy of survival and the irony underlying human endeavor. His third novella, *Return to Haifa*, which is also a rather sophisticated study of the problems of identity and loyalty, remains well within the more unsophisticated reader's grasp. It was as if, instinctively, Kanafani wrote at times with the larger audience in mind, and at others for the more highly cultivated reader. *Return to Haifa* describes the dilemma of a Palestinian couple who return to Haifa when the borders between Israel and the West Bank have been opened following the 1967 June war, to discover that the son they left behind when they fled from their home in 1948 has been brought up as an Israeli by a Jewish couple. It is a touching story of conflict between contradictory loyalties, and Kanafani flouts the expectations of the audience by having the young man choose to stay with those who have brought him up; it is not simplistic nationalism that counts here, Kanafani implies, but lifelong association; not the ties of blood, but the cultural and human aspects of life.

In his short introduction to *All That's Left To You* Kanafani demonstrates his full awareness of the intricate structure he has chosen. The novella has five main characters (the Israeli soldier who comes onto the scene at the end of the story being a minor sixth): Hamid, Maryam, Zakaria, Time, and the Desert. There is a sophisticated and successful attempt at fusing Time and Place, and in the author's own words, "there appears to be no clear distinction between places far removed from each other and between different time frames, and sometimes even between time and place at a single moment." Kanafani describes the world of the story as a "jumbled" world that has to be delivered to the reader "in a single burst."

It is unclear whether Kanafani's apprehension of the phenomenon of place as a crucial existential entity in Palestinian life stems from any awareness of the same phenomenon in classical Arabic poetry, where the "desert" plays a major role in the poet's symbolization of man's tortuous journey through life. In his first two novellas it is again the desert that plays a major role in determining the fate of his protagonists. In *Men in the Sun*, the desert, with its blazing sun—described many centuries ago by Dhu al-Rumma as a permanent fixture in the sky, humming inside the traveler's head and dominating him—that decides the fate of protagonists. Dhu al-Rumma's traveler, though, always arrives, however emaciated and fatigued, at his destiny, thus symbolizing man's capacity to endure; in *Men in the Sun*, desert and sun fatally conquer the Palestinian. In *All That's Left to You* we encounter the desert at night, another frightening phenomenon for the classical traveler, with the desert thickly cloaked by valleys and steppes that "merge in complete oneness with the pitch-black night," and where the voices of the night echo, heightened by the all-engulfing silence around.[65] In this novella, however, Kanafani has the Palestinian face his destiny as an encounter with the enemy summons up all his courage and resolve; we are far removed from his docile acceptance of death in the water tank.

The plot revolves around a family separated during the 1948 upheaval; a brother and sister end up in Gaza with an old aunt while the mother ends up in Jordan. The sister, Maryam, thirty-five years old and much older than Hamid, eventually succumbs to sexual desire and has an affair with a married man known to be a scoundrel for his collaboration with the Israeli authorities. Hamid, discovering her pregnancy, is devastated; the family honor has been defiled, and by a collaborator no less! Maryam now has to marry Zakaria, and Hamid, in his desire to evade the shame Maryam has brought on the family, decides to join his mother in Jordan, crossing the fearsome desert on foot, at night, to evade the heat and the Israeli patrols.

Two timepieces monitor the movement of Maryam's preoccupied thoughts and perturbed memories and the movement of Hamid's footsteps across the desert: a clock hung in Maryam's house where she crouches in anguish next to her husband, and Hamid's own watch. They tick away the time, accompanying the simultaneous movements of the story, and aim to show the unified anguish of the two major protagonists as the account shifts from Maryam watching, thinking, and grieving to Hamid facing the horrors of his journey away from the horror of the reality left behind. There is a considerable use of flashback as the two protagonists weigh their present situation against the events of both the immediate and the more remote past. Periods of time intertwine, but the one great permanence is the desert, with its throbbing heart against which Hamid lays his head. Three voices speak in this work, marked visually by a change in the type-face: Hamid, Maryam, and the Desert itself. The Desert interposes itself to explain the present moment and to provide another dimension to the events assailing Hamid: "He'd strayed a long way from the road. He wasn't conscious of how the night was slipping away. I wished I could say something to him, but I'm committed to silence."

Then two finales take shape at once, despite the spatial distance between them: Zakaria orders his bride to choose between an abortion and a divorce, and Hamid encounters the Israeli patrol guard. Maryam is completely at the mercy of fate. Pushed against the wall, humiliated and alone in the world after her brother's departure, she can find no way of preserving the life within her except by taking away the life of the man who has caused her so much sorrow. Hamid, too, knows he can only survive by killing the Israeli guard. A long and very moving interval passes as he watches over his foe; then the two knives, Maryam's and Hamid's, plunge simultaneously into their victims. Kanafani's inner decorum evidently causes him to hesitate before allowing the killing of the Israeli guard to take place. When it does, it is against the sounds of other Israeli guards coming onto the scene with their dogs. The Palestinian is doomed here, Kanafani is telling us, but at least he has not died cringing. He has made a last stand.[66]

The work of Jabra, Kanafani, and 'Azzam, all three living in the diaspora, dominated Palestinian fictional output before 1967. The fiction of Palestinians living either in the West Bank, then under Jordanian rule, or in Israel proper during the fifties, exhibited signs of weakness both in form and content. The sixties, however, saw the emergence of a new fictional tradition in these areas, which was to develop greatly within a few years and blossom in the work of several now well-recognized writers.

On the West Bank, such writers as Mahmoud Shuqair, Khalil al-Sawahiri, Rashad Abu Shawar, and Yahya Yakhlif rose to fame in the sixties. After 1967, when the West Bank was occupied by Israel, many writers either left voluntarily or, as in the case of Sawahiri and Shuqair, were deported by Israel—a testimony to the influence their writings had begun to wield on the audience around them. Such influence had, it will be noted, formerly been the prerogative of poetry.

In Israel proper, the fictional activity of the fifties focused, as before 1948, either on translating western fiction, or, when original stories were attempted, on direct imitation of western models. The late sixties, however, saw the emergence of Emile Habiby, a prominent political writer and an active member of Rakah, the Israeli Communist Party, who was later to become one of the most famous writers of fiction in the Arab world—mainly on the strength of *The Secret Life of Saeed, the Ill-Fated Pessoptimist* (1974),[67] one of the most original novels in modern Arabic. Other writers who emerged during this period were Tawfiq Fayyad, Muhammad Naffa', and Muhammad 'Ali Taha. With the exception of Fayyad, who left to live in the Arab world, all these writers, and others with them, have continued to dominate the fiction scene in Israel up to the present time.

Habiby's small collection of short stories, *Six Stories of the Six Day War* (1968), caused a stir both in Israel proper and in the Arab world. The collection was inspired by the consequences of the Six Day War of June 1967, when, as a result of the Israeli Occupation of the West Bank and the Gaza Strip, Palestinians were able to travel the whole of their original country after nineteen years of separation. Families were now able to seek reunion with members from whom they were rent apart by the 1948 war and to revive contacts and memories. The theme of reunion forms an internal rhythm in the collection, a thread of unity binding otherwise very different stories. The collection is like a prism on which many aspects of the same experience are carved, and special feelings are evoked only fully possible for people flung apart by history's great upheavals as they find themselves recrossing the temporal distance that had separated them. Time in this collection is mutable and fluid; it caused the tragedy of separation and is still capable of bringing about a reversal of tragedy, once the newly occupied land has been redeemed from occupation; the only immutable entity is the land of Palestine itself. The different protagonists are forever seeking solid roots that will give them security, yet they know that, beneath the dark cloud of defeat and occupation, such security remains a faraway hope.

However, it was with his novel, *The Secret Life of Saeed, the Ill-Fated Pessoptimist* that Habiby came to be recognized, first on a pan-Arab scale, then in both Israel and the West when his novel was translated into Hebrew and other languages. The novel first appeared in 1974, ran into three printings in the first three years, and was reviewed and analyzed in many periodicals and books in the Arab world and Israel. It spans some twenty years of the life of the Palestinians in Israel itself; then, like his collection of short stories, it brings the two parts of Palestine together, and reunions take place. The main character in the novel is Saeed, the Pessoptimist fool, whose quest for survival under the harsh terms of Israeli occupation is reminiscent of that of Schweik in the Czech writer Jaroslav Hašek's famous novel, *The Good Soldier Schweik* (1923); Habiby acknowledges his indebtedness to Voltaire's satirical masterpiece, *Candide* (1759), but the similarity with *Schweik*, the wise fool, is in fact greater. It is worth pointing out here that Habiby would have had ample opportunity to discover Schweik, as he several times went to live in Czechoslovakia where the novel is very famous.

Saeed is another wise fool, a comic hero who is an informer for the State of Israel. However, his stupidity and cowardice, and his outspoken candor, turn him into a victim rather than a villain. Never wholly successful in his attempts to please the Zionist state, he finally reverses roles to become a supporter of Palestinian resistance. There are several erotic situations in the novel, the most moving being Saeed's undying love for his first love, Yuaad. He marries Baqiya and has a son by her, Walaa', who becomes a freedom fighter, and dies with his mother as he defies the Israeli authorities. Despite his grief, Saeed, being the cowardly fool he is, continues to try and please the state; but an idiotic blunder on his part lands him in the Shatta prison, one of Israel's most notorious, where, expected to be a seeing eye in prison for the State, he is brutally beaten by the Israeli guards, then laid out beside the heroic young Saeed, Yuaad's son. The older Saeed is highly impressed by the young man's fortitude; while young Saeed, mistaking the Pessoptimist for a fellow freedom fighter, awards him the respect due to heroes. Once out of prison, profoundly moved by the experience, Saeed finds that he can no longer collaborate with the state. The dilemma in which he finally finds himself is symbolized by the impaling stake on which he sits at the end of the novel, and from which only a miracle, in the form of an extraterrestrial figure, a man from outer space, saves him.

Wit, irony, oversimplified candor, double meaning, paradoxes, and plays on words are juxtaposed in this important work, with some sections depicting the most profound tragic and heroic experiences of life: death, martyrdom, dangerous undertakings, valiant resistance, immutable faith. The comic representation of events is hilarious in places, and the heroic and tragic apprehension of experience, and even the simply human, such as Saeed's life-long friendship with Jacob, an Arabic-speaking Israeli informer, is sensitive and deeply moving without ever falling into mawkishness or sentimentality. The novel ends in the fantastic, when no exit seems possible for Saeed but a savior from outer space. The comic hero, Habiby realizes, must be saved somehow, for he cannot, despite his reversal, be turned into a martyr for the cause. This is one of the finest technical achievements of the novel.[68] The unanimous welcome that the novel received did not stem primarily from its revelation of the wretched experience of Palestinians under Israeli rule (although this was an added influence); the novel was praised because on the artistic level it represented a challenge to the existing models of long fiction in Arabic, resorting in a most skillful manner to an ironic mode in which the comic, heroic, and tragic all find a place.

The foremost Palestinian novelist to rise to fame in the diaspora was Jabra Ibrahim Jabra. After his short story collection was published in the fifties, he turned to the more difficult form of the novel, as being more suitable for the broader, richer spectrum of experience he wished to portray.[69] He began experimenting with the form in the fifties and has published six novels. His first, *Screaming in a Long Night*, which appeared in 1955, immediately revealed the quality of thought and scope of vision which continued to be in evidence in his work. His second novel, *Hunters in a Narrow Street*, was written and published in English in 1960, its Arabic translation appearing in 1974. However, his reputation as a novelist was established with *The Ship* (1970),[70] then firmly reinforced when *Search for Walid Masoud* appeared in 1978.[71] The experiment of co-authoring a novel with the Saudi Arabian ʿAbd al-Rahman Muneef, a latecomer to the field who had quickly won acclaim for his daring novels on subjects of major social and political concern,[72] led to *A World Without Maps* in 1982. The book suffered predictably, however, from the basic, irreconcilable differences in the style and vision of the two authors, and is not regarded as one of either author's better works. Jabra's last venture into the realm of the novel is *The Other Rooms* (1986), a work of strange paradoxes where a person is both witness and accused, actor and spectator. It is written as something of a black comedy, based on a reality which, as the cover of the novel states, "seems more impossible than a dream."

The main distinctive element of Jabra Ibrahim Jabra's novels is the shimmering eloquence of his style. In all his novels he demonstrates great linguistic flexibility, irrepressible energy, poetic flair, and a fine choice of vocabulary. He writes poetically and emotively, yet is never mawkish or sentimental; while his style is always limpid, he can be intimate or cerebral as the situation demands, without ever losing his characteristic fluency and polish. However, he is a modern and, as such, does not write in the grand, rhetorical style of inherited Arabic literature; he is well aware that such a style will not suit the more discursive, more intimate language of the novel. Interestingly, his prose poetry does not maintain the magnificent sweep of his prose. Here, as if afraid the poetic theme will lead him into mawkishness, he carefully avoids the emotive, and even the intimate, in favor of sotto voce style, often rather dry and uninspiring.

In fiction Jabra's unique style reinforces the inner significance of the work, confirming that it is the particular quality of the writer's mind that dictates his or her choice of both style and theme, the one symbiotically attracting the other. Most contemporary Arab novelists are more interested in subject matter than in style; there are, it is true, a few others, such as the Syrians Saleem Barakat and Haydar Haydar, who are great stylists as well, but such figures do not seem to have had much influence on other writers of their age. In this, prose has proven more intractable than poetry. The poetic style—difficult, pervasively inventive, and with very complex metaphorical representations—that dominated Arabic (including Palestinian) poetry throughout the sixties and seventies spread like wildfire among the younger generation, so that poets felt they could only be successful if they adopted the more dominant styles of poetry in the period.

In fiction, however, Arab writers have maintained their own personal styles; most of them, including the Arab world's foremost novelist, Najib Mahfouz, have opted for correctness and clarity, writing usually in a plain and discursive manner. Jabra's great linguistic dexterity and fluency of style have been important factors underlying his popularity as a novelist.

In his novels, as in his short stories, he mainly reflects the life of the intellectual elite. In fact, his predilection for the expounding of ideas (often ideas reflecting major preoccupations within the Arab world) can sometimes be irritatingly exaggerated and inflated, as when he has two fourteen-year-old boys in the Jerusalem of the 1930s philosophically discussing, among other topics, a painting by Botticelli and the writings of Anatole France—something unimaginable at the time for boys of this age, and all the more so when the boy who rigorously introduces the highly erudite conversation on Botticelli lives in abject poverty in one of the Jerusalem slums. Jabra's habit of intellectualizing everything is irrepressible.[73]

The Ship is a complex structure, mixing the events of the present with a lingering past that lies at the root of the emotions, dreams, aspirations, and despair of the protagonists. It is a novel about exile, memories, and nostalgia; about physical struggle, inner conflicts, and intellectual deadlock. Time in this novel recurs in constant flashbacks, so that the past overlaps the present and the present is determined by the force of the past, reflecting the past's pervasive presence in the consciousness of the protagonists. There is no way of summarizing the story in a few lines, since much of it is intermeshed with memories and subplots that converge on events and play their part in leading to the dénouement. There is tragedy in the book, for one of the major characters commits suicide at the end, yet the story closes on a positive note, as if the death represented a way out for the author and some of the other major characters, blunting the edge of tragedy with a promise, if still uncertain, of a better life for the others.

Three of the main protagonists are Iraqi, the architect 'Isam Salman, the surgeon Falih 'Abd al-Hasib and the beautiful, educated Luma; the fourth major character is a Palestinian businessman, Wadi' 'Assaf, working in Kuwait. The intricate plot involves 'Assaf with a Lebanese woman doctor, Maha al-Haj, to whom he is engaged, and involves the surgeon in two triangles: he is married to Luma but in love with Emilia Fernizi, while Luma is in love with 'Isam Salman. All these characters, except Maha, meet on board the *Hercules*, a cruise ship travelling from Beirut to Naples. The meeting, however, is not gratuitous: Luma has persuaded her husband to accompany her on the cruise when she knows that 'Isam is travelling on it, while her husband has secretly planned the trip with Emilia—who, in turn, has (as she believes) persuaded her friend Maha to travel with her fiancé.

What lies behind all this is the complex characters of the protagonists. 'Isam is running away from Baghdad, unable to face two problems: Luma's marriage, which he finds unendurable, and a tribal feud over some land that has caused his own father to kill a relative of Luma's and spend his life in exile. It was in fact this old feud that precluded 'Isam's marriage to Luma, whom he had met while the two were studying in England, with the result that Luma, out of desperation, committed herself to a marriage of convenience with the brilliant and well-to-do surgeon.

Apart from his love for Maha, the Palestinian Wadi' 'Assaf also cher-

ishes the dream of going back to Palestine. If 'Isam is running away
from problems created by a feud over land inherited from his forefathers
and finding his solution in a final relinquishing of ownership and attachment in connection with it, Wadi'''s whole raison d'être is to reacquire land in Palestine, thus reflecting the Palestinian attachment to
their country handed down by so many generations of forefathers. He
has amassed some wealth and has actually bought some land in Palestine, on which he plans to build a large house where he will live with
Maha. Maha, however, reluctant to curtail a successful career in Beirut,
regards him as a romantic dreamer, and it was a fresh quarrel over the
matter that made her decide at the last minute not to accompany 'Assaf
on the cruise.

'Assaf also holds on to another attachment: his poignant memory
of the death, during the upheaval in Palestine in 1948, of Fayez, a gifted
boy from Jerusalem's slums who loved to paint and with whom the
young 'Assaf had formed a strong friendship. The two friends fought
the Zionists side by side, and though Fayez was killed he lives on in
the memory of his friend, who vividly recalls his artistic gifts, his warm
friendship, and the knowledge and intelligent ideas he was so rapidly
acquiring in the Jerusalem of the thirties and forties.

Explosive situations develop during the trip on the *Hercules*. One
evening Luma rouses her husband to fury by dancing on the deck, and
he forces her to go back to the cabin with him. A storm makes everyone
seasick except Emilia, Falih, and Wadi', and it is then that Wadi' realizes
the other two are lovers (we know that the two have been meeting
clandestinely when Falih has paid several professional visits to attend
to Emilia's faked illnesses).

When they dock at Naples, a trip to Capri is planned, but not everyone goes. Luma pretends to be sick, then sneaks out with 'Isam into
Naples, where the two are seen by Falih and Emilia (who had done the
same thing) leaning happily on each other's arm. Falih's day is ruined,
and his arrangement to enjoy the liaison with Emilia in a hotel room
he had booked for the purpose ends in frantic despair. Back on the
ship that evening, he commits suicide.

Beside the empty pill bottle is a letter to Luma that shows that Falih
had actually been planning this suicide for some time, so that the
decision did not in fact spring from shock at his wife's duplicity. On
the face of it, there is no *apparent* reason for the suicide at all. He
seemed to have everything an educated Arab man, living in this oil-
rich part of the Middle East at this particular time, might want: success

in his profession, a beautiful wife, money, women, and social prestige. Such had indeed been the dream of thousands of Arab professionals during this period, when substantial financial opportunities were opened up and there was a general frantic thirst for pleasure and material possessions.[74]

Again, the fact that he had been contemplating suicide for some time[75] precludes any suspicion that Falih might have killed himself as a result of his sudden realization—he being a pessimist and a morose intellectual—of how ironical life is, and how the knife of duplicity can be double-edged.

Suicide is not, it is true, common for an Arab man, but in every culture there are those whose temperament, disposition, and intellectual makeup flout the general rule; Falih's very character and way of thinking are not in fact usual. In a case like this, therefore, one would expect a behavior pattern where his "differentness" would reemerge as a reaction to his wife's duplicity, especially when he himself was, at that very moment, practicing the same kind of deception. His earlier near frenzy at Luma's voluptuous dancing on the deck with everyone eagerly looking on is, basically, no more than the usual jealousy and possessiveness of the Arab man of his wife, whether he loves her or not. It is common knowledge that, no matter how sophisticated the Arab male may have become, his reaction to the erotic has remained, more often than not, traditional; and a traditional reaction would not usually lead to the protagonist killing himself rather than punishing his wife. In his suicide letter to Luma, Falih declares that when he saw her dancing in that enticing way he wanted to kill her then and there, but that he let her be and decided to kill himself instead. This last intention, which reflects a highly "different" reaction, is not convincingly discussed by the author.

Given the ideas and personality ascribed to him earlier by Jabra, it would have been more convincing if Falih had said that Luma's exuberance, her firm grip on life, and her passionate grasping of all the pleasures that affluence can bring, has confirmed for him the futility and emptiness of a life (in the upper echelons of Arab society) devoted to trivia and incapable of struggle—this being in fact how he had previously described their life. But Jabra fails us drastically here, relating the doctor's suicide not to this, but to his quasi-metaphysical reaction to the unrestrained passions of his wife and to the writhing beauty of her voluptuous body as it flaunts its temptations to the world.

Technically *The Ship* is not a tragedy; for a novel to be such, there should be a greater centralization of the tragic character, and a greater sense of the consequentiality of his or her life in the context of the work as a whole, so that the death is seen as *tragically* affecting the events. There is a sharp and overwhelming finality to tragedy. But Falih's death can only change the course of events for the better; it does not really touch the lives of other protagonists tragically. For all Luma's apparent anguish, the reader knows that the future is all in front of her, full of promise and possibilities; while, as for 'Assaf, Maha decides that life with him is her priority and the novel ends with their happy reunion in Naples.

Falih's suicide is interesting from another point of view, in that it involves the objective depiction of a character not only outside the author's personal life and experience, but also diametrically opposed to them. Jabra has a strong tendency to depict something of himself and, even more, something of what he would have liked to achieve, in his main characters. Wadi' 'Assaf in *The Ship*, Walid Masoud in *Search for Walid Masoud*, and Jamil Farran in *Hunters in a Narrow Street* are all three Palestinian like himself, and he depicts them as successful, urbane, energetic, sophisticated, passionate, captivating, engaging, and, above all, *having a strong grip on life*. They are never morose or acrimonious, never sullen or malevolent. Their anger and sorrow over the fate of their people turns into a positive determination to fight in one way or another. A Palestinian, who has a cause to fight and live for, a horizon to reach, and a battle with an external aggressor, is never depicted as a nihilist or a defeatist, and certainly not as self-destructive. These three protagonists, like Jabra himself, live in the Gulf area, somewhere between Baghdad and Kuwait, sharing exile from the same region in Palestine (Jerusalem or Bethlehem) and succeeding eventually in entering the upper echelons of society (in Baghdad or other parts of the Arab world). All three celebrate the Palestinian struggle for liberation and carry sharp personal memories of tragedies that have afflicted them as a result of this struggle (Farran's fiancé, 'Assaf's friend, and Masoud's son all die at some point in the Palestinian struggle for liberation). They also cling to a great dream: to return to their lost country, and reacquire land and roots there. All three carry within them deep Christian emotions, portrayed in glowing, highly sophisticated spiritual and intellectual terms, reflecting Jabra's lingering passion for the Christian philosophy acquired during his early upbringing. Finally, all three are passionate men strongly drawn to the other sex and, in some instances, as with Masoud, possessing an insatiable sensuality which is, nevertheless, highly sublimated.[76]

Falih can also demonstrate passion at times, as when he describes his first meeting with Emilia in his suicide letter to Luma in terms reminiscent of the passionate experiences of both Masoud and 'Assaf; but, unlike them, he finds this passion failing him in certain instances as he becomes victim to an existential nausea and despair. He bears the mark of a general spiritual fatigue, the fatigue of Arab intellectuals who feel utterly helpless to fight the internal, tyrannical, unenlightened systems of their own countries and have no hope of any remedy, in the foreseeable future, for the chaos and maladministration imposed on an Arab world that has suffered for centuries from all kinds of conspiracies against its freedom. In this kind of system struggle can be not only fatal—death has its nobility and its appeal for the fighter—but also stigmatized and made suspect. Falih suffers from an anomaly that freezes the impulse to struggle, an utter incapacity either to leap up and confront brutal authority or to deafen his ears to the abject rhetoric filling the world around him. And in his case nausea brings him to the verge of an intellectual and emotional deadlock.

The Ship is particularly important in this respect because of the radical, if implicit contrast it constantly points out between the personality of the Palestinian and that of other Arabs, the suicide at the end signalling the end of all quest, but *outside the world of the Palestinian*. Possibly Jabra did not think this out, but it is certain that he would never consciously have chosen a Palestinian to be a lost soul at breaking point, embodying the doubts, torments, and utter despair that Falih so fatefully demonstrates.

There is no space in this introduction for any prolonged discussion of Jabra's second major novel, *Search for Walid Masoud*. Suffice it to say that it is a magnificent edifice of style, ideas, patriotism, and erotic scenes, in which Jabra, for all the apparent sexual indulgence of the main protagonist, manages to ennoble passion and elevate the erotic. Like *The Ship, Search* is not without its flaws. Nonetheless, this complex and fascinating novelist conveys a sense of excitement and relish and provides a degree of intellectual and esthetic stimulus that lingers long in the reader's mind.

One of the most promising novelists now rising to prominence (he is also a poet) is Ibrahim Nasrallah, whose novel *Prairies of Fever* (1985)[77] represents a major experiment in modernist literature. The story revolves around the life of an Arab teacher working in one of the most isolated and remote outposts in Western Saudi Arabia (the kind of situation suffered by hundreds of such teachers). *Ustadh* Muhammad's story is one of deep alienation and extreme loneliness: he suffers from phobias, hallucinations, and nightmarish dreams and is totally exploited and victimized. The novel describes a backward place, completely lacking the essentials of modern life and dominated by taboos and hangovers from medieval times, where rigidly observed inherited mores and the blind machinery of the state combine to deprive the individual of the simplest requirements of normalcy. There is a disorienting absence of woman, who becomes an unattainable phantom, a vague, unrealizable dream. But the main achievement of this novel is the cohesive relationship between form and content, and the temporal parallelism of events, memories, and dreams. As in Kanafani, the desert constitutes a main feature of the novel, a force so strong that time becomes dislocated, running off in all directions, mingling the past with the future, while emphasizing the present that becomes a harrowing, unbearable chasm over which the sterile desert endlessly broods. This is a novel about the extreme anguish suffered by thousands of young people who, since the discovery of oil, have ventured into these still closed, remote desert lands of the Arabian Peninsula in search of subsistence. A unique creative endeavor, it flouts yet another of the more pervasive conventions of modern Arabic literature, which almost invariably preserves (often without consciously striving to this end) a constant relationship between author and audience that itself forms part of the creative process.[78] Nasrallah, in this novel, is one of the few authors to write without constantly taking into account an audience whose appreciation he seeks. With its nonlinear narrative technique and multidimensional perspective, this is a difficult novel whose logic and significance are not easily perceived on a first reading.

The appearance of a woman novelist on the West Bank, Sahar Khalifeh, has been a welcome event. No other Palestinian writer of fiction has equaled her capacity to reproduce the rhythms, intonations, vocabulary, and cast of mind of the Palestinian urban classes—menial workers and intellectuals alike—and she reveals great artistic decorum in the way she varies her language according to the status and education of the character she is delineating. Her descriptions of their lives in the area of Nablus (her own home town) where they usually live and interact is graphic and minutely faithful to reality, but also portrayed through an artistic medium that preserves the necessary economy and tension needed for the success of a work of art. She concentrates on two central issues: the Palestinian struggle and the feminist struggle, both for liberation. Between Habiby, with his description of the situation of Palestinians under Israeli rule inside Israel (particularly in his *Pessoptimist*) and Khalifeh, with her description of their living conditions following the Israeli occupation of the West Bank (particularly in her two novels, *Wild Thorns* [1976][79] and *The Sunflower* [1982]), the whole issue of the tortuous and beleaguered existence of Palestinians in their own country has been covered. Her best feminist work is her latest novel, *Memoirs of an Unrealistic Woman* (1986), which probes the issues of feminist aspirations and limitations, again employing a language that presents the particular platter of women's talk in her region, exposing cultural values that are internalized and reproduced; she demonstrates, particularly in *The Sunflower*, the symbiotic relationship between political and feminist struggle. She also shows great skill in depicting both those characters who must, by force of the circumstances around them, undergo a change in their attitudes, and those who represent immutable prototypes. In *Wild Thorns* Zuhdi and Usama respectively represent these two types.

Akram Hanniyeh is one of the more interesting writers among those deported from the occupied West Bank some years ago. A very original writer, he represents reality through symbol and fantasy. In "After the Siege, a Little Before the Sun," the story selected for this volume, the Aqsa Mosque, one of the holiest shrines in Islam, has disappeared, and the story details the reaction of many types of people to this imaginary event. In another story, "That Village, That Morning,"[80] a man who had died long before the establishment of the state of Israel wakes to discover how radically the world has since changed. The story recounts the anguish and bewilderment of an innocent discovery of the Arab/ Israeli situation; for the reader, it provides a searching rediscovery of the systematic aggression and coercion suffered by the Palestinians.

Mahmoud Shaheen is a fiction writer of great promise. From a bedouin background, he carries within his memory all the traditions of a rooted bedouin society. Both a novelist and a short story writer, he shows the tendency, also found in Jabra, to treat a whole mesh of tangled events and complex emotional situations within a single short story. His brilliant story, "Ordeal by Fire,"[81] is a panoply of customs, beliefs, and attitudes skillfully set against a background of intense individual and collective passions; it portrays a clash between deviant emotions and desires on the one hand and established mores and convictions on the other.

Opposed to the enticing voluptuousness of the lovely young wife of an ever-absent shepherd is the abiding virtue of the young man who attracts her, a faithful husband and father whose resistance eventually costs him his reputation and well-being. She lures one of her cousins to her bed, but they are surprised one evening by the sudden arrival of her husband, and it is then that she finds her opportunity for revenge against the virtuous 'Ali, screaming that the masked man seen hurriedly leaving her house that evening was 'Ali himself, come to force her. One of the most poignant scenes in the story shows her father-in-law, who knows she is lying, nevertheless succumbing to her seduction; while punishing her severely for what he knows in his heart has actually happened, he cannot restrain his own aroused desire and makes passionate love to her. 'Ali, however, is subjected to ordeal by fire, and is found guilty.

Thus, the completely predictable resistance of 'Ali, as a man who upholds tribal honor, to the almost irresistible seductiveness practiced on him by the sensual and love-starved young woman, is set against the deviant reaction of the father-in-law. The real poignancy of the story and its superior artistic quality lie in the fine detailing of events, and the sensitive delineation of the intricate psychological reactions of the various protagonists. The story is so packed with events that it could be made into a feature film of normal length; it is, therefore, not so much an inflated short story as an elliptical novel, dealing with an intrinsically explosive and complex situation, but demonstrating at the same time the compression and intensity of the short story.

Shaheen's short story "Sacred River," included in this volume, is another complex account of the reactions of this same Palestinian bedouin community that figures in so many of his stories of the Israeli occupation after the June War of 1967. A tragedy, it provides a poignant description of a life under siege, of a new, restricted experience utterly removed from the splendid freedom of those remnants of the old bedouin community still at liberty in many Arab countries east of the Mediterranean. In their proud isolation from the mundane preoccupations of a settled country and city people in the Arab world, these remnants have traditionally enjoyed a life free of fetishism, political intrigue, competitive ambitions, and the passionate quest for wealth and ownership; now, under Israeli rule, they have fallen sad victims to a new order that has intimidated them, robbed them of their once noble freedom, and corrupted some of their members.

Limitations of space preclude discussion of many more of Palestine's growing circle of fiction writers. Yahya Yakhlif's experimental work in the short story and the novel, although of an uneven standard, has produced some very sensitive writing; his story "That Rose of a

Woman" is an endearing portrayal of the relationship between a young boy and a lovely young woman who champions him and looks after him at his workplace, but who falls victim to injustice and the exploitation of her poverty, without, however, losing her dignity and her will to resist. Yakhlif is the first Palestinian writer to venture, to any real extent, beyond the immediate sphere of Palestinian politics and describe the horrendous reprisals practiced by repressive, fundamentalist regimes in some Arab countries towards those who rebel against them. In his well-known novel, *Najran at Zero Point* (1975), he gives a vivid and minute description, unique in modern Arabic literature, of the near-ritualistic beheading of a group of rebels in Najran.

One of the major characteristics of recent Palestinian literature, both in the diaspora and at home, is its lack of major involvement in the larger Arab scene, a situation that has tended to become ever more marked with the years (this was not the case in the fifties and sixties, when Palestinian poets in particular reacted to the larger Arab situation as strongly as to the Palestinian experience).[82] This estrangement is especially pronounced in relation to the Gulf countries, where Palestinians, together with other Arab nationals, went as teachers and to build the infrastructure of the newly rich states awoken, by the advent of oil, to modern times.[83]

With the aggravation of the national dilemma following the June War of 1967, Palestinian literature tended to become more and more introverted. However, those diaspora writers living in such countries as Iraq and Lebanon have always found greater affinities with the Arab scene there: Jabra's novels, for example, portray a cross-section of Arab intellectuals from Lebanon and Iraq; in her lovely three part collection, *A Balcony over the Fakihani* (1983), Liyana Badr portrays a Tunisian revolutionary living in Beirut and fighting and dying for the Palestinian cause;[84] and Rashad Abu Shawar, in his memoirs of the Israeli invasion of 1982 entitled *O Beirut!* (1983), introduces personalities from various Arab and non-Arab countries. These works involve a general identification with others, not simply with nationalities, and it is clear that Palestinian writers will identify with the revolutionaries, the poor, the exiles, and, as in Jabra's work, the intellectuals. However, even though so many Palestinian writers lived and worked in the Gulf countries for so many years, there is no identification with the nationals of these newly rich countries and the pictures given of life in the Gulf have been consistently negative. The few writers who have included protagonists from the region have depicted them as culturally lagging behind their other characters; we find this, for example, in Nasrallah's *Prairies of Fever* where the main character is surrounded by a world of ignorance, cruelty, and backwardness, and, again, in Yakhlif's *Najran at Zero Point*.

Another interesting point to emerge from a close reading of diaspora literature is that there is very little attachment to the new places where the Palestinian has been territorialized. There does not seem to be any hope, in this literature, that Palestinians will be truly reterritorialized anywhere outside their own country. A poet, Maryam Qasim al-Sa'd, who lives in the United States, reflects a state of perpetual longing for her roots. In her short poem, "Vision," she says:

> Years pass and
> the waiting continues
> Unwavering faith remains
> a halo illuminating generations
> The vision stays alive.[85]

Beirut, Sidon, Tyre, and the rest of the South of Lebanon may be the exception, for they are often mentioned affectionately. But the mention of Amman, for example, where the civil war of September 1970 (Black September) took place, immediately conjures up traumatic experiences. Neither Cairo, Baghdad, nor Damascus are the subject of any really positive allusions in this literature.

It is relevant here to speak about the attitude of Palestinian writers toward the city generally. "The city" has been a prominent theme in modern Arabic literature, especially in poetry, and it is the negative aspects that have been particularly stressed. It is not possible to go into the details of this rich subject here, but the theme has been a part of the modernist direction ever since al-Sayyab poured out his invective against the city in the fifties, describing its streets as "coils of mud [which] bite into my heart," and moaning: "my right hand: no claw to fight with on the streets of the city . . . no grip to raise up life from the clay."[86] The city here is a solid wall that cannot be penetrated, a labyrinth where the poet is lost. Other poets have seen in it a place of corruption and menace, of social squalor and political complicity. It is cactus land, a mill, a wilderness, a bottomless sewer where the alienation of the poet is complete. This has been one of the best treated themes in Arab modernist poetry, with the personal experience of the poet at large in the forbidding city becoming merged with the communal experience of seeking a deeper interpretation of the clash between city and country.

The one exception to this attitude is found in Palestinian literature. The Palestinian city is never a Thamud, a Sodom, a Gomorrah, never a source of menace or a repository of sordidness and corruption; it is, rather, a victim city. No alienation is ever experienced in it; it is portrayed either as besieged and occupied by usurpers, or as lost to its own people—and there can be no alienation in such situations. The terror connected with the Palestinian city is an "external" terror inflicted on it, not by its own people as in other Arab cities, but by alien forces of aggression. And it is not only a victim city, but also a place of heroism, a bed of resistance, a home for patriotic struggle. In one of his poems Rashid Husain (1936–1977) has the Hour of Resistance strike in the City of Jerusalem, announcing the birth of truth.[87] Samih al-Qasim describes how

> At the corner of the street
> at the outskirts of town
> the children of long histories
> were gathering books,
> picture frames, and tent pegs,
> to build a barricade
> block the path of Darkness.[88]

This is not the city of defeat that haunts the rest of Arabic poetry, but the city of resistance after the defeat, which has, in the words of Mahmoud Darwish, "burst with anemones." He exclaims,

> Stare fully in the face of defeat,
> Oh noble City of ours!
> The cement of your streets has acquired a pulse now
> and every arch a braid.[89]

Darwish sees not only in his own city, but in Beirut too, the last stronghold, the last remaining anchorage for a people denied the shelter of their own city. And Jabra, after his initial attack on the city in his short stories, described above, portrays Jerusalem in his novels as a city of great beauty and desirability; nor does he see other Arab cities like Beirut and Baghdad as places of alienation.

Expatriate Palestinian literature displays a very heightened sense of place, an attachment often set in contrast to scenes from exile. As the writers focus on the reappropriation of a fixed place—their own villages or towns—they do so against the moving background of exile, afloat in a world that is often hostile. One sees, in this literature, a constant image of space, open and dangerous, through which the poet forever moves towards a confined place of anchorage and final settlement. This again conjures up glimpses from classical Arabic poetry, where endless stretches of desert, depicted by the poet in vivid and awe-inspiring terms as open and dangerous, full of treachery, drenched in the scalding heat of the sun, lead on to a desired destination. These stretches of desert land are now compared to the diaspora, where the exiled Palestinian has to carve out an existence for himself or herself while awaiting return to the small fixed spot on the map; between the two lie the horrors and terrors of the arduous journey across the wilderness.

And because of a constant but consistently mobile exile, new images appear in poetry, evoking the placelessness of the Palestinian. Darwish describes this state of existence/nonexistence in the most telling terms:

> I give my picture to my lady:
> "Hang it up, if I die, hang it up on the wall."
> "Is there a wall for it?" she asks.
> "We will build a room."
> "Where, in what house?"
> "We will build a house for it."
> "On what spot of exile?"[90]

For the Palestinian in his post–1982 poetry—the poetry, that is, written after the Israeli invasion of Lebanon and the Palestinian exodus from Beirut—place narrows frighteningly, so that, in Darwish's words, "we have to dismember ourselves to pass." A strangled state of being is portrayed in Darwish's poetry, and also in that of Zakariyya Muhammad, Mureed Barghouthy, 'Abd al-Latif 'Aql, and others. The Palestinian people are portrayed crowding airports, looking in vain for a small place to consummate a marriage, travelling endlessly in caravans with their children and bundles of clothes, dying without seeing their loved ones, suffering the loneliness, desolation, and torturing heat to carve out a living in some country of exile.

Poetry After 1967

The contemporary Palestinian literary scene boasts a profusion of poets. Despite the steady development of Palestinian fiction in all three regions where Palestinians live—the Occupied Territories, Israel proper, and the vast, sprawling world of the diaspora—and for all the peaks of achievement attained by some specific works, fiction has been unable to keep abreast of events taking shape in poetry. Both in quantity and quality, Palestinian poetry of the eighties reached levels never approached before. However, this eventual success came only after a period of many failed endeavors in the seventies, on the part of scores of poets. Even the great achievement of Mahmoud Darwish, which came to full bloom in the seventies, was unable, for all its riches and artistic value, to alleviate the situation of much Palestinian (and, in fact, of much Arabic) poetry of the time. Between the achievement of poets in the fifties and sixties and that of the poets of the eighties, Palestinian poetry passed through a dishevelled phase, venturing on an experiment which was as all-pervading as it was breathlessly hectic. Many poets appeared on the scene in the seventies, only to disappear thereafter, or to survive merely on the strength of their patriotic statements. This situation merits further elucidation.

There are two major points to consider when discussing the poetry of the seventies; the first involving the esthetics of the poem and the second its semantics. The first is the great adventure in language and metaphor on which the whole of Arabic poetry (including Palestinian poetry) embarked in that period. There was a metaphorical exploration in Arabic poetry unprecedented in its long history, even in the very sophisticated experiments carried out by both Abbasid and Andalusi poets in medieval times; the leader in this venture was the Syrian poet Adunis who, at the start of the sixties, exploded the potential power of the image and produced luminous and complex metaphors in which the relationship between the image and its object was often remote. He also insisted on originality, sought strangeness, and displayed great skill in culling metaphors from all areas of life. The experiment became a focal point for many younger poets and proved to be highly infectious. Improvization in language and metaphor often became an end in itself. At its best, this was an oblique and distilled experiment, one which veered away from visible forms around the poet and in which metaphors were esthetic necessities that corresponded with the poet's own vision. Thus was ushered in an era of high esthetic self-consciousness, characterized by a very high degree of deliberate mannerism. These markedly modernist features apply more distinctly to the visual arts, but would appear in poetry in the highly adventurous treatment of the metaphor, where the image does not aim to represent reality but is crystallized and realized in its own form and for its own sake. This differs from the conventional use of metaphor in realistic literature, where it was either an ornament or a means of enhancing the direct semantic intention of the poem.

What made it possible for this adventure to take off was that the poetry of the sixties, the heir to so many varied experiments during the previous six decades, from neoclassicism, through romanticism to symbolism, neorealism, and some attempts at surrealism, proved to have acquired sufficient elasticity to accommodate the new venture. Whether really successful or not, poets were now able to mold the material in question and to play with language and metaphor with little resistance either from the poetic tools themselves, which had clearly become highly malleable, or from any conscious reverence for inherited poetic principles and methods, which had now become shaken. The experiment was also greatly helped by the fact that Adunis's own language had, for all its fresh and inventive vocabulary, retained strong classical affinities, preserving the resonance, the sublimity, and the *rhétorique profonde* of the old poetic diction; and in fact, for all the prevailing mood of rejection, a residual attachment to linguistic sublimity and elevation did linger on, so that neither poets and critics on the one hand, nor more enlightened readers on the other (the complexity of the work was an obstacle to the ordinary reader), felt that poetry had been totally torn from its roots—as they must, for example, have felt with the poetry of Salah 'Abd al-Sabur and its often conversational tone and lackluster, even slangy language.

Moreover, as has been mentioned above, Adunis began, at the outset of the seventies, to preach the doctrine of modernity, which proved very attractive to contemporary Arab poets. There is no doubt whatsoever (again as noted above) that the adventure in language and metaphor that Adunis introduced, together with his will to destroy and his call to poets to abandon the old concepts and style of poetry, were all genuine modernist features. However, at the risk of repeating myself here, I would reiterate that any truly worthwhile movement of modernity in the Arab world should have emphasized a transformation in the *Weltanschauung* of modern Arab poets, parallel to the esthetic revolution in form, diction, and metaphor. There was also a great need for a change both in tone and in the concept the poet had of him or her self. For all the attempts to discover a new language for poetry, much poetic diction, particularly that of such pioneer poets of the fifties as Adunis and Khalil Hawi, did not cease to be, in Richard Sheppard's words, "the tool for asserting human lordship."[91] Many of these poets remained, in their own eyes, heroic and liberating saviors who could stand outside society and judge it as if they were not themselves the product of the time they deplored. Stephen Spender gives an apt description of these kinds of poets, saying they embodied the "Voltairean

I," i.e., "the confidence that they stood outside a world of injustices and irrationality which they judged clearly ," whereas the genuine modern "I" is acted upon by events outside the poets themselves, who, even as they indict and struggle against their era, realize that they have its destructive forces in them.[92] Hence, modernity at the hands of the former was only half achieved.

This situation of only partial modernity was nourished by the second highly influential factor for the development of contemporary Palestinian poetry in the seventies, namely, the rise of the Palestinian resistance. Resistance poetry had been part of modern Arabic poetry since the turn of the century, and, with the exception of the early symbolists and of some (though only some) romantics of the twenties and thirties, there was no major poet who did not add his or her voice to the refrain of protest and rejection. However, "resistance," which was one of the important themes of Palestinian poetry in the fifties, became *the* major theme in the seventies.

This was due, first, to the welcome discovery in the second half of the sixties (discussed above) of the existence of a strong, ongoing movement of resistance poetry by Palestinian poets inside Israel, whose tones of noble defiance and patient endurance helped restore the spirit of an Arab world that felt betrayed following the 1967 defeat. A telling example is the poetic exchange between Fadwa Tuqan and Mahmoud Darwish. After the lifting of border restrictions following Israel's occupation of the rest of Palestine in the June War of 1967, Fadwa Tuqan crossed over to Israel, met with the Palestinian poets there, then wrote to them a highly charged poem in which sorrow and faith were mixed. And in one of his finest poems before he left Israel to live in the Arab world, Darwish wrote, addressing Fadwa:

> Needs no reminding: Mount Carmel is within us
> On our eyelashes Galilee's dust is blown
> Do not say, "I would run to her like a river!"
> Our country is flesh of our flesh, bone of our bone.
>
> Before this June we were not nestling doves
> Among the chains love did not crumble away
> Sister, for twenty years we had no time
> for writing verses, we were in the fray.[93]

Second, this mood was cemented by the specific rise of the Palestinian resistance at the end of the sixties, which, following a period of numb disbelief and angry rejection of all the ramparts of Arab society, brought in new hope and faith. Palestinian poets, wherever they were, found great catharsis in the reiteration of resistance themes that expressed a determined belief in the outcome of the struggle and in the necessity of standing up for usurped rights.

Most other themes then disappeared from Palestinian poetry. The mood of the seventies needed this therapeutic focus, particularly after the 1970 Civil War in Jordan, which brought death to thousands of Palestinian fighters and civilians and resulted in the expulsion of the resistance from that country. On the artistic level, however, this near-total preoccupation with the theme of resistance was bound to present complications. One was the danger of poetry falling victim to mere repetition with respect to a subject matter (resistance, redemption, self-sacrifice, adulation of heroism, and noble endurance) that, by its very nature, had little scope for expansion and innovation[94]—such a danger being particularly great in view of the unprecedented number of Palestinian poets now emerging all over the Arab world. As a reaction to this, poets instinctively concentrated on being original, if not in subject matter then in their use of metaphor and diction. No period of Arabic poetry had ever known such an impetuous diligence, such a craving to cull so many rarefied images in the same poem. Thousands of images were coined, chiseled out of the imaginations of scores of poets, Palestinian and others; no realm was left unexplored, as the whole of nature, the whole of history, the whole of life itself was summoned to help devise complex metaphors. However, this great artistic audacity was not always responsible or artistically successful, and many of the images were contrived, inapt, and often totally erroneous or at least totally redundant. The compulsive tendency, in many of these metaphors, to the alienation of the image from its referent (i.e., with the two sides being remote from one another) was often an added complication.

All this ushered in many problems. First, not every poet is an instinctive image maker, able to pack lines successfully with metaphors; whereas Adunis, influenced by major French poets and himself a poet of great skill, succeeded brilliantly most of the time, many of the younger venturers failed lamentably to realize the inner logic that all good metaphors, even those that shun external logic, must have. Poets vary in their dependence on particular poetic tools. Moreover, the creation of images can never be so totally *conscious*. No matter how determined a poet may be, on the conscious level, to seek out new and original images, there is always something unconscious in the process of creating a good image, something illuminated by an inner meta-

phorical apprehension that good poets instinctively possess. Second—
and this is even more crucial—the attempt to combine the communal
theme of resistance, aimed at a wide audience, with this kind of difficult,
complex metaphorical representation brought utter chaos in its wake.
If these two strange bedfellows seemed to fare well together in the case
of some poets, such as Mahmoud Darwish (certainly one of the greatest
modern Arab poets), the experiment was a disaster for most, and critics
and writers began to speak of "the crisis of contemporary Arabic poetry," without, however, offering any new theories or guidelines to
remedy the apparently hopeless situation. Darwish himself protested
against this particular situation, saying, "The abstractions of this poetry
have become so rampant that it has turned into a nonpoetic phenomenon where parasitical creations devour the essence."[95]

There was no way, moreover, for tone in poetry to come down from
the high pitch that themes of anger, frustration, and heroic resistance
naturally induce. Nor could the poets' vision, focused as it was on the
notion of heroic grandeur and on celebrating an enduring challenge
to injustice, allow them to see, in their own lives and in the lives of
those around them, the disintegrated and humiliated existence of men
and women rendered gratuitous victims to coercive regimes. As citizens
poets knew well enough that terror and suffering determined their own
and other people's destinies, making them all, together, the victims
and not the heroes of their times; as poets they ignored this. Poetry in
the immediate aftermath of 1967 had to wage its own battle of resistance, to stand on the side of the self-sacrificing hero who does not
admit defeat, and the popular spirit of the period demanded the continuity of such a stance in poetry. Poets in general had not yet discovered (as the generation of the eighties later did) that standing up for
justice and freedom, itself a heroic stance at any time and in any place,
does not necessarily entail explicit heroics or a need for the poet, in
his or her quest for what is right, to assert his or her own role as leader,
sage, and prophet. All the heroic motifs, inherited from centuries of
adulation of brave champions and national redeemers, and the resounding tones of bravado and defiance that pervaded the poet's work, delayed the process of modernization.

It is necessary to consider these general problems in an introduction
to Palestinian literature, first because a great many Palestinian poets fell
into these traps, and second, because the problem was created, in part,
by the Palestinian dilemma itself, which caused other kinds of conventional subject-matter to be regarded as almost heretical and imposed

on poetry the dominant theme of resistance, which was in essence a Palestinian theme. This period challenges several generally accepted theories. First Buffon's famous dictum "Le style est l'homme même" is conclusively defied here. Not only does it become impossible to distinguish the style of one poet from another, but even to tell to which Arab country a certain poem belongs: all linguistic and stylistic categories became virtually identical—a happy indication, indeed, of the basic unity of Arabic culture, but hardly a healthy direction for poetry. Next, Puttenham's suggestion that "men do choose their subjects according to the metal of their minds" is similarly rejected, for surely this vast number of poets writing in the same vein could not all have the same basic "metal" of mind. Third, the idea that style is not detachable from content has also been challenged, for there is often very little affinity between the main subject matter, i.e., the popular resistance theme, and the complex, highly symbolic style in which poetry was written. One felt that many words, phrases, and passages were not a spontaneous part of a unified whole, but an arbitrary, inchoate implant.

The seventies seem to us now like a battleground where Palestinian and other Arab poets were competing with each other in ever greater audacity and inventiveness, and falling in their dozens along the way. There was something of a taste for the grotesque, for the greatly heightened, and a feverish, haunted atmosphere dominated. It must be emphasized, though, that we are not dealing with a multitude of mere pseudopoets; many among them were, unquestionably, highly gifted poets who wanted nothing more than to write good poetry. I have outlined above some of the factors that drew them to this experimentation—the attraction to ideas on modernity; the fascination with the new; the birth of a new will to experiment; a strong surge of rejection vis-à-vis inherited modes and patterns; the superior output of some poets among the generation of the pioneers—all coupled with a lack of good, healthy, insightful criticism. From the early seventies on, the Arab literary scene came to be divided into camps that transcended geographical boundaries and rather rallied around certain poets or certain poetic styles, so much so that the literary pages of dailies and monthlies all over the Arab world began to contain sharp invective against what writers described as the abhorrent domination of "literary cliques," groups that seemed to be, on account of their vociferous support for each other, rightly or wrongly, most effective and constantly visible in the public domain, and not only within the Arab world. Much criticism started to be written, in Arabic, English, and French, for or against particular experiments, both in poetry and prose, but there was very little attempt at supplying literature with a well-informed critical treatment that aimed to guide poets and point out their errors in a mood of sincerity and reverence for good art. It should be emphasized that, where such errors did occur, they sprang from a sense of public duty and were committed in the cause of necessary innovation. There were, undoubtedly, many talents lost to poetry, but quite a few of these poets were, most happily, able to reassert their artistic integrity and emerge armed with new skills enabling them to reestablish their control over their poetic tools.

However, the frenzied experiments of the seventies were destined to end suddenly and unexpectedly. Poetry, like all art, has its strange and unpredictable equations. The Arab world of the seventies was brimming with creative talent and with an artistic curiosity fed by contact with numerous and widespread poetic experiments worldwide; and in such an environment some positive outcome was inevitable eventually. It was as if an inner dynamism in the poetic art of the period wrenched it free from chaos and misdirection and into a clearer air. The very pervasiveness of the decade's heated experiments was leading poetry to the point of esthetic fatigue, and this point was reached in the early eighties when poetry had finally exhausted all its technical resources and endless repetition and similarity had led to a stalemate. It became, quite simply, impossible for poets to go on as they had been doing; what had started as a genuine, heartfelt departure had become a fashion, and fashions have a genius for disappearing suddenly, leaving little memory behind them. Just as in the mid-sixties serious poets could no longer use the fertility myths so fashionable in the late fifties, so by the end of the seventies the new thematic and metaphorical fashions suddenly lost their allure. Meanwhile, the poets themselves, as a result of the unrelenting competitive experimentation of the seventies, had finally come to feel masters of their poetic tools. Other dynamics were also unconsciously at work. If some continuities persisted, there were also many final ruptures, particularly with established linguistic and metaphorical patterns. There was a craving, in the words of the committed young Palestinian poet Ghassan Zaqtan (b. 1954), for "a new corner from which to look" at the poet's surroundings, and there was born, in Palestinian and other Arab poets alike, the will to "destroy heroism . . . as one destroys a rotten egg, together with valor, sorrow, love, chivalry, and all the other dinosaurs."[96]

By the eighties, then, a great spiritual fatigue had come to reign over the poet's world. The stamp of authority had never been heavier, the internal political order never more coercive, external aggression and global conspiracy never more intense. It became impossible to endure the repeated national disasters with the same kind of bravado, and the situation drove many men and women into either silence or exile. But certain things endured: a literary creativity sharpened to its highest point, a faith in the creative power of words, and a great pride in a newly achieved artistic independence from the immediate past.

Poetry was quickly able to rid itself of the negative aspects of the seventies while at the same time retaining the audacity that had characterized the decade and the firm break with a number of traditional features. New poets now came upon the scene, writing a different kind of poetry; but, as said above, some poets who, for better or for worse, had made a name for themselves in the seventies, succeeded in shaking themselves free from the decade's negative tendencies and now armed themselves with modernist tools. Three major examples of the latter may be found among the Palestinians: Khairi Mansour (b. 1945); Mureed Barghouthy (b. 1944); and Ahmad Dahbour (b. 1946). After publishing several volumes of poetry steeped in heroic motifs and the spirit of bravado (the first two especially—Dahbour always kept some kind of balance), these poets reemerged with different voices in the eighties. What must have happened to them, as to a number of others like them, was an unconscious fermentation within their creativity as poets. And no sooner had esthetic fatigue set in, in the poetry of the time, than these poets came into their own.

The new poets had several splendid and mature experiments in Arabic poetry from which to learn. The pioneer poets of the fifties—such as Adunis (whose effect, as we have seen, was both positive and negative), Badr Shakir al-Sayyab (1926–1964), Khalil Hawi (1925–1982), ʿAbd al-Wahhab al-Bayyati (b. 1926), and above all, Salah ʿAbd al-Sabur (1931–1981) and Muhammad al-Maghut (b. 1934)—continued to exert their influence. And now, too, poets of a younger generation were becoming very influential, most notably Saadi Yusuf (b. 1943) and Mahmoud Darwish (b. 1942).

Of all these, the greatest "godfather" of the poetry of the eighties was Saadi Yusuf, indeed a poet of our times; it is his work, undoubtedly, which lays the firmest foundation for the present-day modernist experiment. Mingling simplicity with sophistication, directness with obliquity, inventive imagery with simple language, and a stifled anger with the "low" tones of the modernist poet, he is magnificently free of sentimentality and false heroics. His stance is a fundamentally tragic one, reflecting a disintegrated world whose heroes are fallen heroes and whose victims are the helpless millions of the Arab world, among whom the poet himself is to be found; yet it is a vision resorting, often, to the tragic/ironic mode to delineate human experience. What is also very important about Saadi Yusuf's experiment is that—unlike other successful avant-garde poets before the eighties such as Darwish and 'Abd al-Sabur, who spoke of great universals (the latter particularly; Darwish, whose genius never stopped developing, did concentrate a little more on the ordinary individual in the eighties)—Yusuf portrayed the little things in life, the small everyday experiences of ordinary human beings who live and toil and suffer from the evil assailing their world just as do the heroes and fighters heretofore so loudly extolled in poetry. Yusuf proclaimed the birth of the "little" man in Arabic poetry; and, in the context of a poetry used for centuries to celebrate the great, the magnanimous, and the mighty, this was a major step forward towards a true climate of modernity.

What is important here is that the new sensibility was not simply demonstrated by the less politically involved poets of the Arab world but also by those poets whose lives were most bound up with the socio-political dilemmas of their age: the Palestinians, and also the Lebanese, the Iraqis, the Syrians, the Yemenis, and others in North Africa and Egypt. As for the rich Gulf region, (an area of the Arab world generally insensitive, in many other ways, to the real predicaments of contemporary Arab life) it is when a poet joins the dissident poets of the Arab world, sharing their rejection of rigid institutions and autocratic rule, that his or her poetry (the Gulf region boasts several avant-garde women poets) undergoes a serious process of modernization (the proestablishment poets in this region still, it must be said, continue to write within the conservative tradition). All over the Arab world new voices are rising, speaking with a different accent, looking at the world with different eyes; and wherever one goes in the dispersed world of Palestinian exile, there is at least one Palestinian poet helping to create the new principles of a modern art. Never before has Palestinian creative talent produced such a rich harvest.

The amazing thing is that these dramatic changes have taken shape silently and unassumingly, without the help of theories and polemics. No manifestos were offered, no forced, narrowly particularized proclamations of how art, poetic diction, and other artistic aspects should be.

This is how we have come to possess such a splendid diaspora poet as Waleed Khazindar (b. 1950), one of the finest poets of the younger generation and probably of modern Arabic letters as a whole, whose rigorous economy of style is unsurpassed by his contemporaries, whose metaphorical representations are both precise and highly complex, whose gemlike choice of words is selective yet smoothly natural—sometimes almost colloquial—and whose dynamic variation of theme is informed by great delicacy and a sensitivity too refined to allow any place for the loud, emphatic depictions of life found in earlier poetry. Khazindar's thematic approach is as personal as it is collective, as Palestinian as it is universal; he is one of the outstandingly promising Palestinian poets of the late twentieth century.

Then, too, we have Ghassan Zaqtan (b. 1954), with his deep personal feeling for the tragedy of others, his luminous vocabulary, his elevation of homely experience to sophisticated poetic heights, and his original selection of themes culled from the life of simple people around him but yet made memorably universal. We have Zakariyya Muhammad (b. 1951), who, above all others, has more radically broken with the old heroic stance, the stance of the poet as hero and liberator shouldering great national responsibilities. Instead we find a new, ironic, self-critical poetry:

> I cannot . . . materialize as a prince that rides
> the crest of the waves.
> I am a palm tree that's heavily bent.
> All eyes, yes, all eyes have rebuked me.[97]

He writes a poetry that is confessional, intimate, almost self-deprecating, but weighted, nevertheless, with the great collective consciousness of his people. He mourns, ceaselessly but in the quietest of tones, the passage of Palestinians from one tragedy to the next and from one exile to the next; his latest poetry trembles with the tragic but totally unsentimental voice of a poet who has reached the end of his endurance and finally realized how the world around the Palestinian has completed its conspiracy.

There are numerous others: Ibrahim Nasrallah (b. 1954), as fine a poet as he is a novelist; Yusuf ʿAbd al-ʿAziz (b. 1956), a devoted patriot, but dedicated, too, to the quest for a personal happiness that endlessly eludes the Palestinian; Rasim al-Madhoun (b. 1947), with his unforgettably sensitive portrayal of family love and his representation of the constant, heartbreaking loneliness of exile; and Taher Riyad (b. 1956), with the classical purity and strength of his diction, his terseness and complex symbolization, and his profound sense of spatial and temporal categories and of how people are affected by the passage of time. There are too many to name them all here.

The already-mentioned dramatic change in the poetry of Mansour, Dahbour, and Barghouthy reflects the enigmatic nature of esthetic integrity and resistance. Dahbour, like Mansour and Barghouthy, is a verse poet, but he has, more than any other poet of his generation, shown a predilection for formal experimentation, opening up the potential of conventional metrics and using them to very unconventional poetic effect. Dedicating his official services to the Palestinian revolution probably meant a partial suppression of his very refined sensibility[98] in the interests of a more direct political address—but only a partial one, for his poetry pulses with a profound, almost instinctive apprehension of the universal significance behind the pathetic and the tragic in contemporary Palestinian life.

Mureed Barghouthy's superior experiment of the eighties stems from a new attitude towards both technique and the apprehension of contemporary experience in the Arab world. Gone are the loud exclamations of tragic protest and the articulations of anger, invective, and bravado, to be replaced by a sophisticated urbanity expressed sometimes in a quietly tragic manner, and sometimes, as he inveighs against the internal and external political orders, in a subtle, ironic tone that is quite distinctive. Thus the guards of the king in his poem "The Guards" are themselves kings with kingdoms and majesty, while the tribal members in "The Tribes" vie with each other in sexual prowess and material possessions. The Mona Lisa is hung on the velvet-covered walls of their tents, facing a tablet with inscriptions to ward off the evil eye and alongside the diploma of a son, framed in gold and covered with dust! The poem ends by noting that

> Our tribes retain their charm
> Now that the tribes are out of date.[99]

Mention should also be made of Muhammad al-As'ad (b. 1944) who has scrupulously shunned all the pulls and pitfalls of poetic fashion,[100] remaining loyal to a self-contained, highly controlled form of expression. He is a poet of great artistic integrity and is the possessor of an unfaltering poetic instinct that enabled him to sustain his own lucid vision through the frenzied period of the seventies and to preserve linguistic and metaphorical frontiers solidly closed to gibberish and false adventurism. Al-As'ad's poetry, marked by a sophisticated urbanity and a language as fresh as it is natural, strikingly attests to the way art works in the creative instinct of certain individuals. For some poets the domain of art is well defined, its frontiers instinctively recognized; yet it is also a very fragile domain, whose integrity, as we have seen, can be violated instantly if a poet shows signs of responding to the loud call of direct socio-political commitment. No poet, it should be said at once, is more committed than al-As'ad: the very nature of his sensibility stems from the fact of constant exile and sustained injustice, and from the curtailment of potential that his Palestinian nationality implies. At the same time, however, his work is striking proof that poetic technique does not necessarily derive from thematic involvement, but stems rather from the poet's own artistic and attitudinal makeup and from the extent to which his or her sensibility will either resist or succumb to the spuriously attractive artistic compromises of the age. All through the period of frenzy al-As'ad, with his refined urbanity and artistic restraint, quietly rejected the "legitimate" social expectations of the period and continued developing his art.

The particular urbane tone of his poetry does not reflect anything in his simple upbringing. He came originally from a village in Palestine, which he left when four years old, growing up thereafter in a refugee camp in the south of Lebanon; his memoirs give us secondhand memories of his childhood and of the exodus, as collected from the accounts of older members of his family. In such a camp he was neither in touch with an agricultural nor with a strictly urban environment, but rather hovered between many kinds of environments, none of them likely, one would have thought, to produce the distinctive urbanity characterizing his poetry. The forces at work in the creativity of this and other poets are many and not always explicable.

The Rise of Mahmoud Darwish   In a field of teeming poetic talent, Mahmoud Darwish stands apart, shining with a curious creative power; a poet of our times and of all times. One wonders, as one contemplates his work, whether his special situation as poet-spokesman of his people, committed to the Palestinian cause to the exclusion, almost, of all other poetic concerns, has been his bane as a poet or his road to ascendency. Has the strict confinement of his theme denied him, and Arabic poetry generally, the versatility and unbounded possibilities inherent in his poetic genius, or has he rather been able to demonstrate that, even within these limits—as enduring as the Palestine tragedy itself, and, like it, penetrating every aspect of experience—his creativity could wander freely, with ever-renewed originality and addressing itself to an ever-growing world audience?

The eventful nature of Palestinian political life since Darwish began his poetic career in the sixties has allowed Palestinian political poetry certain variations on the theme. Punctuated by tragedies and disasters and pervaded by a constant quest for a solution to a dilemma growing ever deeper and ever more intractable, recent Palestinian history dictates a changing role for the hero and calls, generally, for a different means of handling the situation; and Darwish's poetry, more than that of any other in the generation between the pioneers of the fifties and the poets of the eighties, mirrors this changing role. What remains constant in his verse, however, is a pervasive suffering as personal as it is communal, vindicating Camus' statement that in a revolution suffering is a collective experience ("I rebel, therefore we exist"). Yet for all the very personal voice in his poetry—unique and, in a special way, solitary—only rarely do motifs from his personal life creep in.[101] His imagination may often be ablaze with originality, but most of the time he remains in control of his art; while sensing a personal satisfaction with his role as poet one also feels he is permanently undermined and often distraught by the Palestinian situation. Whatever a poet does or fails to do on the personal level is irrelevant if he shoulders, as a poet, his or her full collective responsibility in a time of revolution. And Darwish succeeds (where many poets of the pioneer generation would have failed) in remaining inside the disintegrated world of the Palestinian and being a unifying factor not only on the political level but also, more importantly, on the cultural level. The Palestinian enclave hems him in with the others; like them, he remains somewhere on the borderline of hero and victim.

Palestinian society at home or in exile is basically a tragic one, and it is impossible for a literature mirroring the experience of a people in a constant state of siege to avoid a tragic apprehension of experience, even if this is sometimes mixed with the comic or the ironic. Yet, as said above, a great dignity pervades this literature, a resistance to annihilation, to drowning in one's own blood; and Darwish (like many other Palestinian poets and writers of fiction and personal accounts) has been vociferous in asserting this dignity. His poetry mingles agony and ecstasy, pride and despair, heroic resistance and recognition of the dominating evil that foils heroism so that the victim lurks beneath the hero's garb. Since the Tel al-Zaatar massacre of 1976,[102] when several thousand Palestinians were killed by Lebanese Phalangist forces, and the sequence of catastrophes befalling the Palestinians thereafter—the Israeli invasion of Lebanon in the summer of 1982 that targeted the Palestinian resistance, the resultant exodus of thousands of Palestinians from Beirut, and the Sabra and Shatila massacre, again by the Lebanese Phalangists in 1982—his voice has been tinged with the proud sorrow of a poet who knows that courage, the abiding will to fight for freedom and justice, and the readiness to redeem the cause with one's life are no longer enough to assure the triumph of the hero in a world dominated by technological superiority and global power politics.

In his poem "Ahmad Zaatar," on the plight of the Palestinians following the Tel al-Zaatar massacre, the subtle mixture of hero/victim motifs appears clearly for the first time in Darwish's poetry, together with an overriding feeling of compassion that will become a constant thereafter—compassion of a sophisticated kind, mixing tenderness with pride, and pain with tenacity and resolve. It is a dignified kind of compassion, focused upon the multitude among whom the poet himself is to be found. Yet there is absolutely no self-pity in either the personal or the collective sense; for this would vitiate the nobility and justice of the struggle; it would mean negating the spontaneity and gratuitous nature of the sacrifice and cringing before the uncompromising responsibility of resisting injustice. In his elegy on Izziddin al-Qalaq, assassinated in Paris in the seventies, the hero recognizes his imminent demise, yet shrugs his shoulders, cracks a joke and continues on his way:

> Every time he came to me he would laugh as he said goodbye.
> He would see me in his funeral
> and peer out of the coffin:
> Now do you believe they kill without reason?
> I said: Who are they?
> He said: The ones, seeing a dream,
> prepare the grave for it, the flowers and the tombstone.[103]

Darwish's heroic victims may let out a moan at the hour of death, but they will persist in defending the rights and honor of their people, entering, in Raymond Williams' words, "the heroic deadlock in which men die still struggling to climb."[104]

The universal quality of Darwish's poetry (and prose) stems primarily from his abhorrence of ideology—a precondition, indeed, for all great poetry. At the center of his work is not the "ideology" of the Palestinian struggle, but its tragic necessity, the inevitable need to stand defiantly against the radical disorder that has assailed the lives of Palestinians everywhere.

Darwish has benefited enormously from the metaphorical revolution of the sixties and seventies, the change probably being reflected more in his work than in that of any other poet. The urge to untrammeled inventiveness in the seventies spurred his fertile imagination to new-found freedom; there are moments, indeed, when he seems carried away, and, losing some of his control over the metaphorical representations in the poem, produces a careless image here and there. Such occurrences are, however, rare. Usually, his images are luminous and memorable (how can one forget "Earth scrapes us, pressing us into the last narrow passage, we have to dismember ourselves to pass"?)[105] Concrete, kinetic, olfactory, full of the colors, the flavors, and the sounds of his country, Darwish's images can be dazzlingly strange or totally familiar, and in either case equally capable of transporting the reader into the space of the poem. His language pulses with life and warmth and intimacy, and, at times, with a special childlike tenderness.

Darwish eludes being placed within any particular period. His talent, nourished by the decade's poetic adventures in diction and imagery and fired by the deepening tragedy and rising hopes of his people, bloomed in the seventies. He then became an integral part of the on-going modern movement and continued to develop; despite many differences in his poetry from the avant-garde poetry of the eighties, he shines across borderlines and periods. If one feels, now, that the work of the pioneer generation has became rather stale and dated, Darwish's output, in both poetry and prose, has resisted the passage of time and continues to surprise us. He is as fresh and relevant now as he will surely continue to be in the future. His services to Palestinian literature are boundless and have brought honor to his people both in the Arab world and on the international scene. Along with the cultural achievements of other Palestinians all over the world, Darwish has affirmed the reputation of the Palestinians as contributors to the living culture of our times.

Inside Israel, Samih al-Qasim continued a poetic career that, like Darwish's, is almost completely dedicated to the Palestinian cause; their names in fact are commonly linked. Al-Qasim, however, has established different techniques for overcoming the potential danger of tedious repetition. He realizes that he must continue to feed a public whose appetite for therapeutic poetry has proven to be insatiable; the political theme therefore remains the pivot of his relationship with his audience and any major change away from it would indeed be a defection or betrayal. However, he escapes the trap in two ways. In the first place, having written a substantial amount of political poetry (in which he excelled), he felt able to concentrate sometimes on other themes, such as love for example. This poet has a playfulness about him, a dexterity and an ease with himself and others that Darwish, with his particular makeup, could never accommodate. In the second place, al-Qasim has contrived a way of guaranteeing audience participation within the actual declamatory process of poetry, making the public itself, in some of his experiments, an integral part of his poem; he can be playful on the platform, asking his audience to join him in voicing refrains or, sometimes, in clapping. Darwish, in contrast, takes himself very seriously, preferring the way a poet has always addressed his audience in the Arab world: facing them like a prophet and delivering his poetry like an oracular pronouncement while the spellbound audience hangs on every word and, relating to the message of the poem, erupts periodically in sudden, emotional bursts of acclaim that provide a much-needed catharsis.[106]

Al-Qasim wanders between several modes in his poetry, moving from the tragic to the comic with the greatest ease, and also reflecting at times an apocalyptic vision conveyed not simply through imagery and thematic treatment, but through a tone which becomes at once both sonorous and terrifying.[107] There is, moreover, a postmodernist quality to his work, manifesting itself first in his concern with the active participation of the audience in the declamation of the poem and second in his occasional attempts at pastiche. In 1983 Al-Qasim published a small volume entitled *Collage*, which was a medley of various kinds of writing, ranging from poetry to poetic prose to journalistic statements. In this volume he uses language and rhythms that vary from rhetorical utterances reminiscent of classical poetry to the semicolloquial reminiscent of Palestinian folk songs; the tone alternates between the tragic and the ironic or comic. In the same year he also published a larger collection, *Dimensions of the Soul*, again characterized by some of these elements, but maintaining a greater eloquence than in *Collage*.[108] His rich poetic output is experimental in a way uniquely his own, and he is probably the first Palestinian (and, as far as I know, the first Arab poet) to exhibit some of the qualities of a postmodernist trend in poetry.

For Palestinians, Tawfiq Zayyad (b. 1932) represents the epitome of unending struggle; solid, constant, and firm in his vision of justice. His poetry has changed little since he began writing the earthy, poignant poems in the sixties that are the warmest, most pertinent expression of the Palestinian spirit. Many of them have been put to music

and sung. There are no Palestinians who do not memorize some of
them or hum them to themselves, and no Arab groups, from Boston
to Bethlehem, that do not sing them together at their meetings. His
poetry answers the need that he perceives exists for a firm expression
of faith and determination in the face of aggression; it is not written
primarily for its own sake, for Zayyad's commitment to his country's
cause is probably more sacred to him than the art of poetry itself. At
the same time, however, it is not written merely as a means to an end.
He writes because there is a deep need in him and in his countrymen
to speak out, poetically, on what they feel is politically slippery, vague,
and full of complicity. It is at once a rejection and an affirmation of
his people's precarious situation; the harsh political reality engenders
emotions and aspirations that are, in their turn, transformed into
poetry.

It is impossible to write about all the many poets who have enriched
the tradition both within Palestine and in exile. Some mention should
be made, however, of the richly symbolic work of 'Ali al-Khalili (b.
1943), a highly cultivated poet from the West Bank whose experience
of the wretched political situation there is portrayed in distinctively
modern poetic terms. A particular feature in his work is his use of
short, staccato jets of utterance that reflect the deep anxiety of the poet
and produce an often incisive and vigorous effect:

> Attention, stop, ready, ease up, roll
> green cabbage head.[109]

and:

> Erupt
> fear, snow, cities, forgotten heroes,
> closed windows, emigrant exiled workers,
> landless peasants, songs without lips.[110]

The hyperbole of his poetry points to what he feels to be the absurdities
of life around him, which hems the Palestinian in, not just inside Israel
but within the Arab world as a whole. But there is also, in the midst
of these heated tones, a pertinent search for calm and for an answer to
nagging problems: "Of what purpose is this music, flowing beneath
glorious feet?"[111] And every so often, through the incessant complex
expressions and richly strung images, a simple, piercing statement
gleams through:

> Arab oil was a roof—it collapsed.[112]

or:

> We're the salt of the earth, but this earth
> means clothes, medals, earrings,
> paints, rugs etc.
> for the new generals.[113]

The last passage is characteristic of the poet's ironic perception. Other places reflect a global preoccupation with human experience, especially in its aspect of suffering:

> And to what end is the laughter of decapitated heads
> stacked in Riyadh, Cairo, Morocco, Khartoum, South
> Africa, Chile and the forbidding display of show windows
> in New York?[114]

With this kind of audacity avant-garde Palestinian poets keep the spirit of experimentation active though still guided by a strong control over their tools. This poetry is artistically burgeoning all the time but is never oblivious of the historical reality faced by the Palestinian people at present. It is interesting for contemporary critics to observe how the compulsive hold of political immediacy over the creative energy of these poets has not led them astray as it did the poets of the seventies. This points to a new esthetic maturity governing the poetry not only of a handful of talented Palestinians writing at the moment but also of equally creative and masterful poets all over the Arab world.

Personal Account Literature

Personal account literature by Palestinian writers is perhaps the greatest witness to the age of catastrophe. Most of it represents an affirmative stance in the face of the disadvantages imposed on the daily life of the individual, and of the negative publicity applied to the Palestinian cause with impunity over the decades, unchecked by certain well-known historians and specialists, and unquestioned by ordinary citizens.

Memoirs, reminiscences, diaries, and autobiographies alike reveal a burning wish to establish the identity of the protagonists and delineate their personal experiences. However, the inner life of the individual does not function in a void, and this is especially so in a period of communal upheaval, where no good personal account literature can ever be strictly "personal"; inevitably it will spring from the age that produces it and from a communal identity defining the contours of life around the writer and reflecting the social and political preoccupations of the time. It is thus tied to perceptions and situations that transcend individual life; and this, indeed, is where its significance, poignancy, and appeal lie.

In the case of Palestinian writers, this situation is accentuated by the special environment within which they function. More often than not, Palestinian writers of personal account literature are more mindful of the "external" forces at play around them than of their own private introspections or idiosyncrasies—even when very personal emotions are brought to the fore, the writing usually defines a social context. In his personal memoirs on the Israeli invasion of Beirut in 1982, Mahmoud Darwish's anguish is all the more overwhelming because of the significant events, so vividly recorded by him, that are taking place outside; in fact the war arouses memories and stifled desires that would not have surfaced (at least not in writing) without the poignant proximity of danger. Muhammad al-Asʿad's memory of his dead young brother, although depicted in highly personal terms (the foreboding of a child witnessing death and mourning for the first time, reflected here as a very private inner experience buried for years in the grooves of almost subconscious memory), is also presented in the context of a young death taking place in the loneliness and desolation of a Palestinian refugee camp in Lebanon, in a world of bitter exile and humiliation that seems to double the tragedy of the death. As for the heroic endurance reflected in Salah Taʿmari's account of his solitary confinement in an Israeli prison cell, political heroism has always carried a communal message.[115]

Deterritorialized literatures tend to share a number of common aspects. Two of these, which figure explicitly in Palestinian literature, particularly within the personal account genre, are the political immediacy of the writings in question and the way everything takes on a collective value. A third aspect is a frequent concern with "national identity"; this is a major incentive in Palestinian writings of the genre, for it is this very problem of identity that has been highlighted by the continuing malaise and that lurks behind the varied experiences and special suffering that has been the hallmark of Palestinian life since 1948. Palestinian personal account literature is conceived as an eyewitness account of contemporary Palestinian life, presented with the view, first, of grasping a sense of identity within the chaos of the communal tragedy, and, second, with the view of speaking out to the world. The latter has been a pervasive, almost compulsive need during the second half of the twentieth century; for, since the catastrophe of 1948, part of the Palestinian malaise has been the presence of an almost impenetrable wall blinding the world to the Palestinian cause and its ever-widening implications. A welter of cynical propaganda, filled with delusions and fabrications and almost universally disseminated, has obscured the whole Palestinian question, clouding the justice of the cause and often, even, frankly bestializing Palestinians in the eyes of the world. As a result, Palestinian writers have felt an urgent need to reject this isolation, to beat a path into the consciousness of others by simply telling the story over and over again, piecemeal and in all its myriad aspects, as experienced by single individuals.

The urge in this genre of Palestinian writing is toward a proclamation of the true state of affairs in many areas of life. There is, for example, the need to contradict the picture of backwardness and primitiveness disseminated by negative propaganda by proclaiming the existence of a rooted urban culture in Palestine. In the description of his youth in Jaffa, Yusuf Haykal mirrors the complex, well-established upper class life-style of the turn of the twentieth century, reminding the world that Palestine was not merely a barren and backward desert but rather a country with an advanced urban life, together with a cultivated landscape fertile with orchards, gardens, and green fields. In his description of his young days in Jerusalem, Dr. Subhi Ghosheh depicts a rooted middle class, organized around an abiding social and moral code, with well-defined habits and customs. Then there is the proclamation of intellectual life lived to the full, a life reflected by Khalil al-Sakakini in his voluminous diaries begun late in the nineteenth century, and celebrated by Hisham Sharabi in his description of the two poles around which his early life revolved: the liberal pursuit of knowledge and a genuine aspiration towards progressive change. We have the proclamation of the way a Palestinian woman can transcend the impossible and achieve international stature so sensitively described by Fadwa Tuqan. There is the depiction of a rural life tested by time, as portrayed by Jabra Ibrahim Jabra, with the mesh of warm human relations he so vividly describes, and a style of life which, if full of hardships, still abounded with love and goodness and with ancestral folklore and song.

Last but not least, there is the proclamation of the tragedy. It may be the suffering of children on the exodus, slaking their thirst by licking the dew from the leaves of trees, as we read in Muhammad al-Asʿad's notes; or the tragedy of men maligned and brutalized by the constantly coercive authorities of the Arab countries that controlled their destiny after 1948, as depicted here by Muʿeen Bseiso; or the testimonies of war and aggression and the lonely suffering of men and women fallen victim, in one way or another, to the vicissitudes of savage modern warfare, as we read in the 1982 war memoirs of Mahmoud Darwish, Mai Sayigh, and Rashad Abu Shawar; or, finally, of the fate of brave individuals forced to face the enemy and his machinery of torture, as described in such touching terms by Salah Taʿmari.[116] Many other writers, besides those selected here, have born witness to the Palestinian experience,[117] and many more will undoubtedly do so in the near future; for Palestinians know well enough that if they do not announce their experience to the world, the world will be ready to forget them. Quite apart from the external benefit it can achieve by forging links with the "other," personal account literature is a comfort and support to the Palestinians themselves and a source of healing for those who read it.

Most personal account literature has to rely on memory, which is a very selective process. However, some Palestinian literature of this kind, such as Muhammad al-Asʿad's moving account of the exodus in 1948 and of life in Palestine before the exodus, relies on the memory of others; this account was collected, as noted earlier, from the narrations of older members of his family and community. It is also characteristic of deterritorialized writings that they negotiate between memory and nostalgia. Yet deterritorialized Palestinian literature also has ancient roots; classical Arabic poetry is filled with the theme, established early in pre-Islamic times when the Arabs were still a nomadic people and thus had a constantly "deterritorialized" existence. Indeed, the Arab spirit has, since time immemorial, been torn by nostalgia and revived by memory—two inseparables that also mark Palestinian literature. It might have been thought that, as new generations of Palestinians grew up without actual personal territorial memories, they would slowly relinquish their claim to the land of Palestine and become absorbed in the landscape and life of the countries where they lived and worked. This anthology shows how totally erroneous such speculation would be: for even among Palestinians who were born outside their own country, who have succeeded and prospered elsewhere, the same nostalgia persists, lingering on in borrowed memories. Palestinian children in the diaspora sit around the winter fires, demanding from the grown-ups, from those who preserve the memory, more descriptions of the country they have never seen; as they grow, they are nourished by these memories.

Contemporary Palestinian literature makes a rich and potent contribution to modern Arabic culture, a contribution vibrant with life and creativity. In the realm of fiction, it has developed along the general lines of modern Arabic fiction, with some of its avant-garde experiments, such as those of Kanafani, Jabra, Habiby, and Nasrallah, contributing most constructively to the experiments constantly taking place in the Arab world; in some cases, Palestinian fiction has produced unique treatments matched nowhere else in Arabic, such as Habiby's novel *The Secret Life of Saeed, the Ill-Fated Pessoptimist* and Nasrallah's *Prairies of Fever*. Experimental work in fiction is still, moreover, in full swing.

The particular circumstances of the Palestinians, their history prey to distortion and their identity subject to constant suppression, have instinctively led many Palestinian writers to produce various forms of personal accounts, and this genre promises to provide a major creative addition to the already very rich corpus of modern Arabic literature.

However, it is in the art of poetry that the contemporary Palestinian literary scene is so immensely well-endowed, with Palestinians prominent in the flourishing avant-garde movement within Arabic poetry wherever they are found. This is especially exciting for the critic in view of the political compulsions imposed upon poetry by the very nature of Palestinan life. The general Arab malaise has been traumatic for most Arabs throughout this century, but for no people more than the Palestinians who have, as the critic Ferial Ghazoul wrote once, "the collective portion of everyone; they stand where all swords meet: the swords of the enemies, those of the friends, and those of the brethren." Ghazoul then quotes Mureed Barghouthy addressing the exiled Palestinian:

> To every citizen there is one ruler.
> You alone are favored with twenty
> in twenty capitals.
> If you made one of them angry,
> the law would claim your head
> and if you honored one of them
> the rest would want you dead.

Yet, Ghazoul adds, "For all the occupation of Palestinian land and the fact that the Palestinians are beleaguered and their rights obscured, for all the attempts at exterminating them, at annihilating them physically, psychologically, and culturally, their voice still rises, surmounting all barriers."[118]

What is involved in this literature, however, is not simply a political situation that has to be expounded to the world. Literature would lose its immense value if restricted to polemical narrations or to propaganda, and perhaps the greatest achievement of contemporary Palestinian poetry is its subtle and esthetically sophisticated portrayal of a genuine existential situation. What we are rather concerned with here is the question of justice and human happiness. Palestinian literature is primarily about the suffering and the struggle of a particular section of humanity caught in the toils of a well-engineered political situation imposed on them without their consent and through no fault of their own. The story of Palestine is one of initial innocence encountering a global strategy which, in the early decades of the twentieth century, took plain advantage of this innocence to implement a policy of aggression and fear, from which many thousands of personal tragedies have sprung. It is these individual experiences that are food for literature; and, viewed in the context of the fearful disaster whose dimensions have never ceased to widen since 1948, the high spirit one finds in this literature, the faith and resilience, the compassion and love, the courage and endurance, and the abiding steadfastness, must surely touch the sensibility of readers and lead them on to identify with its values. Freedom and justice are not divisible; they are universals. And tragedy, wherever it happens, and whoever is touched by it, is timeless and has the same face—a human face. It moves us across the centuries when we read of it in classical literature, and it should continue to move us now; for it is in literature that the story of human suffering and human endeavor is best told.

NOTES

1. See Salma Khadra Jayyusi, *Trends and Movements in Modern Arabic Poetry* (Leiden: Brill, 1977), 1:5.

2. See also Arnold Hauser's four-volume book, *The Social History of Art* (London: Routledge and Kegan Paul, 1956). And see my *Trends and Movements*, 1: Introduction, for a fuller discussion of this aspect of literary history.

3. See René Wellek, "The Theory of Literary History," in *Travaux du cercle linguistique de Prague*, no. 4 (1936); and Wellek's essay "Periods and Movements in Literary History," in *English Institute Annual* (New York: Columbia University Press, 1940).

4. See my *Trends and Movements*, 1:5; and see my essay "Vision and Attitudes in Modern Arabic Literature," in Robin Ostle, ed., *Studies in Modern Arabic Literature* (Warminster: Aris and Philips, 1976); my essay "Three Types of Hero in Modern Arabic Literature," *Mundus Artium*, 10, no.1 (1977); my introduction to *Modern Arabic Poetry:*

An Anthology (New York: Columbia University Press, 1987); and see my chapter "Modernist Poetry in Arabic" in M. M. Badawi, ed., *Cambridge History of Arabic Literature*, vol. 4 (Cambridge: Cambridge University Press, in press).

5. Such as the abundant "personal account" literature that Palestinian writers regularly produce. This includes autobiographies such as Fadwa Tuqan's *A Mountainous Journey* (Arabic version, 1985), translated into English for PROTA by Olive Kenny (London: The Women's Press, 1990) and (St. Paul, Minnesota: Graywolf, 1990); Hisham Sharabi's *Embers and Ashes* (1978); and Jabra Ibrahim Jabra's *The First Well* (1987); diaries such as Khalil al-Sakakini's *Such Am I, O World* (1955); Rashad Abu Shawar's *O, Beirut!* (1983); memoirs such as Mahmoud Darwish's *Diary of Ordinary Grief* (1973) and *Memory for Forgetfulness* (1986); Muʿeen Bseiso's *Palestinian Notebooks* (1978); Mai Sayigh's *The Siege* (1988); and reminiscences such as Subhi Ghosheh's *Our Sun Will Never Set* (1988) and Yusuf Haykal's *Days of My Youth* (1988). See the excerpts from all these in this anthology. There are other books as well, such as Laila al-Saʾih's memoirs on the Israeli invasion of Beirut, *Roots Do Not Depart* (1984). We were unable to use an excerpt from this delightful book because of its late acquisition.

6. See Sahar Khalifeh's novel *Wild Thorns*, translated for PROTA by Trevor LeGassick and Elizabeth Fernea (London: Saqi Books, 1986), which speaks of the plight of these workers and the fate of Palestinians in the West Bank. See also, in this volume, Ghareeb ʿAsqalani's short story "Hunger" and Muhammad ʿAli Taha's "Faris Rateeba."

7. The historical land of Palestine, to which Palestinians at large relate, includes the lands appropriated by the Zionists in 1948 and turned into the state of Israel, as well as the West Bank and the Gaza Strip, occupied by Israel since the June War of 1967. When the occasion demands the designation of a geographical locale, I shall of course provide it. This would be appropriate, for example, when one is speaking of differences between the literature written by Arabs inside the state of Israel proper and that written in the West Bank and Gaza; or, alternatively, when speaking of writings that deal, thematically, with the specific problems of Palestinians in Israel or Palestinians in the rest of Palestine. Prime examples of such writing are Emile Habiby's *The Secret Life of Saeed, the Ill-Fated Pessoptimist*, which is an account spanning some twenty years of the lives of Palestinians who remained in the state of Israel in 1948; and Sahar Khalifeh's *Wild Thorns*, see note 6 above.

8. This is not to say that those Palestinian writers who have interacted with the Hebrew language and Hebrew literature have lost any of their Palestinian cultural identity to them. "It is striking," says Hannan Hever, one of Israel's young critics, "that the more the Arab minority in Israel reinforces its identity, the more it makes its presence felt within the majority Hebrew culture," "Israeli Literature's Achilles' Heel," *Tikkun*, 4 (5):30. In this article the writer also states that "publishing houses have also shown an increasing interest in bringing Hebrew translations of Israeli Arab literature to the attention of the Israeli public."

9. Khalid ʿAli Mustafa, *Modern Palestinian Poetry*, p. 24.

10. See my *Trends and Movements*, 1:25–45.

11. Muhammad Salim Rashdan, "Literature in Palestine," *Al-Risala*, no. 684 (August 13, 1946): 897. See also Nasir al-Din al-Asad, *Modern Literary Trends in Palestine and Jordan* (Cairo: 1957), p. 28.

12. My *Trends and Movements*, pp. 34–35.

13. Growing up in Palestine in the thirties and forties, I myself experienced this deprivation of a real literary life. The deepest commitment in the area of literary expression in Palestine was to political invective. Ibrahim Tuqan (1905–1941), the greatest Palestinian poet during the twenties and thirties, and ʿAbd al-Raheem Mahmoud (1913–1948) won immediate fame through their political poetry. Fadwa Tuqan's nonpolitical stance in her

early career led to domestic struggle on her part, as is well explained in the excerpt published in this volume from her autobiography, *A Mountainous Journey*.

14. Particularly Habiby's original novel, *Pessoptimist*, see note 7.

15. One can see this, for example, in the output of two highly gifted brothers, Mahmoud and Zaki Darwish. Mahmoud Darwish's poetry developed quickly after he left Israel in the early seventies to live in the wider Arab world, mixing with avant-garde poets and absorbing all the varied influences firsthand in a way that transformed his work and pushed him to the heights of esthetic accomplishment. Zaki Darwish, in some of his short stories, shows a brilliance and a purity of talent that is also rare; but he is little known in the Arab world as a whole, and I feel he has not developed his immense artistic potential to the full as Mahmoud Darwish has done.

16. See below his poem "Intensive Care Unit," a rare example of his "deviation" from the political theme, speaking as it does with great beauty and eloquence of his experience of a heart attack.

17. From my introduction to Habiby's *Pessoptimist*, p. viii. One could add here that tradition in literature tends to perpetuate itself, and that the tradition of Arabic *poetry* in general (the above-mentioned humorous tradition in classical Arabic was displayed mainly in prose genres such as the famous assemblies or *maqamat*—see note 28) has tended mostly toward a serious tone. In pre-Islamic times, when life was rooted in nomadic norms and customs, the poet, who was the spokesman of his tribe and its defender in its numerous feuds, had to assume a serious and direct tone to suit a mentality that had not yet acquired urban subtlety. Later on, with urbanization in the Umayyad period and the change in the central issues of poetry, there were some early demonstrations of a comic representation of experience (see the discussion on Umayyad satire, especially Jarir's, in my chapter "Umayyad Verse" in *The Cambridge History of Arabic Literature* [London, Sydney, New York: Cambridge University Press, 1983], 1:409–13). However, this early experiment was later superseded by the poet's growing importance as the eulogist of the ruler. Eulogy became a major, if not the major, art in poetry, and there can be no irony, sarcasm, or humor in this kind of verse, bent as it is on the celebration of the grandeur, the benevolence, and the authority of the ruler or mighty prince.

18. Poets such as Ibrahim al-Dabbagh (1880–1946), Jiryis al-ʿIssa (1906–1943), Badawi al-ʿAlami (1901–1958), Iskandar al-Khouri al-Betjali (1890–1973), Burhan al-ʿAbboushi (b. 1911), and others.

19. For these excerpts from his work, see my book *Trends and Movements*, 1:470–71. All excerpts are translated by Christopher Tingley and me.

20. See my chapter "Committed Poetry, *Al-Iltizam*" in *Trends and Movements*, 2:574–83, and see a fuller discussion in Arabic in the *Review of the University of Khartoum*, 1, no.1, 1972.

21. See in this volume, under his name, his poem addressed to Prince Saud ibn ʿAbd al-ʿAziz on the latter's visit to Palestine in 1935. See also his poem pledging his life for his country.

22. A case in point is the poetry of Zakariyya Muhammad, one of the new generation of poets, where the heroic motif has disappeared and a sophisticated, subdued tone predominates.

23. See my discussion of his poetry in *Trends and Movements*, 1:298–302.

24. This final, feminine triumph of self-assertion against all the odds of a hostile, reactionary world is beautifully exemplified in her poem "I Found It" (i.e., "she found herself"). For a translation of this poem, see Tuqan, *A Mountainous Journey*, pp. 213–14.

25. See ibid., p. 107.

26. The Umayyad period abounded in oral tales of love based on real-life personalities. The story of the famous poet Qais ibn al-Mulawwah, whose unrequited love for Laila ended in the tragedy of madness and death, and that of Qais ibn Dharih, whose divorce of his beloved wife, Lubna, at the insistence of his father, also ruined his life, are only two of the most famous. The *Book of al-Aghani* abounds with such tales.

27. These are allegorical stories translated mainly from Persian by the eighth-century writer Ibn al-Muqaffaʿ, whose lucid writing, easy to read but very difficult to imitate, laid down the rules of style for his and several subsequent generations. Most of the stories in *Kalila wa Dimna* are of Indian origin, but some are original Persian and a few are Arabic. Great wisdom, virtue, and skill are expressed in the exchanges between various kinds of animals.

28. *Maqamat* are entertaining, compact, picaresque-style short stories in rhymed prose, revolving around the adventures of an unscrupulous, witty rogue or trickster who earns his living by taking advantage of the gullibility of others. The two most famous assembly writers were Ahmad ibn Husain al-Hamadhani (967–1007) and Abu Muhammad al-Qasim al-Hariri (1054–1122). This genre, with its particular format and its rhymed prose, is unique to Arabic.

29. By the Andalusi philosopher Ibn Tufail (d. 1185).

30. Khalil Baydas founded his famous *Al-Nafaʾis* in 1908 in Haifa, then moved it after two years to Jerusalem where it continued to appear until 1913. It was then suspended before resuming publication for one year in 1919. It was devoted mainly to the publication of fiction. Ahmad Shakir al-Karmi worked in journalism before founding his own journal, *Al-Mizan*, which existed in Damascus from 1925 to 1926 and was suspended owing to his illness and early death. Jamil al-Bahri founded two literary journals, *Zahrat al-Jamil* and *Al-Zahra*, in Haifa in 1922, the latter devoted to the publication of fiction and drama. His early death in 1930 put an end to a flourishing career marked by a rare energy and great dedication to the dissemination of the new literary genres of fiction and drama.

31. Most of al-Bahri's books were, unfortunately, lost to the family after the 1948 exodus and the upheaval that accompanied it. Writers are consequently not very clear as to the exact sources of his work or their years of publication. What is clearly known, however, is that he published most of these works in the journal *Al-Zahra* before bringing them out in book form.

32. See the preface to his short story collection, *Vistas of the Mind* (Cairo: Al-Matbaʿa ʾl-ʿAsriyya, 1924), p. 9.

33. Ibid., p. 12.

34. Ibid. pp. 12–14.

35. See Ahmad Abu Matar, *The Novel in Palestinian Literature*, pp. 23–28.

36. See the preface to his play, *Prisoner of the Palace*, 2d ed. (Haifa: Matbaʿat al-Zahra, 1927). (According to the *Index of Palestinian Arabic Books* [Jerusalem: Matbaʿat al-Liwa, 1946; present edition published by The Arab Cultural Committee in Palestine], its first edition appeared in Beirut, 1920.)

37. *The Index of Palestinian Arab Books* lists another short story collection, *Dreams of Life*, and mentions that it was in press in 1946. Unfortunately, I have not been able to locate it.

38. See a critical account of this novel by Faruq Wadi, *Three Milestones in the Palestinian Novel*, 2d ed. (Acre: Al-Aswar, 1985), pp. 20–23, and by Ahmad Abu Matar, *The Novel in Palestinian Literature*, pp. 48–49; and see Nasir al-Asad, *Khalil Baydas*, pp. 64–87.

39. The relative aridity of Palestinian literature at the time was sternly criticized by certain Arab authors in the forties. The review *Al-Adib* in Beirut published a criticism by ʿAbd al-ʿAziz al-Gharaballi, a writer from the Gulf area, who stated that "Palestinian men of letters did not bother much about publishing," *Al-Adib*, no.12 (December 1944). To this a Palestinian writer, Ishaq Jarallah, heatedly retorted that Palestine was in dire

straits, "exposed to great dangers that threaten[ed] its Arab identity. Despite the fact that the [cultural] field was wide open for a literature which could instill enthusiasm in the masses, no one thought of writing while others were waging a bloody strife. The field here," he asserted, was "not for writing, but for oratory." He also mentioned that (British) government censorship was harsh and was a major factor in the general literary stagnation, ibid., no. 1 (January 1945). Another writer, Michel Jubran, wrote in the next issue of *Al-Adib* in defense of Jarallah, pointing out that most writers "put their energy into the writing of patriotic political articles," ibid., no. 2 (February 1945). And in the March number of the same year, Ishaq Musa al-Husaini asserted that prose writings in Palestine were more in the form of essays and articles than creative writings, suggesting that the ordeal that the country was experiencing might be the cause, ibid., no. 3 (March 1945).

40. I would have liked to include an excerpt from this novel in the present *Anthology* but was unable to obtain the author's permission during his lifetime, probably because I was unable to communicate with him directly.

41. *A Chicken's Memoirs*, 1st ed. (Cairo: Iqra' Series, Dar al-Ma'arif, 1943) p. 157.

42. See the incisive criticism directed at this novel by Faruq Wadi, *Three Milestones*, pp. 26–30, and by Ahmad Abu Matar, *The Novel in Palestinian Literature*, pp. 33–39.

43. Such as the attempt by Muhammad al-'Adnani in his novel *In the Bed* (1st ed., 1946; 2d ed., Aleppo: Matba'at Sa'ad, 1953); and Iskandar al-Khouri al-Betjali's *In the Heart of Things* (Cairo: Maktabat al-'Arab, 1947). The first criticizes medical treatment in Egyptian hospitals and describes other negative features discovered by the author when he went to Egypt for treatment. It also includes a description of his voyage to Italy and Berlin after his cure. The second is a criticism of traditional ideas about love, marriage, the patriarchal system, and the pain caused by continued adherence to such ideas. Al-Betjali is credited with earlier attempts at novel writing such as his novel *Life After Death* (Jerusalem, 1920), which described events during the First World War. This and many other books of fiction, both written or translated, were lost in the upheaval of 1948, when, as a result of the mass exodus of Palestinians, some had to leave large libraries behind. It is also interesting to note that several novels were attempted by Palestinians who were major figures in other fields. A novel by the well-known historian 'Arif al-'Arif, for instance, was published in Cairo in 1947, under the title *Dancing Hall of the Blind*, and another very famous historian, Muhammad 'Izzat Darwaza, is said to have written a novel, *The Brokers of the Land* (or according to another account, *The Angel and the Broker*; see Abu Matar, *The Novel in Palestinian Literature*, p. 51, note 52), attacking the land brokers who tempted some Palestinian landowners to sell their lands to the Jews. There is conflicting data regarding the publication of this novel, some accounts stating that it was indeed published in 1934, while the author himself refers to a lost manuscript with a similar title. What is significant here, however, is that this seems to be the first novel written directly on the political situation in the country. Another major political figure, Jamal al-Husaini, is credited with two novels, *Thurayya* and *The Railroad to Hijaz*, published in the thirties. It is interesting to find the names of a few women authors and translators during this early period. The most famous is Asma Tubi, who enjoyed a prominent status as a woman writer in Acre in the thirties and forties, translating fiction, writing about moral behavior, and later, when she was in exile in 1955, publishing a collection of her own short stories, *Words from the Heart*. The Lebanese-born 'Anbara Salam al-Khalidi produced a translation of the *Iliad*, which she published in Jerusalem in 1946, giving example and encouragement to rising Palestinian women writers. Another Lebanese-born woman writer living in Palestine was Jamal Sleem Nuweihed who, in 1922, published a serialized novel in the review *Dunya al-Mar'a* entitled *Fatina, Daughter of the Moon*. Later, in 1932, she published seventeen short stories in the Jerusalem-based review *Al-'Arab*; between 1943 and 1944 she wrote about fifty short stories that were

broadcast from the Jerusalem radio station. A rather retiring woman, Jamal Nuweihed published only two of her many novels, *Procession of Martyrs* (1959) and *Estrangement in the Homeland* (1987). A third, *Wedding in Paradise*, is now in press. Many of her novels revolve around the Palestine tragedy and the upheaval accompanying it before and after 1948.

44. Mostly, but not always. Some folk romances were improvized to uphold morale following a national upheaval. A case in point here is the folk romance of Sayf Ben Dhi Yazan, on the exploits of King Sayf of Yemen and his victories over his enemies. This was put together in fourteenth-century Egypt after the experience of national calamities and defeat. Other folktales, however, are really meant to amuse and entertain.

45. For a discussion of the earlier experiments in free verse, see my *Trends and Movements*, 2:534–60.

46. See ibid., pp. 542–50 and 557–60.

47. See my chapter "Commitment" in my *Trends and Movements*, 2:574–83. Although the call for commitment in modern Arabic literature adopted many of the ideas of Jean Paul Sartre in his famous collection of 1947 articles, *What is Literature?* trans., Bernard Frechtman (London: Methuen, 1950), it did not embrace his idea that poetry could be exempted from the commitment demanded of other genres. As the earliest and most popular art of the Arabs, poetry was regarded as the first genre that should participate in the battle for freedom and dignity.

48. See my preface to Mahfouz's *Midaq Alley*, trans., Trevor LeGassick (Washington D.C.: Three Continents Press, 1989), pp. ix–xii.

49. See my chapter "Platform Poetry" in my *Trends and Movements*, 2:583–94.

50. See this and other translated poems by Abu Salma in ibid., 1:298–301.

51. See, for example, her poem "I Found It," on the triumph of her long search for identity and self-realization (for reference, see footnote 24).

52. From my preface to Tuqan's autobiography, *Mountainous Journey*, p. xii; see also her poem, "In the Flux" in my *Modern Arabic Poetry, an Anthology*, under Tuqan's name.

53. See *Mountainous Journey*, p.ix, for further elaboration on this matter. And for further discussion of her role as poet, see my preface to *Mountainous Journey*.

54. See the section "Traditional and Modern" in my *Trends and Movements*, 2:594–95.

55. The Lebanese poet Yusuf al-Khal, who in 1957 founded the avant-garde *Shiʿr* magazine dedicated exclusively to poetry, gave a public lecture in the same year detailing what he believed were the criteria of "modern Arabic [he specified Lebanese] poetry." These criteria gave a coherent outlook to how "modern" poetry in Arabic should be, without, however, touching much on any of the modernist criteria in literature. The major criteria in this lecture, which was quite important for its time, were that poetry should be the expression of a lived experience; that the structure of the poem must be based on the unity of experience; that its first objective should be man (a criterion laid down by the Arab emigré critic in America Mikhaʾil Nuʿaima as early as the second decade: see my *Trends and Movements*, 1:113–14, and Nuʿaima's *Al-Ghirbal*, 7th ed. [Beirut: Dar Sadir, Dar Beirut, 1964], p. 25); that a change must take place from an old diction which had exhausted its vitality; that Arabic metrics must be developed to suit the new context; that the poet should use the living image, not simple similes and metaphors; and that images "should present a challenge to logic." It is this last stipulation that can be regarded as an initial approach toward a modernist point of view. For a fuller discussion of this lecture, see my *Trends and Movements*, 2:570–72.

56. From my section on him in my chapter "Modernist Poetry in Arabic" in *Cambridge History of Arabic Literature*, vol. 4.

57. The Egyptian poet Ahmad ʿAbd al-Muʿti Hijazi has described the European city (in this case Paris) where alienation and solitude are rampant. He has long dealt with

the theme of the city. However, when he wrote about the Arab metropolis (specifically Cairo) he wrote from the point of view of the poor country boy who finds himself a stranger in the big city, without venturing into the realms of spiritual alienation and morbid sterility. These he reserved for the European city and its many lonely individuals caught in the grinding monotony of the city's daily routine. See his poems "Secrets," "Elegies on the Stations of the other Time," and "The Lonely Woman's Room" in my *Modern Arabic Poetry*, under his name.

58. The publication of this collection in the mid-fifties coincides with the time avant-garde poets in the Arab world—influenced by such modernist poets as Eliot—also began to attack the city. The first major poet to incorporate the theme of the city into his work was the Iraqi Badr Shakir al-Sayyab, who emigrated from his village, Jaikur (perhaps the most famous village in Arabic literature), to study in Baghdad, staying on there afterward as a government employee. With his great openness to existential experience, together with the revulsion he felt at the political corruption of the metropolis, his well-digested reading of Western poetry, and, above all, the authentic experience of a young, poor village boy of genius and great sensitivity at large in the city, he produced high-level poetry that added deeper dimensions to his experience. He clearly felt crushed by an urban order hugely at variance with his simple origins and was also influenced by an egalitarian socialist ideology that lent greater meaning to his hatred of the city. If his expression of alienation from the city was perhaps immediately influenced by Eliot and other modernists, this influence only helped give expression to a natural and legitimate state of mind. It remained, moreover, on the level of concise, oblique, and restrained poetic expression, never venturing into the absurdly lengthy and detailed discussions of the foulness of city life that Jabra's early work exhibited. The same may be said of other poets from the age of the pioneers, such as Khalil Hawi.

59. 'Azzam has published five collections of short stories: *Little Things* (1954); *The Tall Shadow,* (1956); . . . *And Other Stories* (1960); *Man and the Clock* (1963); and, post-humously, *The Feast from the Western Window* (1971). In all these, only seven short stories are specifically built around the Palestinian experience.

60. Published in my anthology, *Modern Arabic Fiction: An Anthology* (New York: Columbia University Press, in press).

61. Quoted in Victoria Glendinning, *Elizabeth Bowen; Portrait of a Writer* (London: Weidenfeld and Nicholson, 1977), p. 54.

62. This novella was translated, with six other short stories of Kanafani's, by Hilary Kilpatrick (Heineman: London, 1978; Washington D.C.: Three Continents Press, 1983).

63. Translated for PROTA with ten other short stories of Kanafani by May Jayyusi and Jeremy Reed (The Center for Middle Eastern Studies, University of Texas, Austin: 1990).

64. For more on Maghut's experiment, see my introduction to PROTA's volume of Maghut's poetry in English translation: trans., May Jayyusi and Naomi Shihab Nye, *The Fan of Swords* (Washington D.C.: Three Continents Press, 1991).

65. *Cambridge History of Arabic Literature*, 1:429. For more on desert symbolism in classical Arabic poetry see pp. 429–31.

66. Another collection of nine stories by Kanafani, *Umm Sa'd* (1969), is regarded by some critics as a novel because of the unified interdependent theme of the stories. How-ever, the various short stories in the book are self-sufficient and this highly committed work can only with reservations be called a novel.

67. A PROTA book, translated into English by Trevor LeGassick and me, 2d printing (London: Zed Books, 1986).

68. For a fuller critical analysis of *The Pessoptimist*, see my introduction to its English translation.

69. See Faruq Wadi, *Three Milestones* p. 145.

70. Translated into English by Roger Allen and Adnan Haydar (Washington D.C.: Three Continents Press, 1987).

71. Translated into English by Adnan Haydar and Roger Allen, modified by Christopher Tingley, and still unpublished.

72. Muneef's works have without doubt touched the very roots of the contemporary Arab malaise; they have been incisively critical of the negative aspects of the new order in the Arab World, as shaped by competitive commercialism, coercive autocracies, and, most important, by what he regards as the malevolent consequences of the advent of oil in the less enlightened areas of the Arab world. This occurrence has led, in the Gulf Region, to the urge to amass wealth—sometimes by any means—and has also given rise to new life-styles, work ethics, and traditions of human interaction. Although Muneef extols what is noble, chivalrous, and proud in the bedouin society, his greatest emphasis is on the negative consequences of the oil economy. He describes in great detail what he sees as the medieval, obscurantist vision of a bedouin class suddenly made sovereign, fabulously rich, and free to control this new "oil-oriented" world with the help of willing, highly paid officials "imported" from the more advanced areas of the Arab world (the latter portrayed as always clever and subservient, and often corrupt and irresponsible). His five-part novel, *Cities of Salt*, is a most daring piece of invective directed against this new order in the Arab world. The first part of this comprehensive saga was translated into English by Peter Theroux (New York: Random House, 1987). The difference between this writer's vision and that of Jabra (see above) is evident.

73. See his novel *The Ship* (Beirut: Dar al-Nahar, 1970), pp. 56 ff.

74. Even with their dreams of seeing their country liberated and their pervasive sorrow over its affliction, the principal Palestinian protagonists in Jabra's two major novels, 'Assaf in *Ship* and Masoud in *Search*, are not immune to this lust for wealth and pleasure (Masoud in *Search* is a formidable womanizer, for example), even if this is mitigated by intellectual curiosity and sad, nagging memories of their lost country.

75. See his conversation with other characters in the novel *Ship*, pp. 128–35.

76. See Faruq Wadi for an excellent treatment of this analysis, *Three Milestones*, pp. 154–60.

77. Translated into English for PROTA by May Jayyusi and Jeremy Reed and shortly to be published by Interlink Publishing Group, New York.

78. For a full discussion of the role of the audience in the creative process, see my chapter "Platform Poetry" in *Trends and Movements*, 2:583–94. It should be noted, however, that platform poetry represents probably the most extreme form of this phenomenon.

79. Translated into English for PROTA by Trevor LeGassick and Elizabeth Fernea (London: Saqi Books, 1986).

80. Translated for PROTA by Lorne Kenny and Jeremy Reed, it is included in my forthcoming *Modern Arabic Fiction*.

81. This has been translated into English by May Jayyusi and Anthony Thwaite and included in *Modern Arabic Poetry, an Anthology*.

82. Cases in point are the Algerian war of independence and the Suez war of 1956, when Palestinian poets were among the foremost to celebrate the Algerian revolution and to indict the tripartate attack of Britain, France, and Israel on Egypt.

83. The same applies to writers from other Arab countries who lived in the same capacity in the newly rich oil states. The great exception is 'Abd al-Rahman Muneef in his five-part novel, *Cities of Salt*. See note 72 above.

84. The story of the Tel al-Zaatar massacre, published in this collection, is one of the three stories in her collection. The whole book has been translated for PROTA by Peter Clark and Christopher Tingley and published by Interlink Publishing Group, New York, 1992.

85. From her collection, *Earth and Stars* (London: Aurora Press, 1991), p. 61.

86. From his poem "Jaikur and the City." See a full translation of this poem by Lena Jayyusi and Christopher Middleton in my *Modern Arabic Poetry*.

87. From his poem "Jerusalem . . . and the Hour." See a full translation of this poem in *Modern Arabic Poetry*.

88. From his poem "The Children of Rafah," translated by Naseer Aruri and Edmund Ghareeb in *Enemy of the Sun*.

89. From his poem "The Abyss of the City" in his collection *Birds Die in Galilee* in *Diwan Mahmoud Darwish, Complete works of Mahmoud Darwish*, 7th ed. (Beirut: Dar Al-'Audah, 1980), 1:401-2.

90. From "Horses Neighing on the Slope," translated for PROTA by Lena Jayyusi and Anne Waldman.

91. Richard Sheppard, "The Crisis of Language," in Malcolm Bradbury and James McFarlane, *Modernism: 1890-1930* (London: Penguin Books, new ed. 1987), pp. 325-29.

92. "Moderns and Contemporaries" in *The Idea of the Modern*, ed., Irving Howe, (New York: Horizon Press, 1967), pp. 43-44.

93. Translated by John Heath-Stubbs with my help. For a fuller translation of this poem by Lena Jayyusi and Christopher Middleton, see my *Modern Arabic Poetry*.

94. It should be noted here that I am speaking only of one aspect of the political theme: the poetry of resistance. The political theme itself has far greater ramifications than just this one topic.

95. Mahmoud Darwish, "Save Us from This Poetry," *Al-Karmel*, no.6 (Spring 1982).

96. Ghassan Zaqtan, "First Words Are Fascinating and We Shall Remember Them," *Al-Fikr al-Dimoqrati*, no. 3 (Summer 1988), pp. 192-93.

97. See his poem "Apology" on page 224.

98. Dahbour told me that in his early youth in 1963, he (whose scanty educational background was restricted to the refugee camp school in Southern Lebanon) happened to get hold of Tawfiq Sayigh's first collection, *Thirty Poems*, and was prompted, by Sayigh's modernist experiment, to send a letter to the poet through his publishers. Then in 1964, when Dahbour's first collection, *Beasts and Children's Eyes*, came out, he sent it to Sayigh with the dedication, "It is enough for me to say, 'I have lived in Tawfiq Sayigh's times.' " Sayigh, who must have found Dahbour's early admiration an oasis in a desert of neglect, sent the poet a telegram with these words: "Ahmad, you made me cry!"

99. This is a long way from Nizar Qabbani's famous invective against the same party, when he attacked in direct, angry, and ringing terms what he regarded as the lust and backwardness of some of the newly rich dignitaries in the Gulf countries; see his poem "Love and Petroleum," *Complete Political Works*, any edition. The subtlety of Barghouthy's indirect address, which mocks the same things, gives rich food for thought on radically changing poetic techniques and attitudes.

100. See, in this connection, my comments on Muhammad al-Maghut in my introduction to his collection in English, *The Fan of Swords* (see note 64 above).

101. See his poem "Intensive-Care Unit" on page 157.

102. See on pages 398-416 Liyana Badr's story "A Land of Rock and Thyme," where the Tel al-Zaatar episode is vividly and successfully described.

103. From "The Last Conversation in Paris," translated for PROTA by Lena Jayyusi and Jack Collom.

104. Raymond Williams, *Modern Tragedy* (London: Verso, 1979), p. 100.

105. From his poem "Earth Scrapes Us," translated by Lena Jayyusi and Christopher Middleton in *Modern Arabic Poetry*.

106. See my chapter "Platform Poetry," *Trends and Movements*, 2:583-64, where I fully discuss the technique of platform poetry and the way the audience forms part of the poem's making.

107. See his poem "After the Apocalypse," translated by Sharif Elmusa and Naomi Shihab Nye in my *Modern Arabic Poetry*.

108. See, for example, his poem "Second Song" in *Dimensions of the Soul*, 2d ed. (Jordan: Ladiqiyya, 1984), pp. 9–10, which is a mélange of colloquialisms and elevated vocabulary.

109. From his poem "Display Windows" translated by Hanan Mikha'il 'Ashrawi.

110. From his poem "Ardor" translated by 'Ashrawi.

111. From "Display Windows."

112. From "Display Windows."

113. From his poem "Tongue," translated by 'Ashrawi.

114. From "Display Windows."

115. See selections from these writers and those mentioned in the following paragraphs in the "Personal Accounts" section. The excerpts selected may, however, have been chosen from different editions in the works of these authors.

116. See note 5, and see also others, such as Laila al-Sa'ih, *Roots Do Not Depart* (1984) and Nasir al-Din al-Nashashibi, *Do You Know My Beloved Jerusalem?* (n.d. but after 1980).

117. To the best of my knowledge, the most recent example of personal account literature by a Palestinian is to be found in the reminiscences written by Mahmoud Rimawi about his ten-year experience in Kuwait, serialized during the autumn of 1990 in the daily *Al-Quds*, which appears in London. These reminiscences are due to appear in book form in 1991.

118. Ferial Ghazoul, "Beautiful Language of Opposites," *Fusul*, no. 1–2 (1986–1987): 192–202.

POETRY

Yusuf 'Abd al-'Aziz *(b. 1956)*

Yusuf 'Abd al-'Aziz was born in Beit 'Inan near Jerusalem, obtained his degree in the humanities from the Arab University in Beirut in 1986, and then a diploma from the Teacher's Training College in Na'ur, Jordan. One of the young experimentalists, he is active in the literary life of Jordan and has published several collections of poetry. Among his highly acclaimed collections are *Haifa Flies to al-Shaqeef,* published in 1983 immediately after the Israeli invasion of Beirut, and *The Stone's Song,* published in 1984. His sensitive and lively work makes 'Abd al-'Aziz one of the more impressive twentieth-century poets. He is included in PROTA's forthcoming anthology, *End of the Century Poets, New Voices in Arabic Poetry.*

The Traveler

He visits the station,
buys a ticket, and goes away.
He dreams of the unblinking sun,
of inns by the sea,
and the woman like a lily.
      He drinks her kiss
in bed
near a quiet window.

Always he had gathered his days
as the sea gathers its waves at twilight.
He watched them closely, then departed
for inscrutable destinations.
  —Did you find the right departure date?
  —No, I found the road that has severed the river
from its source.

  —translated by May Jayyusi and Naomi Shihab Nye

The House

When I met her by chance
she was a woman whose lips and braids
radiated.
She plucked a flower from my ribs
and flew to the fountainhead
where she built her house from its shining silk.

When I kissed her,
she ran like a gazelle
shimmering across God's open country.

I said, "Who are you, mare of the water?"
and she said, "I am queen."
When I embraced her
she engulfed me with her waves
and lit my spirit's stars.
I said, "Who are you, velvet flower?"
She said, "I am the down of the nightingale,
the milk of kisses."
When I gave her my sweetest embrace
and performed my ritual prayer,
she stormed through me, through every cell and vein
and erected on my dead body
a house for life.

—translated by May Jayyusi and Naomi Shihab Nye

A Place

At this late hour
when the sky oozes heavenly calm,
when everything goes to bed
and sleeps:
    the fighter to his dream of freedom
    the moon to its pillow of clouds
    the lover to his woman's waves
Where will I, the poet, find rest?

—translated by May Jayyusi and Naomi Shihab Nye

Mist

(to Poetry)

Welcome, you wolf slinking into the chambers of calm.
Welcome to you, ancient bird,
to you, murdered daisies.
Welcome to you, my enemy
of very few words.

Was it for this illuminated dust
that you dragged me one day
then dropped me into darkness?

—translated by May Jayyusi and Naomi Shihab Nye

A Song

A woman who rose
from the voice of the first stone,
from the roses of singers,
from the mountain's stream,
and pierced my heart like a spear,
only to disappear into the distance.

A woman of wine and honey . . .
she unnerved me like the hand of God,
and I embraced my death,
saw blood water the earth
and birds tumble down
into the massacre's cauldron,
saw the sea awaken from its solitude
and fire oozing through the veins
of the tree.

A woman, precious light of the eyes . . .
The earth bore her in the month of June.
She stretched her hands out to me
and we embraced at the gateway of defeat,
breeding fighters in all directions.

—translated by May Jayyusi and Naomi Shihab Nye

The Shaqeef Moon[1]

For an evening laden with prophets
for thirty-three gardens
for the red seed bursting in the rock
for the rock that pierces the clouds
and for the free sun

I shall tune my strings to the wind
and sing.
For those who burned like morning birds
I shall sing.
The blood that springs from their bodies flows from mine.

And the blood that runs in the southern plain[2]
is wine flowing from the heart of Beit 'Inan[3]
Let the shepherds spread out in the hills
around Jerusalem
Let the flocks of village women
seek the beautiful colt.

May a wedding stretch from Damour[4]
to the trees of Fawwar[5] near Hebron.
And Haifa, let your hair be for them,
a burst of mint and pure field grasses.

[1] The *Shaqeef* is the famous fortress in southern Lebanon where thirty-three Palestinian fighters fought heroically against the invading Israeli army in 1982. The Israelis lost many men, including officers. All the Palestinian fighters fell in battle before the fortress eventually capitulated. It was regarded as a major position, and after its fall, Menachem Begin, then the prime minister of Israel, came and handed the fortress with his own hands to Saad Haddad, the leader of one faction of Christian forces fighting against the national and the Palestinian resistance in the south.

[2] The southern plain is a reference to southern Lebanon, where warring Lebanese factions engaged in many battles against each other, and where Palestinians also fought side by side with national Lebanese forces and against the invading Israeli army.

[3] Beit 'Inan is an Arab village near Jerusalem and the poet's birthplace.

[4] Damour is a town in southern Lebanon where fierce battles with the Israeli army were fought by both Palestinian and Lebanese resistance forces.

[5] Fawwar is an Arab refugee camp at the outskirts of Hebron in southern Palestine.

For an evening laden with prophets
for thirty-three gardens
wear your blue waves, Haifa.
Illuminate your red bricks
and stretch
      to the summit of the song.

    —translated by May Jayyusi and Naomi Shihab Nye

Khalid Abu Khalid (b. 1937)

Born in the Palestinian village of Silat al-Dhahr, Abu Khalid lived and worked for some time in Kuwait and Beirut. He now lives in Damascus. A poet of firm beliefs, with a steadfast outlook on life, Abu Khalid has participated fully in serving his people and has dedicated much of his poetry to the Palestinian cause. His first collection, *A Medal on the Breast of the Militia,* appeared in 1971; since then he has published seven more collections, the most recent being *I Call You the Sea, I Call my Hand the Sand* (1990).

Prayer to the Tremor of the Final Evening

For Beisan, my little girl

For the bird which will flutter on my final evening
I spread two wings from my heart's pavilion.
Casting my song into her hands, she cries
and points to the wall, toward a blank window,
a songless bird,
and lost dreams of dancing in this moment of tears.
I return to her,
a vision cast down from the sky
and we share a tender hour . . .
An hour lapses in a sad dialogue of love and death
two teardrops unite us, binding questions and recollection
till she plunges into a weeping full as song
and between the sobbing ruins arises the refugee camp
            slaughter of people,
a mirage rising before us
and dissolving in the fog
I drop, defeated, towards my shadow . . .
The road narrows as I leave, it narrows
so I remove my head,
my heart,
my skin,

remove my name,
planting my song in the soil
ascending towards the final evening
as though I had not left.
And pain's presence ascends within me.

Beirut has two faces
the face of destruction and the countenance of beauty
Amman has two faces
one wretched and one glorious
Haifa's faces unfold within us glossing the fields with dew
    and the blazes of battle
And love has two rhythms
the rhythm of exile and the rhythm of origin
Damascus has two faces, exile and departure
and between Palestine and me lies the season of slaughter.
Between you and me, a dove-like murmur,
and the whinnying of horses before they burst
into the warring field.

Now who knocks at the door?
    Autumn's bird laden with grief . . .
Even she can feel the siege
so she picks at a wool thread
patiently whistling her melancholy tunes
Faces scatter their sorrows before the coming winds
Where is the gleaming pearl of morning which once
        gave hope?
I dismounted between the clouds
    and the palm trees' friendly stare
plunged deep
I lamented with a lemon tree until
its own veins extended into my blood
We were one, trembling, touched, and
    my voice emerged from a point in nothingness
      a single droplet
        just a tear

I remembered that we had been friends from a time
    laden with wounds
extending from the first tyrannical shelling forward

through all the beginnings and endings of our lives
We had been friends from the time of patient trees
till the bitterness and fear of the long march
We had been friends since we met
You used to bring water to the basil plant
I send you now an apple, a celebration of
        friendly roses
            I send gentle grass
a bird to companion your sensitive weary eyes
May it be your friend
as I cross this pavement toward the shriveled trees
                faded graves and dust
Leave my corpse in the deserts
searching for us
Enter into a time, into a state of being
of a weary man who loiters among newspapers
        in the wind,
who enters the broadcasting stations seeking a cheering item
            of news
and exits from them slain
who drinks his coffee bitter . . . and dissolves.

She is the orange that colored the final evening
the fragrance of jasmine bursting into the gloom of water
                of blood and road
the sign
    the light
            the banner, moon and sea
                flame, and poetry
the fresh face of the martyr
I beckon to her now to open for me
before I die from the heat, the sorrow and cold

Who knocks at the door?
    Two childrem—a boy and a girl
            The phantom of a kiss hovering between them
    Notebooks arrive
                ink, and carriages
Oceans and boats come to her surrounded by song
Letters come, the weary ones
and I come

a rose upon my forehead, a book clutched,
and my breast hiding questions within my clothes
   —Why?
   —What?
   —And how did the exiled villages scatter?
   —How is it that we burned up in vain in the deserts?
   —How is it that the road to Jerusalem is closed off,
         and the shady roads that led to harbors
            have disappeared?
   —Who will kindle a fire for the traveler in the desert haze,
         or offer him some bread and salt?
   —Who will trade pulse for pulse?
   —Who will plant promises between the first step
         and the final anchor?
   —Will the vagrants' lives go unharvested by every season?
   —Who will share night's ceiling with the refugee camp,
         or roses with martyrs?
   —Who will limit the slaughter of childhood?
Follow the moment of conception to the terrible terrible end.

To her now I raise the fighter's arch, bowing down
         on a singular and solitary pain
dividing its chords among us
From my blood I grant her a wave, that she may sing
She unfolds her estrangement, opens her hands,
         and within her the vast wilderness unfolds
She flings open a wide window for the stranger,
         the wounded stranger stopped by shells
releases a memory brilliant with the blaze of cornstalks
releases all the unsaddled horses
To her I now declare her own trembling within my blood
I declare that the mountains shall erupt
the sky rain victory wreaths
over the roads that have suddenly opened up
         in the siege

   —translated by Lena Jayyusi and Naomi Shihab Nye

Yusuf Abu Lauz *(b. 1956)*

Born in Jordan, Abu Lauz studied at the Higher Teacher Training Institute in Amman, graduating in 1977. Since then he has worked as a teacher in such Arab states as Algeria, Saudi Arabia, and the United Arab Emirates, where he still lives. Active in literary circles, he joined both the Union of Jordanian Writers and, later, the Union of the Writers of the United Arab Emirates. He is one of the editors of the latter Union's literary review, *Literary Affairs*. He has published three collections of poetry. His first, *Fatima Goes Early to the Fields* (1983), demonstrated his originality and his passion for experimentation with new forms and styles; his third collection, *Blood Texts,* appeared in 1986, and showed the growth of the poetic inventiveness that has brought him well-deserved acclaim.

From Trees on Maryam's Sleeves

Maryam in the Grass

You smoked more than ever
that evening on the street beside the sea.
Your lips poured out rivers of poems,
then you broke down on the pavements.
You left,
coatless and alone
coatless as the frost stripped bare the city,
and you waited at the window.
Perhaps a hand would wave in your directon.
Perhaps a bird would light on a tree.

In the cities of the earth you had suffered,
exchanging one affliction for two,
dipping your hard bread in salt.
Despair was your cloak.
Yours was the ancient oak
the strewn leaves, fallen like lovers' hearts.

Yours was the fire, the waiting.
And when you arrived at the distant room
shrouded by quinine trees,
Maryam met you at the door.
She prepared you for the grass of the bed
and lit the fireplace.

—translated by Sharif Elmusa and Naomi Shihab Nye

Trees of Words

Waiting for my woman with hands like spring,
the time passed slowly.
I took refuge in words, preparing my madness for her coming.
I thought of slapping her when she arrived.
I thought of forcing her to dance,
or to sing like African tribes,
like the lovers of Qairawan.[1]

Then I thought of making her untie her hair
under the fountain in the garden
and feed the birds with her slim hands.
I did not fetch a chair, or a book
to read together. I did not buy her
a honeycomb, or a basket of pears.

Suddenly, like lightning from the northern jungles
she entered.
My waiting, my doubt,
all my little plans dissolved in the presence of her eyes.
I forgot to stretch out my hand
to greet this whole city rising from the wheat fields.

That moment,
I felt the sky had swallowed my room,
a dizziness afflicted my papers and books,
I collapsed like an old earthenware jug.
But this was not the end of the story.

[1]Qairawan is a medieval Islamic city in central Tunisia.

As we crossed the road, hands joined, she said,
"I love you."
We stood before a red light. "To love, one must have
a country to bless his love."
But she answered, "Our homeland flows in
    our blood. We carry it with us in this world, wherever we go,
    no matter how far."
I said, "Even this is not enough."
We did not agree, and the problems of streets, and lovers
    remained an unfinished story
    at an unfinished crossing.

—translated by Sharif Elmusa and Naomi Shihab Nye

Your Talk or the Vodka

It's alright,
We have time for a bottle of vodka
and a short conversation.
We have time for the snow on cypress trees.

Don't stop quickly at the door,
water the roses on the balcony!
Woman born of winds
the Barada River[2] breaks in your palms
and trembles in my presence.
Let's fold up our crisis,
return to the first lilac,
announce the reasons for our joys.
Let's pluck the body's ripe fruits.
Something is dancing at the gates of earth.
Something awakens rebellion in us.
Something grants us the terms of our marriage.
It's alright.
We still have time for embarrassing questions
and quiet dialogue.
Who'll go first?
Who'll begin?

—translated by Sharif Elmusa and Naomi Shihab Nye

[2]The Barada river flows through Damascus.

Abu Salma (pseudonym for Abd al-Kareem al-Karmi) (1907–1980)

Abu Salma's family came from the area of the city of Tulkarm in the region of Bani Saab. He moved to Haifa where he practiced law until Haifa fell to Jewish factions in 1948; he fled to Acre and then to Damascus where he lived until his death. His poetry was dedicated to the Palestine cause, and he came to be called "The Olive Tree of Palestine," an allusion to his firm psychological and cultural identification with his country. Abu Salma published several volumes of poetry and was central in representing Palestinian literature at conferences and cultural meetings. In 1978 he was granted the Lotus Prize for Literature by the Union of Asian and African Writers.

My Country on Partition Day

On November 29, 1947, the United Nations approved the partition of Palestine despite the disagreement of many states which voted against it.

My country! Live in safety, an Arab country,
may the jewel of your tradition continue smiling
Though they've partitioned your radiant heart
our honor denies partition.
We've woven your wedding clothes with red thread
dyed from our own blood.
We've raised banners on the Mountain of Fire[1]
marching toward our inevitable destiny!
History marches behind our footsteps,
honor sings around us.

Rise, friend, see how many people
drag their chains of dented steel.

---

[1]The city of Nablus and its suburbs and nearby villages were all called the Mountain of Fire, because the region was a seat of rebellion against the British Mandate and its application of Zionist policy.

Behold the serpents slithering endlessly among them!
They've prohibited oppression among themselves
but for us they legalized all prohibitions!
They proclaim, "Trading with slaves is unlawful"
but isn't the trading of free people more of a crime?
In the West man's rights are preserved,
but the man in the East is stoned to death.
Justice screams loudly protecting Western lands
but grows silent when it visits us!
Maybe justice changes colors and shapes!
Live embers scorch our lips
so listen to our hearts speaking,
call on free men in every land
to raise the flag of justice where we stand.

—translated by Sharif Elmusa and Naomi Shihab Nye

We Shall Return

Beloved Palestine, how can I sleep
when phantoms torture my eyes?
In your name I greet the wide world,
but caravans of days pass,
ravaged by conspiracies of enemies and friends.
Beloved Palestine, how can I live
away from your plains and hills?
The valleys call me and the shores
cry out, echoing in the ears of time!
Even fountains weep as they trickle, estranged.
Your cities and villages echo the cries.
Will there be a return, my comrades ask,
a return after such long absence?
Yes, we'll return and kiss the moist ground,
love flowering on our lips.
We'll return some day while generations listen
to the echoes of our feet.
We'll return with raging storms,
holy lightning and fire,
winged hope and songs,

soaring eagles,
the dawn smiling on the deserts.
Some morning we'll return riding the crest of the tide,
our bloodied banners fluttering
above the glitter of spears.

—translated by Sharif Elmusa and Naomi Shihab Nye

I Love You More

The more I fight for you, the more I love you!
What land except this land of musk and amber?
What horizon but this one defines my world?
The branch of my life turns greener when I uphold you
and my wing, Oh Palestine, spreads wide over the peaks.

Has the lemon tree been nurtured by our tears?
No more do birds flutter among the high pines,
or stars gaze vigilantly over Mt. Carmel.
The little orchards weep for us, gardens grow desolate,
the vines are forever saddened.

Whenever your name sounds in my ears, my words grow more poetic
planting desire for you on every stoop.
Is it possible these words could be torches
lighting each desert and place of exile?
Oh Palestine! Nothing more beautiful, more precious, more pure!
The more I fight for you, the more I love you.

—translated by Sharif Elmusa and Naomi Shihab Nye

Zuhair Abu Shayib *(b. 1958)*

Born in the Palestinian village of Dayr al-Ghusun, Abu Shayib obtained his B.A. in Arabic Literature from Yarmouk University in Jordan in 1983. He then worked as a teacher and journalist in North Yemen for a year, before returning to Jordan where he works as a graphic designer. He is greatly interested in painting and calligraphy and publishes criticism on the Arab literary heritage in various Arab newspapers. His two collections of poetry are *Geography of the Wind and of Questions* (1986) and *Situations* (1987). In his poetry, Abu Shayib demonstrates a deep involvement in the Palestinian experience, sharing the suffering of other Palestinian creative writers and their unanimous protest against the injustice that has befallen them. His original and varied approach to his subject makes him one of the most promising young poets now writing in the Arab world.

Fever of Questions

For how long will you amuse your
    wild wound
    with images of the Hanging Gardens?

And for how long will you remain patient for horses
    to come
and the jungle moon
    to shine
You, whose innocent coffin
hangs in the winds?

For how long
will you postpone writing
and imprison your eyes in a cloud?

   —translated by May Jayyusi and Jeremy Reed

Probabilities

From what source of light
does the day occur?
Does the earth propitiate itself
and the seas catch fire?
By what light
    do we shell the roads until daybreak?
    And the sound is bearable
    and the salt is bearable
    and the morning, like the bullets, is bearable.

Stop, you tall handsome one
we pass from our blood to our blood
    and never arrive
and take flight to our blood
    and the siege pursues us
The wound in our suitcases
    bears our features
    while it is carried by the sea.
        And death is bearable
        and silence is bearable
        and the morning, like bullets, is bearable.

—translated by May Jayyusi and Jeremy Reed

Handsome and Tall
(after midnight)

At the first hour after midnight he stretched
buttoned two stars over his wounds
    and lay down.
Horses were galloping in his wrists
conquering the east.
But at this first act of the day
his courage lacked temerity

At the second hour
the tall handsome one lay down
and buttoned two stars

over his wound.
There was nothing in his chest but
     two bullets
Twice he thought of dying
     then turned over and tried to alight.

In the third hour he stretched
and when he washed his two stars with blood,
he tied his arms to the clouds
     and broke the air
     striking a flame in the woodfire of the stars,
and again tried to get up.

    —translated by May Jayyusi and Jeremy Reed

Martyr

They found him
     luminous, green, in the field.
When they raised his hands
the grasses under them had turned to hearts.

It is said:
     wheatstalks bloomed beneath his sleeves.
It is said:
     The birds carried his blood
     to his beloved cousins.
          He shall return
     blossoming with volcanoes,
     and fill again his mother's breasts.
When they found him green as light
they shrouded him with rose buds,
they spread out the sky to lay him on
and made the sun his pillow.

    —translated by May Jayyusi and Naomi Shihab Nye

Psalm

Ah! The words I never said
           pain me
And those which I have spoken
           also pain me
My own words in the mouths of others
           pain me
Ah! How my voice cracks and divides
How the wind arrests my song!

—translated by May Jayyusi and Naomi Shihab Nye

Taha Muhammad 'Ali (b. 1931)

Born in Saffouria in the district of Nazareth (a village razed to the ground by the Israelis in 1948), Taha Muhammed Ali now lives in Nazareth. A Palestinian poet and short story writer, he is a self-taught man who worked all his life as a teacher and began his poetic career late. He writes a poetry profoundly motivated by the fact of Israeli occupation of his country. Though his poems are extremely popular among the Arabs of Israel, the occupied West Bank, and Gaza, his work is relatively unknown elsewhere. This is due to the rather poor literary communications that exist (with few exceptions) between Arab writers in the occupied territories and the rest of the Arab world. However, the ardent sentiment and the apt metaphorical representation of a devastating experience that is reflected in his poetry must inevitably bring his work to the attention of a larger Arab audience. Taha Muhammad 'Ali published his first collection, *The Fourth and Ten Additional Poems,* in 1983; it is now in its third printing. His second book of poetry, *Tricking the Murderers,* appeared in Haifa in 1989. He is now preparing his third collection for publication, *A Fire in the Convent's Graveyard.*

Thrombosis

A child I was
when I fell into the abyss
But I did not die
I was very young
when I drowned in the pond
But I did not die
Nowadays one of my habits—God preserve us—
is to knock against scores of land mines
      on the frontiers
and for my songs to be dispersed
as the days of my youth are:
here a flower, there a scream
But I do not die!

They slew me upon the threshold
Like the lamb of the feast
—petroleum coagulated in my veins
—In God's name—
Thousands of times they slit my throat
        from ear to ear
yet each time my blood would swing
like the feet of a hanged man
and settle like a rose mallow
large and crimson, a mark
to warn ships
and point out the sites of palaces and embassies.

And tomorrow!
—God preserve us!—
A telephone will not ring
in palaces or in brothels
or in one of the Gulf Emirates
except to offer a new prescription
for my extermination
But . . .
Just as the rose mallow tells
and as the frontiers expect
I shall not die!
Shall not die!!
I shall remain a splinter of shrapnel
the size of a penknife
lodged in their necks
I shall remain
a blood stain
the size of a cloud
on this world's tunic!

    —translated by Lena Jayyusi and John Heath-Stubbs

Exodus

The street is empty
like the memory of a monk
and faces explode in the flames
like an acorn
and the dead crowd all the doorways
they crowd the horizon
and no vein can bleed
        more than it has already bled
no scream can rise
        higher than it has already risen
We will not leave!
Everyone outside is waiting for the vehicles
laden with hostages and honey
We will not leave!
The shields of light are breaking in the face of this siege
in the face of these ill-matched forces
From outside, everyone wants us to leave
But we will not leave!
Ivory white girls hide themselves
from the glare of captivity
and everyone outside wants us to leave
We will not leave!
The big guns rake the jujube trees
and destroy the dreams of the violets
they blunt hunger, but sharpen thirst
they parch lips and souls.
And everyone outside says:
"What are you waiting for? All warmth is denied,
the very air is confiscated,
so why don't you leave?"
Masks fill the pulpits, the brothels and the places of ablution
Masks cross-eyed with surprise
do not believe what is obvious
and fall, astonished and writhing
like worms.

We will not leave!
Are we inside here merely to be outside?

Leaving is only for the masks, for pulpits and for conferences
It is only the siege within that should go outside
the siege which the bedouins of the deserts have brought on us
the siege inflicted by brethren tasting of the sword
and the stink of carrion birds
We will not leave!
Those outside are closing the escape routes
and giving their blessings to the imposter
Praying, petitioning the Almighty God
for our deaths.

—translated by Lena Jayyusi and John Heath-Stubbs

Laila 'Allush (b. 1948)

'Allush has been a citizen of Israel all her life. A poet from occupied Palestine, her poetry has been colored by the fact of occupation and by the frustrations of life as a second-class citizen in her own country. Her first collection of poems, *Spices on the Open Wound*, was published in 1971; her second, *Years of Drought, My Heart*, in 1972. Though her poetry is dominated by a tone of regret over Palestine's fate, it is illuminated by glimmering faith in the inevitability of resurgence and victory.

The Path of Affection

On the startling road seized from the throat of new accounts
On the startling road seized from this century's earrings
reaching the bloodied neck
On the surprising road seized from old Jerusalem
and despite the estrangement of signs, shops and graveyards,
I gather my fragmented self together,
to meet my relatives in the New Haifa.

My companions on our smooth trip in the minibus
know nothing of my suffering
But I am an authentic face, well-rooted,
while their seven faces are alien.

This land is still the old land
despite pawned trees on the hillsides
despite green clouds and fertilized plants
and water sprinklers spinning so efficiently
On the startling road seized from the throat of new accounts
the trees were smiling at me with Arab affection
In the land I felt an apology for my father's wounds
and on all the bridges,
the shape of my Arab face
echoed there in the tall poplar trees,
in the winding rings of smoke.

Everything is Arabic still, despite the change of language
despite the huge trucks, and foreign tractors.
Each poplar and the orange grove of my ancestors
laughed to me, my God, with Arab affection.

Despite changes, dismissals and revisions,
despite the modern tunes,
commercials slapping visitors' faces
despite the flooding seas of light, despite technology
the many psalms, the many nails
and all the goings and comings of foreign peoples,
the land continued to sing an affectionate Arab tune.

Even with propaganda wavering in the air
languages mingling, multiplying,
around the strange outgrowths
of modern buildings,
the land was gently defying it all.
Oh my grandparents, even in the stark light of noon,
the red soil was shining
with Arab modesty
and singing, believe me,
affectionately.

—translated by Lena Jayyusi and Naomi Shihab Nye

A New Creation

I was born in June
that's why my brow is branded with thorns,
why I await for dawn to clear
the painful night from my eyes.

I was born in June
That's why the executioner keeps trying
to change my name
He trims his moustaches and fortifies
the cracks in my prison
leaving the open field free for the beasts
       that crave my flesh.

In June I was born
That's why they constructed a thousand
scarecrows which they clad
in my stolen clothes
          my shoes,
          my coat
impaling them on poisoned arrows
          in my land
hiding my grandfather's sword
selling his remains
          before my eyes.

In June I was born
In June I came alive again
This is why I await the dawn
          with nerves
          and flesh
          and eyes
And this is why I still
beget children.
Guarding my loaf from the pouch of the beast
          in the torturous night
and this is why
my ancient olive branch
was awakened after twenty years
by the tremor of creation, becoming
a whip of fire in my hand.

          —translated by Lena Jayyusi and Naomi Shihab Nye

Naji 'Allush (b. 1935)

Poet, scholar, and critic, 'Allush was born and educated in Birzeit in the vicinity of Jerusalem. After teaching in Jordan for a year, he moved in 1956 to Kuwait where, as an Arab socialist, he found considerable sympathy with his political and revolutionary ideas among other expatriate Arabs. 'Allush concentrated on studying contemporary Arab thought and wrote his first book on the subject, *The Contemporary Arab Revolutioinary* in 1960. He has lived in various Arab cities, including Beirut, and now lives in Damascus. He has spent his life in the service of Arab and Palestinian causes and his poetry devotes itself to the political situation all over the Arab world. One of the most committed of contemporary Arab poets, he used the two-hemistich form until 1957 when he began writing in free verse. He has published four collections of poetry: *The Road of Wounds, A Little Present* (1967), *Windows Opened by Bombs* (1970), and *Bridges of Yearning*. These were published in a single volume entitled *Complete Poetic Works* in 1979.

On the Shore

1

The ocean pauses at the shore,
grows quiet,
quiet,
releases its abundant dreams . . .
Fields of wheat and palm trees
flow out like a field of cornstalks
and quietness reigns . . .

2

Then it stretches into the horizon,
the length and breadth of it,
and reaches out beyond . . .
It grows limpid
and my eyes drown

in the breezes that awaken buried yearnings.
Then the sea grows turbulent . . .
In the ample horizon
horses surge up and gallop,
a tender drizzle
of spraying foam
comes into my place of exile,
and the wind immerses me in damnable kisses.

3

It is
the ocean
coming . . .
It is the ocean coming.
Fields of wheat and palm trees,
palm trees and wheat . . .
Sometimes it comes as cornstalks
sometimes as clusters of ripe grapes
and thickets of trees . . .

4

And I
where sea and sand are joined
am walking towards my thirst,
am searching for threshing floors
that will accept me,
for grapes that will not mock my hunger . . .

5

And I
where sand and sea are parted
am standing, am watching
the palm trees and the wheat
from the sea's tranquility . . .
it comes . . .
and against the anger
of the breaking foam
that approaches, row after row,

harvest after harvest,
that comes in thickets.

6

And I
where sand and sea are joined
call out to the sea on behalf of the sand,
implore mercy for the thirsty
houses
and the sorrowing trees . . .

7

And I
where sand and sea
are joined . . .
One time, the sea's calm spell calls to me
and another time
the sea's anger draws me
so I go to the sea
ecstatic
and leave the sands . . .

8

Then it is the sand
and eternal thirst
that call to me . . .
I leap seething
with imagination
back to my country

9

And where the sea and
sand are joined
I store up an eternal thirst
and carry from my country
the throb of captive hearts.

10

Here I stand
for centuries
pursued by sand and drought
and by eternal thirst.
Currents leave me exposed . . .

11

Sometimes the sea stops and the sand
does not
or sometimes the sand stops
and the sea does not
And sometimes I seek the sea
and not the sand
or sometimes I seek the sand
and not the sea . . .
And one time
the flowers in my body
want the sand
and do not want the sea
or want the sea and do not want
the sand
And sea and sand are parted . . .
I am one . . .
Within me are the sand and sea
lightning and thunder
rain and eternal thirst . . .
Who then will solemnize the marriage?

12

It is the ocean . . .
It stretches out
                    and out
                            and out
embraces the sand on Jaffa's coast,
frolics with the houses in Asqalan . . .
And here I am
standing stock-still.

I do not give my heart up to the sea.
I do not brave the water and its proud eddies.
Here I am
chained by the city . . .

13

Stand still, Sea . . .
Stand still, Sand . . .
My heart radiates with sadness
and with captive regrets.
I love the wind, and the water,
and the damnable kisses . . .
Stand still, Sand,
I am coming with sweeping torrents.
Move on, Sea,
I am riding the untameable horse.

—translated by Lena Jayyusi and Thomas G. Ezzy

'Abd al-Latif 'Aql *(b. 1942)*

Poet, dramatist, and scholar, 'Aql has had an active career both as an academic and as a man of letters. Born to a poor family in a village near Nablus, his father died when 'Aql was a child; he had to struggle throughout the years to achieve his educational goals. He studied for his B.A. in Damascus, then obtained an M.A. at the United States International University at San Diego, California, and a Ph.D. in psychological anthropology in 1979, at the same university. In 1983, he obtained another doctorate in clinical psychology from the University of Houston, Texas. He taught at the University of Bethlehem and then at the Najah National University in Nablus, where he is now vice-president for academic and cultural affairs. In his sensitive and melodic poetry, 'Aql skilfully mixes love with nationalism—a nationalism full of dignity and enduring love, but also full of the regrets of one who has known tragedy and seen tremendous suffering. He has published seven collections of poetry, including: *Poems on a Love That Knows No Mercy* (1975); *Children Chase Locusts* (1976); and *Dialogue of the Same Love* (1985). His four academic books include his book in English, *Agony in Limbo,* published in 1985. He writes extensively for Arab periodicals and participates in many conferences on education, politics, and literature. He was a visiting professor at the University of Wisconsin from 1987 to 1988.

From "From Jerusalem to the Gulf"

Write to me
Here I watch the ebb of the Nile in the valley of treason
Watch Pharaoh play chess in Washington
resting in the shade of the impossible.
Write to me:
The colt flees from Acre to the memory of time
     which flees from my sleepless eyes
     to the beautiful shore of your eyes
Write to me, even a word or two,
of a pearl's yearning, when it has been forced out of its shell.
Once it was hid in the safe harbor of the heart

Write to me about Oman and Dubai
about the palms where the sands hid
      a bedouin sorrow
Write to me about Bahrain, about the wound
      that joins your hands to mine
      about the colt that runs in the desert
      blindfolded,
      that roams this savage time.

Write to me, tell me how, when surrounded
by palm trees and oil wells
you weep when you remember
Jerusalem and Jericho's honied crops
How, surrounded by all that sand,
you weep when the news of young students
facing enemy bullets with books and a thousand rods
      arouses you

In your hesitant writing my Palestinian sorrows meet
with the sorrows of the Arabian Gulf.
Write to me and ask
how people can walk in the square
planted with the limbs of young girls
torn by the occupiers' savage vehicles.
The doves we knew so well in Station Street
do not coo as usual
and the bashful flowers that witnessed our love
are no longer dewy.
Ramadan is over, but I did not go out to sit in
any cafe,
the gunfire that signals the feast did not ring out this year
it was silenced by military orders.
My house is no longer the refuge of butterflies
that had once fluttered on your lips
The birds that once flocked to you
have disappeared,
but their abandoned nests still cling to my roof.
Ah, you will never know
      my longing,
I wish you could come
      some long cold night
      on the wind

or on the feather of a bird wounded by love
There's nothing like love to mitigate
the dark cold of winter nights.

Write to me
The glass loves the vine and lovers, the caravans
Orphans love warmth
and the bird seeks the ear of wheat
Write to me
My heart is tired of politicans, of the politics of normalization,
of parcelled wars.

Write to me a few words
The lamps of love can burn away the endless night
          of Occupation
One letter of love can turn
a cramped cell
into a wide horizon,
into a field and a running stream,
and transform that irascible warden
          into a human being

Write to me
One letter of love can release
          in the prison and the prisoner
          the flowers of hope
and on the walls of Jerusalem
          thousands of ears of wheat.

Write to me, do not write to me
A Time has begun in us
          a Time ends in us
          What use are letters?

—translated by Sharif Elmusa and Dick Davies

On the Presence of Absence

(To "A," whom I haven't seen for twenty years)

Suddenly the cafés and the sands of the Gulf
made peace with me.
Birds craned their bloodied beaks
toward the wound in my side.
I drank a coke, iced with unhappy conscience
Two planes and some settlers were attacking my home in Jerusalem
I tried to find out
        the secret of his cool smile.

I gazed at his picture twice. Between
the glitter of tears and tears
      a country was dying,
      poems, and a loss that orphaned me
      at birth. No,
      he hasn't died, he has only slept in my memory.

Suddenly capital cities meet in us; oil tankers
raise their flags over us, and bitter Time
is contracted to an immeasurable moment.
I ache with longing
For how can I meet him now in the cities of exile
when our promised meeting place
was Nazareth?

Just as we were twenty years ago; the flood of tears in Amman[1]
is our witness: he used to go and collect the news of Ma'rib
discover the footsteps of Abu Dhur, the rebel slain for justice
and I stayed behind
like an olive tree in the mountains of Galilee
recording with blood and tears
his ever present absence.

We're just as we were: he would feed me when hunger
devastated him. I would raise him if he fell

---

[1]The reference to Amman here is to the Black September Civil War in 1970 between
the Jordanian army and Palestinian fighters. Thousands of Palestinians were killed during
that war, and the fighters of the Resistance were either captured or had to take refuge
elsewhere.

in the mud, imbue his heart
with Jerusalem's anger and despair.
Zeal would kindle in his Arab heart
and our rainy days would shine with the sun.

We lost the road. He carried his possessions, riding
his fear through the night
Tribesmen did not discover him at the borders
He went in disguise
And I, on embers, waited for occasional news from him
never leaving Jerusalem in twenty years
fighting the invasion of armed locusts
drawing the picture of the Eagle of Quraish[2]
repainting the minarets green.
In every hour of truth the maps turn against me
Amman tortures me in Jerusalem, and Baghdad
denies Beirut in my name
Damascus kills me in Cairo.

Suddenly Time gives birth to love poems on a page.
There is a delicate line between love and death
O, outlawed poets! arise from the grave
The Caliph
—may God protect him—has embroidered some of your poems
on the sleeve of his magnificent cloak.

—translated by Sharif Elmusa and Dick Davies

---

[2]"Eagle of Quraish" refers to 'Abd al-Rahman I, a member of the ruling Umayyad
dynasty in Damascus. The Umayyads ruled from 661–750 A.D. when they were overthrown
by the Abbasid dynasty and massacred almost to the last man. 'Abd al-Rahman I, later
called "the Immigrant" or the "Eagle of Quraish" fled from the Abbasids and was able
to enter Spain in 756 A.D., oust the governor, and proclaim himself the Prince of the
Muslims. He was one of the greatest Arab rulers of medieval times and was responsible
for laying the foundations for a flourishing Muslim civilization in Spain.

Quraish is the tribe of the prophet and of the two dynasties, the Umayyads and the
Abbasids, and, in modern times, of the Hashimites of Jordan and (formerly) of Iraq.

Muhammad al-Asʿad *(b. 1944)*

Born in the village of Um al-Zeinat near Haifa, Palestine, al-Asʿad's family became refugees in 1948 and eventually settled in Basra, Iraq, where the poet received his early education. Despite great financial difficulties, al-Asʿad was able to complete his studies and move in 1968 to Kuwait, where he worked as a journalist. He now lives and works in Cyprus. Al-Asʿad's poetry is rich in sensuous imagery and emotion and reflects the poet's involvement in the themes of personal love and the collective suffering of Palestinians living in the diaspora. In addition to a book of criticism, *Poetic Diction,* al Asʿad has published several collections of poetry, the last of which is *To Your Shores Come the Birds Today* (1980). An autobiography of the poet's childhood, *Children of the Dew,* was published in London in 1991. His work is included in PROTA's forthcoming anthology, *End of the Century Poets, New Voices in Arabic Poetry.*

Personal Account

You awaken in cities you don't know
Beneath a sky you don't know.
Ghost and event split your loyalty
    You are the hour and the transient cloud.
A moon face
Rises at the far end of the earth
Sets. . .
Come to me.
There where the desert is steeped in eternal time
Hard, dead mushrooms sprout
Multiply
Sprawl
Are called cities.
People are snails grown old.
Roads are circles
Coiling
Coiling
Coiling.

Come to a corner of this planet.
Let us drink wine.
Let us contemplate a past sealed around kingdoms
                         we have not known
The joy hiding in other cities
Shorelines yet unformed.
Come
We shall awaken in a stupor.
We shall share
Cups of coffee on a winter morning.
Look before I do
For a necktie, a shirt and a book.
Precede me to the street brimming with Quranic verse.
You will talk to me then
Of a sun dawning for the first time
Of sea-shells
Gleaming now
Making the walls of the heart tremble
Of roads we awake
To see them extending,
Extending
Extending.
Come, desolation overwhelms me.
A crowd of events divides me.
I am the machined hour and the transient cloud
A moon face
Rising at the far end of the earth
Sliding down
In this rocklike night.
The bells of the spirit ring out.
The dazed body is inflamed
By other bodies
And unseen,
Is submerged by a flood of sleep.
A thousand stony cities
Over the darkness and the desert simply
Float.

Once again
Cities collapse.

An arrow shoots into space
But does not return.
You try to figure out forgotten words
Fumbling for the first sound.
Once more you live in estrangement.
Once again
Snares are snatching at your hands.
How alien things are
When you forget their ways.

What will come next
Will be even darker.

—translated by May Jayyusi and Jack Collom

A Song

When we remember things
One string rings out.
Woman alone
Plays on all the strings
With one stroke
Because she is the entire homeland.

—translated by May Jayyusi and Jack Collom

Prophets

Someone
Will stumble across our prophecies.
We're the foolish prophets
In tonight's alleys.
Where will those words be?
In which museum?
What portions will remain forever obscure?
We're the poets
Annihilated

In the language
In history
And in love . . . ?

—translated by May Jayyusi and Jack Collom

Singers

A deep plunge into the darkness
Merits golden birds
Red roses
And a band all ready to play.
But we the singers in the Arab night
The night of low-profile stars
And eternal sands
We scorn the reward
And cannot take it in.
When the faces of the judges peer down on us
We weep a botanical pain
Picked up in meadows, weep
The blue of waters
And the beauty of deer
Running in our valleys.
When sentence is passed down
In our absolute absence
We will be content with a smile
Or perhaps a sneer.
We are
Not of
This
Kingdom.
Who comprehends the bewilderment
of the last bird
In a blazing forest?

—translated by May Jayyusi and Jack Collom

The Earth Also Dies

With what faith
Can stars
Sparkle?
And naked trees
Cast shade?
With what faith
Can our echoes
Reverberate
In alleys after we leave
For home
And shut the door, saying
That those who bear witness to us
                    speak for our times?
With what faith
Can we deposit ourselves
In language
In talk
As though we were not alone
As though
Others
Newspapers
Television
And airline schedules
Share our coffee with us?
The earth also dies
As do desert roads
Solitary houses
In lonely countrysides
Mysterious city lights
In the depths of night.
The earth also dies
And university degrees
Daily beverages
And the faint evening gloom.

Anxiety is not only
In the nerves
It is in this smooth, unruffled calm

That heaps up on desks
Home furniture
Coffee spoons and
The quiet cradle of the little one
In the corner of the room.

Why are we suddenly left
Without seasons
Without skies
Without mothers?
All dwindle
Fall out of
Our windows
Our papers
The edges of our conversations.
All
Leave us
To return alone
Facing museum gates
Shopping malls
Closed harbors
Deserted pavements
And withering grass
At the end of summer.

The earth also dies
Cannot take us
As martyrs
Or prophets
We who are deleted
Without a sign of identification
To mark our absence,
Who are spread out
Like untranslatable tenderness,
We wanderers
Like nights astray
Over otherworldly deserts.

—translated by May Jayyusi and Jack Collom

When the Inhabitants of Planets Converse

Vast
Beyond number
Like wild honey
Apples in the forest
Ripe figs
In abandoned gardens
Like houses
Destroyed and overturned
Under endless stars
Of beings no one mentions
Like a sea for which
We attempt to find
A history
Like a desert
Forever prelife
For which we attempt to find
Some seasons.

—translated by May Jayyusi and Jack Collom

Who

Who is it that writes the history of this nebula
Which lives nowhere
And nothing lives in it?

—translated by May Jayyusi and Jack Collom

Mureed Barghouthy *(b. 1944)*

A Palestinian poet living in the diaspora, Baraghouthy has lived in many countries of the Arab world, including Egypt, which he left in 1979 after the peace treaty between Egypt and Israel. After living for several years in Budapest, he recently went to live in Amman, Jordan. Barghouthy's earlier poetry was patriotic and full of heroic motifs. In the late seventies, his poetic sensitivity and great originality led to a more modernist approach and produced some of the most compelling poetic experiments among the Arab poets of his generation. He has published several volumes of poetry, including his well-acclaimed *Poems of the Pavement* (1980), which marked his shift into the modernist mode, and *Endless Estrangement* (1987). He is one of the poets included in PROTA's forthcoming *Poets of the End of the Century (New Voices in Arabic Poetry)*.

The Tribes

Our tribes regain their charm:

Tents and more tents
tents of tranquil stone, their pegs are tile and marble
inscriptions on the ceiling, velvet paper covering the walls
the family portraits and "La Gioconda"
facing a tablet with inscriptions
to repel the evil eye
beside the diploma of a son
framed in gold, coated with dust.
Tents, and a glass window
it is the trap for young girls, who look out from it and tremble for fear
their young sister or brother might tell the grown-ups.
Vapor rises from the tea, whiskey and soda
and "I do not like wine" and "excuse me"
"did you manage with the fourth wife?"
Tents and more tents
the chandeliers illuminate opulent furnishings
flies of speech dance through them

in and out of brass gates draped with chains
Our tribes retain their charm
now that the tribes are out of date!

—translated by Lena Jayyusi and W.S. Merwin

The Guards

The guards of his royal majesty, the King
some of them stand on the towers
some of them sit on the saddles
they stand straight
and bow humbly at entrance and exit
some of them watch the food
and some of them watch the servants
some of them guard the others
and some of them dictate the newspaper to the newspaper
some of them compose the poem
and some of them direct applause at the King's speech
they all have style
and a buoyancy, touching the weapon at their side
they are exemplary in gait and manner
and all of them have kingdoms, and all of them have majesty
and all of them are kings.

—translated by Lena Jayyusi and W.S. Merwin

Desire

His leather belt
hangs on the wall
the pair of shoes he left behind has turned brittle
his white summer shirts
still sleep on their shelf
his scattered papers
tell her that he will be gone a long time
but she is there still waiting

and his leather belt
is still hanging there
and each time the day ends
she reaches out to touch a naked waist
and leans back against the wall.

—translated by Lena Jayyusi and W.S. Merwin

An Official

His hand toys with the soap suds and their scent rises
his hand trims the moustache before an elegant mirror
his hand smooths the silk necktie over the starched white shirt
the traingle sits in the middle, not leaning to right nor left
and he stretches out his hand to the sugar bowl,
two and a half pieces
he stirs the fragrant tea, drinks it down
kisses the little girl, and the boy,
embraces his wife, she hands him the briefcase
he says: "and the handkerchief"
in the blink of an eye the folded white square was there in his hand
and he's off to work. . .
A handsome well-groomed man sitting in the back seat
one of his duties
is to conduct lovers
from happy clouds
to the hangman's noose.

—translated by Lena Jayyusi and W.S. Merwin

Liberation

Now all my guards have deserted me
my freedom and death
have become one.

—translated by Lena Jayyusi and W.S. Merwin

Certainty

Slow is the hand of evening as it closes the gates
slow are the girl's hands as she closes the window
draws the heavy blinds
and gathers the ashtrays overflowing with stubs.
She draws her face close to the mirror for a minute
"they are late . . . they are very late" . . .
the clock on the wall ticks in the ordinary way
slow are her steps to bed
cold is the evening
the touch of the blanket.
She pulls the cover over her body
and leaves the lights on in all the rooms.

    —translated by Lena Jayyusi and W.S. Merwin

Exception

All of them arrive
river and train
sound and ship
light and letters
the telegrams of consolation
the invitations to dinner
the diplomatic pouch
the space ship
they all arrive/all but my step toward my own country . . .

    —translated by Lena Jayyusi and W.S. Merwin

I Run toward You . . . I Run with You

We grew up at the cross-road of exile and exile
Where the roads came together childhood fell from our hand
as the wind knocks over an umbrella with one gust
this is my bow to what will remain

and will defeat the wind, your love
which cannot be put off nor given its time, how
tall my figure grows in it, O ceilings of exiles
—and you are the low ones—
I framed a window out of my branches
and looked out towards the distant country
toward the soil of my birth, toward the gentle faces
I said: What will come we will bring on ourselves
or we shall hold it off, these are the same hands
that pass the cups, either for a death almost upon us
or for the nectar that cures all ills
these are the same hands reaching out to close a window or
to fling it wide to green space and a hand waving
this is my bow to your hands
I, the one leaping through the ages toward particulars:
the address of a house, a roof, a guest, a neighbour to be visited,
a stroll in streets which my footsteps long for,
a friend's knock at the door, not the night police.
Draw your robe about me
and spread the greens of earth around me
So I can hide my footsteps and the green of my body and they will be
    blind to me,
So that we may wait, and remain secret, and continue this long pursuit.
I see us running after what cannot be reached in two lifetimes
Let us remain friends with the wilderness.
I come to your palms for refuge, O dream that wears its garment of
    daybreak
drinks its coffee out of my hands, whose home is my home.
We will walk together toward what was lost,
overcoming the drought of exiles
I call to you not to be afraid
even endings say goodbye to our beginnings within us
and in our footsteps fields keep their secrets.

—translated by Lena Jayyusi and W.S. Merwin

A Vision

O lifetime of ours, go on! Parents!
Give our children plenty of milk
Prepare what light for them you can,
save for them every matchstick
keep the lanterns, and the oil
For the night means to inhabit us for a long time.

—translated by Lena Jayyusi and W.S. Merwin

Mu'een Bseiso (1927–1984)

An active poet and essayist, Bseiso was born in Ghaza and did his early studies there. He was studying at the American University in Cairo when the 1948 catastrophe took place. He later lived in Ghaza for some time, but had to take refuge in other Arab countries because of his Marxist affiliations. Wherever he lived, he was a political activist, for which he suffered exile and imprisonment. Though he worked mainly as a teacher, he was also a journalist and, in the last years before his sudden death, an advisor to the Unified Information Bureau at the Palestine Liberation Organization in Beirut. In 1982, he had to leave in the Palestinian exodus that followed the Israeli invasion of Lebanon in that summer. He has published several volumes of poetry, including *Palestine in the Heart* (1965), *Trees Die Standing* (1966), and *Now Take My Body as Sandbag* (1976). He is one of the Palestinian writers who write at length about their lives as exiles and victims of the struggle. His book, *Ghaza Memoirs,* about his life and the details of his imprisonment, appeared in 1971, and his essays were collected in his well-known volume, *Palestinian Notebooks* (1969). Bseiso's poetry and prose had a salutory effect on his contemporaries, and he is sorely missed in Palestinian literary circles.

Aladdin's Lamp for Sahba'[1]

I'll give you the phoenix, my love,
the engagement ring,
the giant's treasure
    masked by clouds
and all that enemies and friends have given me
the snakes' eggs I've collected
    on the road
the green foxes' bracelets
and the birds,
if only I should return

---

[1]Sahba' is the poet's wife.

from the island of ogres!
But the rook bird
has flown, my love,
without tossing me even a feather!
Clouds have migrated with their treasures
and the genie repealed our engagement ring.
Still I wait
for the jagged rock to offer up
flowers from its heart,
for thorns to release
the last fruit.
On the bunch
one grape still hangs.
I believe a drop of rain must linger in the clouds,
a ray of light in the lamp, my love,
a single ray of light!
Whoever said the rook bird must be sterile
or these waves would not give birth?

    —translated by May Jayyusi and Naomi Shihab Nye

Diary of Old Man Defector

I said that the palm could not wound the sword
I said if the people's god were a calf
and men offered him grass,
with your own two hands you had to feed it.
If the sultan ordered you to milk the snake
    then milk the snake!
But you did not believe me. You said the palm
    could be sharper than the sword.
You slew the calf,
and stifled the ten commandments
with mud!
What now, old man who's abandoned
    the volcanoes in my hands and run away?
Escorting the executioner to the bottled genie,
    you found the genie had fled

carrying Solomon's secret
like embers in his hands.

—translated by May Jayyusi and Naomi Shihab Nye

The Vinegar Cup

Cast your lots, people,
Who'll get my robe
after crucifixion?

The vinegar cup in my right hand,
the thorn crown on my head,
and the murderer has walked away free
while your son has been led
    to the cross.
But I shall not run
from the vinegar cup,
nor the crown of thorns
I'll carve the nails of my cross from my own bones
and continue,
spilling drops of my blood onto this earth
For if I should not rip apart
    how would you be born from my heart?
    How would I be born from your heart?
    Oh, my people!

—translated by May Jayyusi and Naomi Shihab Nye

Sailor Returning from Occupied Shores

If only my poems could live, love,
as long as the olive trees and rivers
If only the vines,
could bear fruit twice a year
If only I could return
from the island of winds

and lie on the banks, love,
with my wound, and oars,
carrying in my breast all the wonders of the seas
carrying sails,
fruit baskets, grass, fishes, shells,
a bouquet of clouds,
and sands from our shadeless shores . . .
But I've been fated to perpetual travel!
A wave arrives from the sea,
clutches at my sails,
and will not let them go,
The winds clutch
at my thirsty heart,
and the blood of my wounds
remains fresh for each new morning.

—translated by May Jayyusi and Naomi Shihab Nye

Footsteps

Brother! If they should sharpen the sword on my neck,
I would not kneel, even if their whips lashed
     my bloodied mouth
If dawn is so close to coming
     I shall not retreat.
I will rise from the land that feeds our furious storm!

Brother! If the executioner should drag me to the slaughterhouse
before your eyes to make you kneel,
so you might beg him to relent,
I'd call again, Brother! Raise your proud head
and watch as they murder me!
Witness my executioner, sword dripping with my blood!
What shall expose the murderer, but our innocent bleeding?

At night their guns kidnapped him from his trench.
The hero was flung into the cells' darkness
where, like a banner fluttering above chains, he stayed.
The chains became flaming torches,

burning the ashes which coat our shining future.
Now the hero lives, his footsteps ringing triumphantly
within the closed walls of every prison.

—translated by May Jayyusi and Naomi Shihab Nye

I Was Already Dead

When I said to the lion
You'll die when the blue dove
falls into the trap,
ants will swarm your eyes, pegs will plunge deep,
the ropes that drag you into sleep
will knot forever,
your den's door be blocked by stones
and the trees
plant their branches in their heart and die . . .
All trees after you shall die!

—translated by May Jayyusi and Naomi Shihab Nye

Hasan al-Buhairi *(b. 1921)*

Born in Haifa, al-Buhairi is a self-educated man who, when forced to leave his home in Haifa and join the long trail of the Palestinian diaspora of 1948, chose Damascus as his new home. Here he made friends with Syrian and other Arab poets, including poet-dignitaries from the Gulf area, who shared his preference for the old style of poetry with its symmetrical, two-hemistich forms, its terse constructions, and its strong echoing resonances. He has published several collections of poetry, dedicated mainly to the Palestinian situation and expressive of a deep nostalgia for the lost homeland. Among his collections are: *Twilight and Dawn* (1943); *Haifa in the Heart* (1973); *To Palestine I Sing* (1979); *The Thirsty Rivers* (1982); and *Rose Paradise* (1989). In 1990 al-Buhairi was awarded the Jerusalem Medal for his literary achievement.

Orange Blossoms
(A Palestinian Song)

Do you ask about the orange blossom,
its charm, and all its magical delight?
How dawn arrests the caravan of morning
to catch perfection of it, shimmering bright?

About the fragrance when the stars restore
wine to the reveler through the midnight hours
about the dew drops and about the nights
which string the pearls around the budding flowers

for necklaces which paradiseal gems
covet for their celestial treasury?
Do you ask about the flowers that blossom, rich
with gems excelling heavenly harmony?

It was *our* sky that warmed and fostered them
with purest sunshine that could give them birth
and that which nourished all their grace and beauty
and all their fragramce—was our native earth.

—translated by Salwa Jabsheh and John Heath-Stubbs

The Malady and The Cure

Dire is your lot and the fair light of day
which shone upon you once has drained away.

The hills are awed, they hear the wild winds cry,
and mustering clouds are banked up in the sky

While elsewhere new light pours—and there is life
surging with passion and with eager strife.

But you I see besotted and disgraced
owning but words in party talk debased

Life just as pleasure's overpluss you hold
You feel no shame although your country's sold.

It calls for help, you show a niggard hand
When pleasure calls alone you understand.

Your facile spokesman mounts the rising wave
he climbs the rostrum—words race on and rave

but while he bellows, conscience is stone dead
the people's suffering trouble not his head.

A game of cheating words—loud plaudits sound
Your eyes are blind to what besets your ground

You weep hot tears, but you must learn ere long
that tears alone have never righted wrong.

Who resolutely charge can seize their right
who've cast out fear and are resolved to fight.

—translated by Salwa Jabsheh and John Heath-Stubbs

Ahmad Dahbur (b. *1946*)

Dahbour was born in Haifa, but his family had to flee to Lebanon when the city fell to the Zionist forces in 1948. Because of the great poverty of the family, Dahbour had no formal education, but he read avidly. His highly sensitive poetry is dedicated to the Palestinian cause, mixing themes of heroism with a deep recognition of the dangers and tribulations of the contemporary Palestinian experience. He has published eight collections of poetry, including: *The Story of the Palestinian Boy* (1979), *Mixing Night and Day* (1979), and *Twenty-One Seas* (1980).

New Suggestions

Out of what lair did the earthly tyrants escape?
Nero burned Rome twice, then composed a discordant tune
he went on playing till the city sang with him.
Holako who inherited that melody
    set fire
    to the world's library, the river ran
    with ink, and from the ashes was born
    the language of locusts which rose
                to thank the madman.
After the salutations to madness, Hitler came
    and fashioned soap-bars from the dead;
    but unable to be appeased,
          had to include the sea
          in his vital destruction,
    and war at sea, turmoil on land,
        combined in their angry conflagration.

I too have seen a tyrant—
whose power diminished the other three.
He has committed every atrocity,
and yet: in his day,
there were five poets,
who took to silence.

—translated by Lena Jayyusi and Jeremy Reed

The Terms of Ambition

I assemble my points of ambition—
to drink tea at dawn, and spin freely
in the city
of my buried treasures,
and to correspond with her
who has lightened my stress.

In order to achieve this,
I need to establish in the city of my soul:
time, and a safe land.
Hardly the requisites of an agitator?

For the sake of tea, a dawn, paper, and stamps,
I need armed fortresses,
weapons to help me stand and defend.

   —translated by Lena Jayyusi and Jeremy Reed

From "I Do Not Renounce Madness"

No, whether near or far, high or low, her heart will not change
But I have one condition to state: ask the question:
Who is the enemy?
The shaken sky-sieve sprinkles delicate death
Who is the enemy?
The rest of the white clouds are lit with thunder
and have split into boats, while exiles were preparing to leave
Who is the enemy?
The sea is treacherous
the sky is treacherous
The enemy extracts the essence from olive trees
but the essence is in the eyes and the roots
and we shall not die!
God's camping grounds are vast, and His exile, so full of traps,
      is loaded with police reconnaisance
but we do not die
we generate new life in wombs and the dead
      return and multiply,
between the wind and explosives they prevail
and under their clothes a spirit asks: Who is the enemy?

The Enemy is the Enemy
These locusts are the Enemy
This siege is the Enemy
Equal divisions as they split the camp between them
But the camp does not die
and here the children carry the bomb and wheat stalks, and
the good is abundant in this world, and chains aren't sufficient
to close the playgrounds, and one clear day, the children shall
return in the same boats. Come Laila, come!
Your eyes are black and I love black eyes!
I have died so often before
but when I promise to return, I always return
And perhaps we believe the white night has never been?
But we prepare for it, and forgive no mistakes
I have dreamt that I dreamt
and woke up from consciousness, and when the day returned I was
    split:
My voice was there, my ears were here
And I saw you and did not see you
Forgive me, sad lover . . . but I don't regret
there's no time for that . . . but when I promise to clear
the rains and the past and not to journey far
I do it. I'll tell the trees to unite
I'll tell the sorrows to join forces
I'll tell the motherland to unite
and I promise
    to do likewise

Laila is with me
We walk on rubble, and weep like this, in public,
laugh, like this, in public, and make fun of the word "Why"
No, we shan't return to our childhood
From here, the new begins, and childhood shall return to
Laila's womb, be born in the camp, and the camp shall grow
and grow, then it will run
in the direction of the water spring
and engender a world

And I shall have time to write a different poem.

   —translated by Lena Jayyusi and Jeremy Reed

NOTE: As with other Palestinian poets, Dahbour is alluding in this poem to the
"neglect" and sometimes to the "coercion" Palestinians feel they have received from
other Arabs.

Our Country

Who is it who calls like this?
Who are you, Sir?
It was as if I had heard a voice that knew me, and perhaps for
you it was the same? Or am I mistaken? If I am, I ask your
forgiveness, Sir. For what reason do you think I would contrive
this dialogue? Believe me, I have no ulterior motive. But
let us assume I have faked this dialogue; my aim was to
declare that the day . . . Please listen, and don't go away.
On our land exists a wall which we would like to have converted
into a room, only we weren't granted building permission.
What can I say? Are these utensils sold in the market place?
I put it like this: friend, to everyone who . . .

Do you think that I am in the secret police? Then why are you
afraid of me? I'm only interested in words. So let it go if
I expressed myself badly. It is my country.
Don't we have the right here to shake hands?
To form a friendship of sorts?
An adversary? A pal who forgives?
Or a passer-by who calls our name?
Don't we have that right?
Isn't it our country?
Did you hear a voice? Who is it who calls like this?
Who is it who calls our name?

—translated by Lena Jayyusi and Jeremy Reed

The Hands Again

No seas in books
I seek oceans, but they don't respond
No bed in the tree
whenever I want to rest, its dangerous branches awaken
No dialogue in language
their words only reach my lips, never my inner nerves
No fields in the clouds
only blood that tries to give its news to horizons

No Seas No Books
No Bed No Tree
No Dialogue No Language
No Fields No Clouds

Grow strong, my hands; if you should,
they'd pay attention, then.

—translated by Lena Jayyusi and Jeremy Reed

The Sparrow Told Me

A sparrow alighted on my wrist.
Black or white?
I don't remember,
or perhaps it was brown
I can't specify the colour
but it touched down on my wrist
and the air vibrated with its singing.

You there, lover, you who are here:
will you tell her who loves?

The cold doesn't feel
and the speeding road has no memory;
it alighted on my wrist
without fear of my worn face,
but who is there to understand
or witness this in the blue dusk?
If someone else had seen
I'd know I wasn't dreaming.
Rather I uncovered the secret of the closed skylight
and its green voice, distilled, came to me,
rose higher, bent over
and disclosed: "together
we'll take flight in the lily's crimson hue
and eradicate the hangman's noose."
I questioned: "Together?" "Together" it said, "that's how we'll invent
   the dawn
and conjure up the spirit

drink space by our conquest.
How easy the game could be!"
But the false witnesses
failed to see,
so the bird's voice returned to its origin
and I carried nothing on my wrist—
you'll tell me I'm dreaming?
But it was a sparrow that alighted on my wrist
I heard it . . .
I saw it was not afraid
A wind rose from the East, so I told it my story
and the wind replied: Is it love?

You there, lover, you who are here
tell her who loves
perhaps it was here
        or there
It is white
brown
or perhaps the grass lent it colour
and the air vibrated with song
You there, lover, you who are here
so long as this is possible
then it is possible to be safe
your love is possible
and your child will be crawling soon.

Why then does war recur?

—translated by Lena Jayyusi and Jeremy Reed

Mahmoud Darwish (b. 1942)

Born in the village of Berweh, (a village razed by the Israelis after the 1948 War), east of Acre in Galilee, Darwish lived as a refugee in his own country and entered the political struggle early in his life, joining the Israeli Communist Party, Rakah. As a result of his politics, he suffered constant harassment and repression at the hands of the Israeli authorities, including imprisonment and house arrest. While in Palestine, he lived in Galilee and for some time edited Rakah's Arabic newspaper, *Al-Ittihad* (Unity). Darwish left Israel in 1971 and went to live in Beirut where he maintained his reputation as the foremost poet of the resistance. Several of his poems have been put to music as emblems of the Palestinian struggle. His poetry developed great sophistication with the years, and he has gained international fame and recognition as one of the greatest Arab poets writing today. He has produced more than twelve collections and several highly sophisticated prose works mainly in the form of memoirs. He now lives in Paris and Tunis and is editor-in-chief of the prestigious literary review, *Al-Karmel.*

From: Poem of the Land

This poem refers to the Day of the Land annually celebrated by Palestinians on March 30. It began in 1976. the Israeli army fired at the student demonstrators and five young girls were instantly killed. This poem is in their memory.

In the month of March
      in the year of the uprising
            earth told us her blood secrets
In the month of March
      five girls at the door
         of the primary school
Came past the violet
      came past the rifle
         burst into flame

With the roses
     and thyme
          they opened
the song of the soil
     and entered the earth
          the ultimate embrace
March comes to the land
     out of earth's depth
          out of the girls' dance
The violets leaned over a little
     so that the girls' voices
          could cross over
the birds
     pointed their beaks
          at that song and at my heart
. . . . .

I

I name the soil I call it
     an extension of my soul
I name my hands I call them
     the pavement of wounds
I name the pebbles
     wings
I name the birds
     almonds and figs
I name my ribs
     trees
Gently I pull a branch
     from the fig tree of my breast
I throw it like a stone
     to blow up the conqueror's tank

2

In the month of March thirty years and five wars ago I was born on a heap of luminous tombstone grass. My father was a prisoner of the British. My mother nurtured her braid and my space on the grass. I loved the anemones and filled my pockets with them. At noon they

wilted. Bullets flew across my lilac moon and it did not break. But time
passes over my lilac moon and inadvertently it drops into the heart

In the month of March we stretch out in the land and the
land spreads out in us
Mysterious dates
A simple celebration
We discover the sea beneath our windows
the lilac moon over the cypress trees

In the month of March
We enter the first prison and the first love
Memories shower down upon a fenced village
That is where we were born
Never to pass beyond the quince-tree shade
. . . . .

II

My country: distant as my heart from me
My country: close to me as my prison
Why sing of one place
While my face is in another?
Why sing
To a child asleep over saffron
A daggar in the margin of sleep
My mother giving me her breast
My mother dying in front of me
In a gust of ambergris

3

And the horses waken in the month of March
My lady earth!
What song after me will walk on the undulations
                                    of your belly?
What song is right for this dew and this incense—
As if temples asked now about the prophets of Palestine
And about her continuous beginning
This is the distance greening and the reddening of stones
This is my song

Exit of Christ from the wound and from the wind
Green like plants that cover his nails
                                  and my chains
This is my song
This is the ascent of the Arab boy to his dream
and to Jerusalem.
. . . . .

III

As if I returned
            to what has been
As if I walked
            in front of myself
I restore my harmony
            between the trial and the verdict
I am the son
            of simple words
I am the martyr of the map
            the family apricot blossom
O you who grip the edge
            of the impossible
From the beginning until Galilee
            Return to me my hands
Return to me
            My identity

4

And in the month of March come the silken shadows (and without shadows the invaders). The birds come mysterious as the confessions of girls . . . Five girls conceal a wheatfield under their braids. They read the first words of a song about the vines of Hebron. They write five letters: Long may my country live . . . Five girls at the door of a primary school break like mirrors

they were the heart-mirrors of the country
Earth in the month of March
set fire to her flowers

IV

I am the witness of the massacre
I am the victim of the map
I am the son of simple words

. . . . .

5

In the month of March we come to the obsession of memories and the
plants grow upon us ascending toward all beginnings. This is the growing of *reminiscence*. I call reminiscence my ascent to the *Zanzalakht*[1]
tree. Thirty years ago I saw by the sea a girl and I said: I am the waves.
She receded in *recollection*. I saw two martyrs listening to the sea: 'Acca[2]
comes with the waves. 'Acca departs with the waves. They receded in
remembrance. Khadija leaned toward the dew and I burned.
Khadija! Do not close the door! Nations will enter this book and the
    sun of Jericho will set without ritual.
O country of prophets: Come to your fruition!
O country of planters: Come to your fruition!
O country of martyrs: Come to your fruition!
O country of refugees: Come to your fruition!
For all the pathways in the mountains are extensions of this song.
All the songs in you are extensions of an olive tree that swaddled me.

V

A small evening
A neglected village
Two sleeping eyes
Thirty years
Five wars
I witness that time hides for me
an ear of wheat
The singer sings
Of fire and strangers
Evening was evening
The singer was singing

[1]*Zanzalakht* is the Arabic name for the china tree *(Melia azedarach)* which is one of
Palestine's larger trees.
[2]*Acca* is the Arabic name for Acre.

And they question him
Why do you sing?
He answers them as they seize him
Because I sing

And they have searched him:
In his breast only his heart
In his heart only his people
In his voice only his sorrow
In his sorrow only his prison
And they have searched his prison
To find only themselves in chains
. . . . .

6

. . . . .
Khadija! I have seen
        my vision. I have
                believed my vision. She
Takes me into her
        distance and she
                takes me into her love. I am
The eternal lover,
        manifest prisoner.
                The orange adopts.
My greenness. The orange
        becomes Jaffa's haunting
                thought. Since I have known
Khadija I am the land.
        They did not come to know me
                so that they might kill me.
. . . . .
This soil is my own
        this cloud
                my own and this
The brow of Khadija. I
        am the eternal
                lover, the manifest
Prisoner. The smell of the land

[3]*Mountain of Fire* is a name given to the city of Nablus and its surrounding villages

                in early morning
                        awakens me, my iron chain
Awakens the land in the early
                evening. This
                        is a going out into a new life.
One's own,
                not regarding one's life
                        only the land: has it
Arisen? My child the earth!
                Did they know you to kill you?
                        Did they chain you with our dreams
To drag you down into
                our winter wound?
                Did they know you to kill you?
                        Did their dream chain pull you
Up toward our springtime
                dreams? I am the land:
                        O you who go to the wheat seed
In its cradle, plow my body,
                O you who go
                        to the Mountain of Fire[3]
Pass over my body,
                you who go to the Rock of Jerusalem[4]
                        pass over my body
You shall not pass:
O you who pass over my body
I am the land in a body
                you shall not pass
                        I am the land awakening
You shall not pass
                You shall not pass
                        I am the land but you
Who walk over the land
                in her awakening
                        you shall not pass.
                        You shall not pass.

—translated by Lena Jayyusi and Christopher Middleton

[4]*The "Rock"* is the Rock of the Dome in Jerusalem, one of Islam's holiest shrines.

Homing Pigeons

The pigeons fly off
the pigeons alight

—Prepare the land for me that I may rest
for I love you to the point of exhaustion
your morning is fruit for song,
and this evening is golden.
We belong to ourselves when a shadow enters its own shadow in marble
I resemble myself when I hang myself on a neck that embraces only
    the clouds
you are the air that goes naked before me like the tears of the grape
you are the first of the family of waves
when they cling to the shore feeling like foreigners
I love you, you are the soul's beginning and the end.

The pigeons fly off
the pigeons alight

—My love and I are two voices with one pair of lips
I am for the sake of my love. I am. And my love is for his wandering
    star
we enter into the dream—but he is late so we do not see him
when my love sleeps I wake up to guard the dream from what he sees
I cast out from him the nights that passed before we met
with my own hands I choose our days
as he chose for me the rose table
sleep then my love
so that the sound of the seas may rise to my knee
sleep my love
so that I may descend into you and rescue your dream from an envious
    thorn
sleep, my love
with my hair over you, peace be on you.

The pigeons fly off
the pigeons alight

—I saw April on the sea
I said: I forgot the vigilance of your hands
I forgot the chants over my wounds . . .
how many times can you be born in my dream?

how many times can you slay me, so that I cry out: I love you so you
    may rest . . .
I call to you before speech
I fly with you, holding your waist even before I reach you
how many times can you put my soul's addresses
in the beaks of these pigeons? And vanish like the distance on the slopes
    so that I may realize that you are Babylon, Egypt, and Syria.

The pigeons fly off
the pigeons alight

—Where do you take me, my love, away from my parents
from my trees, from my little bed, and from my boredom,
from my mirrors, from my moon, from the closet of my life, from
    where I stop for the night, from my clothes, from my shyness?
Where are you taking me, my love . . . where? You kindle the wilderness
    in my ear, you make me carry two waves,
(you) break two ribs, drink me then ignite me and abandon me on the
    road to you . . .
Take pity . . . take pity.

The pigeons fly off
the pigeons alight

—Because I love you, blood flows from my side
in my pain I run through the nights swollen by the fear of what I fear
Come often, disappear a little
come just a little, disappear slowly
come come do not stop. Aah from a step that is never taken!
I love you as I desire you, I love you as I desire you
and gather together this light ringed by bees and a fleeting rose
I love you, curse of my heart
Because I fear for my heart, I fear for my desire if it were to arrive.
I love you as I desire you
I love you, body that creates memories and kills them before they are
    finished.
I love you as I desire you,
I tame my soul to the shape of your feet—the shape of your cheeks
I rub my wounds with the edges of your silence and your storm
I die so that words may sit upon your hands.

The pigeons fly off
the pigeons alight

—Because I love you the water cuts me and the sea-bound roads cut
  me
In the light of your hands the morning call to prayer cuts me
my love, I call to you through my sleep, I fear the waking of words
I fear that words would wake to a bee that weeps along my limbs
because I love you the shadow under the lanterns cut me, a bird
in the distant sky cuts me, the fragrance of the violet cuts me
the sea's beginning cuts me
the sea's end cuts me
if only I did not love you
if only I did not love
so that the marble could heal.

The pigeons fly off
the pigeons alight

—I see you . . . and escape from death. Your body is a harbour
with ten white lilies, ten fingers
the sky departs to a blue that it had lost
and I take hold of this marble radiance
I take hold of a fragrance of milk concealed in two plums on marble,
        then I worship whoever grants a refuge
to sea or land
on the shores of the first salt, the first honey
I shall drink the juice of your night, then sleep
above golden corn that breaks the field, breaks even the cry of
        desire, making it rust.
I see you . . . and I escape from death. Your body is a harbour
how can the land turn me out through the land as a beggar
how can the dream go to sleep?

The pigeons fly off
The pigeons alight

—My love, I fear the silence of your hands
rub my blood so that the mare can sleep
my love, the female birds fly to you
take me a wife . . . or a respite
my love, I shall remain with you
till the nuts of my breast grow with you
and the sentries uproot me from your path.
My love, I shall weep for you, for you, for you

because you are the ceiling to my sky
and my body is your land in the land,
my body is your shrine.

The pigeons fly off
the pigeons alight

On the bridge I saw the Andalus of love and institution
over a wilted rose
he gave her heart back to her
and said: Love charges me with what I do not like
it charges me with her love.
The moon went to sleep
over a ring breaking
and the pigeons flew off . . .
On the bridge I saw the Andalus of love and institution
through a desperate tear
she gave his heart back to him
and said: Love charges me with what I do not like
it charges me with his love.
The moon went to sleep
over a ring breaking
and the pigeons flew off.
Over the bridge and the two lovers darkness alighted.

The pigeons fly off
the pigeons alight

   —translated by Lena Jayyusi and W.S. Merwin

Guests on the Sea

Guests on the sea: Our visit is short
our talk is notes from the past shattered an hour ago
from what Mediterranean will the creation begin?
We set up an island
for our southern cry. Farewell, small island of ours.

We did not come to this country from a country
we came from pomegranates, from the glue of memory

from the fragments of an idea we came to this foam
Do not ask us how long we will stay among you, do not ask us
anything about our visit. Let us
empty the slow ships from the remains of our souls and our bodies.
Guests on the sea. Our visit is short.
And the earth is smaller than our visit. We shall send another apple
to the waters, circles within circles, where are we to go
when we leave? Where are we to go back to when we return? My God
what is left of the resistance of our souls? What directions are left
What earthen frontiers are left? Is there another rock
over which to offer a new sacrifice for your mercy?
What is left of us that we may set out once again?

Sea, do not give us the song that we do not deserve.

The sea has its ancient craft:
ebb and flow;
woman has her first task: seduction
it is for poets to fall from melancholy
it is for martyrs to explode in dream
it is for wise men to lead a people on towrads happy dreams

Sea, do not give us the song that we do not deserve

We did not come to this place from the language of place
the plants of the distance have grown tall, the shadow of the sand
           has grown long within us and spread out
our short visit has grown long. How many moons have given their
   rings to one who is not of us. How many stones
has the swallow laid in the distance. How many years
shall we sleep as guests on the sea, wait for a place
and say: In a little while we shall leave here.
We have died from sleep and have broken here.
It is only the temporary that will last in us, age of the sea.

Sea, do not give us the song that we do not deserve

We want to live for a time, not for nothing
but just that we can set out again
Nothing of our ancestors remains in us, but we want
the country of our morning coffee
we want the fragrance of primitive plants
we want a special school
we want a special cemetary

we want a freedom
the size of a skull . . . and a song.

Sea, do not give us the song that we do not deserve

we did not come just for the sake of coming . . .
the sea tossed us up at Carthage as shells and a star
who can remember how the words lit up into a homeland for those
   who have no doorway?
Who remembers the ancient bedouins when they seized the world . . .
   with a word?
Who remembers the slain as they rushed to break the secrets of the
   myths?
They forget us, we forget them, life lives its own life.
Who now remembers the beginning and the end?
We wish to live for a time just to return to something
anything
anything
to a beginning, an island, a ship, an ending
a widow's prayer, a cellar, a tent.
Our short visit has grown long
and the sea died within us two years ago . . . the sea has died within
   us.

Sea, do not give us the song that we do not deserve

—translated by Lena Jayyusi and W.S. Merwin

Intensive-Care Unit

I whirl with the wind as the earth narrows before me. I would fly off
and rein in the wind, but I am human . . . I felt a million flutes tear
at my breast. Coated with ice I saw my grave carried on my palms. I
disintegrated over the bed. Threw up. Lost consciousness for a while.
Died. Cried out before that short-lived death occurred: I love you, shall
I enter into death through your feet? And I died . . . I was completely
extinguished. How serene death is except for your weeping! And how
tranquil if it wasn't for your hands pounding my breast to have me
return. I loved you before and after death, and between the two I saw
only my mother's face.

It was the heart that strayed for a while, and then returned. I ask

my love: In which heart was I struck? She bent over me and covered
my question with a tear. O heart . . . heart, how is it you lied to me
and disrupted my climax?
We have plenty of time, heart, stabilize
So that a hoopoe bird may fly to you from the land of *Balqis*.[1]
We have sent letters.
We have crossed thirty seas and sixty coastlines
and still there is time in life for greater wanderings.

And O heart, how is it you lied to a mare that never tires of the
winds. Hold on so we can complete this final embrace and kneel in
worship. Hold on . . . hold on. Let me find out if you are my heart or
her voice crying: Take me.

—translated by Lena Jayyusi and Jeremy Reed

Psalm 9

O rose beyond the reach of time and of the senses
O kiss enveloped in the scarves of all the winds
surprise me with one dream
then my madness will recoil from you

Recoiling from you
in order to approach you
I discovered time

Approaching you
in order to recoil from you
I discovered my senses

Between approach and recoil
there is a stone the size of a dream
It does not approach
It does not recoil

[1]Balqis or Balkis is Queen Sheba of Yemen who visited King Solomon in the tenth
century B.C. The poet refers here to North Yemen where many of his Palestinian friends
and compatriots went after the exodus from Beirut following the Israeli invasion of
Lebanon in 1982.

You are my country
A stone is not what I am
therefore I do not like to face the sky
nor do I lie level with the ground

but am a stranger, always a stranger

—translated by Lena Jayyusi and Christopher Middleton

We Went to Aden

Before our dreams, we went to Aden, saw the light of the moon
on a crow's wing. We turned to the sea and asked,
for whom are your waves tolling? Are they beating the rhythm of time-
    to-go?

We went to Aden before our history, we found Yemen
still grieving over Umru'u al-Qais[1], chewing *qat*[2], erasing the pictures
Friend, don't you see we tried to get through to the Caesar of our age?[3]

To the pauper's paradise we came, opened windows in stone.
The tribes have laid siege to us, friend, disasters have laid us low,
but we have not traded the enemy's loaf for the bread of our trees.

Do we still have a right to believe in our dreams, and mistrust this
    Arab homeland?

—translated by Lena Jayyusi and Anselm Hollo

[1]Umru'u al-Qais was a great pre-Islamic poet from Yemen who died c. 540 A.D. He is said to have led a life bent on pleasure and wine drinking until the death of his father, the chief of the Kinda tribe, after which he lost his patrimony. He went to Constantinople to persuade the Byzantine Emperor to help him avenge himself, but his trip was a failure; he died on his way home while wearing a poisoned shield given to him by the Emperor as a punishment for his liason with a Byzantine princess.

[2]*Qat* is a stimulant chewed in Yemen as a daily routine. The more tender leaves of the bush are chewed, usually in company while sitting and conversing. Although men are the main addicts, women also use the drug on a lesser scale.

[3]The Caesar referred to in the poem is in the Byzantine Emperor, here used symbolically to denote any autocrat past or present.

Muhammad al-Dhahir (b. 1951)

Born in the 'Uqbat Jabr Refugee Camp in Jericho, al-Dhahir obtained his diploma from the Teacher Training College in Amman. However, he has chosen to work in journalism and has been correspondent to various Arab newspapers and reviews including the Iraqi *Al-Aqlam,* the Kuwaiti *Al-Bayan,* the Saudi *Al-Majalla.* He has done translations and television dramatizations, and has written many books for children. al-Dhair has published his poetry in journals and in two collections; the appearance of his second collection *I Was Not Asleep, It Is the Dream-Reality* (1980) won him acclaim in Jordan.

Three Short Letters

I

The dream gasps in the chest
and the heart suppresses it.
Here where the road begins,
my footsteps pound the streets
looking for a homeland
steeped in sorrow,
for questions that have quarreled with answers.

II

What can I say?
You guide my face on its journey through illusion.
In you, illusion and truth mingle and blend.
You are the bullet, the death,
the secret of this heavy evening.

III

I shall be brief:
You are the transformation
through bouts of bewilderment.
You are the wonder of fields,

the ripest season,
the beginning of time,
the censor of silence,
the distance and arrival.

I shall be brief,
shall leave you bleeding on the shore of the heart,
reading the map of wishes and the nautical guide
to the grass,
opening all suitcases
for those emerging from death
and those entering the impossible homeland.

—translated by May Jayyusi and Naomi Shihab Nye

Joy

She is my only homeland
The only vessel containing my blood

Nothing else have I,
My flowering pride,
Its resonant scent

None but you, the poor of this land
Supporting me

This is how the one I desire
interpreted my life.
She cloaked me with words,
observed my fear—
then slept beside me.

My time will end
my blood will cease,
but she will never end.

—translated by May Jayyusi and Naomi Shihab Nye

The Little Girl

I tell her:
speak to me—she holds her breath
and draws a circle of suffering
      a circle of soldiers
           a circle of guns

She lets down her ropelike braids
I tell her:
    Plough my body
        travel in my palm
           and give me a sign

She gazes at me like a little child,
opens her album,
pointing to the map of the big Arab homeland
writing in blood the names of the tribes

I tell her:
    Draw a moon for proof
She slams her album shut
and enters me to sleep within my ribs
Out comes a troop of children,
a bouquet of wheatstalks,
and her voice, whispering:
—All others but you are enemies
and every god but you, an intruder.

    —translated by May Jayyusi and Naomi Shihab Nye

Waleed al-Halees (b. 1952)

Born in Gaza, al-Halees now lives in Sweden. After suffering incarceration at the hands of the Israelis from 1969 to 1974, he went to Egypt to resume his studies, and later moved to Beirut, where he obtained a B.A. in philosophy and psychology from the Arab University of Beirut. His poetry is one of the most promising contributions to Palestinian literature, and he is highly regarded by several Arab critics, including Hanan Mikhail-Ashrawi and Ferial Ghazoul. He has published one collection of poetry, *Going Early to Death* (1980), and has since published his poetry in many periodicals all over the Arab world.

Days in the Life of a Palestinian Boy

Hoping for continuance, my father joyfully cast his seed
into my mother's womb as he lay
over her, shivering like a stallion. Then he slept,
dreaming he'd have a boy,
hoping for life, chanting even in sleep,
"I'll beget a male child,
the future ongoing, a boy!"
Later I surged from my mother
toward life,
I left the warmth of her womb
to drown in icy roads crowded with people
and dead fish,
icy roads, dangerous death,
I left her to live on the icy roads!

Where's my father so I might tell him
his seed is not content merely with life,
a faint hope for life?
that a warm womb
is equal to all kinds of life.
Where's my father now?
So we might join hands
and laugh, spitting, gripping life with force

(no life can be had but by force)
—I swear I've lied to God just now
for life taken by force only equals
all the warm wombs of women.
Forgive me, Mother,
Slowly I became the wise child of this life!

Semantics and forms perplex me
possibilities dodge me wherever I turn.
But love's strange secret has guided me to you.
Don't ask me about love—
A moment ago I saw my friend overflowing
with it, surrounded by soldiers
and dogs,
at every bend, a dog!
In each eye two dogs were mirrored!
Yet his eyes were full of that strange light
which shuns all dogs.

Shine on me so I may see you,
Let me have a little light.
I beg the sky that's covered with blood,
with pain
I beg the sky that's covered with Jerusalem
with Mt. Carmel, child of the mountains,
to preserve all the little boys born
into catastrophe hoping for life
There they go, down the icy roads
striving, darkening, weeping,
and laughing aloud
as they seize the grass, and water and the forced belonging.

On a lovely rock in Galilee
I remembered Ghassan,
the lad who tried so hard to come to you,
rising to welcome you
lighting stubs of candles on feast days
patiently extinguishing their nubs later,
dedicating all candles to your eyes—

For whom does earth remove its human robes?
Our bleeding country

is bound by bleeding bodies
Our brothers, our foes
pierce us with bullets
and swords
Why do the eyes of madness turn away?
For whom does the night bird cry?

And how shall I come to you?
On the last night of love your beauty
grew monstrous,
a frightful thing,
creating and destroying a world,
killing and resurrecting at once!
On our last night of love your beauty
grew monstrous!

With no hope for life my father joyfully cast his seed
into my mother's womb as he lay
over her, shivering like a stallion. Then he slept
dreaming of a son.
With no hope for life, he swore, "I'll beget a male child,
forget continuity! A male child!"
I surged from my mother
not hoping for life.
I left the warmth of her womb,
I left the warm wombs of all women,
only to find the womb of life hounding me
with secrets.
Joining hands with my comrades,
we laugh, spit, and seize the sun!
No sun if you don't seize it!
I'm the child of this life!

—translated by Lena Jayyusi and Naomi Shihab Nye

Sulafa Hijjawi (b. 1934)

Born in Nablus, Hijjawi lived most of her adult life in Baghdad and was married to the late Iraqi poet, Kazim Jawad. She obtained a B.A. in English literature, and M.A. in political studies from the University of Baghdad, and worked for many years in teaching. She was also one of the editors of the *Review of the Center for Palestinian Studies* at the University of Baghdad and remained in this capacity between 1974 and 1980. She now works and lives in Tunis. She has been active in translating material from and into Arabic, publishing a collection in English translation of Palestinian poetry titled *Poetry of Resistance in Occupied Palestine* (1969), and translating C.M. Bowra's *The Creative Experiment* and David Sinclair's *Edgar Allan Poe* from English into Arabic. She has published many political articles in various periodicals in the Arab world. In 1977 she issued her collection of prose poems titled *Palestinian Songs*.

Elegy on an Estranged Husband

Departing ships have raised their sails
death has drawn the curtains
the stranger has sealed the gap
between embers and ice.

Absent one! Wait a minute!
How did you startle the sunset
How did silence harbor you
without talk or argument
or song?
Are you tired of blaming?
The brutal dialogue of vein against vein?
I thought you eternal
like storms and winds
building, destroying, and building
just like life's mysteries,
stabbing raindrops with pointed tips
a touch saddled with affection
for what comes after death!

Departing ships have raised their sails
death has drawn the curtains
and the road,
that sibyl of birth and death,
now awakens.
Love's story has ended, and left
as irrevocably as youth gave way to age—
all is ended.

Now my heart pounds
while yours stays silent
Between us stretches
a bridge of sorrow
an arch, a door
closed by the winds.
Go then
like sparks vanish after flames
It is your habit
not to settle down after a trip
but calm down a minute, if you can!
Your heart is silent and between us
a star fades
a moon breaks and falls
As if a dream has rusted,
    and crumbled
    into the unknown
But the morning wind returns it as an echo
trembling, like knocks at the door.
Once two hopeful stars bloomed
in one shared dream
The earth, a forest of doves
People rose, gentle as mist
the sun brilliant on the slopes
and the door open to every road.

But now you've dropped your broken wing
and hobbled into the night
leaving your tall shadow to the earth
leaving love, memory, song
Departing ships have raised their sails
death has drawn the curtains

Our ending, like our beginning
is sealed with a groan.
So go, if you must,
or if death wants it
and leave me with my anguished heart,
forever tortured by longing.

    —translated by May Jayyusi and Naomi Shihab Nye

His Picture

His picture still hangs on the wall
warm and bright
while his corpse dangles from the scaffold in the wind
An open sign to wind, please listen!
Oh wind! When you graze the wounds in his body
departing for the four corners
do not wake the children from their sleep
Or tell the waiting stars
his pictrure still hangs on the wall,
warm and bright
while they have hanged him there
on the road of slaughter.

    —translated by May Jayyusi and Naomi Shihab Nye

Death Sentence

At night, orders came to the soldiers
to destroy our lovely village, Zeita.
Zeita! Bride of trees,
of blooming tulips,
spark of the winds!

The soldiers came in the dark
while the sons of the village
the trees and fields and flowerbuds

clung to Zeita
hugging her for shelter . . .

"Orders demand that all of you depart
Zeita will be destroyed before the night ends."

But we held tight, chanting:
Zeita is the land, the heart of the land,
and we her people are its branches.

That's how people fall—
a few moments of resistance,
so Zeita remains an eternal embrace across the nights
In moments she was rubble,
not a single bread oven remained.
Men and stones
were pasted and powdered by enemy tractors,
scattered forever in the light of the impossible.

now in the evenings
in the song of our wind,
Zeita arises, igniting its scarlet spark
upon the plains
And by morning
Zeita returns to the fields
as tulips do.

Night is morning in Zeita,
Night is morning.

    —translated by May Jayyusi and Naomi Shihab Nye

Ahmad Husain (b. 1939)

Born in Haifa, Husain moved back with his family to their village, Musmus, after 1948 when Haifa fell to the Jewish forces. He pursued his secondary studies in Nazareth, then obtained a university degree in history, psychology, and Judaic theology. He has worked as a teacher all his life, and now works as a teacher in Musmus. He has published two collections of poetry, *Time for Fear* (1977) and *Song of the Expected God* (1978), and one collection of short stories, *The Face and the Buttocks* (1983).

A Souvenir Vendor in Nazareth

"Sorrow"—such a useless, pretentious word!
How ridiculous that a little seashell, no bigger than
    a coffee cup,
should dream of containing a gushing river!
As for pain:
    that little grey woman whom you see
    night and day
    on the bends and corners of streets,
    at stations and gates of refugee camps—
it is less conceited,
but also less useful.
What they say is true:
the flower is not a garden
and the tree is not a forest.
When you suffer, you are
no more than a prisoner who carries
his evening meal, walking
toward his seat in the long hall.
Yet there must be a name for that thing
which permeates like the fragrance of a woman's perfume
in a lunatic asylum
or the rank air of a bedchamber
for military detainees

seeping into your nostrils
or suddenly assaulting your senses
while you are
    at the peak of involvement selling
    an olive wood camel
or a Bible sheathed in
    shining metal
or while you're speaking to a tourist woman
    as old as Herod
    or Julius Caesar . . .
Then what can anything mean?
Suddenly you want to go deep
    into remote times,
to become an inscription on the walls
    of an Assyrian temple
to die accepting your death
or begging for crucifixion
as bread is begged for
on the summit of a real mountain
1978 years Before Christ.

Overwhelmed by a sudden feeling that you are an imposter,
perhaps deceived yourself,
or at least you're Barabbas,[1]
and you weep,
images pouring from your eyes
one after another, racing each other to alight
on a distant rim of time which your eyes
have never really imagined.
Yet everything there seems perfectly known to you:
tents, temples, statues of the gods,
streets, inscriptions, even people's names,
a rope of bodies coiling riverlike around you,
songs in languages you suddenly know.
In a street in one of the cities
you meet a man you know
and a woman you love
carrying a jar of honey on her head,

---

[1]Barabbas was the bandit whom the mob demanded Pontius Pilate release from punishment, instead of Jesus.

a pure white cloth draped over it
and the road at her feet spread
with sand, pebbles, desert flame.
A woman linking snow and fire!
—Do you remember me? You ask.
But the woman moves on without seeing you.
She slides through and around you as easily as a whisper,
disappears.
And you remain, a shore submerged in the tide.
When the man laughs,
you could hit him!
—Where are you from?
—Chicago . . . The Old City.
—Go away, you fool!
But who'll sell olive wood to the Americans?
And when the man vanishes
from your eyes . . .
("Old City, you son of a bitch!")
authentic tears pour out.

—translated by Lena Jayyusi and Naomi Shihab Nye

Rashid Husain *(1936–1977)*

A poet from the village of Muslims near Haifa, Husain first worked as a schoolteacher, but was dismissed by the Israelis for his political beliefs. An organizer of the Al-Ard party in Israel, which was founded in 1958 and later banned, he spent many years in Israeli prisons. He became an editor of the Arab journal *Al-Fajr* (The Dawn), which was banned in 1962. He translated selections from Hayyim Bialik's poetry from Hebrew into Arabic and translated Palestinian folk songs into Hebrew. After the June 1967 war, he chose exile and lived in poverty in New York City, dying in a fire in his apartment. Husain's poetry is mainly concerned with the predicament of the Palestinians under siege both in Israel and in the diaspora. He has three collections, the last of which, *I Am the Land, Don't Deprive Me of the Rain,* is his best.

Damascus Diary

You come to Damascus
and later are reborn there
growing twice your size in minutes
Poetry tosses stars into your hands
Roses root in you
and you envy the love that children know
When sudden war erupts
you are ashamed not to be one of its heroes
War explodes in the mountains and sky
while you sit writing poetry
In Damascus?
By what right?
By what right?
You were born and you grow
like love, roses, children and beauty
            in Damascus
By what right?
Clouds build in my mind
till the answer rains down
Like them I am born and I grow

with, before, and after them
for I'm not here as a tourist
I am Palestine
and through my love . . . I am also Damascus

Beloved, I am ashamed to love
in the warring moments of Damascus
for the most beautiful men have gone
to the trenches of the north
My trenches are newspapers
My guns—the articles I write
I am ashamed to love in the absence
of the most perfect men
Nor can I enter cafes
where each chair protests to me:
Here sat a fighter
who now lives in the mountains!
Beloved, if you see my father, ask him
why he taught me the art of poetry
instead of how to fight—
by what right?

Men, women, beautiful boys and lovely girls
all conspire to cleanse my blood
I am the Arab exhausted by humiliation
asking that my blood be purified
with luminous light and simplest love,
purest kisses
So what do I give in return
but these poems, Damascus?
If my blood pours with torrential love
how can I share it
except in print?

—translated by May Jayyusi and Naomi Shihab Nye

Against

Against my country's rebels wounding a sapling
Against a child—any child—bearing a bomb

Against my sister studying a rifle's components
Against what you will—
But even a prophet becomes powerless
when his vision takes in
⠀⠀⠀⠀⠀⠀the murderers' horses
Against a child becoming a hero at ten
Against a tree's heart sprouting mines
Against my orchard's branches becoming gallows
Against erecting scaffolds among the roses of my land
Against what you will—
But after my country, my comrades, and my youth were burnt,
how can my poems not turn into guns?

⠀⠀—translated by May Jayyusi and Naomi Shihab Nye

First

From the play "The Interrogation"

Interrogator: In this poem you are clearly saying that my wife loves
⠀⠀you.
The Poet: I am speaking of my land, I say I was there
before you, and she will always think of me first.
Be her husband—so what!
I loved her before you did
and have first place in her heart.
Even if you buy her perfume,
purchase her the finest clothes . . .
it's for me she will wear them.
I smoked on her lap long ago,
startling her with my earliest cigarettes.
I'll even enter your bed
on your wedding night, and come between you . . .
though you are her bridegroom
she will embrace me, desiring me most.
I will always be between you—
I'm sorry—but I was first.

⠀⠀—translated by May Jayyusi and Naomi Shihab Nye

Jabra Ibrahim Jabra (b. 1920)

Novelist, short story writer, poet, painter, and critic, Jabra is one of Palestine's most distinguished authors. Born in Bethlehem, he studied in Jerusalem and Cambridge, England, where he obtained an M.A. in English literature. After the debacle of 1948 in Palestine, he sought employment in Iraq and settled eventually in Baghdad, where he took Iraqi citizenship. He has written several volumes of literary criticism, among which *Freedom and Chaos* (1960) and *The Closed Orbit* (1964), mostly on contemporary Arabic poetry, have been some of the more valuable contemporary works of Arabic criticism. His work includes: two collections of prose poetry, *Tammuz in the City* (1959) and *The Agony of the Sun* (1981); one collection of short stories; and six novels, one of which, *Hunters in a Narrow Street* (1955), was written in English. His two major novels, *The Ship* (1973) and *Search for Waleed Mas'ud* (1978), have been translated into Engliish by Roger Allen and Adnan Haydar, the second with some help from PROTA. Jabra has himself translated numerous works into Arabic from English. His most notable translation was part of James Frazer's *The Golden Bough,* which he published in 1957 under the title *Adonis, A Study in Ancient Oriental Myths and Religions.* This book greatly influenced some of the leading poets of the fifties, helping them to introduce fertility myths in Arabic poetry with success. His most recent work is an autobiographical account of his childhood in Palestine, *The First Well* (1987). In 1989 Jabra was awarded the Saddam Hussein Prize for Fiction, and in 1990 the Sultan Uweis Prize for Literary Criticism, and the Jerusalem medal for literary achievement.

From: *"Zero Hour"*

I

I saw the moon caught
tonight in a net of branches, a fish
neither known to fishermen
nor to sultans
Stunned on the uptake, I shout: "The night is so brilliant!"
How marvellous the houses and gardens,

and how spellbinding the trees
that describe arabesques on the night's face
and appear to drag the moon into their branches,
and commune with it.
Is this moon, this magnanimous night, love?

A voice among the trees pesters me
I try to elude it, but it persists:
"So you've finally achieved it—
grown ecstatic at a scene
that's repeated every night.
You're besieged—
a cloudlike black water settles on your eyes
day after day
You're mislead by your vision
and your ears are susceptible to the point of deafness.
Your life has the shallow transience
of a daily paper.
You've used up your reserves of inner depth.
You're without tears
and your life is open to strangers
like a hooker's.
They listen in to your telephone calls
and the whispers in your letters,
the feverish pulse in your throat,
and your mind's subterranean thoughts—
which all amount to a deficit.
Have you seen the moon tonight
and felt enraptured?
What vaccine's been injected into your veins?
Is it a book you've read or picture seen
that's dislodged the dark membrane from your eyes,
the armoured shield from your senses,
and the chastity belt from your loin?
Is it in the entanglement of branches
that you've seen love as a pearl-bright moon
beckoning you from the four corners of the night?
Has a universal secret
taken form inside you,
a new spring erupted

mitigating death's seduction—
the one who tries for your favours in bed?

4

Who says that tomorrow or the day after
I would be stunned again by the likes of
what I have seen tonight?
Only the gift of vision persists—
the countdown continues
and the wind streams with hallucination.

O distant voice
were you more than a voice—
the one I knew before you died—
I'd have found in my words the solace
we derived from our dialogue,
for a month a week a day,
until pain was resurrected.
But your going has left only an echo
for which I search through your valleys and mountains
which I chance upon only on rare nights of marvel.
My pain returns in your absence,
and words don't penetrate
the shield you've made of death.
It was almost premonitory the way you said—
"I'll stop here, I've had enough.
Let my deep suffering become yours;
neither man nor Christ extended a hand to me."
Are there hands for those who cry out in the void?
With daring and speed we could not match
you crossed to the other bank.
From the first to the twentieth round,
you knew that words were no use.
Nor tears. Nor screams. Nor silence.
Even love was of no value.
I see the moon caught
tonight in a net of branches, a fish
neither known to fishermen
nor to sultans.
stunned on the uptake, I shout: "The night is so brilliant!"

I want to forget its colocynth,
and that morning's as bitter,
and every hour is a century,
and every minute is a knife aimed at the wrist.
Is this how you felt
when you went to that hollowed rock
and saw your shadow challenge you?
Had I to wait twenty years
to know what you had known,
to meet this horror face to face
this loneliness that roars more violently
                    than the sea?

Is this why we saw visions
and accepted the agony of belief?
And why we shouldered the cross across the world
certain that after the crucifixion
comes the resurrection?

5

I see the moon tonight and I'm stunned.
A mad pit yawns at my feet,
and night's summits extend beyond the hills,
silence thunders, the earth is torn by thunderbolts
and wild boars rush roaring from their caves.
My countdown—haven't I reached the zero hour?
How have I jumped it? What hand has given the signal
and stopped the execution?
Whose fingers grow erect before me like a lofty tree
and show me a world
that still resounds with labor pains,
ringed by dancers and lovers?
How splendid is the night
the way it consumes the hours,
and, as it did over the ancient poet,
lowers its dark veils to blind me.
To end, but won't end.

—translated by Sharif Elmusa and Jeremy Reed

For Socrates

Why did they order you to drink the poison?

We repeat the question
though we know the story;
how you spent the final days
with your disciples, consoling them
so they might prepare for your imminent departure
(as if poison was the god's will),
and how in solitude you amused yourself
by remaking Aesop's Fables
(as if wisdom was an antidote to poison),
and in the end
you didn't forget Aesculapius's ritual—
and asked for the sacrifice of a cock to him
(as if poison demands propitiation of guilt).
All this was more than the rulers could take,
as they could not tolerate the doubts
you disseminated over Athens,
your teachings threatening their traditions.
They rewarded your inquisitiveness with poison.
But without so much as questioning them
you lifted the hemlock to your lips,
swallowed it,
and killed them all.

Who today remembers the names of your judges?

—translated by Sharif Elmusa and Jeremy Reed

Love Poem

Your voice fills my head with song
Wherever I turn I hear you say:
"Would you like to kiss me?"—
Do I just want to kiss you?
I want to contain you
as a storm the turbulent waves—
I want to spin with you

like a hurricane lashing the sea.
You're the sea
that attracts:
O my splendid horror,
that I might drown in you
the way a storm sinks,
and the way a drowned sun erupts in tumultuous fires.
Is my love so bestial?
It's more a delectation
like your breast cupped in my hand,
or the sweetness of your lips
which, as I gulp them,
I fear separation and thirst.
I wish you'd write
with my own blood
your name on my wrist.
Seeing it, I can endure my thirst.

But your song reverberates in my head,
and triggers a storm in search of the sea.
You, you're my own sea.

   —translated by Sharif Elmusa and Jeremy Reed

Salma Khadra Jayyusi

For her biography, please look under "The Translators Biographies."

Khartoum

Taunt me with the sun and sand of Khartoum?
Have you not seen her stars whispering love to me
and her tender heart ever wounded by love?
Her Nile overflowing
    with milk and honey
        and the soul's wine?
Khartoum, City withdrawn behind mystic songs,
keeping eternal watch over memories,
over secrets and ties of the heart
    she holds loyally.

I came to her alone, like a naked spear,
my eyes sore,
my hair a tangle, my breast closed upon hell,
stumbling across the wilderness in my soul
as all winds died down
and the hands of the clock stood still.

With silken cords she lifted me up
extinguished the live coals in my head
and paved my road with lilies and elder blossom.

I entered her gates as one entering life
Her moon loved and suckled me on its warm milk,
her palm trees taught me patience;
and I departed without ever leaving her.
And look! The navel cord is forever uncut,
and the table is lavishly laid
with the blessings of the spirit.

Khartoum and Um Durman
Majdhoub and Zainab

Khadija and Ishaq[1]
Faces of nobleness and truth
Calm hearts that restored my stolen hours to me!
What has become of you?

—translated by the author and John Heath-Stubbs

The Woman

I

Shall I talk about S?
Woman rapt to heaven's seventh circle
Straying among the stars
Divided eternally between father and son
Strung by her hair to the mother tree
Mad with love, with the whistling of the wind.

One day the leopard came saying
"With you time stops,
All searching is over!"

But she drove him back to the jungle, saying
"Go without fear;
Your covenant's safe with me."
And the green world swallowed up
S's magnificent leopard,
The sightless beast struck his heart
and killed him, freed her
to wed the wind.

Waste no regrets on S
Fixed on the star's deception
She brought the art of death in life
To perfection.

[1]Um Durman is one of three towns which make greater Khartoum. Majdhoub is the late Sudanese poet, Muhammad al-Mahdi al-Majdhoub, the foremost poet of his generation in the Sudan; Zainab was his wife. Ishaq is the Sudanese dilettante and poet, Ishaq al-Khalifa Sharif, and Khadija is his wife.

II

You were pure joy once, now
you are everlasting sorrow that never dies,
slamming shut the windows of my heart tyranically
blue-eyed phantom, with the words of Ibn Dharih[1]
on your lips.

How could you endure it so patiently
when, with those stars, your eyes,
you tempted S, then gave up the fight?
Instead defeat, defeat her contrariety
with the royal passion of your embrace.

She betrayed you with inkwells and rosaries
Ravished everyday by the eternal priest,
eyes like arrows chanting wordless songs.

He snatched her away morning, afternoon and evening,
turned her away from you
with the savagery only the righteous can inflict
addressed her charms in words that forced
　　her flowering buds to close,
knotted her hands with rosaries,
bound her in prayers and incantations,
gave her water of lotus to drink
drove the rainbow from her eyes,
and dragged her to the pools of ink.

Priest and lover without end!
Wily hierophant who drove
you both into the wilderness,
Eternal Priest!
Lord who gives and withholds
Anchorite burning with eros
Hermit worshipping the flower of passion
Lover, Traitor,
Provider of all things,
Denier of all things,
Eternal celebrant now paying homage
to the flame of a memory,

---

[1]Ibn Dharih (Qais ibn Dharih, or Qais Lubna, after his beloved) was a famous Platonic love poet who lived in the Umayyad period, 661–750 A.D.

cut off from life in a distant corner of the world
his eyes rediscovering sainthood.

Behold the London
October second drives fear into,
turns it to a dragon's lair,
a den to grieving beasts,
Evelyn Gardens becomes a pool of tears
hot, enduring, welling from heart and guts,
from the pores of flesh,
in despair made new,
bedewing neck, cheek, hand
and the void of time and space
Tears, seal of all joy,
Tears of the timeless covenant,
Censor of all love to come,
bringing to the heart ice and frozen sleep.

One Evelyn Gardens:
House of madness,
breaker of heart and mind,
whose cell-walls collapse
on your image and name
and the fires of memory blaze.

   —translated by the author and John Heath-Stubbs

Songs for an Arab City

I

Among your palms I find my familiar mist
painful division I discover walking beside your river
fighting memories but your waters are deceptive
greeting me playfully, yet when I reply
they hold their mirror up to my face.

II

You linger, unsure of me
although I am a palm tree
rooted in your sky

commanding with a voice like yours.
I bear your countenance
wherever the airports may scatter me
Do you know me? Your heart is
full of the love which I
like all my people,
love and deny.

III

I weary of minarets
tugging at me whenever I make for the west
as if I were stumbling and falling
pursuing me after each prayer
as if I were guilty of blasphemy.
The minarets haunt me.

IV

In you I beheld my own face mocking me
veering away as if it did not recognize me
as if when I went away
I had never left, you were
still there for me.

In you I heard my own voice disputing with me
sometimes in a whisper, at others a shriek
tempting, nagging,
my voice talking back set me free.

In you I saw my grave
deserting me.

V

Haroun al-Rashid's magnificent steeds
    have multiplied in you
and mosques gird you round.
City! What are you?
A monastery?
An armed camp? When will you be ready
for the storm
to rise from you?

—translated by the author and John Heath-Stubbs

On June 5, 1968

Last June severed the ultimate vein in my heart
Have you heard about my death?
About my embarrassed funeral?
The farce is that the dead are proclaimed
        borne in the street, entombed!
I wish the coffin would vanish
like youthful dreams!
Have you heard about my death?
That viper cup
that death in love with death?
Yes, you have:
Your undertaker saw me buried as they
laid him at my side.

—translated by the author and John Heath-Stubbs

The Three of Us Alone

I

Deep in death's shadowy domain
now foreign to my life,
you are freed from my kisses, from your own
tender skin,
you're bonded to permanent shade;
you've made steadfast sand your pillow
and learned the secret of mutation
You gave your heart to silence!
Still you are beautiful.
You set me free only to emblazon
your face on every pathway I take
Your presence hems me round, extends into
        and beyond me
like my own shadow
        it stretches before me
Like the dawn it surrounds me
beautiful and alive.

II

And you too are beautiful and alive!
You beseech God to shield your scars
the daily relics of a past
from which you retreat.
You set me free
to commit me to endless crossing
scudding before the winds of uncertainty
Ah! How you have changed!
You strayed away only to
imprison yourself in a labyrinth
to bury your head in shifting sand
to inhabit a wasteland, to eat the bread
of tyrants, and go to bed
with a deadly death-watch beetle black as night.
Yes, you have changed.

You are beautiful and dead.

III

And you?
You cling to the talons of an eagle that ranges the universe.
Your earth is water, your land inhabited by lighting
Weightless, yet with an Achilles heel,
you explore the cold of harbors.

Your shadow grows in your footsteps,
shrinks as time recedes from you,
and lingers beyond you
　　　It waxes, it wanes,
and lingers beyond you
While death lurks among the harbors
stalking you
You skip away, a whirling caprice.

You turn to the right: A face leaps out
　　　　　　　　　from death's domain
　　　　　　　　　alive and beautiful

You turn to the left:　A face vanishes
　　　　　　　　　into the quagmire of death
　　　　　　　　　alive and beautiful.

A triad that never breaks a date

You three alone forever

Yes, forever alone.

—translated by the author and John Heath-Stubbs

Salem Jubran *(b. 1941)*

Jubran was born in al-Buqai'a in upper Galilee and studied English Literature and Middle Eastern History at the University of Haifa. In 1962 he joined Rakah, the Israeli Communist Party, and worked at *Al-Ittihad,* the Party's Arab periodical; he later edited the journal *Al-Ghad.* He has published *Words From the Heart,* Acre, 1971; *Poems Not Under House Arrest,* Nazareth, 1972; and *Comerades of the Sun,* Nazareth, 1975. Jubran's greatest involvement is with the predicament of the Palestinian people who live under siege. He expresses this involvement in a poetry as simple as it is effective.

Refugee

The sun crosses borders
without any soldier shooting at it
The nightingale sings in Tulkarm[1]
of an evening,
eats and roosts peacefully
with kibbutzim birds.
A stray donkey grazes
    across the firing line
in peace
and no one aims.
But I, your son made refugee
—Oh my native land—
between me and your horizons
the frontier walls stand.

—translated by Lena Jayyusi and Naomi Shihab Nye

[1]Tulkarm is a town on the West Bank near Nablus.

Singer of Wind and Rain

You can uproot the trees
    from my village mountain
    which embraces the moon
You can plough my village houses under
    leaving no trace of their walls
You can confiscate my rebec,
    rip away the chords and burn the wood

but you cannot suffocate my tunes—
for I am the lover of this land
and the singer of wind and rain.

    —translated by Lena Jayyusi and Naomi Shihab Nye

'Ali al-Khalili (b. 1943)

A poet, short story writer, novelist, and scholar, al-Khalili was born in Nablus, where he studied up to secondary level. He then took a degree in Business Administration from the Arab University of Beirut, graduating in 1966. He worked as a teacher and journalist till 1973, when he left the West Bank to work as a journalist in the Arab world, returning home to the West Bank in 1977. He now works as editor-in-chief of the newspaper *Al-Fajr* and as general editor of *Al-Fajr Literary Journal.* He is also one of the chief founders of the Union of Arab Writers in the occupied territories. Al-Khalili is a prolific writer who has so far published more than twenty books. He has also published two novels, *The Keys Turn in the Locks* (1980) and *A Light in the Long Tunnel* (1983). Some of his scholarly research is dedicated to the service of national culture: he has written two books on the popular songs of Palestine, *Songs of Children in Palestine* (1980) and *Songs of Work and Workers in Palestine* (1979). He has also written a book titled, *The Palestinian Folk Heritage and the Class System* (1977), a study of class concepts as reflected in Palestinian folk proverbs. Al-Khalili's poetry volumes, ten in number to date are some of the truly experimental works in contemporary Palestinian poetry; his poems demonstrate his deep involvement with the existential problems of life under siege, and of the experience of coercion and repression which Arabs in the West Bank encounter daily. The poetry contains a subtle mélange of the communal and the personal, of the general problems of life around him and the private strife of the individual facing and reacting to those problems. His first collection, *Dialectic of the Homeland,* was published in Beirut (1976). Some of his other collections are, *Nablus Goes to the Bridge* (1977) and *Alone, Then the Garden is Suddenly Crowded* (1985).

Dialectics of the Homeland

1

Beyond the rainy cloud, the rose, and the pagan dream
are remnants of the old pledge.
The lovers are no more the lovers
And the murderers are similarly transposed,

O homeland, drowning in mystic symbols and in blood,
Lost homeland!
Teach us to exist in the age of lost things
Teach us to unlock barred doors
To fertilize a barren land
Discover in you the cloud and the rose
Illuminate the tired masses.
Homeland of lost things,
Teach us to conceive trees and children,
When the promised sun and the promised wind
Are concealed or revealed
Teach us that the murderers are visible in you
And the murdered invisible.

2

Glory to the dead, who dispersed among the people
who burned:
—Who ploughs fire?
—They plundered all secrets.
—Now?
Apes huddled around the tended fire.

3

The blocked horizons rained.
Who can dam a river between one finger and another?
Who steals a moon that blossoms at a marriage of simple peasants?
Homeland of the newborn mother,
We have concealed a wound, exposed another
Witnessed blood as water, water as blood,
We did not fall,
Beyond the rainy cloud, the rose, and the pagan dream
bridges extend,
beyond the noose is the lily
green corpses pressed in the books of simple people
and in the memory of the struggling masses.
The peaks of death are torture and the taut tones of the voice
The peaks of death are magnificent, for who can possess
his own death lacerated by
obstructed paths?

4

They passed at the twilight of revolution and lost things
Who owns the truth of death?
The customary slates are split:
Death without death
Voice without voice
Homeland without homeland.
Only the poor, the workers, the outcasts,
the elect at the dawn of revolution
remain loyal to the wound, to the truth of death,
to the meaning of the song.

—translated by Hanan Mikha'il Ashrawi

From "What is Your Purpose, Murderous Beauty?"

Mud on the Shoes

Peaceful spirit,
Take your ornaments to every sultan and kneel down
a rump of fat a rump of fear.
The massacre involved students, workers,
wretched intellectuals.
The gates were closed.
And it's alone that you imbibe the mud
of their tattered shoes
And without warning enter a vacuum
To be transformed into a rodent.
Alone, alone peaceful spirit
From fat and fear you procreate
a generation of wall posters
and hot water tapped for the master's bath.

Words

Metonymy, ambiguity, simile, metaphor,
Trope, paradox, pun,
Rhyme, apposition, rhetoric—Arab eloquence—
I've taken up your evil

Let's storm the tapestries of those kneeling in prayer,
I've learned your magic
Take vengeance, then, language—words
Words, words, words, on the mud of traveller's shoes.

Display Windows

Attention, stop, ready, ease up, roll
green cabbage head. Roll, rump of a man
Recently hung.
Roll, bastard.
Then he related:
Arab oil was a roof—it collapsed,
Legendary gold was a platform—it was effaced
or coated with my blood.
Beggars dispersed word by word, and it was said
Bite by bite
in the great Friday sermon in Jerusalem and Mecca—
The treasury house doesn't enrich—contentment is a treasure—
Nor does the plague willingly withdraw.
O beauty,
Of what purpose is this music
flowing beneath those glorious feet?
And to what end the laughter of decapitated heads
stacked in Riyadh, Cairo, Marakesh, Khartoum, South
Africa, Chile and the enchanting display of show windows
in New York? What purpose does the Nile have when
it dies? What is your purpose, murderous beauty?

Tongue

We can no longer indulge in the diversion of meteors and falling stars.
We are the salt of the earth which symbolises clothes, medals,
earrings, brooches, paints, rugs etc.
for the new generals.
When salt dissolves, the earth recoils beneath
sheets of brass and steel.
I restrain my tongue from hallucinating
And say I wish I had died before this.
The earth prevents its tongue from hallucinating
And says I wish I were the resurrection.

The fire grips us and we burn,
We go on repeating I wish I wish I wish, until
Another voice emerges from the fire and utters
What we cannot say.

Ardor

The aperture constricted in the lock
Iron is all this death, steel and brass
The eye's unawareness is sleep
Passion infuses the millions.
Then flow down
Erupt, you
Naked mountain peaks into the burned ruins—
A strangled earthquake
Escapes my breast—
Erupt
Fear, snow, cities, forgotten heroes,
Closed windows, emigrant exiled workers,
Landless peasants, songs without lips—
Flow down.

—translated by Hanan Mikha'il Ashrawi

Departure

Departure, eternal departure
When will the exiles sit
around one table
and a family rejoice
knowing
    that despite sorrow
    it is our homeland!

—translated by Salma Khadra Jayyusi

This Country

At the last hour
of his last day
the prisoner spoke to the executioner
    in clear words
about his country, the most beautiful
    in the world
about this country,
this country
The executioner was stunned
as he turned around him once and again
saw nothing but darkness
blood and chains!

    —translated by Salma Khadra Jayyusi

Waleed Khazindar *(b. 1950)*

One of the finest Palestinian poets living in the diaspora, Khazindar was born in Ghaza where he did all his pre-university studies. He then went to Beirut for his higher studies and obtained a degree in law in 1978. He lived in Tunis for a few years before moving with his family to Cairo in 1991. In his crisp, economic, nonmetrical poetry, there is artistic precision and a well-measured mélange of emotion and semantic intention, of tension and calm, and of a metaphoric originality matched by a novel thematic approach heretofore unprecedented in Arabic poetry. Although Khazindar has published only one collection of poetry, *Present Verbs* (1986), he is already recognized as one of the leading modernist poets among the younger generation. He is included in PROTA's forthcoming anthology, *End of the Century Poets, New Voices in Arabic Poetry.*

Belonging

Who was it fractionally moved the vase
and was here in the room in my absence?
And the picture of the slain knight on the wall
someone has tampered with it.
My papers show disorderly edges
from a hurried reading.
I never leave my pillow this way
nor the abandon of a soiled shirt.

Who was it visited my room with me
away, who can it be?
What new assertion of calm will restore the vase to its place?
What reconciliation impose on the dead knight
his old deameanor, his symmetry on the blank wall?

What will restore to my pillow and my shirt
the aroma of the citizen?

—translated by Lena Jayyusi and Jeremy Reed

Houses

The cloud of migrations is in his eyes,
and in the leather briefcase the book, the pencil, the family photograph
The rust of benches on his hands, the rust of bannisters and doorknobs,
the rust of handshakes on his hands.
The briefcase propped against the wall—
will he take out his souvenirs first, or will he
like a magician take out a country:
a house,
a street,
a capital.
He closed his eye, lay back against the shoulder of familiar habits.
He will not make friends with another vase,
he will not confess to a bed that will blow up in the next war,
he will not make tea or sing.
He will pace back and forth for a long time between the porch and
        the kitchen
and he will listen hard for a sound coming from the garden gate.
But there is only the crunching of leaves under feet
passing
then
going on;
there is nothing but the hum of talk in the houses next door.

   —translated by Lena Jayyusi and W.S. Merwin

At Least

If you would smash the glass against the wall
if you would wake anyone you please, now at two in the morning,
if you would just say what you wrote yesterday, secretly, on the
        cigarette box,
"It has rained, spring has come
and the murdered man is still lying in the garden"—
if only you would do something, friend:
cut something down with your scythe, fling dust around!
Because when you sit like that at the edge of the sofa,

hands between your knees,
after your fourth glass, saying nothing,
I feel a jar breaking inside me.

—translated by Lena Jayyusi and W.S. Merwin

Brambles

What frightened you—an empty cage?
A letter folded there on top of the wood stove?

Something in the scent of those same jasmines in the hedge warned
     you,
the brambles signalled their warning as you passed;
how did you fail to notice?
You turned your key in the door as though a year had not passed,
as though the dust in which you left your footprints
from the bottom of the stairs, had not spoken.
Now suffer the roses, all killed in the vase,
suffer the hands of time on the wall,
and look around you:
it is not just the window shades
nor the mirror, the telephone, the table,
but even the bedsheets have shuddered,
and those pink paper handkerchiefs
with the picture of a boy and a girl in the corner.

—translated by Lena Jayyusi and W.S. Merwin

You Will Arrive: Bewildered

A little before the doorbell rings

they will arrive in a minute
holding waves in their open hands
and they will fill
the corners of the living room with their loud laughter
and go on talking, following you into the kitchen

but if they come on into the bedroom
how will you explain things to them?

You will arrive with wine, embarrassed,
claiming that you were asleep when the bell rang,
and that when you woke up you found all those wings,
those wings that, when the door opened,
each one who came in
thought nobody else had seen.

—translated by Lena Jayyusi and W.S. Merwin

That Day

Nothing about him has changed.
His chair and the table are on the balcony.
His book is open at the last page.
His ashtray, his papers.

Whenever he felt pain he would draw a sprig of basil
when someone was killed on the radio he would draw a bird,
and after his second drink
obscure, inscrutable figures.

Nothing about him has changed
but since that day he has not returned to his chair
nor to his sudden alertness
when the merciless boots pass,
and since that day his contagious laugh
has not been heard in our house,
his reckless, mournful laugh.

—translated by Lena Jayyusi and W.S. Merwin

Absence

Her empty room
A black leather chair to the right.
A black leather chair to the left.

A green-black sweater
exhausted, heavy with love, on the window's marble sill.

Nothing: her empty room.
No wind, not a sound.
The violets hide away in the wall
and the clouds burrow past the window
into the inscrutable blue.

All at once
footsteps, shuffling in the corridor.
All at once
her absence
deep, overwhelming
floods the room.

> —translated by Lena Jayyusi and W.S. Merwin

The Storm

Her silk catches on a thorn,
on a smouldering tardy ember from the first chestnuts
The fluttering of the story still lingers in her fingertips,
and the tone of voice holds much unsaid.

Under a tepid sky she is ablaze
Somehow this fruit has escaped its climate
so the sap was confused
and the petals confounded.

To her soiree a star never came
For two youth spans she's been teaching him the light
The waves, whose blue she is, don't comprehend her helm
She knows, yet she grieves, she storms.

She storms away the reasons and whatever will come
The embers and the silk alike
And also me, when I come late,
or show up before she anticipates
If I don't detect, from the oar's first echo
        the direction of her boat—
And even if I do.

She storms the words, and the time,
and when she calms, a storm breaks
    consuming her.

   —translated by Anton Shammas and Naomi Shihab Nye

Rasim al-Madhoun *(b. 1947)*

Al-Madhoun was born in Askalan in southern Palestine, from which his family was driven to Gaza in 1948. He emigrated again, to Cairo, after the 1967 June War, then moved on first to Amman, then Beirut, then Damascus, where he still lives. He has worked all his life in journalism and broadcasting. Al-Madhoun's work covers the experience of families and individuals living in the diaspora; he often writes about this experience in an intimate and moving personal voice. Among his collections of poetry are *Sparrows of Roses* (1983) and *Copybook of the Sea* (1986).

One Thousand and One . . . Nights

The time has come for me to remove
the cop's hat
and meet you at the artificial door
There's no running away from death
so I'll meet him in public
in the middle of the day,
and, as we start our usual morning bickering,
I'll spend all you wish
of my elusive patience
breaking the rotten egg
    (you'll shake your head,
    smile,
    and your eyes will whisper,
    "You won't break the rotten egg")
but I will
I will place my palm on yours
so you may wipe out my deed
    and go to sleep as a cold tremble
        overtakes you
Did I enter your dream?
I know I'm an idler
and do not step into dreams
    (at least that's what you've said to me)

still I'll ask
how was I in the dream?
What did I see?
The mirage of the country that hid us
and went to sleep?
Or the blood from the rotten egg?
But you smile,
　　　your eyes whispering,
"You haven't broken the rotten egg—
it was only your leap into illusion
your imagining
and you've made an error
for a thousand and one times."

—translated by Sharif S. Elmusa and Naomi Shihab Nye

Family Poems

I Giyath[1]

When you joined us, sure and smiling,
on our somber journey,
I forgave the world.
With the nest of childhood supporting me,
I inhaled its sweet fragrance and felt refreshed.
Maybe your newness
would grant us peace,
the blue calm of your eyes give us strength
to scuffle with life.

There you are, laughing,
while exile awaits you,
your grieving father, the map
of plundered Palestine, and the dreams
of all our friends who passed away.
All this inheritance is yours,
this pain nestling in my chest.

[1]Giyath and Mihyar are the poet's sons. Um Ghiyath (i.e., mother of Giyath, her first born) is the poet's wife.

I know I disrupt the innocence of your blue eyes
but it is they who have disrupted everything
while you were still a wish in your father's heart.

My beautiful son,
the truth is they arranged the world
before you were born
and placed you at a crossing
to find the Future's worthy road.

—translated by Sharif S. Elmusa and Naomi S. Nye

II Mihyar[1]

Here we are together, you and I,
braving the biting cold, cheering diffidently,
with half-shut eyes.
Today is the first of your fifth month,
what they call the month of consciousness.
What are you conscious of?
On the verge of speech,
what impedes you?
Our greedy diesel stove, ever thirsty,
triggers your smile. It sets up
your calendar of colds and shivers,
joy and sleep. It ceases
without warning, and the house
quivers. You fall silent,
I curl under the quilt, and
your mother goes to bed early.
But when that murky foul-smelling fuel
whets the thirst of the heater,
our house hums with warmth,
with your soft child's babble.
The stove, you, my heart . . .
God! How can we be together
and not be struck by feverish joy!

—translated by Sharif S. Elmusa and Naomi S. Nye

III Um Giyath

She sleeps with half-shut eyes, ever vigilant,
like all mothers, a star dreaming of the permanence
of night. Her pulse races,
faster than the pulse of other women,
her hands contract from cold water, soap,
the endless scrubbing of kids' clothes:
this is her daily journey, the round wheel
of her mill.
Earthy as a spike of wheat,
tender as a young girl pressed against
the chest of her lover,
some days sober as a mother
who thinks of her faraway son.
She sleeps with open eyes.
Her hands contract from the cold,
the water, the soap.
Trembling gently, her fingers close and open,
gripping something red as cherries
something tender: my own heart.

—translated by Sharif Elmusa and Naomi Shihab Nye

Peace Be Upon . . .

A flower under siege,
a lily withering in the blaze of exile,
a sad scarf waving from a train window.
That is our rose,
the naked exiled to stone.
Then what?

Details are burdensome.
Beginnings have no doors.
Signatures are erased by the cool morning.
Are you a flower under siege?
A premature lily?
A window in a passing train?

On the evening of the massacre,
Giyath slowly circles between the window screen
and our tears, singing without words.
(What do the children of Palestine sing
when they witness a massacre?)
He bites his fingers, circling and circling.
Giyath is three, three years of drought and grief,
all lost in biting his fingers
as he witnessed the flesh of our brethren
strewn in the streets.
Three years of drought and grief,
Giyath is asking who killed the uncles,
who tore the skin, who made them bleed.
He persists. Can three years of drought and grief
swallow our river of whys?

Is poetry of any value in the alleys of massacre?
Are words of use when the veins burst?
Giyath can circle between the screen and our tears
questioning, wondering.
As long as the massacre masters the scene,
our spiced and graceful words
stand struck on the sidewalk of Time,
waving to those who flee the knife,
naked of everything save remembrance,
grasping at air.
Peace upon those who leave and those who return,
peace upon the blood of victims
speckling the streets of the hungry
peace upon a future liberator who will emerge
from a house of straw and sweep away corruption,
peace upon tomorrow's children,
    who will reach adulthood
    without witnessing massacres,
peace upon Time woven together
with joyful songs and the locked hands of lovers,
peace upon the easy world
waking from late morning sleep,
peace be to God blessing his righteous people.

—translated by Sharif S. Elmusa and Naomi S. Nye

'Abd al-Raheem Mahmoud *(1913–1948)*

Born in Anabta near Tulkarm in the West Bank, 'Abd al-Raheem Mahmoud is the foremost Palestinian poet-martyr and is deeply revered by generations of Palestinians. His secondary education took place at the Najah school (now the Najah University) in Nablus, where he subsequently taught Arabic language and literature until 1936. However, when the 1936 uprising began, he left teaching and joined the fight against the British, while at the same time writing fiery poetry that called his people to the fight for Palestinian rights. From 1939 to 1942 he enlisted in the Military College in Iraq, graduating as an officer. He was then invited by the Iraqi government to teach, first in Baghdad, then in Basra, where he joined Rasheed 'Ali al-Kilani's rebellion against the British. He later returned to Palestine and, until 1948, was active both politically and in the poetic field. He joined the fighting that took place in Palestine in 1947–1948, following the partition decision, and fell in battle on 13 July 1948. His poetry, with its prophetic vision and its noble and enduring patriotism, is memorized by thousands of Palestinians both inside Palestine and in exile.

The Martyr

I shall carry my soul on the palm of my hand,
tossing it into the cavern of death!
Either a life to gladden the hearts of friends
or a death to torture the hearts of foes!
An honorable man's spirit has two aims:
to die fighting, or to achieve victory.
Otherwise, what is life? I want no life
if we're not respected in our land;
if our response is not feared,
if our words are not heard
echoing in the world!

By your life, I see my own death,
but I hasten my footsteps.
No greater wish than to die defending stolen rights
and my country,

My ears love the clashing of swords,
my soul is proud of martyrs' blood.
Behold the martyr's body
sprawled on sands, attacked by vultures,
his blood tinting the earth crimson,
haunting northern breezes with its scent.
His radiant brow covered with dust
only seems more luminous.
The smile on his lips
mocks this earthly life,
and his dreams of eternity,
shape blissful visions.

I swear this is how men *should* die
for how can I tolerate the harm of my enemy's malice,
how can I endure his aggression?
Would fear stop me if it is easy to sacrifice my life?
Am I humble? I simply can endure no scorn!
With my own heart I'll fight the enemy;
my heart of steel, my ravenous flames,
I'll stalk my land with the blade of this sword
so my people know I'm their defender.

—translated by Sharif Elmusa and Naomi Shihab Nye

Call of the Motherland

The slain motherland called for our struggle
and my heart leapt with joy.
I raced the winds, but did not boast.
Isn't it my simple duty to redeem my country?
I carried my soul in my hands asking
any who feared death: do you hesitate
before the enemy?
Would you sit still when your country begs for your help?
Would you back away from facing the enemy?
If so, then go hide in your mother's bedroom!
May your hesitation humiliate you!
The motherland needs mighty defenders

who meet aggression
but never complain;
true lions on the battlefield.

People of my country, our days of sacrifice have arrived;
they shine, radiant, across the hills of this holy land.
Redeemed by our young men too proud
to endure oppression,
what can we do but fight bravely
when the fire's kindled?
March on, to the field! Pour fire
on the heads of the enemy everywhere.
Nothing's humbler than a people who shun the fight
when their country calls for it.

Neighbors, brethren, arise from your sleep!
How can you sleep through this oppression?
Never stop even if the sky should grow dark!
Never retreat even if the sandstorms flare up behind you!
Don't give up even if the world should face you
with weapons from every direction
unite, unite everywhere!
If Palestine should be lost while you still live,
I'll say: our people have
abandoned the path.

—translated by Sharif Elmusa and Naomi Shihab Nye

The Aqsa Mosque*

(A salute to Prince Saud Ibn 'Abd al-'Aziz when he
visited the poet's town, 'Anabta, on August 14, 1935.)

Honorable Prince! Before you stands a poet
whose heart harbors bitter complaint.
Have you come to visit the Aqsa mosque[1]

*This poem gained great fame later on because of its prophetic words about imminent
loss of Palestine.

[1]The Aqsa mosque in the old city of Jerusalem is the third holiest shrine in Islam,
the first being the Kaaba.

or to bid it farewell before its loss?
This land, this holy land, is being sold to all intruders
and stabbed by its own people!
And tomorrow looms over us, nearer and nearer!
Nothing shall remain for us but our streaming tears,
our deep regrets!

Oh, Prince, shout, shout! Your voice
might shake people awake!
Ask the guards of the Aqsa: are they all agreed to struggle
as one body and mind?
Ask the guards of the Aqsa: can a covenant with God
be offered to someone, then lost?
Forgive the complaint, but a grieving heart needs to complain
to the Prince, even if it makes him weep.

—translated by Sharif Elmusa and Naomi Shihab Nye

Haydar Mahmoud *(b. 1945)*

Born in Haifa, Haydar Mahmoud has an M.A. in general administration. He has been general director of culture and arts in Jordan, consultant to the Prime Minister, and is now Jordan's ambassador to Tunisia. He was the recipient of the State Prize for Merit from the Jordanian government (1990) and won the Ibn Khafaja Prize from Spain (1986). He has published five collections of poetry to date: *This Night Shall Pass* (Amman, 1969); *Apology for Sudden Technical Fault* (Dubai, 1977); *Oleander Trees on the River Sing* (Amman, 1980); *From the Sayings of the Last Witness* (Amman, 1986); and *Waiting for Ta'abbata Sharran* (Amman, 1990). Mahmoud's *Collected Works* was published in 1990.

From: *"The Last Witness"*

On whom do you call
O stubborn fighter
No one remains
in the vast desert
    but you to bear witness?

The expanse is barren except
    for humiliation
Every plant that the sands bring forth
    is shrivelled up.

And every breeze that blows from
    each corner
is a dissembler,
heavy with rancour

What runs in its veins
is not blood
That which it engenders
is not human.

There is no throbbing in the pulse
that you would excite.
The well you seek water from
is dried up.

Those spears you hoped would be chivalrous
are mere toys.
The horses on the course
do not race.

On whom do you call?
The age of chivalry is no more
The high exchanges of thought
are silent.

Each way we turn
we face the talons
On each road we take
there is an ambush.

On whom do you call
disaster follows disaster
Your enemies are like
swarming ants

The whole world is in league
against you
You alone are the enemy
it harries.

They say: "He is a stranger in this place
an interloper, a newcomer."
And they say: "He is a stranger in these times,
supernumerary, unnecessary."

So come forth, young men
from the forest of the jinns,
from the rock of determination,
from the thunder.

He who does not requite in
kind, and double,
is dead. He who does not ward off death
is himself annihilated.

—translated by Salwa Jabsheh and John Heath-Stubbs

Two-in-One

One part of me is not
from the other part estranged,
although the whole wide world
against myself is ranged.

How can I cancel out
details of what I am
How can my pulse deny
pulse of its own bloodstream?

How can I myself
from my own self separate
when what within me is one
with that which is without?

One with myself, my eye
gazing sees only me
wherever I may go
it is myself I see.

—translated by Salwa Jabsheh and John Heath-Stubbs

The Palestinian Ayyub

Do you know young Ayyub?[1]
Once, when he passed,
it was like the wedding of the birds.
He was the most beautiful among us.
No Arab mother had born a son
    of such sweetness.
His eyes those of a prophet, his brow
    like the expanse of space,
his arms strong as a volcanic rock.

Ayyub was lyrical as a song
on the lips of the bewildered

[1] Ayyub in Arabic is the biblical Job. The Palestinian in this poem is compared to the old Prophet of patience and endurance.

and the poor. He was
the morning star guiding those
who sought their inner resources
to find relief from the sordidness of life.

But Ayyub's life was sought by his kin;
they tugged at the reins of their tanks and marched
against his suffering body–like devils
they marched.

And he was lost to them! Oh
what a gallant man they have lost!
All places of banishment are his home now,
one place of banishment hands him over to the next.
  A prisoner without prison!
If his breast should escape the enemy's arrow
his back would receive
his kinsmen's myriad knives.

They want him alive, but with no life
They want him dead, but unburied
so that the bargains struck
for his suffering
should remain open.

O patience of Ayyub! Grant us the fortitude
to endure these times.
I proclaim that the world can only be saved
by madness.
My nails must tear my own flesh,
my angels must turn devils.

I proclaim that the new wind will soon be blowing.

  —translated by Salwa Jabsheh and John Heath-Stubbs

'Izziddin al-Manasra (b. 1946)

Born in Hebron, al-Manasra left his hometown in 1964 to study and work in other parts of the Arab world. In 1981 he obtained a Ph.D. in Slavic Literature from the Bulgarian Academy of Science and has worked as editor of some major cultural reviews, such as the important Palestinian monthly, *Shu'un Filastiniyya*. He has published many volumes of poetry and is regarded as one of the foremost Palestinian poets of protest and resistance. His first volume, *Grapes of Hebron*, appeared in 1968; other volumes are *Departure from the Dead Sea* (1970), *The Moon of Jarash Was Sad* (1974), *No One Will Understand Me Except the Olive Tree* (1976), and *Jafra* (1981).

At Night

At night I come to you,
at night I tempt you,
and your memory wounds me.
I weep for you
traveling toward your vineyards in my dream,
towards your mountain paths.
I slide onto your sandy roads like a snake,
leaving my traces before I die.

At night I speak, bringing the sea
to the mountain, reconciling thorns with lilies
    and night guards
with people awaiting seaborne barbarians
or desert strangers, coming from oil wells, coming.
I yearn for you at night but green cities do not merge
with cities of flame; you never leave your exile
and I never enter it.
How can I reconcile our exiles with the
cities of green? Those cities we love.
Hanged with the noose by the blue guards.
Guarded by rubies, oil, and gold.

—translated by May Jayyusi and Naomi Shihab Nye

Dawn Visitors

At the entries to capital cities I met him,
distracted and sad,
a man with worry lines
    that weighed him down
like a cypress tree, drooping and silent,
    despite the winds that ruffled him
whispering in the evenings—
    but he would not answer the wind.

At the gates of capital cities—I cannot name them
but I sing their Arabic names when troubles reign—
I call on the capitals when shells are slaughtering my people's
    children. I call on them, I scream, but no one
        answers.
They've all travelled west, and north. I wish
    they'd gone east, I wish
    they'd become stars in exile, servants to strangers.
At harvest time they sang under the pine trees
but none of the harvest was theirs . . .
    it is for those hard-hearted men
    who owns the lands of exile
Don't bury me in any Arab capital, they've all tortued me
    for so long,
giving me nothing but death and suffering and poverty
and the martyred neighbors of my grave,
those new kinsmen, for every stranger is kinsman to the stranger.
No, don't bury me in any Arab capital
    at the mercy of this ordeal!

At the gate of the capitals I met him
his head forever bent,
immortal as the earth of Hebron,
proud as the mountains of Safad.[1]
He was soft like old wine when it steeps inside the body.

I would have tempted the stars
    to accompany his beautiful departure,
a star to guard him, and one lovely maiden
    to tend him forever.

    —translated by May Jayyusi and Naomi Shihab Nye

[1]Safed is an ancient city situated in the mountainous region of Upper Galilee.

The Inheritance

My father showed me his will.
In it, Sir, I received
a letter prophesying a new exile for me,
a new exile, Sir.

—translated by May Jayyusi and Naomi Shihab Nye

Khairi Mansour *(b. 1945)*

Born in Dair al-Ghusun in Palestine, Mansour lived on the West Bank and studied in Cairo. In 1967 the Israeli authorities deported him from the West Bank. He went first to Kuwait, then to Baghdad, where he worked as a literary editor of *Al-Aqlam*. He lives now in Amman. Mansour's poetry reflects a great preoccupation with age and the passing of time on the personal level; on the communal level it reflects the sorrows of the Palestinian experience, as well as the faith and hope that have dominated much of the poetic expression of Palestinian poets in recent times. He has published two collections of poetry: *Gazelles of Blood* (1981); and *The Seas Are Narrow* (1983). He is included in PROTA'S forthcoming anthology, *End of the Century Poets, New Voices* in Arabic Poetry.

A Nonpersonal Account

I stayed two weeks
in a damp room in the hotel
that sleeps near the bridge,
reading a novel until dawn,
about a man resident in a leaning hotel
in a room in which the walls
are painted with ink.

I spent countless days
in a windowless room
of a hotel that sleeps under water,
reading until death
a novel . . . in which the heroes are composed of silence
    and its events of silence,
with its half-erased title, "This Epoch."

—translated by May Jayyusi and Jeremy Reed

Echo

I might have forgotten it in my first suit
    (but it had no pocket!)
—No, not in my first suit.

Perhaps I forgot it in an abandoned office
    in that first room
    (but it was without drawers or cabinets.)
    Its broken chair now
    grows longer in its loneliness
—No, I didn't forget it in that first room.

Perhaps I forgot it in the first kiss
    (it had no lips!)
—No, I didn't forget it with the first woman.

—I saw it tonight, a little child,
eyes askance, body paralyzed

That was my first poem.

    —translated by May Jayyusi and Jeremy Reed

Two Old Ages

1

When he laughs, his lips bleed with pain,
when he cries he sees
    everything round him liquefy.
He would sit or lie down,
    or pace the long room to and fro,
        and at dusk
drink unsweetened tea,
    and bite the inside of his cheeks from boredom
    anticipating the ritual time for his medicine.
He would stay up all night among the blood-splashed birds
    that have fallen around him
    and upon his shoulders.
He'd open the door at the end of the night

—How many stars remain in the sky?
and how many fruits are left in his basket
    for women?
He shuts the door
and takes out his teeth
and soaks them in a basin.

     His future is his past
and all the seasons are winter.

2

She counts her rings before going to sleep
and returns her pendants
    to a wooden chest,
reads old letters yellowed with age,
    the ink almost erased,
    and in each of them the promise:
    I may see you soon.
She is seventy
her first pendant is fifty
her rings
have never been taken off
    fingers emaciated now with age.
She contemplates drowsily, in noisy silence
    a hoary bone comb
    a toothless comb
and falls asleep.

    —translated by May Jayyusi and Jeremy Reed

The Road

The road might be long to Córdoba[1]
the road might be lost,
but longing for Córdoba
will see that the sail is worked
    and the horse's reins loosened

---

[1]Córdoba was one of the major cities of Muslim Spain. It was famous as a center for learning and represents a nostalgic symbol of past achievement for contemporary Arabs.

to a room
and a wall
    decorated with the saddle of a colt
    and a sword . . . gazing at bookshelves.

    —translated by May Jayyusi and Jeremy Reed

Poetry

It's a language for the stone
when it sits naked under its own name
and is hurled by the wind over the slope.
It's a language for the trees
    when the seasons forsake them
    and their fruits perish.
It's a language for the rain
    when two people embrace beneath an umbrella
    or hurry
        to a corridor or an elevator.
It's a language for people
    when they cry or laugh
    and when they are truthful.

    —translated by May Jayyusi and Jeremy Reed

A Forest

The unarmed forest
    its stones are paper
    its tigers illusory

The unarmed forest
    its woodcutter is a mouse
    its sunlight shadows

The unarmed forest
    comprises embers drowned in water.

    —translated by May Jayyusi and Jeremy Reed

Zakariyya Muhammad (b. 1951)

Born in the rural district of Nablus, this poet studied Arabic literature at Baghdad University and benefitted enormously from his association with Baghdad's vibrant literary community. On leaving Iraq he returned to Jordan where he worked in journalism and began to publish his poetry in 1979. His first collection *Last Poems* was published in Beirut in 1982, but was totally lost because of the Israeli invasion; he is now preparing his second collection *Art Work* for publication. Zakariyya's poetry is one of the great examples of modernist Arabic poetry, in which the inherited spirit of heroics and self-assertiveness, so rampant in the old poetry and in much of the poetry of the older generation of Arab poets, has totally disappeared, and where language is modernized, echoing the real pulse and rhythms of contemporary Arab life. He is included in PROTA's forthcoming anthology, *End of the Century Poets, New Voices* in Arabic Poetry.

Apology

(for my sister)

I was never a knight
nor a fruitful tree
I never gave to those who love me
    any shade
        by way of refuge,
I have induced sorrow in the heart
salt on the lips
a hand dedicated to harm.

I cannot offer you wine or a hat,
nor materialize as a prince that rides
    the crest of the storm,
I am the sky-pointing ladder of apology,
I am a palm tree that's heavily bent.
All eyes, yes, all eyes have rebuked me,
take this smear of blood as a sign
    and my hand as witness to the dryness
        of my branches.

It's not that I'm elegizing myself,
rather asserting my self-respect,
and patching up a garment in which eyes
    have bored many holes.
I've never been promising
Why then did their eyes
        engage me with
        their secrets and hopes.
And why can't I be
    just a word that's never been said,
    just a spark of madness?

What flowers have I carried in my basket?
What birds have perched on my shoulders?
What dust engrains my face?
Amongst flowers I'm the blameworthy one,
On my shoulders I carry a crooked bird.
The dust of fear lies on my lungs
    and on my shoes.
I hesitated when I invented my hand
I hesitated when I asked my questions
I hesitated when I thought
    that hesitation was my pivot
    and my virtue.

I slipped through my own fingers
and conceded to flow across the earth.
My fist is easy, easy
My forehead beads with sweat
    drop by drop I dissolve
I turn saline under my shirt
I have never leaned on a support
and one day
    I will die on the wind
        in whichever land
rebuking my death
and apologizing for my life
authorizing my funeral to be at night
    so that no-one attend it.
I'll walk in it alone
I'll be the only mourner.

I am the bell of sustained waiting
my hand never signed anything
my mouth never said a word,
  other than to express bitter regret
  and shy apology,
I am a bell that never rings.

I'm like water
  that takes the shape of things,
I never claim a definite space for myself
  when the winds buffet me
I'm soft and pliable,
constantly trembling, like a dying dog.

Alone I shall feel shame,
yes, the contrition
will persist till the day I die,
or until I turn into a banner
  wind-beaten into repentance.

From my grief I shall make a palm tree
whose shade will provide you with refuge,
  and when you go away,
  vanishing entirely,
  I shall wear it and I, too, shall disappear.

  —translated by Lena Jayyusi and Jeremy Reed

My Things

The place I inhabited
The horse that I led
The friend through whose lungs I breathed
How did I lose them?

Everything

What wind, then, didn't break my hands?
What gust didn't fly off with my shirt?
Under what millstone wasn't I a grain?

A Tavern

Here the dead are carousing
Here they shake their heads
to the music of shroud bells.

—translated by Lena Jayyusi and Jeremy Reed

Emigration

They're all gone
    towards that place in the North
    where the grasses grow
        to the height of their breasts
They left behind them
    tattered strips from their children's clothes
    and the pegs of their tents
They're gone
Their children on the backs of mules
Their youths carrying baskets
    and their sheep's bells
They were like a cloud
    climbing up to heaven
The more they penetrated the land
the more their shadows expanded
and returned towards the camps
Their dogs were mute
    They would surpass the migrating crowd, then sit down
    their eyes watching
        the moving shadows
    as they ran backward
    like a dark river.

—translated by Lena Jayyusi

The Cafe Mistress

She makes coffee from the sun's leaves
and buries in it the smell of wine and regret
The lady is hatless
    the white flowers of her hair shyly cover her ears
The lady has no farm
    where she can smell the night scented flowers
    and the fruits of the seasons
What can the cafe mistress do?
She makes coffee in the morning
    and at noon
    and in the evenings she washes the glasses
        etched with tree branches
What does the lady intend to do?
Collect river water for her coffee
and count the cups and the faces
        of customers?
What can a woman who lives under shelling do?
One who lives in a time that collects
    like a dust-film on the shelves
How can memory's fan
    expel the bees of regret?

When she drank a glass of milk
two glasses of remembrance
nausea shook her hands and the towel
    and the china
The cup broke as she held it
A smoke-bird floated on the ceiling
The beaks of sleeping words awoke

The cafe mistress is gentle,
the cafe mistress is skillful
and without a rival in elegance!
But when night falls,
    she contemplates her loneliness
    and breaks the long silence
        with her tears.

—translated by Lena Jayyusi and Jeremy Reed

A Woman

The Circassian woman with light ash on her eyebrows
was weeping, her round face
    resembled something looking for itself
and multiplied in the mirrors that lined the narrow room
    and it enlarged when her fantasy flew
        beyond the mirrors.
        She was weeping
Each tear formed a droplet that fell gently
        like divine inspiration
And seeing this my defences were broken,
        all my pretences
I leaned over her weakness
and we cried together
        from the night, from fear, from poverty.

—translated by Lena Jayyusi and Jeremy Reed

Khalid 'Ali Mustafa *(b. 1936?)*

A poet, literary historian, and scholar, Khalid 'Ali Mustafa is professor of Arabic literature at al-Mustansiriyya University in Baghdad. He is active in the literary life of the city, which, despite the war years with Iran, has become the center for pan-Arab literary activity. His first collection of poems, *Basra-Haifa,* appeared in 1975 and reflected the poet's attachment to his homeland as well as his involvement with, and orientation to, Baghdadi life. His book *Modern Palestinian Poetry* (1978), discusses not only the thematic aspects of this poetry but also its general technique with respect to form, diction, imagery, and style. It is one of the best literary histories on the subject.

Circling

You had to keep turning round,
in front of me,
and I had to keep on turning behind you.
If I should slow down
       You'd be behind me
and so we keep revolving,
       I don't see your face
and you don't see mine.

But inadvertently,
in our revolving round the circle's radius
our two faces confronted each other suddenly,
dividing time by that action.
Was it your face turned round
    while you were in front of me?
or was it mine that swung round when
       you were behind me?

We saw the clock intervene,
making us its respective hands,
which of us is the hour hand
    and which dictates the minutes?
We never knew . . . but when the hands
    separated,

the heart stopped,
            the blood froze at their resounding clash.
Our two faces were liberated,
we resumed our circling,
I without seeing your face
and you without seeing mine.
Perhaps a new time piece
will redeem us again
            without a wager!

—translated by May Jayyusi and Jeremy Reed

Meeting of Two Wounds

Your wounded woman's voice—
from where did it come?
I searched other people's profiles, the land of exile,
     the delegations of the wind,
but found no trace.
The thirsty years engraved my face.
I hugged my own shadow, waiting
for the wounds in your voice
to inflame my own
and satiate my yearning.
How deeply I heard your wounded woman's voice!
From where did it come?
From my brother's wound?
From the lost wounds wandering in my body?
From the cloak of night that covers my country?
Corridors of love carried you into my life,
     centered you in my blood,
and I recognized: the voice of my companion. I knew it—
in the olive trees whispering to the bells on the wind,
in the waves washing their child, Haifa
in the fields which teach harvesting children the lessons of
     exile, letter by letter,
in my mother's sorrow as she spoke to my father's grave.
Your wounded voice visited my heart
igniting the deserts of love.

My voice drank you in and
I shouted, Here is my hand!
How did you gather the reins of silence into
      your eyes?
Wait: the cities of pleasure that claimed
      my early years
now vanished behind me, drying like sap
I embody the essence of those years,
how did you ever find my table?
Your wounded voice penetrates my breath,
washes the silence of exile from my lips.
So listen: My wound kisses yours. Beware!
The sea's cloak blazes with us!
We flew above waves building villages,
children to whose feet the grasses prayed.
In our blood the book of water found its voice.
Attention! Both of us fly with wounds as our guides,
over waves swirling with sea nymphs, banners for our eyes.
Houses briefly touched us, then were swallowed by
      the mirrors of the sea.
Shall we raise our hands, wave goodbye?
Should we hope for a new era?
Or lock the doors, letting our sea become
      a barren field?
Inside our hearts the sea celebrated,
inviting all the drowned cities to a dinner party.
You were the one visitor I glimpsed
      entering through the door,
your tentative smile greeted me
      and we flew . . .
over the sea toward a bandaged sun,
still pouring light!
A bird landed on my sorrow, plunged its beak
      into my blood, and taunted me.
Among all those faces, your wound was silent,
and my own felt orphaned, scattered among the corridors,
losing fire.

Could it be that two wounds really met
      in the shade of an oyster?
Night hunted us down with the eyes of our own loved ones

communing with the secrets of death.
Your voice made my wound travel through my body,
making space for your first absence.
And I saw that I was exiled from you, to you!
Could it be? How do such doors open to fugitives?
I felt that a shirt woven by your hands
had alighted on my body
and filled me with clouds.

—translated by May Jayyusi and Naomi Shihab Nye

Taha 'Abd al-Ghani Mustafa (b. 1937)

Born in Qalandya near Jerusalem, Taha 'A. Mustafa obtained a diploma from the Teacher Training College in Jerusalem and has taught English at elementary and secondary schools for thirty-three years. He now lives and works in Abu Dhabi. He writes poetry using the old two-hemistich form with resonant rhymes, and his verse is dedicated to the Palestinian cause. He has published several collections of poetry: *The Volcano* (1983); *Zaatar* (1985); and *The Journey of Pain* (1986).

Reverse Journey

Tired of being lost in life,
tired of endless journeying,
constant moving and shifting,
the winding of the exile's road,
tired of waiting for sunrise
with unfulfilled promises
anchoring our days.
Finally we've risen to create our own fate
spinning a new sun from
the light of the struggle.

Let the tents of humiliation burn!
Braving the battering storm,
we enter the realm
of the impossible!
Fashioning a new road, and
new songs of resistance
whose melodies millions will breathe
marching repeating:
To our land we return
to sit beside our own hearths
toasting bread and remembering

We'll renew old times when life was radiant
and listen to the old relating ancient tales,
of the brave ones who rejected humiliation.

Return to Galilee, to Hebron
to Ghaza, to Jericho!
Ride the impossible, return to stay
Your country calls you, don't look away.

—translated by Salwa Jabsheh and Naomi Shihab Nye

Kamal Nasir (1922–1973)

K. Nasir was a poet who wielded his pen in the struggle for the liberation of his people. During his relatively short life, he experienced exile, imprisonment, and constant harassment before and after the Palestinian revolution of the early sixties, whose ranks he joined. In 1973 he was assassinated by Israeli terrorists who infiltrated Lebanon at night and murdered him in his own home in Ras Beirut. The poem translated here was an answer to a poem by Fadwa Tuqan, which she sent him while he was imprisoned in the West Bank in the fifties.

Letter to Fadwa

If my songs should reach you
despite the blocked skies around us,
it is because I've spread my wings
to embrace your tortured span,
because we share tragedy
and dark destiny,
and together we partake of
memories, wishes, dreams.

I am what you've wanted me to be
and what hardships have decreed.
Rejecting humiliation,
I've claimed my foothold over the clouds,
bleeding till my wounds
tinted the summits with red.
I've loved my homeland, so my heart
aspires joyously to brave the tides.
Regret or cease? That could not be!
Since when did a poet seek honor or regret?

Sister, today your letter arrived,
bright with your lofty spirit,
bringing glad balm to my wounds
and stirring my dormant pen to reply.
Yes, I recall, I do recall
our happy evenings, our carefree friends

beneath the shading jasmine bushes,
our wings open to joy, or folded
with melancholy . . .

We talked until a dream took hold of us
and we grasped its slumbering mirage.
Yes, I remember how you spoke your poems,
resplendent, proud and free on everyone's lips,
more beautiful than the impossible.
Your songs, like sunrays in our country,
feed us with desire and hope
awakening to the sounds of struggle,
the fluttering of banners raised high.

I am still as you hoped I would be,
sun's rays kissing my forehead as I walk,
even alone, toward my goal.
Desire for freedom is my cross;
I thirst, though the cup is in my hand!
Life seethes in my youthful veins
yet I wander naked, seeking life for
my wounded people, that they might live
with happy pride, building their world.

And you? Should my letter arrive
and you find tears scattered among the lines,
do not worry—great hopes must weep
as they struggle to reach the heights.
Tomorrow the night shall withdraw, humiliated,
from our land, and the people abandon illusion,
discovering their strength.
Millions shall swear never to sleep
while there be yet one foothold left for wolves,
and through all the suffering they will yearn
for that moment of reckoning truth.

If my songs should reach you
despite the narrow skies around me,
remember that I will return to life,
to the quest for liberty,
remember that my people may call on my soul
and feel it rising again from the folds of the earth.

—translated by Sharif Elmusa and Naomi Shihab Nye

Ibrahim Nasrallah *(b. 1954)*

A poet and novelist, Nasrallah was born in the al-Wahdat refugee camp in Amman, Jordan, and studied at the UNRWA schools, then at the Teacher Training College in Amman. After graduating he worked for two years as a teacher in the Qunfudha region in Saudi Arabia. He turned this experience into an impressive novel, *Prairies of Fever* (1985), in which chronology is absent and the plot is a mixture of hallucinations and memories and of great torment and alienation. The novel won wide acclaim in Jordan and has been translated for PROTA by May Jayyusi and Jeremy Reed. After returning from Saudi Arabia, Nasrallah returned to Jordan, where he still lives and works as a journalist. Nasrallah is one of the most promising Palestinian literary figures to rise to fame in the diaspora. He has publisehd several collections of poetry to date, including: *The Rain Inside* (1982); *Morning Songs* (1984); *The River Boy and the General* (1987). These collections have been highly praised and he has three times been the recipient of the Union of Jordanian Writers' Prize for the best volume of poetry. His new novel *'Aw* was published in 1991. Nasrallah is included in PROTA's forthcoming volume, *End of the Century Poets, New Voices in Arabic poetry.*

Flight

Tonight I walked out overpowered by you,
an indistinct bird circling in my head,
a swinging cypress took my form
and a space opened
    and closed within me
plains ascended at my will
tonight
I submitted my body to an entrancing vertigo
to endless footsteps
I opened the windows wide,
opened my blue shirt
and my heart
and let the wind disperse me
tonight

I was docile like tranquil waters
and wandered like a desert gazelle
Tonight
I crossed more than one street
and more than one song
and knocked at every door
looking for a friend
    I hoped wouldn't be there!

Woman
this night
is yours
I walk with the flood of you
with your hair
and the smell of your clothes
I make inroads into countries
intoxicated with the surprise of you!
Who loves the winter as you do?
and is fascinated by trees that resist the wind as you do?
And who like you perfects life
with such innocent joy?
God!
If only you were with me now
I have prepared everything
the chestnuts and the fire,
I have pulled back the blinds
and raised my prayer to the gypsy rain
pleaded that it persist in its discord
and eternal rites
God!
If only you were beside me now!
I have prepared my poems
and reclaimed my hand
from the combat of the street
from the merchants
and the brokers
and the guardsmen,
and a frost that has tried so often
to squeeze you out of my heart
from bullets that have repeatedly aimed
to swallow up the ring of your voice

as you commune with the buds
or kindle the fire
God! Had you been with me
we would have sung our song now
    the one which the wind almost uproots from my voice
each time I sing it alone.

    —translated by Lena Jayyusi and Jeremy Reed

Passageway

Lift your sadness
so the soldier can pass through his blood
so the day can flow toward his wound
    a star
        or a cloud
and remove your shadow
for an evening which wings
toward a stab-wound at sorrow's outposts
allow me a space
in which to draw out an exile becoming this torment.

    —translated by Lena Jayyusi and Jeremy Reed

A Woman

Tired man
what can you say
to a woman who perfects her presence,
and is adept at arranging the world
in the space of your perpetual ruin.
What's to be said
to this woman, this child,
as she spontaneously fashions new flights of joy
new birth-rites
and secret paths for the winds,
a variable green for the trees,
and what's to be said

to two intimate braids
which have delivered her to the succulence of fruit,
the scent of jasmine?
And what do you say
to a morning that's never complete without her
and an evening that never closes down
before she shuts her eyes?

—translated by Lena Jayyusi and Jeremy Reed

The Hand

It is the hand
day's beautiful branch
blossoming with fingers,
soft as the dove's cooing,
that neither catches the wind,
nor arrests the water.
But it takes in space
and embraces the earth
from the wild flower
to the palm tree.
It is the hand
comforts us when we are broken,
consoles when we cry,
offers solace to our tiredness.
It is the hand
dream's miracle
legend of creation
columns of light   .
or a handful of embers
that quicken or subside.
It is the hand
a field, and a posy of children's songs,
and a planet.

The hand isn't a book, or lines.
Don't scrutinize the details
Don't read its silence

nor its contours
    you will find nothing.
All the lines that have invaded it
all the bends
are our fault
from the first aberrations
    to the advent of misery.
It is the hand
do not read it
read what it will write
read what it will do
and raise it
raise it
till it becomes a sky.

   —translated by Lena Jayyusi and Jeremy Reed

Thread

Autumn
Winter
Spring
and, catching the carnations unawares,
Summer invades us
Seasons distributed through life and death
flower and as quickly fade,
touching the edge of a final extinction.
Then they shed off dusk
and return to us with their impossible star.
But a cosmic thread connects them to life,
always to life
and we, perpetually wrestling with sadness,
don the silence
then write in the notebook of time
The elderflower has fallen
and the green forest has burnt down
the wind has broken the interlacing vines
and the songs celebrating the day are extinguished.
Yet that cosmic thread connects them to life—

always to life.
I am a man lost in my seasons
there is a season for weariness
a season for joy
and one for defeat
and a flowering season
and there is a cosmic thread which connects me with life—
there is all of you!

  —translated by Lena Jayyusi and Jeremy Reed

Song

Oh! from a country
whose windows are guards and bayonets,
O from a country which has no gates,
    from a country
whose chairs don't end in the clouds.

  —translated by Lena Jayyusi and Jeremy Reed

Jamal Qa'war *(b. 1930)*

Qa'war is a poet who has had an active and productive career among the literary community of Palestinians living in Israel. Born in Nazareth, he studied at various universities in Israel, obtaining a Ph.D. in Quranic studies from the University of Tel Aviv. He now works as a lecturer in Arabic language and literature at the University of Haifa and at the Arab Teacher Training College in the same city, and is president of the literary branch of the al-Saut organization for the enhancing of Palestinian consciousness. He also edits the *Al-Mawakib* cultural review in Nazareth, where he lives. Qa'war writes a poetry firmly characterized by the well-knit style and terse sentence construction of inherited Arab poetry and has published ten collections, including *Songs from Galilee,* (1958) *Dust of Voyages* (1973); *Beirut* (1982) and *September* (1985).

At the Doorstep of September

What words
would you utter, September,
if you were to sing?
Oh perennial prophet of loss,
is this why you return?
Tales are told in a book
titled with blood's calligraphy,
their echoes grow hoarse:
those who close their ears
will kneel, bereft of dignity.

My sail groans,
battered by angry wind,
my boat will never make it to shore.
Look! Over the expanse of harbor
hovers a mirage, breath of the unknown,
the scattererd stars of hope
and the lost compass.

A dark shadow
gathers over the eyes

lamenting those who fell—
offerings for September.
Drink, friends,
the wine lacks spirit
for the exiled,
drink, but don't let September
kill the promise,
and never forget.
What words
would you utter, September,
if you were to sing?

—translated by Sharif S. Elmusa and Naomi Shihab Nye

Kamal Qaddura *(b. 1961)*

One of today's promising young poets, Qaddura was born in a refugee camp in Baalbak, Lebanon, and studied liberal science at Beirut University College, with special emphasis on advertising techniques, fine arts, graphics, drawing, and photography. Graduating in 1985, he worked in design and advertising with the Middle East Advertising Company before moving to London, where he still lives. He has published a number of book reviews in various periodicals, as well as translations of poetry including *The Bed Book,* a translation into Arabic of poems by Sylvia Plath. Qaddura writes a new kind of poetry demonstrating great audacity in the use of imagery and diction; his first collection of poetry, *Land of Slumber,* was published in London in 1991.

All of This Is Strange, Like Everything

They closed every door of escape on him
and slept, slept
before winter entered
through the hole in the window
carrying a bundle of clothes
and the sword of pain
They slept
with the dead for company
before winter entered
carrying a bundle of clothes
and the isolation of wide corridors.

When we sleep
and sleep beckons us to the gap
navigators run away
from the dance of water
to their last death
to the vortex of sleep
the one that never loses consciousness.

I have a rendezvous with sleep
sleep that has no sleep in it.

I sleep like I did before,
like I shall do tomorrow.
I have a rendezvous with sleep.
Blue sleep will put kohl on my eyes
the blue which melts in sleep.

Is this sleep enough?
it seems to stay in my feet.

Like every heavy thing
we sleep.
Like waves we sleep on other waves
settle on a surface of water
of water.

We sleep, sleep
sleep
All this sleep.

   —translated by May Jayyusi and Jeremy Reed

Language

Signs transmitted by the mind
my prison that vanishes under the weight of dream
the feverish states of my annihilation
the stormy game between me and myself
my hungry fingers
the roving of bloody metaphors
a labored birth that settles on the day's fearful cycle
a tangy smell
toward the screen that separates color from touch
a desert wet with space
and a deficient world.

   —translated by May Jayyusi and Jeremy Reed

Fragrance

What screens us from the moment
in which one death's no different from another,
What separates us from color and its glitter
between one mask and another,
the fragrance that differs each morning,
the scent that dissipates over forms
and has us walk backward
to the bitter point of recession
to what lies behind the senses
and death.

   —translated by May Jayyusi and Jeremy Reed

Part of a Wall

A black broad line
red dots fleck its edges
a cutting horizontal line
thin and also black
at its end a dead fish sleeps in the bottom
The scene occupies part of a wall
and everything is dead cold.

   —translated by May Jayyusi and Jeremy Reed

Dead Memory

today in the morning, the morning of today
I fired myself on a dead memory
everything was extinguished
on a road that led away from the rain
Death turned into wet rosy footsteps
that don't recognise time.

   —translated by May Jayyusi and Jeremy Reed

Cold

I feel things are cold
I feel things are cold
but desolate language warms my ears
the light that I don't know slips from my hands
this flat thing that flows in my blood
dark and blind.

—translated by May Jayyusi and Jeremy Reed

Race

Who can find me in the race of wings
    toward the waves so they can catch their breath?
Who can find me
    in the face of the winds
    that subdue their fires to create only ashes
Who?
Who can find me in visions that penetrate the void
    and can then find meaning in my presence?
Like a horse my corpse drowns in oblivion
and death floats as a surface stain posing a question
Who?
Who can find me in the race of wings
    toward the wave so they can catch their breath?

—translated by May Jayyusi and Jeremy Reed

Overflow

This overflow that precedes the word
or checks it
that destroys it or silences its uptake
the salt that burns the void
so that language can evaporate in a sea of grief
This overflow that precedes the tremor

or cuts into it, dwells in it or cancels it
The tears that predominate at evening
keep beauty hidden in a sea of grief
a sea of grief
a sea
of grief
of grief.

—translated by May jayyusi and Jeremy Reed

Muhammad al-Qaisi (b. 1944)

Al-Qaisi was born in Kufr 'Ana near Jaffa. After 1948 he lived in refugee camps. There he learned many of the folk songs that his mother and other women had memorized and that left their influence on his poetry. He has a B.A. in Arabic Literature and worked as a teacher in Dammam, Saudi Arabia, for two years. The next four years he spent between Baghdad, Damascus, Beirut, Kuwait, and Benghazi, before returning to Amman, Jordan, in 1977, where he still lives. He is one of the more prolific poets of his generation and has published at least eleven collections including *A Banner in the Wind* (1968); *Mourning Is Worthy of Haifa* (1975); and *Houses on the Horizon* (1985). In 1987 a collection of all his poetry to date was published under the title of *Poetic Works*. He subsequently published two more collections in 1989, *The Dispersion of a Single Man* and *The Book of Hamda*. Al-Qaisi's poetry is varied; he uses the two-hemistich verse as well as the free verse form and occasionally includes literary and historical allusions and folklore in his work.

Vision

I see the faces change their complexion
peel off their outer skin
I see faces divested
of makeup and masks
and I see an empty stage
the spectators denying their own images
in the third act.
I see a poor man rise
and dream of recreating order.
He doesn't frequent the idlers' cafes.
The papers don't carry his pictrure,
news agencies don't relay his words.
He carves the image of his absent love
on the ceiling of a mountain cave
and sings.

—translated by May Jayyusi and Jeremy Reed

Love Poem I

She's the first words
She's the most beautiful wound
She's added my soul to her album
and given me a gift of conquerors
She is all the shells that have gathered at the
          sea's bottom
She's the first to visit the water well
the first to encounter the heart's alcove
She's the ancestral tear
which has sprung in my chest
and her nocturnal sorrow flowered
and covered me.

How can I ever fear?

   —translated by May Jayyusi and Jeremy Reed

Love Poem IV

In the early morning
where do you think the lovers go?
How can they gather their songs in a single place?
They look for a seat
they ask for a hand of friendship
they seek the road they dreamt of
They seek and seek,
          but do not find.

   —translated by May Jayyusi and Jeremy Reed

Love Poem XII

I feel it so, Sir, life is short—
How can twenty years,
which are all that's left for me
in her handbag,

be long enough to say what goes on in my mind
and in the complexities of the heart
which have been there
since the earth was shaped,
since God created things,
perfected humans and told them:
know each other
the nearest among you to me are the lovers.

Ah, Sir,
how I feel the short duration of my days
and how many joys I miss
and how green this land
green, green, green,
and desolate!

—translated by May Jayyusi and Jeremy Reed

One-Day Vacation

I exempt Monday morning from music
I exempt the radio
I exempt my hand from all its chores
I exempt my ribs
I exempt the day from all earthly cares
I stifle all pain
I exempt silence from all declarations
I exempt the door from the key
and I set the winds free.

—translated by May Jayyusi and Jeremy Reed

Samih al-Qasim *(b. 1939)*

Al-Qasim is one of the foremost poets of Palestine. Born into a Druze family, he was educated in Rama and Nazareth and took up a teaching position in an Israeli public school, from which he was dismissed because of his political views. He has also been imprisoned and held under house arrest several times on account of his poetry and his political views. He is a prolific poet whose poetry deals with Palestinian captivity and struggle. By the age of thirty he had published six collections of poetry that were widely read throughout the Arab world. He has also written several plays. His current concerns are to establish a Palestinian theater with a high artistic and intellectual mission, and to impart a political message of great poignancy to the world. He has developed in some of his poems a unique new kind of satirical verse, which he performs on stage, and which demands active participation from his audience. He has read to many audiences not only in his country but also in London, the United States, and other places abroad. Al-Qasim has published over twelve collections of poetry to date, from which quite a few selections have been translated into English. His first collection was *Processions of the Sun* (1958). Other collections that reflect his continuous experimentation with language and tone are *I Love You as Death Desires* (1980), *The Dark Side of the Apple, the Bright Side of the Heart* (1981); *The Dimensions of the Spirit* (1983); and *Persona Non Grata* (1986).

The Clock

My city fell to the enemy,
Yet the clock continued ticking on the wall
Our own neighborhood was demolished,
The street fell,
Yet the clock remained ticking on the wall.
My house crumbled to ruins,
Even the wall fell,
But the clock remained
ticking on and on.

—translated by Sharif Elmusa and Naomi Shihab Nye

Bats

Bats on my window
suck in my words
Bats at the entrance to my house
behind newspapers, in corners
trail my footsteps,
observing every movement of my head

From the back of the chair, bats watch me
They trail me in the streets
watching my eyes pause
on books, on young girls' legs . . .
they watch and watch.

On my neighbor's balcony, bats,
and electronic gadgets hidden in the walls
Now bats are on the verge
of suicide

I am digging a road to daylight

—translated by Sharif Elmusa and Naomi Shihab Nye

Ashes

Don't you feel we have lost so much
that our "great" love is now only words,
that there's no more yearning, no urgency,
no real joy in our hearts, and when we meet
no wonder in our eyes?
Don't you feel our encounters are frozen,
our kisses cold,
that we've lost the fervor of contact
and now merely exchange polite talk?
Or we forget to meet at all
and tell false excuses . . .
Don't you feel that our brief hurried letters
lack feeling and spirit,
contain no whispers or dreams of love,

that our responses are slow and burdened . . .
Don't you feel a world has tumbled down
and another arisen?
That our end will be bitter and frightening
because the end did not fall on us suddenly
but came from within?

—translated by Sharif Elmusa and Naomi Shihab Nye

Love Poems

1

When I pass people,
they jeer at my whisperings and laughter.
They pity the passing stranger,
squandering his youth in such madness.

Let's forgive them, my love,
they do not see you walking beside me.
Let's forgive them!

2

Teach me how to see you
for you are inside me.

Teach me how to embrace you
if I am inside you.

How can I make your sorrow
reel into joy?
All blessings be upon you.

Take my hand flowing toward you
like a river.

Great love is a divine word.

3

I bled all my time—
My blood was tumultuous.

I bled my place
my blood was in turmoil.
Still my pride remained with me
because you shared my elegies
and blessed my songs.

4

I love you
I whisper "I love you"
I scream "I love you"
Be the beginning of time!
Be the end of all space.

5

Your hand in mine
Your eyes in mine . . .
The motherland is a train
disappearing behind the collapsed horizon of time
leaving behind a whirlpool of dust
and newspaper shreds
leaving behind a returning man and woman
surrounded by stacked suitcases
of sorrow and waiting.

—translated by Sharif Elmusa and Naomi Shihab Nye

You Pretend to Die

(In memory of Mu'een Bseiso)

A *kufiyya* flutters in the wind.
A tuft of your pagan hair fluttering
and the nightingale of your soul
flaps to escape the ribs of your chest
that can no longer contain the storm.
Oh, you ancient mariner,
you are swamped.
What a star has fallen in the woods,

what a rose pulsating on the waves,
your heart.

Groom of lemons and almonds,
how is your bride in her bridal white,
suspended in exile?
Who performs the marriage rites?
Do you still remember us?
Do you recall the rhythm of
your obstinate youth,
the spirits that erupted from your palms?
Is there a fortune teller on your secret planet
to bring you the news?

Here's the latest:
A child's doll had its legs severed;
on the charred porch a lady
gathers burning clothes from a line;
a missile aims for an orchard.
Are you listening?
The coyboys' symphony
played by a mythical band
on the brass chords of your heart . . .
with speeches by corporations, stock markets, barracks.
Can't you see God's rope being lowered
from a helicopter to the drowning land?

You scared away birds that flap bad omens,
You threw a stone into the well of madness.
The stone split into fragments
in the terrifying ripples. You sang of faith
without seeking the masters' favors:
you sang until you despaired.
Now I sing for you, my rascal friend,
grant me a quiet pause.
Who am I to be continually burdened
by Ghaza's pains?

Your coffin has room for two songs.
one says, "I'm the shroud" and the other:
"I'm tired of roaming from exile to exile,
tired of being a shriveling homeland

cut off from its source."
My friend, your coffin has room for
two gypsies.
How could you pass away
leaving us behind?
Couldn't you have waited
two more minutes, two drinking bouts,
two more poems, two roses?
. . . A massacre.

Do you say you want your own tomb
like everybody else's?
Do we live, die, like the rest?
In safe places they are chewing our bones.
Be humble! I ask you in the name of the God—
Who blessed the knife that slew you
Who has given endless rope to the butcher
Who has created and neglected you—
Do you want your own tomb?
Yours is the trench of the rebels
in a country you prayed would not forget you.
How many prophets made false promises?
How many gods fed your empty hope?
You've got no tomb, my friend,
no tomb.

I tried to reach you
when your heart burst in the bed
of that faraway hotel, the last hotel.
I tried to reach you, to hold your grieving head,
but a poor poet finds the fare expensive,
the region of death expensive—
I tried to reach you,
to apologize to your death
for my life.
How could I reach you when Cairo's gates
are sealed by the star of David?

The jasmine emits its fragrance;
the mothers of fallen men sit,
however they wish, at evening's door.
And you, still humoring us—

we know it, your Palestinian black humor.
Don't do that. You only pretend to die.
Love flew you from one country
to a farther country
You only pretend to die.
Say that's true, surprise us
with a fresh song!
Rise, saint,
go on living you bastard!
We have no time to die,
if we diminish, our enemies multiply.
Rise with graceful heart and steps
and walk among us.
We still fill the daylight
we still prod history, and men.
My comrade, rise,
you know how much we love you,
you know
how much we love you.

—translated by Sharif Elmusa and Naomi Shihab Nye

I Do Not Blame You

Your wings are small for this storm—
I do not blame you.
You're good, and frightened, and
I am the hurricane. I used to be a wing
struggling in the storm
but then I became the storm,
lacking light, shade, or a wise language.
And now I confess
to be a lost planet circling a lost world
and I do not blame you:
What has tender mint to do with the storm?

—translated by Sharif Elmusa and Naomi Shihab Nye

Drunk

Many seas, but one sailor—
Bless me, Mother.
Many winds against one banner—
Sister of mine, weep for me.
One life and many deaths—
Beloved of mine, forget me!

—translated by Sharif Elmusa and Naomi Shihab Nye

'Abdallah Radwan (b. 1949)

Born in Jericho, Radwan now lives in Zarqa, a town near Amman, where he is the principal of a school. He spent an unhappy, poverty-stricken childhood in the refugee camps of Karama, Salt, and other Jordanian towns, but managed to graduate from the Jordanian University and enter fully into Jordanian literary life. As a member of several literary societies, he has participated in many pan-Arab conferences and represented Jordan in several world festivals, visiting Prague, Moscow, and Bandung. He has published four collections of poetry, including *Lines Over the Signpost of the Homeland* (1977); *I Do Not Relinquish the Homeland* (1979); and *I See a Joy Rampant in the City* (1984). His work is characterized by a tone of mixed regret and hope, and, like many other Palestinian poets, he dwells on the themes of nostalgia and torment, keeping alive the memories and hopes of an uprooted but resilient people.

The Fall

Your voice, sweet as the river's, is asking,
    "Why do you circle around me, then leave?"
I exclaim:
    "Here are your eyes, paving for my eyes
    a road to knowledge.
    Down with knowledge!
    We need transformations to the opposite
    to death, rancor, and desparate moments."
Your eyes beseech—
and I glimpse a light in them
that views transformation as something strange.
I answer their question:
    "When the distance between truths is a sea
        of falsehoods,
    I declare I have lost the truth
    because I cure my cowardice with cowardice.
    I neither advance nor retreat
    but travel by staying in my place

fighting a sea of death
and yearning for the decisive moment!
Between darkness and truth
I struggle for balance
on the edge of the deadly chasm.
Behind me, there's the end of something gone.
In front, the end of something that will begin.
And so I remain, struggling at the point
    of beginning,
struggling with a frightening thing."
I need the courage of a child to advance . . .
But I am no more a child!

    —translated by Sharif Elmusa and Naomi Shihab Nye

Deformed

The night here, my love, is deformed.
Love is deformed,
Death deformed,
and God—
Even God is deformed!
Yet you ask about my life story—
Dear friend, I have no life!
Because I was born
    into a deformed night
    in a tent, my love,
    at a deformed hour
Because I grew up deformed
    in my family
    in my tent
Because I have loved
    within a deformed society . . .
This is why you find me
    deformed!

    —translated by Sharif Elmusa and Naomi Shihab Nye

To the Children

This country suffering under the waves of dying—
who can recreate it?
Who can return the love of the sun to us,
the love of our country?
Who can bury this fear dark as night?
Who
besides the little children of my country?

—translated by Sharif Elmusa and Naomi Shihab Nye

You Are Everything

(For Palestine)

I saw in you a mother, a sister, a wife
I saw in you my family
The warmth of the tribe was on your lips
telling the tale of a heart
    dead for many years
    but growing now
    as a child in your arms

—translated by Sharif Elmusa and Naomi Shihab Nye

Harun Hashim Rasheed *(b. 1927)*

Born in Gaza, poet Harun Hashim Rasheed witnessed, as a child, British soldiers demolishing his and his neighbors' homes in reprisal against Palestinian rebels, an incident which left a deep mark on him as a poet. After obtaining a Higher Teacher Training Diploma from Gaza College, he worked as a teacher until 1954. He then became director of the Sawt al-Arab broadcasting station in the district of Gaza. After the fall of Gaza to the Israelis in 1967, he was harassed by the Israeli occupation forces and was eventually compelled to leave the region. He now works in Cairo, representing Palestine at the League of Arab States. His poetry is among those contemporary writings most committed to the Palestinian cause; he describes in his simple, direct, balanced, and highly expressive verse the plight of Palestinians uprooted from their homes, their inner torment, and the deep feelings of loss and alienation that they have known throughout the years. The appearance in 1954 of his first collection, *With the Strangers,* was a great event in the history of Palestinian poetry, as he was perhaps the first poet to address himself to the question of the physical and spiritual alienation of the Palestinians. Since then he has published sixteen other collections, the most recent of which, *The Rebellion of Stone,* appeared in 1988. Rasheed has also written plays, a novel, *Years of Suffering* (1971), and several studies on poetry and politics.

Poem to Jerusalem

For the sake of a city that's imprisoned,
for its Dome and Aqsa Mosque,[1]
for the annihilated sanctuary
where Muhammad's feet once stood,
for all this city has endured,
and for all it has preserved,
for Mary and Jesus,
for all the beings she has known,

---

[1]The Aqsa Mosque is the Mosque of Omar, the third most important shrine in Islam, situated in the old city in Jerusalem. The Dome is the Dome of the Rock in the area of the Mosque and is one of the most beautiful Islamic monuments.

for my city's sake,
raped and abused,
on its wounded brow
God's words are effaced.

I call on all our dead
and all our living
with verses from the Bible
if only they could hear
with verses from the Quran
in the name of God
calling the young among them and the very old
calling them from my depths
to every brave fighter
I tell them the struggle is for Jerusalem
I call on them to resolve and have faith
tell them how Jerusalem's sanctity is wounded
I call upon them all to help Jerusalem
She cannot wait any longer,
she overflows with grief.

From the Atlantic to the Arabian Gulf
I call upon you in the name of God
with the purity of anger I beseech you
for the city with the humiliated eyes
I call you in your name,
I call my Arab people.

—translated by Sharif Elmusa and Naomi Shihab Nye

After occupying the city of Gaza, the Israelis began searching houses and forcing men and women to stand next to the walls and raise their arms. Often they shot at them. The poet had this experience.

Raise Your Arms

—Raise your arms . . .
they aimed their guns at me . . .
—Raise your arms . . .

I stood, my eyes flaming
and scorching with anger
as an insistent film of events
assailed me.
Can defiled cities be
the outcome of our struggle?
Have years of suffering,
long days of vigilance
in trenches, on hills
and in tattered tents
led to this?!

The world blackened in my eyes
my hands on the wall
as guns were pointing at me
I wished the wall would fall on my head
My comrades and I waited
for their bullets,
for their bullets

They walked away, and the wall
remained, gazing back at us
waiting for a fiery volcano, for the flames.

—translated by Sharif Elmusa and Naomi Shihab Nye

Taher Riyad *(b. 1956)*

Born in Amman, Jordan, Riyad was unable to finish his university education because of financial difficulties. After living in Damascus for some time and participating in the city's many thriving literary activities, he moved back to Amman. Riyad has translated works by T.S. Eliot, Dylan Thomas, Samuel Beckett, Ted Hughes and others. He has also participated in many literary conferences, particularly in the Mirbad Poetry Festival, convened in Baghdad and Basra every year and regarded as the meeting place of poets, critics, and creative writers not only from the Arab world, but from the world at large including the United States, Canada, and Australia. Riyad has benefited from these meetings a great deal both as a poet and as co-director of Dar Manarat, a promising publishing house in Amman. Riyad is one of the most original poets of the younger generation; he writes a poetry that boasts of the terseness, economy, and eloquence of the best in classical Arabic poetry combined with the thematic, attitudinal, and metaphoric adventure of the best modernist poetry written in Arabic today. He has published three collections of poetry: *The Wind's Desire* (1983); *Mud Ritual* (1985) and *The Lame Staff* (1988). He will be represented in PROTA's next Anthology, *End of the Century Poets, New Voices in Arabic Poetry,* forthcoming.

From "Signs"

I

I am not the shade who upholds the bare tree
    against its dissolution,
I'm not hunger to strap stones round my belly and suck
    your emaciated breast.
I'm thin like the figure of fear,
I contain the thirst of embers
    to transform themselves back to branches,
I do not pray for what's to come
—nothing will come—
and I don't concede to reverence.

It is a chain of ants that raised this earth
  and now erodes it slowly.

III

Your face is purer than the mirror,
  luxurious and more eager.
Colours rejoice around your head, rejoice
  and Ah, they suffer.
Offer death a libation for the past,
  it may accept and stay.
And it's the same: your destroying a lover
  or your destroying things out of love.
Now the mirror's clouded for you; break it
  and say: "My eyes see better."

V

I just forgot
nothing more
I forgot
      the salt of creation scorches my eyes
      and the sands of insomnia
I try to remember:
Does water describe the shape of fountains,
their pattern of fluidity,
and indicate the day's greenness,
or does water have
      the shape of drowning?

VI

Rejoice twice:
when you see the sand turn wet and soft
and when it becomes water

Twice rejoice:
tomorrow will be overcast
and shade compose a sky

And hide just once
for a scoundrel might inherit the earth
and scratch the living.

VII

Why do you grow narrow as my vision widens?
and how is it that you hover around me
when there's no news charging the air,
no celebration in the fields?

You consign me to anticipation,
I know I'm without horses,
and that we've missed the dew
between the fear of walking
and the mirage of arriving.

Why do I become narrow as my vision expands?
I'm addicted to drinking you in secret,
    and my thirst is constant.
I see you eluding me
and I pursuing your absence
    lame and blind.

XXII

Like all of you my tongue carves the wall
    of hallucinations.
And like you I chisel the water,
and like me, fear has you imprison
    Time
        in bottles.

XXX

For a tree whose greenness crosses all frontiers
For a tree
that departs at dawn
    and never returns,
I burn my torn limbs in its fire,
and without its noticing me,
sit apart from it,
and play with a little twig.

XXXVI

How late you are!
I'm now driving eternity
to death's summit.

I wish you'd searched more carefully,
before asking for help
from those who have abandoned it.

If only you'd been there a little!
You might have stretched a hand
to your demolished house.
How late you are!
and you ask my permission?
Pass yesterday . . . or pass tomorrow.

—translated by May Jayyusi and Jeremy Reed

Laila al-Sa'ih *(b. 1936)*

Al-Sa'ih studied psychology and philosophy at the Arab University in Beirut and has worked as a free-lance literary journalist in Kuwait. She writes her poetry in a prose medium that reflects her sensitive approach to major events pertaining to the Palestinian expeirence; she also writes on love and the liberation of woman's spirit and mind. Her collection of prose poems, *Copybooks of the Rain,* appeared in 1979. Her latest work is her diary on the 1982 Israeli invasion of Beirut, *Roots That Do Not Depart* (1984).

Intimations of Anxiety

You do not know how hard it is,
transfiguring blood into ink—
emerging from one's secret dream
to voicing the dream.
Perhaps I need years to understand
what swirls within me when we meet.
Do you know that constellations of cities and paths tangle
restlessly in the sand?
I do not know the name
for such sweet incandescence.
Even now I have not discovered all the stars
fanning out in the soul and body
like eloquent shining symbols.

Under a mass of snow
a violet is patiently waiting.
Each opening rose partakes of
the patience of ages.
These are the things we must share,
and how the word takes shape within me.
Pulled between a world that created me
and a vaporous world I wish to create,
I begin again.
Each time you transform me

into a haze,
Wait for my anxiety
for this nameless creature thumping
in my breast.
I begin again
with your book,
from your book,
reading the first pages
over and over, dazzled, amazed,
enveloped by vast days and puzzling depths,
saying: The moment will come
in which I discover language,
voice of the sun's fruits,
dialect of waves engulfing my heart.
Maybe then I will be able to add
a single syllable to this existence—
this arduous impossible task.

—translated by May Jayyusi and Naomi Shihab Nye

The Ever-Deferred Moment

A warm tremor flickers in the chilled body
as a fire glows in darkness; and a rising voice
envelopes silence—let us transcend extinction
to find out what remains in us.

Am I more in need of myself these days?
Yes, I am,
needing to gather up all the moments that
    slipped the heart's duration
For only in the heart's duration do I find you,
immense, powerful, luminous as a million stars
    or a thousand suns.
No longer are you a corporal body—
since your essence penetrated my being,
blending with my cells,
no longer can we be close—
now you inhabit me.

Look at them, who eye the season of silent brilliance
without understanding.
They witness the union of sky and earth,
the merging of rain and autumn evenings,
without comprehension.
I say:
Have you seen my beloved?
But they don't see.
You say:
Have you seen my beloved?
But they don't see.
If you are no longer a corporal body,
if your essence now inhabits me,
how could they understand?

Did I ever mention
you are the language bridging
the possible and impossible,
your love is companion
to the indescribable?
I never told you
the moment forever deferred
the moment forever awaited
is what makes our love its own language
bridging possible and impossible
and our mingled sorrow huge as eternity.
The deferred moment will be an embrace
of imaginary presences and real absences,
an embrace of the nebulous now
and the future point of light that will arrive
when the plant is reconciled with earth,
when all arrows return to their bows,
when branches mingle with their roots
and the glowing universe is once again new.

—translated by May Jayyusi and Naomi Shihab Nye

Waleed Sayf *(b. 1948)*

A poet, short-story writer, dramatist, critic, and scholar, living in Amman, Sayf was born in Tulkarm in the West Bank and studied for his B.A. in Arabic language and literature at the University of Jordan; he then obtained his Ph.D. in linguistics at the School of Oriental and African Studies of London University in 1975. He subsequently lectured at the University of Jordan for three years, before leaving to free-lance in television drama; since 1987 he has been director of educational production at the Jerusalem Open University, whose initial program he helped to organize. His television dramatizations often draw from the rich, classical Arab heritage, but he also writes both plays and essays on the current plight of his own people. *The Long Road* is a serialized drama on the life of several generations of a Palestinian peasant family. Sayf's poetry quickly drew attention through its originality of theme and approach, and many poets in Jordan acknowledge his influence. He has published three volumes of poetry: *Poems in the Times of Conquest* (1969); *Tattoo on Khadra's Arm* (1971); and *The Estrangement of the Children of Palestine* (1979).

Death at Night's End

When they wakened me, the moon
was limpid like the eyes of a young girl
with her hands waving a last farewell
    and the trees passing on
    by strange balconies;
It was a time of stinging rain
    and the place was a festival.
When they wakened me from sleep
    and my blood cringed at the rancorous helmet
they asked me about the arriving cloud
about the sun, how it turns into a butterfly
about the rain
    when it fills the night with longing
        for intimate talk
They asked me about my love's name

her address
her contours
When they wakened me from sleep
the northern winds were ravaging the dew
from my love's eyelashes
Imagination crossed over the wound to the frontiers
of the impossible
where a cat-and-mouse game went on
where the gallows
was an abyss towards my love's home
where my love's eyes
were an explosion over the inert oasis.
When they wakened me from sleep
the day was a living amber among the ashes of myth
a beautiful inferno behind the wall
The face of day was a mare
in children's songs
It was a suitcase which someone's hand
had lost on a train.
. . . . .

When they came for me and the door burst open
the silver moons of grief were pulsing in the depths
where mermaids were braiding a wreath
the color of dawn
and where my love was playing her drums
on the green crystal path:

"Singer! Sing of him
in the dance with circling feet
whose moustaches are so neat
like a line that's finely etched
on white paper, in black pencil sketched."

A mare was leaping in the vision of the world
when the sycamore tree becomes
a tree of myth and wonder
of cloudy sorrow

When they came for me, and the door burst open
the fragrance of my love was everywhere
and the scarlet berries hung low

The vast sea drew near like my beloved's eyes
My love was in my mind climbing
     ascending through the blood-stained night
     toward the blazing stars
     toward the wounding silence
The night patrol followed her footsteps
When they breezed in her my forbidden scent
and saw my name, like a tattoo, on her hand.
My love was playing her drums
on the green crystal path:

"Oh you musician, sing!
of my beloved and bring
people in a ring.
Be patient, horse, and why
Your horseman has passed by."

Then things acquire the bitter taste of tragedy
stinging rain and greenness become
a nightmare that stifles the breath of the Civil Guards
rings them round with the faces of the dead
become like savage birds
that grow more and more each minute
     and wander by secret paths.
When they came for me
and the door burst open
primordial snow and wild horses
     filled my breast
My love ran among the dense trees
     chasing a butterfly
     and the promenade was filled
     with the feet of sailors and children
The evening turned warm and intimate
like the stories of grandmothers.

When they came for me
the world was going its daily round
and longing for my love
     drowned me in a drizzle of light
     and warned of imminent death.
The neighing of a blood-flecked steed

came to me from all the high places
    leaving me the taste of wild thorn bushes
    and the taste of tepid fire.
When they came for me and the smell of scorched grass
    smouldered in my nose
(My love's foot slipped in the stairway and I fell
Pigeons crooned with sorrow and I replied
All rivers poured into my heart and I wept.)

When I woke up from dim sleep
and across the night their barren faces loomed
(like deserts without color, without water)
When their shaggy uniforms appeared
Khadra was being born in my head
    with a star of blood on her hands
    so I could become in a moment
    a bough in this jungle.
    (which stretches from Jordan to Granada)
    across the eyes of children
    and across the frontiers of myth
When they came for me and I woke from sleep
all the women of the world were my mother
and my wife
All things broke loose
in the open breast of the universe
    like my love's wound
and became a symbol in the sea of fire
where pure virgin language
    multiplied like savage grief
My love took on the aspect of my homeland
    that very hour
When from all directions, Khadra's arms stretched forth
watching for my next awakening in her arms
drenched with sea spray
    kindled with bitter fragrance
When they came for me, and led me away that night
the village moon was full
    over my love's brow
the longing for my love kindled me
    warned me against the coming death
    sprinkled me with the spray of desire

and I became braver
When they maliciously turned my back
Khadra was rooting out of my face all the weeds
    of stale time
    and removing from my supple body
the masks of ancient silence
and with all the wonder of loving persistence
she uncovered for me all secrets
A live ember fell
and before their bullets whined
I was there, entering it, my own country
across the contours of my kindled body
uniting with it
without a passport.

    —translated by Sharif Elmusa and John Heath-Stubbs

Mai Sayigh *(b. 1940)*

A poet and writer born in Ghaza, Palestine, Sayigh graduated from the University of Cairo with a B.A. in sociology in 1960. She has since dedicated her life to the cause of freedom and has a particular interest in the women's liberation movement. Since 1971 she has been president of the Union of Palestinian Women and has served on numerous panels at feminist meetings the world over. She has published three collections of poetry: *Garland of Thorns* (1968), *Love Poems for a Hunted Name* (1974), and *Of Tears and the Coming Joy* (1975). Her prose account, *The Siege,* on the Israeli invasion and siege of Beirut in 1982, was published in 1988.

Elegy for Imm 'Ali[1]

Don't go away!
Across the distances you kindle our fires,
deliver joy, ignite our dreams
Leaving was never your style; you were always
    about to arrive
Now the flower vendors close their shops
    under the blitz, and
darkness prepares to depart
This city you loved,
crowded with history, iron, and anger,
braids her joy with fatigue
    and threatens to fall into oblivion
She huddles over its newborn dawn
planting stars in that hopeful sphere,
and repressing her tears in the songs
      How could you leave us
      with no goodbyes?

You, who always repressed your tears
from you I learned how basil grows

[1] Imm 'Ali was a Palestinian woman who worked in the Resistance and was killed.

how the sky descends
    to rest in your arms
You wiped the sorrow away from
    its brow!
From you I learned how the heart can be
    a live coal, a burning flower
Now the dignity of your great death
    opens up wounds
that even trees bleed,
and poems.

    —translated by Lena Jayyusi and Noami Shihab Nye

Departure

In this the moment of departure,
point your red arrows,
disarm the lightning, and open wide
the gate to my exile.
Close the sky's open face, and ride away.
I long so deeply that the shores unfold their seas
and horses bolt!
Hooves have trampled my heart a thousand times,
a thousand waves have broken over it!
Now I'll carry the roads and palm trees in my suitcase,
I'll lock my tears in the evening's copybooks
and seal the seasons.

Let's begin our song: here is Beirut *wearing* you
    like her own clothes.
You must sit well on the surface of her glory
abandoning tears
In her blue froth
she contains you like eternity
like the sense of beginning that comes with certainty

—How can you be dead, yet so absolutely present?

Let the rivers abandon their sources,
the winds abandon their skies,
and the seas dry out!

Everything in the universe has an end
except my spilt blood . . .

Each time I think of it
you remain as large as your death.
The war planes choose you, discover you, plant
their blackness in you.
From all those clouded last visions,
how will you begin the story of harvest?
War planes select you,
at the start of your sleep,
at the end of your sleep.
How often did the sky explode over you
        with hatred?
How often were you taken aside?
How many massacres did you survive?
Now you collect all the wounds, taking refuge with
        death,
wearing dreams as wings.

—translated by Lena Jayyusi and Naomi Shihab Nye

From Beirut under Siege

A last letter to my son

Son!
This war breaks the heart
steals lives,
halts the stars in their orbits,
extinguishes day.
I beg you to remain a witness
to this siege.

Son!
Beirut, that fortress in the flames,
will not succumb to fire's touch.
She lives like a cactus flower.
Pomegranate blossoms unfurl from her wounds,
and birds build new homes.

Son!
Fire baptizes our awakening!
I would not object if one day soon
you wake up to find my martyred face
     on a poster.
But in the darkness of the grave I shall wait
for a new red bullet from your gun
     to reunite us.
I won't forgive you if you dally
or throw your hands up to fate.
Son, be careful,
hypocrisy has a whole cast of actors,
as do compromise and caution.
But you are meant for danger,
     winds and rains
smearing the sky with spring
     and martyrs.
Then the moon shall rise
     over our savage night
Son, beware!

War gobbles the heart,
rips life from my hands,
halts the stars in their orbits,
extinguishes day.
I urge you to resist, to remain witness.
I urge you to join your brothers
and resist the siege.
Son, please!

    —translated by Lena Jayyusi and Naomi Shihab Nye

Tawfiq Sayigh *(1923–1971)*

Born in Southern Syria, Sayigh grew up in Tiberius, where his family had acquired Palestinian citizenship. He studied at the Arab College and the American University in Beirut before going to Harvard to study English literature. After that he went to Cambridge University where he taught Arabic. Between 1962 and 1967 he was editor-in-chief of *Hiwar,* a bimonthly cultural magazine. When *Hiwar* folded he went to teach at the University of California at Berkeley. He published several translations from English literature, including T.S. Eliot's *Four Quartets.* Sayigh wrote prose poetry whose language and images have great precision. It reflects an anguished soul torn between sorrow and alienation he experienced as a Palestinian refugee, his ungratified love for K, and his deep metaphysical conflicts, some of the best manifestations of the Christian faith within Arabic literature. He published three collections of poetry. *Thirty Poems* (1954), *The Poem, K* (1960), and *The Ode of Tawfiq Sayigh* (1963).

Poem 28

The night I put on my good suit
fixed myself up, cut my hair
and dined at the Copacabana
with my girlfriend,
my friends, and their girlfriends,
we strolled on the dark Corniche[1]
and instructed the sea—
"Go ahead with your rhythm and break,"
and to the stars,
"Ooh la la"—
our lips going wide of speech.

I picked up my pen to write
a song to my love;
I scrambled inconsistent rhymes,

[1]The Corniche is Beirut's sea side; with its many quaint cafés and restaurants it was the haunt of writers, poets, businessmen, and lovers.

and the pen fluttered from my hand,
perched on the ground and screeched into my face:
"There you are
a single strand of hair
in the head's abundant growth!
What right have you to sing?"

And the day I gave my resignation
to the director
(I never refused any of his demands.)
The sun scorched me
before disappearing at noon.
The day I got tight at the bar
and the one-eyed barman evicted me,
I reached into my pocket
and grabbed my small change
to keep it from slipping
through my pocket-hole.
I found a piece of paper
and inked it with curses
profuse enough to cover every sea;
but the paper flew away
before my verse had scorched it
and questioned me
in a wise ringing tone:
"There you are
a white hair
on a young man's head.
How dare you sing?"

At this I sheathed my pen,
wrapped my belongings in the paper,
kissed my beloved,
without the song.
I cursed the barman
and the director
in the same fireless style.
I oscillated, a single hair
in search of a bald head
to take root in.

    —translated by Adnan Haydar and Jeremy Reed

To Enter a Country

Edging closer, but without admission,
it goes on and you never reach your aim.
Your lacking a passport means
statelessness, no entry.

Water surges in your ears—
your mouth and belly take turns.
You knew the ocean
as mood and color;
your transient companions
exhaust you.
Tomorrow they will sleep
while you toss and turn restlessly in bed.
They'll feast,
you'll vomit.
They'll tell stories and recount adventures;
you'll be left conversing with ambiguous fish
from a great distance.

You come close to deliverance
then it slips between your fingers.
The hills smile for you at times.
And occasionally the young women
wave their scarves in the air for you.
In the morning, you are enthused
by songs and applause;
you pick up your bundles
and scramble along.
You stash your wallet
in the pocket of a nearby sailor
only to see
in the evening
a handsome, intimidating giant
rise upright before your eyes,
a face that's terrified you before
in a thousand ports,
a thousand countries.

The mountains darken;
buttons and flagstaffs glitter;

joy is temporarily suspended.
Holding the book in his right hand,
he bellows:
"Your passport?"
No passport—
No entry
If you don't have it,
get out.

One group descends
another ascends
the officials change
people hurry forward
and dead embers shine again in your head.
Passports are stamped.
Everyone hurries in:
murderers, traitors and spies,
one holding a green passport,
with a black one in his wallet;
others lean on the rickety gangplank,
finding that after completing their short journey
they have to embark on the long one.
Some are carried on board
without sense of a homeland or voyage.
You cry out, pray, supplicate:
"My papers are in order;
I have a degree in every pocket,
why have they not issued my passport?
Who or what informed on me?
What are the charges against me?
I can answer to anything.
There are no embassies in the ocean."
"And which is your embassy?"
"I used to know it
and visit it regularly.
But I've forgotten its name now."

The seamen hit high spirits:
two days on shore
make two weeks at sea bearable;
two weeks subtracted from time.

The ship plows the sea
leaving a sluggish wake.
Their laughter backtracks insultingly
and you wonder on which shore you will dock?
Will you be met with applause?
or demonstrations?
or silence?
And you wait anticipating
a redoubtable giant's confrontation
and the chanting of those who greet you
with power irrefutably stronger
than you or the sea,
a force that exceeds their own desire.
They mutter their incantation:
Welcome, welcome,
but the law is the law . . .
the fire blazes on the heights
and the smoke traces these words around it:
"Our needs to see you are like yours
but the law is the law
No passport
No entry
If you don't have it
There's no way in."

You puncture your ears
with stoppering fingertips
not wishing to hear;
but the temporal whisper continues:
"I am hospitable
a new guest doesn't bother me;
I am rich,
I afford comfort to the visitor.
I am beautiful
and you yearn for beauty
my arms are permanently open.
I am magnanimous,
that is my virtue."

—translated by Adnan Haydar and Jeremy Reed

From "The Poem K"

Detours and evasions
and no way forward.
The rain never slackens
it pours over London's
white on white faces.
A London of dark skies, walls, and stone hearts
one large
unquenchable lavatory.
My chest weighs
with the nightmare of days
and their corresponding nights;
and I fumbling about in London's streets
alone
alone with K's shadow
and K's love penetrates me,
works through me
like the city's sewers

. . . . .

Every night I'm pursued and tried.
I am tortured, led to the guillotine.
Every morning I attack
but there's no one to chase
I search,
but there's no cup to assuage my thirst.
I proceed, leaning on my staff,
but there's no shrine in sight.
I beat around in a void,
untiring, untouched by the cold.
I'm powerless
no family
Crippled
and no healing Christ.

Who can save me
from the idolatory of dreams?
I mumble while my eyes
are still half-closed
only to see that the night strokes me with a whip

and the gesture's repeated during the day.
They feed my day with nails
then feed the nails my own blood.

Every night, every day,
I am re-widowed,
re-orphaned.
I grieve over a death
with no promise of resurrection;
Death, resurrection, death.
My mother's iron shield
is a cutting sword of fire
K's iron shield
is a cutting sword of fire
The two swords met
in the shape of a cross
on which I was hoisted.
No women to mourn
No women to lay me out
No-one to roll the stone.

My mother,
I lost her to death
K,
I lost her to life
Death is my enemy
Life is my enemy
I hang
between life and death:
In a state that's neither life nor death.

Whale, return it to me.
Return it to me.
I pursued you
I dashed my drums to pieces
I roared, racking my brains
but no vein stirred in you.
What's it to you?
An innocuous meal?
Something indigestible?
Give it back to me;
it's my only light:

I live in a blackout,
while other people's nights are lit:
It's my only confidante
with whom I discourse softly
against the inhuman roar.
Return it to me, Whale
Return it to me
O, usurper
I both loathe and idolize;
You who unite
the secret and divine
like an ark of covenant.

Two conflagratory swords
never let up
They clash but never fall
from the hands of the two Maryams
The Maryam of sorrow and the Maryam of sorrow
The Maryam of tranquility and the Maryam of discord
The Maryam of sowing and tending
of safe harbor and solace
and the Maryam of hammer and axe
who sows pustules
Maryam of talons that flay
the loved one's flesh
before the enemy's,
destroys the self
before the loved one.
The Maryam of charity and protection
and the Maryam who demands a victim every day
The Maryam of the heart
and the one of the flesh
The Maryam of sorrow and the Maryam of sorrow
The Maryam of love and the Maryam of love.
Two that are one.

The two blazing swords dance,
contend.
They flash through the air,
rebound.
They guard the two gates

to my summer home, to my winter home
At the time when blood rages and nerves flutter
they force sweat out of me
and leave my flesh shriveled,
my left side paralyzed.
I shift my eyes from door to door
waiting for either guard to close his eyes
(Yet when they close, the swords grow eyes)
I go from one entrance to the other,
propping myself up, dragging my corpse along
but I am barred wherever I go
and I look up
I lift my arms
I utter prayers whose endings I've forgotten
and I find the ceiling lower
and more deeply fissured
than I remember
and I lift my arms
my heart and my voice:
"Help me, help me."

—translated by Adnan Haydar and Jeremy Reed

Umar Shabana *(b. 1958)*

Shabana was born in Amman where he still lives. He has a B.A. in Arabic literature from the Jordanian University and now works as a literary correspondent for the Lebanese newspaper *Al-Hayat*, which comes out in London. He is an experimental poet whose main emphasis is on Palestinians' conditions of life, particularly on their life in exile and the resistance they face in their efforts to achieve their human rights. Shabana's first collection, *The Windows' Celebration of the Storm,* was published in Amman in 1983.

Evening Balcony

A foggy street
a rainsong
where lovely girls lie spread out on balconies
I bare my breast to the flame
waiting to see her balcony
made ready for song
waiting for the hour to change instantly into night
while others fall asleep
all except one
that opens a hand to the wind
while another dares the light

—translated by May Jayyusi and Charles Doria

From: The Book of Songs and Stones

o star of the mountains
and song
have the rifles left you?
planets of the coasts
for how many days must we wade in our blood
returning our bodies to the river

where the mountains glow with our martyrs' blood?
they rushed to the hills
to the valley of the Jordan searching for fire
for a blood moon

they fanned out through the hills
that decline toward Jericho
to hunt down monsters
carrying stones in their innocent hands

they spread out through the deserts
that hug the sea beside orange and almond groves
between us the river flowed
gazelle, don't hate us
our land is straight and narrow
wolves snap at our heels
dogs harry us

for furious gazelles we wait
do not hate us,
gypsy, do not reproach us
you the herald of our pains
tell our story to the girls:
"be fire, we'll be the wood"
say to the children in every house
to every child who will repeat our tale
"glory to you
and to every mother
for the fire kindled from a stone"
lovely songs!
what country will embrace our dream?

star of the mountains
we begin now in the songs of south Lebanon
the singing south where bullets zing
the prophet south where we begin
but shall not end

for the road passes here
you who march for our blood
in stone the sea tells our tale
this is blood for Palestine
which now gleams in a stone

in Jerusalem's hand
or the hand
of a little girl from Jenin[1]

for Palestine, a woman
who has joined her blood with her lovers
giving them the secret and the charm
she whose hands hold the trembling
roses of her lovers

her blood is here
quivering, now boiling
for whom none sing save her lovers
come, let us gather her sorrows
and sing

—translated by May Jayyusi and Charles Doria

Khulud

I begin alone
my footsteps lose themselves on the road
I find shelter in my pain
the river comes back to me
I find shade in it and am set on fire
looking for her I return to the river
where she baptizes her pain
we met
once more poverty unites us refugees
in the alleys of the camp

she comes
I am alone
she sees me
together we walk the alley singing
the camp listens surrounding us
like a bullet we carry it in our blood
it turns to rain and fields

[1]Jenin is a town in the West Bank not far from Nablus.

I shout, "the camp grows great in our blood
contains us
walks with us to the land
birthplace of our woe"

free the rein of the houses
lightning starts from the pain of the poor
give wheat stalks their due
labor starts from buds that break into flower
    above our tin houses
come come
behind the camp let us pray

   —translated by May Jayyusi and Charles Doria

Mazin Shadeed (b. 1945)

A poet and a writer for radio and television, Shadeed was born in 1945 in Acre; since the 1948 debacle he has lived in the Arab world at large. He obtained a B.A. in philosophy and psychology from Cairo University in 1972, and after working in Kuwait for several years he eventually settled in Jordan. He works as public relations officer in the Jordanian Phosphate Company and edits *Development,* a scientific journal published in Jordan. Three collections of his sensitive and versatile poetry, *Writings on the Gate of Sorrow* (1978), *I Am the Gypsy, I Call You* (1983), and *Thus Spoke 'Irsan, Thus About the Gazelle* (1985), have so far appeared.

The Caravans' Departure

It's a sad wind that blows
over the ruined houses
around the roofs of the city
and beats on every door,
    enters through the windows
to etch a signal sorrow,
and tells us in departing
that we were worthy of the fall,
and that a land invites defeat
where the neighing of horses has turned into a whimper,
and from which the rain withdraws
neglectful of the seasons.
What harbor will embrace a nameless child,
and from where will joy come to us?
Where have the rainbow and the caravans
disappeared to, in what direction
have they gone, will they travel?
In what place will the horses regain voice?
And for how long will the caravans keep searching
    for their shadows in the dark?
restlessly awake all night
until sleep comes at daybreak?

—translated by Sharif Elmusa and Jeremy Reed

Love Song

He sat alone
under the branches of the night
and liberated his birds for me,
called my name aloud, and waited
as I dropped down to him
like the sun's curtains open on the universe.

Through the wave-orchards
his persistent call reached me,
accompanied by his horses.
He stretched out glowing fingers
that broke into soft elder flowers
from which joy emanated,
flooding through my body
as I ran to him, ringing bells.

We walk together, like two happy songs,
we ran together, like two gazelles,
and radiated like two stars
before we fused
  like two shores
  like two waves
  like two springs
  like two light rings on fire

He planted a wheat stalk in my open hand,
He told me: "Come to the valleys
let's wander like two gold roses
  among our lanterns
  and our mirrors
Where I look I see you"
"—And I see you where I look."
"We'll walk together
spinning our roses
and I'll release my birds
to climb towards your cloud-high forehead."

Under the star-throne, under the sky-vault, under
   the branches of the night
we sat together

Then he opened my palm and said, "Joy begins with you."
And I said, in return, "You grant me ecstasy."
We embraced, and before he kissed me, he said,
"You're both the beginning and the end of the dream."
He sprinkled fragrance on me, in return for dew.
I said, "Give me your colors, and I'll transform you with mine."

He plunged into my mirrors
and in our union
we reappeared as two reborn.

   —translated by Sharif Elmusa and Jeremy Reed

Anton Shammas *(b. 1950)*

A poet and fiction-writer, Shammas was born in Fassouta in Upper Galilee. He differs from all other notable Palestinian writers by virtue of the fact that he writes in both Arabic and Hebrew and has gained worldwide recognition for his writings in Hebrew. He studied art history and English and Arabic literature at the Hebrew University in Jerusalem and in 1981 attended the International Writing Program in Iowa City. In 1987–1988 he was a Rockefeller resident fellow at the Center for Near Eastern and North African Studies at the University of Michigan, Ann Arbor, and has been teaching at the same university since then. In 1974 Shammas published his only book in Arabic, a collection of poems entitled *Prisoner of my Wakefulness and Sleep* which reflected his innate control over his literary tools and his early consciousness of the modernist apprehension of experience. All his other publications have been in Hebrew, including two volumes of poetry, *Hardcover* (1974) and *No Man's Land* (1979). In 1986 his major work to date appeared, a novel in Hebrew entitled *Arabesque,* which won him international fame.

Then How Will the Poem Come?

I

Just as desire sprouts
among the shivers of the flesh,
melancholy sneaks between my fingers at night's end.
I bury my face in your neck and lament
all the swans that departed to strange islands to die.
On the shore I chase after them, arriving
after their beaks have been planted in the sand
like surrendering flags
and their whiteness withers on the rocks.

Then how will the poem come?

IV

I open the map of the world
searching for a village I lost,
searching in the pockets of a grandfather I never got to know
for fragments of tales and rare fragrances.
I encircle him like a butterfly,
I cling, breathing his passion into my lungs.
If he'd had blue eyes he would have draped them
amulets around my neck.
I swing, feeling the drowned shrines
in the palms of his hands.
I ask him to color my eyes with departure
and return me to legends, wearing a cloak
spun from the wings of northern gulls.
I swing, asking him to drape me across a swan's neck,
to rove about all the islands before being born
where I wish.
I know the dreams one by one.

Then how will the poem come?

V

And I ask, how do all these days,
like lemon fragrance, pass through me?
I fear my words will drop from me
into the streets one day.
Children will pick them up,
turning them into tails for their kites,
and covering the gaps in their dreams.
I fear I may die before all the words chasing behind
can catch up with me, and no one will remember me.

Then how will the poem come?

—translated by Ferial Ghazoul and Naomi Shihab Nye

An Evening of Poetry Reading

I try to remember who said it, in vain. Outside,
no doubt, the wind brushes past walls like a cat's tongue
on a rasp. All that I recall:
Sorrow is a one-way street.

Behind you, walls. Before you, the audience:
They take aim
and clap.

When I stood up, a woman raised her coat collar
and bent her head. She might have remembered the wind
that brushes, no doubt, past the walls outside.

A woman shields herself from the cold with a collar
and a newspaper.
Silence between us is a rasp
being licked by the poem.

—translated by Ferial Ghazoul and Naomi Shihab Nye

Seven Poems

I

It's five o'clock in the morning
and the city is a crusader in search of the City.

Dawn's dew on helmets and children's shoes,
the horses' neighs, moist with hymns,
and dreams rising from windows like kites.
Wakefulness clips their strings and they alight.
(Who will clip this string from my neck?)

And I fear standing, I fear
becoming a stone filled with time's bubbles, a nail
on the big Gate, or an inscription
on a saber's handle.

Tell the guitar player at Jaffa Gate
all the houses of the city will tumble down if he stops.

II

If you walk at night
beneath the street lamps,
beware!
Of your shadow slipping away
or getting stuck on the wall.

III

You were two poems away from me, or
even closer
within my lips and my reach.

But when the climbing paths wound
toward the childhood behind me,
the wilderness poured down on me suddenly, and my sadness
dashed forward.

So I became the minaret of vacancy.

And you ebbed away like dawn's call for prayer.

IV

"Haven't we met before?" said the lip to the finger.
"Of course we did," the finger said, "in the station of desire."

V

Street lamps doze off with their lights at the end of night;
their foreheads touching the asphalt and sleep.
Allah yawns and lights our way with his little lantern
like an usher in a theater aisle.

VI

I open the door,
and hang my face on the rack.
I strip in the dark,
and lie on my bed.

If sleep comes, he won't recognize me.

VII

Two doors of myself I know. One
for the exit of yesterday. Another
for two entrants only: you and the poem.

The third, where I stand alone,
opens up on my death.

—translated by Ferial Ghazoul and Naomi Shihab Nye

Sa'adeh Sudah *(b. 1952)*

Born in the Nayrab Refugee Camp in Aleppo, Syria, Sudah was educated in various Arab countries and obtained a B.A. in Arabic literature from Beirut Arab University in 1977. He has worked as a journalist in several Arab countries, and since 1983 he has lived in Cyprus where he is one of the editors of the journal *Filastin al-Thaura.* An avid reader of Arabic literature, both classical and modern, Sudah writes a poetry of questioning, wonder, and almost metaphysical bewilderment in the face of life's vicissitudes and ambivalences. His work is firmly divorced from the loud, self-assured political themes and attitudes that dominated much of the Arabic poetry of the seventies. He has published one collection of poetry, *Song of Fatigue* (1980). A book of his essays, *Difficult Questions in the Time of the Uprising,* was published in 1989.

A Ring

On my lips lingers a woman
of whom I do not tell

I do not tell of her

She took my hand in her hands
admitting that tears spring up easily
since our last encounter

glimpsing a wilted ring
shining on my finger
mute pain flashed across her face
a flood of pain
and I realized I had lost
the mischievous boy within me

She danced with many men that night
holding a glass of wine for a final toast
I held my own
we did not come together

Now tears well up in me too
when I glimpse on my finger this wilted ring
and realize I have lost the mischievous boy
within me.

—translated by Lena Jayyusi and Naomi Shihab Nye

Your Hands

Your hands,
two clouds shading
the arid desolation that stretches
between my immense affection for this life
and the longing that bids me search among tombstones
for the secrets of the tides.

—translated by Lena Jayyusi and Naomi Shihab Nye

Prophecy

A star informs me
that my mantle circles
between two points
one marking the beginning
(from where do you begin?)
one marking the end
(if only the harbors could shelter you)
. . . You're destined to walk and grow thirsty,
gradually wearying,
until the sad throbbing ceases
and you grow still.

—translated by Lena Jayyusi and Naomi Shihab Nye

A Poem to Tayseer Saboul[1]

My own face has left me stranded.
I grow naked in the presence of your memory,
struck wordless, impotent . . .

Now you sleep deeply
letting go of the primal questions
or forgetting them.
You become a child who knows only sleep
not wondering about meanings
or why anyone might be fasting today . . .
not even the puzzle of impotence could preoccupy you now
for you are reduced to simple presence,
you enter the heart of the mystery.

Now you sleep deeply
and my own wakefulness seems too deep to bear.
My muteness paralyzes as I contemplate
your first journey and that other one,
filling with tears, for you have grounded
all my questions in mystery.

—translated by Lena Jayyusi and Naomi Shihab Nye

[1]Tayseer Saboul, Jordanian poet and writer, committed suicide after the June war of
1967.

Khalil Touma (b. 1945)

Palestinian poet from Beit Jala near Bethlehem. Unable to complete a university education for lack of funds, he worked in a Jerusalem hotel as a receptionist. In 1966 he was elected to the administrative committee for the Union of Hotel Workers in Jordan. Following the Israeli occupation of the West Bank, he resumed work at the same Jerusalem hotel. In April 1974, he was placed under administrative detention by the Israeli occupation authorities. His first *diwan, Songs of the Last Nights* (1975), appeared while he was in prison, and during the twenty-two months of his imprisonment he completed his second collection of poetry, which was published in 1976 under the title *Star over Bethlehem*. A third collection of poetry will soon be published.

Between the Wound and Its Bleeding

Night lit by Muhammad's face . . .
It is time for us to pluck you
    from our depths
    to fling you outside this earthly sphere
For the sky now attempting to rise
    slowly, a serene bride
      in her new gown,
    is looking for her groom
She spreads her arms
    and rivers of blood pour over the barren earth
She gazes eagerly;
vases are filled from her glances
and the veins of the poor and miserable injected
    with strength
She looks for her groom. O sky!
    Gaze on us through the smoke and ashes
    Watch when the earth rolls round becoming
    small as a prison cell
    When the sunrays pale
    and harden to whips in the investigator's hands
You will see Muhammad as an apple tree

trampled down in the caves of barbarians
Look on us as you search for your groom
Stretch your hands through the grills and bars
and see Muhammad's body like clay
  taking the shape of the motherland
Stretch your hands to the locks
to the cold iron
the walls filtering dampness
to the land still opening its breast
for his young and tender body,
    so he can rest awhile
     before he resumes the journey of suffering
Stretch your hands to him, and when you rise,
  soaring onto the horizon, like Palestine's flag,
  remember that his youth melts a little every day
  as it wipes their spittle off your beautiful face.
Look, as you advance on the saddles of anger,
You are definite like death,
  beautiful as a garden full of children.
Muhammad used to raise his fists
calling to the wayward mare of the winds
and she would respond, submitting her back to him.
When his comrades would ask him to wait awhile
  he would point with his eyes
  to the far distance where waves had ebbed
  and the sun's shadow elongated like tent poles.
He was the horseman
  and sleeping eyes would awaken to the hooves of
   his mare.
Those who were deaf heard him clearly.
The road would rise behind him, running on and on
  to new worlds.
You who comes now, like death, like the morning,
  Look!
He has tied his steed and entered the cave a little
but same as the flash of time between the wound
  and its bleeding
he will return again
to resume the journey.

  —translated by Sharif Elmusa and Naomi Shihab Nye

Fadwa Tuqan *(b. 1917)*

Born in Nablus, Palestine, Tuqan was introduced to the art of poetry by her brother, the famous poet Ibrahim Tuqan. Initially a Romantic poet skilled in the traditional forms, she turned to free verse at the outset of the movement and wrote on a variety of personal and communal subjects. She was one of the first major poets to work toward emotional veracity, laying the foundation for feminine explorations of love and social protest. When her birthplace fell to the Zionists in the June 1967 war, resistance themes predominated in her work. Since the publication of her first *diwan, Alone with the Days* in 1952, she has published several collections of poetry, including *I Found It* (1958), *Give Us Love* (1960), *In Front of the Closed Door* (1967), *Horsemen and the Night* (1969), and *Alone on the Summit of the World* (1973). Her well-acclaimed auto-biography, *A Mountainous Journey* (1985), details her childhood, youth, and growth into poetic maturity, and ends with the Israeli occupation of the West Bank after the June 1967 war. It has been translated by Olive Kenny for PROTA and was published in 1990. Fadwa Tuqan is now writing an account of her life from the Israeli occupation to the present. In 1990 she was awarded the Sultan Uweis Prize for Poetry, and the Jerusalem Medal for literary achievement.

The Sibyl's Prophecy

1

On my twentieth birthday
the eternal soothsayer told me
"The swishing winds
have prophesied,
Evil spell around this house . . .
this house shall stay divided
until a certain horseman arrives . . .
a stately serene man, neither slow nor downhearted.
The winds tell me he shall come
on a road cleaved open by thunder
and lightning."

"Oh Sibyl! Won't you ask the winds
for a time *when* will this horseman arrive?"

"When rejection becomes
a blazing fire, a Golgotha,
then the womb of the earth shall birth him."
But the winds also said,
"Beware of your seven brothers!
Beware
of your seven brothers!"

Under the cracks of this warped ceiling
I stood by the unhinged balcony
waiting for his hooves
listening to the pulse of buried seeds
bursting quietly inside the earth
and the heart of the wheatstalk
Oh, chemistry of life and death,
when would rejection become
a blazing fire, a Golgotha?

2

When he came, his footsteps were bells
echoing in the vaults of darkness.
The wind was the horse running under him,
shaking every ruin he passed.
He pulled me up behind him, saying,
"Dear one, your love protects my naked back,
hold fast, don't fear the night or wolves.
Love knows no fear."

When we mounted our horses
our songs flashed
like glittering daggers
unsheathed against the night!

On the shores of night
the trees grew high
flowers, and fruits ripened.
And the stars:
each time a star plummeted

in hurricane season
our windswept trees sent forth
new constellations.

That day we rode the horses' backs
our brows shone radiant with sun
shimmering vision wreathed our eyes
flowers carpeted the lips of meadows
on lowlands and river bank alike.

(Inner Voice):

But within me the winds nagged,
"Beware!
your seven brothers!
Beware!
your seven brothers!"
till it became a roar,
"Beware!
your seven brothers!"

If only we had spoken softly,
contained our agitation
If we could have continued walking
      slowly, stealthily,
      behind the fences

If only the moon
retired to its quiet cave in the mountains
      drawing its curtains . . .
but I feared the light exposing us, my love.
I feared hounds chasing us on the road,
going mad when the moon's blades gleamed against the dark
"Your love protects my naked back,
cling to me, darling, for love is no coward."

(Inner Voice):

   But the blowing winds chanted
   "Beware your seven brothers,
   Beware your seven brothers!"

3

Cain appears everywhere
knocking at doors
    climbing balconies
    and walls
leaping, crawling, hissing serpent
with a thousand tongues
Cain frolics in squares
swirling with hurricane
blocking paths, flinging open
    the gates of perdition
With his bloodied hands
    he drags the fiery coffins
Cain, the mad god burning Rome
death waxing large
as crystalline red willows
draping across horizons, and the thresholds of houses
Death, a giant growing bigger everywhere,
permeations of death and red Cain.

Sorrowfully, I stretched out my hand
pleading,
"Brothers! don't kill my beloved!
Don't twist the young neck
I beg you, in the name of love, kinship,
compassion,
don't kill him,
don't kill him,
please, don't . . . !"

4

When death reposed
and the branches of silence wove themselves around me
over him I bent, heavy with grief
cleansing his broken chest
with love and tears
collecting his limbs twisted with blood
    and smoke and pebbles
gathering his night black hair

the torn petals of his lips
the jewelled eyes
      (Ah, those eyes once the home
      for visions and dreams!)
      now stitched to the seam of night's jungle!

I gathered him limb by limb,
bouquet of flowers,
and gave him over to the winds
saying, "Plant the shrapnel of this body
on mountain slopes and summits,
in plains and lowlands and riverbeds
Scatter him across the body of our homeland."

5

September keeps me pinned to the cracks
    of my divided home
Still the sibyl of winds knocks at my sad door
whenever morning breathes,
repeating,
"The seasons complete their cycle
and the festivals of rain will bring him back . . .
March will bring him back
riding a chariot of flowers."

    —translated by Naomi Shihab Nye with the help of the Editor

Enough for Me

Enough for me to die on her earth
be buried in her
to melt and vanish into her soil
then sprout forth as a flower
played with by a child from my country.
Enough for me to remain
in my country's embrace
to be in her close as a handful of dust
    a sprig of grass
        a flower.

    —translated by Naomi Shihab Nye with the help of the editor

During the first weeks after the June 1967 war, foreign papers and radio stations slanted news in a way that gloated over the misfortune, as if the end of the Arab people had been decided by this relapse. From this situation the following poem was born.

The Deluge and the Tree

When the hurricane swirled and spread its deluge
of dark evil
onto the good green land
'They' gloated. The western skies
reverberated with joyous accounts:
"The Tree has fallen!
The great trunk is smashed! The hurricane
leaves no life in the Tree!"

Had the Tree really fallen?
Never! Not with our red streams flowing forever,
not while the wine of our torn limbs
feed the thirsty roots,
Arab roots alive
tunneling deep, deep, into the land!

When the Tree rises up, the branches
shall flourish green and fresh in the sun
the laughter of the Tree shall leaf
beneath the sun
and birds shall return
Undoubtedly, the birds shall return.
      The birds shall return.

—translated by Naomi Shihab Nye with the help of the Editor

Song of Becoming

They're only boys
who used to frolic and play
launching rainbowed kites
on the western wind,
their blue-red-green kites
whistling, leaping,
trading easy laughter and jokes
duelling with branches, pretending to be
great heroes in history.

Suddenly now they've grown,
grown more than the years of a normal life,
merged with secret and passionate words,
carried love's messages like the Bible or Quran,
to be read in whispers.
They've grown to become trees
plunging deep roots into earth,
stretching high towards the sun.
Now their voices are ones that reject,
that knock down and build anew.
Anger smouldering on the fringes of a blocked horizon,
invading classrooms, streets, city quarters,
centering on squares,
facing sullen tanks with streams of stones.

Now they shake the gallows of dawn
assailing the night and its flood.
They've grown more than the years of a life
to become the worshipped and the worshippers.

When their torn limbs merged with the stuff of our earth,
they became legends,
they grew into vaulting bridges,
they grew and grew, becoming
larger than all poetry.

—translated by Naomi Shihab Nye with the help of the Editor

Ibrahim Tuqan *(1905–1941)*

Ibrahim Tuqan was the foremost poet of his generation in Palestine and devoted much of his poetic energy to the Palestine cause. He employed a terse and poignant phraseology and his themes ranged from the strictly personal to the broadly national. His tone could be ardent and gentle when delineating a personal experience, grand and ceremonial when speaking of the national struggle, and sarcastic and ironic when attacking national ills. His poetry was published in Arab newspapers and was widely quoted. After his death it was collected in a single volume, *Dīwān Ibrāhīm Tūqān.*

Commando

Do not consider his safety—
He bares his life on the palms of his hands.
Worries have substituted
A pillow for his shroud
As he waits for that hour
That ushers in the terrible hour of his death.
His bowed head disturbs
All who glance his way.
Within his breast there is
A throbbing heart afire with its purpose.
Who has not seen night's charcoal blackness
Set on fire by his spark?
Hell itself has touched
His message with its fire.
There he stands at the door:
Death is afraid of him.
Subside, tempests!
Abashed by his boldness.

Silent he is, but should he speak
He would unite fire with blood.
Tell whoever faults with his silence
Resolution was born mute

And in the man of resolution
The hand is quicker than the word.
Rebuke him not for he has seen
The path of righteousness darkened
The foundations of a country
He loves demolished
And enemies at whose injustice
Heaven and earth cry out!
There was a time when despair
Almost killed him . . . but

There he stands at the door
And death is afraid of him.
Subside, tempests!
Abashed at his boldness.

—translated by Lena Jayyusi and John Heath-Stubbs

From "Dead Hearts"

Those who sell the land have drenched it with their tears
    but the plains and hills still curse them
The brokers who hawk my homeland
    obviously don't fear God for selling it
wearing their gaudy clothes
    stuffed with the lowest hypocrisy
tinted expressions that never blush
    and breasts like dreary graves
for their dead and buried hearts

—translated by Salwa Jabsheh and Naomi Shihab Nye

From "Brokers"

My country's brokers are a band
    who shamefully survive
Even Satan went bankrupt
    when he realized their temptation
They lead an easy, splendid life
    but the bliss is the prize of the country's misery

They pretend to be its saviours,
    whatever you say, they claim to be its leaders
and protectors! But they are its ruin
    it is bought and sold through their hands
Even the newspapers
    shield them, though we know the truth!

    —translated by Salwa Jabsheh and Naomi Shihab Nye

From "Lest We Lose"

You're the ones loyal to the cause
    You're the ones who carry its burden
You're the ones who act without speech
    God bless your strong arms!
A declaration from you equals an army
with all its military might
Your gatherings restore
    the glory lost since Umayyad conquests[1]
But we still have bits of country left in our hands
    so rest awhile, lest we lose what remains.

    —translated by Salwa Jabsheh and Naomi Shihab Nye

From "In Beirut"

In Beirut they say: You live affluently
    You sell them[2] land, they give you gold.
Neighbor, relent: since when is it bliss
    that thousands die to make one rich?
Those who give this gold know well that
    one gives with the right hand, receives with the left.
But it is our country! What are their treasures
    or gold that they can equal it?

    —translated by Salwa Jabsheh and Naomi Shihab Nye

[1]Reference here to the Arab conquests during the Umayyad period which began forty years after the advent of Islam and continued for ninety-two years. During this flourishing period worldwide conquests were accomplished.
[2]I.e., You sell the land to the Jews and they make you rich.

'Abd al-Raheem 'Umar *(b. 1929)*

Born in the village of Jayyous near Tulkarm, on the West Bank, 'A. 'Umar now lives and works in Amman, Jordan, participating fully in its literary life and representing Jordan at many Arab conferences. He is one of Jordan's leading political commentators with daily columns in such Jordanian newspapers as *Al-Ra'y, Al-Dustur,* and *Al-Akhbar al-Urdiniyya,* and he has written six verse plays. He has published four collections of poetry, the most recent of which is *Songs of the Seventh Exodus* (1985).

Songs of the Seventh Exodus

What are you up to?
Now the passages have narrowed.
All that is left for you
is wilderness and your rendezvous
with death's dragging pulse.
No family to comfort you, no salvation, no horse
is heading your way:
only silence looms along the sky.

What are you up to?
The bitter choice is carved on the stone.
What does a man do when he can't
auction his love, his fragile dignity,
when the world teems with commerce
and the market with cunning eyes?

From "Sinbad Faces the Storm"

—translated by Sharif S. Elmusa and Naomi Shihab Nye

Plea

We journey
toward a tree standing tall,
toward a perfect oasis.
Fated to hope,
we cup the dew in our palms.
A brilliant light beams on our foreheads,
a flute orders our steps.
Still, the road is ribbed with fear.
Will this caravan ever settle?
Will our trek ever end?

—translated by Sharif Elmusa and Naomi Shihab Nye

From "The Siege"

The fathers would have built
a great wall between us and the road,
the waves of the vanquished sea
would have turned into stone,
had they known we'd become refugees.
Who could know our tents would be strewn
across the sands?

Long times passed, longer, long.
During nights of exile,
conquerors filed into our world.
Could our slender bodies ward them off?
Could we really have sung in such
interminable dark? We learned
the low hum of exile, nothing more.

Now Abel lies among ruins,
disintegrating, while a crow tells the tale
of a brother who killed his own.
Long times passed, longer, long
Conquerors filed past—
Kufr Qasim, Sabra, Shatilla.
And our own brothers, the ones

who speak our mother tongue,
had forsaken us.
Between the ocean and the gulf,
the gulf and the ocean,
between the weak and the strong,
the strong and the weak,
stretches the long arm of our siege.

—translated by Sharif S. Elmusa and Naomi Shihab Nye

Ghassan Zaqtan *(b. 1954)*

One of the finest young Palestinian poets, Zaqtan was born in Beit Jala, a village near Bethlehem. From 1960 until 1967 he lived in al-Karama refugee camp east of the Jordan river where he received his early education. In 1967 his family moved to Amman then to Rusaifa where he finished his secondary education and obtained the diploma of the Teachers Training College in Naʿur, Jordan. He then worked as a physical training teacher between 1973 and 1979 before moving to Beirut where he worked with organizations of Palestinian youths. In 1982 he had to leave Beirut in the Palestinian exodus and now works in Tunis as editor of the literary review, *Al-Bayadir*. A member of the Union of Jordanian writers, Zaqtan received its poetry award in 1977. He has published five collections, one of which *Old Reasons* was not distributed because of the Israeli invasion in 1982. Zaqtan has clearly transcended his immediate predecessors who led the course of modern Arabic poetry since the early fifties. He belongs to that group of young Arab poets (among whom there are many Palestinians) who show the authentic marks of a modernist outlook and technique. His poetry abounds with luminously dazzling, fresh imagery; it deals with sensitive subjects ranging from the universal themes of life and death to the particular themes that run through contemporary Arab life in general and Palestinian life in particular. He is included in PROTA's forthcoming anthology, *End of the Century Poets, New Voices in Arabic Poetry*.

Another Death

Prostrate in front of the door,
her corpse where she used to stand.
Remember her singing at night,
the glitter of her silver comb,
her knee that semaphored lightning
at us, like her glass rings;
her hennaed hair, the pagan motion of her head,
and her laugh in front of the door.
We knew the meaning of her hair bound or worn free,
as we cycled through the lamplit alley,
bells tinkling, horns blaring, her heart would dance . . .

(her head's supported by two paving stones.)
Her outstretched arms reached along the door,
five fingers, nails crested like scythes,
our confrontation with her cosmetics,
the fringe of her hair,
the perpetual awe with which she viewed the world,
and our wonder at the sight of her open shirt.
Useless to say, Good morning . . .
Your face and hands are cold.
. . . Good morning . . .
You will always be alone now.

Your journey is solitarty through the street,
without your glass rings, the flash of your knees.
Voices will build to a roar around you,
the torrent hidden in the rocks will growl,
the cars cruising the big market will scream,
and the boys' reflections will flash
in the windows as they run.
. . . . .
   . . . You will go out alone into the road,
without the keys to your rooms,
or your mother's advice,
and the road will open to your footsteps,
and on a sudden you'll surprise the river that shines
like a crystal thread suspended by a god.
. . . . .
   And as you pass, light will sleep in your hands,
the river finds the contours of your fingers,
the torrent will pool itself in your palms,
the rocks rest their foundations in your hands.
The place in the courtyard where you washed will shine.

You go by yourself down the road,
restoring the earth, melting the stubborn salt,
and you'll be shy; you were always shy.
Wind will bring fragrance from the ridge,
a stork cry overhead,
and the carrion crow will preside over all,
bringing us children from the streets,
as we follow it, shouting, rejoicing.

—translated by Lena Jayyusi and Jeremy Reed

An Incident

I saw a hand waving from the river,
it quivered before it disappeared,
wiped off something—a luminous trace of air,
scent of carnation.
The fingers continued to play, wavered,
drew desparate words on the surface,
grew tired, and went under.
How we rejoice alone,
while beneath the water,
there are sunken forests of desires—
the province of the losers.

—translated by Lena Jayyusi and Jeremy Reed

How Did They Inform on You?

How did words like lilies find your heart, 'Ali?
From what distances did you apprehend
their ringing echoes, as you bent, singing
like a bow of fire over the heat-dried mud,
between the jaws of noon and sunset?

From what distances did their ringing find you,
and despite the incandescent blaze of noon,
draw you to the festival's seething crowds,
your naked back glistening in the heat,
while the girls' eyes glittered, and a palm tree
flared in your soul, and shone through your clothes.

From where did that ringing come to you,
and the inspired note take hold of you?
Possessed, you would pull the wedding from its horns
towards the madness of your voice,
or make it dance on your shoulders like a well-trained bird,
interpreting the rhythm more leisurely
when fruit smells invaded from the river.

From where, and how, did they inform on you, 'Ali?
so that returning home, carried, washed, and in a shroud,

you looked embarrassed, exposed like the first field flower,
surrounded by an envelope of dust.

—translated by Lena Jayyusi and Jeremy Reed

A Mirror

Two faces loom in the catastrophe—
my father and his horse; a little moon
that we will capture sails above our house.
If only we could regain our childhood,
we'd imprison that moon a while between our hands,
and when our hearts opened, let it fly away.

—translated by Lena Jayyusi and Jeremy Reed

Tawfiq Zayyad *(b. 1932)*

Zayyad is a poet and a political writer. Educated in Nazareth and later in Moscow, where he studied Russian literature, he has worked in public life and struggled for the rights of the Palestinians in Israel through the Communist organization, Rakah. For several years he was the elected mayor of Nazareth, where he has been very influential. Apart from his translations from Russian literature and his translation of Nazim Hikmat's major works, he has himself published several collections of poetry, among which *Warmly I Shake Your Hands* (1966) is regarded as a landmark in the history of the Palestinian struggle against Israel. It includes many poems of courage and resistance, some of which have been adapted to music and have become part of the lively tradition of Palestinian songs of struggle.

Here We Shall Stay

As though we were twenty impossibilities
In Lydda, Ramla[1], and Galilee

Here we shall stay
Like a brick wall upon your breast
And in your throat
Like a splinter of glass, like spiky cactus
And in your eyes
A chaos of fire.

Here we shall stay
Like a wall upon your breast
Washing dishes in idle, buzzing bars
Pouring drinks for our overlords
Scrubbing floors in blackened kitchens
To snatch a crumb for our children
From between your blue fangs.

Here we shall stay
A hard wall on your breast.

[1]Lydda and Ramla are two towns between Jaffa and Jerusalem.

We hunger
Have no clothes
We defy
Sing our songs
Sweep the sick streets with our angry dances
Saturate the prisons with dignity and pride
Keep on making children
One revolutionary generation
After another
As though we were twenty impossibilities
In Lydda, Ramla and Galilee!

Here we shall stay.
Do your worst.
We guard the shade
Of olive and fig.
We blend ideas
Like yeast in dough.
Our nerves are packed with ice
And hellfire warms our hearts.

If we get thirsty
We'll squeeze the rocks.
If we get hungry
We'll eat dirt
And never leave.
Our blood is pure
But we shall not hoard it.
Our past lies before us
Our present inside us
Our future on our backs.
As though we were twenty impossibilities
In Lydda, Ramla and Galilee
O living roots hold fast
And—still—reach deep in the earth.

It is better for the oppressor
To correct his accounts
Before the pages riffle back
"To every deed . . ."—listen
To what the Book says.

—translated by Sharif Elmusa and Jack Collom

A Million Suns in my Blood

They stripped me of water and oil
And the salt of bread
The shining sun, the warm sea
The taste of knowledge
And a loved one who—twenty years ago—went off
Whom I wish (if only for an instant) to embrace.
They stripped me of everything
The threshold of my home
The flowerpots on the balcony.
They stripped me of everything
Except
A heart
A conscience
And a tongue!

In their chains, my pride
Is fiercer than all arrogant delirium.
In my blood a million suns
Defy a multitude of cruelties.
My love for you
You people of boundless tragedy
Lets me storm the seven heavens
For I am your son . . .
Your offspring
In heart
Conscience
And tongue!

Our hands are steady and enduring.
The hands of the oppressor
However hard
Tremble!

—translated by Sharif Elmusa and Jack Collom

What Next?

What next? . . .
I do not know.
All I know
Is that
The belly of space and time
Curves with child
That truth does not die
And usurpers cannot enslave it
That on this land of mine
Conquerors never lasted.

—translated by Sharif Elmusa and Jack Collom

Pagan Fires

At my ease
I pull a youthful shoot of light
From the field of night.
I tend the nursery of dreams
At the wells of abundance.
I wipe away the tears of my loved ones
With a cloth of jasmine
Plant the brightest, rarest oasis
Amid the burning sands
Build for poor bastards a life
Fragrant, good and just.
Should I stumble one day on the way
My roots will set me right!!
At my ease . . .
For I am not a match
Burning once, then dying . . .
I am like pagan fires.
I burn from cradle to grave.
I burn from my ancestors to the child invisible down the
    road.
Wide as the horizon is my breath.
I perfect the tiny industry of ants!!

At my ease . . .
For the function of history
Is to unfold as we will unfold
At the oppressors of this earth.
We have prepared an end.
We shall reward them
With that which they have preserved.
We give them enough rope
Not to prolong their sticklike lives
But to enable them
To build their own noose!

—translated by Sharif Elmusa and Jack Collom

All I Have

I never carried a rifle
on my shoulder
or pulled a trigger.
All I have
is a lute's melody
a brush to paint my dreams,
a bottle of ink.

All I have
is unshakeable faith
and an infinite love
for my people in pain.

—translated by Sharif Elmusa and Charles Doria

PALESTINIAN POETS
WRITING IN ENGLISH

Hanan Mikha'il 'Ashrawi

For her biography, please look under "Translators Biographies."

Metamorphosis

Ramallah, June 10, 1989

The Day Yasser was shot his mother turned
to stone; draped with the flag, his makeshift shroud,
she held her ground at the deserted town
square. Each chilly dawn she clutched a torch
of modest flowers—jasmine, daisies, and roses
from her garden—while bewildered soldiers
driving by, returning from their night shift, wondered
at the mist—clad apparition vaguely
reminiscent of a statue somewhere.

The Night before Raja was shot the lights
went out; his mother lit a lamp muttering
in anger at her superstitious fear
of omens. A hastily painted name on the Martyr's
Wall, next day, unraveled his substance before
her very eyes, and she reached out and touched his absence.
Carved out, hollowed/hallowed in her dark—filled womb
she turned and shed what little remained and calmly
transformed herself into a night vision.

Women and Things

Women make things grow:
Sometimes like the crocus,
surprised by rain, emerging fully
grown from the belly of earth;
Others like the palm tree with

its promise postponed
rising in a slow
deliberate
spiral to the sky.

Women make things light
afloat
like the breathless
flight of soap bubbles
shimmering in the eyes of a lone
child in a forbidden schoolyard;
And heavy
like the scent of
an overripe fruit
exploding at the
knowledge of summer-hardened
soil on days of siege.

Women make things smooth
to the touch
like the kneading of
leavened bread at the dawn of hunger;
And coarse
like the brush of a
homespun coat on
careworn shoulders and bare
arms barely touching on the night of deportation.

Women make things cold
sharp and hard
like a legal argument thrust
before the threat of search and detention;
Or warm
and gentle like
justice in a poem,
like the suggestion of
the image of freedom
as a warm bath and
a long soak, in an undemolished home.

Women make things

And as we, in separate
worlds, braid
our daughters' hair
in the morning, you and
I, each
humming to herself, suddenly
stops
and hears the
tune of the other.

Night Patrol
(An Israeli Soldier on the West Bank)

It's not the sudden hail
of stones, nor the mocking of
their jeers, but this deliberate
quiet in their eyes that
threatens to wrap itself
around my well-armed uniformed
presence and drag me into
depths of confrontation I
never dared to probe.

Their stares bounce off stone,
walls and amateur barricades, and
I'm forced to listen
to the echo of my own
gun fire and tear gas
grenades in the midst of
a deafening silence which
I could almost touch, almost
But not quite.
I refuse to be made
into a figment of my
own imagination. I catch
myself, at times, glimpsing
glimpsing the child I
was in one of them. That

same old recklessness, a daredevil
stance, a secret wisdom only
youth can impart as it hurtles
towards adulthood. Then I
begin to take substance before
my very eyes, and
shrink back in terror—as
an organism on its long
evolutionary trek recoils at the
touch of a human hand.

If I should once, just
once, grasp the elusive
end of the thread which
ties my being here with
their being there, I
could unravel the beginning . . . no,
no, it was not an act
of will that brought me
here, and I shall wrap myself in
fabric woven by hands
other than mine, perhaps
lie down and take a nap.

Should I admit then into
my hapless dreams a thousand
eyes, a thousand hands, and allow
unknowingly the night's
silence to conceal me, I
would have done no
more or less than what
thousands have done before, turning
over in sleep clutching my
cocoon of army issue blankets,
and hope for a different posting
in the morning.

June 1988

*In February 1988 Israeli soldiers buried alive four young men—
Isam Shafiq Ishtayyeh, Abdel-Latif Mahmoud Ishtayyeh, Muhsin
Hamdan, and Mustafa Abdel-Majeed Hamdan—from the village
of Salem, near Nablus. They were dug up and rescued by the
villagers after the soldiers had left.*

Death by Burial

This plot is not one
fit for planting.
Here the earth is
hard, dry, grating—
Needles of dead leaves
scratch.
I close my eyes, dust
chokes my throat,
I never knew earth
could be so heavy,
perhaps were I to
raise one arm
someone would come across
my grave one day, and,
as in late-night horror movies,
see a lifeless hand, an open palm,
fingers half-curled . . .
and scream.

I did not die that day—
Something else did
And it still lies in
that putrid grave
fermenting its knowledge of darkness.

June 1988

Rasha Houshiyye lost an eye in March 1988 when she was hit by a rubber bullet shot by an Israeli soldier. At the time, Rasha was standing on the balcony of her grandmother's house in Al-Bireh, near Ramallah. Then two children (both 9 months old) lost an eye in the same way. By the beginning of the 7th month of the intifada, *around 40 people had suffered the same fate.*

From the Diary of an Almost-Four-Year-Old

Tomorrow, the bandages
will come off. I wonder
will I see half an orange,
half an apple, half my
mother's face
with my one remaining eye?

I did not see the bullet
but felt its pain
exploding in my head.
His image did not
vanish, the soldier
with a big gun, unsteady
hands, and a look in
his eyes
I could not understand.

If I can see him so clearly
with my eyes closed,
it could be that inside our heads
we each have one spare set
of eyes
to make up for the ones we lose.

Next month, on my birthday,
I'll have a brand new glass eye,
maybe things will look round
and fat in the middle—
I've gazed through all my marbles,
they made the world look strange.

I hear a nine-month-old
has also lost an eye,
I wonder if my soldier
shot her too—a soldier
looking for little girls who
look him in the eye—
I'm old enough, almost four,
I've seen enough of life,
but she's just a baby
who didn't know any better.

June 1988

Sharif Elmusa

For his biography, please look under "Translators Biographies"

A Little Piece of Sky

Marvelling today at the Safeway's abundance
of tuna fish cans,
I thought of my friend Hussein.
He was the genius of the school.
He breathed in history, grammar, math
as easily as the dust of the camp.
He had a pyramid's core. Books
would've sprouted from his head,
but he had to live, and to live he
apprenticed with a carpenter,
and later on flew his skill to an oil country
where he made good as a contractor.

His father had been killed the spring he was born
in a familiar war that made us refugees
and tossed us on the moral map of the world.
His mother was a woman of meager means,
could look at a word for a year
and not recognize what it was.
And so it was:
poverty wagged him everyday.

One afternoon
I met him walking home from the store
holding, with his thumb and forefinger,
the upright lid of a half-opened
tuna fish can, humming a tune
about holding a little piece of sky.

In Balance[1]

(For my father)

I was powerless against you then—
you noticed only my violations.
Now we stand in balance
in the brass pans of the scale,
and I sit next to you,
marvel at how the sun baked your face
black, simple, tenacious,
and how from the good earth,
the earth you made good,
your heart grew tender
as the hands rough.

Father, this apricot tree so lush,
climbing madly toward the sky,
bears no apricots.
She must be infatuated with herself.
Father, the grapevine in Uncle's garden
speaks no grapes.
She must be in mourning
over his death, he planted her.
Father, why don't you like the city?
I like to look undistracted
at the sky, to see the face of God.

Camel Fragments

I love her
and she loves me
and my he-camel
loves her she-camel.
These most perfect love words
were said in Baghdad, 1200 years ago,

---

[1]Appeared in *Cedar Rock,* Spring 1985.

by Abu al-ʿAtahiya,[1] who knew
that words have their roots in the text
of the world, that a dog or cat
can't bear the honor of this verse.

In a vanishing tribe
the young woman tattoos her thighs
in a pattern like the brand
of her lover's camel.
She calls the act *binding*.
She shows him her tattoo
only in the nocturnal hour of *riding*,
when the membrane of being softens
and the five million doors
of the tamed body open
and they ride, not knowing
who's the rider and who's the mount.

Somedays I wonder what kind of karma
must I earn so the camel's soul
may migrate into mine. The camel labors
without fretting before mirrors
whose business is to mock.
He does not go about networking,
hiding his infirmities behind the veil
of a career. In his desert he thrives
on wild artichokes on cacti
on hard cabbage hearts.
His belly swells on all sides.
He curves his neck against gravity
not to gain perspective
not to curse or praise the gods
just for the freedom of the curve.
He strides with autonomous gait
as if the earth still feels his weight.

[1] Abu al-ʿAtahiya (748–828) was a medieval Arab poet who lived in Baghdad. He wrote
a spontaneous kind of poetry with a simplified diction and metaphor.

When Slippers Mingle

The Persian painter paints
a man and a woman
lying under a silk sheet
exchanging some intense
whispers.
He keeps their slippers
outside the frame, separate:
one pair in the lower left corner,
one in the lower right.

The Persian painter knows
that when a male's and female's slippers mingle
everyone loses interest.

The Beggar

My tools are a palm,
          a cupped wound,
and a trickle of words:
          frail, correct.
I haul them every morning
and claim them as my own.
For hours I repeat my refrain
and add up my sighs. When
I tire I stalk a bench
that can hold the weight
of a humbled man.

Sometimes I get lost
in the hum, the sway of the street,
and see a sky, blue and benign,
and feel I could act on the world,
clutch a briefcase in the shape of will,
my shoes firm, their soles
cantaloupe-colored, whole.
But soon the quest thwarts
my dark enchantment.

Why do I beg?
It could be politics or dice,
the drunkard father, or the mean street
that the green, hidden hand
doesn't touch.

But why do you turn away your eyes?
Are you afraid
your dole will go to booze?
Does my sight humble you,
remind you of life's
            precariousness?
I must live somehow.

Lena Jayyusi

For her biography, please look under "Translators Biographies."

Poem of Opposites

The Klezmer plays.
Later, on the small screen
    in the empty living room
    there is Beirut
    awash in bullets.
Mind heaves,
    the question burrows in
    finding no anchor.
What are they to each other
    musician and soldier
    the sweet clarinet
        and Beirut's ruins?

Month's end
    crescent's beginning
cycles ever circling
around our lives.
I saw the music player
    walk out of a low hut
    to stride across the sea
    to an olive-filled country
        that was mine
"I have prayed and wept for my people,"
    he said
"Why not you for yours
    what have they to do with me?
Mine is now to live
    whichever way
    bury my past
    in whatever fashion
        move on.
You and I are not of a kind."

I listened to Klezmer music.
Later, watched
    Shatila's dying
    on the screen
    in my silent living room.
Flinching mind spills over.
I saw the young woman
    dance with her lover
    then weep for her kin
    on the anniversary of Babi Yar
    but when I spoke to her
        at the airport
    leading to my country
she would not recognize my voice
led me
    to a separate room
        for questioning.
How is it the same fingers
    shape the melody
    can coldly wrap around a trigger
        point it at the heart?
Am I alone to hang
    on the pendulum of opposites?

The longing river winds on
    carrying more exiles across its hump
        each month
    feet travelling one way
    memory branching the other
        like a stubborn vine.
The music player still plays the Klezmer
    weeps
the young woman
    still dances
    points to her memories
    sometimes weeps
and they still guard
    the gateway of my country
        against me.

February 27, 1990

At the Limit

*On the events of my daughter's birth, three months early,
on March 11, 1982.*

It comes
> as they describe it
> glacier colliding with glacier
> in your vein
> storm-chill
> exploding in the limbs
> pain thrusting at the throat
> air resisting the windpipe
> the point of the knife still twisting
> in your womb.

It comes
> with the hum of machines and voices
> that reduce you to object size
> numerical dimensions
>> slicing up your life in segments
>>> kidney functions
>>> liver
>>> pulse
> the infinitesimally small
> casting you to an infinite friendlessness
> unfamiliar figures and sounds
> turning you stranger to all
> huge round light staring you into submission
> And what's the use of fighting it?

It comes
> riding on the hump
>> of other happenings
>> a trickster
>> taking you unaware
>> as you dream up the next day's small events
>> sort the minutes neatly into kinds
> and what's the point of fighting it?
>> the one thing you want to know
>> is hidden from you
> "Was it a boy, or a girl?"

What is this past tense
    that shatters hope's eardrum
    folding the long grey road
        into an accordian that plays from memory
        letters that will not be answered
        beginnings that hang shadowy
a simple word
    that turns the room
        a wastebasket of crumpled paper.

It comes
    unlooked for
        in the middle of the night
        as you turn inwards
        looking into dream
floods you
    like blood
        like placental waters.
Of all the things that flood
    fear in the wolfing hour
    longing that hacks your breast
    childhood's remembered hurts
this is the one that finally
        drowns you
        washing away even the debris
            of its trail.
September 4, 1987

Breadmother

The flour is measured
    its mound hollowed
She pours yeast-water
    to bring it to its age.

Plunges both hands in
    rubs substance and fluid together
    urges them to solidity.
A wrist begins to harden.

She kneads the pale mass
    presses into it
    ten hungry mouths look up
        from the imprint of her knuckles.
Punches, rolls, fights with the thing
turning it to her will
    pliant, smooth, elegant.
    The shoulder begins to stoop.

Leaves it to rest.
Divides it into equal measures, allots each
    its share of space on the darkened tray
        obedient rows
            waiting for her touch
Rolls each portion round
    and out
    a perfect circle
    zero to zero.
A line appears across her face.

Next thrusts each
    into the furnace
    burns it to an earthen gold
    the very stuff of life.
Her colours drained, only a fire-flush
    across her cheeks,
the eyes begin to dim.

And then,
        she starts again.
Is this what happened
        to the ancients?

December 6, 1983

Death of Enver

To My Mother

It is all over
I am sorry
The dawn has fled the night again

The night lies huddled in a polythene bag
The sun turns on itself, suspended in its heat.
It is all over;
only on the grey cement is there any movement
a faceless trickle running after itself.

All over.
Only in the grey silence is there any growth
The day flees from itself
The day scatters into the distances
The day has quietly exploded.

Wintering Alone

Wintering alone
 I walk the bleak steppes of imagining
brown-streaked snow cover
   of the field
     behind the house
       beckons
clumps of bush
 assertively rising
thin branches of a tree
 wearily fanning out.

Wintering alone
 my heart becomes
   this landscape behind the house
   seeps, bleeds into it
   lies bared beneath sky's cover
here I am—
 your woman, horizon
 of endless end
 graying over mind and body
encircled.
The years have taught me what to see,
 when to give in.

But
    there

        look
        a child goes tripping
        between the brown weeds
            over the graceless elevations of the field
        thinking of Christmas
            a handful of days away.

December 12, 1989

Aminah Kazak *(b. 1960)*

Born in Hamilton, New Zealand, Kazak now lives in Canberra, Australia. She studied in New Zealand and has a B.A. in political science. Her interests include painting, calligraphy, music, and languages.

Deportation

Before they came for me
I took my voice and hid it under the dawn
so they found only my bleeding mouth, my broken
    hands, my eyes empty of vision

They traveled
to every corner of my country,
frustration building
The sound of my voice split their heads like thunder,
my agony pumped through their veins

Later they took my bleeding mouth, my broken hands,
    my eyes empty of vision
and threw them past the horizon
So I left them with a voice
singing its song of love for my country
which they will never understand
never embrace and never possess.

My Last Day with Aisha

All I can remember now are the words we didn't speak
The winds tossed them high into the night sky
And the moon sat counting the stars
You had so much to say, but the silence deafened us
We sat, stilled by pain
and watched Jerusalem bury her children.

I laid my hand on the small grave and let fall a single tear
Small as it was we both noticed it
I wrapped the sparrow's broken wings and bloodied
     head in my muslin scarf,
and turned it to face Mecca
As the call of the *muezzin* broke on the shore of Jerusalem's grief.

Unlike the sparrow now silent and still
you had never been free to return
in that night's dark loneliness
You laid your aching body upon the horizon
letting your love of Palestine ignite the sky.

All I remember now are the words we didn't speak
The winds tossed them high into the heavens
and the moon sat counting the stars.

Naomi Shihab Nye

For her biography, please look under "Translators Biographies."

My Father and the Fig Tree

For other fruits my father was indifferent.
He'd point at the cherry trees and say,
"See those? I wish they were figs."
In the evenings he sat by my bed
weaving folktales like vivid little scarves.
They always involved a fig tree.
Even when it didn't fit, he'd stick it in.
Once Joha was walking down the road and he saw a fig tree.
Or, he tied his camel to a fig tree and went to sleep.
Or, later when they caught and arrested him,
his pockets were full of figs.

At age six I ate a dried fig and shrugged.
"That's not what I'm talking about!" he said,
"I'm talking about a fig straight from the earth—
gift of Allah!—on a branch so heavy it touches the ground.
I'm talking about picking the largest fattest sweetest fig
in the world and putting it in my mouth."
(Here he'd stop and close his eyes.)

Years passed, we lived in many houses, none had fig trees.
We had lima beans, zucchini, parsley, beets.
"Plant one!" my mother said, but my father never did.
He tended garden half-heartedly, forgot to water,
let the okra get too big.
"What a dreamer he is. Look how many things he starts
and doesn't finish."

The last time he moved, I got a phone call.
My father, in Arabic, chanting a song I'd never heard.
"What's that?" I said.
"Wait till you see!"

He took me out back to the new yard.
There, in the middle of Dallas, Texas,
a tree with the largest, fattest, sweetest figs in the world.
"It's a fig tree song!" he said,
plucking his fruits like ripe tokens,
emblems, assurance
of a world that was always his own.

Shrines

Only the bleat of a terrified ram broke the stillness
that hung over the camp as I walked among the
remains of so many lives.

—Walter Wisniewski
  Sabra Camp, Lebanon.

We cannot build enough shrines.
My friend's hands tremble
as he unfolds his poem about Lebanon,
the bomb planted on his uncle's farm.
Newspaper chats: "A plastic bag
of flat Arabic bread lay on the gravel
along with the contents of El-Burgi's pockets."
For a moment, there is no light
at the end of anywhere.

How we go on being mild-mannered,
speaking of restaurants and movies,
is the worst miracle of the modern age.
Courage! To answer the woman in Berkeley
who said, "They deserve it,"
to find words where words don't live,
in the blaze of anger, the ram's long tear.

If we light candles, we must light a million.
Lebanon, Salvador, Palestine, here.
If we bow in remembrance
we must weld our lives
to the earth which holds us so briefly
chanting, this, for those, who had less than that.

Blood

"A true Arab knows how to catch a fly in his hands,"
my father would say. And he'd prove it,
cupping the buzzer instantly
while the host with the swatter stared.

In the spring our palms peeled like snakes.
True Arabs believed watermelon could heal fifty ways.
I changed these to fit the occasion.

Years before, a girl knocked,
wanted to see the Arab.
I said we didn't have one.
After that, my father told me who he was,
"Shihab"—"shooting star"—
a good name, borrowed from the sky.
Once I said, "When we die, we give it back?"
He said that's what a true Arab would say.

Today the headlines clot in my blood.
A little Palestinian dangles a truck on the front page.
Homeless fig, this tragedy with a terrible root
is too big for us. What flag can we wave?
I wave the flag of stone and seed,
table mat stitched in blue.

I call my father, we talk around the news.
It is too much for him,
neither of his two languages can reach it.
I drive into the country to find sheep, cows,
to plead with the air:
Who calls anyone *civilized*?
Where can the crying heart graze?
What does a true Arab do now?

Arabic Coffee

It was never too strong for us:
make it blacker, Papa,
thick in the bottom,

tell again how the years will gather
in small white cups,
how luck lives in a spot of grounds.

Leaning over the stove, he let it
boil to the top, and down again.
Two times. No sugar in his pot.
And the place where men and women
break off from one another
was not present in that room.
The hundred disappointments,
fire swallowing olive-wood beads
at the warehouse, and the dreams
tucked like pocket handkerchiefs
into each day, took their places
on the table, near the half-empty
dish of corn. And none was
more important than the others,
and all were guests. When
he carried the tray into the room,
high and balanced in his hands,
it was an offering to all of them,
stay, be seated, follow the talk
wherever it goes. The coffee was
the center of the flower.
Like clothes on a line saying
you will live long enough to wear me,
a motion of faith. There is this,
and there is more.

The Words under the Words
(For Sitti Khadra, north of Jerusalem)

My grandmother's hands recognize grapes,
the damp shine of a goat's new skin.
When I was sick they followed me,
I woke from the long fever to find them
covering my head like cool prayers.

My grandmother's days are made of bread,
a round pat-pat and the slow baking.
She waits by the oven watching a strange car
circle the streets. Maybe it holds her son,
lost to America. More often, tourists,
who kneel and weep at mysterious shrines.
She knows how often mail arrives,
how rarely there is a letter.
When one comes, she announces it, a miracle,
listening to it read again and again
in the dim evening light.

My grandmother's voice says nothing can surprise her.
Take her the shotgun wound and the crippled baby.
She knows the spaces we travel through,
the messages we cannot send—our voices are short
and would get lost on the journey.
Farewell to the husband's coat,
the ones she has loved and nourished,
who fly from her like seeds into a deep sky.
They will plant themselves. We will all die.

My grandmother's eyes say Allah is everywhere, even in death.
When she talks of the orchard and the new olive press,
when she tells the stories of Joha and his foolish wisdoms,
He is her first thought, what she really thinks of His name.
"Answer, if you hear the words under the words—
otherwise it is just a world with a lot of rough edges,
difficult to get through, and our pockets full of stones."

My Uncle Mohammed at Mecca, 1981

This year the wheels of cars
are stronger than the wheels of prayer.
Where were you standing when it hit you,
what blue dome rose up in your heart?

I hold the birds you sent me,
olive wood clumsily carved.
The only thing I have
that you touched.

Why is it so many singulars
attend your name? You lived on one mountain,
sent one gift. You went on one journey
and didn't come home.

We search for the verb
that keeps a man complete.
To resign, to disappear, that's how
I've explained you.

Now I want to believe it was true.
Because you lived apart,
we hold you up. Because no word connected us,
we complete your sentence.

And the house with wind in the windows
instead of curtains
is the house we are building
in the cities of the world.

Uncle of sadness, this is the last pretense:
you understood the world was no pilgrim,
and were brave, and wise,
and wanted to die.

Fawaz Turki *(b. 1940)*

Born in Haifa, Palestine, Fawaz Turki is a poet, and the author of fine prose accounts of his life as a Palestinian in exile and the lives of other Palestinians. He has published several books in English, including his autobiographical accounts *The Disinherited: Journey of a Palestinian Exile* (1972) and *Soul in Exile* (1988). His book of prose poetry, *Tel Zaatar Was the Hill of Thyme,* was published in 1978. He has read at several poetry forums in the United States and other countries, and his work has appeared in a number of poetry journals. In the United States, where he now lives, Turki has been active on behalf of the Palestinian cause, a writer-in-residence at the Virginia Center for the Creative Arts, a professor at the State University of New York in Buffalo, and a frequent speaker at conferences and panels dealing with the Middle East and Third World Poetics. Since 1987 he has devoted himself exclusively to his writing.

The Seed Keepers

A Recital

Burn our land
burn our dream
pour acid onto our songs
cover with sawdust
the blood of our massacred people
muffle with your technology
the screams of our imprisoned patriots,
destroy,
destroy
our grass and soil
raze to the ground
every farm and every village
our ancestors had built,
destroy every city and every town
every tree and every home
every book and every law,
flatten with your bombs

every valley,
erase with your edicts
our past
our literature
our metaphor,
denude the forests
and the earth
till no insect
no word
can find a place to hide.
Do that and more,
I do not fear your tyranny.
I guard one seed
of a tree
my forefathers have saved
that I shall plant again
in my homeland.

Beirut

Beirut is a dead rat
lying motionless
in the pocket of the Third World
speaking with a heavy French accent
as she pronounces her Arabic ownhood.
In the river beds of affluence
the waters have dried up
and disinherited selfhood
walks in rags
looking for a Western wedding to attend.
At night she goes to the casino
to place her bets on the roulette table
using a fistful of classified ads
from *France Soir*.
At night she returns home,
to her pocket,
and the darkness frightens her
as she drives

on Artificial Road
where the mirage of a mule appears
and she runs her car off a cliff.

Dusk in Galilee

On Request

A feast of colors
is the sunset in Galilee,
a silent orgy
in the horizon of our
West Bank,
silver grey stars
quivering in the sky
speeding to hug one another
body and soul
like erotic grapes of sorrow,
the wind
and the desolate music
of the *oud*
are a theater of sounds
on the west bank
of our ancient river
and the evening will unfurl
exquisite delights
in Galilee.
The military governor
tells his guests
all this has come to pass
because he issued an edict
and his soldiers used their guns
to make it so.

Osama Jibril of Jerusalem

As he played backgammon
in the side street cafe
in the back streets of Jerusalem,
where he felt safe,
because our culture had pierced
the walls of the Dome,
our music hung in the air,
our *muezzin* bespoke of history,
our workers
(begrimed by the work they had done
for our oppressors)
were home—
the military governor
issued an edict
for the arrest of Osama Jibril.
I am afraid
he said,
to return to that savage abyss
of dark night.
But before I feel the blows
of your whips,
before I feel the dampness
of your dungeons,
before I feel the crush
of your torture,
before I am cowed
by your threats,
I want to tell you
that you can not wrest from us
the blood of our martyrs,
the vision of our patriots,
the memory of our homeland.
We will resume our journey
muttering cruel prayers
and drinking rain.

In Search of Yacove Eved

Yacove Eved was an Israeli.
In the summer
Yacove Eved always sat on the rocks
in the park at Mount Carmel.
Yacove Eved loved the harbor
and the boats
and the colors as the sun
set in the horizon.
Whenever I saw Yacove Eved on the rocks
whenever I passed him in the park
I always said
Salaams Yacove
and Yacove Eved
always waved both his arms
and said *Shalom Shaaer.*
Yacove Eved is like me
he knows all the stabbed dreams
all the ones who died
and who now keep company
with their gods,
so Yacove Eved and I
we sit and talk about this
and we watch the harbor.
Sometimes Yacove Eved
sees me at the port
fishing for the sunken images
and Yacove Eved says *Salaam Shaaer*
and I say *Shalom Yacove.*
Yacove is like me
he knows all the lonely travellers
all the ones who never returned
whose ships are lost at sea.
Now I do not know where
Yacove Eved is
and I do not know where to find him.
I have never known anyone
by that name
but these verses are for him.

PROSE

Short Stories

Ibrahim al-ʿAbsi *(b. 1945)*

Al-ʿAbsi was born in the village of Dawaima in the district of Hebron, but grew up in the refugee camps of Jericho, where he gained his primary and secondary education. He then joined the Teacher Training Institute in Huwwara near Irbid, graduating in 1968. From 1968 to 1989 he worked as a teacher in Jordan and is now the cultural editor of the Jordanian paper *Saut al-Shaʿb*. He participates fully in the literary life of Jordan and has been to many literary conferences in the Arab world. Al-ʿAbsi writes skillfully about the misery of life in the refugee camps, describing its harsh conditions and cruel deprivations. He has so far published two collections of short stories, *The Grey Rain* (1977) and *The Third Choice* (1981), and was awarded the M.S. Irani Prize for the Short Story in Jordan in 1985.

What Happened After Midnight

"Shaikh Hamid, it's ten o'clock now," Abu Alush was saying. "You have to make your nightly rounds."

Breathing heavily, his mouth wide open, Shaikh Hamid was dozing off on a cane chair by the door of the large shop. As Abu Alush's voice reached his ears, he moved sluggishly in his chair. When he opened his eyes slightly, he was surprised to find that the men had already gone from their evening get-together. Only Abu Alush was left, sitting across from him and smoking with relish a hand-rolled cigarette while he listened to the small radio that lay at the shop's entrance.

Shaikh Hamid felt around in his pants pocket and took out a round yellow watch. He brought it close to his eyes.

"It's ten o'clock sharp," he murmured. Then he uttered a long sigh and put the watch back into his pocket. He gazed at a beam of light that was coming from inside the shop, stretching out across the dusty outside porch.

"I swear, they're lying!" Abu Alush said irritably. "The news is a bunch of lies! The UN is lying, and no one cares about us!"

Immediately the chair beneath Shaikh Hamid began to tremble. He kept his eyes on Abu Alush's face. Soon Abu Alush stood, picked up the small radio, and went inside.

"Get up, Shaikh Hamid, and trust in God," he said.

Shaikh Hamid felt uneasy. As he bent down to pick up the thick stick that was lying near his feet, anxieties grew inside him; Abu Alush's voice seemed calm enough as he went inside the shop, but he was quite capable of flaring up or calming down in a matter of minutes.

"Be watchful, Shaikh Hamid. Nights are long in the summer, and the camp is full of thieves. Bear in mind that the warehouse is stacked to the ceiling with rations, and that tomorrow distribution begins."

Shaikh Hamid was about to say something; however, bitter in his frustration, he stood there with his eyes lowered, looking at the ground beneath his feet. It was not long before he rose and passed through the beam of light and into the dark street.

When the camp overseer said, "Shaikh Hamid, I have chosen you to be the warehouse watchman," Shaikh Hamid's face went blank. For a moment he'd stayed staring bewilderedly at the overseer's face.

After recovering from his astonishment, he was about to tell the overseer that he was too old and too physically frail to stay up late at night. The overseer had patted him on the shoulder, and Shaikh Hamid had not said a word.

To himself he said, "Surely, the camp overseer must be deluded; I'm not competent for such a job." However, after he remained silent for a little while, his imagination began to resound with the ring of the ten dinars he was to receive at the end of every month . . .

Shaikh Hamid paused near the whitewashed building that stood in a corner of the camp. Catching his breath, he peered into the faded gray night that covered the camp. From a distance the camp's shacks looked like strange plants growing in a desert.

"May God's curse fall on these times!" he said, feeling sunk in despair.

Then he went on, quickly and cautiously walking around the chalky building.

The shacks of the camp looked asleep, drowned in deep silence. From a corner came the strained barking of a dog, and a black column of smoke was rising from the camp's incinerator.

That morning, the camp overseer had said to him, "Be careful, Shaikh Hamid, don't let me down. The warehouse is full of supplies. You must remain fully awake."

Idris, the camp policeman, laughed, saying, "Shaikh Hamid is the Lion of the Night! Don't worry—I'll stop by every now and then."

Despite the warmth of the evening and the heat from the ground, Shaikh Hamid was shivering all over with cold. He stood with his back against the wall, grinding his teeth. Then he began to sing an old folksong; sadly, with feeling, he sang it over and over in the stillness of the night.

It was midnight when he heard a voice screaming, "Shaikh Hamid!"
Quickly grabbing his stick, he sprang away from the wall.
"Who's there?" he shouted, trying to make his voice sound as hoarse and as harsh as possible.
Idris' voice came insinuating into his ears; it was as hoarse as a dog's bark: "You're a lion, Shaikh Hamid."
In anger, Shaikh Hamid spat and closed his eyes irritably, while his veins throbbed rapidly and violently. When he'd calmed down, Idris' footsteps were fading in the silence of the night. He suddenly felt fatigue in his limbs. He slipped down to the ground and stretched out his legs in front of him.

After midnight a cold wind rose in the dirt roads, followed by some loud noises which quickly died down. Shaikh Hamid was puzzled by the sudden, unexpected, blowing wind and the noises. He listened carefully but could not distinguish anything out of the ordinary, so he let his head droop and closed his eyes.
The moment his grip on the stick relaxed and hot, troubled breaths were coming out of his mouth, the drone of a car's engine came from a distance. Like the buzzing of a bee, the car's droning pierced his ears and made his eyelids tremble rapidly. But when he tried to open his eyes they were too sticky to open.
"It must be a truck on the road," he whispered.
But the roar of the car was getting closer to him, and a beam of bright light pierced the darkness. At that moment, Shaikh Hamid stirred and grabbed his stick.
"Who's there?" he shouted, in a strained and feeble voice.
Immediately the car's roaring ceased, and the light vanished. As the place became drenched in heavy silence, there was a feeble smile on Shaikh Hamid's face, and he said, faintly, "The truck must have gone away . . ."
Then he closed his eyes again.
A few moments later, loud, noisy movements began to grow around him. He could make out the stamping of feet and a faint, rapid whispering that sounded like it was coming from a defective cassette player.

Soon afterwards a distinct, familiar smell pervaded the area: it was the smell of flour in the air!

Immediately Shaikh Hamid stood up.

"Who's there?" he shouted.

Through the darkness he could see men running and disappearing into the building. He picked up his stick and screamed, "You! Stop there!"

He heard a soft and distinct laugh, which he was well acquainted with. He froze on the spot; cold shivers ran down his back. At that instant, his hold on the stick weakened, and he said in a feeble voice, "The overseer! It can't be!"

In the morning Shaikh Hamid was in a white bed, covered with a white blanket. As he stared at the people around him, there was an expression of blankness on his face.

When he saw the overseer's face, and Idris standing next to him, he shuddered and opened his mouth to scream, but the sounds would not come.

"The poor man's gone senile," the overseer said.

—translated by Admer Gouryh and Thomas G. Ezzy

Salih Abu Usba' *(b. 1946)*

Short story writer, scholar, and critic, Abu Usba' obtained a Ph.D. in literary criticism and comparative literature from Cairo University in 1977, and worked as a lecturer on Arab literary criticism first at the al-Fatih University in Tripoli, Libya, then at the al-Ain University in the United Arab Emirates. He then left teaching in order to direct the Arab Institute for Literary and Artistic Output, a pan-Arab institution based in Rabat, Morocco. His collections of short stories include *Naked on the River* (1972), *The Trial of the Tall Man* (1974), and *The Princess of Water* (1977). He has published three books of criticism: *Palestine in the Arabic Novel* (1975), *Readings in Literature* (1978), and *Palestinian Poetry* (1979).

Mirage

'Abd al-Mawla was driving alone in the desert when his engine stalled. Utterly inexperienced, he pretended to try to fix it. At his wits' end, he climbed back inside and rested his head on the steering wheel for support, dozing off briefly. Suddenly his head sent out a blast from the horn and he started up in alarm, shouting as if someone were present: "Who do you think you are? Why do you stand there like an idiot, singing children's songs, what is this?"

'Abd al-Mawla was furious.

"Why all this exuberance?? I want my car to start, but you stand there pleased, gloating over my misfortune . . . Tell me what you want! I don't find you funny!"

He thought that throughout its entire existence the desert itself has never been the final goal of any traveler, even of one as frustrated as him.

What brought you to anchor in this wretched harbor, 'Abd al-Mawla? What terrible luck placed you in the desert's gaping mouth that swallows camels, cars, and people? What fate is it that casts you in this desert with a madman . . . ?

The madman stood bewildered outside the car. 'Abd al-Mawla imagined that he had never ridden in a car before, so it fascinated him. He was circling it, feeling its sleek dark roof, but the blazing metal burned his hand and he went back to staring at the windows, then staring through them . . .

'Abd al-Mawla watched him in silence . . . After his frustrating episode attempting to fix the car, he felt exhausted. He sat behind the steering wheel wondering if anything would turn up.

"Why are you looking at me like that?"

Having shouted this loudly and resolutely, 'Abd al-Mawla rubbed his eyes. The scene before him shimmered like the last shadows before sunrise. Watching him closely, 'Abd al-Mawla closed the car windows.

What will you do, 'Abd al-Mawla, if this stranger sees something that appeals to him and wants to get hold of it? What if he does something stupid? Will you defend yourself to the death? What death are you speaking of? Isn't your life a living death every day? Do you consider this living? You live in the desert leaving your family thousands of miles away; alone in the desert you pile one piastre on top of another . . . And when you return to your village, the simple inhabitants think you are a millionaire! But if they knew how you save your piastres, one by one; ah, if they only knew! . . . Then they'd realize that you are a corpse inside a living body.

"Look! look!"

The man beat loudly on the car windows. 'Abd al-Mawla imagined his pounding might shatter the glass. His face seemed infantile and distressed, his thick lips parched, and he panted as if he had run nonstop for many miles . . .

Suddenly, he grew taller, his eyes bulged, and his lips hung down. *How can I win him over?* 'Abd al-Mawla smiled and reached for the thermos of water . . . *Perhaps he's thirsty* . . . he was thinking. He opened the car door and the man lunged forward. Without waiting for an invitation, he began gulping the water . . . *How thirsty he is!!*

'Abd al-Mawla gave him some biscuits from a tin he had with him, and the man devoured them instantly . . . *How hungry he is!!*

His facial expression changed and his body shrank to its normal height. Even his eyes and lips resumed their natural looks.

'Abd al-Mawla wondered, *Have I misjudged him? Perhaps he isn't evil, or a criminal, or a highway robber* . . .

"What's your name?" he asked him.

The man laughed long, then began singing some cheerful children's songs. 'Abd al-Mawla wondered, *How can I communicate with him?*

"Do you want some water?"

He shook his head no.

"Do you want to eat, then?"

Again he shook his head no.

"Where do you live?"

He motioned with one hand to make 'Abd al-Mawla understand he inhabited the whole universe.

"Do you want to get in the car with me?"

For this 'Abd al-Mawla received no answer. The man simply climbed in onto the seat.

"It is hot in this desert . . ."

He nodded his head in agreement.

"Are you married?"

The movement of his head did not tell 'Abd al-Mawla anything.

'Abd al-Mawla tried to light a cigarette, but with someone watching he felt too clumsy. The man picked the radio transistor, fiddled with the dial, bringing in some distant news. He listened with such concentration that 'Abd al-Mawla asked; "Do you understand?"

He nodded and 'Abd al-Mawla realized, then, that he was an Arab like him. *If this man would just speak . . . All he knows is children's songs and how to shake his head; what world has he come from? Does this desert that swallows a man swallow their tongues too?*

"As you can see, my car's broken down," 'Abd al-Mawla said.

. . .

"I can't understand why it stalled."

. . .

Still no answer. But 'Abd al-Mawla decided to keep talking to him.

"Do many cars pass through these parts? I work for a big company, it's well respected. I have some money . . . These desert journeys are really exhausting . . . but I make them anyway . . . Life isn't easy, is it?" Still the man said nothing.

'Abd al-Mawla reached out for some biscuits and began devouring them one after the other.

"Won't you have one?"

The man neither answered nor moved.

"I'm starting to feel dizzy . . . All these endless hours in the faceless desert! If it weren't for this radio, I'd feel completely cut off from the world" . . .

"My family lives a long way from here . . . My father told me I should always be polite to people I don't know."

. . .

"My father taught me that, do you hear!" 'Abd al-Mawla was almost screaming now.

. . .

"My father taught me it's good manners to answer when someone asks you a question!"

. . .

"I'm speaking to you! Don't make me lose my self-control . . . Speak to me like I'm speaking to you!"

'Abd al-Mawla raged; his nerves felt shattered; night was enclosing him and he could neither see nor hear anything. His brain rambled, *The water won't last for days, nor will the biscuits sustain me for long . . . From where will my deliverance come in this desert's gaping mouth? Won't it swallow up those who are searching for me too?*

Thinking he might inspire some thread of hope if he wandered about, 'Abd al-Mawla climbed out of the car and began stumbling through the darkness. He raced east, west, north, and south. He ran in swift desperate circles, returning to his car worn out. Throwing himself behind the steering wheel again, he went on talking: "Did you see how tired I became? Aren't you going to guide me to someone? . . . Why don't you speak?"

He turned on the radio . . . An enchanting melody flowed out to his ears, launching his imagination . . . He was holding a gorgeous young girl in his arms; they danced and teased and ran toward the sea . . . She was splashing water on him as he splashed it back on her . . . They raced each other, they laughed, they plunged into the sea together, they drank cold drinks under a sunshade, they built sand castles, sand, sand, and now here he was, drowning in sand. He awoke from his reverie when the music stopped suddenly, and a broadcaster's hoarse voice interrupted: "Missing in the desert is 'Abd al-Mawla Muhsin. 'Abd al-Mawla traveled alone on a regular assignment into the desert and . . ." The announcer did not say that the desert had swallowed him. The voice continued: "Search for him is being carried on by helicopter, over an area of one hundred square miles . . ."

'Abd al-Mawla exclaimed joyfully: "They're searching for you, 'Abd al-Mawla; they're searching for you, do you hear? East, west, north, and south."

His feet felt worn out, his whole body fatigued. Hearing a noise off in the distance, he realized the rescuers had arrived. He thought of his family. He thought of the beautiful girl running into the sea and the sand castles they had built together . . .

With a sudden start he realized the one who had been with him had vanished!

"Where are you; where are you?" he called out. "Come back! Where are your childish songs? Where's your joyful, mad face? They're coming to save me!"

But no-one answered ʿAbd al-Mawla . . . His voice echoed out into the vastness of the desert. He stared hard for the stranger but could detect no trace of him. "He has melted away," he said.

He looked down to see his water spilled onto the car floor and his biscuits crumbled . . .

He slumped on the seat . . . The roar of the plane's engine grew closer, but ʿAbd al-Mawla heard nothing at the time.

—translated by Olive Kenny and Naomi Shihab Nye

Ghareeb 'Asqalani *(b. 1948)*

Novelist and short story writer 'Asqalani was born in Majdal 'Asqalan in the south of Palestine. He now lives in Gaza, where his family was forced to move because of Israeli occupation in 1948, when 'Asqalani was an infant. He grew up in one of the Gaza refugee camps and his early education took place in the camp's schools. After pursuing his secondary education in Gaza, he went to Egypt and obtained a B.S. in agricultural engineering from the University of Alexandria in 1969 and a Higher Studies diploma from the Institute of Islamic Studies in Cairo in 1983. He worked for some time as an agricultural engineer in Syria before returning home to Gaza. His short stories have been published in various prestigious Palestinian and Arab magazines. His first collection of short stories, *Breaking the Silence*, appeared in 1979 and his second, *The Alphabet of Death*, in 1987. His first novel, *The Overflow*, was published in 1979 and his second, *Time of Vigilance*, in 1987. He has also done great service to Palestinian literature produced in the Occupied Territories by collecting and publishing two anthologies of Palestinian short stories, the first appearing in 1977 and the second in 1982.

Hunger

Sa'id adjusted his headdress until nothing of his face was visible but his eyes which were filled with worry and anger. He sighed bitterly, and clenched his teeth to keep his agonized exhalation from reaching the face of his wife, who was standing beside him and urging him to hurry up.

All last week he had made an effort to leave home before dawn like the others, but at the last minute he would kick the door angrily, throw down the packed lunch his wife had prepared for him, and go straight back to bed, to wake up only at the redness of noon. His wife did not realize he was rolling on hot coals that were burning all his insides. Today he had no alternative but to go. He had resisted greatly; he had hoped to find some solution for hunger, but it was biting hard.

Already he had sold all his wife's jewelry, and his own few personal possessions had passed into the hands of others in return for a few liras. These had staved off hunger for several days only; afterwards, the screams of his children began to pierce his veins, and he ran out, in a mad frenzy, to look for a job in the city. But the city had been busy with its own affairs and many more workers were offering their services than there was work available. He had dragged his feet from one store to the next and had been repeatedly turned down.

To the usual question came the usual answer: "What do you do?"

"I don't have a specific skill, but . . ."

Their looks of sarcasm pierced him and kept him from going on, while their smirking lips hastened to say, "Sorry, but we don't have anything that will suit you."

"Sirs, any job will do."

"What we pay is too little. It won't be enough."

"I'll take anything—just anything."

They fell silent, and deep down he knew that there was no hope of a job; but still he stood there, mesmerized, until the answer hit him: "We don't have any jobs."

Some of them would go further, saying with distaste and condescension, "Why don't you work in *Israel?*"

While others, if there was any room for teasing, would toy with him sarcastically: "What is your profession, young man?"

My profession! God! If only you knew what my profession is! . . . It isn't something you'd be able to do! You scoundrels, I've practiced it to the marrow of my bones! I've left all traces of it behind the bars.

And he would disappear, disappear to far beyond the bars.

There you left them, making the future. You have been released out into the sunlight, to let hunger get its grip on you and to find the world turning its back on you. If only my comrades knew! There, all matters were studied with precision; duties, both immediate and long term, had been assigned, and a full program had been prepared. Boycotting work in Israel had been a basic and most urgent issue. But there had been other issues that they had not been willing to stop and consider in depth.

He flailed the air angrily, for his thoughts had touched off anew the sadness and bitterness in him.

Behind the walls, the meals, meager as they were, had come with regularity, so that one did not notice them any more. As days went by, classes and lectures were given constantly; discussions grew heated, voices grew loud, drowning out the screams of the children and the fatigue of the wives and mothers outside. For a beautiful tomorrow was a brighter prospect than all the bread one could get. One day you could come out into the sunlight with expectations.

The law of hungry days requires this, in order to keep the smiles on the children's faces, for a child's smile is a pressing matter always . . . And your beautiful city winks at you whenever it sets eyes on you. Others rush to it, glutting it with kisses and deceit and money. All along the roads, your footprints are guns and bombs and shrapnel. Today your first steps search for bread and distract themselves with hatred for those who love your shameless city, their own hypocrisy. And here you are, tightening the kufiyya *around your face for fear that people might recognize you. At any rate, the issue is simple. The queue of workers will only get longer by one today, you will be given a job in a factory or a brothel, what's the difference? The penny you earn will be blended with the filth of the whole world. But the children's cries will quiet down, the hardened tears of the bereaved wife will flow down her cheeks, in thanks.*

"Rely on God, Sa'id. You're neither the first nor the last."

He came back to reality as he heard his wife's apprehensive voice. He patted her shoulder lightly and kissed her sad eyes. "I'll be going today, my dear, for I'm not—" And he went away quickly, fearing that she might feel a tear falling on his tightened cheeks.

The car dropped him at the Majdal intersection. Mastering his emotions, he joined the other workers. He observed the various physiques and ages of the men, and tried to assess how sleepy and how much in need of rest they were. He was surprised to hear some of the younger men laughing, but was stunned and taken aback by the worry and misery he could see dwelling inside them, deep as their inmost cells. . . . Then he saw them rush towards a car—a Peugeot—that was slowing down close by. He heard several voices calling, "Shlomo! . . . Shlomo! . . ."

This spectacle absorbed him. He looked around and met the eyes of an old, slender man standing beside him.

His direct look encouraged the old man to ask, "Why aren't you rushing like the others?" Then he added, trying to make his question sound more appealing, "With Shlomo, you might be lucky."

"Who is Shlomo?"

"A contractor, who chooses the stronger ones to carry stones and bags of cement."

He understood that his muscles made him a candidate for such a job, and did not feel like pursuing the conversation any further. To cut it short, he said, "A man's fate is decided by chance."

He was struck by the man's confident reply: "God expects you to do the seeking. He'll do the guiding."

A volcano erupted inside him. Was this what God meant by "seeking"? How miserable it was, when a person became a slave, displaying himself to be sold on pavements! He stood watching the flow of slaves as they surrounded the man, who was getting out of his car, his lips in constant motion around a huge pipe.

Through snake-like coils of pipe smoke, which was blown into the defeated faces and which the warm morning rays broke up as soon as it hit it, the man inspected them.

As the man was scrutinizing their faces, his eyes and Saʿid's met for a moment. Saʿid looked back defiantly, opening his eyes as wide as he could and staring into nothingness. He didn't notice the gesture the contractor made to him as well as to some of the others who hurried over to the car. He felt the old man nudge him.

"Hurry up! What's wrong with you? Are you in a different world?"

"What are you saying?"

"The *khawaja*[1] has signaled you to go."

He looked incredulous, but the old man urged him sympathetically.

"Go on, son . . . You might not find another job today."

He followed and threw himself into the back seat of the car, where he found himself squeezed in among men and objects. He felt the smallness of the place. He took off his headdress and felt the urge to smoke. From inside the spirals of smoke he started watching things, oblivious to the men around him. He avoided looking at them as the car cut its way to its destination—the job, about which he knew neither where it was nor how long it would take to get there. Together with his cigarette, he lost all awareness until the car entered the construction site and slowed down close to the skeleton of a building.

The workers jumped out of the car, and some of them started unloading the equipment. Saʿid's eyes went up the height of the building. It was an engineering web of bare cement columns. He assumed that he was to help fit out this skeleton with walls and other necessities until it turned into apartments and offices that would house a new flood of Jewish emigrants from across the seas, by which time he himself would have become a skeleton withered by the wind. No choice—one

[1] *Khawaja* is a foreign gentleman.

of the two had to be a skeleton; no choice, for the building had to be completed—it *had* to. . . .

"The *menahel*!"[2] said one of the men, pointing to a man who was coming towards them. As soon as he got to where they were standing, he started allocating duties to them.

The *menahel* pointed at him and asked, "What's your name?"

"Saʿid."

"You, go and work with Abu Mahmoud on the second floor."

He pointed to one of the entrances to the building. Saʿid went straight there without asking any questions; the process of outfitting the building required that he should go to Abu Mahmoud, and that was where he would go.

"Hello, Abu Mahmoud . . ."

The man, who was hanging on to the scaffolding, was startled and dropped the measuring tape from his hand. Saʿid bent to pick it up as the image of Abu Mahmoud came into his memory. He was overcome by a wave of such fear that he shook all over and the measuring tape was about to fall from his hand. But he strengthened his grip on it.

Is that you, Abu Mahmoud? He cursed silently this wretched day and the surprises it hid. *Abu Mahmoud, am I going to be sharing with you in the dressing up of this skeleton?* He remembered vividly the look of terror in the man's eyes the day he had torn up his work permit and thoughtlessly thrown it in his face. He had never attempted, that day, to hear his own stuttering, frightened words, nor had he sympathized with the terror he felt in his own heart. He had never realized, on that day, that the pain in children's eyes was stronger than a work permit and a measuring tape—stronger even than cement columns. They had no choice . . . He shook his head violently to throw off the stream of past memories, trying to live in the present moment. Forcing a pale smile to his lips, he looked towards the man. "God give you strength, Abu Mahmoud."

"And you, my son," he murmured in a low, wary voice. "How are you?"

"All right, thank God. I'm at your service." Saʿid smiled to relieve the tension. "The *menahel* sent me to you. I'm working with you to-day."

"Very well, my son."

"What can I do?"

---

[2]*Menahel* is Hebrew for supervisor.

He spoke with sincerity, and Abu Mahmoud relaxed and smiled incredulously. Was Sa'id really going to be working today? In construction? With the mixer and brick molds as his equipment? Abu Mahmoud wandered no further with his thoughts, but looked at the young man seriously. "You can either mix the stuff up and carry it here, or hand me the bricks."

Suddenly a pail full of cement appeared in between them, carried by the trembling hand of a man around forty years of age, who weighed scarcely more than that number in kilograms. Sa'id could hardly believe that this human skeleton was able to move, but was soon ashamed of his thought as he noticed the man's protruding veins, which were silently defying the heavy weight. Abu Mahmoud took the pail from the man and spoke to him. "Azra, this is Sa'id. You'll be working with him today."

Azra shook hands with Sa'id, while Abu Mahmoud answered Sa'id's unspoken question. "Don't take him lightly. This Yemeni Jew speaks Arabic better than you do; don't let his work be better than yours."

The Yemeni winked and laughed, saying, "Abu Mahmoud is the best foreman on the building! He's a man of gold."

He went down, followed by Sa'id, as Abu Mahmoud watched them with affection and sympathy. It was a cold autumn morning; the cold air harassed the bones brutally, its effect showed in the creases of faces, and in eyes.

Now Abu Mahmoud is hanging on to the scaffolding on the fifth floor, treating a wall that belongs to someone else. And the poor Yemeni has left his flocks at the borders of Sanaa, and abandoned the rich milk and the damned qat,[3] *and has come to play around with cement mix and suffer under its weight all the way up and all the way down, while you like a machine hand over the bricks and watch them being transformed into walls that rise higher, and Abu Mahmoud's skill does not allow you a minute to take a breath. And every second the building grows higher and you rise with it while the fields of Majdal spread out below you like a green carpet that is forbidden to you. You wish you could sleep in the shade of a tree around the well whose water you were first washed with and by whose edge your mother swore to wash your circumcision wounds so that you might be continually replenished and remain as fresh as the water of the well.*

---

[3]*Qat* is a kind of plant chewed by Yemenis as a stimulant, in sessions that sometimes last for hours.

What has happened to these wishes? And your small feet running around the well—where have they gone? You have no time to remember. Work lasts from early morning till nightfall. At night you're exhausted, and your dreams fade away into a deep sleep, in preparation for the next day. The bed holds you in such an embrace that you are unable to respond to your wife's advances. She comes closer, twists and turns sensuously, and even dares to try to stimulate you, while you pretend to be asleep, fearing that your weary muscles might fail you. The woman's body writhes, the smell of sex is in your nostrils, and yet you feign sleep.

You can't even satisfy your wife any more, but, after all, the screams of children are stronger than the desires of the body. But sometimes you get fed up and give her all the remains of your manhood. Then you go back to work. Every day you pass the well and the sycamore trees on the road and if you were young now, and climbing the tree, you'd be dragged to the police station and accused of violating a blessed tree and spoiling its curative milk. And poor Azra, his nails torn from scratching the sycamore tree for its milk, hoping that his daughter's boils might be cured after all the doctor's medicines have proven useless. And the poor child withers away from her wretched illness, and Azra withers away from looking for a solution until his pockets have dried out but the flow of boils on his only child's face has not. He's desperate for help because his daughter has to get into a hospital, and therefore he must look for another Shlomo, and another job as well. At night the vegetable market is his other world. Here stands Azra, torn between night and day; the night engulfs him as a carrier of crates of vegetables, while the day possesses him as a carrier of pails of mixed cement. And his pockets are always empty, for the hospital is a drain. And the child cries and Azra screams. He curses the blasphemous day and the sycamore tree.

The autumn morning is cold, and Abu Mahmoud is a good man, and his hand is blessed, and he earns his penny honestly. Under his hands the walls rise, and he covers over the skeleton of the building, and I can hardly catch my breath as I hand him one brick after another, while your veins, Azra, do not have a second to relax before they tense again under the weight of the pail so as not to interrupt Abu Mahmoud's pace. Abu Mahmoud, the kind man, the best foreman on the building, the man of gold. Health suffers while the eyes of the boss become acquainted with the pace of our work from the spasms of your veins and the scratches on my scabbed hands from the sharp bricks. While Majdal is too busy to pay us any mind, and the vegetable market is full of people and peddlers, and the sycamore tree is blessed and bears fruit several times a year, and the beautiful day isn't necessarily followed by another that is lean . . .

As he saw Abu Mahmoud scrambling down from the scaffolding, Saʿid came back to reality.

"Saʿid! The Yemeni! God help us . . ."

"What's happened?"

"He's collapsed! He's collapsed, my son! God help us!"

Not understanding what had happened, Saʿid hurried down after Abu Mahmoud. All he knew was that Abu Mahmoud's words were those of agony and grief. They rushed up to the man, who was slumped over the cement mix, face downward.

They carried him and laid him down on his back in the shade of the wall, away from the draft. His hands were limp on the floor; his dark veins were all twisted, like a crushed earthworm. Froth from his mouth mingled with yellow mucus from his nose and spread down to his jaws, carrying with it black particles of the cement that covered his face. He was breathing heavily; his ribs quivered with the pain that showed in his black eyes that stared at the sky. Abu Mahmoud began to flex and unflex his stiff legs, while Saʿid gently massaged his chest and listened to his weary heart.

Like an animal who's just been slaughtered, Azra moved his limbs. Abu Mahmoud breathed deeply and said, with an unsteady voice full of emotion, "Thank God! Thank you, God!"

Azra stood up and walked around the men, who were murmuring in unfinished sentences, as though addressing someone from another world:

"Almighty God! . . ."

"Merciful God! . . ."

"Out of pity for Azra's child you've spared him, Almighty God."

Saʿid wiped off the dirt and spittle on Azra's face. Azra's eyes followed the movements of Saʿid's hands and his lips moved, but his voice was inaudible. Saʿid patted his forehead encouragingly, but Azra burst into silent tears. Saʿid tried to soothe him but stopped suddenly. Azra's limbs grew limp, and he gazed far beyond the black walls through his flowing tears. . . .

There's no difference, no difference at all. Today it's Azra, just as yesterday it was Saleh. Saleh of Bir Sheba, and the dark walls, and the bags of cement, and the stones. And the prisoners of Bir Sheba built more prison cells for more friends. And the summer wind hit their faces and wrung from their innermost cells a sweat that condensed as salt on lips waiting for break-time to come. . . . Saleh with his thin body beneath the weight of the heavy stones, carrying them to the second floor, a sardonic smile on his lips, fighting his own fatigue and lack of strength. When his smile could no longer moisten the bitterness of the salt on his lips, he collapsed, and the stone he was carrying fell on his chest and was blown away by the desert wind; but today it was a cold autumn wind that congealed the froth on Azra's forehead.

Saleh's friends had put down what they were carrying and formed a circle around his body, fuming angrily, roaring fiercely. There had been shouting, and frightened soldiers with clubs and rifle butts.

To no avail. Saleh's sardonic smile had been transmitted tenderly by the desert wind. While Saleh still lay there they had gone on strike to demand the necessary medical help for him; there had been the will of youth that translates itself into pamphlets and decisive steps. Today Saleh is lying in Azra's eyes, and his friends shed a stream of tears. . . .

Get up, Azra, you're the stronger one! Get up. He held Azra's hand tenderly, but a strong blow hit him from behind and knocked him to the ground. Sa'id looked around him. Shlomo was glaring down at him and waving his fist angrily. "Back to work, you ass!"

Abu Mahmoud rushed in to explain: "Sir, Azra collapsed. We came down to help. The work is fine, it hasn't suffered."

Shlomo spit disgustedly. "The work is terrible! *You're* all terrible!"

With the urge to strike him, Sa'id jumped up and headed for Shlomo. Fiercely, Abu Mahmoud threw his arms around him and held him back. "Calm down, son," he begged. "We're not his equals."

Sa'id was kicking out with his legs and trying to get free of Abu Mahmoud who was trying to push him away from the contractor.

"We're not on his level." Abu Mahmoud pleaded. "He's a bastard, a pimp! To him, the whole world is money, but he can't buy everyone."

Azra crawled over to Sa'id. He got to his feet with difficulty but soon fell down, panting heavily. "Calm down, Sa'id," he said, "I beg you, calm down. All this has happened on account of me. Calm down."

Shlomo felt the seriousness of the situation. He walked backwards, his apprehensive eyes not leaving Sa'id, until he reached his car. He jumped in and shouted furiously, "Abu Mahmoud, you're fired!"

"So what?" answered Abu Mahmoud in a clear voice. "God damn you and your job! Get out of our sight!"

Shlomo started the car and spat with malicious joy, pointing at Sa'id and Azra. "Those two asses are fired too!"

Sa'id broke free of Abu Mahmoud's grip and raced toward the car like a bullet, but the car sped away, leaving behind a cloud of smoke. A thick dust enveloped the three figures, making them cough profusely.

—translated by Salwa Jabsheh and Thomas G. Ezzy

Samira 'Azzam *(1925–1967)*

'Azzam was born in Acre, Palestine, and became a refugee in Lebanon in 1948. She worked most of her life in radio broadcasting and journalism, either as an employee or as a free-lancer. Her short stories, many of which revolve around the Palestine experience in the diaspora, are characterized by precision and control. The stories stem from a realistic modern experience in the Arab world, portrayed with skill and compassion and spun around a single point of action or idea. Three collections of her stories were published in her lifetime: *Little Things*, (1954); *The Long Shadow*, (1956); and *And Other Stories*, (1960). Her fourth and fifth collections, *The Clock and Man* (1963) and *The Feast from the Western Window* (1971), were published posthumously.

Bread of Sacrifice

When Ibrahim handed him the tobacco-filled pipe, he wished he could break down and cry like a child. He felt tears welling in his eyes and turned his head aside to wipe them away on his sleeve. In an attempt to hide his sorrow, he raised his head to peer over the barricade, but when he turned back to face his companions their grief-stricken silence brought the tears back into his eyes. The night, presided over by a distant, cloudy moon, seemed to grieve with them; everything in the universe seemed to know his story. He longed to be able to give himself up to the luxury of sorrow, but could not. He longed to shake his friends, to throw away the armor of toughness and cry—cry without shame. He raised his sleeve to wipe his eyes and felt the woolen shirt irritating them, reminding him of that talisman of hers he was wearing, that would protect him—as she once said—from every treacherous bullet.

Yes, he could remember that night.

It had been a night of stinging cold like this one, with a thin crescent moon. He had been ordered to guard the small hospital the Arab Legion had set up in a town house that consisted of four stone rooms and a small garden. The eight hospital beds were occupied by eight wounded men brought in following a battle between the Jewish Nahariya settlement and the Arab villages around Acre. Yes, it had been cold that night, and neither his *kaffiyyeh* nor his heavy overcoat were enough to shield him from the biting chill, so he had taken to walking about in order to keep the blood from freezing in his veins. When he tired of this, he returned to lean against the hospital wall, near the door, gazing at the distant houses of the city which slept uneasily, fearful of sudden attack. He did not know what time it was exactly. The only remaining lights were the streetlamps on the main thoroughfares, and the night was silent save for the sound of a distant jackal.

Yes, he did not know exactly what time it was when he sensed her standing near him in her white nurse's uniform, asking him whether he wanted a cup of tea. He had not given thought to tea, nor to anything else; nevertheless, he felt it would be nice to have a warm object to hold against his chilled fingers, and accepted her offer gratefully. When she returned with the tea, he finished it off in four gulps so as not to oblige her to wait long, and gave her back the empty cup, murmuring some word of thanks. And after she left, he thought it would have been polite if he had talked to her a little more. He turned his head, searching for her shadow behind the window. He saw no one. He decided to thank her in the morning—but who could she be? There were two female nurses, and he had seen nothing of her except her white uniform. The second night he was determined to be less rigid when she brought him tea. He waited a long time, but she did not come. He told himself that she must be too busy with those who really needed her care to see to his tea. Why shouldn't he, therefore, knock on the door and ask for his own tea? He hesitated, not wanting to be a nuisance. The lights went out, the city slept, leaving him and his comrades the responsibility of keeping vigil. It was about this time last night that he drank her tea. He flexed his fingers, frozen by the gun-barrel, and wished for something to bring them warmth. No sooner had he lifted his hand to his mouth to blow on his fingers than her white uniform suddenly appeared at his side and he heard her saying, "I've brought you your tea without asking; you won't refuse it, will you?"

He raised his eyes, looked at her, and extended his cold hand to take the cup. He decided it would be nice to speak to her before drinking. "Don't you find the work here hard?"

With a gravity he had not expected, she replied, "Do you think I'm not good enough for duties like this?"

"I . . . No, not at all . . ."

At a loss for words, he raised the cup to his lips and drank quickly, scalding his throat. He returned the cup to her without a thank-you, and when she had moved a few steps away, he called out, "Miss"— why shouldn't he ask her name? There was no harm in that. She stopped, and he approached her. "Excuse me, I wonder if I might know your name?"

She laughed before replying: "And why not? We are all comrades here. My name is Su'ad."

"I am Ramiz. My buddies call me Sarge. Should we shake hands?"

She laughed and gave him her hand, then slipped away as lightly as she had come.

Su'ad. How strange—another Su'ad. He seemed to have luck with this name. Some days ago the Acre Women's Committee had presented a gift of hand-knitted woolen shirts and blankets to the Arab Legion. In the pocket of each was a card bearing the name of the young woman who had knitted it, along with a word of encouragement. He still kept his. He felt for it in his pocket, pulled it out, and lit a match by which he read the words "Su'ad Wahbi," and below the name "May this shirt be worn by a hero."

The match went out and the words vanished. He put the card back in his pocket. Could it be her? If it were, wouldn't that be a pleasant coincidence? He turned to the door, and found it locked.

The third night he arranged to begin his shift of guard duty earlier in order to have an opportunity to enter the hospital and ask after the wounded. The door was open, and he went in. He saw her carrying a dinner tray to one of the soldiers. He greeted her and asked if he might visit them. She replied, "Why not? I'd like you to meet Hassan so he can tell you the details of the battle. I've heard it myself dozens of times, but it won't hurt to hear it once more."

He followed her.

He stood next to her in front of Hassan's bandaged head, and they both laughed to hear the wounded man say; "Su'ad is a strict nurse who wants me stretched out like a corpse. She won't even let me sneak a cigarette."

As she laughed, Ramiz noticed that her teeth were very white, and her eyes shone with an indomitable will. The mood in the room encouraged him to ask; "Still, you'd agree with me that she's a good one?"

"Good? She's the best of them all. She's better than my old mother. She's always around, giving this one something to drink, that one something to eat, answering the bells that ring in all the rooms. If ever she finds a moment to rest, you'll find her sitting by the door with her knitting."

"Knitting?"

He remembered the shirt. His hand moved, finding the thick buttons of the overcoat that covered it. Opening the coat to show his shirt, he turned to her and said, "Do you recognize this shirt?"

"Yes. So you were the one who got it."

"Don't I deserve it? I still have the card. This way I will always remember my duty to perform as a hero."

A persistent bell summoned her and she left him with Hassan, who asked him for a cigarette which he promised not to smoke until Su'ad gave him her approval.

Two weeks went by, and the wounded began to recover and leave the hospital, all except one who was transferred to another hospital. Ramiz's guard duty there was over, and he returned to his job training recruits. He would meet new recruits and release others until darkness fell, then he would take his rifle and go for his nightly guard duty. Only when dawn lit the sky did he go home and throw himself on the iron cot in his one room house. There he found time to think about her.

An entire week went by, during which he did not see her. Where could she be? Why did he feel driven to think about her, and to treasure the shirt she had knitted? Yesterday morning he had discovered something as he got dressed. She had knitted and knitted without knowing who would wear the shirt. Maybe she had a picture in her mind's eye of what the man who wore it ought to look like. Obviously she wished him to be tall, with broad shoulders—a man she hoped would be a hero. He turned to look at himself in the mirror on the wall and felt his muscular arms. He laughed at his own foolishness as he gazed at himself. But what harm would it do if he acted a little silly, burying his face in the shirt, for example, or kissing it?

On the eighth day he chanced upon her in the street. She was not in her nurse's uniform. He stopped her, saying, "I almost didn't recognize you out of uniform."

She shook his hand and said; "The hospital has moved and I couldn't think of anything to do today. What are you up to?"

"Training recruits during the day, and guard duty at night—nothing much! And no tea!"

Her silvery laugh rang out. She caught him gazing at her and blushed. She started to walk away, and he rushed to speak to her before shyness overcame him. "I hope you don't think I'm being out of line. Couldn't I meet you somewhere?"

"Our town is too small for that."

"But we're comrades in arms. I train recruits, both men and women. Come to the Port Club. We can talk a little bit after I'm finished with drilling."

They agreed to meet there at three. He was in the middle of demonstrating to a women's squadron how to stand firm holding a heavy rifle without faltering, when he caught sight of her. He continued with his job, and did not talk to her until the exercise was completed. Then he dismissed his class and turned to greet her, offering her a chair.

"Aren't you exhausted?" she asked.

"Who isn't? But once I realized what sort of mobilization and preparations are going on in the Jewish settlements, I wished there were sixty hours in a day. We have a tough job ahead of us."

"Are you afraid?"

"Wary. It won't be easy. I think the Jews have stockpiled a great many weapons in their settlements. We've found out many things."

"Have you gone there yourself?"

"Yes, I used to go a lot before relations became strained. Now I can't go. I'm on their blacklist."

He saw her observing him. Presently, her lips parted and the determined look flashed in her eyes. "You know, I'm starting to believe that you are something of a hero."

"A hero? No way, though your card has given me the inspiration to be one."

"Do you still have it?"

"Here it is."

He handed it to her, and as he took it back, he pressed her hand briefly then released it. Then, to give her a chance to conceal her embarrassment, he looked out over the blue sea in front of him.

It was spring. Springtime in this part of Palestine is a sparkling sea, traversed by white sails during the day and lit by the twinkling lamps of fishing boats at night. The fragrance of the orange groves fills the air. That spring, Ramiz learned about two things—love and war—and the first gave meaning to the second. War was not simply an enemy to kill voraciously. Rather, it was the assertion of the life of the land he loved and the woman he loved. Palestine was not only a sea with fishing boats, and oranges shining like gold, and not just olives and olive oil filling the big oil jars. It was Suʿad's black eyes as well. In Suʿad's eyes he saw all of Palestine's goodness. He saw the image of a happy home for him, and a wife who would bear him young heroes and make her love the meaning of his existence.

Each new day her image accompanied the news of battles in the morning papers. The battle of Qastal.[1] The Palestinian counterattack from the Triangle of Terror[2] on enemy settlements. His and his comrades' raids on the infiltrating Jewish armored vehicles rolling down the road from Haifa to Acre to Nahariya. The heroism of his people in Salama, in every town and village.

Then came the fall of Haifa.[3]

He would never forget that evening.

He was busy training the recruits. When he turned toward the sea, he saw dozens and dozens of boats filled with refugees. The people of Acre gathered at the city walls to learn about the new situation. They had been aware of the battles that were being fought in Haifa, and they knew that the British authorities had secretly helped the Zionists with fortified positions. Although the British had publicly declared that they would not leave Haifa until a few months after the end of the Mandate Period, they now suddenly announced that they had to leave the city.

The terror poured down Mount Carmel[4] onto the Arabs who lived on the slopes. The British authorities spread terrifying rumors that caused panic. At the same time, they opened the port, and made their ships available to carry off anyone who wished to flee. So people crammed into them while gunfire spat out at them from the mountain.

---

[1]Al-Qastal or Qastel was the battle waged on April 8–9, 1948 between the Zionist forces in Mandatory Palestine and Palestinian forces led by ʿAbd al-Qadir al-Husaini who was killed in this battle. Al-Qastal was a hilltop village on the road between Jaffa and Jerusalem. The fighting along this major road was planned by the Zionists to cut Jaffa off from the capital. This battle also had other dire consequences, for the Irgun and Stern Terrorist Gangs (led by Menachem Begin) attacked the nearby village of Dair Yasin and massacred 245 civilian inhabitants. This attack has become one of the major incidents that the Palestinians and many other Arabs regard as flagrant symbols of atrocity and terrorism inflicted by the Zionists on the Palestinians.

[2]The Triangle of Terror: these are the towns and villages in the Tulkarm-Qalqilya-Tireh district, near Nablus, which gallantly stood in the face of attacks by the Haganah Zionist forces. Both Tireh and Qalqilya repulsed their attacks on May 13, 1948.

[3]Haifa fell to the Haganah Zionist forces on April 23, 1948. Acre, where the story (based on a true account) takes place, fell to the Haganah Zionists on May 17, 1948.

[4]Mount Carmel is the mountain overlooking the Mediterranean on which part of Haifa is built.

The boats dumped them on the shore of Acre, a human mass, some stunned by their wounds, others by hunger, still others by terror.

The homes, the mosques, the monasteries, the plazas of his city were jammed with them.

They brought his small city the burden of providing food and shelter for so many.

That night he saw Suʿad with dozens of women volunteers, receiving the wounded at the port and assigning them to hospitals and homes. At the same time, the war of rumors began to play on everyone's nerves.

He awoke the following day to a loud knocking at the door. He opened it and was astonished to see her there. She was crying.

She said that her brother had got hold of a truck, loaded it with everything that would fit, then crammed his wife, his children, and himself onto it and drove to Lebanon. Twenty families in her neighborhood had already done the same thing. Her brother had tried to make her come with them, but she had refused. She had argued with him and he had slapped her on the face. All she could do then was run away.

She would be the last to leave.

He was startled and remained silent, not knowing what to say to her. When she tapped against his chest with her fist he asked; "Have you done this because of me?"

She blurted out; "No, not because of you. Yes, I love you, it's true. Still, you're not everything!" And she left.

He opened the door and went out into the city. Dozens of cars, both large and small, full and empty, were speeding off like the wind. Baffled, he did not know whether to weep or shout or start pelting them with stones.

After a week the city was empty, except for the fighters, a handful of woman nurses scattered among the small hospitals, and refugees from Haifa or the surrounding villages. There was no more time for meetings with Suʿad. To the north and south, the enemy was lying in wait for a chance to attack. By day he slipped into the villages to gather rifles and ammunition; his nights were spent with five others crouched behind barricades set up on the roof of a disused cigarette factory. The city had to hold fast until the Mandate ended and the Arab armies could come in to fight the battle.

These were his duties as assigned by the National Committee of Acre. When he had time to rest, he thought of Suʿad, wondering how she was living and under what circumstances. One day he was startled to see her suddenly; he stopped in his tracks.

She was wrapped in a coat and was carrying a large basket.

He did not know how to greet her, but she solved the problem by opening the basket and directing her words to all his comrades. "The National Committee was afraid you might run out of food, so they sent me with these things."

There was bread, cigarettes, and candy in the basket. Her eyes were filled with love. He wished he could embrace her in front of all his comrades.

He felt he alone had the right to walk a little way with her on her way back, and to take her fingertips in his trembling hand. Then he raised her hand to his lips, begging her not to do such a crazy thing again. She went off, and he stood watching her until a bend in the road swallowed her.

She visited them repeatedly.

She always stayed just a few minutes, but they were enough to arouse his emotions in a way that made him both tired and happy.

Until the beginning of the week.

The fighting grew more intense, with shelling going on for an entire day and two nights, and for part of a second day.

The enemy's armored cars were advancing along the main road to Nahariya. The fighters had to ambush them with artillery placed on the roofs of houses near the road.

The battle did not subside until three the next afternoon. Some of the men lay on the barricades to rest, and others lay on the ground. He went down to wash at the garden faucet before heading to the city to find out what plans the Arab Legion had for hauling the wrecked cars into town. His face was covered with soap, when he heard the sound of a bullet, then another. As he quickly wiped the soap from his eyes, the sound of her voice rang in his ears.

Turning toward the garden door, he saw that she had darted in. Her basket was in one hand and she held the other against her chest. At the beginning, he did not see anything wrong as she was standing, but then she fell into his arms and blood began to flow from her chest. He stopped her wound with his hand and called out to his comrades, who quickly threw their shirts to him to absorb the blood that came pouring out.

She opened her mouth to speak, but a rattle in her throat choked her words—then, with a single groan, it was all over.

It happened so fast he could not believe it. A single horrible instant put an end to everything. How could time not have stood still, how could it have marched on, allowing her to die? Why did she not revive under his kisses and his anguished cries, and how could those eyelids not tremble with life as he whispered his love to her?

She was dead. How, when the fragrance of her hair still lingered in the air, the warmth of her hand could still be felt on his palm, and he could still taste her lips against his own? Her eyes had never spoken of death, only of love and the promise of life.

Rubbing his eyes to banish the nightmare, he gripped the pipe Ibrahim had handed him, so that his fingernails would not bore into his palm. He stared at his comrades.

"Yes, she is dead," their eyes seemed to say. We must take her from you and bury her on the hill over there. We'll mark her grave with a flag and proclaim her a heroine.

She loved you and became a symbol for all of us, Ibrahim, and Wadeeʿ and Salih, Ahmad and ʿAbdullah.

A thin yellow moon and a few stars. Nothing but the darkness and the glowing ends of cigarettes. Behind the barricade they had neither food nor drink, and they had not slept.

The rest of the night passed peacefully except for a skirmish or two at dawn. Then things grew quiet, and the tired heads surrendered themselves to a sleep broken by hunger and fear.

At dawn ʿAbdullah rubbed his eyes and looking over to the piles of wooden boxes nearby asked; "Isn't there anything to eat?"

Wadeeʿ replied, "Sure, there's our hunger."

He fell silent.

There were Suʿad's loaves, stained with her blood. What a wretched dip for their bread!

Their hunger became unbearable, and they were soon unable even to stand up.

Ramiz felt that the situation was turning into a humiliating ordeal, and that he alone of his comrades could dare to consider eating the loaves.

He covered his eyes with his hands. Could anything be worse than his being forced to feed her blood to his friends?

He looked over at his comrades. ʿAbdullah lay on a blanket, as did Salih. Ahmad sat on a sandbag, pressing his hands against his stomach.

They were ready to eat a dog's corpse, but no one reached for the loaves baptized with blood. He would have to set things in motion. What would he say to his comrades? Take it, for Suʿad has given us the bread and the dip?

He bowed his head for a moment, then dragged himself to his feet. If the idea was too awful for him, he must go to the city and get them something to eat.

He tried to stand up, but he was too weak. His comrades realized what his going to the city would entail. Any bullet would catch him like a little bird—the open countryside between their post and the city center was wide and exposed. Armored cars protecting themselves by spraying out bullets in all directions could be expected to pass at any moment. So Salih took him by the shoulders and made him sit down.

He sat down, and once again the battle between the blood soaked bread and their hunger began.

There it was, still piled in the corner, in the basket, just the way Suʿad had brought it. It would hurt, but it would save five lives.

What price would he pay? Could he bear to see the hands tearing off a piece and the teeth chewing the bread she had stained with her blood? His eyes clouded over—no, it would never happen, even if they all had to die. They weren't any better than she had been, so what if they, too, died? She had died carrying bread to them, but they would die because they would not touch her bread. Her death would not save their lives. They would be rejecting the bread of sacrifice, offered to them to test their humanity, or his own humanity at least. What had they done that they should starve? But what if they did starve? They could just forget the bread was there. In any case, they were not considering it. They had abstained, willing themselves to wait for another source of nourishment, or to die—and with them would die the chance to avenge her death.

Revenge? Yes, how could he have forgotten that? How could he choose to die of hunger like a dog, and to let five others die with him? So many encounters with death had inured him to the thought of it. But if he could choose the death he wished, he would not choose to die of hunger. Suʿad herself would never allow that of a hero.

He shuddered in pain.

He realized that throughout this last night he had thought more about his hunger than about Suʿad. Hunger had suspended all other sensibilities. What a horrible experience!

He called to his comrades, and they were barely able to open their eyes. He would call them one by one: Ibrahim and Wadeeʿ and Salih and Ahmad and ʿAbdullah. They would form a circle around him. Then he would rise and bring the loaves of bread. As he put his hand out to open the basket he would tell them an ancient story known to this land and its people, the story of the redemption of life by flesh and blood. Then he would bring the loaves and, with all the solemnity of an Eastern Orthodox priest offering the bread of Jesus, he would tell them: "Eat, for this is my body; drink, for this is my blood." He would also eat some himself, and something of Suʿad would remain in him. How did this thought escape his attention before? Something was now nudging him, shouting and demanding, reminding him that he had to do something for that body now buried in the corner of the garden.

He pulled himself up and walked to the other corner, his movements followed by five pairs of eyes. He could feel their gaze fastened on his legs. With a trembling hand, he took the basket, opened it, and brought the bread to his lips. Then he approached his comrades, fell to his knees, and handed the loaves out, saying; "Eat . . . Suʿad would not have wanted us to die of hunger."

Then the world grew distant, and he fell senseless to the ground.

—translated by Kathie Piselli and Dick Davies

Liyana Badr *(b. 1950)*

A novelist and short story writer, Liyana Badr was born in Jerusalem to an educated nationalist family. Her father, a doctor, was
incarcerated for many years during her childhood because of his political views. When out of prison, he did a great amount of patriotic and
philanthropic work, opening his practice to the Palestinian refugees in
Jericho's three refugee camps. Her mother joined in her father's struggle, and the family's constant exposure to the scrutiny of the secret
police has led them from exile to exile. Despite this very unsettled life,
Liyana Badr was able to finish her education and obtained a B.A. in
philosophy and psychology from Beirut Arab University. However, she
was never able to finish her studies for an M.A. because of the Lebanese
civil war. She was an editor on the cultural section of *Al-Hurriyya* review
and undertook collective work in the Union of Palestinian Women in
Jordan and in the Sabra and Shatila camps in Beirut. These experiences
are reflected in her 1979 novel, *The Sundial*, which was published in
English by the Women's Press, London, in 1989. She has published two
collections of short stories, *Stories of Love and Pursuit* (1983) and *I Want
the Day* (1985). Her collection of three short novellas, *A Balcony Over
the Fakihani* (1983), contains some of the most touching and poignant
accounts of the plight of Palestinians in Lebanon. It described the
notorious 1976 Tel al-Zaatar massacre by the Phalangists where Palestinians and poor Lebanese, the inhabitants of the camp, were besieged,
bombarded, and starved out, and at least 15,000 were killed in the Israeli
invasion of 1982. This book has been translated into English for PROTA
by Peter Clark and Christopher Tingley. Liyana Badr now lives and
works in Tunis.

A Land of Rock and Thyme

> For hands of rock and thyme
> This song . . .
> "Ahmad Zaatar" by Mahmoud Darwish

1   The Picture

I dreamt tonight we were walking together. He always comes to me in my dreams. We were both walking along the road near the Martyrs' Cemetery, but I'd no sooner seen him than he went off. He leapt up, began to move among the graves, then ripped his picture from one of them. I don't know where he went then. I looked round at the graves with their white headstones and the garlands of withered flowers on them. The fresh green grass of spring was all around. I looked for him but didn't know where he'd gone.

My mind's full of the picture, and I was impatient for the photographer to finish it. I'd intended to go and put it on his grave in the Martyrs' Cemetery. But the situation was tense; fighting had broken out again. Who, these days, would dare go to the Martyrs' Cemetery? I had a long argument with my sister Jamila, who finally took the large-size picture from me and locked it away in the cupboard. I was pregnant, she reminded me, the baby was due at the end of the month, and it would be difficult to run if there was sudden shelling. What should I do then? Wait? My whole life had been spent waiting and waiting— but I hadn't expected to marry a man who'd love me and want me, wait with me, then leave forever and never come back.

They used to call him "the Indian" in the Damour camp. When I first saw his swarthy features and black eyes, I thought he really was Indian. When we first talked about it I asked him, "Are you Indian?", and he laughed and laughed, till he almost fell over.

"Indian?" he said: "Me? I'm from the village of Jamaain near Nablus, Yusra." It amused him afterwards to remind me that I'd been misled by the nickname and thought he really was Indian.

2   Damour[1]

After we'd left al-Zaatar we lived for about a year at Damour. Our house was at the side of the road, an eerie house with no doors, no windows, no floor and no sanitation—a big house, burned inside like the rest of those in Damour. Stripped of its tiles, the floor was just sand and gravel. The first thing we did was clean it, which took about a week. Mother whitened it with lime, but it was only half white because of the grime

---

[1]Damour was mainly inhabited by Christians, and when it was shelled its inhabitants fled eastwards to the Christian area. Ironically it was the Tel al-Zaatar survivors fleeing from the east who took refuge there.

and smut. We brought in empty gun boxes that my brother made a door from, and we put up plastic sheets for windows. At night the winds came straight into us because we were close to the sea, and Mother would sit up all night, too frightened to sleep as the wind beat against the flimsy sheets with a sound like shelling. Always she was anxious and frightened, frightened in the winter and frightened in the summer. Mother was the only one who was frightened.

When the Israelis started their airstrike, Mother's nerves were already shattered and we just couldn't stay in Damour. Life there was utterly dreadful. The houses were a long way from one another, whereas we'd been used to having lots of neighbors around us. The shops were a long way off, too, and the vegetable market even further away. There was no running water in the house. In time we managed to attach an electric cable to the streetlight and fix a lamp to it inside the house. But mother was still frightened. We didn't like Damour, and we finally moved to Beirut, into a flat left empty by its owners who'd fled the fighting.

3   Water Has a Memory

During the final raid on the Tel al-Zaatar camp, I was at the water tap, which was in the last part of the camp they attacked and captured from us. Each day, throughout the siege, Jamila and I would take the lower path that led to al-Dikwana. Usually we couldn't even get two jerry cans of water. The water was cut off early in the morning and came on again in the afternoon or the evening. We used to wait eight or ten hours for our turn at the tap. Sometimes our turn came, and sometimes an attack started, with shells falling on us like rain. Then the water would be cut off and no one would get any.

In the beginning, at the start of the siege, we used to fill our cans from Jinin School, near the George Matta metalwork factory, and we used to sleep in the broad cellar of which the factory was part. The place was filled with over seven hundred people, who shared it with bits of metal and huge pieces of machinery. We'd lay our bedding out amongst piles of rods and various pieces of machinery used for cutting, smelting, and casting, just able to find a place among the chairs, beds, and metal cradles that were stacked one on top of the other. Our blankets would be laid on the floor and our belongings put out to the side. We couldn't sleep because of the pungent smell of the metal that got into our nostrils and choked us.

We stayed at George Matta's for about a month. It was a dangerous spot because it was near the Monastery of the Good Shepherd. Every day the women swept the workshop floor and sprinkled water on it; they'd bake bread on a metal sheet on a kerosene stove. People would knead dough, make bread, go to sleep, and get up again in this shelter. In the first days we were sometimes able to go out and fill sandbags to strengthen the defenses of the camp. Even Mother, a month after giving birth, went with the women to fill sacks. Everyone did their best.

From time to time some *fidaain*[2] would pass by the shelter, reassuring us and keeping our morale high. "Don't be afraid," they'd say. "There's no danger." In the last ten days of the month their visits stopped. None of us any longer had the courage to stick our heads out of the door of the shelter.

The enemy was right on us, and anyone who peeped out would be instantly shot at by snipers. They got very close to us. Only one street now separated us from them; we were at one end and they were at the other. Five people were killed by snipers, although, in the first period of our refuge there, no one was wounded except once, when a shell fell near the door of the shelter and injured several people.

One day a girl popped her head out of the door and saw them sneaking up on the shelter. We didn't hear a sound, but we knew their next attack would be directed at us. We knew the Fascists had entered the shelter next to George Matta's factory and killed a hundred and twenty people, including seventeen from the Shuqair family alone. As the snipers seized the front entrance, our people opened an exit in the back wall, and so got safely away.

We left at five o'clock with only the clothes we were wearing; everything else was left behind. The next day, before the Phalangists[3] could complete their occupation of the district, I went back to the shelter with a group of others to get whatever supplies we could carry. I had to get a tin of milk for my baby brother because Mother's breasts had run dry and she couldn't feed him any longer.

Many people were injured as we left, shot down as though they'd been standing right in front of the rifle. As the snipers fired, the dead dropped one after the other. Those who got out in one piece were the lucky ones.

[2]*Fidaain* are the freedom fighters sworn to fight and redeem their country with their blood. The root of the word is *fada*: "redeemed with his life"."

[3]*Phalangists* are another Lebanese fascist faction.

4   In the Middle of al-Zaatar

After the assault on the Good Shepherd Monastery district, we moved
to the middle of the camp; there was no space left in any of the shelters,
where people were already packed one on top of the other. At the side
of the main road, we found an amusement room with table games
named "Flippers," and we reinforced the entrance with lentil sacks and
sand, and settled down in the place. It was opposite the Red Crescent
clinic, which had now been turned into a hospital and was used for
preparing the food there. Flippers had only one, normal-sized room,
in which the machines had been placed on one side, and we shared it
with these and the clinic's cook. People who saw us used to ask how
we could possibly install ourselves opposite al-Dikwana, in such an
exposed position. But what else could we do? Mother would answer,
"God is our refuge." The simple truth is that there was nowhere else
to go. The lentil sacks weren't much help as reinforcement; shells from
the 500-mm cannons simply passed over them. Once a shell came and
hit the inside wall, and shattered all over the place, one splinter sinking
itself into the stomach of my eleven-year-old brother, Ali. It buried
itself under the skin and black salve was no use for getting it out. Mother
tried to take him down to the Red Cross, so that he could be evacuated
to the western area with the wounded, but she wasn't able to.

Here, in the middle of the camp, Jamila and I would go each day
to fetch water—two jerry cans, which was barely enough for so many
of us—there was Mother, Father, three girls and six boys (five after the
fall of al-Zaatar). Living as we did across from the emergency clinic,
we'd sometimes have patients coming to us for a drink, and at times,
too, the cook would take some of our water. Sometimes a hundred
people used to gather at the water tap, at other times rather fewer,
depending on circumstances. The tap was in a narrow alley, flanked by
houses that were all empty, for the area was constantly exposed to
snipers. We'd put our jerry cans down in a long row, then hide in the
rooms nearby. When the water came on, usually some time after two
or three in the afternoon, there'd be chaos as people rushed towards
it; nobody kept their place in the queue. One day when I went with
Jamila, the day Father was killed, the water came on at two o'clock.
There were people, and there was water. We went to it as soon as it
came on, but Jamila left, saying she wanted to be home by six in the
evening. A neighbor standing near me asked after my father. I didn't
know anything. "He's fine," I said, and I laughed because the man

lived next door to us and I was surprised to hear him asking after Father when he saw him every day. Half an hour later Jamila came back, her eyes red and swollen.

"What's the matter, Jamila?" I asked.

"Mother hit me," she said, "because I wouldn't come back here and fetch water." Jamila knew that Father had been injured, but thought the wound was a minor one. We were still waiting for our turn around midnight, and it didn't finally come till three in the morning. It was beginning to get light and we were still at the tap. The neighbor came back. "Still here?" he said. "I think you'd better go home."

He didn't want to tell me what had happened. "By God," I said, "I'll stay till I've filled my jerry can if I die doing it! We don't have a drop at home." I cried that night, I cried a lot. It was chaos. Anybody with a weapon would fill up before us; it made me feel bitterly angry. But finally, at about three, we managed to fill up two jerry cans and leave. At home I found Mother sitting up with my Grandmother, which was unusual.

"What's the matter?" I said. "Why are you still up?"

"We're sitting up," they said.

I gazed straight in front of me. Then I looked around. "Where's Father?" I asked.

"He's been wounded in the foot, dear," said Grandmother.

"No!" I said. "I want to see him, now!"

"Go to sleep," she said.

I insisted on seeing him. "Where is he?" I asked. "Has he been hit?" Jamila put her jerry can down and fell asleep at once.

"Didn't Jamila know what had happened? What is it? What's happened?"

Jamila heard nothing, she'd fallen asleep from exhaustion. I received the shocking news: Father had been wounded soon after we left and had lived on for another four hours. He saw everybody else, but when they asked him, "shall we send for Yusra?" he said, "let her get the water for her brothers and sisters." That's what really hurt me. If only I'd been able to see him, to talk to him—one word—while he was still alive. He spent four hours talking normally with them. He'd been wounded by a bullet from a machine gun and had bled internally. There was no first aid available; all the medicines had run out, and there was just salt solution to disinfect the wound. This had no effect.

Mother was at his side and he talked till he died, his wound bleeding. He died at about eight in the evening.

Death had become familiar: there was nobody in al-Zaatar who didn't anticipate his own. There were two taps where we filled up with water. Once, when I was standing there, I suddenly became aware of a man next to me, crying out: "Aah! Aah!" I looked at him and saw that he'd rolled over on the ground and died. Shells often bounced into the middle of groups of people, and the only ones who survived were those protected by fate. All you ever saw was people carrying other people. Our home being by the emergency hospital, we saw most of the wounded. Everyone expected death; no one in Tel al-Zaatar thought to live out his natural life. When father died the condolence people offered was the heartfelt wish that we ourselves should survive.

Nobody knew what would happen any more. You'd be standing next to someone—and an hour later, you'd hear he was dead! There was one young man, I remember, who said, "When I die, put me in this coffin." They made coffins from cupboard doors and there was a door ready. "I'll measure it against my body," the young man said. A moment later a splinter of shrapnel struck him in the back and killed him on the spot. So they did put him in the coffin he'd measured himself for. I'm amazed I've never been injured myself.

It was like a dream. You'd talk to someone, and an hour or two later you'd hear they were dead. Nada, a friend of mine, was killed by a sniper, and she was a volunteer nurse. Death reached even her.

I remember Father. He worked on a building site at first, but he was hit in the eye several times when chipping stone, and in the end he was so badly injured he couldn't work any more. In the last part of his life he started up a shop inside our house, selling small articles.

I remember Father. Once, when we were in the middle of the camp, people discovered a water tank in one of the houses. We had a heavy metal barrel that held one and a half jerry cans, and I would always take that with me to make sure the trip would be worthwhile. But on the way back I felt as if my heart had stopped beating from exhaustion. A metal barrel! When there was an explosion I'd run and run, yet feel I was staying in the same place. Then I'd go on walking with the barrel still on my head. It didn't matter how violent the explosions were— I'd hide behind a wall or in a doorway, but it never fell off my head and there was never a single drop spilt.

But too many people discovered the water tank and they emptied it of water. I went there after that with my brother Jamal, who was killed later, and we were there for about half an hour, scooping up what was left of the water till we could fill the barrel and half the jerry can Jamal had brought.

Then, almost as soon as we'd filled up, the shelling started. Young *fidaain* rushed round us and I felt as though my feet were walking backwards. When we were almost home I simply felt myself being thrown to the ground; I'd fallen over and the barrel of water had fallen with me. I started crying. What else could I do? The tears I wept were not from pain but from frustration. I scooped the water up with my hand, but when I got home there wasn't a drop in the barrel. I remember Father said: "What's the matter? Have you been hit?"

"No," I said.

"Are you hurt," he asked.

I said that I wasn't, weeping over the lost water. My knee was bruised and my body ached, but I was weeping out of frustration for the lost water.

5   The Exodus

When we left the camp they said we'd be surrendering. People set out together. Some at night, some in the daytime. Some people left on the Qalaa road and some on the Dikwana road. We were on the Dikwana road, and what a terrifying experience it was!

We set out in the daytime, quite early, at about eleven in the morning. The *fidaain* went into hiding, then withdrew from the camp at night, but when we set out, we no longer knew what was happening in the camp and those who stayed behind didn't know what was going on outside. One of our neighbors was sitting in her house when the Phalangists burst in; she thought they were *fidaain*. "Up and out of here!" they shouted. She shouted back: "I'm not going! Where can I go?" They killed her together with her son and her husband. Her daughter fled and told people what had happened. Her son—what a waste of life!—was fourteen years old.

At first nothing happened on the road we took. Then, in groups, we passed through their posts where they stood on the two sides of the road, and they started killing people left and right. We didn't look at them; if you looked at them and met the eye of one of them, perhaps you might be dragged away. I never looked. They'd come among us and pick out whomever they wanted, then simply kill him. On both sides of the road there were Landrovers and armed men with crosses on their necks.

A man was walking next to me, his shoulder brushing mine. They grabbed him by the shoulder. "For God's sake," he said to them. "Which God?" they replied. Before I knew what was happening, he'd fallen to the ground; there was a revolver and a single shot to the temple.

We set out in a crowd, with everyone mixed up; a mother didn't even know where her own child was. I seized the hands of some of my brothers and sisters and Mother grabbed the hands of the others. Only Jamal was cheerful. "Load up!" he said lightheartedly, as we got ready to leave the camp. "Load up! We've got to take everything with us. Don't let's leave anything behind!"

He longed for the sea. Why did he long for it? He loved the sea passionately. He couldn't wait to reach the western district. We had an aunt who lived by the sea in al-Awzaai, and he used to go swimming when he was there. He couldn't believe his luck, because he'd be going there, going to the sea. When would we be starting? Before we set off we all warned one another how, if you're questioned, you must answer: "I'm Lebanese." But he was a young man in the first flush of manhood, in his fifteenth year. People had become weak with hunger during the siege, but his face had grown round and healthy. He'd gotten taller during the siege and his body had shot up in a quite uncanny way. On the way one of them stopped him and asked: "Lebanese or Palestinian?" "Palestinian," Jamal answered. A bullet to the head, just like that.

We passed by him—he'd gone on ahead of us because he was impatient. I just glanced at him, receiving such a shock my feet could no longer move forward or hold up my body. My nerves shattered, but I couldn't stop or lean over him and touch him with my hand. If any of us were to stop by somebody who'd been killed, they'd pick us out and finish us off at once. I couldn't. We moved on, right past him.

I looked at him, stretched out there on his back, as if he was asleep or had fainted. There was no blood at all. Then because they . . . So I *didn't* bend over him. I *didn't* stop. I *didn't* touch him with my hand.

My mother wasn't with me at that moment. When she saw him she fell into the ditch, with my baby brother whom she was carrying, in an indescribable state. She was a mother, the mother of Jamal who lay stretched out on the road as if asleep or in a faint. She couldn't stop by him either.

We went on, everyone totally stunned. I don't have any clear memory of it. Death hovered over us all. No one could look to left or right. I can't remember it clearly.

They started picking out the young men who were with us and

rounding them up. There were some cars and people who came to get money rather than kill. Mother found a car, paid the driver four hundred pounds and the family was crammed in. She didn't know how or where she was going, and we lost our old grandmother who was left behind. "Go and find her," said Mother.

My brother Nimr was with her in the car. He was a young man of eighteen, but they didn't notice him. He'd been with the *fidaain* who'd tried to leave the camp by the mountain road the night before. They hadn't been able to break through, and he'd left with many other young men, by the Dikwana road. He hid himself in the crowd, and so got away. While I was looking for my grandmother, the car moved off; I came out of the crowd, but couldn't find it. I found my grandmother. "That's it," I thought, "Mother's dead and so are my brothers and sisters. There's no way out. Everyone's going to be killed." I was terrified.

Suddenly I noticed a man in army uniform, one of the *Ahrar*[4] or Phalangists, I don't know which. He was the one my Mother had haggled with about hiring the car. I went up to him and somehow summoned up courage. "You're the one who fixed up the car for my mother and brothers and sisters," I said. "Find one for me and my grandmother too." I don't know how I managed it, but I talked to him. "Let's have some money," he said. I didn't have any on me, but grandmother had fifty pounds and we gave him that. "Get up on this lorry," he said. It was a dustcart. "I can't get up on that," I said. "Why, isn't it good enough for you?" he asked sarcastically. Then he came back and arranged a car for us, and I got in with grandmother. Then a woman came with her family, looked inside the car and saw us. "Do I have to pay for you?" she said. She wouldn't believe we'd paid, and said she wanted us to pay the same amount she had. The soldier got into the car with us and took us along the Jisr al-Pasha road as far as the Samaan Gallery, where there were some orchards. "Get off," he ordered, and as we did so some men came by. "Where are you taking them?" they asked him. "Take them away quickly, or they'll kill them and throw their bodies in the orchards." We got back in the car and were taken to the Museum area.

There were people all crowded round, and we newcomers joined those who'd already arrived and stuck to them. We couldn't have gotten away from them in any case, because we were united by sound, or

---

[4]*Ahrar* is a Lebanese fascist faction.

rather by sounds—the sounds of weeping, wailing, shouting, sobbing, and beating of cheeks and breasts. Everything round us was normal— cars, people, ordinary petrol stations—whereas we'd supposed that doomsday had come. It was as if we'd been reborn, but where had our minds gone? Nobody knew. Life was extraordinarily normal around us—so normal it made you crazy.

I rushed madly into the museum, looking for Mother. I searched among the people there. "Have you seen my mother?" I asked every- where. I said to grandmother: "That's it. My mother and brothers and sisters must be dead." My hands beat helplessly against my cheeks, and I wept, no longer knowing anything, except that the Phalangists were detaining people and settling old scores as they chose. Then: murder.

The final slaughter happened in the Museum. I looked and saw a room with a broad display window; it was packed with young men imprisoned inside.

There were a number of killing stations on the way, the last of these, apart from the final one, being the barracks near the Hotel Dieu. Only those destined for long life left there alive!

I saw a woman dressed in deepest black, more than forty years old. She was hitting a man over the head with a piece of wood with a nail on the end of it, and a young man, perhaps a relative of hers, came up and helped her. She was taking her revenge on us. I heard another woman, who was carrying a pistol, say, "I want to pick out the hand- somest young men and kill them."

It was summer, and most of the Phalangists were in their sleeveless undervests. It was hot, really hot. They wore crosses and had black bands tied to their foreheads.

The Phalangist who got us through—or was he one of the *Ahrar*, perhaps—said to us, "You chose Junblat. We had nothing against you till you joined the international left."

"Grandmother," I said, "I can't live for a minute without Mother and my brothers and sisters. I can't live by myself, can I?"

"Be patient, darling," she said "You're sure to find her."

But nobody had seen her. Mother wasn't there.

Someone, I don't know how, got us to the lorry. The Arab Deterrent Force was around us, Saudis and Sudanese. "Thank God you're safe," they were saying. I cursed them in my mind. God damn you, I thought; They kill people right under your noses, and you just stand there as if nothing's happened! The lorry belonged to the resistance and it took us to West Beirut.

In West Beirut, I found her. We met. She wept; I wept; but we met.

She'd been told, she said, that we'd been killed in al-Dikwana after she left, and that flesh had spattered the walls in the Hotel School where we'd been separated. During her trip her car had been constantly stopped by young men who'd come forward and demanded money, so that the few pounds she'd had left had disappeared.

And my little brother needed hospital treatment! At the hospital it was difficult to prick his hand with the serum needle because his veins had shrunk from hunger; he was only six days old when we went into the shelter, and the milk had dried up in Mother's breasts because she couldn't get any nourishment. She'd boil lentils for him, then grind them, mix them with water and get him to drink it. When he went on crying and crying, we'd rock him in our arms so that he wouldn't miss Mother's breast. In the shelter I'd lift him up and walk up and down with him, and one of the young men in the camp thought I was married because the baby spent so many hours in my arms.

Everybody left hungry and weak, and many children died. There was nothing to eat except lentils, chick peas and a few tins. Cigarettes ran out and it was a real hero who could get hold of a full packet of them. Some of the young men would wrap *mulukhiyya*[5] leaves or tea leaves in newspaper and smoke that.

Even Father, who had had a few cartons of cigarettes in the shop, had craved tobacco and longed for a cigarette as he lay dying.

I remember . . . No.

He was forty-six when he died and he had some kind of premonition of it. I once heard him say to Mother, "My time's coming. I'm going to die."

"Of course you're not!" said Mother hotly. "I'll die before you do!"

He told her he'd die as his father had, and at the same age; and so it happened, according to his premonition. My grandfather had been killed by a stray bullet during the exodus from Palestine in 1948. He was forty-six-years old.

6   Ahmad

They learned, finally, that Ahmad hadn't been on the plane that blew up in midair on its way from Bombay to Beirut. At the glass doors of

---

[5]*Mulukhiyya* is a vegetable with large green leaves which are chopped and cooked with meat or chicken. It is a popular dish in Palestine, Lebanon and Syria, as well as in Egypt, but virtually little known in the rest of the Arab world.

Kuwait airport was a middle-aged mother, wearing on her head a white cotton scarf embroidered on the fringes with tiny flowers, and dressed in a long, black village gown. Her hand was against her cheek and her muscles trembled with fear and apprehension, presaging the arthritis to come.

She wanted to scream, but was quite unable to. Ahmad had just graduated, and his family was waiting behind the barrier in the arrival lounge but neither he nor his plane appeared. Five years abroad and a diploma specializing in radiography. When they heard the news of the crash and Ahmad wasn't there, they thought . . . But Ahmad had enlisted as a volunteer and gone direct to Beirut, to the Damour camp.

"Five years of India! I won't say five years of crushing loneliness and being away from home because I was a member of the resistance and the Students' Union. But I was convinced all that had no kind of value while I was abroad. Did you know that, Yusra? I felt isolated, apart from the world. It was as if I was on one of the peaks of the great Himalayas. I was ill for a long time, and once I fell off a motorbike and was badly bruised. Ill, with just a few Arab friends, in a small village in the middle of India, hundreds of kilometers from the capital. India? What a place! Indian films are one thing, but the country's another!"

They'd called him "the Indian" at the camp, and one day I asked him: "Are you Indian?"

He'd laughed and laughed at my question, which he hadn't thought of before. "Oh no! . . . Would you believe it? Is it possible? Oh no!" He just didn't know how he'd managed to complete five years there.

And I'd asked him, "What? Is it true you're Indian?"

"Yusra, do you know what it means to be away from home, there, in a remote part of the world? It's a very real feeling. As real as I am now. Diaries. Look here, at the top of this page: '18 December 1975. Today some friends and I were wandering round the market place and one of us went to buy a box of matches. It turned out to be a surprise and a joke at the same time. The box was sealed, but when I opened it I found all the matches had been used. That just sums up India.' "

I pointed to one of the pages and asked him about an expression written in English. He read it out to me. It was from Tolstoy's *War and Peace* and it said that the factor establishing an army's morale is hard to quantify scientifically, because it isn't related either to the number of soldiers or to any other obvious cause.

On another page I saw curving lines that he'd clearly drawn himself.

It was a miniature map of Palestine. I read what he'd written by it: "Remember. This must be turned into a reality." I found nothing else of any interest in the diary; just appointments noted here and there, names scattered about, accounts of monthly expenditure, and records of money received and remittances sent through the post.

Ahmad told me about himself. His father was dead, he said, and his mother was remarried in Kuwait to a Palestinian who worked as a van driver, carrying goods during the day and people who were too poor to afford a taxi at night. Often, as he sat in front of me, he'd become distracted, his thoughts wandering to the West Bank, to his town. He told me about his childhood days and about his married sister Aisha, who was still there and who he hadn't seen since the day he left the West Bank. He thought about her constantly and kept coming back to her. He went on talking to me about her, about the country, and about the spring flowers there.

"You're lucky!" I said "At least you've seen the town you came from."

A town of olives and almonds—that's how I imagined it. He had a tree there, he said.

"What kind of tree?"

"Almond or mulberry, I can't remember exactly."

They had a house on the top of a hill. "We want to build one or two more rooms," he said. "For the two of us. There's an orchard here." He'd draw a plan of his town as he spoke, sketching it out on paper or dust or sand. He hoped to go back; and kept on telling me the 1980s would see us return. He was pretty sure this would happen.

Ahmad was transferred from the camp to work in the administration of the medical department. Then he requested a military training course outside. We'd become engaged before he left, and our letters thereafter were full of love. Before he left I gave him three Fairuz tapes; Ahmed loved Marcel Khalifa[6] and Fairuz[7], but I've sealed his tapes with red wax now.

The engagement was to last fifteen months; he was a fighter in the

---

[6]*Marcel Khalifa* Another Lebanese musician and singer who has gained great reputation since the seventies for the firm stance he took, in his progressive songs, against fascist aggression in Lebanon directed at both the Lebanese and the Palestinians. His songs are some of the finest songs of the resistance to the coercion and injustice in Lebanon and the Arab world.

[7]*Fairuz* Lebanon's foremost singer, loved all over the Arab world for her crystal voice and the progressive content of her songs.

resistance and we didn't have much money for extras. We'd planned to marry in the first month of 1981, but he decided, finally, that this should be brought forward. He told his mother and his family to come, and they arrived in October, before I'd had time to get myself ready. We drew up the marriage contracts, and I prepared some clothes. His stepfather and his mother, who wanted to take him back, begged him to leave Lebanon, but he wouldn't agree. I couldn't find a house, and they said they'd only return after our wedding. His mother wanted to take pictures for her family in Kuwait, so they'd know her son was now married.

The house. It was simple, he said; there were no problems about it. A week before we got married I told him I wanted to see the house, and off we went. "God preserve us!" I said. "Is that a house?" It was an abandoned house, isolated amid open country, near an army camp which was one of the centers of the resistance in the South. Around it, as far as the eye could see, were orchards, agricultural land, banana and orange plantations; an empty stone house with no furniture. I was confused and tense. "Is this the house you've been telling me about for the past year?" I asked in astonishment. But I went back, cleaned it and put it in some kind of order inside. "It's all right," I told him. "There's no problem."

We got married there and lived in the house for about ten days. Then his family left, and I went back to my mother's house in Beirut because my leave from work was over.

I stayed with my family for three months and at last found a vacant room we could have moved into—two days after his death. I was a new bride in my parents' home; an embarrassing situation to say the least.

He usually came on Saturdays, because he knew that Sunday was my day off, and the last time he came he gave me part of his salary for the first of the month. I was cold and wearing his field jacket. I put my hand in the pocket and found some cash. "Is that all that's left from your salary?" I asked him. He tried to conceal things, then explained. There'd been an error in the accounts for the sales of the organization's monthly magazine, and he'd paid the difference out of his salary. There was only three hundred pounds left. I tried to show him this didn't worry me. "There's no problem," I told him. We went out to the cinema.

Finally, one Thursday, two days before he was due home on the Saturday, he was killed in an Israeli air raid, from a wound to the head. I'd heard about the raid on Damour and Sidon that same day, but I'd thrust the possibility aside, banished the nightmare from my mind. I didn't think he'd die, that he could possibly die; it never occurred to me even once. The Israelis' surprise raid got him when he was in the camp near Sidon.

This happened during the daytime of Thursday, 29 January 1981.

In the first month of the year.

At two o'clock in the afternoon.

7　And Then

Two o'clock in the afternoon, four o'clock in the afternoon, twelve midnight, dawn. It was all the same.

A wooden door, painted gray like everything else in the building. A short ring at the door, and then . . . To the left was the sitting room of Jamila's house, with the chairs still folded up on the table, as if no one had thought of using them for a long time. Since when? Since the news arrived. And where was Yusra?

The martyr's wife lay on her bed, utterly broken, shaken by fits of weeping so intense that they took away all her strength. "How?" she shouted. "Why?" Faintness took hold of her from time to time, and the women would come to her, bringing rose water and eau de Cologne, massaging her temples and her flushed face. Blackness is the sign of a martyr's wife, blackness rising up on all sides with the stammerings of the women calling for calm and patience. Her sudden sobbing shattered the stillness and they gathered round her trying to soothe her. Patience! Is there anything in death to be patient about?

Her dull eyes moved round the corners of the room, and the few pieces of simple furniture: the double-doored cupboard with its top loaded up with cases and bags, the chairs in a circle round the bed. In them were women, old and young, dressed in black. Concern, and sad, silent contemplation.

In the midst of this Yusra lay on the bed in an agony of grief, her head on a square pillow with colored patterns of gold and silver flowers and oriental designs on the black silk of the pillow case—a present from Kuwait, made in Hong Kong.

They brought her orange juice, but she refused to drink a drop. They pleaded with her, loving and insistent: "Yusra, you're going to have a child."

The child! What had he done wrong? Yusra drank a glass of juice, becoming more aware of the presence of the three-month-old child inside her. Quickly, decisively, she considered the matter. Three months in the womb. Six more to complete the pregnancy. Another person would be born. It would be a Palestinian, from its first moment in the world.

Yusra's mother tried to persuade her to stop her choking sobs and eat something. Everything, she told Yusra, is fate and chance: God decrees the span of each of our lives from the moment of our birth. It was enough that she, Yusra, had got out of Tel al-Zaatar and was still alive. Her mother also said something about a wall on which Yusra had stood and about the dozens of dogs scavenging among the bodies thrown at the foot. She talked about the need to go on with the living of her life.

Yusra screamed, her voice becoming louder; her swollen eyelids becoming redder. "Don't talk to me about forgetting!"

Her mother leant her worn face over her, her tears falling, her handkerchief tied round her chin in two strands that fell down on to her bosom. She stroked her daughter's hair. Yusra screamed again. "Don't talk to me about forgetting!"

He was gazing at her, smiling out of the small photograph she'd immediately hung up on the opposite wall.

8   Scenes

Beirut was like a box full of matches. It was transformed now into a vast land of volcanic ashes and flowing molten tar, and it was crumbling minute by minute. He hadn't liked Beirut, had been irritated by the heavy traffic there. "I was ill when I got back from India," he'd say. "I had a headache. For the first week my head wouldn't clear."

He'd fall silent and his thoughts would stray. "What's wrong, my dear?" I'd say: "What are you thinking about?"

"I was miles away," he'd say; and when I asked him where, he'd say, "the West Bank." I'd get horribly depressed sometimes because his thoughts were always there. He'd talk to me at length about his village and the days he'd spent there.

He loved taking photographs of natural scenes, and I'd say to him, "What sort of pictures are these? Take a picture of us!"

He loved Maghdusha. We went there and took pictures of ourselves among the trees, near the huge white statue of the Virgin which seems to rise up to Heaven on the spiral staircase that surrounds it.

Photographs of the sun descending from the gray clouds, like a red apple falling into the sea. White clouds flying at sunset, like locks of hair. Two lonely daisies in a field of green grass.

Anemones, wild thorns the colour of violet, tarragon flowers, and a statue of the Lady of Love, with treetops that seemed to embroider the fringes of heaven.

I remember how he photographed a vine in a corner, with a natural scene stretched behind it. Then there was the child of Jamila—who got married after we left Tel al-Zaatar—his teeth not yet appeared, running happily in the grass. There was a picture of all of us together, our hands clasped beneath the huge lilac tree that cast its shadow on our faces. I was puzzled by the picture he took of his soldier's cap as it lay amid the grass and the flowers. How strange! What made him take a picture of a cap lying happily among the grasshoppers and small pebbles and roses? Just a soldier's cap? He used, too, to love taking pictures of the sun when it was close to the earth, at sunrise or sunset; and he always managed to capture its golden light, making me feel that everything linked to him overflowed with a shimmering light of a glimmering sunrise. Ahmad came from a town of olives and almonds, and he radiated joy; that's why, when I see pictures of him, he's always laughing.

The last time he visited me, I remember, I'd had a dream which I shall never forget. I dreamed that he and I were sleeping in our house, which was on a rock high up on the top of a mountain, with a deep valley beneath us. Asleep on this rock, we were about to fall, and the rock, huge but unsteady, was about to tumble down with us.

The dream unsettled me and I told him about it. "You're anxious about getting a house," he said. "We'll soon find one to live in."

Now I always see him in my dreams. The last time I saw him, he was asking me to heat some water so he could take a bath. The last bath he had was at the base, just before he met his death; but in my dream he asked me for hot water. I was wearing dark clothes, black on black, in mourning for him. I felt happy, and rejoiced. I was almost wild with happiness. I woke up, and knew it had all been a dream. My grief was unbearable.

The clothes I sleep in are as black as all the rest. I've forgotten many things but I still remember the white wedding dress we hired for his mother to take a picture of us.

The woman's pregnant and dressed in black. I am that woman in black. He was anxious for me and told me of his concern for me and the birth. "You really care for me that much?" I'd ask him tenderly. From the first month he started to plan for the upbringing of this child I now wait for alone.

When he died, I felt my life had ended, that everything had come to a stop at once and there was nothing left in the world.

I'll try to live . . . to fight against the sadness weighing down on my soul, leading me, sometimes, to feel that I'm losing my sanity. I'll try—but it's not easy at all.

But I will try.

When I remember, I weep. I open the album and look at the photographs. I come upon the sentence he wrote inside:

"These pictures make me feel I've become a professional—an expert photographer. I've taken them to embody phases of a life: phases of darkness, and phases of light. There are times of bitterness and there will be times of beauty and tenderness and light.

"Those times will come."

All I remember apart from that is his smile.

—translated by Peter Clark and Christopher Tingley

Riyad Baydas (b. 1960)

A short story writer, Baydas was born in Shefaᶜamr in the Galilee, where he completed his elementary and secondary schooling. He then spent three years at the University of Haifa studying history, philosophy, literature, and art history. His collections of short stories include: *Hunger and the Mountain* (1980); *The King* (1985); *The Path* (1985); *The Wind* (1987); and *Preliminary Plans* (1988). His main area of concern is, as he himself puts it, "to explore the problem of human existence by means of the general relationships found in our society." He tends toward a stark realism in his depiction of these relationships, and his writing technique is characterized by an experimental variety of form and approach.

Hunger and the Mountain

From a distance the village appears silent, submissive, and forlorn. Yet once you enter it and roam through its streets and the tiny pavements that hug the flanks of its narrow roads, you can feel that sticky heat that flows down the faces of its inhabitants and of the visitors who come to our village in the summer. The smell of onions is abundant in its streets and alleys. The sight of garlic whets your appetite for a piece of that lamb liver that hangs outside the butcher's shop, to be fried with crushed garlic. But you'd wipe off your mouth and swallow your saliva while you stare open-mouthed at these sights, which, despite yourself, are arousing your appetite. It is not a consolation, either, after seeing all this glorious food laid out and delicious; for not being able to have any of it, is to watch one of those foreign films at night and see how dead easy it is for *them* to consume it.

Early in the morning, my mother shouted, "Get up and look for work!"

I yawned. I raised the quilt, then brought it back down over my whole body. My mother went on muttering. But I was not overly bothered by her words, for the night before I'd been drinking with

Ibrahim a few glasses of lousy arak[1]—the cheap kind, without any appetizers—and now I could feel my stomach shot through with pain and my head reeling and still heavy with a hangover.

I felt sleep once more tickling my eyelids. I was not thinking of anything at all—only imagining meals I wished I could be eating that day with my mother.

But she would not leave me alone to breathe in that expansive atmosphere, which exuded the aromas of good, rich food.

"You're slacking! You're not doing a thing!" she shouted again, angrily. "Get up and water the tomato seedlings, they're drooping! Get to them before they wilt! In a little while, tomatoes will be more precious than gold!"

With the tips of my fingers I pushed at the quilt. It fell back. My face appeared in the mirror opposite, sallow and pale, and ravaged by fatigue. My hand slid down to my stomach and pressed on it. I felt an acrid taste filling my mouth . . . Bitterness. Nausea. The mirror reflecting my image arouses nausea and disgust. The bed, a hell. The night, a whore I lie down with once every twenty-four hours. Good food seemed to me one of the Seven Wonders of the World, impossible to attain. My throat is a flaming cinder. My stomach heaves. I press on it. My hand goes up as high as it can and comes crashing down on the mirror. This mirror, mottled with black splotches and some sad, painful memories that my mother is always talking to me about, is all that remains of my father's legacy. It shatters. Its fragments rest quietly on the floor.

My mother rushes in. Stupefaction fills all the angles of her face. Her eyes are staring. She beats her breast. "God have mercy! . . ."

Hell is killing me. There is a Hell on earth . . . Yes, contrary to what they taught us at school, where they told us there was no such thing . . . This Hell I live is merely a smaller version of the Hell up there— or, perhaps, is even worse. If my father had not been a stonemason, then I would have had the chance to continue my studies and to get a clerk's job or something of that kind. Then, Hell would have been something quite different, different from what I experience now. Then I'd have stamped out this nausea; I would not be in it. The night would not have been a whore that I get tired of embracing. The heat and viscosity would have receded from me and from my village . . . My father was a stonemason and my mother a housewife. As my mother

---

[1]*Arak* is the famous liquor of the Middle East made up from grapes and anise.

told me, his love for his village was excessive, in a terrible way. For that reason he never had money, not even once in his life. He has distorted the meaning of life in my eyes. Had I known him, my view of him might have been different. But I never knew him, for he died on the day of the Catastrophe; he insisted on not abandoning the village, on not submitting to the will of the enemy. My mother and I are what's left of his shadow. We fled our village and took up residence in another. My mother still repeats what he said once during the days of the Mandate to the Bishop, who was trying to reconcile him to the British: "If Christ's grandfather were an Englishman I would stop worshipping Him! I don't want them, and I don't want to talk to you either!" Angrily, he'd slammed the door behind him.

My mother breaks in on the record in my head: "Shall I make your tea with mint or with Persian thyme?"

"I don't want anything."

Once again, the record starts spinning in my head. I burp. A rather disgusting odor spreads across the room. I shut my mouth tightly. My pupils dilate. They become live coals, and I feel them radiating a thick and sticky heat. My mouth fills up with liquid, I run to the toilet. I discharge the remains of last night. I feel fatigue sapping my strength. The disgusting stench spreads everywhere. My mother brings the tea. I open the tap. I gargle. I spit out weakly. I go back to the room.

"Man searches for perfection, but ultimately he fails . . ." This is what Ibrahim told me last night. In foreign films people may achieve some levels of perfection, but here a person never dreams of attaining any; he thinks only of making sure he can eat every day, and that in itself is one big load. Ibrahim claimed that all his experiments had failed miserably because of the harshness of life here, and he asked me to test out his idea of running around the huge mountain ten times. I laughed and went on drinking arak with him.

My mother brings the tea. She pours it. I down the cup quickly. I strip off my pajamas and throw them down in the middle of the room. I put on my new pair of pants—which I bought three years ago—and go out.

Last night I spoke to you about the notion of perfection, isn't that so?
I want to have good food!
If you run around the mountain ten times, you'll win.
I want to gobble up a tomato, with a delicious loaf of bread and thyme!

You will be the first of my human experiments. Here, animals strive harder for perfection than man himself ever does.

I want my home to be full of the aroma of grilled meat and good arak!

Whatever the conditions, it is our duty to seek perfection.

I want to go to bed with a rich woman!

It will all happen for you if you run around the mountain ten times for five consecutive days.

I want not to be bored with this life, and to not be hungry!

As I told you, I'll give you the sum of two thousand liras if you run around the mountain and prove that you have the ability to face a challenge. . . .

I felt a heavy load fall off of my shoulders and smash to bits. The familiar street became like a very beautiful tulip. People became different. That thick stickiness that I felt every day did not engulf me any more. One day my dream would come true, and I would succeed in not going hungry for a whole week. The night would no longer be the whore it was on all other nights. No, for a whole week, I won't go hungry. Joy would fill my mother's heart as she saw me coming, staggering under a load of rice, lentils, flour, and a few delicious tomatoes to tide us over till the plants in our garden ripened. I'd buy a quarter pound of lamb meat, and we'd savor its delicious taste. We'd celebrate and make jokes. We won't lose our tempers. We'd dance beside the fireplace as logs crackle inside it. We'd dance in circles around the fireplace in our small kitchen. It'd be a genuine, authentic *sahjeh*,[2] more authentic than any *sahjeh* at a wedding celebration. . . .

I'll not surrender to the mountain. Tonight, I'm going to pray a lot so that I can stand firm in the face of its might and its massive size. It will not be able to challenge me. It's either the mountain or my nausea, hunger, aimlessness, misery, and sorrow. I'll imagine it as the most beautiful object I could desire in the whole world. I'll run and surge forward, sing and pant, blowing out the air of sorrow, melancholy, and boredom. Compared to two thousand liras, five days are nothing. I'll be more than some human experiment on perfection . . . To hell with perfection! It'll not change a thing in my life. Perfection of what? . . . If everyone learned to think like Ibrahim thinks and behaves, then no

[2]*Sahjeh* is a special dance accompanied by song that the men chant as they dance. It is performed mainly in the countryside.

evil would touch this world; there would be no spread of unemployment as terrible and dreadful as this. The hunger game would end with the mountain . . . It is certain that I'll either overcome the mountain and run around it or fail. The game will end either with my finishing off the mountain or with it wearing me out and making me fail. One or the other—no more, no less. The important thing is that the mountain should take on a significance different from the one I'm familiar with. No, the mountain is not a mountain is not a mountain: it is not inorganic at all. It throbs, it has a heart, it feels, loves, hates; it has a sense of solidarity and sharing; it feels sorrow and joy. So why, O Mountain, don't you stand on my side? Tomorrow I'll be running ten laps around you. Don't let me down. Don't frustrate me just to show how strong you are. If you want, we'll share the money . . . Tomorrow the game begins. With my lean body I'll overcome the mountain . . . *Should you succeed in the first test, we can think about taking the matter further. The mountain will become a source of livelihood for you, and you will become a source of research and experiments!*

Good. What a splendid idea, that the mountain should become the means by which the fangs of hunger will lose the strength to consume my entrails. Through the mountain it will be I who devours hunger. Perhaps one day the idea of hunger will become a trivial idea, which I'll no longer be able to comprehend. As the others say, earth can become a paradise. Hunger is a terrible thing, and he who doesn't get used to the fangs of hunger, to viscosity and many other things, goes mad or beats his head against alley walls. His eyes get tired from staring at plates of delicious food heaped up in cafés. Perhaps he'd kill himself, or maybe flee to the mountains and become a vegetarian. A queer idea, that—but not unreasonable, in its own way. I shall reflect on tomorrow's event with extreme seriousness.

"Till we meet tomorrow, Ibrahim . . . You and I, and the mountain. And, after five days, the two thousand liras . . ." As I hurried outside, I sang in a loud voice: "You and I, the mountain and the mo-o-ney!" I made my way home in silence.

I'm all set!
Be careful of the mountain. It's steep, and its rocks are slippery.
Don't worry. I'll think of it as a beautiful whore, lying back calmly waiting for me, its trees her beautiful erect breasts. Brilliant idea, don't you agree?
Diabolical also.

It's a very simple proposition: the mountain or the whore or both will bring me luck as long as I can hold my own against its steep slopes and sharp rocks by thinking of it as a wonderful whore. That's the difference between a hard, miserable life and a life of luxury. It is in accordance with the dangers of this mountain that no one before has climbed to its summit or even dared look up at it. This is not simply because it is dangerous, but because all those who've tried to climb it and challenge its great might have fallen and died. For from it emanates constantly the putrid stench of black death. If my mother knew that I intended to run around this towering mountain and climb parts of its dangerous slopes, she'd be furious and would forbid me to take on this insane venture which only the craziest people on earth would undertake, simply to prove their rightful worth in the face of the monotony of this contemptible world. But hunger and unemployment make madmen out of ordinary people. Or, let's say, bring them to the brink of madness—there's no difference whatever between dying and living in boredom, hunger, and viscous heat. Defeat begins the minute you shrink back from the dangers of this steep-sloped mountain . . . No, I'll not capitulate to its holy might. Not only in scaling a lofty mountain does danger lie; it lies, rather, in an essential point of weakness in man himself, and that is his hunger. Hunger is truly terrifying: that inner terror that sweeps through the spaces of the self, accompanied by fears and turbulent conflicts deep within. Something truly frightful pushes you to resist hunger, however high the cost; you feel something falling through your stomach, your heart, and your lungs inside you. Hunger has no mercy. Neither do others have any mercy whatever . . . O Father, if you had not been a stonemason, I'd not be preparing now to destroy myself so readily. If you'd been well-off, I'd not be taking such risks. I'd be sitting in my office, calm and content . . . You never liked them because of their meanness and cruelty, and they returned your feelings. I feel the same way about them. There is no difference between your feelings and mine. We're both in the same boat, except that you were a mason, with steady work, while I—I can hardly get my daily food. It's not my fault, Father. There is heartless unemployment. More than thirty times, I signed on at the unemployment office. The official there took no notice of me. The reason is very simple, Father. It is because I'm like all the others. He sees hundreds like me waiting for one specific job. He knows nothing of my hardships, or of the mean and violent feelings that assail me. Once I planned to tell him about my life—about its misery, its harshness, its viscosity—but, when confronted with his laughter, which rang throughout the room, I withdrew. "Ha! Ha! Ha!" I slammed the door behind me. He shouted, "You're like all the others, young man!" I didn't hear the rest . . . This village has killed me, Father. There is no spot in me where it has not deposited its intense and clammy boredom. Every day it kills me. It unsheathes thousands of daggers to stab me with even as I stand still in my place, not making a move. I have no strength to scream. This guy Ibrahim searches for the knowledge of human perfectibility, and I search for a bite of bread. Yesterday I saw him throw a tasty piece of bread, spread with genuine French cheese, to his dog. My mouth watered. I wished he'd go inside for a while so that I could jump at the dog, tear it to bits, and rip the bread out from its mouth. Ibrahim felt I was staring too much at the dog: "Poor, hungry dog," he said tenderly. That's right. "Hungry." He was hungry, and he deserved such luxurious food. In my mouth gathered a big gob of spit: "Fie. Fie . . ."

"What's happening with you?" Ibrahim was shouting. "Are you still putting on your shorts?"

"I'm ready. I'll be right down. I'm on the other side of the hill."

I arrived at his side.

"Let's begin," he said firmly.

The game has begun. Will you, O Mountain, collapse in the face of my persistence, or will I collapse in the face of your might and arrogance? I don't know . . . That thing whose domain I now intend to explore is an unknown. The mountain is rugged and I will be stronger than its ruggedness, its steepness, its slippery rocks. My throat goes dry. My breathing accelerates. The burning sun stirs up in me a strong feeling of viscosity, and the mountain appears as calm as a hero in one of the ghost stories I used to read as a child. A hot flame is almost leaping up inside me. I urge myself to be calm in climbing its slopes. I have to run ten laps around it. I have to. If this mountain were Hell, I'd have to go into it, just to get the two thousand liras . . .

I begin.

Remember what you were imagining yesterday. Your hungry mother resisting the ferocity of this life . . . No matter how complicated things get, I can always eat tomatoes . . . But things will not get complicated. It's almost impossible that I should surrender to the mountain. Sisyphus himself will not prove to have been any stronger or braver than I . . . I *am* Sisyphus. Don't say I'm not. To earn my food, I might even become a test area for nuclear experiments in this village. Or, become a mouse in which they search for cancerous cells. If ever they inform me that they are interested in conducting experiments on me with regard to the complexities of cancer, I will be totally ready. I will not refuse . . . Unemployment and boredom are killing me. My mother's hunger terrifies me . . . It's quite likely that my father, when he entrusted me to my mother's care, reassured her that once I grew up to be a man she would not need anyone's help. That I would honor and cherish her . . . I only wish I could, Father, but the matter is not in my hands. I've done all the things that please her. I've planted the plot next to our house with onions, tomatoes, garlic, cucumbers, and potatoes. I've tried in every way possible to honor her, but lack of work has made me a failure. Don't be too sad. I'll become an experimental testing ground for all the sciences. I might become a boon to science and mankind. It's possible that my name will be recorded in books and official reports . . . At this moment, I'm happy. The mountain is getting more rugged before me. I blow out my breath, gasping with difficulty. I am swept by a sudden desire to throw myself into the lap of this mighty mountain. The meager food I ate yesterday is not enough to sustain me for ten laps. I might collapse . . . I look back. Ibrahim is exhaling the smoke from his cigarette, looking anxious and impressed. Tenderly he strokes the hair of his foreign dog . . . I run, racing along between some sharp rocks. I will not give in. I will not collapse. The mountain will. . . .

The first lap is over. Ibrahim claps with joy.

"I'll prove to the world that we are not what they claim we are!" he shouts out.

I wipe the sweat that rolls off my body as I run. I don't stop. The mountain seems to be making itself larger, resisting. The ground heaves under my feeble legs. Shrubs vibrate, become sharp knives. Its rocks are like volcanoes, apt to erupt at any second. I trip on a stone. I fall on my face. Blood oozes calmly out. Resignedly, I lift my weary body and go on running.

Ibrahim claps his hands. "Try not to give in! Two thousand liras is a lot of money . . . If you succeed today, you'll get two hundred liras in advance!"

Remember what you were thinking about yesterday? How much you felt like going to bed with a whore? The mountain is a soft, smooth whore, waiting for you. Its shrubs are not knives but mellow breasts, that need to be stripped bare of mountain mist . . . A little energy returns to me. The second lap is over. The mountain is a whore, a plump prostitute that goes to bed only with me. Its breasts are in need of tender hands. I'm the One, O Mountain! Don't dump me in the ditch of failure. Don't brand my forehead with cruel failure, or this viscosity will invade even further corners of my being. Nausea, boredom, and deep sadness will afflict me . . . How am I to blame for my unemployment? I'm not responsible for my own and my mother's hunger!

Tears are splashing onto the smooth rocks.

No! No! . . . I will *not* surrender! . . . Damn! My breast is rising and falling like the swelling of stormy, angry sea-waves. I give up! . . . Restrain your might, Mountain, I no more can! . . . My feet are stumbling on the rocks. For the second time, I fall on my face. I try to get up. The sun beats against my face like sacks of cement. My back! . . . The mountain is a mountain. No matter how much I imagine it to be the beautiful things that are dear to me, it will not change. It will not surrender. For a second time I try to continue my run, and fail. Minutes pass, and Ibrahim comes up to me sadly.

"I'm sorry. You've failed completely . . . I'll give you two hundred liras as a gift. Don't be too disappointed . . ."

"A difficult life . . ." I said, panting. "We must continue living it, moment by moment." Brushing off the dust that clung to my face, I continued: "There's no one solution. Why not just go on?"

Both of us went our separate ways.

—translated by May Jayyusi and Thomas G. Ezzy

Zaki Darwish *(b. 1944)*

Born in Berweh in the Galilee, which was razed to the ground after the 1948 debacle, Darwish now lives in Judaideh, where he is the headmaster of the Shi'b secondary school. He obtained a B.A. in Arabic Literature and education from the University of Haifa, and has been very active in the literary life of Palestinians in Israel, heading the cultural department of the Union of Palestinian Writers in Israel. He also edits the *Aswar* review and is editor-in-chief of the paper *Nida' al-Aswar*. He began writing his short stories early in life and has had at least four collections published: *Winter of Estrangement* (1970); *The Bridge and the Deluge* (1972); *The Man Who Killed the World* (1977); and *The Dogs* (1978). In 1983 he published his first novel, *Exodus from Ibn Amer Plain*. Zaki Darwish's style is robust, vivid, and gripping. His characters have depth and intelligence, and his plots are original, even haunting. Some of his work has been translated into Hebrew and is popular among Israeli readers.

Horses

I. Foreword

I have a special feeling for horses. I no sooner hear the word *horse* than memories wake in me, vivid and intense, like a wall blocking out all other pictures and thoughts.

"What's wrong with that?" someone might say. "We all have particular memories that live on in us."

II. The Horse My Father Killed

I felt that I was to blame and I returned home with my personal tragedy weighing on me. My father's guest room was the usual mixture of old men with fertile memories, who recited what they could of Quranic verses, and recalled fragments of memories unconnected by time or place, with nothing in common except for the general agreement they inspired that what used to be was so much better than what is, in spite of everything—a viewpoint with which I was never prepared to agree.

I told them the story of the blue-gray horse.

"It's not worth making yourself so miserable over it," my father said.

"Why not?" I answered, "when I've lost the most beautiful thing I had?"

"You've nothing but books and book learning," he said. "But I once lost a real horse, a pedigree horse that I helped bring into the world one rainy winter night. I watched him grow day by day. I studied a few years at school, where they taught us a lot about horses, but I never knew a more beautiful horse than mine. Do you know, I once crossed the whole Ibn Amir plain on his back, till I reached the Bisan depression? I galloped along the shore to Jaffa and Gaza and climbed the mountains of Galilee on his back, entering the races on occasions like weddings and feasts. I jumped fences and went through ravines and valleys. He never failed me. Through rain and summer heat and darkness, he never once failed me."

"Yet you killed him," someone said.

"That was when he did it," he continued, "I mean when he finally did fail me. He did it in a situation which needed the utmost initiative and resolution."

"How was that?" we asked.

"It was during the 1936 rebellion," he answered, "and the horse had to climb the hills to the village of Miaar by way of Shi'b. We'd learned that the British were planning to attack Miaar, looking for the rebels they were told were there. The road to the village wasn't particularly difficult, and in any case it wasn't the first time I'd ridden him up it. He'd never stopped or shown any signs of tiredness the other times, and I was pretty sure I'd be able to reach Miaar before they did. I once raced a British car along the road from Acre to Birweh, and got several meters ahead of it. I only stopped when they shot over my head from the car.

"That day the horse seemed to be going even faster than usual; those who saw us on the outskirts of the village said we seemed to be flying—the horse wasn't simply running, they said, but skimming along, with his feet hardly touching the ground. My *kufiyya* was spread out in the air like the sail of a boat on a stormy sea.

"My horse and I were galloping through the valley between Shi'b and Birweh, when suddenly the horse stopped as if pulled up by some powerful force. I looked around. There was a peasant plowing his field with the help of a worn-out old mare; he'd stopped for a moment to rest himself and the horse. I noticed my horse smelling some fresh dung, then he raised his head high and beat the ground with his hooves, neighing hoarsely. I tried to push him on, but in vain. I used the whip and the spurs, which I'd hardly ever had to use before. I tried talking to him, first harshly, then kindly, but he stood fixed in his place, then took a few slow steps to where the mare was standing. He put his head over her neck, whispered something into her ears, then began smelling all over her body.

"At that very moment the first British car appeared on the Halazoon valley bridge. A real rage took hold of me now, an indescribable anger that I couldn't control. I opened my legs, then closed them savagely on the belly of the horse till I felt the spurs piercing his sides; but the horse was desperately smelling the mare's body. Then I lost all control of myself and knew that I'd reached a pitch of anger from which there was no return. I jumped off the back of the horse and looked for the nearest thing at hand, but found only an old plow lying in front of me. I picked it up, raised it high above my head, then, with all the strength of my pent-up rage, plunged it deep into the horse's neck. The warm blood spurted over my face and chest. The horse first raised his head high, then raised his front feet, then, standing on his back feet, rose higher and higher. He was a sublime sight as he stood there, rearing up between the earth and the sky.

"Now the British cars, five of them, were parallel with where we were standing. I threw a last look at the horse. He was still rearing up in the air, and I ran eastward toward Miaar."

"And did you get there before they did?" we asked.

"I did, but that's another story. The important thing is that I never owned a horse after that, and never even rode one again. It was said that when the mare saw the horse rearing up between earth and heaven, she took fright and ran out of the field, dragging the plow behind her. The peasant himself was terrified. It was also said that the horse remained rearing up in the air till he lost his last drop of blood."

One of those present said that when my father left his horse rearing like that, he put the end of his garment between his teeth and ran, heedless of everything. They also said that a mighty wind blew and thrust him before it towards the east. And others said that he was sometimes flying—or rather, not so much flying as speeding on with the leaping run of a hare.

III. Horses and the Sea

Mustafa al-Salih had never been known to lie, and never prophesied anything that didn't come true. It's true that he used to disappear sometimes until people forgot him, but he'd always reappear, suddenly, sooner or later.

However, what he related at the end of his long life was beyond all normal belief. That day, a day of scorching summer heat, he crossed the streets of Acre—or rather its old alleys to the south and the west that smelled of salt and fish—one after the other; he even crossed those next to the wall in the north and east. He'd performed his dawn prayer at al-Jazzar mosque, and when the noon *adhan*[1] sounded, he found himself in front of the Zaituni mosque, where he entered and performed the noon prayer. Then, in the evening, he found his preferred corner at the mosque near the fisherman's harbor, and related his strange story immediately after prayer, as people sat in a circle round him. That's why it's impossible that the man could have been telling lies.

He told his story half reclining, with his eternal staff, which he'd never been parted from since he lost his leg, lying beside him.

The story of his leg is another strange one. He'd jumped his horse, from a great height, into the body of a British tank in al-Kasayir, entering like a huge rock hurled down by a raging torrent. The horse was killed, flying over the back of the tank like a bird. It was only then that he discovered how unequal the struggle was between a tank and a horse. That night they asked him, perhaps for the thousandth time, about the three days in which he'd lain unconscious, but they didn't expect anything more than his usual answer:

"I don't remember."

This time, though, a strange light shone in his eyes. It was said later that a radiance covered his face, rising from his very heart and lighting up the whole mosque. His features had a repose they'd never shown before.

"I was there," he said, pointing toward the southern window of the mosque.

"Where?" they asked.

"In the depths of the sea," he answered. "You know I usually only swim after the dawn prayer; that's been my habit ever since I learned to swim, and no great waves or storms or heat or cold ever hindered me. The depths of the sea are always warm, my children, like a tender mother; it's only the surface that's cold. That day I plunged into the depths, and perhaps I went further and deeper than usual, or further and deeper than my age allowed. A huge wave bore me up, higher and

[1]This is the Muslim call to prayer, performed usually from the minaret of a mosque five times a day (dawn, noon, afternoon, sunset, and night).

higher, till I imagined I was being raised to a height from which there was no return to the sea. But just as I was beginning to believe I was flying, I found myself falling again. Then another mighty, towering wave engulfed me, and thrust me, lower and lower still, into the depths of the waters. I confess that I felt afraid. But the strange thing was, my children, that the depths of the waters were lit up, as if it was the middle of the day. But where did the light come from? Not from the stars, certainly, and there was neither sun nor moon in the sky. Finally, I found myself in a large cavern, where I breathed pure, dry air. The waves would reach the mouth of the cavern, then retreat, just as they do along the walls of Acre. I saw clearly that the sand on the floor of the cavern was completely dry, and so were the walls. Then I saw the wonder of wonders. A white horse approached the mouth of the caverns, peered inside for a moment, then went away. I was astonished: could horses breathe under the water the way a fish does? I could still see the horse. He had a great wound and blood was pouring from him, so that the depths of the sea were tinged with it. As I expected, the sharks rushed at him from all directions. But the horse took on a dignified pose, and didn't need to use his hooves, because the sharks first froze where they were, then approached to pay him homage and lick the wounds on his body dry. And, strange to relate, a single lick from a shark was able to stop the bleeding at once.

From a great distance I could see the clear outline of shores, with clouds of smoke rising above them and fires blazing on them from one end to the other. From here a mighty progression of horses rushed, horses of all colors, white, black, light brown, and gray, pedigree horses beyond doubt, all wounded, but still bearing the mark of their distinction. Balls of flame would pursue them, till finally they'd vanish into the depths of the sea. I continued to watch, utterly fascinated, especially as the wounds of these horses would heal with such unusual speed. And the strangest thing of all was how the sharks showed such friendliness to the horses, wiping away their blood, and giving up the kingdom of the sea. Then I saw the horses mate and procreate, multiplying at remarkable speed, till I thought the sea would become too small for their swelling numbers.

On the third day the horse that had first appeared, returned and stood in front of the cavern. I approached him and felt that I knew him. If I'd had any faith in reincarnation, I would have said that it was he, my old horse who'd attacked the tank. I put my hand on his back and he bent his neck a little. My old yearning returned. I mounted him, and he turned and carried me like lightning, without any guidance from me, till he finally set me down on the shore of Acre. But how in heaven's name did he know the place?"

Those were Mustafa al-Salih's last words. He then said, "Excuse me, I must go on an errand." He never came back after that.

"Does this man partake of things that are forbidden?" someone asked.

"God forgive us, no one's ever known it happen," several people answered.

"Was he dreaming then?"

"Do the pious dream?"

"Was he delirious?"

"But he's as strong as a horse."

"What was it then?"

"God only knows."

—translated by Lena Jayyusi and Christopher Tingley

Najwa Qaʿwar Farah (b. 1923)

Born in Nazareth, Najwa Farah studied at the Women's Training College in Jerusalem and worked as a teacher. She married a religious minister in 1950 and lived with him and their four children in several cities in Palestine, as well as in Beirut. She now lives in London. Her life has been dedicated to serving the cause of her people through her short stories and her many articles and talks. Her work is known not only in the Arab world, but also in such countries as Australia, Sweden, and the United States where she and her husband were invited for the purpose of acquainting audiences with the Palestinian issue. She published her first collection, *A Passer-by*, in 1954, and has published at least five other collections since. The following story was chosen from her collection *For Whom Does Spring Come* (1963).

The Worst of Two Choices; or, *The Forsaken Olive Trees*

Recently, Salim abu-Ibrahim had withdrawn from other people. The villagers only saw him at dawn, when he went to his olive trees. Women got a glimpse of him when they opened their shutters to let in the morning air, or when they went to the chicken coops to feed their hungry broods.

"We've seen Abu Ibrahim going to his olive trees," they would tell their husbands as they brought them their early morning cups of coffee.

The men would shake their heads knowingly: "There is no strength or power except in Thee, O God! . . . He was a lion, a pillar of strength in the village . . . A man of few words and much dignity . . . Tall in stature, with strong features that commanded respect . . . A worthy man. . . ."

The withdrawal of his wife, Imm Ibrahim, was another matter. She dreaded most those moments when he would break his silence and give vent to his pent-up feelings: "Your constant grumbling and nagging has wrecked our peace! . . . You want to see our children, and your heart is torn apart. Is it easy for me to leave, to become a refugee in a strange land,[1] at my age? How can I abandon everything here? You don't care, because you haven't worked on the land as I have, and you forget the long years of toil it's taken to build it up, by my father and his father before him . . . You just want to see the children. Of course, you're their mother, but are you the only mother here whose children are across the border? The man who listens to a whining woman is a fool—and I more than anyone else!"

"Please, listen to me, Abu Ibrahim," she implored. "I haven't asked you to move . . . If you think it's a mistake, well, don't go! . . ."

He let out a sigh that was almost a groan. Rising to his feet, he began to stride up and down the room, while his wife murmured faintly, "It's true, I do long for the children. Aren't they *our* children, a part of *us*? Ibrahim, ʿAbla, Jamil, and Sami . . . Little Sami, who left when he was four years old . . . It's as though they were dead! One year passed, then two, and now seven, but we're still saying, 'This year we'll see the end of it. Peace will come and we'll see them again . . .' But it's no good. Will life begin again for us? Isn't it truer to say that the end of our life is getting nearer all the time? Have you forgotten how ill you were last winter? Won't death catch up with us before we see them?"

"That's enough!" shouted Abu Ibrahim. "I told you to stop!" To escape his wife's voice, he wound his *kaffiyyeh* around his head and left the house . . . The olive trees were still there, waiting for him.

Imm Ibrahim breathed more quietly. She had begun to look forward to Abu Ibrahim's visits to his olive trees. She wanted to cry for her lost motherhood, but she didn't dare cry when he was there, watching her every thought and action, listening to what she said to the neighbours. She wanted to dream about the children and the carefree past. She longed to talk about Ibrahim and his young wife. They said she was pretty. She wanted to talk about ʿAbla, who was still looking after her unmarried brothers. ʿAbla was a motherly child, and truly devoted to Jamil and Sami. She had refused offers of marriage so she could care for them. But Jamil—poor Jamil! . . . He had lost a hand, sliced off by a paper-cutting machine at the printing press. The thought was too painful to Imm Ibrahim. And little Sami . . . She remembered how he'd used to sit on his lap after the noon meal: soon he'd be unable to keep his eyes open, they were heavy with sleep, and he would doze off with

---

[1]Under Israeli law, Palestinians who remained on their land were not allowed to go to neighboring countries unless they planned to leave for good.

his eyelids half open. In the village they called this "deer-sleep." He'd had a habit of drawing in his lips when he slept, making a strange little noise like the ticking of a clock. His small body would grow warm as he lay curled on her lap. Later she would carry him to his cot and lay him down. Imm Ibrahim held out her arms . . . No, he wasn't here! They were empty . . . The breeze that was coming through the open door felt cold.

It was summertime. The trees in the garden were heavy with fruit, but the children were not here to see them. Summers used to be so happy . . . She would prepare for their return from school, and the house would ring with their laughter. It had seemed that Imm Ibrahim was always making coffee, and cooking, and their house had been bright and cheerful. But now that joy was gone.

Night provided no welcome rest. She spent its long hours dreaming of the past, and when she came back to reality she sobbed out loud.

"What?" shouted Abu Ibrahim angrily. "Crying again? . . . Crying during the day is bad enough. Must you also cry at night? You'll be the death of me! . . . What in the world are you weeping about? Your children?—Why? Are they sick? Are they dead? Are they in trouble? What do you think the refugees feel like, who have to live in caves and tin shacks?"

"Don't say that! God forbid! . . ."

"Then what are you crying for?"

"Oh, please, Abu Ibrahim! . . . I didn't know you were awake. I've stopped. I've stopped crying . . ."

"You've only stopped because I'm awake . . . Just like a woman—so unreasonable!"

But he couldn't go back to sleep. He got up, sat on the couch, lit the lamp, and began to roll cigarettes, smoking one after the other. Imm Ibrahim also lay awake, though she did not get out of bed until morning.

The dawn was gloriously unaware of their pain. It broke suddenly through a bank of rose-tinted clouds. The stars withdrew bashfully behind their veils. The moon, pale but serene, dutifully awaited the arrival of her lord the sun, then slipped away unseen.

Abu Ibrahim put out the lamp and hurried to the kitchen. Imm Ibrahim was already preparing his coffee. The comforting smell of the newly-ground coffee beans quieted him. This was a moment he had always looked forward to, even long ago, when he was a child and his grandfather sat cross-legged on his mattress on the floor, murmuring through his long beard as his fingers moved slowly from one bead to the next on his yellow *misbaha*.[2] The house would fill with relatives and friends. The village elders would sit on the couches along the walls, sipping hot coffee with loud slurping gulps, piously reciting their beads, and discussing the crops and the condition of the olive trees. Coffee was a gentle friend, that took him back to other days and made him feel at one with his people and their traditions. Its warm odor held deep, old, and very dear memories.

Did he really, in his inner heart, blame Imm Ibrahim? Wasn't he annoyed because she was putting into words his own pain, which he dared not face? Of course he longed to see his children; he could hardly bear to mention them, or to look at the photographs that hung high on the wall in the sitting room, or to set eyes on their clothing, which still hung in the wardrobe. Even Sami's slingshot was there, that he'd tried to hit birds with in the summer, when they were all at home together and the house was full of their chatter. Sometimes at night Abu Ibrahim dreamed about them, and woke up choking down his sobs.

He remembered the day his neighbor's wife had stopped by to say, "I've got good news for you! Ibrahim is married!"

He and his wife had been stunned. Ibrahim, married! . . . He had only been eighteen when he left, a fine young lad . . . And now, he was married!

Although his mouth felt dry, he had asked the woman, "How do you know?"

"Sa'id's son, who works in Cyprus, wrote to his parents and asked them to pass the news on to you and Imm Ibrahim . . . Well? Aren't you happy about it, Abu Ibrahim? You can give them your blessing, even though they are far away . . ."

But instead they had wept, because the house was silent and empty. They didn't even slaughter a sheep to celebrate the wedding. The shuttered windows of the sitting room had remained closed, and no bride came for Imm Ibrahim to welcome with an earthenware water-jug, a piece of freshly-kneaded dough, and a sprig of fragrant basil—tokens that she might bear children and that there might always be enough to eat and drink in her home. Instead of singing wedding songs, Imm Ibrahim had sobbed and felt faint, and the women had gathered around

[2]*Misbaha* is a chain of worry-beads, on which the faithful recite the ninety-nine "names," i.e., attributes, of God.

to help turn her mind to happier thoughts, coaxing her to give them the sweetmeats that are offered at weddings.

The house became so full of women that Abu Ibrahim had felt compelled to go out. He had gone to his olive trees. They consoled him, but they also gave him pain. He felt personally related to each of them. He loved their graceful beauty and faithful generosity. The grove was a holy place for him. He was intimately acquainted with each breeze that rustled the shimmering leaves. Weren't they the children of last summer's winds? . . . These olive trees had witnessed the era of the Turkish sultans. They had survived the British Mandate. They remained now, unperturbed and strong, combating time itself with their silent endurance and devotion. Why couldn't he be like them? Why must he desert them? Why could he not endure steadfastly, as they endured? Why did he have to be a leaf driven before the wind? Life had placed him here. Why should he leave? . . .

He'd been bowed beneath the weight of his inner conflict. Here, was the message of the trees . . . but at home the voice of Imm Ibrahim would depict their children across the border, reminding him that they were part of their parents' bodies, that life without them was desolate, an endless deprivation, and that death, which surely lay ahead, might overtake him at any time. Hadn't he had heart trouble last winter?

The olive trees spoke to him about the land, his beloved earth that belonged to his ancestors who had plowed it, worked on it, gathered its generous yield of fruit, and died content. It was his heritage to guard and cherish. He must be loyal to their loyalty to it. How could he leave it for an unknown, unloved town, where he would be a stranger, a burden on his own children? He thought of his married son, whose new wife might not like him. He could imagine her saying, "Why have you burdened me with this old peasant, your father?" He also shrank from the thought of an unfamiliar house and an unaccustomed climate, a strange bed and an unfriendly pillow, a window that opened out onto an unexplained world . . . He would not be able to hurry to his kitchen every morning as he had done for so many years. The familiar jars of oil and grain, which filled up much of the room, would not be there; nor would the copper trays and pans his mother had used. Even the coffee cups would be of a different size and shape. He pictured himself going into a small, cramped kitchen with complicated electrical appliances. It might be modern and clean, but to him it would be cold and bare . . .

He had become aware once again of the trees surrounding him.

Glancing about to make sure no one saw him, he had flung his arms around one of the trunks, letting the leaves caress his face, and given way to tears. Some spirit within him went out of him and entered the trees. Their voices converged upon him, telling him they belonged to him forever. Lifting his head, through the leaves he'd seen the sun setting behind the violet hills. Its fiery glow warmed his heart. Night had come, hiding the world from view, and the stars had lined up into protective ranks. At their head had risen a full moon.

Abu Ibrahim allowed the tedious travel arrangements to proceed, and the day of departure finally came. It was a sad day for the entire village. The neighbours gathered outside the house to share in the grief of parting. They had always known Abu Ibrahim. They had often gone to him with their problems. The fact that he had not left the village had given them courage to remain. Their disputes had been settled in his house, and they felt it belonged to them too. The place would now seem silent and empty. Was not a home made by those who lived in it?

As they bade his wife farewell, the women wept.

"May God bring you success, but your departure leaves us desolate!" cried one.

"Take us with you, Imm Ibrahim!" implored another.

Old Imm Bakr stepped forward: "Give this *mandeel*³ to Bakr," she pleaded. "Tell him that his mother embroidered it with the last sight of her eyes . . . Tell him that I have kept his land safe, but, if God should take me before I see him, may he think well of me. And, if my body should turn over in its grave when the oil and the olives are being enjoyed by others, it will be because they were not enjoyed by Bakr and his descendants."

The women glanced at each other. "Bakr!" they cried, "Where is he? No one has heard of him since '48. Can he still be alive?"

Everyone doubted it but Imm Bakr, for she believed that every person who went away was bound to meet her son. For her, he lived in all the lands beyond the border. The women shook their heads in resignation. This faith alone gave meaning to Imm Bakr's life.

Abu Ibrahim and his wife got into the car, while a truck moved off ahead carrying their belongings. As the car started forward, the villagers clung to it, and their farewell blessings echoed around the couple long after they had departed. Abu Ibrahim felt that life had gone out of

³*Mandeel* is a handkerchief.

him, and that his friends were mourning his death. It seemed as if he were attending his own funeral. Surely, his funeral procession would have been like this—the black car his hearse, the weeping and calls of farewell, the slowmoving line . . . These were the friends who would have come to his funeral . . . Pain numbed his senses, so that he scarcely felt any physical reaction.

When the car passed the olive grove, he felt like his heart was about to leave its cage. Before the car moved off, he turned towards the grove. The trees seemed to be bowing their heads and drawing him to themselves. Was this really his funeral? Was he at one with them at last?

Alone. Even after he crossed the border and saw his children, who had been waiting so long to embrace him, he was alone. It was not that the reunion had been cold—even the police who guarded both borders had been moved by it. But he remained a stranger, unknown even to himself.

His daughter-in-law proved to be kindly, and made every effort to make him feel at home. But nothing lessened his inner pain . . . It was unbearably strange. He yearned constantly for the land, the olive trees, the village, his daily life. He had hoped to make a new beginning, but he lacked the vigor or desire to do so. Slowly he began to die, as each day bore him further away from what he had loved. His fears had come true. Around him were high, steep hills, like minarets with *muezzins*[4] that craned forward to make sure he was hearing their call—so different from the gentle, friendly hills at home. The new kitchen, also, was as he had feared it would be: white, small, all-electric, and sterile. His mattress was hard and unyielding, even though he used a bolster from home. When he first woke up he would often feel he was back there, but with returning consciousness he would numbly try to remember how he'd come to be *here*. He lived in dread that the jars of oil and olives he'd brought with him should all be consumed, for it was only when he tasted them that his misery would leave him briefly.

One night he sprang up in terror. He had dreamt that he was dead and was being carried in a coffin to his funeral, with all his friends following. Even during the day, the memory of the dream would not leave him.

"This is the second time I have known death," he mused. "I was right about what would happen if I left home."

---

[4]The *muezzin* is the man who calls the Muslims to prayer from the minarets of the mosque.

Soon his family realized he would not see many more days. One morning, they found him still and cold. The doctor said his heart had failed him while he slept. But his daughter said she had seen the shadow of death on his face the day he crossed the border. He alone could have known that now he had died for the third time.

—translated by Ruth Lenox and Thomas G. Ezzy

Tawfiq Fayyad (b. 1939)

A novelist and short story writer, Fayyad was born in Haifa and remained in Israel after its formation. He studied in Nazareth and at the Hebrew University and has a B.A. in communication science. He was imprisoned by the Israelis in the notorious Shatta prison and the prison of Ramla from 1969 to 1974, and was later deported across the Sinai desert to Egypt; he then went to Beirut, which he left with the other Palestinians in the exodus of 1982, and now lives in Tunis. While in Beirut he founded and directed Dar al-Nawras, a progressive publishing firm dedicated to children's literature, which was destroyed by the Israelis when they entered Beirut. He has published three novels, *The Deformed* (1963), *The Group* (1974), and *My Beloved Militia* (1976); and two collections of short stories, *The Yellow Street* (1968) and *The Idiot* (1978). His stories are some of the best fictional statements on Israeli occupation and on the pervasive and multi-faceted struggle of Palestinians as they seek justice and dignity.

The Idiot

Several months had passed and life in the Jenin refugee camps continued its monotonous routine. Ever since the Israeli army invaded it, the few men remaining in the camp wore striped nightshirts and made frequent use of the small chairs of colored straw in Saeed Zir'een's café. The café was situated at the edge of the winding road that cut through the center of the camp. Some men played cards while sipping the syrupy tea that was served regularly on the low, bare, cracked tables, with edges scorched by the cigarettes extinguished on them. Some hugged the decorative hoses of waterpipes, leaning over them with surprising intimacy and tenderness, while the backgammon dice tumbled from one side of the table to the other, scattering like small besieged creatures. The players' deft fingers pursued them across the faded brown boards, cupping them and shaking hard. The hands clicked and rubbed them, then dashed them out again till they clattered against the walls of the board.

Between the tumbling dice and the dealing of cards, the Egyptian army was clashing with heavy cannons and machine guns along the Suez Canal. Palestinian commandos *(fidaain)* set an ambush in the lowlands along the Jordan Valley for an enemy patrol, knocking out their vehicles and engaging them with light machine guns and hand grenades. Meanwhile, Israeli Mirage and Skyhawk planes raided the Irbid area, bombing refugee camps with rockets, burning them with napalm, and pursuing fleeing dwellers with machine guns, mowing them down, then returning safely to their bases.

An argument heated up. The pipes were removed from caressing lips and cards laid aside, for this time neither the double dice nor the queen of the cards were of any value. The numbers of dead and wounded got all mixed up with the numbers of cards and dice. Now the little dice stopped racing, the boards were folded with a bang. Despairing sighs rose from the collars of striped nightshirts. Cigarettes flickered and glasses were lifted toward dry throats. The problem of Palestine was laid out once again. First explained, then solved militarily, then peacefully the West Bank returned to King Husain. It returned to the PLO (Palestine Liberation Organization). It would never return. They became excited. They argued vehemently. They stopped when a military car halted in front of the café.

Eyes hung on the green berets, racing from one Star of David to the next, shining on foreheads, on shoulders. The eyes returned sadly to the cards and spinning backgammon stones. The only other motion was the figure of Saleem the fool, spitting at the soldiers' car and hurling strings of curses at the Israeli soldiers. Why did they insist on occupying Palestine? He stood at the end of the alley hurling stones and old shoes at the backgammon players, raining curses on them too since they never helped him swear at the soldiers. They never helped rescue him, either, when he fell into the soldiers' hands and they beat him for his words. All they did was play cards, instead of fighting the Jews.

One day, in the clutch of his anger, Saleem the fool climbed to the roof of the café. He lifted his short tattered *qumbaz*[1] and pissed on the backgammon players. He wished to insult them, make them feel they were not worthy men, since they only made good their manhood if an issue concerned him personally. When the Israeli soldiers beat and cursed them, however, not one of them dared raise his head. They

---

[1]A *qumbaz* is a straight, narrow robe, with the opening in the front being held tight to the body with a thick belt. It is a traditional attire for men in the countryside and is made of either cotton or expensive silk, according to the status of the man. In Palestine it is often striped but can also be of plain color.

would slink away home like scared sheep. Today he aimed his urine onto the coal brazier of Saeed Zarᶜini's waterpipe, extinguishing it, and Paunchy, as Zarᶜini was called, chased him down with kicks and blows. He determined to take revenge on Paunchy and all his dull customers.

He thought about his brilliant revenge possibilities for days. Maybe he would surprise an Israeli soldier, steal his rifle, and hide it somewhere in the café, then intimate to the soldiers where they could find it. They would kick in Paunchy's paunch and drag him to prison. Except that when Saleem pictured himself whispering in the ear of the Jewish soldier, with the Star of David shining on the soldier's forehead, he felt a chill come over him. He cursed himself for even considering such a wicked idea which would render him a spy and bring him so close to that many-toothed star. He even beat his head with his fist to put the idea out of his mind. But no sooner had he done this than he found himself entangled in an even more complicated idea. He could steal the rifle and lie in ambush for the soldiers at the back of the café. When they appeared, he could fire at them and vanish, leading them to believe that Paunchy was responsible. They'd slit his belly and close down the café. Maybe all the customers would get their own fair shares of blows, kicks and insults—especially Mahmoud "the Moustache" who never stopped twirling his scented whiskers at every girl in the camp.

Saleem pressed his head with both hands to stop the thoughts from running through it. His heart catapulted as he imagined himself holding the automatic rifle. His hands shook and he swore never to think of this again. Should he try it, the gun would surely recoil and kill him instead, which would devastate his beloved "Fattoum." Besides, all the others would really gloat over his ignorance then. He swore to abandon all thoughts of revenge on Paunchy and Moustache.

Still, one day as Saleem walked near the café, he caught sight of the backgammon players and his heart began beating rapidly again. Old plans of vengeance surged again in his head and became so entangled that he barely heard the roar of the military car behind him, blowing its horn. Before he could leap aside, a soldier shoved him with the butt of his rifle, laughing mockingly. Saleem fell forward onto his face in the dust. He scrambled to get up, and spit as hard as he could after the car. Realizing he clutched a round stone in his hand, he threw it hard at the soldiers, but they were already out of range. He tripped and stumbled down again.

Moustache let out a loud laugh. His whiskers quivered like the jaws of an enraged scorpion on his wide shiny cheeks. And Paunchy laughed so hard he almost choked on his waterpipe. His giant belly heaved up and down.

Saleem's eyes were burning. He stood shakily, tasting the blood in his spittle, fixing his stare on Moustache's face and Paunchy's stomach. He brushed the dust from his clothes. As he passed the café, he spit at the men and ran.

As he ran, the idea he had been waiting for flashed in his mind. He stopped, panting, and turned to see if anyone was following him. A wide grin of victory played across his lips.

He rubbed his hands together and scanned the road. His gaze fell on a large round stone. His lips parted and he dribbled saliva from his smile. Looking around to make sure no one was watching, he stooped over the stone and picked it up, stuffing it into his pocket.

At the first alley he turned off and made his way back behind the café. There he lurked, clinging to the wall, awaiting the return of the Israeli patrol. His nerves were alert. His eyes fastened on the orb of the sun, which seemed to dangle at the edge of the camp's perimeter. His eyes watered and it seemed to him that the sun was about to fall onto the houses. His heart pounded as he watched the road.

Finally the patrol car appeared. It was traveling dangerously fast, swirling up dust behind it. Saleem's hand trembled. He pressed his back against the wall. His heart beat wildly and his breathing quickened. He gripped the stone and blew on his hands as the car neared. He pitched the stone at the car as hard as he could and clung closer to the wall, still shaking.

The stone hit a soldier on the head. He let out an awful scream and Saleem's heart toppled.

The car screeched to a halt. The hands of the backgammon players froze. The car reversed with amazing speed and stopped again. Moustache, Paunchy, and everyone else looked stunned.

Before Paunchy could open his obsequious mouth, the soldiers had leapt from the car and without questioning, began to beat the customers with the butts of their rifles and kick them with their heavy boots.

The sergeant stamped on Moustache's whiskers and pummeled Paunchy's fat belly—it was more than Saleem could take. He found himself laughing uncontrollably, which gave him away in his hiding place, and he fled with utmost speed, lifting his robe as he ran and bumping into things on the way.

To tell the truth, Saleem never really thought about the problem of the occupation of the West Bank by the Jews and their refusal to withdraw from it. Only when the patrol drove wildly through the camp, frightening children and startling chickens, did the whole confusion occur to him. The soldiers' laughter and their pointed rifles filled his heart with fear.

Were it not that "the monster's life is long," as Paunchy used to tell him, the car would certainly have run him down a long time ago.

As for the lousy bearded Shaikh ʿAbd al-Raheem, Saleem carried enormous resentment, for he knew the man wished him dead, especially under the wheels of the Israeli soldiers' car. This was the worst. Were the *shaikh* to wish him an ordinary death, Saleem could have accepted it, but to wish him death under the wheels of the Jewish soldiers was intolerable.

And had the soldiers maintained their familiar level of provocation, Saleem might have been content to spit and curse at them every time they passed. He might even have forgotten the whole story of the occupation eventually, had not the soldiers come up with a new story which would never have occurred to him at all.

One day as Saleem sat at the water taps flirting with the girls, a military car paused and a soldier bellowed through a bullhorn that everyone was to go home immediately and remain there, by order of the military governor. Anyone who hesitated, or left his house without permission, would be fired at. Saleem hooted with laughter, believing the soldier was slightly unhinged. When he saw the people around him hurrying off to their homes and the girls departing without filling their jugs, he tried to prevent them. He stood in their way, saying, "Don't pay any attention to him!" Suddenly he found himself the last one in the road. How could people obey this deranged soldier's orders? Why hadn't they listened to him? Bullets spattered around his feet and he fled, the hem of his nightshirt between his teeth. His heart was beating with terror. He cowered in the cave he inhabited in the middle of the camp. For two days he could not leave it, for whenever he stepped out from the opening, bullets rang around him and he would dive back, trembling with fear. He was hungry and thirsty, but all he could do was curse and spit at the soldiers from his hiding place.

Curfews like this happened all the time. Saleem was prevented from going to the water taps to get water for his beloved Fatmeh whom he called, "Fattouma, Queen of All Girls." He wasn't able to run her errands. He never wanted her to get tired. Besides, he loved taunting the other girls in the camp who were unsuccessful in their attempts to win his heart. Not even Aida, who dressed like a city girl in a short skirt, had been able to win him away. She had promised to marry him if he would abandon his love for Fattouma. But he rejected her, even though Fattouma was married and the mother of three children, and Aida was young as a doe.

The story of Saleem the Fool's love for Fattouma, and the loss of his wits, went back more than five years. He had settled in the Jenin refugee camp after previously living in all the other camps. Some even traced the story back further to when Saleem was still a youth, during the first exodus, and Fattouma was still a young girl. He had searched for her everywhere, in all the camps of unoccupied Palestine, and the camps of Lebanon and Jordan.

The strange thing was that he never asked about her. It was as if he waited for some mysterious sign. Perhaps this was why he always sat by the water taps, even after he'd found her.

Some of the refugees said she had been the sweetheart of his youth. Some said she was his sister because of the strong resemblance between them, and the affection she bestowed on him. She nurtured him like a sister, feeding him, washing and patching his clothes. She even cut his hair and nails. Once she had housed him in a tin shack she built for him in the corner of her courtyard. Had it not been for her mother-in-law's disapproval and expulsion of him from that place, he might still have been there, instead of in the cave where kids ran to escape the Israeli raids and men went to urinate. Despite all, Saleem continued to call her his beloved Fattouma, the "light of his eyes."

Often the women attempted to discover the history of this love from Saleem himself, but he always became angry and cursed them. Sometimes he left Fattouma alone for a while after being questioned.

The old women wove intricate stories, but mostly they just wanted to find out one thing; whether Saleem the Fool was a man like any other man or not. They teased him playfully, poking him in his lower abdomen till he collapsed with laughter, stretching out on his back. The women's eyes were hinged to the front opening of his *qumbaz*, hoping it would flop back a little. He seemed to realize this and would hold it down with both hands, teasingly. Then he poked them on their own bottoms, so they feigned anger and punched him harder. Hajjeh

Wafiyyeh would hit him on his thighs, higher and higher towards his groin, and when once he felt her hand was about to reach his upper thighs, he bit her on the arm and fled. He avoided her ever after.

Those who had known Saleem from the village of Zir'een said he had been a beautiful, gentle child. Pregnant women frequented his parents' house, just so they could play with him. Fatmeh's mother had visited his house often while she carried her child. This was why Fatmeh resembled him. They had both spent their childhood in Zir'een till the gangs of the Haganah invaded it, dispersed its people, and set the homes on fire.

Shaikh 'Abd al-Raheem was not convinced by the stories of Saleem's madness, however. He thought it was just a cover-up for his wanton playfulness. Actually, he was envious that the women of the camp were jokingly affectionate with Saleem, while they recoiled from the Shaikh and avoided him. He only ogled their swaying buttocks, pretending to be kind. Because he was so jealous of Saleem, he went around declaring the Fool a dissolute wretch, bound for hell. When Saleem heard this, he felt a chill and closed his eyes to darken the awful image of sizzling skin. He did not believe God could be so cruel. He cursed the *shaikh* for misrepresenting God. One day he caught the *shaikh* peeking through the cracks of the front door at Hajjeh Wafiyyeh's house, gazing at her thighs as she crouched half-naked at the washtub. Saleem shouted and clapped his hands, exposing the peeper and increasing the *shaikh*'s wrath against him. The *shaikh* came at him with his cane. Hajjeh Wafiyyeh hurriedly dressed and burst forth to defend Saleem. She placed herself between the *shaikh*'s stick and Saleem, shouting, "You cannot punish a madman!" The *shaikh* asked the Lord's forgiveness with half his breath, but with the other half insisted Saleem was not mad but possessed by a cursed devil, and should the Hajjeh continue to defend him, her past pilgrimage would lose its grace.

When the invading Israeli forces occupied the Jenin camp and the talk about war and its aftermath dominated people's conversations, Shaikh 'Abd al-Raheem forgot about Saleem the Fool. People lost interest in his love for Fattouma and the women stopped circling around him to chatter. This made Saleem mad at the Jews who had spoiled his life. Had he not chased the soldiers with insults and stones, his neighbors might have forgotten about him entirely. Only the latest incident with the Israelis brought him back into the camp's eye.

He was overjoyed to be noticed. Yet for many days, he avoided the area near Paunchy's café, having heard that the soldiers had almost killed Mahmoud the Moustache, then dragged him unconscious by the hair, thrown him into their car, and driven him away. Paunchy was laid up in bed with two broken ribs while his son Jaber ran his business. Jaber was keeping a lookout for Saleem, planning to break his bones should he pass by again.

And had Fattouma not taken Saleem into her house and hidden him, he might have been killed. The *shaikh* kept insisting that Saleem was an atheist "Commie" who should be exiled from the camp immediately. He swore he had seen him more than once at the Jenin prison with Fatmeh's husband, an avowed communist. He claimed this happened during the time of Jordanian rule, when he had gone to lead the prisoners in prayer. Never once, he said, did either of them join in the public prayer behind him. They were later transferred to al-Jafr in the Jordanian desert, so they could not poison the other prisoners' beliefs. Fatmeh's husband died there and Saleem was eventually released. He started looking for the wife of his old friend so he could live with her in free communistic fashion. This was what the *shaikh* liked to say, hoping to incite as many people as he could against Saleem.

After Mahmoud was released from prison, people flocked to see him, asking if and how the Jews had tortured him.

But Mahmoud refused to speak to anyone, even to his bosom friend Paunchy. He cautioned his mother to keep the door locked. As soon as Saleem heard of his release, he hurried to Fattouma's house and begged her to hide him. He was terrified Mahmoud might seek revenge, especially after he heard the Jews had shaved off his moustache. But Saleem did not think about what this would do to her.

Immediately people stopped passing in front of Fattouma's house. Even the women avoided her when they saw her in the street. Or she would approach a group of acquaintances and they would stop speaking, remaining silent until she had gone on. Even Abu Salih, the shopkeeper who had always welcomed her warmly, informed her he could no longer sell her anything on credit and that she needed to settle her old account. The world darkened in her eyes. She left Abu Salih's shop with tears flowing down her cheeks.

She arrived home still weeping. Saleem was crawling around her courtyard, her children on his back spurring him on like a donkey. They jumped down when they saw her and clung to her dress, while

Saleem rose up slowly. His foolish, staccato laughter froze on his lips when Fatmeh, choking with tears, took her children inside and closed the door behind her. Saleem stared at the door, not understanding. Then he bowed his head and wished he could die.

Saleem withdrew to his cave and kept to himself, venturing out only when he was desperate for something to eat. He would stand outside Fatmeh's door, calling to her till one of her children emerged, bringing him bread and boiled potatoes, or olives. He would retrace his footsteps to the cave, ignoring all the children who tried to play with him.

Occasionally, Fatmeh came out to him, took him by the hand and led him in. He could not meet eyes with her. She would heat water and wash his long hair as she used to do. She would place hot food in front of him and serve him tea. He would eat quickly and return to his cave, to sit again in seclusion and think of the Occupation, how he would get rid of those Jews and force them to withdraw. Then life might return to normal and his happy days with Fattouma could resume.

A whole week had passed since Saleem had been to Fatmeh's house. No one in the camp had seen him. Since people were used to his withdrawal, they didn't really miss him, except for the children who enjoyed throwing stones at him. However, Fatmeh noticed his absence from the third day. She sent her son to find him with some food. The cave was empty, so the boy left the food and went back to tell his mother. She sent him again that evening and again the following morning, when he found cats eating the food he had left.

Now the news of Saleem's disappearance spread quickly throughout the camp. Some said he must have died in the cave, but no body was found. His mattress was missing. Others said he had moved to Fatmah's house in the dark, so he could live with her secretly.

Crowds of old women immediately began visiting Fatmeh, showering small gifts upon her affectionately. No sooner did one leave than another one was at the doorstep. Fatmeh didn't understand what was going on. She was bewildered at the affectionate attention being given her. But as quickly as the visits had begun, they suddenly stopped. The old women asserted that Fatmeh must have hidden Saleem in some magic spot, since no trace of him had been found.

Mahmoud began asserting, with an all-knowing smile on his lips, that what he'd said all along was true: Saleem was a spy for the Jews. Didn't everyone notice how Saleem had disappeared as soon as Mahmoud exposed him? Who knew what camp the Jews had sent him to this time?

Shaikh ʿAbd al-Raheem, while agreeing with Mahmoud's spy theory, held to his view that Saleem was an atheist commie at the same time—weren't all the Muscovites Zionists and wasn't the person who had set up communism in Russia a Zionist Jew? This was why the Russians had helped Israel defeat the Arabs and occupy the whole of Palestine, by giving the Arabs faulty weapons and tanks which could not run in the desert and planes which auto-destructed in midair. Saleem was probably only one of hundreds of spies who had been sent to the West Bank, Syria, and Egypt to provide the Jews with accurate information on the Arab armies. No wonder Saleem had run away when he was exposed! The *shaikh* said similar spies had been planted everywhere in Egypt during the reign of King Farouq. Saleem was probably now masquerading as a *shaikh* in some West Bank village and leading public prayers. No doubt all the commies memorized the Qurʿan and were well-versed in the basic principles of the faith, as if they had graduated from the illustrious Islamic University of al-Azhar in Cairo. They could falsify the faith and induce others to become unbelievers.

As for Fatmeh, she was saddened by Saleem's disappearance. Since she had neglected him, she blamed herself. And she worried terribly about him—were he out in the mountains, he might be killed by a patrol of soldiers. Even if he escaped their bullets, he could be attacked by wild animals in the open country.

Three nights after the discovery of Saleem's disappearance, people woke to the ringing of bullets. Before they could realize what was happening, the Occupation soldiers were raiding homes, pointing their weapons at people's chests, and turning the contents of the houses upside down. They were searching for saboteurs, and leading off men and youths to their military vehicles.

The strange thing was that they examined every axe they found and confiscated it. No one understood this. It remained a riddle till the next morning when word spread that one of the soldiers had been killed earlier that night from an axe blow to the head. He had been stripped of his weapons.

This was the third time the houses had been raided by the Occupation soldiers searching for the *fidaain*. Stories of *fidaain* battles with the occupying soldiers near the Jordan River and in the mountains of Tubas and Hebron had been relayed by radio and in conversation at the café. Yet this time the search was different. This time the *fidaain* were supposedly from the camp itself. The majority of boys and men were arrested and a curfew was imposed on the camp. The soldiers fired into the air to punctuate their seriousness and spread the terror. They even killed Hajjeh Wafiyyeh's goat when it peeked out from the courtyard.

Mahmoud was dragged from his home and pummeled with rifle butts till the blood flowed from his mouth. Everyone in the camp knew he was a proud guy who never let an insult pass without avenging himself. Maybe he had secretly joined the *fidaain*, everyone thought. Since the loss of his moustache and his release from prison, he had given up sitting in the café and making passes at the girls.

This was confirmed when the bloodied axe was found in the alley near his home. In no time, people were whispering about his heroism, imagining he would never confess and would ultimately be released to continue his guerilla activities.

That night people went to sleep half believing Mahmoud had joined the Palestinian *fidaain*. Yet if he had been a genuine guerilla, wouldn't he have used a hand grenade or automatic rifle instead of an axe? Why didn't he wipe out the whole patrol?

That night bullets again resounded. Soldiers were heard shouting and running. Some of the bullets even penetrated closed windows, waking people up in fright, freezing in their beds. Before they could rise, a strong cry echoed through the camp, rising over the roaring of rifles and soldiers, calling, "Fa . . . T . . . T . . . OU . . . M," then dying away.

The people were not sure what had happened. Some said Saleem the Fool had been bounding like a tiger from one alleyway to the next, shooting the soldiers, striking them down. Others said it was not Saleem but Mahmoud, who must have escaped from the soldiers en route to prison and returned to fight them.

Still others insisted it was neither of the two, but a trio of young men who moved like panthers, and could not be recognized because of the checkered scarves masking their faces, and their clothes the color of sand and stone. They passed as noiselessly as the wind, some said.

However, people close to Shaikh 'Abd al-Raheem, who from that night forward confined himself in the mosque and devoted himself to prayer, told another story. The *shaikh* said that when the soldiers dragged him to the cemetery at the foot of the mountain next morning to identify the martyr, he beheld the face of Saleem the Fool, smiling, with a great halo of light shining from his forehead. He said the light was blinding. He became tongue-tied and was unable to speak until a soldier butted him with his rifle between the shoulders. When he stretched his hand out to Saleem's in order to raise the index finger in assertion of the oneness of God, he found he was clutching a bracelet of amber hair, the color of Fatmeh's, that encircled Saleem's wrist.

Hajjeh Wafiyyeh swore by the tomb of the Prophet and her pilgrimage that she had seen Saleem that night in her dreams, dressed like a bridegroom, riding a gray mare led in procession by the people of the camp. The shooting interrupted her dream in which, at that moment, he was crying, "Fat . . . T . . . OU . . . MA!"

As for Fatmeh, her neighbors told the rest. When she emerged in response to Saleem's call as he fell dying at her doorstep, she ripped her dress and began wailing and wailing even after the soldiers dragged her off by her unbound hair and disappeared with her.

—translated by May Jayyusi and Naomi Shihab Nye

Emile Habiby (b. 1921)

A novelist, short story writer, dramatist, and journalist, Habiby is one of the most illustrious Arab authors in Israel; he is highly regarded all over the Arab world both for his creative work and for his political activity. Born in the Galilee, he joined the Palestine Communist Party in 1940, becoming editor-in-chief of its weekly organ, the *Al-Ittihad*. After the fall of his part of Palestine (Nazareth and Haifa) to the Israelis in 1948, he joined Rakah, the Israeli Communist Party, which he represented for nineteen years in the Knesset. He published his collection of short stories, *Six Stories for the Six Day War*, in 1968, and in 1974 published one of modern Arabic fiction's best works, his novel *The Secret Life of Saeed, the Ill-Fated Pessoptimist*. The novel deals with the conditions of Palestinians living in Israel and mingles comedy and tragedy to bring out all the painful contradictions of Palestinian life under siege. The novel has run into many Arabic editions and has been translated into Hebrew; so far two editions of PROTA's English translation have appeared, (1982 and 1985). In 1983 Habiby published his play *Luka 'the Son of Luka'*; in 1985 his novella *Ikhtiyyeh*! (Pity!) appeared in *Al-Karmel* review and afterwards in book form. This novella aroused critical interest by its author's characteristic originality of approach, his success in introducing humor into serious or even tragic situations, and his skillful, mythical use of time through a sense of constant connectedness with Arab history and culture. In 1991 Habiby started a publishing house, "Arabesque."

The Odds-and-Ends Woman

Why did what I said surprise you? Didn't I tell you that a separation of twenty years makes a man forget even himself. And is that a light thing? The poets inside are all the rage now, and the poets outside are basking in the warmth of their resistance and linking themselves with them—you know "these are our standard-bearers," and all that sort of thing.[1] But what kind of reception did they give them before the disaster of 5 June 1967, when our poet recited the Ode of Return:

[1]The poets inside are those who remained on Palestinian soil after 1948 and became Israeli citizens. Those on the outside are the Palestinian poets in the diaspora. The Arab

Ah my country! If only I could see the havens of sanctuary and the cradle of my youth!

"What's that got to do with you, you loafers?" they yelled in our faces. "Didn't you refuse to make the emigration to Yathrib[2] when we did?"

And you, why do you keep muttering now about the odds-and-ends woman in al-Wadi Street in Haifa? Why won't you believe her when she tells you she buys all the pieces of pilfered bedding from the Heights, and every cupboard and chest, in the hope of finding the treasure she's looking for? Totally illogical, you say!

Well, is that the only illogical thing that's going on in this country of ours?

You disapprove of her buying all the sofas from Qunaitra, do you? So why did you keep quiet when the authorities let a contractor with lots of money or influence win the auction on Qunaitra, Qunaitra with all its furniture and coffee cups and *kubbeh* mortars and toothbrushes and insect sprays and books by al-Farabi and toilet rolls! You even let them provide him with a vacant site alongside the police building, with a warehouse where he could display his goods. How could you do all that?

Would the whole thing be more logical if they'd cleared a space for him by the Middle East Showroom, up there in the heart of Tel Aviv?

I realize no one actually decided to boycott this "smugglers' hoard," but it's also a fact that no one ever goes near it, Arab or Jew; the first out of piety and the second out of fear. While yet another group, the women, claim the style's old-fashioned. Meanwhile the contractor himself solemnly swears in all the languages of the Mediterranean basin from Syria to Tatwan in Morocco, that his business is ruined—he doesn't care about the ruined families on the Heights! The only person who didn't boycott his goods, he said, was the odds-and-ends woman.

That's her nickname now, "the odds-and-ends woman." You've started muttering, among yourselves, that she's an old hand at pilfering. In 1948, you say, she plundered all the rugs from Abbas Street and moved into the mansion abandoned by Abu Ma'ruf, who owned the "Ten a Penny" store in the Syrian Market in Haifa in the old days.

---

poets in Israel first became known to the Arabs outside as poets of the resistance because of the poetry of challenge and defiance to Israeli rule that they were writing.

[2]Yathrib is Medina in Hijaz (part of Saudi Arabia now), where the prophet emigrated in A.D. 622 (the first year of the Islamic calendar) when his persecution by his own tribe, Quraish, presented grave danger to him and to his calling. Habiby is speaking symbolically here.

Have you ever seen any "mansions" in Wadi al-Nasnas? The ruins there are lucky enough to be in a valley which protects them from the salty sea air. Have you ever visited the mansions in Old Acre and heard music pounding against the walls, walls which not even the wall of Ahmad al-Jazzar[3] could protect? Aren't you ashamed?

In the old days you'd snatch at the slightest excuse, find any sort of reason to go knocking on her door, and she'd give you coffee and a sweet smile. Among yourselves you called her the uncrowned queen of the valley. Since then she's been looking for treasure in sofas. You never used to see anything wrong with that, so why are you muttering about her now that the treasure chest's opened up for her again? I know her much better than you do.

When her husband left with one of her sons, she insisted on staying behind with her crippled mother; that was at the time of the first exodus.[4] Then, when her mother died five years later, we heard that her husband wouldn't even acknowledge her and didn't want her back. And you didn't believe her when she told you she didn't want to leave her house in any case. You kept making insinuations and saying there must be some love affair behind it all; that, you said, was the only possible reason she'd want to stay behind. Well, perhaps you'd be so good as to tell me why it was so reasonable for all of you to stay behind? I know her much better than you do.

She used to sell the rugs and chairs and mirrors she got hold of, and she'd open up the sofas and look for hidden treasures, then put them back together again and sell them too. Occasionally, she might find something. One day I visited her and found her squatting on the floor with the stuffing from a sofa scattered all round her. She was reading a letter she had in her hand, and sobbing. When I asked her about it, she said it made her think of her children.

"What's this letter?" I asked.

"It's one of a whole pile a young man seems to have been sending to his girlfriend," she replied. "She kept them hidden inside a tear she made in the sofa." She wiped away her tears. "My treasures, my treasures!" she cried.

She used to live on whatever money she made from selling furniture. She'd offer you coffee and refuse all your gifts.

---

[3]The famous wall of Acre, built around the ancient city to ward off attacks by the Crusaders.

[4]The first exodus of the Palestinians took place in 1948 when the Zionists were trying to establish their hold over parts of Palestine and resorted to various terrorist techniques to get rid of as many Palestinians as possible.

If you broached the subject of poetry, she'd enter into the discussion. You used to rush to finish a line if she could only remember the first half of it, and when she recited a whole line and broke the meter, you all murmured malicious compliments. If you started talking about politics, no one was quicker than she was to show keenness or want to do something useful. If one of you were put in prison, she'd be in there visiting you before your own mother got there, bringing in food and washing your shirts.

The fires of twenty years had eaten away at the wood of her boat, as it sailed toward King Solomon's mines. Everything she had was for sale except her treasures. The same fires had taken their toll of her hair, which was white now, but her smile remained as fresh as ever, unaffected by the ravages of time. If only you people had valued her smile as much as you enjoy making malicious gossip about her now!

She knew you'd seen me visiting her just recently. Are you going to gossip about that too?

When I heard you all muttering and grumbling about her, when you whispered together that she was the only one who went to the "smugglers' hoard" where business was at a standstill, when I heard that the uncrowned queen of the valley was being called "the old odds-and-ends woman" now, I rushed over to see her.

She welcomed me as though nothing had happened. Sofa stuffing was scattered all over the floor of the lounge.

"Have you taken up upholstering again?" I asked.

She gave me her beaming smile.

"Do you weep on your own?" I asked.

"I'm not alone any more!" she exclaimed.

"You mean you have your treasures?"

"No," she exclaimed. "It's their owners I have. They're coming back, again and again."

"Do you realize," she added, raising her head proudly, "that they need me now, after twenty years of oblivion?"[5]

She raised her head again, as if to apologize this time. "Do you realize," she asked, "that they need me now?"

And how about you people? Do you imagine I'd write about her without her permission? If that's what you think, you're wrong, I assure you!

[5]These are the almost twenty years between 1948 and 1967, the date of the Arab Israeli June War. It was then that the two parts of Palestine, that taken by the Zionists in 1948 and that taken by them as Israelis in 1967 (which constituted the whole of Palestine at that point,) became open to each other.

You don't know, for example, that she found one of her sons jailed in Ramla prison on a charge of distributing pamphlets in Old Jerusalem. And you don't know, either, that her husband came across the bridge from Lebanon to talk to her about how she might be able to help get their son released. The son is a dedicated doctor, but when she's talking about his dedication, she's even keener about it than he is, as if she wants to say: "These are my children!" How do you measure up to her?

She always talks about her husband with love and admiration; after all, he brought up their son, the dedicated young doctor.

She talks admiringly about herself as well, and says she's reached an understanding with the bankrupt contractor who owns the "smugglers' hoard"—she can take all the stuff she wants on a fifty-fifty basis. She sells it, she says, and then uses the proceeds to feed herself and visit her son in jail; she's even paid for the services of a lawyer with connections. She visits her son, takes him cigarettes and washes his shirts for him, "just as I used to wash yours too."

Then she asked shyly, her eyes lowered: "Have you met the roving spirits?"

"Roving spirits?"

"Men and women, from the Gaza Strip, the West Bank, Amman, even as far as Kuwait. They cross the bridge, then they walk through our alleys without saying anything, staring up at the balconies and windows. Some of them knock on doors and ask, politely, if they can come in, look around and have a drink of water. Then they go away without a word. The places they asked to go into were their homes.

"Some of the people living in the houses greet them with a sympathetic smile, but with others the smile's a wry one. Some people let them come inside the house, while others simply won't open the door.

"Then there are those who don't knock on doors, but keep looking around for a passerby with a dark complexion.[6] When they find one, they stop him and ask him whether there used to be a house made of dark-rimmed stone standing on that particular spot. Sometimes the passerby will stop to try and remember, then start reminiscing; sometimes he'll say: "I was born after the disaster, Uncle."

"These roving spirits don't come to my house. They haven't heard about my treasures. Why haven't you written something about my treasures in your newspaper?

---

[6]An Arab, as contrasted to the numerous Ashkinazi Jews living in the area.

"Go on, write something! Write about the treasures from the inside of my sofas. I've got whole bundles of young people's treasures here: first love letters, poems hidden by boys in the pages of school textbooks, bracelets, earrings, bangles, chains with gold heart-shaped pendants that you open to find two pictures inside, his and hers. I've got diaries in shy, delicate handwriting and others in broad, confident hands. They're full of questions: What does he want from me? And full of binding oaths for the homeland.

"Will you promise to write about my treasures, so the roving spirits can find their way to me here?"

When I'd given her my word, she got up, went over to an old box, and took out a bundle of old papers that she handed to me. "Take them," she said. "This is a present for you."

"What are they?"

"Letters I used to write but never sent to the person they were meant for. They'll help you realize why I stayed here in the valley."

"But why are you only showing them now?"

"Because it's only now that I can be with you all. You're my children, so don't leave me again."

When we were young, we never used to go to sleep until my grandmother had told us one of her stories. She was over ninety and always got everything mixed up. She used to start the story about Clever Hasan in the middle: "Clever Hasan grabbed hold of his magic wand and beat the evil giant with it . . ."

"What magic wand, grandmother?"

She never paid any attention to our shouts, but just carried on telling the story. Never once did we manage to stay awake till the end of the story, and she always fell asleep before it was finished, so that none of us know the beginning or end of the story. When we grew up, we used to reminisce about my grandmother and that story of hers (which we called 'the tale without a tail'), and all start laughing helplessly.

This presupposes, of course, that it's the logical thing for a story to have a beginning and an end. But is that really the rule? And even if it is the logical thing, is it logical in this country of ours?

So why should I tell you the things I read in the letters the old odds-and-ends woman gave me recently? Shouldn't it stay a secret between the two of us?

And so this story will remain 'without a tail' till you and I can write one for it together.

—translated by Roger Allen and Christopher Tingley

Akram Haniyyeh *(b. 1953)*

A short story writer and journalist born in Ramallah, Haniyyeh studied English literature at the University of Cairo, then worked in journalism, becoming editor-in-chief of *Al-Sha'b* newspaper in Jerusalem in 1978. His creative writings as well as his work as a Palestinian journalist under occupation worried the Israeli military rulers of Jerusalem and the West Bank, and Haniyyeh was hounded, prohibited from traveling, and in 1986 imprisoned and deported. He now lives in exile. His fictional work reflects great originality and sensitivity to the problems of Palestinians everywhere. His first collection of short stories, *The Last Ship . . . the Last Harbor*, which appeared in 1979, won him immediate recognition. It was followed by other collections, including *The Defeat of Hasan the Clever* (1980); *Rites for Another Day* (1986); and *When the Jerusalem Night Was Lit* (1986).

After the Siege, a Little Before the Sun

The first to notice what had happened were four people who by chance arrived simultaneously, on that lovely summer morning, in the alleys of the Old City.

The van full of workers going to the Israeli factories had stopped and let Amineh out at the western end of the city. She had to head in the direction of the Damascus gate, where she was to occupy a strategic spot for the sale of the fresh figs she was carrying along on her head. Each day she left her village early to catch the trade of the workers and the morning influx of people to the Holy City—a crowd that included all races and nationalities, and especially the visitors to the holy shrines in the city.

Abu Mazin was still drowsy as he went to pick up his quota of morning newspapers to distribute to the small retailers. Later he would return and spread out his goods in Saladdin Street.

Sulaiman was hurrying across the street towards the bakery in al-Musrarah where he worked, to collect his allocation of flour and bake his cakes before the streets became congested with workers and students.

The fourth person, Haj Abu Fu'ad, had, as was his custom, arrived at the city at this hour to perform his morning prayers in the Haram.[1]

All four noticed it at the same time, but from different spots in the city. It was a strange and unbelievable sight. Their eyes dilated with surprise and horror at what they saw, and each of them resorted to prayers and supplications for the Day of Judgment, and invoked the name of God against the devil. They rubbed their eyes incredulously, but once convinced of the reality of the situation, they sent out screams that reverberated in the quiet Jerusalem dawn.

With screams they would not have believed themselves capable of issuing, they gave voice to their horror. "The Dome's[2] been stolen!" . . . "Come quick! The Dome's gone!"

As their voices echoed in the empty alleys of Old Jerusalem, they were greeted by curses and vilifications uttered from behind closed windows. Then, slowly, came the sound of keys being turned squeakily in old gates. The Old City's alleys and streets began to fill with people coming to see what the noise was about.

Within minutes the city had awakened, and the residents came running from all directions, looking for the source of alarm, dumbfounded, and asking confused questions. The streets swarmed with people, and the panic of women and children was audible as they looked for a path through the crowds.

They came running from Damascus gate, Jaffa gate, and the gates of Hutta and al-Sahira and al-Silsila. They arrived from Khan al-Zait, from the Christian quarter and the Armenian sector. They came from Takiyya track, the Mufti track, from the Saʿdiyya quarter, the Wad street, the Khudayr barrage. Some of them arrived in their nightclothes, with unwashed faces, and all had anxious disquiet visible in their eyes.

Immediately, the border guards, soldiers, and police took up their usual positions at the Jerusalem Wall and the Gates, without, however, daring to step into the inner alleys. When the inhabitants saw them, they realized that something had happened. The news was passed from one person to another, and the mass of people began to flow towards the Haram. Their shouts grew to a confused cacophony, and none of them believed or wished to believe what had happened.

When they reached the Haram, the truth became apparent: the Dome

[1]The mosque of Omar or al-Aqsa Mosque, the Mosque of the Dome, and the huge courtyard around them are all known as al-Haram, or sanctuary. When someone prays in al-Haram, it usually means that he is praying either in al-Aqsa or the Dome Mosque.

[2]The Dome of the Rock in the *Haram* area is one of Jerusalem's most beautiful monuments. It is shown in almost all the pictures and postcards taken of Old Jerusalem and is one of the first sights a visitor arriving at the city would see.

of the Rock had disappeared, as if spirited away by some magic power, and there was no vestigial trace of earth or stones to indicate how it had happened.

The screaming rose in volume as the crowd pushed and elbowed one another in their haste to kiss the ground which was the site of the Dome. Many fainted; others fell under the feet of the stampeding masses. Children became hysterical at the sight of the distraught men and women, while those who had retained their calm busied themselves with carrying the women who had fainted, or torn off their clothes in mourning, to the corners of the Haram.

After a short time, a party of men emerged from the gates of the Haram. They were the members of the Highest Islamic Council, and of the Waqf,[3] and of the Sermons and Guidance, and other religious institutions. All of them stood silent; shock and amazement had overwhelmed them.

Also gathered there were old men and women who usually attend the Friday prayer in the Haram. And there were beggars too, most of whom slept in the Haram courtyard. Everyone felt the loss of something dear to his or her heart.

Comments poured out:

"They may be planning to put a new settlement in its place."

"Or build a new quarter."

"Perhaps they found fighters inside, and took it to keep them prisoners."

"Maybe Arab planes were sent to seize it and take it off to one of the capitals. That way the Arabs won't feel they've got to liberate Jerusalem and all the holy monuments here!"

"We'd better stay in the Haram and Holy Sepulchre tonight, in case they try and steal something else."

"There'll be an Islamic summit!"

"And an Arab summit!"

"And they'll proclaim the holy *jihad*."[4]

"And ask for an immediate meeting of the United Nations Assembly."

---

[3]Waqf is an Islamic institution into which property and monies are put in trust—either for charity and then regarded as a pious endowment, or for specific members of the family as in family *waqf*. In the latter case a supervisor is appointed to administer the fund for the beneficiary or beneficiaries of the trust. In the Sunni sect, women do not inherit outright, but have to share the inheritance with male relatives. In the absence of brothers, these may be uncles or cousins, even remote relatives.

[4]*Jihad* is Holy War in the service of Islam against aggressors.

"Statements and declarations will come down like rain."

"The Israelis will accuse some insane minority."

"They've put paratroopers and border guards everywhere!"

"What will King Khalid's[5] reaction be?"

"And the pious president?"[6]

"Where could they have hidden it?"

"They must have dismantled it piece by piece."

"Where were the guards and custodians?"

"Will they change the name of Jerusalem now?"

"Where will they celebrate the Mi'raj and the Isra'?"[7]

People continued to converge on the Haram from all quarters and suburbs of Jerusalem. Many of them traveled by side or mountain roads to avoid the barriers set up by the border guards.

At the various entrances to Jerusalem, and the streets leading to them, accidents were frequent. Cars had been allowed to enter the city before the roads were blocked. Almost instinctively, drivers lost control of their wheels, as soon as they discovered something missing in the familiar layout of Jerusalem.

That day, after the initial reaction had subsided, the general scene in the Old City was disquieting. The village women who always sat at the side of the road, or on the stairs of the gate, in order to display their fruit and vegetables, now sat pensive, unwilling even to return to their villages. Even the waiters in the cafés, usually so garrulous, moved quietly amongst their thoughtful customers, and pickpockets refrained from preying on the few tourists who had gone down to the Old City that day. The young men of the city gave up their feverish chase of women tourists, and the owners of souvenir shops and bazaars shut their shops and sat down in front of them. There was conjecture as to how the incident would affect tourism. No one heard the shouts of porters as carts obstructed the free passage of the narrow alleys. The

---

[5]King Khalid of Saudi Arabia who was reigning when the author wrote the story.

[6]This is president Anwar Sadat who, when he visited Jerusalem in 1978, said that his deepest desire was to pray in Al-Haram.

[7]Mi'raj is the place from which the Prophet limped all the way to heaven on the night of Isra'. Isra' means night travel. Muslims celebrate the anniversary of this holy event every year at the Dome Mosque, and elsewhere. The rock inside the Dome, which looks as if it is flying toward heaven, is believed to have attempted to rise in pursuit of the prophet's Isra' and stayed hung up in space.

smell of grilled kebabs and cakes and *falafil*[8] and *za'tar*[9] bread and spices and *kinafa*[10] completely disappeared, as did the background music from shopkeepers' radios.

Amineh, one of the original four who first noticed the loss, sat pensively on the stairs leading to the Damascus Gate, staring into space. She hardly bothered to chase the flies off her unsaleable figs. She was recalling the first time she ever came to Jerusalem. She was only seven and her father had brought her with him on the last Friday of Ramadan. Her eyes filled with tears as she remembered how her father had bought her a new pair of shoes, and a dress enmeshed with golden threads for the Feast.[11] She recalled how they had entered a sweet shop and eaten *kinafa*, and how her father had left her at the shop of one of his greengrocer friends and gone to pray at the Haram. Yes, she remembered that first visit in all its minutiae of detail, and her subsequent trips to the city with her father, which were occasions of joy. Another memory flashed in her mind: that of a visit to the Holy City with her husband, who was also her cousin, to choose necessities for their new home. She remembered how they ate together in one of the restaurants, and how, on her return, she had told her close friend of all she had seen in the metropolis.

A tear escaped from her eyes . . . Her cousin . . . her dear husband . . . everything had changed after the war,[12] and her husband had to give up his job, and work in the Israeli factories. He used to talk enthusiastically about the demonstrations that took place in the cities, and the explosions which reverberated from time to time . . . An inscrutable anxiety would overcome her. Then her husband was arrested and sentenced to four years in prison, after he had been accused of assembling a bomb to be placed in one of the streets. After that, she

---

[8]A delicious snack made up of ground soaked chickpeas mixed with onions, parsley, cumin, and other optional ingredients and made into balls and fried.

[9]Thyme. *Za'tar* bread is bread dough on which is spread pounded *za'tar* prepared with other ingredients, including roasted sesame seeds, and mixed with oil. Thyme is one of the wild herbs of Palestine that grow profusely on mountain slopes; it is eaten a great deal for breakfast or snacks and has become, with the orange, a symbol of Palestine and of Palestinian attachment to the land.

[10]This is a sweet and expensive dish made of a special dough and lined with sweetened cheese, drenched in butter, baked, then drenched with sugar syrup. Nablus is particularly famous for this dish.

[11]The Feast of al-Fitr or Ramadan, the month of fasting. This is one of two major annual feasts which takes place after the completion of Ramadan, the Muslim month of fasting, and is called "The Small Feast." The other is the Adha Feast or "The Big Feast," and takes place after the completion of the annual pilgrimage.

[12]The June War of 1967.

had no choice but to take produce from her family's land—figs, grapes, and tomatoes—to Jerusalem, to support herself and her two children. She realized, too, that the city had lost its enchantment for her, and become linked in her mind with her imprisoned husband, the sexual advances made to her by customers, and above all the thought of her two children awaiting her return.

She looked around her . . . The streets were empty of cars and buses. There were a number of village women gathered around her, who had entered the city before the decision to close the gates. A group of men were sitting on the stairs of the Damascus gate. "Do they love Jerusalem as my husband does?" she wondered. Then she lowered her head and wiped away the tears that her memory had evoked.

As for Haj Abu Fu'ad, he sat down near one of the gates of the Haram. He needed a long time to be convinced that what had occurred was in fact a reality, and that the receptacle of his prayers, hopes, and entreaties to God had disappeared. For over forty years he had come here to pray, and had learned to distinguish every stone in the place. At times of anxiety, annoyance, or exasperation, he would sit under the canopy of green cypress trees, open up the Quran and read. But with the disappearance of the Dome he felt uprooted, felt that his relationship with the past had been severed. He remembered the Ramadan nights and the night of qadr[13] on the twenty-seventh day of Ramadan, and the feast prayers. He recalled the day the Aqsa mosque had caught fire, and how he had experienced a great rush of energy to his body as he had helped carry water to the site to extinguish the flames. "They don't fear God," he murmured to himself, "but . . ." He realized suddenly that in the confusion of events he had missed the dawn prayer. "But many other things have been lost!" he reflected, and wiped the tears that trickled down his cheeks into his beard.

The Haram was crowded with people divided into different groups, all sitting on the ground. Silence predominated over the sound of distressed weeping. Haj Abu Fu'ad stared at the diversity of faces. He regained some of his inner strength and whispered, "Praise be to God, we are still here."

In Saladdin Street Abu Mazin sat in the place where he always dis-

---

[13]Qadr Night is the night of the twenty-seventh of Ramadan, the fasting month. Regarded as the holiest night of the year, it is a normal night to most people but to a select few, believed to be especially blessed by God, it is a general belief among Muslims that it can suddenly reveal a flood of light and that those persons' wishes, expressed during that fleeting moment, will always be answered.

played periodicals, and felt his eyes blaze with tears. There were no newspapers, magazines, or books on show, because he could not even complete his trip to the printer's to bring over his consignment of newspapers. A few customers enquired about the morning papers, and whether they were carrying a report about what had happened, but he merely shook his head and waved his hand with fatigue and exhaustion.

Every day, winter and summer, he left his house early in the morning with his head well wrapped, on his wife's instructions, against the bitter morning cold. He would look at his sleeping wife and children, open the door quietly, and go on his way. Whenever the Dome of the Rock rose into view, he would repeat, "Oh God, the Giver, the Knower," and would add a number of prayers. This practice had grown into an inveterate ritual, but as from today the morning would be different in its prospect and he would be compelled to adopt a new pattern of conduct. "But," he asked himself, "hadn't the rituals already changed a few years back? And the city air? Don't the very streets protest under the weight of alien boots? And haven't I myself felt a stranger in these streets in which I know every inch?"

The picture of his son, Mazin, leapt in front of his eyes. "That young devil . . . what's he doing now, I wonder? Has he maybe gone out on a demonstration with his fellow students and been arrested? Will I have to pay yet another fine and bail him out?" He felt his heart throb, and then a flicker of joy cut across his sadness. He looked towards the proud Jerusalem wall and whispered, "Ah, those youngsters! They love Jerusalem even more than we do."

As for Sulaiman, he never completed his trip to the bakery. He sat on a chair in one of the coffee houses in the Jaffa gate. "I don't think anyone wants to eat this morning." He took out a cigarette and was about to light it, when he remembered that he hadn't had anything to eat or drink since he woke up in the early morning. He thought of asking for a cup of coffee, but noticed that all the customers and waiters in the café were sitting in silence. He changed his mind and lit the cigarette.

Sulaiman had only prayed once in his life, and that was in the holy Haram. Yet this didn't prevent him from recognizing the value of the sacred object of which the city had been bereaved that morning. His visits to the Haram had been a regular feature since childhood. He would go with the groups of schoolboys to listen to what the teacher was explaining, or with friends, or would be assimilated into the crowds at prayer on occasional Fridays and Feast days. He never prayed, but he possessed a special reverence for the Haram and was proud that he lived near it in the Old City. Now he felt that an integral part of his past had died and that something of importance had been subtracted from his daily life. It seemed to him that the covered alleys and cobbled paths of the old city were no longer infused with the same character and inspiration. Even the ancient Jerusalem Wall had lost its usual glamour. He whispered to himself, "For the past few years I've felt an alien here. This isn't the Jerusalem I've always known."[14] He scrutinized the silent crowds. "Even the Dome which disappeared this morning isn't the same one I've known since childhood." He threw the butt of the cigarette on the floor in front of him and lit a new one. He felt as though he was choking. "Life passes," he thought, "and I haven't achieved anything yet."

He felt bitter and remembered how the financial situation of his family had stopped him completing his university education, despite the good average he got in his examination. As a result, he spent years going from one Israeli factory to another, until in the end he took a job in the bakery owned by one of his relatives, and there he had remained to this day. He stamped on the ground with his foot. He had often considered emigrating, only to change his mind at the last moment. His life was tied to this land by inseparable roots. "Life passes too quickly," he reminded himself again, and every day he found himself overtaken by the routine of going to the bakery in the morning and finishing his work at noon. On some days he would be given additional duties at one of the companies. His mother always asked God's help for him every morning when he woke up early, and earnestly entreated God to guide him in life. But there he was, and still nothing had changed. He looked up at the Jerusalem walls where the guards stood with arms at the ready, and said, "This isn't the life I meant to lead." Then he added, as an afterthought, "I haven't been positive enough."

When night came, the inhabitants of the Old City began to move from their places. Many went to sleep in the Haram court; the rest, especially the women and children, returned home. The soldiers maintained their vigil on the walls, but the stars shone lucently in the sky. The alleys echoed with the drum of sure footsteps.

—translated by Salwa Jabsheh and Jeremy Reed

[14] i.e. since the 1967 June War when the Israelis took hold of the Old City of Jerusalem.

Mahmoud Sayf al-Din al-Irani (1914–1974)

Palestine's foremost pioneer in the short story and a man of culture and style, al-Irani was born in Jaffa. He moved to East Jordan in 1942, where he worked as a secondary school teacher before being appointed first as inspector of schools, then as assistant to the deputy minister at the Ministry of Education, then as counsellor for the Ministry of Information in Amman. He has published many volumes of short stories, among which are *With the People* (1956) and *Fingers in the Dark* (1971). In 1985 a prize for the best short story volume was initiated in Jordan in al-Irani's name, in recognition of his influence on the development of the short story in Palestine and Jordan.

Garbage

I knew he was greedy; it was reflected in his eyes. He would look at you with a questioning stare, with a persistent inquisitiveness, replete with utter impudence.

I have never seen such eyes before, relentless in their consuming focus, devouring the bread you eat, the air you breathe, and even the shoes you wear. Eyes that swallow faces, skies, water, cobblestones, flowers, everything, even the garbage.

He arrives early in the morning, and knocks on the door with his fist, completely ignoring the electric doorbell. He doesn't think of tapping lightly on the door. Thumps are always his way of announcing himself, as if the electric doorbell never existed. He impacts his impudence into his fist and thumps on the door till I come out to him with the garbage can, and he takes it away surlily, without offering so much as a good morning. I then close the door, leaving him alone with the garbage can.

Once my curiosity was such that I was compelled to watch his movements. Would he simply empty the contents of the can into the large sack and go away? He didn't! He carefully examined them, sifting through them with his fingers, all the time peering with his omnivorous eyes.

He would rummage curiously through the garbage until he found something, which he would then place in his pocket. However, I have never succeeded in learning what sort of thing he retrieved from the rubbish. Most of all, I disliked making contact with his eyes; they completely overpowered one's defenses and trapped one in their web. It was as if those eyes always demanded something of you.

Once I did give him a coin. His gaze thereafter grew more insolent, more penetrating. And after I gave him money for the second and third times, I realized he had come to exploit the situation most vilely. Perhaps he knew intuitively that I could not withstand his stare, and that, in all possibility, I was afraid of it.

After a time I realized my error in offering him money. I took to avoiding any eye-to-eye contact and watched him discreetly from behind the window without his being aware of me. I would follow his movements with my eyes; that slow walk of his, with the sack slung over his back, his greedy eyes researching each detail of the road, missing nothing. I became obsessed with his perverse behavior and kept asking myself what it was he could be looking for amongst garbage, and what was the nature of the thing he invariably slipped into his pocket?

Could it be a piece of dry bread? I asked myself, or some jam left in the bottom of a jar? Perhaps a piece of rotting cheese or of canned meat? I wondered whether it was a partially eaten orange. And then again, I reasoned, what would be his purpose in extracting these things? It couldn't be that he was starving. But on one occasion I was able to get a clearer glimpse of the object of his search which he pocketed with such adroit cunning. He had searched through the garbage at some length that day, and because there was so little wind, he began to perspire profusely. Then I saw his fingers fasten like a clamp over something; and with surprising agility, he succeeded in conveying it to the pocket of his ragged pants. He then stood there and wiped the runnels of perspiration from his forehead with the tail of his tattered headcover. After that he wiped his moustache with the palm of his hand. He tightened his lips and licked them as though he relished the salt taste of his sweat. What I managed to glimpse him take was a small teaspoon. Of course, he must make similar discoveries every day. Perhaps the occasional spoon, a fork, a knife, and other miscellaneous ephemera. Children, servants, careless women, any or all of these could account for the negligence on which he preyed. For if the remains of food are deposited in the garbage, so it must be that items of cutlery and plates and saucers must follow in like fashion. And he had made it his business to unearth these things, searching through the remains of fruit and vegetables with the accomplished skill of an expert in such matters. He is careful to unpiece everything, and to be sure he discards nothing of value.

I once saw him pick up an object from the side of the road. He dropped the load from his shoulder, and placed it on the ground at a distance, as though he resented its existence. He then bent down by slow degrees and picked up the object. It was a coin, a piaster . . . five piasters . . . who knows? It glistened as he studied it in the palm of his hand, before slipping it into his ragged trouser pocket. He rested for a few seconds, sitting on top of the large garbage bag, and then repeated the same actions of drying off his forehead with the tail of his head cover, wiping his moustache with his hand, and licking his lips. It fascinated me why he should act out this ritual whenever he had made a discovery. Then it occurred to me that a cat does the same thing after stealing a piece of meat or a chicken's leg. Once it has torn the flesh apart and eaten, it proceeds to lick its lips as a mark of satisfaction. But, our insolent dustman adds to it by wiping his moustache with the palm of his hand, as though congratulating himself and delighting in the prospect that there is no end to this spoil.

I realized a long time ago that he was greedy. I imagined that he collected knives, forks, spoons, and plates in order to sell them. It seemed an easy and profitable trade, and one about which I was sure he felt no shame. The parasitical instinct within him must have condoned his actions.

I longed for a day when he would knock on the door and, without impudence, say: "I found this in your garbage." Had he done so, then I would have felt sorry for him. I would have recognized that he worked with honesty, and that the food he got was soaked with the sweat of his labor. I would have recognized, moreover, that it was my duty to help him every now and then with a small tip. But this was impossible. His avarice stood in the way, that and his determination to make a business out of what he found. There was no end to his pickings and he knew it. Yet above all I resented his devouring glances which sank into the depths of one's being. And there was my other grievance which I've had occasion to mention—the way he maintained no respect for privacy and thumped on the door with his naked fist, completely ignoring the electric doorbell.

I got dressed since it was past nine o'clock in the morning. When I went out into the street, it occurred to me to look carefully at the ground, the stones, every detail my eye picked up on. It seemed to me that if I looked hard enough I, too, might find the coins that he pocketed. But where were they? And where did he find them? He reminded me of snake charmers who succeed in conjuring snakes and vipers from cracks and piles of stones.

I quickened my stride; I didn't wish to be late in meeting my friend Abu Muhammad. It was at this hour that we sat down together over a cup of coffee, and it delighted me to watch my friend smoke his water pipe. He never forgot to offer me some of the luxurious cigarettes which he kept especially for his friends. Abu Muhammad is a good man, a respectable trader, and a decent friend. Every piaster he earns, he does so lawfully. I am impressed by his honest earning of money, and even more so by his astute, professional mind. And if he wasn't these things, he would never have been able to make a place for himself amongst such competition, nor earn such a secure reputation in the wholesale business. He puffs quietly at his water pipe and emits an aura of self-confidence. And when he writes you out an invoice, he does so with the meticulousness of one who undertakes the gravest responsibility. He then orders one of his employees to prepare a bag here and a sack there. And when you settle the account and pay him, your mind is completely at rest. You think to yourself: "Abu Muhammad is a respectable man." And even on that day when the Persian tobacco was missing from the market, it was through his efforts that the crisis was solved. He made available what he had stored, and that day he heaped up a handsome, lawful profit. I remember saying to him at the time. "Who would have thought that this would happen? Your sound judgement has saved the market."

"By God no . . . The matter was just a coincidence, no more and no less," he answered me modestly.

How astute these men are! Take, for example, my other friend Abu Elias, who works by commission. His credentials are a pen and paper, and a foreign language that he speaks fluently. Whenever I see him, he is busy writing letters or, rather, typing them on his typewriter to send abroad. And in return he receives samples of canned food, perfumes, pens, kitchen utensils, socks, handkerchiefs, ties, combs, pins, all kinds of toothpaste, shaving creams and ladies' skin-care creams, keychains, razors, objets d'art, and a multitude of items that go to fill up his warehouse. There's a constant demand for these products, and his profit is reflected through his busy trade.

When you enter his house you feel immediately relaxed. His home is beautiful, built from the profits of his work. Once, as we were sitting in one of the corners of his neatly arranged garden and drinking tea he said to me, "Simplicity is the secret of beauty."

This concept of simplicity impressed me deeply; it was apparent everywhere in his house, even in the luxurious armchairs he had ordered from Italy. These chairs are so comfortable that you literally sink into them, and correspondingly feel elated, caught up in a world of dreams. And you find this simplicity in the garden, with its vined paths, its flower beds shimmering with color and fragrance, and its luxurious fountains that arrow upwards and descend in a rain of droplets on the surface of the marbled pool. This idea of simplicity completely overwhelmed me, reminding me of my friend's particular cleverness and of his persistent hard work in the warehouse, where he sits taking orders by telephone, and then arranging for samples to be packed and dispatched immediately to prospective clients. He once presented me with a necktie, imported from Paris, and when I offered to pay him for the article, he expressed surprise, saying, "What? Surely the loss of a dinar is nothing compared to pleasing a friend!"

These are men who don't devour one with their eyes, or penetrate one's depths with their stare, or knock on the door with a heavy fist beat. These are the men who impress by their gentle smiles, their kind words, their enjoyable company, their fine conversation, and unconditional loyalty. And if it wasn't for Abu Elias's friendship, my money would have been taken in front of my eyes by my pernicious nephew.

After his father had died, I took it on myself to educate and look after my nephew. One day Abu Elias said to me, "And what guarantee do you have that your nephew will repay even some of the money you are spending on him?"

The question startled me into an awareness I should have realized right from the start.

"What do you suggest?" I ventured.

"Get him to sign a power of attorney in your favor for the land he inherited in Jabal Amman. It is, as you once told me, a quite valuable piece of land."

"An authorization?"

"Yes. It is a guarantee for your expenditure. I know he is your nephew and you are his uncle, but in this world there is . . ."

"Life and death."

"Exactly. This document is simply your guarantee . . ."

And so the boy agreed to sign a power of attorney, and I maintained him for the next two years. But when he felt able to take care of himself, he turned his back on me and refused to acknowledge my claim to compensation. He endeavored to turn my friends against me and requested his inheritance. Abu Elias told him, "You should be ashamed; he is your uncle." And Abu Muhammad reinforced this by saying to him, "This is your uncle, you should treat him like a father." But he was an ill-mannered and ungrateful boy. The court hearings did him no good. And if it hadn't been for a friend's advice, I can see he would have bankrupted me. He is avaricious and has impudent eyes. When they look at you, they are like nails being hammered into your chest. Whenever his fingers touch my hands I shiver, for it seems that their one obsession is to incessantly search for something, some secret, or some gain. I take refuge in God. But it's not easy to forget such ingratitude and such calculated malice in refusing to recognize my legal rights. Damn him, I think, and how closely he resembles that garbage man who is forever searching through litter. God damn that one as well. He has spoiled my day. But starting tomorrow, I'll show him. Yes, I'll clear him out of the place, make no mistake. I won't fear his eyes nor that dirty fist which pounds on my door. I will tell him that he is a thief, stealing people's knives, forks, spoons, and plates. I will expose him for stacking up stolen possessions in his house and selling them. And that unlawful money goes into his pocket, an easy profit made out of the likes of you and me. He feels neither fear nor guilt. Such impudence. Yes, as from tomorrow I will boot him out. I will expel him, and I will no longer have to tolerate his devouring, hungry eyes, nor his snake-like fingers that are forever unsatisfied in their rummaging. And my God I will not fear his fist.

—translated by Salwa Jabsheh and Jeremy Reed

Ghassan Kanafani *(1936–1972)*

A novelist, dramatist, and short story writer born in Acre, Palestine, Kanafani's most vivid memories of his boyhood sprang from the 1948 war in Palestine, which led to the eviction of the Palestinians into the various Arab countries. Kanafani became a refugee with his family, and it was this experience which formed much of the substance of his fiction. He lived for several years in Damascus, where he joined the Arab Nationalist Party (later, the Popular Front for the Liberation of Palestine.) After working as a teacher in Kuwait for a few years, he returned to Beirut in 1959 and became the spokesman for his Party, writing prolifically in both literature and journalism. He met his tragic death in 1972 when his car was booby-trapped in Beirut. A politically committed and popular writer of originality and style, he published five novels, two plays, and five collections of short stories. His novella *Men in the Sun* (1962) was made into a film and translated into several languages, including English. The film was banned in many Arab countries for pointing an accusing finger at the treatment of the Palestinian refugees and reflecting their sometimes blind and desperate search for survival in the face of terrible odds. Another brilliant novella, *All That's Left to You*, is one of the earliest and most successful modernist experiments in Arabic fiction; it again revolves around the plight of the Palestinians. This novella, together with a collection of Kanafani's stories, has been translated by PROTA and published by Texas University Press, (1990).

The Little One Goes to the Camp

It happened during the war—or rather, during the time of actual fighting, the time of constant grappling with the enemy. In wartime a peaceful breeze sometimes blows up, and a fighter has a chance to breathe, a truce, a moment of rest, time to retreat. But in the constant heat of battle, the enemy's always just the distance of a gunshot away, and you're all the time dodging, miraculously, between two bullets. This, as I said, happened during a time of continuous fighting.

I was living with seven brothers, all tough and unruly, and a father who didn't love his wife, perhaps because she'd borne him eight children during the fighting. My aunt also lived with us, together with her husband and five children, and so did our old grandfather, who, whenever he managed to find five piasters on the table or in a pocket of the many pairs of trousers left about, would go straight out and buy a newspaper. He couldn't read, of course, and this meant he always had to confess what he'd done, so that he could have the latest news read to him (loudly, because he was deaf) by one of us.

During that time—but before I begin, I ought to say that it wasn't a time of real, literal fighting, as you might think, because it wasn't a true war—in fact there was no war on at all. It was just that there were eighteen of us, of all ages, living in a single house. None of us had managed to find a job, and hunger, which is something you've only heard about, was a daily worry to us. This is what I've called a time of fighting; and in fact there's really no difference at all. We'd fight to get food, and then fight about sharing it out, and then start fighting all over again. Then, when things were calm for a moment, my grandfather would bring out his carefully folded newspaper and look at us all out of his small, apprehensive eyes. This meant that five piasters had been stolen from somewhere or other—from someone's pocket maybe—and that a quarrel was going to break out. My grandfather would cling hold of the paper, facing the uproar with the calm of an old man, a man who'd lived long enough to know that all this noise wasn't worth getting excited about and didn't need an answer. Finally, when the voices had quietened down, he'd lean over to the nearest boy—he didn't have any faith in girls—and thrust the newspaper into his hand, though still keeping hold of it for fear it would be snatched away.

Issam and I were ten at the time. He was bigger than me, as he still is, and regarded himself as the leader of his brothers who were my cousins, just as I considered myself the chief among my own brothers. After much effort, my father and uncle managed to find us a regular daily job. We'd carry a large basket between us and, after about an hour and a quarter of walking, we'd reach the market place just after dusk. Let me describe the vegetable market as it was then: the shops would just be closing, and the last trucks, filled with unsold vegetables, would be getting ready to leave the crowded street. Issam and I had a task that was easy in one way and difficult in another. We had to find vegetables to fill our basket: vegetables lying in front of the shops or behind the lorries, or taken from the stalls if the stall owner was dozing or he'd gone into his shop.

It was a time of struggle and fighting, I can tell you! You can't imagine how the fighter dodges between two bullets all day long! Issam would dart forward like an arrow and snatch a bruised cabbage, or a bunch of onions, or perhaps an apple from between the wheels of a truck that was just moving off, while I'd take on the enemy—the other children, that is—if they tried to pick up an orange that I'd seen first in the mud. We'd work right through the late afternoon, and we'd quarrel with all the other children, and the shopkeepers, and sometimes with the police. The rest of the time we'd quarrel with one another.

All this happened during the fighting; you wouldn't dream how the world's turned upside down at times like this, and certainly no one expects it to be virtuous—that would be ridiculous, because living however you can, by whatever means, is an extraordinary triumph of virtue in itself, and when a person dies his virtue dies as well, doesn't it? Let's agree, then, that at a time of constant battle, the virtue you've got to acquire is the main one of keeping yourself alive; everything else comes second. And as the battle's a constant one, there isn't any second, because you're never finished with the first.

Once the basket was full, we had to carry it home between us—and that was everyone's food for the next day. It was, of course, completely agreed between Issam and myself that we'd eat the best things in the basket on the way back. It was an unspoken agreement that we never actually discussed; things just happened that way naturally, because we were together in a time of conflict.

That cursed year the winter was a very cruel one. One day we were carrying a really heavy basket, one I'll never forget—it was as if you'd fallen in a trench during fighting and found there was a bed in it. I was eating an apple. We'd just come out of the gates of the market and we were walking down the main street. For ten minutes or so we'd been walking among people and cars and buses and shop windows without exchanging a word; the basket was really heavy and we were both totally absorbed in eating. Then, suddenly . . .

No, I can't describe it. No one could. It's as if you'd been unarmed and at the mercy of your enemy's knife, then suddenly found yourself sitting safe in your mother's lap.

Let me tell you what happened. We were carrying the basket, as I said, and there was a policeman standing in the middle of the road. The road was wet and we had almost nothing on our feet; perhaps I was gazing at the policeman's thick, heavy shoes when I suddenly caught sight of it, its edge appearing from beneath one of the shoes. I was six meters away, but I knew, probably from its color, that it was more than one lira.

In situations like that you don't stop to think. People talk about instinct. Well, I don't know whether the color of paper money's got anything to do with instincts, but I do know that it's linked with that brutal, murderous force which we all have in the depths of us, which is capable of killing in an instant; I do know that, in a time of constant struggle, a person doesn't think when he's carrying a basket of rotten vegetables and sees money lying under a policeman's shoe six meters away. What I did was throw away what was left of the apple and, at the same time, let go of the basket. Issam must have staggered a little under the weight of the basket he was now holding on his own—especially as he'd seen it just a moment after I had. I rushed forward, driven by the same unknown force that drives a rhinoceros to attack its target blindly, to the end of the earth if necessary. I thrust my shoulders against the policeman's legs, and he retreated in alarm. The effort had thrown me off balance too, but I didn't fall at once—then, in that instant of time in which fools imagine nothing can happen, I saw that it was a five lira note. I grabbed it, then finally fell, but I got up quicker than I'd fallen and started running even faster.

The whole world began to chase after me. I heard the policeman's whistle, and the sound of his shoes pounding the pavement close behind me, and Issam's shouts, and the horns of buses and people calling out. Were they really all coming after me? Deep down, though, I knew with total certainty that no one in all the spinning planets could catch me! With the cunning of a ten-year-old I took a different route, perhaps because I calculated that Issam would show the policeman my usual one. I don't know. I just ran and ran, without looking back, and I don't recall feeling tired. I felt like a soldier running away from the battlefield in a war he'd been forced to fight, with nothing left for him but to go on running with the whole world at his heels.

I reached the house after sunset, and when the door opened I saw what, deep down, I'd known I'd see: seventeen people waiting for me. They studied me, swiftly but precisely, as I stood in the open doorway looking back at them, with my feet firmly planted on the ground and my hand clutching the five lira note in my pocket.

Issam was standing between his mother and his father, and he looked furious; no doubt the two families had been quarrelling before I arrived. I appealed for help to my grandfather, who was sitting in his chair, wrapped in his clean brown cloak and gazing at me in admiration. He was a wise man, a real man, who knew how to deal with the world. All he wanted out of these five liras was a big newspaper.

I waited impatiently for the quarrel to start up again. Issam had been lying, of course: he'd told them he was the one who'd found the five liras, and that I'd seized it from him, then forced him to carry the heavy basket by himself for the whole exhausting journey home. Didn't I tell you it was a time of battle? No one felt any urge to question Issam, because no one was in the least interested whether he was lying or telling the truth. Issam had realized that clearly enough, and, for the first time, had been prepared to debase himself by announcing that I'd beaten him and so shown myself to be the stronger of the two.

His father was looking at things quite differently. He was ready to accept half the amount, with my father taking the other half. His thinking was that if I managed to keep the whole sum for myself, then I'd have the exclusive right to it; but that if I gave up this right, I'd lose it all, and they could share it.

What they didn't realize was the significance of a child holding a five lira note in his pocket in the time of battle. In a tone which, for the first time in my life, carried the threat of leaving the house for good, I told them that the five liras was mine and mine alone.

I'm sure you can guess what happened next. They went mad; the ties of blood went by the board, and they all combined against me. First they threatened me, but I was prepared for anything they wanted to do. Then they started beating me. I could have defended myself, of course, but I wanted to keep my grip on the five liras in my pocket, which made it difficult for me to avoid their well-aimed blows. At first my grandfather watched the battle with interest; then, when he'd grown tired of it, he stood up and faced them, making it easy for me to cling to him. He suggested a compromise. The adults, he said, had no right to the money, but I ought, one sunny day, to take the children of the house somewhere where we could all spend the five liras as we wished.

I stepped forward, determined to refuse what he'd suggested; then, just at that moment, I glimpsed something in his eye which held me back. I didn't follow exactly what was going on in his mind—I just felt that he was tricking them and begging me to keep quiet.

Of course a child of ten, in a time of battle, can't understand the way an old man like my grandfather can. Nevertheless, I realized what was going on. He wanted his newspaper every day, perhaps for a week or more, and because of that he was prepared to please me at any price.

So the family came to an agreement that evening. I knew, though, that my task wasn't over yet. I had to protect the five liras every minute of the day and night, to put off the children, to block endless attempts by my mother to persuade or tempt me to part with the money. One evening she told me the five liras would buy two pounds of meat, or a new shirt for me, or some medicine that was needed, or a book if they should think of sending me to a free school next summer. But it was all in vain. It was as if she was asking me to clean my shoes while I was dodging between two bullets.

I didn't know exactly what I was going to do with the money. Over the next week I managed to put the kids off with a thousand lies. They knew I was lying, but refrained from saying so—though not out of virtue. There was something else that revolved round the only virtue in existence at the time: the five liras.

My grandfather understood all these things, and he wanted his newspaper as the price for the part he was playing in the affair. When the week had gone by, though, he began to get restless. A man of his age couldn't help realizing what was going on: he felt that I wasn't going to buy him a newspaper, that he'd lost his chance and had no way of getting it back.

After another ten days everyone believed I'd spent the five liras, that it wasn't in my pocket any longer and that I only kept my hand there as a ruse. But my grandfather knew it was still there, and one night actually tried to pull it out—I always slept in my clothes now—while I was fast asleep. But I woke up, and he retreated to his bed and went to sleep without a word.

It was, as I told you, a time of fighting. My grandfather was sad—not because I'd broken an unspoken agreement, but because he hadn't got his newspaper. He understood this time of constant fighting and struggle, and, in the two further years he lived, he didn't blame me for what I'd done. Issam forgot the incident too. He was a tough boy, and deep down he understood exactly what had happened. We still made our daily trips to the vegetable market, but we quarrelled less than ever before and even talked a little. It was as if something—an invisible wall—had suddenly risen up between us; he was still in the thick of the fighting, but I'd begun to breathe a different air.

I remember that I kept that five liras in my pocket for a full five weeks. I was preparing a suitable exit from the time of battle, but whenever I decided to carry it out, it seemed to me that what I was doing would be like a bridge taking me back to the fight, not an exit from it.

How can I explain this? Keeping the five liras with me somehow seemed to be a better course than spending it. While it was still in my pocket it represented a key I had in my grasp. At any moment I could open the door and go out of it—yet, I felt if I once turned the key in the lock I'd come face to face with another time of fighting behind the door, a much bigger one than the first. It would be like going back to the beginning of the road.

The rest isn't important. One day I went to the marketplace with Issam, and as I dashed forward to snatch a bundle of chard lying near the slowly moving wheels of a truck, I slipped and fell underneath it. Luckily for me the wheels didn't run over my legs, but stopped just as they touched them. Still, I woke up in hospital, and, as you'll no doubt guess, the first thing I did was look for the five liras. It wasn't there.

I think Issam took it when he was with me in the car that took me to the hospital, but he never admitted it and I never asked him; we merely exchanged glances of comprehension. No, I wasn't angry because he'd been busy stealing it while I lay there bleeding. I was just sad that I'd lost it.

But you can't understand. It was a time of fighting.

—translated by May Jayyusi and Christopher Tingley

Muhammad Naffaʿ *(b. 1940)*

A short story writer from Galilee, Naffaʿ was born in Bait Jinn and did his secondary studies at Rameh. He studied for two years at the Hebrew University in Jerusalem and then worked in many jobs. In 1970 he joined the Israeli Communist Party and dedicated himself to political work. His first collection of short stories was *The Pedigree Mare* n.d.; this collection was followed by *Wuddiyya* (1978); *North Wind* (1979) and *Kushan* (1980). His main themes are the land and the peasant's mystical love relation with that land. He also delineates ways to preserve Arab land and protect it from the encroachment of Israeli authorities.

The Uprooted

1

Some people try their utmost to find analogies between the cradle and the grave, between the palace and the tomb, propounding, with a certain verbal sleight of hand and an unwarranted fatalism, that the palaces of today are the mausoleums of tomorrow.

But is there in fact a resemblance between the ruins of *these* homes and a tomb? All that remain standing are some of the walls; mud roofs, for the most part, in a state of collapse; and the rest overgrown with dry grasses and brambles. Although an odor of decay and desolation hangs over the place, this does not prevent small, colorful birds from landing on the clumps of bramble and patiently, skillfully gathering up the seeds while they punctuate their activity with scatterings of sweet song.

At the water spring grows a large bramble bush, with its green-veined, pointed leaves spotted with white droppings from the birds that come to the water. The birds like nothing better than to burst into song before and after they drink. The grapevines and the pomegranate and mulberry trees have remained green and have continued to grow to the extent that they look wild because of their entangled branches and the other plants that have climbed them at will. Little creepers rustle among the dried grass and straw. The lanes and byways are covered with dust and stones and are overgrown with nettles and mallow. Time has taken its toll of things without having been able to obliterate or efface them, while the good land is being exploited by others.

I followed the stream bed that led out from the spring and wound its way among the ancient trees. Lined with old concrete, it was now dry and filled with leaves and decaying rubbish because the water had been diverted elsewhere. In one of the houses, swallows had built their mud nests on the walls and ceilings, and spiders had woven their webs, in their distinctive manner, at points of their choosing.

I imagined the people who had lived here, tending their fields and orchards, drinking the water they drew from the spring in jars and earthen pitchers whose porousness kept the water in them cool. They would spend their evenings on the rooftops, or in the lanes or court-yards. Children would swing from the trees. Fires would be lit, around which wedding feasts were celebrated while bitter, scented coffee was drunk. In the nooks and corners, mothers would lie, giving birth to their babies: I imagined a woman, her face pale from the pains of her labor, and an infant laid onto a straw mat, announcing itself. Beneath the tangled trees, a tryst had taken place, with hearts throbbing, breasts being fondled, hair caressed, kisses stolen, while tears of love flowed down cheeks.

Conditions were disrupted; the houses and the trees were burned; the children tasted terror; men and women, children and animals were slaughtered as the people were uprooted by war. These stone walls, the dust, and the trees are all that remains of the village of Hittin.[1]

The sun had nearly set, as we left the houses to their quiet. We gazed at them, expecting that at any moment songs of peace would ring out from them.

2

Weeks and months went by. Snow began to fall at daybreak, blinding the birds, silencing the valleys and plains, and immobilizing the drain-pipes. Ropes of ice formed on the clotheslines, while sparrows and skylarks descended on the houses to get their share of life from those who loved life. Without showing any fear or flying away, they picked out bits of lentil and cracked wheat from the leftover *mujaddara*[2] that mother scattered on top of the snow.

---

[1] It was here that Saladin won a crucial victory over the Crusaders in 1187 A.D.
[2] A dish made of rice or cracked wheat with lentils, onions, and oil.

From Radio Amman: "This is Fathia from Jaffa, presently located in a camp near Amman. I send greetings to my sister in Riyadh, my father in Kuwait, and my brother, Hasan, whose whereabouts have been unknown for twenty years . . . Oh Hasan, what's the matter with you? Who have you left me with? Am I not your sister? Who can a sister lean on? Mother, may you have a long life . . ." (She weeps, mournfully.)

I, too, have a sister, Fatmeh is her name. What if she were out in the wilderness without shelter or food? With the wind tearing at her hair, trying to pull it out by the roots, with the snow covering it when she lies down, transforming her into a disfigured old hag at the age of twenty, as her eyes gape to the left and to the right? I imagine her wandering from one place to another, while the snow wipes out her footprints so that she can't find her way. In the distance, thunder crashes; thick white clouds hide the sun and blot out the difference between morning and evening. Her voice is hoarse from crying aloud, and her wandering about has made her emaciated, so that she looks like a ghost. I imagine her face-to-face with some wild animal hunting for prey, its sharp fangs red. It closes on her as she twists and turns, shutting her terrified eyes and raising her hands in surrender. There, where the waters of the canals and ditches converge, snow has drifted onto their surface, making them one with the obdurate earth. It is impossible for her to distinguish one from the other. Her feet, bloody from running away and blue from the bitter cold, slip into the water. She goes under, and comes to the surface. She flings out her hands, trying to save herself, but there is no deliverance.

Who said that Jaffa abhors people? Jaffa was founded by people, so how can Jaffa go on without them?

She scattered more food for the nightingales and sparrows so that they might stay alive, while I searched on the dial for songs of revolution and peace. I repeated to myself: "How beautiful are Jaffa and its people!"

3

Because the winter season is long, and so are the winter nights, I always tell stories about the winter. When I was seven years old, I would go to bed—or rather, to half a bed, since my mother and I shared it. The reason for this was not merely our poverty, but the fact that it was warmer sleeping that way. Nothing was sweeter to me than to bury my hand in my mother's bosom, while my father and sister slept nearby.

They liked lots of sleep, and would doze off quickly on their large sheepskin whose long wool was compacted from being sat on and slept on so much. They preferred sleeping near the hearth, which my mother did not like to do because it gave her disquieting dreams. According to her zodiac, it was better for her to lie with her head to the east and her feet to the west, in keeping with the movement of the celestial spheres.

It was midnight, or later, when there came a violent and prolonged knocking at the door. We all woke up at once. My heart beat quickly, while my mother prayed to God for protection and my sister poked her head out like a turtle. When Father opened the door, a man entered, along with a girl, who promptly threw herself on the floor, crying out, "Oh, Mother!"

The man spoke a few words in my father's ear, and we all got up. They were strangers. Although we had little firewood, because the rain had started early, my parents lit a fire in the earthen hearth, and the house became so filled with smoke that we couldn't see a thing. The girl settled down quietly near the fire without saying a word, though she was breathing hard. When my mother pointed to spots of blood on the floor near her, the man said:

"The girl's family took refuge in Lebanon after the war. However, she wasn't with them when they left, and she's asked me to take her to the border. We've been walking since nightfall. Her shoes were useless, and because of the way things are, I had to move fast. She took off her shoes and dumped them on the road. The mud and the flintstones on the way made her feet bleed. This hurt her; she cried, but I didn't stop. It was very cold—so cold that it seemed to sting our faces like fire. When she collapsed to the ground, I scared her with the threat of hyenas and wolves, which made her go on walking until I was sure she couldn't go any farther. Her five dresses, all that she owns, which she is wearing one on top of the other—were all soaked through. That blood on the floor is from her feet."

Mother brought her some old rags, which she wrapped around her feet. Without any shyness she took off her dresses and stood there in nothing but her underclothes. From time to time, she cried out, "Oh, Mother!" The stranger merely looked at her without saying anything. We had only one room, and no coffee or tea, since we were poor and the 1948 war had put coffee and tea beyond our means. Mother heated some water on the fire and mixed it with molasses, which the girl drank. Wrapped up in the black woolen blanket that Mother and I used as a cover, she became a little warmer. She began to complain of how harshly the man had treated her on the way, and she cried pitifully as she told of her family's absence and her having been left as a vagabond. The man sighed, swallowing. Occasionally, my father put wood on the fire, which produced clouds of smoke; then, he opened the door and let the cold air in, until he got a headache and had to go to bed. Mother busied herself drying out the girl's clothes—her name was Aida—while I listened to her story, looking out of the door on the savage night, where rain, wind, and cold held sway.

The man offered my mother money, which caused tears to roll down her cheeks. It was pitch dark, but they had to get back on their way before daybreak.

Rising to her feet, the girl said, "They killed two of my brothers on the threshing floors. The third is missing. Father and Mother took refuge in Lebanon."

She spoke so calmly and courteously that I thought the tears on her cheeks were due to the smoke. Mother forced some shoes on her; in vain, she and my sick father pleaded with them to stay with us until the weather cleared and the girl's wounds healed. Mother was afraid of what might happen to the girl if she left while it was still night: that she might become a homeless waif, or die.

What I came to realize was that her tears were not from the smoke, and that her return from Lebanon would not be in the dark when peace would come.

4

It was dark when we got into the car from Acre. Each of us was on his way to his village, and we all rode in silence. At one of the villages, a boy wearing pajamas stood on the road, blocking the car's way. We stopped, and he got in. He was about nine years old.

"Where are you from?" the driver asked.

"From Khan Yunis," he replied, while a gloomy silence settled over us.

"What brings you here?"

"Looking for work."

A few piasters were jingling in his pocket. The passengers looked at him with concern; his thin, brown face bore the marks of exhaustion and hardship.

"How did you get here from Khan Yunis?"

"With my brothers," he replied, somewhat anguished.

"Today?"

"No, two days ago."

"Where have you been sleeping?"

"In the lanes under the trees."

"What do you have in the bag?"

"Bread, and an orange."

He searched with his hands in the dirty, crumpled, white cloth bag. The boy seemed comforted by the crackling of the dry bread.

One question after another came from the passengers.

"Do you have a house in Khan Yunis?"

"No—it collapsed."

"Where are your brothers?"

"They went off and left me, so I decided I'd come and look for them in this town."

"Do you have any money?" asked the driver.

"Yes, I do."

"Okay, give me half a lira."

The boy took a handful of coins from his pocket: there were piasters, five-piaster pieces and ten-piaster pieces. The passengers were angry with the driver for taking a fare from the young lad. As for the driver, he paid no attention to this but looked suspiciously and angrily at the bag of dry bread. The passengers were also indignant at the boy's brothers for having left him alone on the roads at night in strange country. The driver, however, turned on the radio and tuned in the news from the Israeli broadcasting station: "Israeli planes have bombed a factory in Abu Zaʿbal.[3] Fifty workers who had just finished their lunchbreak were killed, while scores more were wounded. The Israeli planes returned safely to their base."

We reached the village, but the boy was reluctant to get down.

"Get off," ordered the driver.

"I'm afraid to get down and be in the dark alone."

"Where are you going?" asked one of the passengers.

"I don't know."

The boy had to get off. He did so, swinging his bag. Confused and dismayed, he walked along the pavement. The broadcast went on to say that the Minister of Defense had sent word to the Egyptians, via the Red Cross, that one of the planes had accidentally dropped a 400-kilogram bomb set to go off after twenty-four hours, and that the bomb would have to be dismantled to be disarmed.

[3]An industrial town in Egypt's delta.

"War hardens the heart," remarked the driver. "How could his older brothers have left a boy like this on the roads?"

5

> Shine upon our land, O Wheat,
> Shine over the fields;
> Coat our land gold with your color
> And dance above the fields.

The moon had just set behind the mountains as I slipped away under cover of darkness. Night in the Khait region was like night anywhere else. The broad field seemed to be completely peaceful, and the caves where people slept seemed dark and lonely, with not a cough or any other sign of life in them. As for the shepherds, there was no need to take them into account because after sunset they had gone deep into the pastureland, and the sound of their camels' bells now came from a great distance.

The wet stalks of grain and the grass soaked my legs. I spread a thin layer of wheat on the threshing floor and piled up some straw along the edges. After a few moments, I pricked up my ears: I heard footsteps and a low call. She stole in like a thief. She pulled the overcoat partially over her shoulders since the night was somewhat chilly, and warmth was desirable.

"It's all because of the overcoat," she remarked.

At that time, I was herding cattle from dawn to dusk, because the land was too muddy to be plowed. Because it was heavy, I used to leave my overcoat in the cave and use it only as a blanket at night, on a bed made of chaff and old clothes. One night, when I complained about how bad my coat smelled, I heard her burst into a fit of uncontrollable giggling in the darkness of the cave.

"What a pain in the neck!" came from her father, who was sleeping near her.

I took note of this; and the next day I left the pasture early. Entrusting the cattle to the others, I discreetly went back to the cave. Normally, the girls remained in the caves to clean up under the animals, to do baking, to mend clothes, and to fetch water from the springs of the Arabs or the Rabeed Well, which lay near the Morning Star Settlement. I sat on the rocks that formed the roof of the cave and listened to the girls laughing. Although their talk was silly and immature, I liked it.

When they emerged from the cave, they were carrying my coat between them like a coffin and mourning hilariously. They had loaded it with the rest of the chaff and cow manure, and were using it to carry away the filthy stuff! I got angry, and hastily climbed down to stand at the mouth of the cave.

"You should be ashamed of yourselves!" I scolded.

They laughed in embarrassment, letting the coat fall. As for her—Zumarrud[4]—she blushed charmingly. Confusion and pleading showed in her eyes. I would have loved her to remain that way: confused, embarrassed, taken by surprise. Everything about her was beautiful—even her agitation as she tried to make up some excuse was beautiful.

Over the next few days, I never looked her way, except for an occasional stolen glance. I made a show of having had my honor offended, which disconcerted her. She would make as though she were about to speak and then swallow her words at the last minute.

At night, most of those who were living in our cave would go to the poetry reciter's place, to pass the time listening to stories of Zir Salim and the folk romance of the Bani Hilal. They would come back late, repeating, everyone to a different melody, the poems they had memorized: "I fenced my home against my foes; But a home has no defense, save its menfolk . . ."

For my part, I would pretend to be tired and remain in the cave with a few others, including her and some of the younger boys and girls. On account of the cold, we would bury our feet in the straw. One time, there was a rustling in the straw, and something came close to my buried foot. That something was warm, smooth, and enticing; and in the dancing light of the torch she blushed again in agitation and embarrassment. Thus, I began to regard my old coat as something not to be parted with.

Her face was warm, and her long plaited hair was as cool as basil from the mist and dew that had settled on it. Her breathing was rapid, and her heart pounded audibly. Her lips were full, and her waist was like, not a beech twig, but a bundle of them. I could imagine her face, blushing as usual, the bewilderment showing in her eyes and the slight frown on her brown forehead.

When the night was nearly over, the straw crackled as she got up to look around and check out the area. I followed her with my eyes as

[4]Emerald.

she disappeared into the standing wheat. The rustling of her wary steps lingered in my ears, while I stayed on in my warm spot. Just before dawn, some of the stars began to disappear, and everything fell silent. I didn't realize how much time had elapsed until a nightingale broke into song and a donkey brayed; then came sounds of barking, and coughing.

When day broke to receive the first rays of the sun, the wide plain became visible. Everything seemed normal as I lightly and briskly made my way to the harvest. The sun climbed higher, dispelling the mist, and songs rose up from the throats of the harvesters.

It was mid-morning. Zumarrud was singing:

> Shine upon our land, Oh Wheat,
> Shine over the fields;
> Coat our land gold with your color
> And dance above the fields . . .

And the wheat *was* shining above the plain; with a pleasant rustle, it danced in the breeze.

Then the singing stopped. The people got to their feet, as some men appeared at the top of a high hill. All of them were complete strangers to us. We had no time to think, for right away they opened fire from the hill. A camel went into a foaming rage, then fell down with blood pouring from him; a man screamed in extreme pain. The shooting continued, and flames burst out in various places. The people had no weapons. The strangers' bullets guided the people in bunches toward the road. The wheat, the threshing floor, and the caves were left behind, and the camels were dragged forcefully along. Women wept, and men fumed, but the people realized that Khait had been lost to them.

Today, we might hear one of those fellows say, "What Hannibal's elephants and Ghengis Khan's horses took years to accomplish, Israeli planes have done in hours.

"However, as we harvested the wheat, we were stronger than elephants, horses, or planes. When we stirred up the earth, it smiled and grew green; we sowed life, while they sowed destruction in the earth. Even more, we were *like* the earth, which springs forth every year with each new season, life bursting from the sleeping seed. We know that the wind may blow the seed away, or the waters may carry it off; but wherever it lands, new life will sprout up from it."

—translated by L. M. Kenny and Thomas G. Ezzy

Waleed Rabah (b. 1940)

Rabah was born in Abbasiyya near Jaffa. His family left Palestine in 1948 and he was unable to pursue more than a secondary education. He became a journalist and founded his own monthly periodical, *Al-Ghadab*, in 1988, in New Jersey, U.S.A., where he now lives. His first collection of short stories, *Etchings on the Cell's Walls*, appeared in 1975, followed by *Solo Tunes on the Canvas of the Tent* in 1976. His last collection, *Mischievous Imp of the Camp*, appeared in 1977. His stories stem mostly from the experiences of Palestinians in the diaspora, and delineate with sensitivity and touching gravity the dilemmas experienced in facing a harsh and often antagonistic world. Rabah has also written at least six collections of children's stories.

Solo Tunes on a Zinc Wall

Her hennaed toes are grimy from going barefoot. Her chafed ankles are bloody from the combination of thorns and wheat stalks. Bits of rock, embedded in the creases, work their way at night into the soles of her feet, where flesh blends with pain.

"Woman, try to rest for a day or two," said my father, with increasing agitation. "Buy yourself a pair of shoes that will protect your feet from thorns and the bites of insects."

A warm tear runs down her cheek, working its way into the wrinkles. When it finally stops at the bottom of her chin, it is as cold as summer hail. In their sleep, the children have uncovered themselves; slowly, she crawls over to cover their tender bodies, while my father's eyes mist over like a drizzle untouched by any wind. She hums:

> "You who sleep on pillows are ignorant of what's going on.
> A bird shrieked, announcing separation,
> Would that I were there to see it.
> With my own hand I broke the pen and drank the ink."

Oh, Anger! The bones in my palm pierce like saws in their eagerness to reach out for the ears of wheat and gather them, adding them to the bunch she is holding with love in her arms. Every time I added an ear she said: "And that's another bite to feed a small, hungry mouth. . . ."

Our tent is the wind's plaything. It is like a dry leaf hanging on to the branch of an almond tree on an autumn day—a leaf that clings to its branch, striving to avoid the splattering mud and brackish water. My father hurries along; we follow him, each carrying a heavy stone to secure the edges of the tent. We steady the tent pegs, tighten the ropes, and go back to crouch around the smoke that corrodes our tired eyes. As for her, she is always sitting there, mending a dress . . . or singing . . .

As we scampered in the mud of the camp, she was standing beneath the rain, her body covered by her embroidered dress. She was trying to keep order among the women who were lined up to receive the American clothes that the United Nations bestowed on us refugees. Her dress clung to her sagging breasts. The pouring water seeped through it, down to the hem, from which it dripped into the mud at her feet. Words of rage and bitterness died on her lips, and all I could hear was her lilting, "What a world! They hide behind their chandeliers, while I trudge in mud up to my knees! I used to have a beautiful pair of shoes that I pranced around in every time I went to the meadow on rainy days . . . Now, alas, it is our fate to go barefoot!

> "They've clipped the bird's wings
> and left it dejected."

They looked at her and smiled, but their smiles soon turned into sarcastic laughter. "Leave yesterday's sorrows behind, woman! We all had a pair of shoes once, and we all ate the grain of our own land without having to line up and beg for the flour that comes all wormy, sent to us by the UNRWA . . ."

I used to cling to her dress like a fly, and she would drag me along wherever she went. She would go into the alleyways and become aware of my presence only when I screamed with hunger or asked for a forbidden piece of pastry. I always knew beforehand what she would finally say, but the different ways she had of answering made it worth going on asking. One time she'd slap me on the mouth with the back of her hand, so hard that I'd be unable to speak for an hour or so. Another time she'd feel sorry for me, and kiss me, and promise me things. And a third time she would cry bitterly and try to explain to me that all we had was barely a loaf of bread, so how could we afford sweets?

But I never gave up. Only once did she ever accede to my request. It was the time she went to the city and sold all the wheat she had collected by following behind the harvesters for three days straight. I remember that on that same day we had meat for dinner. Needless to say, it was tough—even the fire had difficulty penetrating its tendons—but it was meat none the less. . . . When she'd gotten back to the tent, we clustered around the fire, my father smiling openly. As she started unwrapping the bundle I was thrilled to see a furry coat. "Keep your back warm," she'd said to my father, "or else you'll get rheumatism . . ." Every one of us got something that day. My share was a huge, oversized pair of pants, whose cuffs filled with mud every time I wore them. In its pocket I found a piece of paper, on which were some Arabic words that looked as if they'd been written in Kufic script. They said: "Child—Whoever you are and wherever you are, I'm giving you my pants as a present. Take care of them, for they are of good material. My father bought them for my birthday two years ago, and I hope that you receive them on your birthday . . . With regards—Young Harold."

As she hurried along she tried to avoid the thorn bushes on both sides of the road. Panting heavily, she urged me to hurry so that we could catch up with the harvesters before they started gathering up the ears of wheat.

I could see the grains of sand embedded in the cracks in her ankles. She sat down and plucked them out with a wheat stalk, or whatever else was handy at the time, and then kept on walking.

I contemplated her tall figure, which reminded me of a palm tree whose roots suck earth for nourishment. A coarse red shawl embroidered with red thread was tied to her waist. On her wrist was displayed a bracelet that she had worn ever since those first ululations had come out of her house on the day of her marriage to that "ill-fated man" (as she called him). As a result of constant rubbing against mud and soil, the hem of her dress was all frayed. She trailed her dress behind her proudly, and refused to wear anything else. The reason she gave was that it held the smell of our soil. "Oh, my son! I wish you'd known the smell of our soil! It is far superior to all the fragrances of the world. It's like—I can't even describe it—it smells like rain on its first day after a long period of drought . . ." However, every time she refused to change her dress, my father would say, teasingly, "Don't you believe her! She keeps it on because in it she can smell our first wedding nights!" And she would hit him coyly on the back: "Be careful of the children, you ill-fated, stricken idiot! They're all ears! . . ."

She took a deep breath and looked toward the horizon. The sun was starting to penetrate the base of the mountains. She looked around, searching for a place the harvesters had passed over to begin collecting

wheat in. Usually she tried to spot an inexperienced harvester and followed him, picking up whatever stalks of wheat he had failed to pick
up himself. What she gathered she held in her arms like a baby. If a
harvester looked back, she gave him a smile and urged me to hurry,
promising me a penny if I collected a thousand ears—a glorious penny,
which I would flaunt in front of my friends and spend only on whatever
was absolutely necessary.

The hours passed while she stooped, scratching up the ground in
hopes of finding an ear of grain that had been accidentally trampled
into the ground by the feet of the harvesters. That day she collected a
lot, which made others envious. And for the first time that I could
remember, she smiled generously and said, "Tomorrow is a rest day.
We've gathered enough today." Then she added, "We've got to keep
on. I've got to make enough to be able to give your brother two pennies.
Poor baby—he went to school today murmuring that his classmates
always have sandwiches to eat at school, while he just looks on longingly
. . . Tomorrow, I'll give him two pennies—just to satisfy his eyes for
once!"

She sat down, panting. The wheezing from her chest pierced into
the air around us. She added another bundle and covered it with her
sash, which she had already spread out on the ground. She stood up,
urging me to help her. I was exhausted, and my body just sank to the
ground. She looked at me compassionately. "Sleep beside our bundles,"
she said. I lay down on my side and fell into a deep sleep.

I woke up to her voice, gusting like rain: "Everybody, listen! I've
been robbed! They've stolen my wheat! Everything I've spent the whole
day collecting is gone!"

The people stood around her in a circle, their eyes filled with sorrow.
Words poured out like splashes of water—more than I could ever quote
here. I remember her on that day, sitting there as though she had lost
a child, or as though my father's pants had ripped. The hot tears that
ran down her cheeks became mixed with sand and dirt; they flowed
down to the base of her neck, where they were soaked up by the fabric
of her dress, which was already caked with dried mud.

She put her right hand to her cheek and began to sing:

> "I'll cry and let everyone cry with me
> for the affliction that has befallen me alone."

"They've robbed us, son; all the day's work will go into other people's bellies," she said.

She was interrupted by one of the harvesters, who carried over a bundle of wheat on his scythe and put it down in front of her. "Here, woman, take this. We've made up what you've lost."

She looked at him with great astonishment. With her right sleeve, she wiped her eyes. "No . . . I'm used to collecting my wheat with my own sweat."

She stood up and started all over. By the end of that day she had collected many bundles, which she kept tied to her skirts, for fear they be stolen.

I could hear women whispering that the harvesters had left ears of grain behind for her deliberately, to compensate her loss.

At the cattle *souk* she sat down on the sandy ground and displayed her merchandise, but no one seemed to notice her.

"Who'll buy my wheat! It's free of stones and dirt! Ear by ear, I gathered it myself! . . . As firm as an eyeball! . . . Grain pure as gold! . . ."

Her wrinkled throat quivered with thirst. She swallowed her saliva until it dried out completely; then she placed a pebble on her tongue and started sucking it, trying to create a flow of moisture in her dry mouth. I could hear it screaking against her teeth, like the sound of rain on the zinc roof of our tent.

"Wheat pure as gold! . . ." As she called this out, her upper jaw revealed the gold teeth that she had tinted her mouth with in the past, when money had flowed freely from her hand.

"Wheat free of stones! . . ." She was like a tree stripped of its green branches. The circles around her eyes as she lay on the sands were thick and black, as though they'd been punched by the fist of a rowdy soldier.

"He asked me to buy him an ounce of red tobacco, so that he can roll a few cigarettes and smoke them while he twiddles his thumbs. So that he can satisfy his craving and get a little precious pleasure . . . 'You know,' he said, 'the day I planted that apple tree in the yard of our house I thought I'd die before I tasted its fruit. But within a year's time it had bloomed, and its fruit was as big as a fat ostrich's egg . . . In the evenings you always used to sit on the north balcony and place a bite in my mouth that burned on my tongue, yet melted like sugar . . . Oh, the good old days! . . .' "

"Wheat! Wheat! . . . Starting tomorrow, I'm going to start following the harvesters and collecting ears of barley instead! It seems that people have had enough of wheat, or have taken to buying UNRWA flour, or maybe they can't tell the difference between wheat and barley any more . . ."

She took a deep breath. Sweat dripped from her forehead. She was beginning to feel suffocated by the heavy air and the heat.

Someone took a handful of wheat and examined it.

"Bad wheat."

Agitated, she answered, "Sir, at home you eat biscuits and butter. That's why you regard this blessing from God as 'bad.' "

He looked at her dubiously. "Even if your wheat was 'golden,' as you claim, no one would dare buy it from you as long as you're wrapped in that filthy shroud."

After looking him over from head to toe, she answered, "May God give us patience!"

For a long time she studied the faces of the passers-by. Then she saw a policeman who was kicking out at whatever he came across. He saw a man selling cakes and turned the tray upside-down on the man's head, causing him to weep and beg the policeman to let him go on with his business, but the policeman gave him a kick and walked on to harass someone else. He threw a large jug of lemonade to the ground. Out of frustration, its owner cursed the government; as a result, he was handcuffed and thrown into a police car that was parked not too far away.

"What a treacherous world! . . . When the British had our village surrounded, I stood up to their tanks and threw sand at their faces. When they asked me about the names of certain wanted men, I answered: 'If you were men as you claim you are, you wouldn't be asking a woman these questions! For once, be what you claim to be! Catch them in an open battle! . . .' There we stood, defying them like quinine trees as they stand mocking the blowing wind . . . What has changed? I don't know . . . The need to make a living? Hunger?"

"Woman, you can see with your own eyes what's going on, and yet you've got your wheat spread out all over the pavement! You know it's forbidden for beggars to spoil the look of the streets, yet you all defy the regulations and show no respect for law-enforcers. Take away your wheat or I'll grind it into powder, and mix it with the sand and stones!"

"Son, this is a blessing from God. How could you trample on it? Aren't you afraid that something bad will happen to you? That you'll go blind? . . ."

"Come on, you fool!"

The rays of the sun were reflecting into her eyes off his silvery, shiny belt. Her eyes dropped from his chest, past the buttons of his coat, and stopped at his shoes.

"Can't you hear? Come on!"

"If I had been there, no one would have dared stop me! But today, hunger has its say . . . He's there, in the tent, lying down. Because of his need for tobacco, any trivial thing turns him jittery as a bull . . . And the little one, my precious love, always clinging to me so I'll reach into my bag and put a pastry, dripping with honey and sugar, into her mouth . . ."

"Don't play helpless with me . . . 'Wheat pure as gold!' You are in defiance of the law and of the police . . . 'Wheat free of stones!' 'I'll exchange the wheat for an ounce of tobacco only' Idiot! No one but an idiot would dare defy me!"

The noises in the background made her numb. She looked aside, then looked back at his shoes and saw the reflection of her tired face. Smiling bitterly, she followed the movements of his shoe as it crushed the grains of wheat into the sand. She remained still as a statue; and when his cane came down on her shoulder, she took a deep breath and said:

"God Almighty, please grant us patience!"

—translated by Salwa Jabsheh and Thomas G. Ezzy

Yahya Rabah (b. 1943)

A short story writer from the district of Gaza. Born in the village of Sawafir, Yahya Rabah was five years old when the Israelis seized his area and forced the people of his village to leave it. He grew up in one of the Gaza refugee camps and obtained a diploma from the Teachers' Institute in Gaza before going to the University of Ain Shams in Cairo for his B.A. in business administration. Since then he has lived in many Arab countries, working in broadcasting and journalism. He has published two collections of stories, *He Who Has Not Traveled* (1975) and *Birds of Affection* (1981). He has also published books on the various aspects of the Palestine revolution, including his book on the famous battle of the Shaqif Fortress.

Death of a Bird Hunter

1

The moment he walked in through the wide glass door, the bar became filled with the drinkers' cheering. He paused for a few seconds at the door to scan the faces, which looked hazy because of the clouds of smoke that filled the room and because of his weakening eyesight. With slow, tottering footsteps he advanced until he reached the middle of the room. Shouts of welcome came at him from all sides.

"Welcome to the bar, Nimr al-Hisan!"

"Gentlemen, now you're going to hear the story of Nimr al-Hisan, the Tiger-Stallion!"[1]

"A hunter—I came to do some hunting, but I became someone's game instead!"

Laughter and cheery excitement resound in the place. Some try to get out of their seats, but their lazy muscles do not respond, so they sink back, while Nimr al-Hisan stands in the middle of the room. On

---

[1]*Nimr* ("tiger") and *Hisan* ("stallion"): The former occupies the position of the given name; the latter, the position of the surname or nickname. Whatever their origin, the qualities of courage and strength implied in these names are meant to have both ironic and tragic overtones.

his face is a smile directed at everyone; his weary glances scan the various faces, searching harshly and sadly for something.

"I am Nimr al-Hisan, the bird hunter! I'm the best hunter in the world! I spot a bird at the highest point in the sky, and I shoot . . . One shot, and the bird is hanging from my game bag. It doesn't matter whether a bird is high in the sky, or over a tree, or hopping in the grass . . . One shot! Just one shot, and the bird is hanging from my bag!"

The drunks' cheers get louder. They raise their glasses in salute. Out of the pocket of his jacket, so old that nothing of its original appearance has remained except its rusty, yellow buttons, he takes a small, odd-looking bottle with a metal base in which he keeps a picture of his wife. Nimr al-Hisan walks around, so that each one can pour a drink into his bottle. He raises it high in the air and gulps it down avidly, one drink after another, until he has completed his round and comes back to the middle of the room, drunk and exhausted, standing like some mythic figure hovering between sleep and wakefulness.

"I am Nimr al-Hisan, the bird hunter! A long time ago, I used to hit the eye of a needle dead center, and I could hit a flock of starlings with one shot! Even today, I say, let anyone dare to challenge me and say he's a better hunter!"

Caution permeates his limbs, and his eyes gleam with defiance. He stretches his arms as though aiming his hunting rifle; he flexes his hand, closes an eye, and holds his breath. His body shudders. His hands shake and then go limp; his features sag, and saliva dribbles over his lower lip, then his entire body trembles and he bursts into tears. Through the tears that become mingled with the cigarette smoke, he scans the faces. Looks of pity, sarcasm, drowsiness, indifference are directed towards him.

He propels his exhausted body out through the wide glass door and plunges into the heart of the city. Nimr al-Hisan resumes his wandering, staggering and swaying, moving in a circle. The cold wind slaps his face; his white hair unkempt, he stops every so often to suck up whatever is left in his odd-shaped bottle, then he continues on his way.

When the night guards spot him, they whisper in their usual pitying tone:

"Poor Nimr al-Hisan!"

"He came to the city one day to sell his birds, and lost himself."

Their whispers reach his ears; they reach him in his daze, which is sometimes interrupted by short periods of clarity. But he never stops his roaming around until he gets too tired to do it any more. He slows down his steps, stops, and falls asleep next to any wall.

2

Nimr al-Hisan had come to the big city many years before. Because he was always out on the streets, he was well-known to the crowds there, and was watched for in the fancy restaurants and cafés and bars. At first they saw him as a handsome young man, a kind of gypsy, with the pride of a fighter who was accustomed to winning battles. He had come to their city to sell them the colorful birds he hunted. He was tall and broad, with thick hair falling on his forehead and bright, shining eyes, as sharp as a hawk's.

He would come in at infrequent intervals, wearing a jacket with bright, shiny yellow buttons, which he had found one day while roaming the hills. When he found it, he had been very pleased. "It may be the uniform of a soldier," he told himself, "One of the fighters who once crossed these hills . . ." Alone with his gun in the hills, he had put it on and taken a few strides, like a soldier on parade. Then he had fired a shot into the air, and laughed and laughed, until he could feel the whole sky resonate with his laughter . . .

Nimr al-Hisan came from a small family of peasants who lived in one of the small border villages. When the war[2] broke out, his family, like all the other families in the village, lost most of their arable land. The young men of the village stayed around for some time, waiting for the fulfillment of the promises that had been made to compensate them for the lands which they had lost. But these promises were never made good, which forced a lot of young men to leave the country to look for work. Those who didn't emigrate went to the nearby cities and worked as shoeshine boys, porters, factory hands, or waiters. Some of them even worked as servants for rich families whose wealth had multiplied after the war. But Nimr al-Hisan's family didn't leave the village. The eldest brother kept plowing what land they had left, even planting trees in the cracks between the rocks. As for Nimr al-Hisan himself, the family bought him a small herd of goats, and he inherited an old rifle that had belonged to his father, who had been killed in the war.

[2]He is speaking here of the 1967 June War, known also as the Six Day War.

That is how Nimr al-Hisan became a shepherd and a hunter of birds. There was nothing to induce the family to go away from their immediate surroundings, not even to the big city, of which many tales were told. There was no need to go there, for every week a big village fair was set up at the crossroads, and everyone from the larger villages came to it to exchange their goods, as well as to stock up on news about the wide world around them.

Nimr al-Hisan used to attend these fairs with his wife, who was deeply in love with him. He would don his soldier's uniform, with its shiny yellow buttons, which he had found in the hills. On his waist he wore a thick metal-edged belt lined with hunting bullets; on his right shoulder he proudly carried his rifle, while on his left he hung his birds, birds of all colors—white, blue, yellow, red, and gray—strung like the flowers on the necklaces that the village girls wore round their necks.

One day, one of his fellow villagers told him, "Nimr, if you take your birds to sell in the big city, you'll earn much more than you ever will here."

At first he was apprehensive, but his wife urged him on: "Go, Nimr, go to the big city. To make a living a person has to be daring, and not afraid of adventure."

And so, Nimr al-Hisan came to the big city for the first time. He was as handsome as a gypsy, as proud and self-assured as a fighter who was used to plunging into battle. He stood at the edge of the main square, in front of a large café. Standing there, tall and broad, with his hawklike eyes and his long rifle, he looked like a figure out of some legend.

"Hey, hunter, come in!" called one of the men inside the café.

Wary and somewhat overwhelmed, he entered the café. A group gathered around him.

"Are these birds for sale?"

"Yes."

"Where are you from?"

"One of the border villages."

"Border? Which border?"[3]

Someone gave him a few coins and took his multicolored birds. Nimr al-Hisan went out into the crowded square. There were all sorts of people, cars, and tall buildings. Noise was coming from everywhere.

---

[3]He is speaking of the new border formed by the Israeli occupation of the West Bank in June 1967, after the Six Day War.

He tried to get a handle on everything that was going on, to set it in order in his mind.

"Later I'll tell my wife about all this," he murmured to himself. "Maybe next time I'll bring her with me."

As time went on, Nimr al-Hisan became a familiar figure in the city. Sometimes he came alone, and at other times he was accompanied by his wife, who walked at his side clinging to him, her beautiful eyes full of wonder. Many of the customers who bought his colorful birds would pay her compliments when they saw her with him.

"You clever hunter—how did you bag such a pretty bird?"

She would lower her head in embarrassment, while he swelled with pride.

Frequently, Nimr al-Hisan would send his wife to the city to sell his birds, and she'd come back to tell him all she'd seen. One day, she left for the city with his birds, but she never came back. He got back from the hills with his herd and waited for her until nightfall, but still she hadn't returned. He asked the police about her, as well as the staff on duty at the hospitals and the faces he knew in the city.

"My wife—have you seen my wife?"

Some kept quiet.

Others answered in the negative.

Others answered, impatiently, "Your wife? We don't know her . . ."

But a fire was eating at Nimr al-Hisan from within. Behind all the answers, he could sense people's mockery.

One day passed after another.

One month after another.

Every sunset, Nimr al-Hisan began to make his rounds in the heart of the big city, and would stop, defeated, at the end of the night. Full of expectancy and of fear, he would throw himself into one of the drinking places. As time passed he became like a living legend that people got so used to that it didn't affect them any more, to the point where Nimr al-Hisan and his story became a regular subject for the chatter of the drunkards in the bars at the end of the night.

Did Nimr al-Hisan forget the wife he lost in the city? Did he lose himself in the process, and start searching for himself? Did hatred of the faces that had taken his wife from him and made fun of him wane? Did he finally make his peace with the big city he'd once come to, strong and proud, displaying his colorful birds, only to have it steal all his strength and turn him into a wingless old hawk?

He made his rounds in the daytime.

He made his rounds in the nighttime.

Nimr al-Hisan would fill his odd bottle with whatever the drinkers' glasses contained, and drink it. The drink and his misery always filled him with agitation, and when the tension reached its peak, his body would shake, and he would burst into tears. Then he would disappear into the heart of the city, and huddle down to sleep next to any wall he came upon.

3

One day, the people in the city missed him. They no longer saw him in the squares sneaking into restaurants to eat leftovers. Late-night drinkers waited for him to pass by so that they could pour some of the liquor from their glasses into his bottle and listen to his stories.

The days passed one after the other. People in the big city were on the verge of forgetting him altogether . . . Until he appeared again.

He walked into the bar through the wide glass entrance. He paused for a few seconds at the door, looking, scanning the faces. On his shoulder hung his old hunting rifle. The drunks spotted him from behind the thick smoke that issued continuously from their cigarettes. Excited, they shouted:

"Nimr al-Hisan! Nimr al-Hisan!"

"Welcome to the bar, Nimr al-Hisan!"

"Here comes the brave hunter!"

"What have you done? Have you sold your bottle and bought a rifle?"

Nimr al-Hisan walked a few steps until he reached the middle of the room. On his face was a smile directed at everyone, while his tired eyes scanned all the faces in that hazy air.

"I'm Nimr al-Hisan—the best hunter in the world!"

The cheers of the drunkards grew louder. Hands stretched out to him, glasses were raised to salute him, while he went on in his semi-conscious state, "A long, long time ago, I used to hit the eye of a needle! With one shot I could bring down a flock of starlings! Whether a bird was high in the sky, or over a tree, or hopping in the grass, or even inside its nest, I'd shoot . . . One shot, and the bird would be hanging from my bag!"

His body was trembling; his hands shook as though they were being driven by some current. With his left hand he held the rifle, and with his right he gripped the trigger. He pointed his rifle at the faces, one face after the other, while the sarcastic screams grew louder. Then there was one moment of stillness, and he fired. The shot burst out, and blood gushed out of someone's face.

The shock became identified with the numbness in the men's limbs. A deathlike silence prevailed. The rifle fell from Nimr al-Hisan's hands. Exhausted, he turned around and left the bar. Every limb in his body was trembling.

When he got outside the wide glass door, he collapsed. When the others got over their shock and caution, they rushed to the door to find him—a corpse.

—translated by Salwa Jabsheh and Thomas G. Ezzy

Fadl al-Rimawi *(b. 1945)*

Born in Beit Rima in the district of Ramallah, Rimawi obtained a degree in Arabic literature from the Arab University of Beirut in 1974 and now works as a teacher in Ramallah itself. He began writing and publishing his short stories at the beginning of the seventies and has co-edited *Palestinian Short Stories in the Occupied Territories* (1977), which is a collection of twenty-seven short stories by fourteen writers of fiction. He is active in the literary life of the region and his work shows a pervasive concern with the situation of Palestinians under occupation.

The Sous Vendor[1]

A silver jug was held firmly on to his paunch by a leather belt. On either side of the jug sat two rows of glasses. He always walked with his head held high and his back straight. At first glance, you'd assume from the way he walked that he was arrogant and haughty; but a closer look revealed the secret: he was only trying to support the jug—the jug that was the source of his livelihood and of his misery. He never rested for a minute. He started out early in the morning, carrying his jug and heading for the main street in town, where the workers gathered and where commercial activity was boisterous.

My own heavy schedule and my many functions in the store where I worked never gave me a chance to get to know him. But one day I saw him walk into the store, hesitantly and with some apprehension.

"Welcome! Come in . . ." I said encouragingly.

He smiled a mournful smile and said, "Please, could I have an inexpensive shirt?"

I gave him what he wanted, and, as a kind gesture, I asked him for a glass of *sous*. I took one sip, then downed it in a single gulp; for, contrary to what I had expected, it tasted wonderful. I put my hand into my pocket to pay him, but he took his shirt and hurried to the

---

[1] *Sous* is a very refreshing soft drink, noncarbonated and black in color, made from sugar and the root of the licorice plant.

door. I followed him outside to thank him and tell him how tasty I had found his drink.

He looked back at me and said with enthusiasm, "We're professionals—I've been preparing this drink for the past ten years, and whoever tastes my *sous* never stops asking for it."

I stayed standing at the shop entrance, my eyes following him as he disappeared into the distance. He seemed to me as if, with every step he took, he was getting ready to plunge into a new bout with the people, the street, and his *sous*. The brass plates in his hands clanged appealingly, and his voice grew louder. "The Original *sous* is here! Cool off! . . . Cool off . . . Quench your thirst before it's too late!"

People gathered around him, asking for a glass of licorice drink. He handed out the drinks quickly and efficiently, and never ceased calling out and clanging his plates the whole time.

"The man must have made a fortune out of selling *sous*," I thought to myself. "He sells each glass for ten liras. If you add up the glasses and the liras . . ."

The next day I heard his voice approaching. I rushed to meet him at the door of the store. I asked him for a glass of *sous* and gave him fifty liras for the drink. He tried to give me my change, but I refused it; he got upset and seemed confused.

"If you want us to be friends you've got to take back the balance of your money," he said. "Yesterday's drink was complimentary, but if you insist on not taking back your change, I'll never set foot in your store again."

I gave up and took my change. I tried to thank him, but he answered, "It's nothing, my son . . ."

As time went by, my relationship with the *sous* man grew stronger. As my interest in him grew, so did his attachment to me. I tried several times to explain to myself the secret of this strong relationship with a man who was twenty years my senior. What was causing this bond? Was it the need for a father figure? Was it the cruelty of life and the circumstances of exile? Or was it . . .? Was it . . .? The questions always ran into each other, so I gave up trying to find an explanation, telling myself that eventually time would answer all my questions.

One midday I noticed, as he walked in to visit me, that he looked tired. He asked if he could sit down. A few moments later the store had emptied out, since a lot of the customers stayed home at that time of day. I took the opportunity to ask about his health.

"Son," he answered, "I know my health is getting worse every day."

"Take it easy on yourself," I told him. "It's very hot, and you keep walking around all day . . . Who would look after you if anything happened to you?"

"Son, you're still young, and you have no responsibilities to burden you . . . People like me have to work all the time! If they don't work all day long they don't survive. I've got nothing in this world—no house, no land! All I've got in this world is a wooden hut in a refugee camp, where eight of us have to squeeze in. Six pounds of tomatoes are hardly enough for a meal for them, and look at the price of things! Everything I earn during the day I spend at the end of it—So, if I have to stop working for one day, that day we starve! . . ."

I tried to interrupt his volcanic eruption, to cool down his sadness and agony. All I could say was, "Be patient, Abu ʿAli . . . Things have got to get better."

"What you're saying, son, is consolation for the helpless. I've been like this for the past ten years. Three years after the Occupation,[2] I was thrown into jail and charged with several offenses. When I was acquitted, I was not allowed to return to work. Just imagine—my job was only as a receptionist in a government office, but even that I was prevented from keeping! What a world! . . . I said to myself, any work in my own country is better than leaving. They were trying to block me from ways of making a living, but I'd find my own way . . . And so you see me, walking all day, here and there . . . Long ago I was strong, so it didn't matter. But my health has deteriorated. I can't run around any longer as I used to. All I'm aiming for is to be able to save a small amount of money to open a small kiosk on the side of the street."

Abu ʿAli looked at his watch and stood up abruptly. He took up his jug, which was lying beside him on the floor, and went out into the street, clanging his brass plates and pouring the *sous*, with no enthusiasm and with words that hardly came out.

Abu ʿAli disappeared into the distance, and I was no longer able to hear the clanging of his brass plates. Then suddenly the air was filled with an explosion.

I looked outside the store. People were running into each other; everyone was trying to get away. I closed up the store and hurried home before a curfew was announced and the place filled up with soldiers. On the way, I caught up with some acquaintances of mine.

[2]He is speaking of the Israeli occupation of the West Bank and Gaza.

"Those sons of bitches!" they were saying, "They've done it again! They want us out—they want us to get fed up and leave!"

"This time they've done it on the main street! Later, their investigation will announce that it was done by 'saboteurs'! . . ."

"The blast caught that poor *sous* man right in the stomach! He was too close when it went off . . ."

I couldn't control myself any longer, and asked furiously, "Which *sous* man are you talking about? Abu 'Ali?"

"Yes, that's him."

"Are you sure it was him?"

"We saw him fall to the ground with our own eyes. The fragments of his pot scattered all around him, and the licorice juice mixed with the blood of his hand, which was torn off, and the blood of the other casualties. People were kind enough to carry all of them to the hospital. We couldn't hang around any longer, as there were lots of army cars surrounding the place. We had to run away."

I went straight to the hospital. A crowd had gathered in front of its gate. People were shouting together, as if in a chorus, "Murderers! Criminals! Abu 'Ali, your blood will not be wasted!"

I took the opportunity to ask one of the well-known doctors, as he passed by, about Abu 'Ali.

"He's still in a coma. We'll do our best to help him. The rest of the wounded will be okay, they've only got minor injuries. Is he your father?"

"No—only someone I care about."

"Don't worry, we care about him too—and about his friends. He's our father, and they're our brothers . . ."

I muttered to myself that there was still some goodness in the world.

I turned back to look at the crowd; it was scattering. I spotted a woman who looked tense and obviously agonized. I thought she might be Abu 'Ali's wife. I felt in my pockets and went up to her. I greeted her and introduced myself. I handed her some money.

"This is your money," I said. "Your husband left it with me to keep for him."

She took it hesitantly, saying, "Just in time, son . . . Thank you very much. Kind and honest people still do exist . . ."

I stood by her side, trying to make her feel better, while the hospital was in turmoil. Doctors and nurses were walking back and forth; everyone was tense and hoping for Abu 'Ali's recovery. Finally, they brought us some news. Abu ʿAli, we were told, had regained consciousness. They allowed us to see him.

He was screaming in agony: "Where am I? Where's the jug? Where are the young men? . . . Murderers! They want to kill me! . . . ʿAzmi, where are you? Where are you, Um ʿAli? Where's the street? . . ."

Silently we stood by, waiting for Abu ʿAli to come out of his delirium.

At dawn, Abu ʿAli came around. We smiled at him. Everyone rushed to congratulate him on his recovery. All the neighborhood people went in, one by one, bidding him to get strong and get back on the street to his job, and saying things like it would only be a few days, or the worst was over. The hospital turned into a place of rejoicing.

"The people in the neighborhood have built you a small kiosk," I told him. "They've got a new jug ready, and everything you need, and they insist that you return to them."

"I will go back, ʿAzmi. Now I'm convinced I'll go back. I won't shirk. I'll stay on the street till I die. I'll come back to you, and the jug, and the *sous*. My brush with death has renewed my determination. I'll make the best *sous* ever. Its taste will captivate you and its color will look different to you. I'll be with you in ten days. My wounds will heal quickly—all the doctors have said so."

On the day that he was due to return, the people were out waiting for him early in the morning. They carried him on their shoulders and cheered him; they danced and sang to celebrate the opening of the kiosk. Everyone was asking for the new *sous*.

Abu ʿAli entered the kiosk, put his mouth to the spout of the jug, blew in it, and said, "Today the *sous* will be given out free. The kiosk is yours. You've bought it, you own it; my job is to make the drink and distribute it."

A convoy of military cars approached the kiosk, and soldiers surrounded the crowd. The crowd stayed put.

"What is it that you want?" Abu ʿAli asked their leader. "The people and I are doing nothing wrong. As you see, I'm giving out *sous*, and the people just love it."

The commander shook his head and gave orders to disperse the crowd, take down the kiosk, arrest Abu ʿAli, and charge him with causing a general disturbance on one of the city's main streets.

A group of soldiers led him to the back of an army car. He got in, proud and unperturbed. Before the car disappeared into the distance,

I heard him calling in a loud voice: "'Azmi, 'Azmi, take charge of the jug and the *sous!* The people must have *sous* to drink, no matter what happens!"

I went straight to the jug. Before going any further, I told myself, "This is a difficult task, but an important one. People must have *sous* to drink. That's what Abu 'Ali wants."

I remembered the store I worked in. I tossed the keys to the owner and picked up the pot. With steady footsteps, I started calling, "Here's the *sous!* Cool off, quench your thirst! . . ."

In combination with the clanging of the brass plates, my voice produced an appealing, melodious tune.

—translated by Salwa Jabsheh and Thomas G. Ezzy

Mahmoud al-Rimawi *(b. 1948)*

A short story writer, Rimawi spent his childhood in Jericho, which he left in 1967 to follow a journalistic career, moving from Beirut to Cairo to Kuwait where he remained for ten years before being deported in 1987. He now lives in Amman, Jordan, working as a journalist and writing a daily political column. An original and interesting writer, his stories reflect the kind of suffering and rootlessness that he has known during his lifetime as an exiled Palestinian. Though his stories reveal a rather pessimistic outlook on life, this is combined with a faith in the ultimate success of the struggle. His greatest concerns as a writer are democracy, freedom from terror, and the situation of his people, the Palestinians, who are, he believes, capable of participating fully in the civilization of the age, but who are denied the means of real self-expression because of their political plight—deprived as they are of a homeland. Rimawi published his first collection, *Nakedness in a Night Desert*, in 1972. His second collection, *Northern Wound*, appeared in 1980, and his third collection, *Planet of Apple and Salt*, in 1987.

A Longing for the Good Land

Removing the *kufiyya* and *iqal* from his gray head, Abu al-ʿAbd tossed them onto the dirty blanket beside him.

He heaved a deep sigh, for the heat was unbearable and he did not dare to strip the Agency uniform off his thin body. The tent had no door, and there were girls and women across the way. Undoing the laces of his heavy boots, he flung them into a corner; then, stretching out his legs in extreme exhaustion, he lay on an old coat, carelessly folded under his head, resting it on the palm of his dry, chapped hand. Of necessity, he tried to rest from the weariness of the ten hours he'd spent in construction work on the neighboring mountain. His wife, Imm al-ʿAbd[1] was at the neighbors' in the tent opposite, talking about the water being perpetually shut off and a life that was more than half spent.

---

[1]Imm (colloquial for *umm*, mother). Arabs call parents by the name of their firstborn male child, and by their firstborn daughter if no male child is born to them. Hence Abu al-ʿAbd and Imm al-ʿAbd in this story.

Abu al-ʿAbd's hapless daughter Khadijeh was out learning to be a seamstress. But his son Hasan, a young fellow of twenty who had finally learned to curse people for no reason, was at this moment smoking and drinking tea while winning and losing at cards.

"Or he may be somewhere else. Who knows? . . ." Abu al-ʿAbd yawned and wiped off the bead of sweat that hung from the tip of his nose. His ears, which were filled with thick hairs, picked up the sounds of a song about Jerusalem coming from a radio whose batteries seemed new. Unable to sort out his true feelings about it, he turned over onto his other side. He felt a pain like a hammer striking the sides of his head, and he said to himself, "Life be damned!" His eyes were heavy with sleep; and so, there being nothing to prevent him, he surrendered himself completely to it.

Ever since leaving the Nuweimeh Camp, where he'd lived for twenty long years, he had been sleepy all the time. Hasan had been born there, and there he had built a three room house with dahlias and a white poplar tree in the courtyard. Some of the wise men in the crowd he spent his evenings with told him that this was an evil and unfortunate disease. Others told him frankly that it would lead to the final sleep. What, however, should this matter to Abu al-ʿAbd? . . .

Little by little, drowsiness overcame his consciousness, so he closed his eyelids while the scorching, dusty breeze played with the things in the tent and sticky sweat covered his haggard face. He heard the clamor of the children outside like a buzzing noise. The air on his face made him imagine he was traveling endlessly, exhaustingly; traveling, but never arriving at his destination. The palm of his hand under his head was soaking wet. He withdrew it. The coat was coarse, made of camel hair; he felt as though he were sleeping on thorns, alone in an unknown land, cut off from the world. The cheese and tobacco had left his mouth so dry that he could not swallow his saliva. Rising sluggishly for a drink, he looked around hopefully for the water jar, afraid that he wouldn't be able to find it. He finally discovered it near the entrance to the tent, but the water, drained almost to the bottom, was warm. Tipping the jar straight up into his mouth, he greedily swallowed the few meager drops. A small pebble scraped his teeth and spoiled his enjoyment of the water. He spit it out, then spit again, but the taste of dust was still in his mouth.

Once again he threw himself down on the blanket, as though he wanted to escape from some unknown thing that was lying in wait for him. He was determined that he would sleep for a long time—even if it did lead to his final sleep. However, the fatigue in his legs thwarted his desire. He tried shifting his legs around into different positions to drive away the discomfort, but all he managed was to annoy and exasperate himself. Convinced that his efforts were fruitless and that he was going to remain suspended between the world of awareness and the world of blissful sleep, he became depressed, fearing that this might be the beginning of some ailment that would come between him and the half dinar he earned from the owner of the building on the nearby mountain. He cursed his son Hasan—that good-for-nothing who did not look for work and was never at home. Mustapha, who'd been working in Kuwait for five years, bore them in mind only at the Two Feasts[2], when he would send a green banknote that Hasan would get his hands on and spend in any way he liked. Then the damn fool would say he was going to get married—when Khadijeh still didn't have a husband to provide for her yet!

Outside the tent the sun seemed to be on the verge of completing its daily journey, and he still hadn't been able to doze off for an hour or two. His mind was so weary and confused from too much thinking and remembering that he had now reached the point where he could no longer think of any one thing or bring any memories back into his mind. This state made him feel better, for usually it led to deep sleep and forgetfulness.

Within a few minutes Abu al-'Abd, and with him the chapters of his sad life, were in a sound sleep. The clearest indication of this was his high-pitched, staccato snores, that sounded like an animal that had just been slaughtered. A huge, persistent fly flitted over his features, making him seem to be, to any observer, totally unwholesome . . .

The way from the Nuweimeh camp to the east bank of the river is long and thorny. And when a whole family travels it, on foot, in the middle of the summer, it becomes a much more painful hardship. There is more chance of dying than of living.

But he had actually covered this ground. There had been something driving them—specifically, from the rear—to move out. Imm al-'Abd, wanting to rest for an hour every half hour, had filled him with exasperation, while the way had been long, the planes had shown no mercy, and the shock had stripped his nerves bare and inflamed them.

Behind them, Jericho had been engulfed in billows of smoke, and

[2]Muslims have two major feasts, the Small Feast to celebrate the end of Ramadan, the month of fasting, and the Big Feast to celebrate the end of the annual pilgrimage to Mecca.

his heart had been so full of grief that he could hardly speak. O God, what a cruel world! What cursed times! How had this happened? . . . Imm al-ʿAbd, on the other side of fifty, had had vaguely dissatisfied questions in her eyes. Hasan, tense and high-strung, had not quite dared ask his father why they weren't staying behind like others. Khadijeh had been afraid, and the blankets on her back were heavy; when she told her mother that she had forgotten the radio turned on at home, the latter had silenced her with an angry look. "Well, did Abu Hal-eemeh's family leave? . . ." Khadijeh had asked, but the weight of the blankets forced her to pay attention to where she was stepping. Despite Abu al-ʿAbd's disbelief at all that had happened, it seemed, as he hurried on his way, that he had been expecting *this*!

Agitated and grieving, the soldiers around them were slinking off, some toward the river and others to the east. In the fighting, life and death seemed to be the embodiment of two diverse energies that might fuse into each other. The battle was not over, and the chances of either dying or living were still strong. It left a peculiar taste in his mouth.

Abu al-ʿAbd had been afraid that the family might get separated—that he would lose Hasan, his youngest, for example, or poor, sad Khadijeh, or his spouse, with whom he had fallen in love one day in Bayt Dajan. In 1948 a bullet had ended the youth of his first-born, al-ʿAbd. For how many years had he been grieving, tormented by night-mares and attacked by misgivings . . .

At the foothills of Suwaylih, a tractor had given them a lift. This was very lucky; the driver had been their neighbor in the camp. As he was getting up into the trailer behind the tractor, his trousers caught on the edge of the door, and he almost stumbled. With bitterness he thought of the gypsies, who never settle down in any home; he felt an instinctive sympathy for them, fearing greatly that in the end his destiny and theirs might be the same. Hot tears had risen in his eyes, but he had mastered himself as he hid them from Hasan's sight. His body was reeling from the effects of the speed, the crowdedness, and the lack of a support; the constant up-and-down motion made him sick.

As the tractor quickly covering ground bore him far away, his eyes had remained fixed on the west. He suffered a great and agonised hatred of those men who cut down trees. When the mountains of Amman came into view, he began imagining how his relatives would receive him, and this had given him feelings of embarrassment and regret. When the vehicle stopped he had jumped down to the ground and, absolutely done in with exhaustion, sprawled on the nearest sidewalk.

The shade of a towering building had given him a sense of great re-laxation, mingled with a longing for some obscure thing that despair had taught him he would never attain.

No-one knew as Abu al-ʿAbd did the details of black days. Nor did anyone understand as he did the impact of the *khamasin*,[3] and how he had wound up owning nothing but a cramped blue tent, symbolic of vagrancy and a transient life . . .

"Hasan hasn't come yet."

"He'll come for sure."

"He may have gone to a movie. Or, he's just hanging around some-where . . ."

"But he was determined to come! He was the most insistent one of us all . . ."

"He may be in the blue tent."

"I went there myself. His father's there, sound asleep."

"Only the one who is absent knows what his excuse is."

"He may be needing us."

"He may have lost his way . . ."

"No one knows how to get here better than Hasan."

"It's been half an hour . . . I'm worried about him."

"My God, when is he going to come? Where can he be?"

"Anything could have happened! Who knows? . . ."

"I say, maybe he's waiting for us now . . ."

"I'm sure that Hasan . . ."

"I dreamed that Hasan . . ."

Until they realised they were wasting their time. They agreed at once that their time was too limited to allow for idle speculation. As if carrying out a prior decision the three of them disbanded, each having in his mind an idea that was simultaneously both clear and obscure; an idea as translucently radiant as a dream. For one intense moment their eyes met, the language of their eyes voicing their agreement. They went on their separate ways, filled with the sensation of a promise that they would meet again.

Abu al-ʿAbd awoke as if he were climbing out of the bottom of a dark well. Darkness shrouded the confines of the narrow tent also, making it difficult for his veined fingers to find the box of tobacco. The fact that the tent was deserted, that no one was there, alarmed

---

[3]Hot, southerly wind that blows usually in spring.

him. This total silence made him realize that something had happened. He got up sluggishly, began searching without much hope for the lamp, stumbled over the kerosene can, and fell to the dry dirt floor.

Again he surmised that there was something unsettling about all this. Ever since going out to work that morning he had been conscious of a bitterness in his mouth, and that he was depressed, not feeling like himself . . . Where was Imm al-'Abd? Hadn't she had her fill of talking yet? And Khadijeh—what was keeping her out until this hour? No doubt she was with her mother. As for Hasan, who could control him? . . .

They had never left him alone before, so what was going on? A sense of stifled sorrow, whose origin was obscure, arose from deep inside him, awakening dark apprehensions in his mind. He got up to go out and ask the neighbors.

Puzzled at seeing the whole camp quiet in sleep, he became aware that it was very late, and his fears increased.

"Abu Yusuf! Abu Yusuf! . . ."

The man rose out of his bed in alarm. After a brief exchange of greetings Abu Yusuf said, "Why did you deprive us of your presence this evening?"

"Never mind that. Where are Imm al-'Abd and Khadijeh?"

"Ah yes . . . I saw them looking for Hasan. Someone said—I didn't see him, but someone said—that he'd been seen sauntering through the camp wearing the uniform of our young fighters, with a weapon on his shoulders. Then, he went into town. Neither Imm al-'Abd nor Khadijeh believed this. Each insisted that he had had an accident, God forbid . . . Why do you find it strange, Abu al-'Abd? My son is with them. Don't you understand that yours is too?"

But Abu al-'Abd did seem to find it strange. Thoughts of al-'Abd, his son whose youth had been cut off by a bullet, and of the long years he had grieved for him came immediately into his mind. He was aware of a burning longing for al-'Abd, and the contours of Bayt Dajan appeared before him as though he were in the presence of a dream. His good land, in faraway Bayt Dajan . . .

He was on the verge of tears, but he withdrew to his tent. This time, the overpowering darkness did not bother him for he was cut off from the place, gazing into his memories. It didn't occur to him to find out what time it was, but he was sure that he had slept a long time, and that morning was near.

—translated by Olive Kenny and Thomas G. Ezzy

Khalil al-Sawahiri *(b. 1940)*

Born in Jerusalem, al-Sawahiri now lives in Amman, Jordan, working as director of Dar al-Karmel Publishing House. He has written several books on culture and politics, mainly on the situation of Palestinians in the West Bank and Lebanon. His books, *Talk of Conquerors* (1982) and *Children of the R.P.G.* (1983), documented the Israeli war of 1982 in Lebanon. His collections of short stories are: *Three Voices* (1972); *The Bashura Café* (1975); and *Evening Visitor* (1985). He has also edited a collection of Palestinian poetry from occupied Palestine and written a critical study of that poetry (1982).

The Spectators

When I succeeded in getting a job, a few months after the Israeli Occupation, I found myself obliged to live in Jerusalem. The point of this was not to live in luxury, but to alleviate the difficulties of traveling back and forth between my village and the city. My work required that I come in early in the morning and go home late at night. I wasn't a clerk, or a manager, or a shop owner, or even a correspondent for one of the news agencies; I was merely a good-looking, well-spoken waiter, with some experience in the art of flattery and in being agreeable to customers. When the manager of the Zahra' Hotel decided to employ me, he did so because I was meek, to the point of servility, and because I was willing to accept the salary he had offered me—namely, 220 Israeli liras, as well as food and an elegant black suit of clothes.

I became totally convinced of the necessity of living in Jerusalem after I'd had several run-ins with Israeli army patrols on my way back to the village at night. Each time, I got clear of them after a lengthy interrogation that made my mouth go dry and took my breath away.

I tried my best to find lodging in Wady al-Jawz, al-Shaykh Jarrah, al-Musrara,[1] or any place else outside the walls of the Old City. My feet got blistered as I went around searching for *any* room, regardless of rent, but to no avail. Finally, I found myself in a miserable room in one of the worst and dirtiest parts of Old Jerusalem, namely the

[1]Quarters in East Jerusalem outside the walls inhabited by Arabs.

Wad District. I had often heard the hotel employees talk about the traffic in hashish, sexual perversion, and gambling that was carried on there.

"I'll stay here for the time being," I told myself. "Until I find another place outside the walls."

My room was located on the roof of a two-story building, in which the rooms were dreadfully jammed in on each other. As I climbed the many, worn-out steps, I had to clear my throat at the entrance of each unit and mutter, "*Ya Satir!*"[2] for the housewives to hear me. I had to call their attention to the fact that I was going up or coming down in order to give them time to cover themselves up.

It was difficult for me to get to know immediately all the inhabitants of this large courtyard, but I learned that there were five families, in addition to an elderly woman who was alone. I noticed that the people of the courtyard generally avoided her, and regarded her with a mixture of suspicion and aversion. Frankly, I myself had no such feelings toward the woman, for her face to me seemed old and familiar, like the face of my Aunt Ni'mah, who had been stricken years ago by an infectious disease that had sapped her vitality. At the time, they had said it was TB.

I must admit that the contempt of the courtyard's residents for this woman continued to perplex and bother me, especially since I had begun to feel a kind of kinship with her that grew day by day. I therefore decided to "lance this boil," in order to clear up the mystery.

One evening, I took advantage of the landlord's visit to collect the rent and asked him, "Who is that woman who lives alone in the room beside the entrance to the courtyard?"

The landlord looked at me for a moment, then winked, saying, "Why do you want to get involved? Let God protect these 'women.'"

The man's words and his wink puzzled me, and aroused my curiosity. So I pulled up a straw-bottomed chair that I would place by the window and lean back in, with my light switched off and my transistor radio turned on, watching the people as they came and went through the courtyard.

"Sit down, Abu al-'Abd," I said to him. "I hope you'll stay to drink a glass of tea with me."

But the man carefully closed his wallet upon the 50 liras rent money, put the wallet in his pocket, and prepared to leave.

---

[2]"O Protector!" This gives the female members of a household time to cover themselves adequately or to get out of sight.

"Some other time, God willing," he said.

Knowing that another time would not come round before the end of another full month, and not wanting to wait that long, I quickly put my hand on his arm.

"Everyone who's lived here before you has asked about this woman," he said. "So I may as well satisfy your curiosity. Everyone says that she's 'respectable,' and that certain men visit her after 10:00 P.M." Shaking the collar of his coat to affect a total lack of malice, he added: "I wash my hands . . ."

This was the last thing I'd been expecting the man to say, since there was nothing to indicate that the woman might be engaged in that profession. Old age had worn her out; she had nothing left to fall back on in such a business, or to attract customers.

"Glory be to God! A wolf in sheep's clothing!" I exclaimed. I was overcome by a sudden feeling of nausea and disgust, though I would have preferred not to believe his words. "My dear fellow, you can't be serious! What's this you're saying?"

"May the Lord forgive me for speaking out," he said peevishly, with deep malice showing in his eyes.

"Do you know her name?"

"They call her Imm Ahmad, but I don't know if that's her real name."

"Where is she from?"

"She says she's originally from Haifa, and that her husband was killed in the 1948 War. She claims to have a son in Kuwait, but in the twenty years she's lived here I've never seen his face."

"Does she pay her rent regularly?"

"Alas, how much do you think she pays me per month? Her rent is only ten Israeli liras. I've tried to evict her several times, but unfortunately there is no proof of anything against her, so I haven't been able to put her out. Nor do I think I could do that now. But it's just a matter of time," he went on in a disgusted and vindictive tone, "in a few months, she won't be able to pay her rent. Israeli prostitutes are filling the streets of Jerusalem, so that there will be no market for Imm Ahmad from now on."

After Abu al-ʿAbd left, I tried my best to forget the matter and drive every bit of interest in her from my thoughts. Although I was not convinced by the man's assertions, I began to understand the reason why the courtyard people shied away from her. Also, certain obscure aspects of her behavior began to make sense to me.

I pulled down the curtain of the window that overlooked her room, and threw myself on my bed and tried to sleep. However, this question kept nagging at my mind until it turned into a kind of nightmare. I sat up abruptly in my bed and turned on the transistor.

"A prostitute?" I asked myself. "So be it. Why am I so concerned with her? I've seen many like her hanging around the hotels I've worked at. Why should I be preoccupied with this woman's case?"

The next evening, while passing through the courtyard gate, I met Imm Ahmad as she was locking her room on her way out.

"Typical of loose women," I said to myself. "They run from one house to the other."

Her face was old and forlorn, as though the undefined wrinkles that lined it were mourning her departed beauty. Her flabby breasts and haunches were like a dusty mattress, worn out with much use. Glancing at me sadly and dejectedly, she put her key into her handbag and went out. At that moment I understood what Abu al-'Abd had meant about her not being able to pay her rent in the future. An idea occurred to me that I might follow her to find out where she was headed, but I felt ashamed to do so. I stayed behind my window to watch for her return. The other doors and windows in line with her room had faded and lost their interest for me.

Imm Ahmad returned at about eleven that night, carrying a few things with her. Through the window I could make her out, sitting near the bed and eating her supper. What if I went to visit her? She certainly knew my face, but would she let me in? And if she did open the door, what would I say to her? That I'd come to have a chat? That would be absurd. And then, what if one of my courtyard neighbors should see me? They'd say that the new lodger had fallen prey. No, I won't go!

Once more I asked myself what was prompting my concern for this woman. Was it because she resembled my late Aunt Ni'mah? Was it out of compassion for her, or because I wanted to find out the reason for her degeneration, the way many of those who visit prostitutes do, pretending to be motivated by humanitarian feelings and nobility of character? I certainly had no desire to go to bed with her; nor would I ever have. Even if I wanted to, the amount I sent off to my father and brothers every month didn't leave me enough for a movie, not even once a month.

The next day I made an effort to return early. I got home at about nine-thirty but did not find her in. It seemed she left her room about that time every evening. When she did return, she was accompanied by a man, who waited outside until she had opened the door. Then they went in. She drew the curtains of her window. Behind them I could see her shadow passing back and forth. Shortly after midnight, the light in her room went out; the door opened suddenly, and the man came out. Now I was certain that she was a virtuous woman. Who was the man, and why had she let him out intentionally in the dark? Was she aware that I was watching her? Did she know that others were keeping an eye on those who came to visit her?

The next evening, Imm Ahmad was still in her room when I got back, but it was another woman's form I could make out sitting on the edge of her bed. I couldn't believe my eyes at first. I tried to find a rational explanation as to who this woman might be. Was she a neighbor in the courtyard? It was possible. Was she a professional crony? Perhaps . . . but they seemed to have a rapport between them, and were deeply absorbed in conversation. How could a woman of this sort have a female friend, even if she were a partner? There's no doubt that every prostitute hates a rival, for there's no love lost between a beggar and his comrade with a full bag, as they say. Why then were these two women so deeply engrossed in talking, as though they were discussing a subject of the utmost importance?

The visitor left at about eleven o'clock. Imm Ahmad saw her to the gate, shaking hands warmly with her as though confirming another rendezvous. Imm Ahmad then returned to sit quietly where her visitor had sat. As the window curtains were open, I was able to observe her serious and preoccupied expression. She seemed absorbed in a daydream, or sunk in profound thought.

"Misery and old age often lead to gravity," I said to myself.

At that moment I felt a sense of tragedy, such as I used to feel on leaving the cinema after watching a sad movie. Those sensations, however, would quickly dissolve and disappear, while my awareness of this woman's tragedy became a reality, a nightmare that persisted in my imagination every night; even during work, as I served soup or plates of food to the young Jewish men and women, I would be overcome by feelings of bitterness and hatred. Whenever I recalled the sad image of the unfortunate Imm Ahmad, and then saw the faces of those young women, I realised the extent of her terrible tragedy.

"Imm Ahmad's time has passed and gone," I would say to myself. "Her situation is like that of the waiter who grows old, and his hands begin to shake, and his back becomes stooped as he serves the food."

I wondered what went on in her mind. Did she regret her lost youth? Did she curse the occupying army that had reduced her to this wretched state?

Having decided to spend my time off that week in trailing Imm Ahmad and watching her movements, I got up the next morning as early as usual. After getting dressed, I sat down by the window. She was moving about with unusual briskness, as though preparing to go out. She went on this way until after 11:00 A.M., when I saw her leave, wearing dark clothes. Before she finished locking her room, I had started down the stairs, though I deliberately slowed my pace a little in order to give her time to leave without seeing me. When I walked through the gate, Imm Ahmad was heading south toward Habs al-ʿAbeed alley.[3] I followed her through that dingy alley, which leads to the spacious courtyard of the many-gated Aqsa mosque.

I wondered where this woman was leading me. Did she really intend to go to the Aqsa mosque? Was it reasonable to think that Imm Ahmad would perform her Friday prayers? Had she been transformed overnight into Rabiʿah al-ʿAdawiyah?[4] Had Abu al-ʿAbd been vile enough to claim that this pious woman was a fallen prostitute? My God, what was I seeing?—Imm Ahmad was entering the Aqsa mosque!

I felt a terrible pain in my head. Never did I imagine that a fallen woman would lead me to this place, or that someone like me would be watching for a prostitute in the courtyard of the Aqsa mosque.

I sat down near the ablutions fountain and decided to perform my prayers in the outer court, so that I could spot her when she came out. I considered going back home to wait for her at the gate; I would greet her and apologize for the wicked thoughts I had been harboring. I chose, however, to remain in the mosque courtyard.

As soon as my prayers were done, I quickly put on my shoes and got up to go and wait among the pine trees of the western passageway. On my way toward the women's section of the mosque, I unexpectedly came across a large group of women crowded closely together. I could see a number of floral wreaths that some of these women were carrying, and I was even more surprised when I spotted some white banners with black lettering being raised above their heads. On the banners, I was able to make out such phrases as: "ETERNAL GLORY TO OUR

---

[3]Literally, "The Slaves' Prison." The name of a street in Old Jerusalem regarded as a secondary entrance to the Aqsa Mosque.

[4]Rabiʿah al-ʿAdawiyah was a famous ascetic woman who lived in the second century of Islam.

FAITHFUL MARTYRS," and "INVADERS, GET OUT OF JERU-
SALEM."

Then, the women's voices rose with cries of: "Jerusalem is Arab and
shall remain Arab!"

Their tremendous enthusiasm increased until the sound of their
shouts rose to a roar. A wave of amazement and confusion spread
through the crowd of men who were leaving the mosque on the eastern
side. Turmoil set in; some made off towards the Dome of the Rock
and the eastern entrances to the mosque courtyard, while others clustered together, dumbfounded, watching the women's procession as it
grew in numbers and density. I stood there gaping with open mouth,
my eyes searching for Imm Ahmad. Suddenly, with the feeling of a
worried child who has lost his mother in the crowd, I found her. I saw
her marching behind the wreaths and shouting, with genuine fervor,
"Jerusalem is Arab! Down with the Occupation!"

What was happening? Had this huge crowd of women, like Imm
Ahmad, lost the source of their incomes because of the Occupation,
or was she the only harlot among them? If so, why were they demonstrating along with her?

Suddenly, I remembered: this was the first anniversary of the June
War.[5] No doubt this demonstration had been organized for the occasion. What a disgrace!—Imm Ahmad was aware of this, and was participating in it, while we wretched, bearded men were neither aware
nor participating.

But how did Imm Ahmad know about this? Most likely, the friend
who had visited her the night before had informed her. But what good
did she think it would do her? Did she think that in this way she could
help drive the lines of Israeli prostitutes off the streets of Jerusalem?

The procession of women kept moving until it climbed the steps
leading to the Sahira gate. Some of the men followed alongside it,
occasionally lagging behind. By the ʿUmariyya School, a few police
officers were gathered. They began to charge at the crowd of women,
but drew back. I didn't know whether it was because they were nervous
about the narrowness of the alleys or because the whole body of the
procession was composed of women.

I sensed that following the procession through the lanes inside the
walls of the city would not be without danger; I was afraid that the

[5]The "June War" is the Six Day War of 1967.

police might suddenly attack. Therefore, I tried my best to go past the procession through another alley, thinking I'd be able to wait in the square outside the Sahirah gate. From there, I would get a better view of the procession, and be less exposed to danger. When I passed through the Sahirah gate, however, I was suddenly confronted by a large contingent of mounted policemen waiting in the square. I walked on as far as the wall of the Post Office opposite the Sahirah gate, and stopped there to watch.

Three women who were leading the procession passed through the Gate first, each carrying a wreath. They were followed by two others with a banner that said, in black letters, "GLORY AND ETERNAL LIFE FOR OUR FAITHFUL MARTYRS." Then came a flood of women and another banner. I could not make out what was written on it, but I was able to see Imm Ahmad clearly as she led this group.

The police did not wait for the rest to come through. Tugging on their horses' reins, they rushed the procession, forcing the women to crowd even more closely together. The horses whinnied loudly as they reared their heads, foam flying from their mouths. The wreaths began to fall to the ground. With shrieks of pain, the women fled from under the hooves of the attacking horses. I heard a loud wail rising from the men who, like me, had lined up to watch the terrifying spectacle.

All at once, a scream of pain rang out. We saw one of the women being thrown to the ground and trampled by the horses' hooves.

A police car rushed up, its siren wailing. Some of the people, stunned, began to gather around the pools and smears of blood and the crushed wreaths, but the police drove them back. I searched for Imm Ahmad among the crowds of fleeing women, but I couldn't find her.

At last, I found myself back at our courtyard gate. I stood in front of Imm Ahmad's room, which was still locked. Midnight came and went, and her room remained wrapped in deep darkness. I stayed awake to watch, in the forlorn hope that light might suddenly burst forth from her window.

Next day, the hotel staff were talking sadly about a woman known as Imm Ahmad, who had met her end under the horses' hooves at the Sahira Gate as she made her way with a procession toward the graves of the Martyrs. Some claimed that her husband had been killed during the June War, while others insisted that it was her son who'd been killed then, since her husband had died fighting in the 1948 War.

As for me, I made no comment. I could not bring myself to repeat what that man had previously told me when he visited me to collect the rent.

I did, however, make a firm decision that I would change my place of residence immediately.

—translated by L.M. Kenny and Thomas G. Ezzy

Mahmoud Shaheen (b. 1947)

A novelist and short story writer, Shaheen had an unhappy child-hood. Since his father took him out of school in the eighth grade to make him a shepherd he had no formal education. Three years later, he ran away from home and spent the next few years working at various strenuous jobs to earn a living. After 1968 he joined the ranks of the Palestinian resistance, and now works for the Palestinian Information Office. He is deeply involved in the traditional and folk music of Palestine and is an accomplished flute player. Shaheen has written a fifteen-hour documentary series on Palestinian life under Israeli occupation, one novel, *Forbidden Land* (1983), and two collections of short stories, *The Visitors* (1979), and *Ordeal by Fire* (1979).

The Sacred River

1

"What's going to happen, Aunt?" asked Wardeh. "If the West Bank falls, will we be thrown out or will we be able to stay here?"

She was holding her baby close to her breast and an image of her husband Muhammad came into her mind: Muhammad, stranded in Amman, who might not be able to reach them if war broke out.

'Aisheh al-'Allan[1] straightened up in front of the loom that she had managed to pack and bring with her into the cave. She had hoped it would keep her busy until the war was over. "No, my dear," she said. "We won't leave our land, and God will settle our accounts with the Israelis."

"But how about Muhammad?"

"God will look after him, my dear."

"What if he stays in Amman and can't come back?"

"Then we'll send you to him," her aunt 'Aisheh answered.

---

[1]'Aisheh al-'Allan also appears in Shaheen's story "Ordeal by Fire" in *Modern Arabic Fiction: An Anthology*, ed., Salma Khadra Jayyusi, Columbia University Press, forthcoming 1992.

The enemy radio declared that the West Bank in its entirety had fallen. People could not believe the news.

In Jerusalem, hundreds went down on their knees in prayer . . . Archbishop Elia knelt before the statue of Jesus in the Holy Sepulchre, fear and sadness on his face. "God, grant us your mercy," he intoned. "Save us from the evil of our enemies. Dear God, protect your precious land." "Amen," replied the congregation. Inside the al-Aqsa mosque, thousands spread their hands upward, toward the sky. Shaikh 'Abdul-Hamid prayed: "God, let there be a wall in front of them and another one behind them, and, dear God, let a black cloud fall before their eyes so they cannot see." "Amen," replied the congregation.

Outside, in the courtyard of the mosque, the sound of machine-gun fire could be heard. Enemy planes flew low over the city, dropping bombs, firing indiscriminately. Pieces of human flesh were scattered about. A little boy, frozen in fear for a second, turned and ran, leaving a small puddle of water behind him. Thousands of people emerged from shelters and houses and headed east, some of them running. One man carried only a light bag, another cried that he had lost his donkey, a third asked that his purse be returned. In the commotion a man called continually for his son, a woman screamed, another tore at her face with her nails. A man suddenly became hysterical and began to beat his wife with a cane: she had not followed his instructions to bring what could be carried, he scolded. But she replied, weeping, that she could not believe the West Bank would ever fall. A woman struggled to balance on her head a huge bread-pan containing some chickens. Her baby screamed from its nest on her back, while her husband, carrying bundles of clothes, drove their other children ahead of him. Still another woman had caught her foot between two rocks and was struggling to get free. The shepherd, Muhammad 'Audeh, hearing the noise from the west, left his herd and climbed quickly to the top of the mountain to see what was going on. Thousands of people were running along the valleys, climbing the mountain tops, pushing down the slopes. He began to beat on a tin plate, frightening his sheep into movement. He took off his cap and began waving it, shouting, "Hey you people, you everyone, the West Bank has fallen into the hands of the Jews, people are leaving; look, look, they are running away."

From the top of the mountain he repeated his cry, to the east and west, the north and south, waving his *kaffiyyeh*, jumping high, occasionally falling down where he would kick the ground in frustration, sending stones rolling and clattering down the slopes.

Hearing Muhammad 'Audeh, people came out of their hiding places, out of caves where they had fled when the war started, trembling in terror and fear. Panic spread among them as through the others fleeing from the west. Wardeh al-'Audeh stood watching her brother jumping and calling and finally rolling down the mountain banging the tin plate, producing a tremendous clatter that frightened the sheep and made them run away.

Voices rose, calling on people to leave the land; other voices cautioned waiting. But when Muhammad 'Audeh reached the valley, his news erased the doubts. "Hey listen," he cried, and climbed to a high rock so people could hear him. "The Arab countries have been defeated, the Jews have taken the West Bank, and Gaza and Sinai and the Golan, too. I'm telling you the truth. With my own eyes I saw people leaving Jerusalem and Tour and 'Aizarieh and Abou Dais, carrying their belongings, their kids on their backs. If you don't believe me, climb the mountain. See for yourselves how they're running from the west, running away like a tribe of cats."

"Will they do to us what they did in 1948?"[2]

"Will what happened in Dair Yasin[3] and Kufr Qasim[4] happen again?"

"Maybe worse things will happen."

"The only way is to leave, to save your lives and your children . . ."

"They're ripping pregnant women's bellies and cutting off children's heads."

"Don't you remember Dair Yasin?"

"Oh! If only we were armed . . ." People carrying clothes and miscellaneous belongings stumbled over each other. A Tarmezian woman

[2]1948 is a reference to the year of what is known as "The Palestinian Catastrophe"; i.e., the year the Zionists took hold of many Arab towns and villages and open land, thereby forming the state of Israel and evicting thousands of Palestinians to become refugees outside their own birthplace.

[3]Dair Yasin is a small Palestinian village near Jerusalem where at least 245 women, children, and elderly people were massacred in cold blood by Menachem Begin's Irgun faction and its sister faction, Stern, on April 9, 1948. The massacre is a theme in many literary works in Arabic.

[4]This is a reference to another notorious massacre by the Israelis which took place on October 29, 1956 in the village of Kufr Qasim. At the behest of higher Israeli army authorities, a curfew was imposed on the village between 5 P.M. and 6 A.M. The order was given to the *mukhtar* of the village half an hour before 5 P.M. and no plea by the *mukhtar* could dissuade the Israeli military from their decision. There were over 400 men and women at work in areas far from the village. Many of these, on returning home after 5 P.M. were massacred in cold blood. Like the massacre of Dair Yasin, the Kufr Qasim carnage has inflamed the imagination of poets and fiction writers in the Arab world. It has also been the subject of a film.

was banged so hard by someone's head that blood flew from her nose
. . . Jamileh Hamdan emptied flour into a piece of cloth and tied it
into a bundle. And Fatmeh, the wife of the crazy mute ʿAli al-Khatib,[5]
struck her hands together. Fatmeh drew closer to ʿAisheh al-ʿAllan, who
sat still in absolute bewilderment.

"What do you think aunt! Should we leave or not?"

"No, by God, life here is death, my child, but leaving means death
as well, so, by God, let's at least die in our own land, that's much
better."

Fatmeh did not argue; for her ʿAisheh al-ʿAllan's advice was the final
word. As for ʿAisheh al-ʿAllan herself, the only thing worrying her was
that her son, Muhammad, might stay in Amman and let his wife, Wardeh, and their child remain with her, away from him.

But thousands of other people were moving on, heading east, exhausted, walking with heavy steps, their tongues dry, their children
crying, dogs sniffing for a drop of water. The June sun beat down
without mercy, perspiration poured down foreheads, lips cracked in
the heat. An old man rolled down the mountain and stopped to rest
in the valley; he moaned and groaned, then fell asleep, an eternal sleep.
A plane opened fire on the crowds of moving people. Bodies fell, some
rose up again and plodded on swaying from painful injuries! Ravens
croaked in the sky, and a wheat field burst into flame as a bomb exploded. A soldier paused and quickly changed into civilian clothes;
another dropped his gun, still another traded his weapon for a drink
of water.

Wardeh al-ʿAudeh's tears fall silently. The woman they call the "crazy
refugee" rushes up from the bottom of the valley. She is wearing the
same sackcloth garment she always wears and she is heading in the
opposite direction from everyone else. She pounds her breast with two
stones. She sings in a sorrowful voice; her tears dry on her cheeks.

ʿAisheh al-ʿAllan says from the depths of her sad heart, "Oh! You
wretched woman, where are you going?" Wardeh looks first at her
husband, then at her son, the shepherd Muhammad, standing close to
his herd. Her face turns sullen and gloomy and she thinks worriedly
about her daughter's future.

From the cave where the family of Ahmad Abu al-Jadayel has sought
refuge, sounds of people shouting emerge. Scattered lines of people

---

[5]ʿAli al-Khatib also appears in Shaheen's story "Ordeal by Fire" (see footnote 1).

are moving between the two banks of the river. A woman is carrying one child in her arms and two on her back. An old man is pleading to God. A flock of frightened pigeons flies up, away from a high wall along the bank. An owl croaks, announcing endless sorrow!! Enemy soldiers are dancing in the Al-Aqsa mosque. And others rape a virgin on the tomb of Christ in the Holy Sepulchre. The sky turns dark. The children in the city's orphanage look around them with puzzled eyes. What is happening? Ropes are stretched across the river between the two banks.

Flocks of sandgrouse are migrating from their homeland. People cross the river holding tight to the ropes. A woman screams as she falls into a whirlpool. Floating on the surface of the river is the dead body of a baby. A shepherd riding a mule crosses the water behind his sheep. The sheep swim hard and climb up on the other bank. A man places his children behind him on a mule and crosses the river. A donkey brays joyfully, discovering that he can actually swim. On the bank a priest stands, watching the scene with tearful eyes. A woman cries for help as the hens she was carrying on her head fall into the river. 'Aref, the son of the Shaikh, exchanges salutes with the invading soldiers. The river carries the drowned hens toward the Dead Sea. A dog climbs to the other river bank, where enemy soldiers are distributing biscuits to the emigrating children. A bag of flour slips from a woman's head and sinks deep to the bottom of the river. Up on the mountain, Muhammad 'Audeh is playing the evacuation tune on his flute; the notes travel across the mountains and fill the valleys.

'Aisheh al-'Allan begins to moan and her eyes fill with tears. Wardeh al-'Audeh cries silently, remembering her husband far away. At the entrance of the cave, Hajjeh Safiyyeh raises a banner of surrender. Hajjeh Zawaba pledges her resistance until death, and old man 'Audeh weeps, his heart shattered by the suffering which life has brought upon him.

2

Difficult, bitter days pass without a word from Muhammad. 'Aisheh al-'Allan is worried. The process of smuggling people to the East Bank has now become a prosperous business. In the beginning, the dealer charged five dinars per head, but the price quickly rose to ten, fifteen, and then thirty dinars per person. Where, thinks 'Aisheh al-'Allan, can she get such a large amount to pay a smuggler to accompany her daughter-in-law and grandson to the East Bank? From across the hills, the wind carries that sad tune of exile to 'Aisheh al-'Allan. Muhammad is playing his flute again. Memories of tragedies fill her mind until the thought of her son crowds out all other memories. 'Aisheh al-'Allan begins to sing and cry as she sits weaving at her loom. Songs of travel, songs of absence, songs of prisoners, songs of lamentation for the dead. At the sound of 'Aisheh al-'Allan's singing, other women shed tears of their own. Wardeh cries silently as she always does, holding her child close to her breast. She sits down close to her mother-in-law; Hajjeh Zawaba joins her. Wardeh gets up to offer the older woman her seat:

"No, no," says Hajjeh Zawaba. "Stay where you were my child, may God rejoin you safely to your husband."

"May God keep you always safe, my mother." Hajjeh Zawaba sits close to her daughter.

"How are you 'Aisheh?"

"I'm okay, God bless you, Hajjeh."

"Then why do you keep on lamenting like this? You don't know that anything is wrong with Muhammad. May God bring good things. Why blind your eyes with crying?"

"I don't really know Hajjeh, may God bless him and have mercy on him and ease the difficulties before him. If only he calmed my heart by sending a word about where he is, if only his wife and son were with him, then my trouble would be lessened. Oh my son! Who is washing his clothes, who is cooking for him, how is he surviving? Is he alive or is he dead? Only God knows."

"May death strike down his enemies! Be patient, 'Aisheh, God helps those who are patient."

Are we to remain patient forever? 'Aisheh asked herself. Here without children and families, we have been scattered about till we are homeless, we are exhausted. I did tell him three months ago, the last time he came before the war, to take his wife and son back. But he said no, he was waiting until he found a decent place for them. Then his hand was bothering him, where he had hurt it with the chisel. May God be with him, she said to herself.

'Aisheh bent down and kissed the flat stone that Muhammad had especially polished for his mother with his chisel and hammer. She sometimes used it as a seat, at other times as a table for the teapot and cups. "May God protect the hand that smoothed it," she murmured.

But Hajjeh Zawaba was thinking, staring at her daughter's face, *I have found a solution.*

" 'Aisha? Let's think of my daughter."

"Yes Hajjeh."

"I have ten dinars. I will ask Muhammad (may God protect him) to take a goat to the market and sell it; see if you can arrange for the rest of the money. Then we'll send her and her child to your son, her husband. In case the occupation continues, it's better if everyone is with their own folk."

Signs of gratitude were clearly seen on 'Aisheh al-'Allan's face.

"Oh, Hajjeh, may God be generous to you. I really thought he would come before now and let whatever is to happen, happen."

"Would you want the young men to come, 'Aisheh, only to be slaughtered like sheep? Have you forgotten what the Jews did in 1948? Why did people leave the land then? If they hadn't feared massacres, they would never have left."

'Aisheh al-'Allan stopped weaving and was quiet. "Who shall we send her with?" she asked.

"With 'Aref al-'Ali. He's been working as a smuggler, ever since the war began. He's taken and brought back many people."

"Isn't there anyone else, Hajjeh? Have you forgotten what his uncle did to us, in the days when the British were here? He would charge five piasters for a tank of water."

"Who else is there, 'Aisheh?"

"I don't know . . . Oh," she sighed, "may God help us against those who caused us all these troubles."

3

"Don't worry, Hajjeh, just put your confidence in me. By God, until we cross the river, I'll protect her like my own eyes. The world is not yet without the virtuous!!"

"How much do you want, 'Aref?"

"Listen Hajjeh, I'll tell you."

"Say it then, my son!"

"Mention the prophet in your prayers."

"A thousand prayers to the prophet."

"By God, only for your sake, Hajjeh, and for the sake of 'Aisheh al-'Allan, will I do it."

"May God protect you, my son. How much do you want?"

"I usually ask fifty dinars a person, but to you I'll offer my eyes, and thirty for the girl and ten for the boy, that makes forty dinars all together. I wouldn't take such a small amount from anyone else."

'Aisheh al-'Allan took thirty dinars out of her cloth purse.

"I swear," she said, "by the life of my son who is the dearest soul to me on this earth that we gathered these thirty dinars with great difficulty. The family of Hajjeh Zawaba sold a goat for ten dinars; I took a loan of five dinars from Haj 'Ali 'Ata, promising to weave two covers for him, and we borrowed here and there until we collected thirty dinars."

'Aref al-'Ali shook his head.

"By God, that's not enough, Hajjeh; it might have been enough if there were a lot of people going, but nowadays one has to risk one's life for five persons at most, and return alone."

'Aisheh al-'Allan replied, "By God, brother, that's all we've got. And after all, the baby will be carried by its mother, you're not going to carry it are you?"

"May God forgive you," answered 'Aref. "Would I carry anyone but myself? Every person carries himself, and God carries us all. I charge by the person and that's that. If the price doesn't suit you, I'll bid you farewell." He paused. "The market *might* go lower," he added. "If that happens, Hajjeh, I promise you I'll take her with me, but now, thirty dinars is not enough."

'Aref walked away, saying to himself: "Now the Hajjeh will call me back."

However, neither of the elderly ladies uttered a word.

'Aref began to think. How can I let this beautiful girl slip through my hands? She's a gazelle, 'Aref, a gazelle, flesh like peeled pistachio nuts, hips, oh! How can you leave all that? Wouldn't you take her even without a fee? She is but a fish, a fish with no scales, and you, 'Aref, are the fisherman. No one has called you back. You better turn around, go on.

'Aref turned back to Hajjeh Zawaba and 'Aisheh al-'Allan.

"Oh God damn the devil, I can't leave this girl, and the child who has not seen his father. Besides, I value your friendship, Hajjeh."

"God will reward you," said Hajjeh Zawaba. "When will you leave?"

"Tomorrow morning, with God's help."

"Here, brother." 'Aisheh al-'Allan began to count the money into 'Aref's hand.

When, in the morning 'Aref appeared alone, 'Aisheh al-'Allan immediately became apprehensive about sending Wardeh with him.

"Good morning, Hajjeh."

"Good morning to you, 'Aref. You're all alone?"

"Yes."

"No one else is going with you?"

"God forgive you, how could I travel alone with one girl? The trip wouldn't be worth it. I've got five other women to take but I left them nearby while I fetched Wardeh."

'Aisheh al-'Allan looked relieved.

"May God guide you safely, when do you plan to cross the river?"

"Tonight, if all goes well. Tomorrow at this time she'll be with her husband."

"May all go well," answered 'Aisheh. " 'Aref, my son, think of what happens when she has crossed the river and is sitting in a taxi on the other side. Don't send her alone, my son. Take her straight to her husband and you'll have performed a good deed in God's eyes."

"Don't worry, Wardeh's like a sister to me, dearer than my own eyes."

"Then there is still goodness in this world, my son," answered 'Aisheh. "May God protect you and make your journey an easy one."

'Aisheh al-'Allan gathered into a large bundle some clothes of War-deh's, of the baby's, of Muhammad's. She put bread and olives and onions into a smaller bundle, "so Muhammad could eat of the olives and onions of his own country and of the bread his mother had baked with her own hands." She filled a canteen with water and she helped her daughter-in-law arrange the bundles on her back. She kissed Wardeh goodbye.

"May God bless you my child, give my love to Muhammad. Take care of him, don't make trouble for him. And kiss him for me. Tell him his mother kisses him. Don't forget to give him the handkerchief I put in for him, my daughter." She paused. "Here are two dinars for you if you need something on the way," went on 'Aisheh al-'Allan. "Tell your husband this handkerchief has the smell of his mother, I've placed it in between the clothes . . . Take care of yourselves my child, may God ease your path, may God blind those who mean you harm, may God find you a friend on every road you take."

'Aisheh hugged and kissed the child, her tears running down. The bundle on her back and the child held close to her chest, Wardeh followed 'Aref, hot tears sliding down her face.

Her mother-in-law's words still echoed in her mind: "Don't forget Muhammad's address my child, may God grant you all his kindness and goodness, give my regards to all our relatives and loved ones, my daughter, tell them our thoughts are with them day and night, and we await their arrival."

Her mother had said: "May God ease your way, and help you reach your husband safely." The two older women watched until Wardeh disappeared over a high hill.

Muhammad 'Audeh left his herd and hurried to his sister, tears filling his eyes. "May God be with you, my sister," he said, holding her close to him, kissing her, and the child. "Give my regards to Muhammad, tell him his brother Muhammad plays the flute all day, and remembers him with every sunrise." He continued, "and as for the enemies who took our land, God damn them, tell him we are not afraid of them. When you get there, send us a word through that radio program[6] . . ."?

Wardeh followed 'Aref al-'Ali and was soon out of sight.

4

'Aref al-'Ali slowed down to walk beside Wardeh. He glanced at her. (Oh, what eyes, lips, cheeks, neck, breasts. She's really a rose, just like her name, whoever called her Wardeh? He looks at her full lips, and a violent wave of lust rushes through his body. His teeth begin to chatter, his mouth goes slack. 'Aref al-'Ali, he says to himself, what prevents you from lifting that dress, touching those hips, planting your fingers there, rubbing the flesh until blood comes . . . you could sleep with her here on the fertile soil of the valley, turn her on her stomach, then on her back . . . there's nobody here, only the sun and mountains and valleys . . . Would she scream? Would she fight back? What would happen then? Would she run back to the village, and spread the news around so you'd lose people's confidence and your business? Or would you rape her and kill her if she tries to get away . . . 'Aref tries to control himself. He looks at Wardeh, who walks along, looking meek and sad. What is she thinking of? Does she think of this man, walking by her side alone in those mountains? A man who never has enough of women? Does she? After all, she hasn't had a man since her husband left six months ago . . .)

Wardeh walks silently along. (Darling Muhammad, am I really going

---

[6]Because of the way Palestinians were scattered and families were split after the 1948 catastrophe and the 1967 June War (please consult the Chronology in this book), several radio programs were initiated in the Middle East by which simple short messages to and news of family members were broadcast.

to see your handsome face? Are you going to hold me in your arms tomorrow night? I won't be shy. I'll tell you how much I'm thirsting for you and want you. Make love to me until morning, Muhammad, till I have had enough of ecstasy. I know what you'll say: 'You shameless imp, that's enough,' but will it be enough? How will you welcome me? I know you'll be happy to see me . . . and look at Faris, what a beautiful baby he is . . . the spitting image of you . . . same nose, same chin, look at the dimple on his chin. Why didn't you come back to the West Bank after the war? You've chosen to work in Amman, you say; well . . . Are you still hammering at stones? How many stones have you polished in your lifetime? Are you laughing? . . . Okay . . . Don't answer that, try this one, how many rocks have you broken on your anvil and turned into beautiful polished stones? And do you still work with Fatah[7] against the enemy? Don't worry, I won't tell anyone, not even your mother or mine. But why didn't you come home? Wouldn't it be better to struggle for freedom here than in Amman?)

Wardeh's hands had grown tired holding the child. She raised the baby to her shoulder, glancing sidelong at 'Aref in the hope that he might offer to help her. 'Aref stretched out his hand. "I'll carry him for you," he said. Wardeh didn't say no. She paid no attention to the hand that touched her shoulder before taking the child.

"Imagine it, Wardeh," said 'Aref. "The English killed more than a hundred soldiers in this valley. When I pass here at night I get so frightened. God almighty! It practically makes the hair on one's head turn white. The ghosts of Turkish soldiers come out and start talking in Turkish and the English ghosts answer in English, you know."

Wardeh said nothing.

"Before I go to sleep, I read the *kursi*[8] verse from the Quran," 'Aref goes on. "One night I woke up to find one of the ghosts was sitting at my head and eating my food. I called on God, and the earth opened up and swallowed him. Now, now don't you be scared. You'll be all right. As long as I'm with you."

Wardeh, struggling to banish the images of the ghosts from her mind, spoke for the first time. "Where are the other women you said were going with us?"

---

[7]*Fatah* is the largest wing of the Palestinian Liberation Organization.

[8]*Al-Kursi* verse is part of the Yasin chapter in the Quran. It is supposed to have special powers of protection for the person who recites it.

(What a beautiful voice, little gazelle, why didn't you say something long ago?)

"We'll soon get to the meeting place," answered 'Aref. "You can wait there till I come back with them."

He pressed the child to his chest, imagining its mother in his arms. But the image of the mother did not come alive into his mind, and the child was too small to fill his embrace. He drew closer to Wardeh until his knee hit her thigh. Wardeh felt the bump, but assumed that it was unintentional.

"You're getting tired, 'Aref? You're bumping into me."

"God forbid! The sun came straight into my eyes, my dear, and I didn't see where I was going."

"What about those ghosts? Is that true?"

"What can I say, Wardeh, every one of them is at least as tall as a telephone pole, may God protect us."

"Do they hurt people, those ghosts?"

"No, only those who curse or hate them. But they are frightening."

The sound of an approaching helicopter gave 'Aref another chance at Wardeh. "Hide, hide," he said, stretching his arm around her waist and drawing her to him. As the helicopter passed low and disappeared behind the mountains, Wardeh was aware of 'Aref's hand running over her hips, but she convinced herself that that, too, was unintentional. But she took the child from 'Aref's arms and walked on along the valley floor.

(She didn't say a word, 'Aref, that means she accepted your advances. I'll wait until we get to the meeting place . . . What a beauty! And then naked under the cliff's shadow! . . . I'll try once more. If she keeps quiet, that'll settle it!)

("Who brought you, Wardeh?" " 'Aref al-'Ali." " 'Aref al-'Ali? I can't believe you've arrived safely, I can't believe it." "Why not? Isn't it me here in front of you?" "Let me see you, Wardeh." "Take your hands out of there!" "How is my mother?" "She sends her love; here, take these, I almost forgot." "Forgot what?" "She's sent you one of her own handkerchiefs." "How nice." "Try the olives and the bread, she baked it with her own hands so that you'd like it." . . . "Oh mother, your bread is wonderful!" "Oh Muhammad, please don't cry; I cried all the way." "Weren't you scared?" "Just of ghosts 'Aref al-'Ali told me about. Nothing else scared me." "Ghosts!! You mean genies?" "He called them ghosts." "Let's forget all that nonsense; tell me about the village, your brother Muhammad's flute, your mother and the young ladies from the village, the Jews, the war!!" "Listen, sir" . . . "I'm listening." "Now, then, you haven't told me about the young ladies of the village?" "I won't tell you about them." "You're jealous, Wardeh." "You're more jealous than I am." "That's true." "Hold me tight." "Hold me tight." . . . "My love." . . . "My love.")

They came to a well and a small public garden. Dung near the well indicated that sheep had been there recently. High cliffs surrounded them, casting a soothing enchanting shadow.

'Aref stood close to the cliff. "Here we are," he said." "We'll rest a bit, and then I'll go fetch the other women. I won't be long." Wardeh put the baby down and asked 'Aref to help unload the bundle on her back. Another unexpected opportunity! 'Aref stood close, and she was certain he was making approaches to her! But she said nothing, preferring to delay the confrontation with him.

'Aref placed the bundle on the ground and lay beside it. Wardeh, exhausted, sat down and rested her elbow on a nearby stone. She allowed herself the luxury of closing her eyes.

(What a coward you are, 'Aref! All you have to do is raise that dress with your hand, and then everything will happen as it should happen. How do you think an exhausted woman will react? Not only is she tired, but she hasn't seen her husband for six months. Why not put out your hand, you animal, you coward, why not?)

'Aref stretched a trembling hand to Wardeh's thigh. She opened her eyes and looked into his flushed face. In a voice that registered displeasure, she said calmly, "What do you want, 'Aref?"

He shook with fear, and stood up.

"I—I—I'm going to bring the other women now," he said. "Be careful of the Turkish ghosts. They may come out while I'm gone."

"Why don't you go then," said Wardeh, in some annoyance. "I'll settle with the ghosts." The truth was that the story of the ghosts had filled her mind.

"Okay, Okay. I'm going, don't shout at me." (Uff . . . what kind of a woman is she?)

'Aref saw it was useless to make further advances to Wardeh; he suspected that she had been aware of his intentions from the very first time he had touched her shoulder, but had controlled her temper. He pushed the idea of rape out of his mind. After all, his family had passed the chiefdom from father to son for a long time; he had a name to uphold within the community. He had a business to maintain. Besides, he wasn't as brave as he pretended. But he did not give up all hope. After all, who knew what could happen?

("Let me tell you, Muhammad." "What?" " 'Aref is a scoundrel, and the son of a scoundrel." "Oh, 'Aref! I thought you were going to tell me about the young girls back home; so what did the despicable 'Aref do?" "Won't you get jealous?" "If you tell me about the young ladies first I won't get jealous." "Okay. I'll tell you—Zawahi, the daughter of Hamdan Abu-Rattah, eloped" "Eloped?" "Yes." "Who did she elope with?" "I know you were in love with her before you married me! She eloped with the shepherd of Hamed Dakhil." "But how?" "He had asked for her hand, but her folks didn't accept, so she ran away to Hamed Dakhil's house and stayed there, and begged him to marry her to his shepherd. The families interfered and they forced her to marry him!" "By force!" "Well sort of, because her parents first had refused her marriage to the shepherd" "What else?" "One girl was made to marry a man of seventy, and another to marry 'Ali Zurra; so-and-so committed suicide because she was not allowed to marry the one she wanted, and . . . and . . . you ask me about the news of the town and its girls as if you've been away for years. It's exactly the same it always was. Nothing has changed." "And the men?" "Well! The Jews imprisoned all those who had arms in their houses, and took those who were members of the resistance and the communist party." "By God! Who have they imprisoned?" "Well, Rizk Abu al-Jadeyel! Mahmoud and 'Ali 'Abd Rabbo and 'Ali al-Khatib . . ." "All right, now tell me about 'Aref al-'Ali, did he joke with you?" "More than that." "Wardeh, are you saying he dared to go further than jokes?" "More . . ." "By God! Tell me, what did that coward do?" "I asked him to help me take the weight off my back and—" "That despicable son of a despicable, I swear by my honor, I'll hang him at the place Muhammad Fadda hanged himself at Sadd al-'Iqab; I'll leave him hanging there forever. I thought he had just tried to make jokes with you . . . oh, that scoundrel son of a scoundrel—" "Calm yourself Muhammad." "No, I won't calm down until I have him hanging by a rope. I won't calm before—")

'Aref climbed the hills, passing the frontier post where a battalion of enemy soldiers was stationed. He drank some tea with them and chatted with Captain Shlomo, before heading on. Five women waited for him in the place where he had left them earlier in the day. Four of the women, three with small children, were on their way to join their husbands—in Amman, Kuwait, and Saudi Arabia. The fifth, a virgin girl, was being sent by her parents to her fiancé who was working in the Gulf.

'Aref walked ahead, and the women followed him to the well where Wardeh waited. He suggested they rest until sunset, since then they would have to keep walking until they reached the river.

The virgin closed her eyes, the woman with two children sighed in a way that expressed the extent of her pain. In his mind, 'Aref undressed the five women and the girl, turning them first on their stomachs and then on their backs.

The sun sank in the west, and darkness spread into the valley. Partridges woke from their siesta and flocked between the cliffs, and pigeons flew up out of the valley up toward the sky.

"Okay, girls," said 'Aref, "time to get moving."

The women shook the sand from their clothes and began to feed the children.

"How far is the river from here?" asked Wardeh.

'Aref stood up. "If we go quickly, we'll get there in about three hours," he said.

The women picked up children and bundles. Their minds filled with anxiety, their footsteps heavy, they followed 'Aref.

One of the women spoke. "How lonely these mountains are at night!" she sighed. "I can't understand why we have to go through all this misery and smuggling and bribery. So we cross the river in front of the Jews. What would they do to us? If we leave our land to them, what more do they want?"

The woman from al-Tour village looked around her, waiting for one of the others to answer. Then she said, "Haven't you heard the horrible story about the virgin who was raped by the guards at the frontier after they killed her brother? They threw her into the valley and left her to bleed to death."

"And then there was that family that was robbed of all their money."

Each of the women began to recount what she had heard about those who had to pass the enemy soldiers. Wardeh said nothing. She was exhausted, and her son clutched her breasts like a cat, his eyes warily looking around him. She coveted the strap with which one of the other women supported her child on her back. But then she realized her baby was too big and would never have stayed quiet on her back unless he were asleep.

The older children walked along, falling down every now and then.

"Mother, where's Father?" asked one.

"He's waiting for us on the other river bank," her mother replied.

"When will we get to the river?" the child persisted,, "Why do we have to walk at night? Where shall we sleep? If we meet the Jews will they kill us? I'm so tired, carry me, Mother, carry me." The mother would pick the child up, carry her for a few moments, and ask her to be quiet.

Wardeh moved her baby wearily from one shoulder to the other. She looked upward, where the moon was rising between the cliffs. Oh, she thought, I wish 'Aref would let us rest a bit!

At the top of the hill, 'Aref stopped. Flocks of partridges swooped in front of him, their wings whirring in a frightening way. The children drew closer to their mothers.

"Come! We'll stop when we see the meadow," he said.

The women sighed with relief as they reached the top and saw the meadow before them. They lay down to rest with their sleepy children.

(Five women, and a virgin, you, the night, the sky and the earth, and you're doing nothing. What a coward you are, 'Aref! Desire is killing you and you'll never satisfy it as long as you live—what was it Shlomo asked you, "what have you got today?" and you answered, "Five women and a virgin." "That's a rich haul!" he'd said. But you won't give way. Why? For your family name. But the image of the virgin who bled to death after you and Shlomo raped her and killed her brother still comes back to you in dreams. And what are you going to do tonight? Look at this full-breasted virgin, how she sleeps on her side—okay, 'Aref, lie down behind her, caress her thigh. Coward, you can't even face doing that—all right, then undress these women in your mind and sleep with all of them at the same time. Let them lie down on their stomachs in the moonlight—this way, that way, how wonderful it will be—it won't be the first time you've undressed women in the moonlight, 'Aref, look at those lovely bodies in front of you—who would you start with? Well, the virgin—and how about the others? Later! Oh, moon, how beautiful you are, and how beautiful the bodies that undress in your magical light.)

The erotic images disappeared. 'Aref came back to the present. He realized that his desire was still unfulfilled. He looked at the women and an agonizing lust rose inside him that made him resentful and made him regret that he had not agreed with Shlomo to rape them. In sudden anger he screamed at the women, "Get up, get up!"

Frightened by his tone, the women stood up quickly, and the children began to cry. Down the slope he ran, the women following with their children and their belongings, wondering aloud about the reason for his sudden outburst. Wardeh said nothing, but she suspected it had something to do with her own encounter with 'Aref's hands before the other women arrived.

Low hills and ravines, a flat stretch of land, this was much easier than climbing mountains. The moon was moving westward; Aref had said they would not cross until after the moon had set.

The moon had gone down below the western horizon and darkness covered the land. The willow trees, oleander, and blackberry trees cast strange shadows in the distance. 'Aref signalled to the women to be silent and follow him slowly. Each prayed that her child might not scream and betray them at a crucial moment.

"They're from our people!" 'Aref suddenly cried, realizing there were no enemy soldiers, but people hiding behind the trees. His body trembled, reacting in fright.

"Who's there?" asked a man's voice.

"A friend." answered 'Aref.

"What kind of a friend travels at this hour?"

"Immigrants to the other side."

"We're coming back from there," said the man's voice.

'Aref drew closer, and a group of women, men, and children emerged from the shadows of the willow trees.

"So you're coming back," said 'Aref.

"Yes, but we don't know our way!!"

"That's no problem, I'll lead you," he offered.

And so as not to lose this unexpected opportunity for a handsome profit, 'Aref declared to the women that his mission was over.

"Congratulations," he said. "You've arrived safely. All you have to do now is go through the trees and cross the river. The water may not even reach your knees . . ."

Wardeh felt as though a heavy weight had been lifted from her shoulders. But something nagged at her. Wasn't the agreement that 'Aref was to cross the river with them and arrange for transportation to Amman?

It seemed that 'Aref could read what was going on in Wardeh's mind. "Don't you believe me?" he asked. "I know what I'm saying. The river is an arm's length from here, and as soon as you cross over you'll find our freedom fighters. You won't get lost, I promise you."

Wardeh forced herself to accept 'Aref's words as she had previously forced herself to believe that his advances to her were innocent. She pushed forward and the other women followed her. As they set off, she heard the newcomers say, "Beware of the whirlpools! Watch—"

But 'Aref interrupted quickly, "Don't be scared, there are no whirl-pools in this area."

Then he turned back to the newcomers, bargaining on the price of his services. Wardeh could hear him explaining that they would not find their way without him and his knowledge of the mountain roads, ravines, and valley, not to mention possible enemy ambushes! He stressed enemy ambushes in case the "returnees" fell into one that would force them back to the East Bank or kill them, so it could never be said that 'Aref cooperated in such traps.

Wardeh, pushing on with her child, sighed in weariness. It was true the river was not too far, as 'Aref said, but it was much further than an arm's length. Already the women had crossed tens of arms' lengths without reaching the bank. Wardeh secretly cursed her position, dependent on chiefs and sheikhs, and the circumstances that made her a shepherdess, the daughter of a shepherd who was the son of a shepherd, until the one thousandth grandfather.

Ahead, the trees and the oleander and blackberry bushes were thicker. The river was near. Wardeh cleared the intertwining branches with one hand and held the baby close with the other. "Here we are," she said. "There's the river." She sat down on the bank, clearing a place for the others who unloaded their children and their bundles. The water looked calm and not too deep.

The childless woman said, "Why isn't the sound of water louder?"

"Because Jesus Christ blessed it when he was christened in it," answered another woman. "He said, 'calm down, you are blessed,' and it did calm down, and since that day the sound of water is low and gentle!"

Wardeh listened, fascinated by Jesus Christ's ability to calm the water. She felt she had blasphemed when she had in the past compared Jesus Christ and the Prophet Muhammad, to Christ's disadvantage. For hadn't the Prophet Muhammad told the holy rock when it went up to the sky, "calm down, you are blessed,"and the rock had done so from that day and remained hung between sky and earth! She started to ask God's forgiveness for her error. Both prophets were surely great.

One of the women said, "Let's go, girls, and trust in God." They all stood up and began to pray, some in silence, some aloud.

'Aref was right, Wardeh thought. The river was not too wide.

"If we had a rope," she said, "one of us could cross and tie it on the other end . . ."

"The water's shallow, and even if we had a rope who would risk herself and cross alone?"

"We can tie it to someone's waist and hold it from one side while she crosses, so if she falls we can pull her out," Wardeh suggested.

The childless woman said, "We did think of the rope, but people told us the water was shallow."

"What if we're caught in a whirlpool?"

The childless woman answered, "Okay. Why don't we just stay here until the Jews come and get us?"

The virgin was silent as death!

Wardeh said, "Trust in God, girls, let's go."

She tied her dress round her waist, placed her bundle high on her shoulder, and held the baby tightly to her breast. She first grasped a willow branch that was trailing in the river, but the childless woman suggested the women hold each others' hands. Wardeh dropped the willow branch, stretched back her hands, and went forward, the women forming a human chain behind her. She walked slowly into the river, swayed a little as her foot slipped on some small stones, but regained her balance and moved slowly ahead. The water was up to her knees.

'Aisheh al-'Allan sat on a piece of sack cloth, carding her wool for spinning, sighing in anxiety.

Suddenly, Wardeh felt that the current was about to pull her feet from under her . . .

Muhammad 'Audeh looked longingly to his flute—Hajjeh Zawaba moved restlessly in her bed—Father Elia knelt, praying before the icon of the virgin in the Holy Sepulchre. The crazed refugee walked back and forth through the alleys of Jerusalem wearing her tattered sack cloth garment, her hair unkempt and dishevelled—Shaikh Abdul Hameed was in his bed, deep in contemplation.

Wardeh steadied her feet on the ground against the pull of the current. The women called on Jesus Christ and all the saints and prophets to help; the virgin looked upward into the sky, silently pleading. Wardeh recited the name of God over and over as she tried to raise her foot. But the current was too strong. She moved forward without raising her feet and so pushed slowly ahead.

Several of the children began to cry.

Shaikh Fayez al-ʿAli raised his glass in salutation, as did Captain Shlomo, *mukhtar* Faleh al-ʿAli, and many others . . .

Wardeh had covered a third of the distance across the river. The water was now above her knees—she had repeated God's name more than a thousand times. Slowly, she pushed her foot forward but felt it suddenly moving in emptiness, the current pulling her strongly. She lost her balance. Now she could neither put back the foot she had moved forward nor steady the other again. At that moment she knew she would never see her husband again. She felt her leg dragged under by the pull of the current. She almost fell, caught herself, but was dragged down and under. Then she screamed, an anguished scream, and pushed her baby into the arms of the woman behind her. Desperately she clutched at the willow branch. Unconsciously, the other woman held tightly to the baby and struggled back against the current. The baby's screams rose and mixed with the terrified cries of the other children. The willow branch broke, and Wardeh sank into the whirlpool. The other women stood petrified staring at the water—the empty space—where Wardeh had gone down. Soon Wardeh's body appeared, pulled along by the river in front of their frightened eyes. In silence, they stood watching the floating body carried away by the river until they could no longer see it in the darkness. Together they returned to the river bank, their fear of the enemy soldiers gone. The childless woman held Wardeh's baby tight to her breasts in overpowering tenderness, while his screams grew louder and louder. "Mama! Mama!"

In Jerusalem, the crazed refugee passed in front of the Church of the Virgin. She struck at her breast with stones, and sang in a sad voice, "Alas, they took her away and left me all alone."

Tears came into Father Elia's eyes as he knelt before the Virgin's icon in the Holy Sepulchre. "Oh blessed virgin, can't you see what has happened to your people? How long must we bear this agony, Mother of Christ? How long will you continue to deny us your blessings and your mercy?"

Shaikh ʿAbdul Hameed was also praying. "God do not place upon us a heavier burden than we can bear. Oh God, forgive us and have mercy upon us. You are our God. Let us be victorious over the infidels . . ."

ʿAisheh al-ʿAllan straightened up over the sackcloth and continued to spin. Tears fell from her eyes and she began to lament in a low, sorrowful voice.

The sound of 'Aisheh al-'Allan's lament brought a sense of deep sadness to Hajjeh Zawaba. Muhammad 'Audeh, close to tears, picked up his flute. The low, sad notes travelled through the night, across the valleys and hills, to all the houses of the village. And those who were awake in the night wept.

—translated by Salwa Jabsheh and Elizabeth Fernea

Sulaiman al-Shaikh *(b. 1943)*

Born in Saffouria near Nazareth, al-Shaikh has lived most of his life as a refugee. After training in Lebanon as a mental health nurse, he studied for a B.A. in history at the University of Alexandria. He worked for some time as a nurse in Lebanon, Kuwait, and Texas, then as a journalist, and then as an employee at the Higher Council of Culture, Arts, and Literature in Kuwait, where he stayed for many years. He then became deputy editor at the well-known *Al-ʿArabi* monthly in Kuwait. He has published two collections of short stories, *The Sycamore Tree* (1980) and *From the Life of Hanzala al-Shajrawi* (1988).

Kadima[1]

"Fire, Hussain! Go on, fire!"

"Kadima! Kadima!"

His commander, Eliaho, was watching the battle through his field glasses.

He heard the order given a second time. "Aim carefully, Hussain!"

He looked round him, and found nothing but sheets of zinc, dust, pieces of wood, broken rocks, and pebbles.

"Go on, shoot, Hussain! Are you asleep?" The voice of his companion in solitude brought him back to reality.

He fired a few shots at random, without focusing on any particular target.

The planes returned, sweeping over the eastern side of the refugee camp.

"The sound of these explosions really is frightening." The words came out of his mouth in a whisper. He found a wall and leaned on it, seeking protection, scared that some splinter might hit him.

A few seconds later the commander's voice reached him. "Hussain . . . Hayeem and Isaac advance to the east side. There are shots coming from the hospital area."

He moved slowly and cautiously, looking round him in every direction.

[1] *Kadima* is a Hebrew word meaning "attack."

A bullet whizzed just over his head, and he threw himself on the ground.

Feverish thoughts passed through his mind. *God bless my father's soul. This is exactly what he warned me about. "Brothers could easily kill one another without realizing it."*

God bless his soul!

The planes returned, spreading terror to every living thing in the area. They were, he supposed, targeting the places the firing was coming from.

Horrendous explosions were heard, very close at hand. He stayed face down. A few moments passed before he heard his orders.

"Batallion Twenty-one, attack. Move quietly and carefully."

He found that Hayeem was by his side. They jumped over the remains of a house that had been completely destroyed.

The artillery began shooting at distant targets.

A bullet whizzed over their heads, and Hayeem fell to the ground. Several more bullets followed and he threw himself next to the remains of what had once been a wall.

Thoughts struggled again in his mind.

Planes bombing. Tank missiles and marine shelling to complete the destruction and desolation. Many dead, no doubt about that, and yet they fight back from among the ruins. Saboteurs! God protect them!

He shuddered, as if touched on a raw spot by the thoughts passing through his mind, as if someone had found out his deepest secrets.

Repeated orders were heard: "Isaac, attack! Hayeem, attack! Hussain, Ibrahim, *Kadima, Kadima!*"

What the hell am I doing here? What has this got to do with me?

In the last war I escaped joining up because of appendicitis. The inflammation was perfectly timed to coincide with the start of maneuvers before the attack on the south of Lebanon in 1978.

I couldn't find any reason or excuse at the beginning of this war. I did consider opening the wound, but that, I thought, would have been too obvious. An operation in 1978, and the wound from it opening in 1982—it wasn't very plausible! I thought of running away, but there were a number of difficulties there.

The shells from the boats were well aimed at the hill where the firing was coming from. He heard the order over the radio, "Batallion Twenty-one, *Kadima, Kadima!*"

"Come on, Hussain, shoot! The saboteurs are close to you on the left and right. Shoot!" He shot at random, in all directions.

He couldn't see them at all. They might as well have been ghosts.

He heard only the whine of their bullets. Trying to jump and hide behind one of the walls, he bumped against a body, then against a second one, then a third. He looked around him more carefully. Several bodies, the bodies of women and old men and children! *What has this war got to do with them?* He felt a lump in his throat; he vomited a little and tears flowed down his face. Bombs exploding, fires burning, houses destroyed, human beings murdered. *God damn me and people like me!*

He threw himself to the ground as a bullet whizzed right past his ears.

The bullet pierced the wall. He shuddered, feeling very frightened. *Just a few centimeters difference and it would have been my head it had sunk into!*

In his ear, he heard his father's words again. *"The father could be killing his son. The brother could be killing his own brother." That's what he always repeated. God bless his soul!*

For five days the planes and ships and tanks had been bombing and shelling, and they'd been attacking, but there'd been no surrender yet. The bullets continued to whizz over their heads or strike them as they tried to advance. And still they were only on the outskirts of the refugee camp.

"Batallion Twenty-one, assemble! Batallion Twenty-one, assemble in the school playground! Batallion Twenty-one, assemble!"

He moved cautiously toward the nearby school, which had been clearly marked on the map before they started the attack.

There he found their commander Eliaho with some others from the batallion.

"We've got to storm the hospital," Eliaho said. "The aircraft and tanks have opened things up for us, and our orders are to take it over because there are still some saboteurs inside. Hussein and Isaac and Shlomo—you attack from the back and we'll give you covering fire."

The three moved to the places indicated, and so did the other men.

The thundering of the bombs added a new, heightened terror to the one he already felt.

How must the people being shelled feel? God bless you, father, you uttered your wise words and died. You did your best to get me out of the army before you died—but it was no use.

"Quick, Hussain, quick!" The order jerked him out from the depths of his thoughts.

The bombardment stopped, then came the orders: "Batallion Twenty-one, attack, attack!"

He moved slowly and cautiously, shooting at random. The voice giving the orders rasped out, "Quick, Hussain, quick!"

He rushed forward. With a big effort, he jumped to avoid the ruins of one of the houses—and found himself standing face to face with the man.

He gasped, and the man jumped at him, holding a long knife. He moved to avoid the attack—but didn't fire. "Calm down and listen!" he shouted. "I'm a Palestinian like you!"

His words surprised the man, who retorted angrily, "A Palestinian, fighting with the Zionists?"

"Keep your voice down," he whispered. "The soldiers of the unit are close to here. I'll make sure you've got a clear path out, but cut me with your knife first."

Amazement showed on the man's face.

"Why?" he asked.

"There's no time. Quick, cut my right hand! And I want you to know I'm not here by choice."

"Why didn't you have any choice?" the man asked breathlessly.

"When they block every possibility of any kind of work or job, and then offer you the chance to join the army as your only way of making a living, what else can you do?"

The man's face grew worried.

"How can I cut you," he asked, "and why?"

"We haven't got much time. Go off to your left, the soldiers haven't got there yet. But cut me first. I'll scream, and then you run off as fast you can. Here, take my machine gun."

"Why?"

"So that I won't be suspected, or be forced to kill myself. Come on, quick!"

He closed his eyes and turned his face away.

"Hurry!" he urged.

He heard a gasp and a breaking voice say, "Oh, brother!"

He gasped in his turn, and gritted his teeth. Then he screamed with pain and fell down bleeding.

When he woke up, he was being carried on a stretcher. He heard Commander Eliaho saying, "This Druze from Asfia must have seven lives. Take him to the hospital."

—translated by Salwa Jabsheh and Christopher Tingley

Yusuf Shruru *(b. 1940)*

A novelist, short story writer, and translator born in Ramla, Shruru went as a refugee to Damascus when his town fell to the Israelis in 1948. He studied for his B.A. in Arabic literature at the University of Damascus and taught at Kuwaiti schools before finally leaving for London in 1958. There he obtained a diploma in International Law from London University; he presently works at the Kuwaiti embassy in London. Early in his stay in London he met Colin Wilson and translated four of his works into Arabic. He has published two collections of his short stories, *A Boat of Blood* (1966) and *One Eye by Day* (1974), and two novels, *Sorrow Also Dies* and *The Time of Snakes* (1988). Shruru's work has special importance as a reflection of the experience of a Palestinian writer who lives in the West and whose cross-cultural experiences have given added depth to his outlook on the problems of his own people and his depiction of their experience.

One Eye by Day

"Just a one-way ticket," I said faintly.

I put down a large bank note and stood there waiting. The old man wiped his spectacles and stared at me in silence, then scratched his head with a finger of his right hand. At long last, he spoke.

"One-way?" he asked, his face a patchwork of question marks. "Where to? What's the name of the city or place you're going to?"

"You choose," I replied. "I just want to feel free again, and see life afresh."

The old man was still now, his eyes calm behind his spectacles. I had no idea what he was thinking about. He smiled, then, after a moment's reflection, he put out his hand and picked up a small yellow ticket.

"The place is called Arabish," he muttered, in a voice flecked with colorful intonations. "It's been completely run down for more than a year now. You'll have a wonderful time."

The railway station was a hive of activity: pieces of paper flying in all directions; trains standing there as if stunned, like whales from the depths of the ocean; a thin face laughing richly; a baby anxiously clutching at its mother's face; a dark-haired girl standing there alone, her tired eyes ravaged by so many hours of waiting; an ambassador singing a drunken song and a policeman trying to keep him quiet; a long whistle announcing the departure of yet another train; a small man followed by a porter carrying a heavy suitcase. And there was me, carrying my ticket, my identity, and a picture of my face; my mind filled with thoughts. My train was waiting there, motionless, with the word "Arabish" written on it in large letters. I'd never heard of the place before.

What am I like? Well, I have a head with thick hair all over it which I've no wish to have cut, and the features of my face aren't very harmonious; they're flabby and suggest a weak personality. I'm twenty-eight, and for six years I studied at a university with a huge dome, which awarded me a degree certificate with a government stamp and a minister's signature on it. I'm tall and clumsy, with a slight stoop. I'm a pharmacist, and when I graduated I went to work in a pharmacy; I wore a white coat and stood behind a wooden counter for hours on end, reading prescriptions with their deliberately awful handwriting. Like some hireling, I'd disappear into the back of the store, then re-emerge with the medicine. I wasn't cut out for this type of work, and I started looking round for ways of making my life more worthwhile.

At university I believed in revolution—in the Abbasid Caliph al-Saffah[1] and Al-Hajjaj[2] and Che Guevara[3]—and I trained myself to participate in lengthy, logical debate. I had a cause and I wanted it never to die. Revolution was truth and power; I was a revolutionary, and revolutionaries should never die. I grew a black beard which I never trimmed, read about wars of liberation, admired Mao Tse-tung[4] and Ho-Chi Minh,[5] not to mention the film *Viva Zapata*, and was carried on people's shoulders during demonstrations.

---

[1]First ruler of the Abbasid Dynasty whose capital was Baghdad and who ruled over a vast Islamic empire. He reigned from 749–54.

[2]Famous general who helped confirm the Umayyad dynasty whose capital was Damascus and who held the power from 661–750. As viceroy of Basra in southern Iraq, a region known for its restiveness, he clamped down with an iron fist and quelled all rebellions and claims of the tribal noblemen to the Caliphate.

[3]Latin American revolutionary who was killed in 1967, but who has lived since as a legend, particularly among Third World peoples.

[4]1893–1976. Founder of the People's Republic of China and of Maoist communism.

[5]1890–1969. Vietnamese nationalist leader and president of North Vietnam from 1954 until his death. He was organizer of the Vietnamese independence movement, the Viet Minh. In his last years he led the struggle of North Vietnam against the United States, which supported South Vietnam.

Now I want to put an end to my present existence. I feel as though my life's binding me with strips of glue to this city of mine, with its cafés and flies. My shell's closed up and won't allow me to slink deftly away, like some cat escaping from its lot to make a new one from its own thoughts. My very existence has become a misery; life's risen to a head and then collapsed, and I don't know where it is any more.

"So why don't you go off somewhere?" a friend suggested sarcastically a few days ago. "Go somewhere a long way away, then you'll know what you really want."

The conductor took my ticket by the gate. "This place of yours has been in ruins for more than a year," he said.

My tall, clumsy frame made its way along the platform, looking for an empty compartment. Every carriage was empty, apart from the boxes full of preserved foodstuffs. The young driver stuck his head out so that he could see the signal to start. There was no suitcase swaying in my hand. A train with just five carriages, a whale that's given birth to a dwarf!

"How long does it take to Arabish?" I asked the driver quietly.

"Just three and a half hours."

I got into the first carriage, sat down on a plush seat, and, seeing my face in the mirror opposite, gave myself a fulsome smile: I'd embarked, with no ties to bind me, on the great unknown journey. I took out a cigarette and started smoking avidly.

Someone, I've no idea who, once said to me, "Staying in a place is hard, but sometimes it's just as difficult to leave it."

Ever since then, the idea of leaving has lent a sparkle to my failing heart and given my bleary eyes a waft of jasmine scent. Leaving is so much better than staying here, where I sit in a glass-fronted café, chattering till dawn. The everyday life of this city seems rather meaningless now. I have to understand myself before I do anything else. I remember once reading a Russian novel and being totally riveted by a single sentence: "The person who walks must finally reach the end of the road." Over many exhausting months and days and hours I'd searched for my road, till moss grew on my forehead and my eyes dried up, till I got a pain in my back and felt crushed like a dried-up leaf that's fallen to the ground. I felt as though I alone was exposed to the charge of standing aloof from the real work of the world in order to develop my inner self. The world keeps going, despite all the lies and the false images and the corpses piled high on the burning desert sands. People move about the streets like frogs, they laugh as they eat, and procreate every night. Why should we think there's a curse on the world whenever a man dies? If I were to be struck down with sickness for a time, the wheels on the buses and cars wouldn't stop turning. I'd simply sit miserably moaning on my bed.

I'm always trying to collect things and keep them; and when I release them or they leave of their own accord, they don't sink into emptiness, but rather stay here living inside me.

"Our days will never die," she once said to me, silently weeping, "as long as there's still a spark in them."

"My heart's delight," I called her. She was twenty-two when she got married, and she'd lived with me for four long years. One Friday night, I tiptoed my way among the beds of sick people crammed into the huge hall to get to her bedside. She didn't give me her usual smile; she was weeping like the sky over a sad city. I sat down beside her, withdrawn into myself.

"What did the doctor say?" I asked cheerfully. "When will you be coming out?"

"You must help me," she replied, her tears streaming down. "I don't want to see you again. We've lived together for a long time as though we were married; let that be enough. You'll never marry me. I want a house, and a husband, and children. I've been happy living with you. When I met you, I was young. We've often talked about separating. We must be strong and take the final decision. Please, please, help me! Stay with me now, I mean, but help me get rid of your chains. Stay with me, but just as a friend. Please, my love, don't come and visit me tomorrow. Go out of my life, if only just for a little while. Some time soon, I'll come to your place and pick up my things. You're still my life, but you'll never make a future for me. Don't say good-bye for ever, just till we meet again like two friends. You'll be the only friend I have."

I left without even looking behind me. The streets were quiet, and the cold air nipped people's faces. I pushed my face right down into the top of my overcoat—and all the while, there she was in bed, crying over a love which had given her two children, both of them dead. She was dreaming about a husband, and a house, and children, all of it without love; it was enough for her to have been, and still be, in love. As for me, I had no idea what I was going to do. The lush green of past days had faded now, and all movement came to a halt in the house where she alone had been my heart's delight.

Just two days before, a huge yellow car had pulled up beside me, and her face, the face I knew so well, leaned out. Alongside her sat her young husband.

"How are you, my dear?" she asked, her eyelids moist with tears. "How's life these days?"

"Be happy," I replied in a joyless tone. "There aren't so many days of real happiness, after all."

The car moved rapidly off, like a small plane, leaving me alone in a street where all the leaves had fallen. Everyone has to find his own way in life, but I haven't found mine yet. It's entirely my own fault. Things have just got away from me, and I'm left with myself. Sometimes I'm even afraid this self will disappear as well.

"Why don't you work out there with the others?" the café owner had asked me.

"Where do the others work?" I asked, turning my eyes away. "Who do they work for?"

"They work out there, in the world," he replied, "as *fidaain*."[6]

I let out a nasty, sneering laugh, then started smoking a big cigarette.

"Being a member of the *fidaain* means sacrificing everything," I told the café owner, "absolutely everything. I don't own anything that I can sacrifice, even my own self."

The café owner started reading aloud from the newspaper: "Life is the most valuable thing a man owns, and it is only granted to him to live once. He should live it in such a way that he feels no pangs of regret over years pointlessly wasted. If he lives it honestly, he can whisper to himself as he lies dying: 'My whole life has been devoted to the noblest cause in our region, the cause of the *fidaain*.' "

He stopped reading for a few moments. "Did you hear that?" he said looking towards me. "That was said by a man working in the mountains out there. But the *fidaain* troops would never take young people like you. You're just a useless chatterer, that's all!"

I looked at my watch. Half an hour and I'd be at Arabish. Then I'd see just how run down the place was, that intellectual sensation which had taken hold of me for more than a year. Why am I for ever questioning myself without ever actually doing anything? The cursed worm still eats at my heart, turning it to a lump of raddled dough. How can youth have disappeared without so much as a question? But who's to say the goal hasn't been defined? Why isn't man born with a goal ready-

---

[6]*fidaain* are the freedom fighters sworn to fight and redeem their country with their blood. The root of the word is *fada*: "redeemed with his life."

made, waiting for him? Our own destiny makes the goals; that much is true. Who was it that said that? Perhaps it was me, in one of my moments of intellectual disquiet.

There was a knock on the door of the compartment. "Coffee or tea, Sir?" asked a man with a languid expression on his face.

"Black coffee with no sugar, please," I replied automatically.

He closed the door politely, and I sat there waiting for him to come back. How I wished I'd bought a paper or brought along a book to read! Journeys are dreadful if you're on your own. Trees never grow by themselves, and people can't live without friends and families and smiles.

The train came to a halt. I looked out of the broad window and read the sign: "Arabish." This was the place, and I rubbed my hand and got out on to the station platform. The place was empty; there wasn't a soul anywhere. It had been swept and looked clean. Arrows pointed toward the exit, and I went down a flight of stairs and up seven more; then my eager gaze took in the wide city street. The old clock in the square showed 3:20; the day was still young. I'll choose a room on the edge of town, I thought, somewhere where I can watch the people and shops, where I can see my own self growing. I have lots of money in my back pocket; I took out my entire month's salary yesterday. I've no family to spend it on, and I don't have many financial ties. I'll buy some clothes from this city—I'd like it to live in me before it slips from my grasp the way everything else always has. My café friends won't even notice I'm not there; their life's just a constant daze of talk. The owner of my apartment will notice, though, because I didn't pay him last month's rent. The owner of the pharmacy will send his driver to inquire, and he'll be amazed when he discovers I've gone.

This city looks dead. Death's still alive and well here! The houses look clean from the outside, and the shops have all kinds of imported goods in their windows. I stood outside a shop to choose myself a tie with a pattern. Looking at my reflection in the glass, I felt as though I were a stranger, as if faces change when places do. The prices were very high. I haven't seen a single other face yet. Where were all the faces in this city? The old man scratching his head at the station had been making fun of me. There's nothing run down here. The streets look clean, and the shops are full of goods. The trees in the houses look fresh and bright, and the old clock's exactly on time.

Suddenly I felt lonely. There were plenty of houses, shops and restaurants in this long street, but for all that, there still wasn't a soul in sight, and I began to hear the sound of my own footsteps on the deserted pavement. The people in this city, I thought, must take a nap after their midday meal. Soon the street and the pavement would be bustling with activity; I'd be smiling at everyone, and might even see a face that liked me, so that I could return the feeling. Love is a fertile soil from which leaves, flowers, and fruits all grow and flourish. I might even open a small corner pharmacy. I still wasn't sure I liked the name "Arabish"—there was no music to the sound of the word. I was philosophizing, as usual. How strange it was! The whole atmosphere seemed oppressive. Pangs of hunger were now eating away at my stomach like a saw. I'll have to look for a restaurant, I thought. I'll cover the table with different dishes and ask for some red wine; then, when I've finished, I'll order some brandy and black coffee—the coffee in the train was foul. I'll ask the restaurant owner about renting a room on the edge of the city. I won't be spending a lot of time chattering to people here. I seem to be the only visitor; there was no one else on the train. I'll start looking for a restaurant and go in the first one I come across. I must have a smoke; smoking helps me think. I wish my own city was as quiet as Arabish! I looked for a cigarette, and cursed myself for a complete fool as I realized I'd run out. I'll buy a large packet of Supremes, I thought, here's the tobacconist's. I pushed the revolving glass door, went in—and found myself pushed out into the street again! Was I dreaming or what? I rubbed my eyes. No, how could it be? Death's still alive, even in small places, I thought. I must have a fever. I'll try another store. Here's a different one. I pushed the door and made my way inside; and once again I was shot back on to the empty pavement like a mortar shell. How could I be seeing visions twice in a row? I went crazy and started kicking at the doors of the shops, poking my head inside, then coming out panting, with the sweat pouring from my forehead. Everything, everywhere, was wasted away. How could a whole city be turned into a ridiculous freak show? I'm going to kill that old man, I thought, and trample his glasses under my feet. Who asked him to choose a place like this for me? I gasped. No restaurants in the whole city! How on earth did they eat?

The young train driver had told me before I left, "You know, there's only one train a day to Arabish."

I'd have to spend the night here, then. But where and how? The faces of the people who live here might eat me up. I must get away, I thought. I'll hide in a cave or the shady branches of a tree. I'm not crazy yet. I started running like a racehorse. Strange animal faces began to peer out through the windows of the shops, and suddenly, as I was tearing through the streets, doors started opening and human forms with different animal features came out and ran after me. I won't let them catch me, I thought. How did destruction come to this city? I'm finding it difficult to breathe, I'm panting, as if I was on the point of death. The people here are the same size as me, and have the same limbs, but their faces are like the faces of different sorts of animals! I'm sure I read the name of the place properly before I got off the train. I've seen people wearing animal masks before, but these faces aren't masked, they're real. I can hear the sound of their footsteps behind me, many of them. Their breath's scorching the back of my neck, my hair's flying in the wind, raw fear's twisting my entrails! I reached the huge city square. The creatures, with their human size and animal faces, had blocked all possible escape routes. Paralysis seized me suddenly; dazed, I stayed exactly where I was and took a closer look at them. One of them had a fox's face with phlegm dripping from its mouth; another short one had the face of a plump chicken; a third, the face of a lean dog; and a fourth was a sparrow, chirping discordantly. But most of them had the faces of white lambs.

There was a sudden silence in the square and the streets around it. All those animal eyes were now aimed at my flabby human face. A body with the face of a black cat started sniffing the ground around me and was followed by a huge police dog which let out a bark. The animal faces moved three steps forward. I felt surrounded. I'd have to surrender; resistance was impossible. Another figure appeared, with a lion's head topped by a white mane, his eyes gleaming with a burning flame. He checked me carefully, circled me twice, then raised his finger as a signal. Three police dog faces stepped forward and escorted me to the Municipal Building, where I stood waiting to hear how their language sounded.

"Burn him alive," a chicken suggested in a language just like my own, "then give him to the city wolves to eat."

Four wolves' faces looked up at once. Their red tongues were hanging out, and they began to lick their chops with relish.

"No!" came the voice of a white lamb, again speaking my language. "He ought to work as a hired laborer and go and gather fresh grass for us from the plains."

Several lambs came forward, not meek at all, their eyes glinting with a mean and vicious spark.

"We'll send him to spy on the houses," barked a police dog. "Some people still don't believe in our new way of life. They plan to stir up revolution against the government of our city."

The old lion with the mane and the powerful eyes looked up and asked everyone to be silent. This particular face was, I was sure, the leader of the city. They all spoke in a language like mine, the one people used in my own chattering city. All eyes were fixed on the leader, the lion whose fires had been cooled by old age.

"Listen, my friend," he said, addressing me. "More than a year ago we suffered a terrible defeat. We thought it was going to be a victory. More than a year ago the houses in this city were reduced to rubble and the bodies of its young men scattered across the pavements. Thousands of carriages and cars were burned and our birds of war had their feathers plucked. The skies afforded no protection; heavy stones rained down, and our birds died in their nests. We were a powerful state, I can assure you, with a strong army, but more than a year ago we were totally wiped out. It was a general defeat. Our eyes took on a wasted look, and just a few steps away a city set about attacking us. It crushed our own history and spat on it, then proceeded to rewrite history just as it wanted; it was the victor after all. The war didn't last long, my friend. It was like the flash from a spark, over before we even realized it had started. We were all stunned, with no idea of how to repair matters. We groped around in a daze, searching for a solution in the general whirling confusion. Then one group of young men started working as *fidaain*, while other groups sought out a way of life without risks, and . . ."

"Do you people here know what being a member of the *fidaain* means?" I cut in.

Some of the animal faces made way for a young tiger with the hair receding from his face, and he stepped forward to answer me.

"Yes, we know," he replied, "but we don't take part ourselves, because we think it's all futile."

The elderly lion addressed me again. "An expert's been to visit us several times," he said, "and he gave us a machine which you'll see in a minute. He suggested we sit behind it for just a few hours, and be turned into animals; or rather have our faces changed into animal's faces; everyone should have a face to conform with his character. We liked the idea. I was the first to sit behind it, and after a few hours this was the face I got. I felt a kind of calm spread over my face and my thoughts were stilled. People started to change. You see, there are lambs, chickens, foxes, dogs, cats, poisonous snakes, and other creatures too, according to the way we were before we were transformed. For example, we're not afraid of somebody with a lamb's face; a person wearing a face like that is easily led and walks behind us with no trouble. But we never listen to what the snakes have to say; they're poisonous, and their sole wish is to plant poisonous thoughts among us . . ."

The young tiger's face stood out suddenly from the other faces surrounding me.

"I have a tiger's face," he said, "and I'm courageous. But I believed courage should be at the service of our city, so I sought peace. The enemy city doesn't attack us any more, and we can't butt its borders with our horns either. We don't want you to keep your human face. It will be like a curse on our peace, like those young men who work as *fidaain* and live in the hills and mountains around our borders. We don't want you to be like a plague, sowing death in our streets. You must sit behind the machine till you take on an animal face of your own. We'll see what sort of personality you carry inside you; you can't deceive us for long."

He gestured with his right hand, and four police dogs came up and led me forcibly, to the sound of singing from the chickens, cats, birds, and lambs, into the Municipal Hall. I tried to protest as a lamb butted me, but a police dog whispered in my ear.

"Try not to use your eyes too well," he suggested. "Be like us. We have one eye by day and at night we close them both to sleep. When we were men, we used two eyes like everyone else, but now we don't any more. One eye's enough during the day."

The huge machine loomed large in the hall, with all kinds of angles on its legs and arms. On the top of it were four electronic eyes of dazzling brightness, and behind it was a collection of comfortable chairs covered in blue velvet. They chose one of these for me and forced me to sit down on it. The animal faces now moved back, and an old fox with foul-smelling breath came over and pressed an electric button. The electronic eyes began to move. I felt feverish, and little by little my senses began to fade. Now I'm going to appear as I really am; an animal face will grow where my human one was. I've lived the life of a coward, philosophizing, chattering on, passively absorbed by the way things are. I was no longer able to hold on to the spark of my life. I philosophized about clutching at things which had slipped from my grasp. I defended nothing with any vigor, had no idea of responsibility. My life was a mere lake of words.

Long, fine whiskers have grown on my upper lip, and my face has become thin and pointed.

"You, the animal lurking inside me," I shouted, "don't show me your face. I'll have the face of a cowardly mouse. I'm just a useless chatterer."

I must defeat the peace in this city. The mouse's face isn't fully formed yet. I've found a goal. I'll escape from the city of emaciation and destruction and safety. I felt an incredible strength surging within me. Being a member of the *fidaain* means sacrificing everything—everything—with no exception. Now I'm in control of my life. I don't want to have one eye by day; I want hundreds of eyes to look out of me. The young men are up there, living in the hills and mountains, and I must run and throw myself into their midst. I've no wish to stay in Arabish, the city of safety and of the curses of some other history against my own. I'll kill the old man and trample his glasses. He's just a collaborator.

By some miracle, I managed to stand and rush out into the streets with the police dogs chasing after me. Their barks burned my eardrums, and the noise of my running was accompanied by the sound of the lambs, chanting in unison as if at a demonstration:

"Let him collect fresh grass! Let him work as a laborer!"

The police dogs were chasing me like fiery arrows; I could feel their hot breath down my neck. The plains around the city grow vegetables, trees, and olives. If the police dogs don't catch me, I'll say this to the young men up there: "Our days will never die as long as there's still a spark in them. Being a member of the *fidaain* is the only spark in this time of cursed defeat."

—translated by Roger Allen and Christopher Tingley

Mahmoud Shuqair *(b. 1941)*

Born in Sawahra near Jerusalem, Shuqair studied for his B.A. in philosophy and sociology at the University of Damascus. He was living in East Jerusalem when Israel occupied it in 1967 and remained there until he was deported by the Israeli authorities at the end of the seventies because of his political writings about the occupation of his country. By that time, he had already gained recognition as a short story writer with his two collections *The Bread of Others* (1975) and *The Palestinian Boy* (1977), both published by the avant-garde publishing firm, Salah al-Din. After deportation, he moved to Amman, where he still lives, participating fully in its literary life and dedicating himself to writing. His third collection, *Rites for the Wretched Woman*, was published in Amman in 1986; it is an original experiment of very short concise sketches, taken from life and written with poignancy and skill.

The Villagers

The summer heat had the village wrapped in languor, and the retreating shadows of the dilapidated walls were announcing the coming of mid-day. The *mukhtar* was walking slowly in his long robe as he approached a number of men who were standing by a wall and seeking cover in its shade. Some were playing *sija*[1] and some were watching, while others had fallen fast asleep.

The *mukhtar* spoke up loudly, and with an assertiveness which he hoped would convey gallant concern. "By God, men, it seems that people have no more pride left in them! There are no more real men! There's no more honor!"

They seemed to understand immediately what he meant. An old man raised his hands imploringly. "Have patience, Abu Majid. May God guide your steps . . ." And in a tone of sympathy, he concluded, "Show some discretion, men . . . And may God show discretion towards all his creatures."

One of the *sija* players pulled his hat down over his head and flat-

---

[1] *Sija* is a popular game played in some parts of Palestine and Egypt, similar to dominoes.

teringly said, "Why should you be bothered, Abu Majid? May God never show us his face again! He's a scoundrel!"

Abu Majid looked as though his blood were boiling. "There's no honor left anymore, men! He lets him assault his wife without showing any sign of rage!"

"No, no," said the venerable old man, nervously. "Be God-fearing, be God-fearing . . . They say he assaulted her, but that she filled the whole place with her screams and he got nothing from her . . ."

"Listen, you, does Khalid al-ʿAli ever lie? He says he witnessed everything!"

"But, my dear friend," said the old man, trying to close the subject, "today he went to court to file a suit against him. The court is looking into the matter . . ."

"By God, this is a question of honor! If it had been a piece of land for which he went to court, we wouldn't have said a thing!"

"Only a vile man would go to court for this," said the man who'd tried to appease the *mukhtar* earlier.

Some of the sitting men remained silent; only their hands moved occasionally, to wipe the sweat off their faces.

Others, however, who had been noncommittal before, made their comments now:

"When Husain Abu Safiyya made passes at al-Jarrash's daughter and attacked her, and she returned home screaming, al-Jarrash attacked the Abu Safiyya family with his gun."[2]

"Brothers," a man who up till now had kept silent was moved to say, "if al-Jarrash kills a man, he can pay blood money to the victim's family. But this is an impoverished man who's down on his luck."

"The woman is to blame for the dishonor," added another. "For without her consent, that man would not have been able to get close to her."

The *mukhtar* stood up. His gaze wandered over the roofs to the old houses, and over the walled barns. He was dreaming of bygone days when his grandfather used to ride his horse through the alleys of the village, and men would bow their heads, and women would cover their faces in deference.

---

[2]The issue of honor is very grave in the Arab world, especially in the countryside. In Palestinian villages (and in many others in the Arab world), a man is stigmatized if he is silent about the misdemeanor of another man toward any of his women folks, whether wife, daughter, sister, or mother. It has not been unusual for such a man to retaliate harshly, even to kill any such attacker of his own honor or that of his family.

The shade had now receded so that the *sija* players were grouped under the fiery sun, while those who were watching moved close to the wall.

Suddenly, the *mukhtar's* attention was drawn to some children who were running down an alley, screaming and muttering unintelligibly.

"What's the matter kids . . . what's happened?"

From all sides the children gathered, each one giving his own version, waving their hands and pointing to a specific place.

"My God, there's a big fight going on!"

"They're pulling each other's hair!"

"And one of the women was dragging the other around!"

The *mukhtar* rushed forward. He felt responsible for the village. His steps were firm and sure as all the others trailed behind him: one was limping, another was throwing his weight on his cane, while others were right on the *mukhtar's* heels. The nearer they drew to their destination, the louder grew the foul words and the screaming. There were women, old and young, standing on the rooftops and alongside the walls.

As the *mukhtar* approached, he saw that one of the women—he was able to recognize her as 'Aziza, even though her hair was scattered all over her face—had gotten hold of another by the hair and was dragging her about.

"Oh, damn you!" he muttered, then rushed forward, striking out at both women until he'd stopped the fighting.

It had begun when 'Aziza's mother was passing through the alley and heard some words directed at her by Imm 'Awwad who was sitting on the front porch of her house:

"May God forsake her! . . . She tempted him until he made advances at her, and now he's the one they've put in prison!"

Blinded with anger, Imm 'Aziza could not let this pass.

"May God forsake *you*!" she'd flung back at Imm 'Awwad, "and your spinster daughters! They've never let a man pass by without having a try at him!"

It was as if a snake had bitten Imm 'Awwad. Screams rang out from all sides.

Although the *mukhtar* disliked the residents of the neighborhood, his feeling of responsibility compelled him to end the quarrel.

"May both your fathers be damned!" he thundered, amidst the bedlam of women's voices and children's screams. "Get out of here! Go home! Damned be the father of anyone who shelters you in his house!"

Although the swearing and foul language continued, there was no more fighting. The men gathered around the *mukhtar*, and he began to tell them about the old days, when a woman would not have dared raise her voice in the presence of a man, and if she met one on the street she would shrink back and lower her eyes to the ground.

One of the men nodded. "Yes, by God, the world has changed. Women were not allowed to leave their houses."

"Take it easy, men," commented another. "The air is filled with scandal and abominations."

The cursing and swearing subsided. A boy came running through the alley. He yelled, "'Aziza, your husband's come! I swear to God, I saw him!"

"Get going, 'Aziza!" one of the men standing by shouted at her. "Have a little shame! Your husband's come!"

Her husband staggered along the barren, dusty road. He was wearing a threadbare jacket with a dangling, flabby collar. The jacket reached to just above his knees, and his patched trousers billowed over a pair of worn-out shoes. He was holding a bag to his chest; his face was covered with a *kufiyya*. And in his eyes was a look of humiliation and sorrow.

How can you cross the alley now? he was thinking to himself. *And if you were to meet any of your fellow villagers, would you greet them? Where would you find a voice to speak with? Suppose you heard them laughing as you turned your back, would you dare to stop and look them in the eye? Of course not. All you can do is keep your eyes to the ground and hurry on your way, wishing that the earth beneath your feet would somehow open up and swallow you, so as to relieve you from this torture and pain.*

He drew nearer the village. The children were playing, but their eyes were fixed on him. Some of them went over to him and gave an account of the fight that had broken out earlier. He paid no attention to any of them, and kept walking.

One of the boys began to sing:

> Up the fig tree she went,
> Up to her usual place she went,
> She swore at me, may God disgrace her!
> Woe to you, girl, your looks are brazen,
> Your womb has a child whose teeth have come out.

It was as if a dagger had sunk into his heart. But he kept on: *God damn her! She's disgraced herself, she goes out into the streets and picks fights with others, and still she feels no shame! But, what can you do? You paid dearly to be able to marry her. And supposing you divorce her, who will bake your bread then? Who will take care of the children and look after the house? And you work from sunrise to sunset, for nothing but a morsel of bitter bread. . . .*

He continued walking, dragging himself through the alley. Some men were sitting in front of one of the shops, while others stood next to a wall. The *mukhtar*'s voice was still resounding, and the men around him still nodding flatteringly. He kept his eyes to the ground and did not greet anyone, but he could feel the sharp eyes that were focused on him like needles pricking his skin. Silence crept over the alley, until nothing could be heard but the faint sound of his footsteps and the low sound of a maudlin song emitted by a distant radio.

He dragged himself down a side alley that led to his house. The needles were no longer pricking his flesh: *"Let them say what they will. I can neither kill nor strike at anyone . . . And as far as honor, manhood, and pride are concerned, I'll leave it all to them. There's no more honor anyway."*

He closed the garden gate. His children saw him and ran up to him, in all their innocence, their eyes looking intently at the bag he carried. His heart leapt as they clung to him joyfully. 'Aziza was sitting down, looking depressed. A stifling silence crept into the house.

For hours, feverish and exhausted, he lay down thinking.

Yesterday night, on his way back home from the city, villagers had been talking about 'Aziza. But he'd never got up the courage to ask her about the details of what had happened. Today he'd come home early, but even now he could not find a way to ask her. Every time he made up his mind to start questioning her, he checked himself, and shrank back. He was still hoping for an explanation that would relieve the piercing ache he felt in his heart.

Finally, the knots which had been holding back his tongue were loosened:

"Woman, tell me the truth! Did anything happen between you and him?"

Suddenly, she felt deep regret. She had often cursed her father for forcing her to marry him; she had always seen in him the cause of her misery and wretchedness; yet, she was now sorry for him.

"Be God-fearing," she replied in a low voice that implied innocence. "You too? What's the matter with you?"

Then he begged her to tell him everything that had taken place. She saw his total helplessness to do anything so evident in his eyes, and pitied him the more for it.

"Go and wash your feet first," she said. "Then I'll tell you everything."

He sighed with a great sense of grief and sorrow. 'Aziza gazed searchingly at her husband, and suddenly the image of 'Awwad sprang into her mind.

She remembered how her heart would swell with admiration when she watched him take part in wedding ceremonies. She would stand by the window, poking her head through among the other women's, so as to watch the *dabka*[3] dance in the main yard. Leading the men in the dance, and singing to the melody of the *shabbaba*,[4] 'Awwad had won the hearts of virgins and married women alike.

Yesterday, while out fetching wood, she had been singing blithely. 'Awwad was grazing his sheep, prancing around, and playing on his *shabbaba*.

As 'Awwad approached her, she felt overwhelmed. Desire was dancing deep inside her.

"Out working so early, with the morning dew still on your shoulders?"

"What else? I have no choice . . . Life is demanding."

When she'd finished gathering wood, 'Awwad had lifted the bundle and placed it on her head.

There was a strange look in his eyes. Her neck throbbed, her body felt all limp, and she gave a frivolous laugh. The bundle fell to the ground.

As he heard her laugh, 'Awwad lost his head. His eyes were lined with kohl, and his good looks were enhanced by his red *kufiyyeh*. He took her in his arms and kissed her firmly on the cheek, then threw her to the ground.

Suddenly, a bell hanging from one of the sheep's neck had rung. Jumping up, she had run off like a scared rabbit. She looked around the open space, but could see no one. With trembling steps, she had returned. All the world around her was hazy.

All at once, behind the trunk of an olive tree, she had seen a fright-

---

[3] *Dabka* is the traditional folk dance in Palestine, Syria, and Lebanon.
[4] *Shabbaba* is a kind of flute.

ening face, as if Fate itself were passing there. She had cried out as loud as she could, and jerked convulsively.

Now, her husband was wiping his hands on a piece of cloth, the pain still deep in his heart. He looked at her tentatively; all he was hoping was that she would diminish his pain through some reassuring words that came out from deep inside her, words that would be warm and tender. He tried to speak, but once again found himself unable to say a word. 'Aziza noticed this.

After a long period of silence, he spoke. "It is your fault. You shouldn't have gone so far from the village."

"I swear to God, I had no bad intentions!"

"Then how could he have assaulted you?"

"I was getting wood . . . He attacked me like a brute!"

"Even so, you could have struck at his head with a stone, damn him!"

"I was paralyzed with fear."

"He threw you to the ground?"

His body was shaking violently now, his voice becoming sharper.

She lowered her head and said, "Maybe . . ."

"What do you mean, 'maybe'?"

"I tell you, I was out of my mind! I was screaming, and it was then that Khalid 'Ali came along."

The pain inside grew even greater. He sensed that his attempt to investigate the matter would give him no peace of mind. He stared at the faces of his children, who were sitting in a corner, and then he burst out angrily, "Answer me frankly! . . . Tell me! Tell me! . . ."

Tears flowed from her eyes. After a while, she said, "By God, no! . . . Have pity! Why are you thinking such evil thoughts?"

He stared at her and tried hard to comprehend the meaning of her tears. But this did not help him reach a decision, and he wept. He cried like a baby . . . The children noticed their father weeping. In their minds, the image of a father who gave them sweets and money, who was stronger than any other man in the village, was shaken; and in turn their lips curled, and soon they also were crying.

He felt poison boiling in his veins, as though he'd been bitten by a snake. Throughout the long night, he could not sleep.

The *mukhtar* was still thinking of bygone days.

Over the village, a strange summer wind was hissing.

—translated by Salwa Jabsheh and Thomas G. Ezzy

Muhammad 'Ali Taha (b. 1941)

A short story writer born in the village of Miaar in the Galilee, Taha's family became refugees in 1948 and lived in the Palestinian village of Kabul. He did his secondary studies in Kufr Yasif and obtained a degree from the University of Haifa. At the end of the seventies, he joined the Israeli Communist party. He has chosen a teaching career but is also deeply involved in a wide range of literary and political activities and attends many world conferences. His first collection of short stories, *For the Sun to Rise*, appeared in 1964 followed by three others: *A Bridge on the Sad River* (1977); *'A'id al-Mi'ari Sells Sesame Cakes in Tal al-Zaatar* (1978); and *A Rose for Hafiza* (1983). His fiction reflects the oppressive conditions of Palestinians under Israeli rule. He has shown particular interest in the life of Palestinians in refugee camps, and has depicted it in terms that are as realistic as they are esthetically gripping.

Faris Rateeba

If, at an earlier time, some stranger had come to our village and asked, at every single house in every street and alleyway, about Faris Sa'eed Abu Arab, people would have shaken their heads in ignorance and asked, "Who?" For the people of our village had known him only as "Faris Rateeba," or "Son of Rateeba."[1] That is what the boys in the neighborhood had been calling him ever since his tender age.

When we were children, we enjoyed calling him by his mother's name because everything that was unusual or peculiar aroused our interest, just as would have the birth of a two-headed calf or a three-legged chicken. We knew that referring to someone's mother's name in any way was not considered proper or respectful (although we never knew why), and whenever we did this it was for the purpose of teasing.

[1]When a person is named after the mother, as is the case here, this is regarded as an insult to the father, as children are named after the father and not the mother. It was only after Faris had demonstrated exceptional gifts of courage and leadership that he earned what everyone would normally regard as his or her natural right: the correct way to be named.

We were ready to answer any kind of question; but not one of us, not even a slower-witted one, however cleverly or cunningly he was asked, would ever answer if asked about his mother's name.

I remember one incident while we were in elementary school. Our teacher, a Christian, came in wearing a starched shirt, white as cheese, and perfectly ironed pants. Carrying his attendance book, he sat down behind his desk and called on Ghadban al-Nimr. Looking apprehensive, the boy came forward. The teacher asked him his mother's name. We laughed in astonishment at the question, and I pinched my friend's leg, whispering, "That son of a bitch! How does he know her?"

Ghadban did not answer. The teacher repeated the question, and Ghadban, anger showing overtly in his dark face, said, "What do you need *her* name for?" The teacher kept asking. In those days, Ghadban's mother was a real dark-skinned, green-eyed beauty, in the prime of her youth; Ghadban stubbornly refused to divulge her name. When the teacher slapped his face he ran out of the classroom, retaliating for his own mother's integrity by cursing the honor of the teacher's mother.

The teacher smoked an American cigarette and calmed down a little. Then he asked for me. Trembling like a goat struck by shivering December cold, I approached him. He asked me my mother's name.

"Faris," I answered, "I'll tell you *his* mother's name: it's Rateeba!"

Faris cursed my mother's honor.

Outraged, the teacher threw down his pencil and beat both Faris and me, saying, "What a bunch of primitives!"

When we complained to the headmaster and asked him what the word "primitive" was, he said it meant that we were backwards; peasants. We resented the Christian teacher even more. A man who couldn't even pronounce Arabic eloquently, and he had the gall to ask about the names of his students' mothers . . . From that day onward, we called him "Mr. Primitive."

I did not understand why Faris should have gotten so furious when I mentioned his mother's name, for everyone in our village knew him as "Son of Rateeba," even though he had a father, a man with a large, strong moustache that looked like two scorpions and who tilled the soil using a white-browed cow and a castrated donkey.

We didn't know who had given him this name, neither did he. It might have been one of his elderly neighbors, or uncles, who wanted to tease him; then, when everyone laughed and the child got angry, the name just stuck to him—and, as in a Catholic marriage, never left him.

At first his mother had expressed irritation and anger whenever we asked her about "Faris Rateeba," and she would curse our fathers. But finally she gave up and began referring to her son by the same name. His father had regarded our calling his son by his mother's name an insult to his manhood. He would curse our fathers and our grandfathers, and would call us by our own mothers' names. He even asked his son to do the same to us, pulling his ears to remind him of the retaliation that was expected of him. But in time, he gave up as well, and began to refer to his own son as "Faris Rateeba."

And why not? . . . After all, he had married his wife out of love, and everyone in the village knew it and kept on taunting her about it. For, to our village, love was something shameful: any girl who fell in love was a disgrace to her father. If he didn't kill her, then he had to strip himself of his own *kaffiyyeh* and walk around bare-headed.[2] Rateeba—as our mothers told us later—had fallen in love with Sa'eed Abu Arab. They were caught meeting behind the cactus bushes, but her father didn't kill her. Nor did he kill Abu Arab, nor strip himself of his *kaffiyyeh*. Instead, he had let the two marry, and Rateeba had left her father's house on a horse, her head held high as any other girl's. Her father believed it was best to bury the scandal; but the people didn't forget it, and so they called Faris by his mother's name, as they called the path behind the cactus bushes where the lovers had met, "Rateeba's Path."

Faris would have been a great fellow—had it not been for his mother. In summer, when the neighborhood children gathered on the threshing floor to wrestle, Faris used to embarrass us all by throwing us down one after the other. Despite the fact that we were all agreed that tripping from behind was illegal, we would always try to cheat in order to throw him down; yet it was he who would manage to throw *us*. Those who were watching would applaud and shout things like, "Hooray for the Son of Rateeba, he's just like his mother!" or, "Your mother took on your grandfather!" Then the boy would get angry and fling his opponent down off the piled straw of the threshing floor so as to hurt him, in revenge for his mother's honor.

Whenever we played and hit our "ball"—converted from a tin can—with our thick canes, and it landed near him, we would sing in shrill voices a song that referred to his mother by such names as "beloved"

[2]Women in Islamic culture cover their hair. When a woman from a conservative background goes out bare-headed, it is taken as a sign that a great calamity has befallen her or her family.

and "fetching." He would become furious and hit the ball very angrily; his oak cane would raise bloody welts on our thin legs. But we never minded, and we would joyfully continue with our singing and teasing.

And we grew older . . .

As for myself, I became a construction worker with the Solel Boneh Company. Ghadban al-Nimr became a stonecutter in Mr. Gold-schmidt's quarry, while Faris Rateeba became a cook in the Hadar Restaurant. He was a good cook; his mother, Rateeba, was very competent, and she helped cook for weddings and funerals, specializing in rice, *kubbeh*,[3] and stuffed aubergines.

But the City, dear reader, is a curse that corrupts the elderly and drives young men mad.

One Friday evening, Faris Rateeba came back to the village for his usual weekend visit with family and friends. This time, however, he came making derogatory remarks about our *mukhtar*.

"The *mukhtar* is a Government agent," he said.

"Everyone knows that," we answered.

"The *mukhtar* is corrupt," he said.

"If you're not a wolf yourself, you'll get eaten by other wolves," we answered.

"The *mukhtar* is reactionary," he said.

We laughed at the expression. What difference did it make whether the *mukhtar* was reactionary or progressive?

Still, the boy had planted a certain amount of worry and insecurity in our minds. Where on earth had he gotten that kind of talk? Who had warped him? How could he dare criticize the *mukhtar* so openly? The *mukhtar* came from a powerful family, and always had his gun by his side . . .

I must admit that, were it not for the fact that I was afraid of the *mukhtar* and that Faris' mother had been caught in her pre-marital tryst with Sa'eed Abu Arab behind the cactus bushes, I might well have voiced frankly my admiration of Faris' opinions. It is pleasant, at times, to find fault with the high and the mighty. Nevertheless, I told myself: "Keep away from the mud, or you'll get mired."

The next week on the bus, I saw him sitting by the back door with

---

[3]*Kubbeh* or *kubaibeh* is a dish made of meat and (soaked) crushed wheat, pounded together and either spread and baked on a tray, or made into hollow balls stuffed with meat fried with onions, then fried or cooked in yogurt etc. It is one of the more expensive and delicious dishes in that area of the world.

the workmen, inciting them by discussing such controversial subjects as national insurance, workers' rights, and the Builders' union.

"Unions! What rubbish!" said Ghadban al-Nimr. "Don't talk to *me* about them!"

We all laughed and made fun of him, saying, "Ghadban has got him there!" But Faris didn't bat an eye. Instead, he began talking about the right to strike.

The bus almost burst with our laughter: Go on strike! Whatever for?

But Faris didn't give up. Sweating profusely, he began to tell us of various strikes by other workers, and of what had been achieved through them.

Then Salim Antar asked him, "Whose side is our superintendent on? The people's or the government's?"

"The government's."

Salim Antar's moustache quivered as he shouted in Faris' face, "God damn your mother, do you plan on fighting the government?"

Furious at hearing his mother cursed, Faris jumped up to slap Salim's face, even though he was still a beardless youth while Salim was a full-grown man. We had to stand between them to calm them down. We advised Faris to get ahold of himself, and not to be misled by dreams and the lies of liars. It was shameful and malicious to talk of strikes, we explained. One should kiss the hand that one is unable to bite; if he didn't like working for one man, then he should look for another to work for. His boss wasn't keeping him against his will. His grandfather may have killed a hyena, we reminded him, but he had not been able to control his own daughter.

But Faris Rateeba paid no heed. A week later he went even farther and started criticizing the Government. The Government was an exploiter, he claimed, that sucked the workers' blood. Arabs had lost their rights. The Government must bring back the refugees and return the land to its owners. "This is our home," he said repeatedly, "and foreigners have come to kick us out."

"But refugees return only after a war," objected Salim Antar.

"Sooner or later, they'll come back," said Faris fervently. All of us liked this "sooner or later"—all except Salim Antar, who retorted sarcastically, "They'll come back on your father's castrated donkey!"

Finally the people on the bus split into two groups, one siding with Faris Rateeba and his "sooner or later" idea, and the other, larger group siding with Salim Antar. Faris Rateeba seemed quite pleased at having won some supporters.

But Hasan the Lisp cursed the moment Faris Rateeba had gotten on the bus. "At the end of a hard day's sweat and toil," he complained, "it's too much to have to listen to Faris Rateeba arguing politics! Politics is for people who have learned about it, in universities and in foreign countries . . . This bus ride has become depressing! Now please shut up, Faris Rateeba, or I'll curse your grandmother's grave!"

But Faris Rateeba did not stop. A week later he came back with a bunch of pamphlets, which he distributed free of charge to the workers. When some of us began reading the pamphlets and found that their purpose was to attack the government, we threw them away, to avoid trouble. To put it bluntly, we got scared.

"Who's behind all this, Son of Rateeba?" screamed Hasan the Lisp. "We need bread to eat, Boy! If you want to fight the government, then God be with you—go to Syria! Now keep quiet, or we'll kick your ass!"

But the young man did not keep quiet. Some time later he came on board with copies of a newspaper marked with a red line and walked along the aisle between the seats, showing them to the workers. When no one dared buy any, he distributed them free of charge, saying that they contained a news item about the *mukhtar* of our village: he was imposing a tax of one and one-half liras on all refugees for the cheese they were receiving from relief agencies.[4]

Two simple-minded workers bought copies. As soon as the bus reached our village and the men had gotten off onto the street, Salim and Hasan threw Faris down on the ground and beat him until he could barely move.

"Hooray for Salim and Hasan!" some cheered.

Salim sat on Faris' chest, put his hands around his neck, and said, "Ha! Are you still a Bolshevik?"

"Leave him alone," someone said. "He won't do it again . . ."

"No!" said Hasan the Lisp. "His eyes are still as rude as the words in that newspaper! He's still a Bolshevik! Maybe it's not his fault, though—his mother's a Bolshevik!"

Some interceded to stop Salim and Hasan. "The boy is still young and immature," they said. "If he had been aware of what he was saying,

[4]These refugees are probably from the '67 war, as a result of which many Palestinians were forced to leave their homes and relocate in other parts of Palestine. The cheese in question had been sent by one of several relief agencies, sponsored by the United Nations or the Jordanian government, that had been formed to ensure the basic subsistence of these refugees. These supplies are charity donations, and are not supposed to cost the recipients anything.

he never would have used words like 'reactionary' and 'sooner or later.' "

The truth is, my own heart was completely with Faris, only I was afraid of the government's retaliation. I was afraid that our village might be destroyed, and, as the proverb says, "If you do not fear a loose woman, fear her offspring."

Faris proved beyond doubt that he was bold, for a week later he began again to show the newspaper to the workers in the evening bus. Subhi, the son of Hasan the cobbler, bought a copy. Salim Antar and Hasan the Lisp were furious, but didn't dare confront the son of Rateeba directly. He had become quite reckless.

"Your tongue is not as sharp as his," Hasan the Lisp told Subhi. "He will get the better of you . . ."

When Subhi started selling newspapers and distributing leaflets with Faris Rateeba, some found this outlandish. "Two scoundrels have found each other," they said. "It won't be long before they land in prison."

Faris Rateeba acquired his own supporters: Subhi ibn Hasan; Salim, the son of the cowherd; and Samih, the son of Yusif the Watchman. So the *mukhtar*, along with a group of village elders, summoned the fathers of these young men and threatened them. But Faris Rateeba did not back down. Nor did his supporters, although Salim had good reason to be frightened, as his father's livelihood was entirely dependent on the *mukhtar*.

Then one day the son of Rateeba did it. He really did it . . .

On a Saturday evening he began shouting into a microphone, "All of you, get up and come out!" Some cursed his mother. The children, thinking there must be a free show, ran about happily. As for us, we decided to keep away from this meeting. "One ear of mud, the other of dough," we said.

Suddenly a Landrover drove up, and a dark young man with flecks of premature white in his hair stepped out and urged us all to show ourselves. No one came. "Come on, everybody, rise up!" he repeated. The children applauded. Then the newcomer came forward to the microphone and said: "Folks! Is this the proper way to receive your guests? By running away? Peasants! Workers! Students! Why didn't you come to this meeting? If you don't want to, then suit yourselves! I'll speak to the berry trees by the spring! Listen, you berry trees . . ."

And the man spoke for over an hour, just like Abd al-Nasser used to speak on the radio. He cursed the Government; he exposed the *mukhtar* and called him a Government stooge . . .

We listened from a distance. "He is talking as a man should," said one of us, and went up to the village square. One by one, we followed him. The square became filled with people, and the speaker went on eloquently, saying more and more. We applauded him eagerly. It is true that eloquent words can entice a snake out of its hole.

The *mukhtar* had warned us that the government was about to burst with anger—had it not been shameful to burst at someone as lowly as the son of Rateeba. But, for all its supposed grandeur, the government *did* confront him. It put him in jail and then set him free. It put him in jail again and set him free again, and again, and again . . .

And the boy became a necessary evil in the village. As people get used to the cold of winter, to the heat of summer, and to the fierce winds of autumn, so did our village accept the son of Rateeba and his group.

"They are atheists!" said the *imam*. "They are the ones God meant when he said in the holy *Quran*: 'These are the people who've gone astray, the people who've incurred God's wrath."

"Bolsheviks! Bolsheviks!" the *mukhtar* said.

"Reds!" said Sergeant Sharon.

We avoided the group, not even daring to talk to them in secret. We had families to think of. Nothing makes a man humble and acquiescent as his responsibility to family and children.

But the government had no wisdom. They pushed their luck too far. They pushed *us* too far, and stripped us of all possessions. After all, we were not snakes that could eat dirt. They confiscated all our lands. The school went to the Governor-General, the *Waqf*[5] land went to *Apotropus*,[6] and other land went to *Minhal*.[7] Nothing was left but Um al-Hijara.

Um al-Hijara is fertile land. On it the watermelon grows enormous, and the wheat grows so high as to hide a camel. The government had designs on it, and so did the *Apotropus*. When they sent old yellow papers to expropriate the land from us, we became incensed. What a government! It was leaving us no way out.

One day Faris ibn Rateeba heard that men from both *Apotropus* and

[5]*Waqf* lands are lands that have been put in trust with the Muslim administration.
[6]*Apotropus* is the Jewish agency in charge of the possessions of the Palestinian absentees.
[7]*Minhal* is the agency for the administration of the lands of Israel.

Minhal were coming to work the land at Um al-Hijara. He gathered his own men first, and they recruited over twenty more, and they got ready. They hid in the rugged Kharoubbeh area north of Um al-Hijara.

The moment the men from *Minhal* arrived with their equipment he gave the signal, and our men started throwing stones at them and beating them with sticks. *Minhal* men are known to be more afraid of sticks and stones than our city neighbor, Yusif al-ʻAli's wife, is of mice. They got a good beating. Suddenly a police car appeared, and out came policemen wearing armour and shields. They lasted only half an hour. Our men were fighting desperately for Um al-Hijara. The policemen abandoned their car and ran away. Five more cars arrived, then another three, and then a car full of soldiers in green berets.

It was the Battle of Um al-Hijara. Faris and his men stood up to them, resisted, and fought them back. When the soldiers tried to capture the wounded, Faris thought that it would be best, both for their safety and for maintaining the psychological and material advantages gained so far, for his men to retreat. He ordered them to do so and stood fighting the soldiers alone. Faris was wounded, captured, and thrown into a blue police car.

When the news spread to the village, Rateeba rejoiced:

> "With our souls we defend you, Um al-Hijara!
> With our soul and blood we fight for you, Faris Abu Arab!
> Mother of the martyr rejoice, for all other boys are your children!"

Everyone in the village was alerted: old men, young men, women, children—even Salim Antar and Hasan the Lisp. Carrying canes and stones, they set up barricades to block the roads and insisted on the release of Faris. Gunshots rang out. The news reached neighboring villages, and their men began to arrive and take part, and fighting erupted again. Then more tanks arrived in Um al-Hijara. Aisha was wounded, and Hanna's leg was broken.

In a procession, men and women carried Faris on their shoulders.
Faris shouted: "With our souls and blood . . ."
And the people answered: "We defend Um al-Hijara!"
"With our souls and blood . . ."
"We defend *you*, Faris!"
From that day onward, his name became Faris Saʼeed Abu Arab.

—translated by Salwa Jabsheh and Thomas G. Ezzy

Yahya Yakhlif (b. 1944)

A novelist and short story writer born in Samakh, a town in the vicinity of Tiberias, Yakhlif has lived as a refugee most of his life, while working for the Palestine cause. For many years he was secretary-general of the Union of Palestinian Writers and Journalists and he still works for Palestinian cultural advancement. He is well read in Western literature in translation and has had many volumes of fiction published. His short story collections include, *The Mare* (1972) and *Norma and the Ice Man* (1978); his three novels are: *Najran at Zero Point* (1976), a novel which brought him immediate fame and recognition; *Apples of Lunatics* (1981); and *Song of Life* (1985). His novella *That Rose of a Woman* (1981), based on a real life story, is one of the most moving pieces of fiction in Palestinian literature.

That Rose of a Woman

I waited for her in the morning. I was carrying good news and I sat on a stone in the street waiting anxiously. I waited a long time before she finally appeared. She put out her hand. Shaking it, I felt I held a breathing bird.

"Why are you sitting here?"

"I've been waiting to tell you good news!"

We had worked together during that long, spreading and harsh summer in the factory that produced Turkish Delight. I was a humiliated, overworked child who carried within him the wrinkles of a much older man. She was a young woman with a calm face and silent eyes. Her hair always hid beneath a red scarf that lit up her face and reddened her cheeks. Working at the factory in front of the oven was nearly more than we could tolerate, particularly during that blazing summer that tasted like hot pepper. No one could stand it except for those who had graduated from the physical fitness course at the refugee camp's youth center. That's why it was impossible for anyone like me, who only ate cooked eggplants in tomato paste, to tolerate the working conditions for more than a few hours without fainting and collapsing, never to return to work again.

In spite of that rough summer, my heart throbbed delicately like the wings of a squab about to fly for the first time. The small boy wearing my clothes walked side by side with Intissar, that rose of a woman, a few years his senior, to the end of the street where the roads branched out. At night, anemone flowers awoke in his heart, and wild birds took off from his chest.

Once someone spilled some of the ground sugar that coats the Turkish Delight onto my clothes. Intissar rushed over to lick it off. I spontaneously held her and licked what rubbed off onto her clothes. We were happy as naked children bathing in a pool.

I waited for her next morning, I was carrying good news. I waited a long time before she appeared, munching an apple. She was curious: "What's up?"

I said, "There is going to be a wedding at our house."

"Whose wedding?"

"One of my mother's relatives is getting married at our house!"

Happiness filled her face.

That same day there were rumors that Ox, the owner of the factory we worked in, was dead. Death made Intissar's face stern. I tried to ease things by saying it was just a rumor, then went on talking to her about the wedding that would happen and the sweet drinks of rose water and raisins and lemonade that we would serve.

She turned round several times like an impatient filly and then asked, "How can a person find your house?"

I was that young boy walking from the tin shacks to town every day, while the hot sun penetrated my head. I was the boy who stayed in bed for a long time each year due to malnutrition and anemia.

I was that small unripe boy who wore open sandals summer and winter and never went out to the swings on holidays because his clothes were always patched.

I was the boy who stood with the bowed head in the line up of poor students, who had to wait his turn to drink a glass of milk during the morning break. I was that child, tearful, unripe, with bowed head, who did not like the cod liver capsules given free at Dr. Dahmash's clinic, who sold newspapers at the Mowahhad Garage or boiled corn cobs at the doors of the cinema.

I worked hard during that long, sprawling summer. I mean, we worked hard together during that harsh, interminably long summer.

In the factory that produced Turkish Delight, I was a child and she a young woman with a calm face, silent eyes, and hair that always disappeared behind a scarf—her name was Intissar—may her heart fill up with joy wherever she is now, that rose of a woman.

The factory was an old-fashioned one still using primitive methods. Our job was to fill up various sizes of cartons and boxes with the small pieces of fragrant sweets and later spread powdered sugar over them.

The factory manager sat facing us from a high place, supervising the flow of work and forbidding us to speak to one another. Most of the workers were from the refugee camp and worked during their summer holidays until it was time to go back to school. There were some elderly women as well, and only one young woman. And there was no end to the prohibitions. It was forbidden to speak to one's neighbor, or to urinate more than once a day. Forbidden to chew anything in one's mouth. Forbidden to snatch any of the tasty Turkish Delights which were soft and smelling of rose water. Forbidden to slip one in one's pocket to eat later or slip it into one's younger brother's mouth.

The factory manager stayed seated while tea and food were brought to him. The water pipe was placed at his side. A shoeshine man arrived before him, as did watermelon and grapes. The wholesalers and retailers came to him. He wrote receipts, received money, and issued IOU notes.

And he was never absent. He always arrived before us and left after us. He counted us one by one, deducting the daily wages of whoever was late, kicking out anyone late more than twice. Crowds of children from the refugee camp gathered at the door waiting for the chance to be offered work. He screened his employees constantly with his eyes, and searched anyone who trembled or paled. If anyone was caught hiding a piece of sweet in his clothes he was slapped and his wages for the day deducted. Then he would be transferred from his job of filling up boxes to working in front of the unbearably hot oven where the dough was made. If you fainted you lost your job forever.

In that same factory overflowing with cruelty, my heart experienced for the first time the delicate flutter of a small dove's wings, opening up for the first flight.

One day we had lunch together during the break. She had placed her lunch on mine, for we worked side by side. We ate boiled eggs and onion and a box of sardines and some salt and dry falafel. We ate and drank water. We had the chance to talk about the back pain we suffered from bending all day, filling boxes. We also talked a little about the bull of a man who never released us from work until after dark, when the pain had already constricted the muscles of our calves. Our blessed luncheon did not last long as the factory warden soon announced the end of break and we returned to our jobs where we whispered without looking at one another. Every hour or so we glanced out the window, impatient for the shadow of the setting sun.

After that luncheon the little boy walked side by side with that rose of a woman up to the end of the street where the roads crossed. And at night the anemone flowers awakened in his heart and birds sprang out of his chest.

One day the Bull Man was absent. His chair remained empty like an opened astonished mouth.

The guard came and told us: "Come on, work!" No one really feared the guard, for his personality and authority had long been swallowed up by the personality of the Bull Man. We started working slowly without enthusiasm.

Later on, Sabir, the handsome young man who worked with us filling up the boxes, started singing aloud. Everyone was surprised at first; his voice was like a piece of clear glass that fell from above into our little repressed domain. But after a while, the singing became contagious—the mood let loose. We ate sweets without fear, we jumped over the sacks. When someone poured some powdered sugar onto my clothes, Intissar rushed to lick it off.

That day Intissar and I licked and played. We felt real joy, and we were like naked children swimming in a pool. That evening, we went home without permission from the guard. At the end of the road going home, we shook hands for the first time. I had to stand on tiptoe to give the impression that I was nearly as tall as she.

Next morning I waited for her.

I was carrying good news.

I sat on a stone at the side of the road and waited anxiously.

I waited a long time before she appeared, munching an apple. She shook hands with me and I felt as if a bird were fluttering in my heart.

"What's up?"

I said, "There's going to be a wedding at our house."

"Whose wedding?" she asked, gracefully.

"One of my mother's relatives is getting married at our house."

"And will there be music and singing and dancing?"

I nodded and joy filled her face.

She overflowed with questions. Is the bride beautiful? Does she have a golden tooth? Has she bought bracelets and rings? Has she bought a white dress and makeup and a pin for her hair? Will they be living alone or with her husband's family?

She asked me questions all the way to work and I managed to find answers.

I was imagining roses unfolding, fields of gleaming wheat, wild horses running in the wilderness, and a clear moon that descended from its place to walk by my side.

I imagined the red bell-like flowers of the pomegranate pinned on young women's hair and their lips dyed crimson from eating mulberries.

She was asking and I was growing happier and happier. And for the second day the Bull Man was absent.

Our friends in the factory sat in circles. No one knew what was happening. Rumors spread that the Bull Man was dead.

Intissar frowned at the mention of death. Sabir said, "If he's dead, why doesn't someone else come to pay us our wages?"

We sat in a corner full of sugar sacks as the older men sorted things out. I kept exaggerating my descriptions of the forthcoming wedding party at our home, and told her of the lemonade and the raisin and rose water that would be offered, and of the almond candies and the other sweets. And I invited her to come.

She frowned and stared at her clothes and her hands. The idea seemed to frighten her. Suddenly, she got up, like a wayward filly, and went to a circle of older people discussing their wages and rights.

Sabir had opened a sack of sugar and was siphoning it into cones of paper, distributing it to the workers and rejoicing, "Drink sweetened tea tonight, make your children *'aseeda*[1] with syrup!"

Intissar was still restless when she returned and asked again, "How can a person get to your house?"

I began describing the way to her. Her expression was grave as if she were looking into a mirror and fixing her hair.

My mother opened the cupboard and removed my white shirt and long navy-blue pants. Early that morning she had swept the two adjoining rooms and the yard and watered the sweet-smelling tree and

---

[1] A dish, sweet or savory, made up of flour or semolina, fried in butter and, when sweet, drenched with sugar syrup.

the mint pots. From her wedding trunk she removed sheets and cushion covers and tablecloths—her precious things that she rarely used. She polished the windows and prepared a meal of rice and boiled meat in honor of the bride.

By afternoon the first celebratory ululations were heard and the bride began to get ready. Neighborhood girls appeared wearing their very best clothes.

My job was to stand in the yard and keep children out.

The fat woman down the road began beating her drum, which signaled the beginning of merriment.

Now the children I had shooed away began climbing on top of one another's shoulders to see what was happening inside the wall of the courtyard. My eyes kept veering away from my task to the road that led to town. When the children tired of jumping, they looked for another game. They made a circle around an old fig tree that had no leaves and had lost most of its branches to old age. On sunny days the women used it for airing out cushions and quilts and door mats.

Finally she arrived, accompanied by an elderly man wearing a blue beret and a worn navy-blue suit. He looked like one of those Armenians who sold sausages and pastrami sandwiches.

She was wearing a red dress, a woolen shawl, and red lipstick on her mouth. She looked ready for an evening of fun. "That's my father," she said, pointing at the man. She said he would come back to fetch her. The man raised his beret and bowed. She entered the door of our house with great familiarity, as if she had been there before. I ran to my mother and told her the friend I had personally invited had arrived. My mother rose and walked towards Intissar, warmly took her arm, and seated her next to the bride.

When I went back to my position outside, the old man was walking away with a cigarette in his hand. He was humming a tune or a song. For some reason he reminded me of the fig tree and its determination to survive.

After the guests had all arrived I stood in the doorway facing Intissar, who smiled at me. She seemed in a spell of happiness.

Did the child grow several years and several inches at that moment?

The fat woman with her heavily madeup face beat the drum ferociously. And girls began dancing. One was skinny and couldn't match the beat, another was in the early months of pregnancy and danced carefully. A third was pale and looked like a fly that had landed on its back and now struggled to right itself.

The bride's mother moved among the guests, offering sweets, making lavish welcomes, and wishing abundant good luck to everyone.

Suddenly the fat woman stopped beating the drum. She asked for the lantern to heat the drum's leather and make it more responsive. As she played harder, the bride's mother pulled Intissar to the dance floor.

She stood there, shy. My face blushed. Moments later she threw her shawl aside and started dancing. The skinny girl left the floor first, followed by the pregnant woman. The flylike dancer had to be pulled by her dress to sit down.

I stared at Intissar, alone on the dance floor, unbelievingly. I looked from one face to another to see what they thought of my moon and my rose. Hands began clapping as she moved her feet lightly and swiveled her waist. Her delicate hands braided the air. How could one woman be so many things? A lioness, a breeze, a hurricane and a tame dove.

Her dance was ferocious. The drum beats grew louder and louder. Hands clapped, and blood flowed hot in the veins. One moment she was like a high undulating wave, then she would recede, her movement dissipating like froth. Her dancing then would have the taste of tears. The bride's mother yelled, "More! More!" Intissar looked at no one as her feet knocked the floor. She was freeing herself of anger, she was spitting out rust! She tended the herd of the clouds. Suddenly she would shiver, smile, and soften. Remembering that she had to please the guests, she would return to the tune. Bridges extended outwards toward the pale girls and fat women, toward the eyes that experienced happiness only once a year.

Toward the end of the evening, the pregnant woman who had danced earlier, announced that her golden bracelet was lost. She shouted angrily, praying to God to break the hand that stole her treasure from her handbag. Argument broke out among the women and joy turned into silence, then dejection.

The pregnant woman accused ten women at once and the bride's mother suggested she search all the guests.

No one objected to this humiliating procedure. But I felt as if someone were looking at my private parts. When it was Intissar's turn to be searched, I wanted to knock the pregnant woman down and step on her head. But I did nothing. The pregnant woman touched her breasts, her hips, and asked her to take off her shoes. Suddenly she held Intissar's purse and shouted, "Here it is! Things bought with hard-earned money never get lost!"

She held onto Intissar's hair, shouting, "This woman is a thief! She infiltrated our camp to steal our bracelets!" Intissar's voice was weak. "I bought that bracelet myself," she said. "It is my very own bracelet." She looked toward me for confirmation. I was frightened. I nodded at her for assurance. The bride's mother came over and guided Intissar toward the door even as she was reiterating her claim that it was her own bracelet, bought with money earned by the sweat of her brow. The bride's mother closed the door behind her, saying, "Thank God the thief was not one of us." She kissed the pregnant woman's cheeks, led her back to her place, and offered her more sweets. She wanted everyone to be joyous again.

When my mother tried to ululate, her voice sounded wounded.

Outside, Intissar walked away behind the old man who had been waiting for her near the fig tree. They were swallowed by darkness.

The bridegroom came to take his bride. The women left, and the bride's mother went home without tasting the rice and boiled meat. Empty chairs and garbage filled the room. The white woolen shawl was still thrown over a chair, like a petal off its rose. My mother left everything as it was and went to bed.

Before that I saw tears in her eyes. (I remember them years later, so vividly, the color of crystal shining.) She spoke as if talking to herself, "God damn us, we never rejoice for very long."

At dawn a hard knock was heard at our door. It awakened my mother. (I had not slept a wink.) That despicable pregnant woman entered, bowed down, and started to cry. "Last night I was wrong to accuse that girl," she said. "When I went home I found my bracelet in my drawer."

She pulled out both bracelets, cried harder, and said, "Look at them! Aren't they exactly alike?"

My mother nodded her head sadly.

The pregnant woman told me, "Take the girl's bracelet back to her and tell her I kiss her hands and her feet. Ask for her forgiveness. I'm pregnant and can't tolerate the curse of an innocent girl."

My mother calmed her down and made her a cup of coffee. The bracelet lay in front of me like a time bomb about to explode.

Why did Intissar accept insult so quietly? Why didn't she flatten mountains and shake the whole world?

The next morning. The last morning. The morning of iron moments. I carried my packed lunch, the white shawl, and the bracelet that only fit the wrist of a woman like a rose.

The door of the factory was locked. That seemed odd. I knocked twice. The door opened and a strange man stood there. His fingers were big and harsh like the hooves of a cow. "What do you want?"

"I work here," I said. He told me to wait. I felt that something was going on inside. I don't know why the place reminded me of a slaughterhouse. When I was admitted, I saw more new guards carrying clubs.

The workers were all standing straight like we would do in school when the teacher walked in. High up there was the Bull Man holding an iron rod.

When I entered all eyes turned towards me but no one spoke. I stood at my usual place next to her. I didn't dare meet her eyes and she gave no sign of welcome. The silence was terrible. Then the Bull Man bellowed, "Doesn't anyone intend to confess?" He called up the guard whom we had all ignored during his absence. He yelled at him, "Who did that to the sugar sacks?" The guard was trembling. I looked at Intissar. Her face was dry and lifeless. Her dancing face had vanished. The Bull Man shouted, "You traitor!" And he brought the iron rod down on the guard's head. The guard swayed and fell to the ground.

Sweat, red and green veins, flowing blood. A thumping heart, a chest that goes up and down. Suddenly Sabir stepped forward. The handsome Sabir, tender as mint leaves. He stepped forward with his pale face and his rich hair, leaving his lunch behind him. Was he trembling? The Bull Man, still shouting uncontrollably, said, "So it was *you* who did it! You son of a bitch!" I saw him raise the rod high, bring it down on Sabir's shoulder. Sabir swayed back and forth with an agonized face, then toppled down.

It was then that Intissar dropped her lunch bag. I stared at her trembling face. She was splintering apart. And she stepped forward, one step, then two.

She let out a piercing scream, a long scream of torment, then scratched the Bull Man's face with her nails. He was shocked and he screamed too. Some of the new guards rushed forward to pull her back. She spat in their faces as they pulled her hair to drag her away.

She spat and swore, again and again, all the swearing words usually used in the Beirut slums. I couldn't keep from following her. They threw her out the gate.

We walked together. She was silent between her tears. Her hair was wild. Her eyes stared straight ahead, penetrating.

Why had she kept quiet last night? She resisted so slightly—Why didn't she flatten mountains and shake the whole world?

At the crossroads she raised her hand to arrange her hair. Her look was telling me goodbye.

The universe shrank. I handed her the shawl and the bracelet. She showed no sign of surprise. She put her hand out to me, withdrew it, turned her back, and walked away.

When I returned to the camp on that hard, hard morning, the people had already left for their daily work. Only children and widows were relaxing on their doorsteps.

The dry fig tree was still clinging to life, and an old woman was draping a baby's diapers over its boughs that spread out like horns.

—translated by Salwa Jabsheh and Naomi Shihab Nye

Selections from Novels

Sahar Khalifeh *(b. 1941)*

One of the foremost Palestinian novelists, Sahar Khalifeh was born in Nablus and has become well known for her feminist stances. As a very young woman, she entered into a traditionally arranged marriage; then, after thirteen years of frustrations and disappointments, she found her freedom and decided to dedicate herself to writing. She resumed her studies and obtained a Ph.D. from the University of Iowa in 1988 in women's studies and American literature. She now works as Director of the Women's Affairs Center in Nablus and Gaza. Sahar Khalifeh has written five novels so far. Her early novel, *We Are No More Your Slave Girls*, made quite an impact because of its advocacy of feminist freedom, but it was with the appearance of her third novel, *Wild Thorns*, in 1976, that she received literary recognition and acclaim. This novel was translated into Hebrew, French, German, Dutch, and, in 1985, into English by Trevor LeGassick and Elizabeth Fernea for PROTA. The following excerpt is from her fourth novel, *Memoirs of an Unrealistic Woman* (1986), a book already translated into Italian and German. In her work, Sahar Khalifeh expresses her deep belief that feminist consciousness is an integral part of political consciousness, and the struggle and tribulations of Palestinian women are shown, in an artistic and convincing manner, to be part of the general political Palestinian struggle for liberation. Her style is sensitive, economical, and lucid; although she writes in modern Arabic, her language is deeply rooted in the Palestinian vocabulary and general idiom.

From Memoirs of an Unrealistic Woman

As the emptiness grew deeper, so would my own sense of inner void. My head would spin as if enclosed within the eye of a needle. The more events crushed me, the more submissive I'd become. Then my submissiveness would lead on to contentment, and I'd pray to God to send me more occasions for it. The virtues of my husband would become clearer to me, and I'd blame myself for not seeing them earlier.

If he brought something new for the house, I'd thank God that he wasn't mean with money; and if he no longer spent repeated evenings out of the house, I'd thank God our life had become settled. If he ordered me to perform some stupid service, I'd thank God he'd come to depend on me in large or small matters. The days would pass and I'd feel tranquil and secure; all memories of his faults would fade, would become mere phantoms, to be driven firmly and decisively from my mind. Then, when he returned to his old ways, I'd be devastated, and blame myself for his waywardness. "If you weren't barren, Afaf," I'd tell myself, "your house would be full of sound and movement, and the children would draw him towards you. If you weren't so listless, he wouldn't have tired of your dull company. If you weren't so plain-looking, he wouldn't have desired other women." In a desperate attempt to repair what life had destroyed, I'd begin to make the house and myself more attractive. I'd turn the house upside down, wash the window panes with soap until they gleamed like diamonds, and scrape the floor till it was like a mirror; lay the coverlets and blankets and pillows to air at the windows and on the balcony rails, and put his suits in the sun till the vapour rose from them. I'd go to the market too, and buy meat and vegetables, taking care to choose the largest and freshest: cucumbers that had kept their first freshness, tomatoes that were still half green, potatoes lovely as a full moon, and okras and green beans and cauliflowers and radishes. I'd come back home proud of my vegetables and my fridge full of good things, and thank God because I lived the best of lives.

Then I'd begin to make myself more attractive. I'd stand in front of the mirror inspecting my clothes. Here was a dark-colored dress which I should change for a lighter one, and there was a light-colored one which I should change for a darker one; here was a short dress whose hem I must let down, and there was a long dress which I must change for a short one, or shorten the dress itself. I'd spend days lengthening and shortening, buying and window-shopping. I'd make a full inventory of all the windows in the shopping center and all the sales going on in town, spend all the money I had. Then, when he'd stopped drinking for a while, and the bags had gone from under his eyes, I'd say, with silly coquetry, wearing my best dress, "Here, Mahmoud, give me some money, I'm broke." I'd throw open the fridge and show him the good things stacked up inside, then lay my new clothes down on the bed until you couldn't see the bedspread under them any more, and go joyfully round them, hoping he'd be glad. He'd smile grudgingly and say, "Is that the best you can do!" And I'd cry, "What's wrong with the way we live? Thank your God, Mahmoud, and don't deny your blessings. Your house is the cleanest and brightest in the neighborhood, your wife's cooking is the best, and you and I are the best of people." He'd dip his hand in his pocket and hand over a stack of dinars. "Take this," he'd mutter, "and be quiet." So I'd take it and be quiet; and, day by day, I'd grow quieter still, till one day I'd break down and cry, then grow calm, and go back to my old listless ways. The fridge would become empty and the house would gather dust everywhere. A windstorm would blow and the windowpanes would become as dirty as sandpaper, and I'd sleep and sleep. I'd beg God to grant me a new light to disperse my darkness even for a few days, so I could gather the strength to continue my trip in the wilderness. God would answer my prayer and things would improve. My husband would smile and the sky would fill with a light that made my spirit overflow, that I'd drink to the depths as avidly as someone lost in the desert. This would provide me with the strength to step further into the burning heat of the wilderness. Whenever I fell back into listlessness, a spark would leap up again, giving me new strength to take further steps, and so on, endlessly.

The more I walked on, the less possible it became to return to my starting point when I was still a young girl toying with painting and reading pamphlets and defying the family. That was all clouded now. Indeed it had vanished, lost in the labyrinth of a shaken memory; it was no more than a remote dream, a mere illusion. Whenever that dream drove me through its many coils, I'd rebuke myself. "Be realistic, Afaf!" I'd say. "Be realistic!"

I often heard my father say that, may God rest his soul; and I'd hear my mother say those words too, whenever I met her and complained to her about my predicament. The same words would come from the women as they gathered round their coffee and read fortunes in the cups. The word "fate" was the refrain of a kind of communal song repeated by the womenfolk. One woman would begin by unburdening her inner soul, revealing the ruin of her life in an intimate gathering, unfolding the contents of her heart and the scrapbook of her sorrows; and she'd cry, and draw on her cigarette, and describe her husband in the ugliest terms, giving him vicious nicknames and calling down curses and misfortunes on him. Then, when she heard the horn of his car outside, she'd pull herself together, wipe her face, smooth her hair and dress, look at the lowered eyes with a kind of shared emotion, then whisper the words of wisdom: "That's our fate!" The words would be repeated by dry lips avidly smoking, and undulate like the echo of a common "Amen."

At the beginning I never said "Amen." But the deeper I went into the wilderness, into the desert of thirst and darkness, the dimmer the starting point became till it was a mere dream and the more I began to believe I should school myself to the realism I was said to lack. Realism meant accepting things as they were, adjusting to them, going along with them to the point of dying to preserve them. I'd remember the stories, some long, some short, that had fixed the whole intricate picture in my mind; the stories of women whom I'd heard, in those distant gatherings, call down curses and misfortunes—death and chronic deformities even—on their husbands. But if one of them became widowed or divorced, or if her husband took another wife alongside her, she'd fill the world with her crying and wailing. Once I phoned to congratulate a woman on her divorce, and she cursed me and slammed the receiver down. I stood stunned near the telephone, unable to believe what I'd heard, persuading myself, finally, that I'd dialled the wrong number or misunderstood what she said. So I rang her again and began the conversation more carefully. She sighed. "Oh, yes, Afaf!" she burst out. "Your heart does you credit, and so do your brains! Good riddance to him, you say? Why good riddance, you fool? He divorces me, and I'm supposed to rejoice? Who'll bring up the children? Him or me? And won't I have to pursue him through the courts, asking him for child support and begging him to leave me this child or that for another year, or even a few more months?[1] And if I should forget about him, would the children forget? And if he takes them away from me and burns my heart with anguish, who will I live for, and where? With my brothers, under the feet of their wives?"[2]

When I heard this, things became clear in my mind. "And you, Afaf," I said to myself, "where would you live? Under the feet of your own brothers' wives?"

I had marvelous brothers, who knew how to usurp a woman's rights. They're actually very respectable men, even though, when our father died, they snatched his inheritance before he was cold in his grave, leaving nothing to us girls except the family name and its good stock.

---

[1] In Islam, a divorced mother keeps her son until he is seven and her daughter until she is nine. Then they go to live with their father.

[2] In Islam, men are responsible by law for supporting their womenfolk. When a woman in traditional society gets divorced, she will be supported first by her father, then, if he is deceased, by one of her brothers; this means that she has to go and live with him and his family, a situation which can engender much tension and hurt. Khalifeh is speaking here of women in traditional society, for whom the ancient law is still applicable. Today, educated women would shun this reliance and opt for independence.

I tried to spur my sisters to action. "What about our share?" I asked them. They repeated, with one voice, "That's our fate!" So there was more than one meaning and tune to the same word! And more than one heavenly reward! Since that time I've learned to repeat the words "our fate" with even greater conviction, and begun to realize their force with utter clarity. And since that time my husband hasn't missed a single opportunity to bring the matter up, to try and stop me taking pride in my family and its great repute, and in the fact that my father was an inspector of schools, more learned than anyone else round about. At a time when fingerprints were people's signatures, my father was writing reports and using the dictionary, looking for the roots of verbs and the meaning of difficult words. My husband used to feel inferior when my father was mentioned, especially when his own was mentioned too. His father was almost illiterate, and was married to two women and had a dozen children, mostly girls, all of them married to men with no money or status—in contrast to my sisters, who were all married to men with good jobs and high social standing; one of them was a deputy minister, and another was a bank manager, and a third was an ambassador. As for my brothers, one was a doctor, the second an engineer, and the third a lawyer. I came, then, from a family of high standing and lineage, and my husband used to regard this as my best quality. But when he heard the story of the inheritance, he was furious and began taunting me with my family, and I had nothing left to boast of.

In a desperate attempt to regain my status with him, I hurried home, crossing the deserts, and the bridge, and the river,[3] and said to my sisters, "Come on, let's go." "Where?" they asked. "Come with me," I insisted, "and you'll see." They followed me out of curiosity—or desperation perhaps—and we sought the counsel of the family elders, who advised us to close our eyes. "Shame on you!" they said. "Each of your husbands is worth a ton of gold!" "And what if we should get divorced?" I said, continuing the argument. A single cry issued from all their throats, including my sisters': "God preserve us from your evil words, God preserve us from your evil words!" Everyone gazed into my sisters' eyes, then my sisters gazed into one another's eyes, then they all gazed at me. I was accused, among other things, of being

---

[3]Afaf is speaking here of crossing the Jordan river to the West Bank where her family lived. It is clear from the novel that she lived with her husband in one of the oil countries. The bridge is one of two bridges across the Jordan where Palestinians visiting their homes or relatives in the West Bank are searched and inspected by the Israelis.

rebellious; that's the way I'd always be, they said, however good my life was. And they agreed that I'd been like that since childhood. I asked what they meant by this, but they didn't deign to answer, and turned to my sisters, ignoring me completely. My sisters were cleverer than me. They absorbed the general mood around them and repeated again, "God preserve us from her evil words!"

We left after I'd been given such a lesson in "fate" that I'd learned it by heart. I began repeating the word in my memory lest I forget it; I'd begin the day, every morning, with the word "fate" and end it with the same, in a whisper at first, then in a loud voice, until with time I became convinced of its wisdom. One day, by chance, I happened upon a political article that greatly impressed me, and, adopting some of its political jargon, said to myself, "It's true, I'm one of the oppressors, not one of the oppressed." My cause was finally lost.

One day I felt a sudden sense of awakening and repeated my protest to one of my sisters. She said, "It would be shameful, Afaf, for us to fight our brothers." The sons of our father deserve his money more than sons-in-law who are perfect strangers. "And what about us?" I screamed. "We're the wives of those strangers," she answered. "And what if those strangers should divorce us?" I retorted. "Afaf!" she shouted. "You're nearly thirty. Grow up! Be realistic!" "Do you think it's so unlikely?" I shouted back. "What guarantee do we have?"

"The only person who can guarantee it is you," she said. "Try and understand. Men need patient handling. What can I tell you? Shall I tell you about my husband's bad temper? About the constant burden of living with him and his violent reactions to the smallest thing? But it's all in the family and hushed up, thank God. Everyone knows your husband spends long evenings out and goes in for certain things, but mine? No one knows about my suffering. We don't let it out!" I clutched her arm. "Tell me!" I begged. "Tell me!" She stopped abruptly, suddenly realizing what she'd said. Then she shot me a look full of suspicion, and I started laughing. I remembered how my mother, sisters, brothers, and all the other members of the family never trusted me with a secret; they used to warn one another, "Don't tell that chatterbox!" The warning was always an encouragement to my nose, ever eager for stories, to start twitching, and I'd begin sniffing around and searching. I'd resort to reading Sherlock Holmes and Arsène Lupin and learning enough to keep looking till I found out. Then I'd stand on a chair or a bed or by the window, and shout, "I've got it, I've got it, at last!" My mother would shout, "God! Take her to You and release me!" "If you'd trusted me," I'd retort, "I wouldn't have said anything. But I will now, I'll let the whole world know!" But I never really revealed things outside the family, because I was always ready to make a deal. I'd agree to exchange one secret for another, and one story for another. That's how I built up such a rich collection of tales and anecdotes.

My sister gave me another suspicious look. I pointed to my nose. "Shall I start sniffing?" I said. "Be quiet," she said in desperation, "all that I need is you! Take it from me, Afaf, some husbands are sugar-coated, and some are open books, and others are stealthy like a snake in the grass." "Amen!" I shouted, as if totally amazed. "Oh, yes, Amen!" She sensed the sarcasm in my answer and shouted back, "By God, if my husband was like yours, I'd get every last thing I wanted! But you're an imbecile a million times over!" I winked at her. "Do you mean blackmail?" I said. As she walked away, she shrugged and muttered, "Call it blackmail if you like. What do you call the situation we're in?"

I rushed to her, laughing as I kissed her. I always laughed when I saw how people's reactions revealed their inner secrets; I was totally the opposite of how I'd been when I was still very young and pure, and refused to compromise with any kind of falsehood and insincerity. In those days, when I discovered a situation like this, I'd go out of my mind and start screaming, and my mother would shout, "God! Take her to You and release me!" But now, as I saw my sister reveal those things we'd discovered on the path of life wherever we found a foothold for ourselves, I couldn't stop myself laughing and laughing until my eyes and heart were drowned in tears.

And so I came closer to being realistic. I no longer thought of divorce as a solution to my problem; in fact divorce was a great source of fear, equaled only by my fear of marriage. For what could I do without the marriage? Years of my life had passed without my having any other profession except marriage, and even this I hadn't mastered according to the rules: I wasn't a fruitful wife who'd filled the house with children, and I wasn't the obedient servant, and I wasn't particularly endowed with beauty, or money, or coquetry. Besides, I wasn't in the least happy. I wasn't happy in my wretchedness, or in my husband's humiliation of me, or in his own self-reproach when he felt ashamed of himself and wanted to change. I wasn't happy in my present state, or happy contemplating the future. The present was a continuation of the past and the future was a continuation of the present. What would I do, in any case, if I got divorced? Where would I live and how? Father was dead, and Mother was old now, living with my older brother. My sister-in-law was hot-tempered and irritable as a reaction to my own brother's temper and irritability. My other brothers were no better, and nor were their wives. Each one, in fact, had his own responsibilities and burdens, just as he had his own "wise and correct" outlook on things I considered pointless. They were so intent and fixed on these things that they had no time to think about anything else. Whenever one of them saw me reading a newspaper or a book, he'd smile and say, "There's our philosopher again!" And I, for my part, would retort, "There's our empty vessel again!" I'd say it silently, with the expression in my eyes. But since the language of the eyes is well-known and easily understood, they always knew exactly what I meant.

So I ended up being realistic and unrealistic at once. Realistic because I knew divorce wouldn't bring any solution, and unrealistic because the thought of it haunted me night and day, in my dreams and in my prayers. Realistic because I kept my house spotless so as not to give him the least excuse to take any final action against me, and unrealistic because (for all his suspicions about me) I remained faithful and solitary. But I wasn't really solitary. I had my cat, Anbar, the sink, the dishes, the kitchen knife, and the clothes lines.

—translated by Salwa Jabsheh and Christopher Tingley

Faruq Wadi *(b. 1949)*

A novelist, short story writer, and critic, Wadi was born in Bireh, near Jerusalem, then went to study in Jordan, obtaining a B.A. in psychology from the University of Jordan. He is very active in the literary life of Jordan and is constantly in touch with men and women of letters in the Arab world. He has participated in many literary conferences and film festivals. His collection of short stories, *Exile, My Love!*, appeared in 1976; his novel *Road to the Sea* (1980) won fame and instant recognition for its deeply penetrating depiction of the human spirit slowly discovering itself, and its reflection of feelings hitherto rarely addressed with such candor and such a decorous approach.

From A Road to the Sea

Father was happy to have finally arrived. He was eating my aunt's food and telling her about my mother. "She's in good health, and will come with us next time. And you, sister, how are you? Miserable? Everything's miserable. Here, and there."

My father had asked me, "Shall we go to al-Muzair'a first, or to Jaffa so you can see the sea?" Time had stopped, waiting for my answer.

My longing was all for the sea, and Father's longing for the land. I paused a long moment, facing the question and the wrinkled face. His memory had fed me stories of both land and sea, and now he was asking the difficult question, adding in a conspiratorial tone what would likely give him the desired response, "From Muzair'a you can see the sea, since it overlooks Jaffa."

He repeated his question democratically: "What shall it be, the land or the sea?"

I said, "We'll go to the land first."

The words slipped across my tongue gently, in a tone bent on fulfilling Father's wish. He seemed relieved, his tension disappeared. An old hope glowed in his face, shining with secret desires, lit up. I consoled myself thinking I would see the sea from there, and the streets burned under the wheels of the car.

We left the gloom of Ramallah behind us in the distance. Ramallah, which had many years ago bidden good-bye to its last summer, always seemed to be huddling into itself, dreaming of another summer. The region called Batn al-Hawa, the Belly of the Wind, on the outskirts of the town, opened up to a rich and pure breeze. For there you could bid good-bye to the town; and it welcomed you back at the same place. From the car window we could smell the rich aroma of cocoa, for the chocolate factories were still where they had been. We used to look for the key to the cupboard that Mother would hide in a secret place that was never secret. We could smell the fragrance of cocoa, while the delicious little pieces melted into our teeth. Mother would scream, "You've eaten them . . . What am I to offer the guests?"

Now our driver was saying, "Batn al-Hawa! The purest air in the world!"

He breathed deeper, filling his lungs, and my father did the same.

Crickets buzzed among wild thickets of trees, their incessant humming scratching the solemn silence of the place.

We passed Betonya. Now the humming disappeared, and silence dominated the village whose houses were scattered to the right of the road, while the fields stretched to the left. I could see the furrowed spaces at the base of the mountain slopes stretching wide, lined with grooves which the sun left in a land that sucked sea water. I could remember the days of the tiny sea. Rain water poured toward this place, from the sky, from the top of the mountain, from the side of the street, or oozed out of the land itself, gathering on the land at the foot of the slope. We would cross the hills under the sun rays that appeared after days of incessant rain, and come to Betonya to see its sea. It was really no sea at all, but we regarded it as such after our feet had been wounded from walking and hopping across the mountain rocks. We would contemplate the "sea" for a moment, then strip off our clothes and jump in to embrace the water. We believed we were embracing the real sea. We would dive and plunge and swim till evening came. Then we would return home, exhausted, across the mountains. Mother would scream from the distance as she saw me coming. "Where were you? My heart was burning up with worry . . . where *were* you?"

My damp, dishevelled hair with mud still clinging to it would expose me.

"I was at the sea!"

"What sea?" she'd return, angrily. "What muddy sea are you talking about?"

"In Betonya."

She would peel the mud off my skin as I stood naked in the basin, surrendering to the water's warmth and the smell of soap and the loofah scrubbing my body raw. I listened to her voice. "What sea is this? There's no sea left? They've[1] taken all the seas. Jaffa's sea, and Haifa's sea, and Gaza's sea and the sea of Majdal. They've taken all the seas. Mud! Nothing but mud! Look at the water under your feet! It's all mud!"

The water under my feet was all mud. They'd taken the seas and left this sea of mud for me. I asked my father about the real sea's color and he said it was more blue than the sky. So it's not just the color of mud then? I asked how big it was and Father said the eyes could not measure it. I knew then that my mother's seas were all one big continuous sea stretching along the country's coast.

And I kept longing for the sea. When I answered his "Land or the sea?" question with, "Land first," I kept my longing secret. "From our village I shall see the sea." The car was still swallowing the distance, crossing roads and villages.

. . . The landscape changed and wilderness rose on both sides of the road. Small houses retreated, and small rocks, and fields, and wild trees. Locusts disappeared and wandering butterflies, and death dominated the landscape. Somehow wonder and enjoyment felt suddenly absent. What was this place? We stayed silent for a long time. Even the car's engine felt muted. The silence prevailed until the driver's voice broke in finding my face in the front mirror and questioning rather defiantly, "Do you know where we are, *Ustadh?*"

I was not happy with that name. *Ustadh* sounded sticky in my ears. But the place remained dry and desolate. I said without pause, "In Bait Nuba."

No trace of the destroyed village remained. Bulldozers and tractors had removed all its ruins after demolishing the houses. How did I recognize it then, despite the fact that I had never visited it? Sometimes I had passed it nearby on my way to 'Imwas.

The driver continued to gaze at me in the mirror, and said, "Bait Nuba! Then you know all the region!"

Father sounded shocked. "Bait Nuba! God, I served in it for six months when I was in the National Guard. But by God, I didn't recognize it now? How could I?"

[1]Meaning the Israelis.

The driver said, "They've wiped it off the face of the earth."

"May God's angels destroy them," Father said.

The driver pointed to the barren summit of a mountain, "That's where Yalu once stood. They've destroyed it too, completely erased. Do you remember it, *Ustadh?*"

I tried to sound assertive as I stared at the eroded black line which used to be the paved road that led to the village. "I remember it. It had an ancient wall that was wiped out along with the houses of the village."

The driver answered, "A wall? I don't remember! Anyway, you must be more knowledgeable than we are in history, *Ustadh.*"

Yes, it had had an old wall. We were silent for a long time.

'Imwas . . . village of wine and holy chants . . . of the plague and Abu 'Ubaida Ibn al-Jarrah's tomb,[2] village of frontiers and fences . . . That's what it used to be.

Before the explosions that had finished the village in June, all the alleys and dirt roads had converged into one paved road. People mingled, a human river out to breathe the summer air near the café and the bus stop by the seminary.

Now we were crossing the street, melting in its nakedness. All the houses and graves and the café and bus stop had been wiped out, while the faraway lands to the east had absorbed the flood of dislodged human beings. That June, they had poured out from the street carrying bundles, belongings, and the burden of defeat, heading toward a faraway land in the east. Now the place seemed desolate and strange without them. My father pointed to the lofty trees behind the wall of the seminary, and the shining windows reflecting the stones of the old building as we passed. He was saying, "They've left the seminary standing. Thank God they've left something standing in the village."

The driver explained, "The Latrun seminary supplies them with vegetables."

"Maybe it was spared because it is a religious place." I said.

"A religious place, *Ustadh!* These people don't know God!" he answered sarcastically.

'Imwas, the seminary, the delicious wine . . . Fragments of memory swarmed my mind, uniting in waves, and drowning me. Just like the Latrun wine which we sipped with relish, its secret numbness taking

[2]One of the early Arab generals who conquered areas west of the Arabian Peninsula.

hold of our limbs after the first glass. We were still discovering our blessed coming of age, our delicious bodily reactions, the flow of the sap and the thrum of the heart, and the secret letters which did not dare to fly from our hands as the wine seeped through our veins and our heads burned with dreams and illusions. Words came to us from books we read secretly, and the world felt so much wider than a camp or two cities, and all the villages and land were ours, as was the sea looming through the remote metal fences across the frontiers at the forbidden areas. Near 'Imwas, we had to cross through the villages of Safa and Bait Nuba and walk up the street to the seminary. We would sit under its cypress trees on a stone bench near some cactus trees. We used to carve our names on the thick leaves of the cactuses, and I would try to draw the face of a girl who had ignored me on the way to the camp and the face would get lost in the stickiness of the cactus pulp. Yusuf would carve his name and Maryam's in a heart pierced by a bleeding arrow. By now the cactus leaves must be dry but I imagine them to have kept our scars. Yusuf would sit under a tree in the seminary's orchard and shout that he could see the sea from there, calling me to climb and look at it too. I'd pull myself up and gaze into the distance but could never see the sea. He'd point and say, "There, beyond the land!" But I only saw tractors digging beyond wire fences, no water. He'd keep saying, "There it is! beyond the land!" But I still could not see it.

In the old cellar under the seminary stood huge wooden barrels and giant hoses. The priest would explain to us the secret of wine and distillation, then give us a bottle of old seasoned wine as a gift that we'd drink under the holy trees, feeling its spirit seep into our bodies. Then we'd carve our names, and those of the girls we loved, and gaze toward the sea as the horizon blazed with twilight, and our head with the blood of Christ. We'd see the distant nearby sea, without really seeing it.

The car swerved onto a new road opposite the seminary. I felt a blood other than my own rush into my veins. Here I was, entering the road of my own village for the first time. The driver said, "Here's where the wire fences stretched."[3]

My eyes searched the ground for some landmark, but could see

---

[3]These were the fences separating the Israel of 1948 from the rest of the Arab countries. They were abolished after 1967 and Israel's occupation of Arab territories.

nothing besides flat stretches of land. The seminary grew smaller behind us, a little green oasis. I could feel the car's wheels madly trampling the old days behind us, all crushed by this new paved road that joined the street of 'Imwas with a road which had been neglected for years. Thorns had grown from its cracks. Once it joined the village with other invaded towns beyond. Now the new street was struggling to connect some lost continuity, interrupted by the thorns and wires. The driver said, "Now we're in the green belt they speak of."

"Where is this belt? The land used to be *always* green!" my father exclaimed.

The speeding wheels were still swallowing the asphalted road, burning away history, memory, the war, defeated armies, names carved on cactus leaves and the bark of cypress tress; and piercing time over a road where memory froze like the hard face of an icy river.

The driver said, "It won't be long now."

We arrived. I stepped out of the car silently, armed with dreams and wonder! I tried to contain my excitement and took a deep breath.

A sour air filled my lungs. The car that had carried us here drove off, its engine melting into the emptiness as it veered far away behind the mountain. Silence with its rough fingers fell upon the place.

We could see the rubble of the village on our right . . . the remnants of a wall and scattered stones of houses. Far away, a small old building the size of a single room remained standing among the debris. On the left the old fields stretched, a million slender green stems going toward the sea.

Our footsteps left the paved road and walked onto dusty ground dominated by thorns and dry wild plants. We crushed them beneath our shoes, making a broken sound which mingled with my father's panting.

He stopped among the debris. I stood behind him, feeling completely bound to him, mechanically reacting to his every move. His eyes roamed the place like two swords, and he looked like an old horseman whose spears had all been broken. The footsteps of his aging horse echoed plaintively on the ground. Then he sighed deeply, expressing emotions which had been suppressed in his breast for many years, devouring his life. "Ah! I never believed I'd live long enough to stand on it again with you! Twenty-five years! What a life!"

What a life that crushed us from one exile to another!

I stared at everything. Merciless misery everywhere. I could not feel my kinship to this land. Where were the threads of continuity that had shaped themselves so beautifully in my mind through many a winter's tale? I wondered in my heart if we had not lost our way, then could not help saying, "This is *it*?!"

I wanted the question to be neutral, perhaps kind . . . but my mouth was suddenly dry. What cruelty could two small words embody? 'This is it?!' and what guilty eyes faced my father's reaction to the question,

He glanced at me hard, as if he sensed in my question the hint of denial of all the beautiful descriptions he had, over the past years, bestowed on this place. What cruelty could make of these two neutral words!

Such a rude and stupid question!

But his face looked simple, transparent as dew as he answered. For twenty-five years I had known this face with its sad wrinkles, its clarity, its tender eyes that examined things with strange compassion. But never before had it seemed purer or more tenderly eager than it did now. Also, it was sadder and more tired than I had ever seen it. His hungry eyes scanned the old dust, the stones, the fallen walls and dry trees, submerging them in that strange tenderness, bestowing on them the longing of a lover who has finally laid his head on the breast of his beloved.

After a long silence he said, almost apologetically, "That's it! But it was not like this."

The apology felt like a stab in my heart. I had thought his face to be answer enough.

I breathed deeply, trying to find some fresh air to inhale. The native son knows his village and surroundings better than I or the driver; even Bait Nuba, which I could recognize after they had wiped it out in its entirety. I could see Yalu's wall that was there no more. I am a teacher, supposed to know history, and a driver who knows no history says they've left the seminary standing because it supplied them with wine. We used to drink wine under the holy trees in the Latrun seminary gazing at the names we had carved on cactus leaves and tree barks. Yusuf would see the sea and I would not, and I'd feel isolated. A driver may know no history but he knows the secrets of geography. Now I felt isolated again, isolated, falling into the second sin because my mother's seas were not separated, were never separated, would always remain one sea stretching along the country. My father's face was answer enough. Therefore his words hit hard, slapping my face, and burdening me with the cruelty of my question, "This is it?!" No, it was never like this, just like so many other places are no longer as they were. The street of ʿImwas used to be a human river on summer evenings, and now it is wiped out. Houses and bus stops, and graves and the café all wiped out. What a sin to feel so isolated, when my mother's seas were one continuous sea . . .

We were walking among the stones, trying to avoid stumbling on them. Father stopped suddenly and I stopped behind him.

Nearby stood a large gully where all the garbage from nearby inhabited districts was heaped. Now I understood that acid smell in the air. Father said, "Sons of bitches . . . Couldn't they find another place to throw their dirt?"

Then he jumped, startled, fixing his eyes on a faraway tree with broken branches. He began scrambling toward it like a chased locust, and I was leaping behind him, curious about what had prompted such sudden energy, what discovery had suddenly burst forth. He ran as if he were young again, dodging stones and approaching a tree against which he pressed his palms, palms worn out by longing, age, and fatigue. He shouted, "This was our new house! May God destroy them! I knew it from this China tree. God! The china tree neither grows old nor dies. Look . . . see this bullet in its trunk? This has been there since the time I learned how to shoot. I was younger than you are now. May God break them, as they've tried to break it. Son, the China tree is strong. If you break it off, it grows again; it remains hard, it never grows old or dies."

His voice sounded amazed, like a surprised, cool wind rising up from the valleys of past life; he pointed at everything, his forefinger piercing the air with great fondness, as if he had just discovered the outlines of the place for the first time. "There . . . there's the Yemen well. We used to call it that. Water? No! it had no water . . . Look, the *zaʿtar* now covers its mouth. God! *Zaʿtar* growing from the inside of the well! Once this well was a storeroom for weapons. And there . . . look . . . there's the shrine of Yahya the prophet . . . that room there. They've left it standing. We used to offer our sacrifices there: mats, and candles, and sheep that we slew at its door. They've preserved it because it's a religious shrine . . . A religious shrine! It's true, these people don't know God. Look, look . . . There used to be the wall of the school, that demolished wall there . . . Those stones heaped next to it used to be a water reservoir. On this side was the old town and our old house was there. And there, faraway, was Lidd.[4] Muzairʿa is in the Lidd dis-

---

[4]The Arab "Lidd" is what the Israelis call "Ludda," where the international airport is now located.

trict. Next to those trees below was Quliya, our neighboring village. In it Hasan Salama[5] taught us how to make explosives from sugar and potassium."

He pointed out the remains of several other villages. Then his voice began to falter a little. I saw defeat weaken his posture. I seemed to hear waves rolling across the green spaces. Distance narrowed, pulling me toward the sea. Then I heard his voice saying, "Our land was famous for its *sabr*."[6]

His fingers peeled the thorny skin of the delicious fruit as I watched. He bent to eat it with relish. A great sadness whose source I could not fathom overwhelmed me. It was a sorrow that arose from gazing into the face of an old man eating his fruit with so much passion, as if by gripping it he gripped life. He offered me a fruit that he had peeled for me. I shook my head, saying I wasn't hungry. In fact, I wanted it very much; but sorrow dominated all desire.

I dug my feet into the ground, leaning against the China tree. My father's voice repeated that the China tree neither grows old nor ever dies. I felt its bark pressing against my back. My eyes gazed out toward the coastal plain and moved toward the sea like a colt bolting abruptly. I realized the sea lay there, covered with fog. My father lay down on the ground, breathing the earth's fragrance. Suddenly, the place came alive for me, overflowing with houses and trees and people who used to be there. The stones rose up in front of me rebuilding themselves, and I could see the place with a different intimacy, a familiarity borne in the bones. I wanted the stones to speak, to carry on a dialogue with me. And I felt overwhelmed by the flavor of cocoa in the belly of Ramallah's valley, by the rich smell of Jerusalem's humidity, and the aroma of *za'tar* breaking up out of the well of Yemen. In the brilliance of the horizon behind the fog I could see my mother's seas all joined. One single sea, to which my eyes were trying to find a passage.

—translated by May Jayyusi; and Naomi Shihab Nye

[5]One of the Palestinian military leaders who trained fighters and himself fought and fell in battle defending Palestinian rights.
[6]A delicious summer and autumn fruit with a prickly skin.

Extracts from
Personal Accounts

Rashad Abu Shawar *(b. 1942)*

A prolific writer who has published many novels, short story collections, children's books, and a book of diaries, Shawar was born in Zikrin, in the region of Hebron; on becoming a refugee in 1948 he lived in many towns and refugee camps before moving to Syria. He has no higher education, but is an avid reader, and now works as director of publishing for Palestinian writings and writings on Palestine. Among his novels are *Days of Love and Death* (1973) and *The Lovers* (1977), and among his short story collections are *Memory of Days Past* (1970), *Trees Do Not Grow on Books* (1975), and, his latest, *The Story of People and Stones*. His diary, *O Beirut*, appeared in 1983, recording the daily experience of Palestinians and Lebanese during the Israeli invasion of 1982 and the following exodus.

From O Beirut

I'd only been in Damascus for a few hours when the bad news came: "They've bombed Beirut. They've destroyed the walls of the Sports Stadium. They've killed and maimed and wounded dozens of people."

That's what they'd done on June 4, 1982. The Lebanese papers arrived. I saw mind-boggling pictures on the pages of *Al-Safir*.

I went for lunch, with my wife, to the house of my friend, the poet Nazih Abu 'Afash. I contemplated the graceful images he creates, and tried to forget; but then the poet Mamdouh Adwan arrived, his face sombre.

"Have you heard the news?" he asked me. He added, "They've started to invade the South."

Silence hung over us. So this was war. It was the fifth of June. Why now, I wondered, why June? I wondered how long we'd be able to hold out; I wondered how severe the blow was. Memories of the month of our defeat in 1967 were rekindled in me.

I found myself jumping up and holding out my hand to say goodbye. Nazih and his wife walked a few steps with us.

"Why all this anxiety?" they said.

I said to myself, Why the reassurance? Why the optimism?

We carried on down the street. Other people were walking in the opposite direction. When we reached the camp, we heard a voice over the loudspeaker calling on people to donate blood.

The voice stopped and then we heard the weeping. We were in the Yarmouk camp, and the camps are one thing and the rest of the Arab world another . . . Here there's blood, tears, ardor, and fury. We saw scores of young men and women going to the Deir Yarmouk Clinic and returning from it.

What now?

Now that the Zionists have started their invasion, let us defend our revolution, our families, our dignity, our future, and our dreams.

For months we'd been expecting this battle, the big one, the biggest and fiercest of them all—and designed, as far as our enemy was concerned, to be the decisive one. We, for our part, hadn't contemplated a decisive battle so soon, with this enemy—an enemy bristling with American weapons, and all the stronger for the vacuum of the régimes around it, which are fierce in their dealings with their own people but have open frontiers for their enemies.

My friend 'Abd al Hadi an Nashash and I live side by side in the camp. We quickly met together and decided to leave. He said goodbye to his wife and children, while I stood at the door with mine.

"This battle will be a terrible one," I said to my wife. "Do you remember how I called our street 'the last street'? Yes, I expect them to reach it . . . in Beirut. I've never stopped writing and saying that. If you hear of my death, keep a firm hold of yourself—mourn, but don't let sorrow take over your life and the children's. Bring them up as you should and help them to study. I remember I've been brave in past battles. I hope I will be again. I'll try, I promise."

"Do you know," said my wife, "Fahd went to the clinic today to donate blood, but they turned him away because he's only twelve. He cried his eyes out."

I've won then. This is Fahd, my eldest son. He knows Palestine and he loves her. Here he is, going to give his blood, stretching out his Palestinian arm, the dark, lean arm that will carry a heavy burden one day.

Goodbye . . . Goodbye, then, to my wife and my children. The Zionists are coming and we're advancing to meet them.

My father once said to me, "Look, Rashad, when we left Palestine our family was just you and me. Your mother, Zainab, and your sister, Ma'zouza, went down with Palestine. Now there are six in your family and eleven in mine. We've multiplied unimaginably."

Yes, we've multiplied. That's good. A single person can give his life. Fahd will still be here, and al-Tayyeb, and so will Ahlam, my Ahlam, the daughter I waited for to make up for my mother and sister. Clever Ghassan will still be here, the youngest, whom we named after Ghassan Kanafani;[1] they blew him to bits, but they couldn't blow up his novels and stories and essays—or his presence.

We reached Beirut at night.

Hello, Beirut. Hello, Fakhani,[2] and, above all, hello, Sports Stadium.

The Resurgence of the Spirit

Where did it come from? From the sea . . .

A tank was hit. Within seconds rockets were launched from the flats—you know them—the Aramon flats. Tanks were burning, and we captured one.

Adham was talking excitedly. The sky was exploding with bullets. They're parading one of those swift white tanks in the Burj al-Barajneh refugee camp.

They were stopped at the Beaufort Heights, they were stopped at al-Rashidiyyeh refugee camp, and they've been held for a long time in the groves surrounding 'Ain al-Hilweh refugee camp and at the gates of Beirut—they'll be held for a very long time!

Begin[3] and Sa'd Haddad[4] hastily took photographs, then the two of them moved far away from the castle of terror, the castle haunted by the Palestinian spirit.

Begin said to the quisling sectarian mayor, "I'll give you Beaufort Castle."

Eitan, his Chief of Staff, declared, "We're fighting the fiercest and

[1]Ghassan Kanafani is a famous Palestinian. See his biography in the Short Stories section.

[2]The quarter in West Beirut where many Palestinians live. It has been a constant target for Israeli attacks.

[3]Abu Shawar wrote his diaries on the Israeli invasion of Lebanon on June 5, 1982 when Menachem Begin was prime minister of Israel. Begin is remembered by the world community as the prime minister who signed the Camp David peace treaty in 1979. However, his history as a Zionist goes back to Mandatory Palestine when he was the leader of the Irgun terrorist gang responsible for numerous acts of terror in the forties. Among their actions were the blowing up of the wing of the King David hotel in Jerusalem where the British civilian administration was housed, killing 91 civilians (July 22, 1946); and, in conjunction with the Stern Zionist gang, the Dair Yasin massacre of April 9, 1948, in which 245 civilians, mostly women and children, were killed in cold blood.

[4]Sa'd Haddad was a major in the Lebanese army, but defected to form his own army in the late seventies. He then allied himself with Israel and was on the Israeli payroll until his death in 1985. His main objective was to clear South Lebanon of a Palestinian presence and to defend the northern Israeli borders from the attacks of the *fidaain*.

most dangerous of our wars, with an enemy we've been fighting for a hundred years."

Oh, this long, bitter war!

The myth fights against sand, water, castles, *Ashbal*,[5] against the groves of Tyre and Sidon, and the deserted homes of the southern town of Nabattiyeh—the myth and the God-given promise. That promise, written in Hebrew mixed with words from other languages, remained an illusion till the Balfour Declaration; then it became stronger and more effective, because it was written in English, the language of an empire on which the sun never set.

The myth fights against the simple Palestinian peasant who doesn't understand computer language. It fights against the Palestinian and Lebanese Resistance, fights against it with F15 planes, with Cherbourg surface-to-surface and surface-to-air missiles, with long-range heavy artillery never before used in Arab-Israeli wars.

But what's to be done when the Palestinian's so stubborn, stubborn in a way no computer can grasp? What's to be done when the Palestinian doesn't recognise either the promise of the God of the Torah or the promise of the English God whose sun has set?

The enemy's occupied Beaufort Castle, but the Castle attacks, ceaselessly. Every two or three days there's a battle, an incursion, a raising of the Lebanese and Palestinian flags.

Begin was taken to Beaufort Castle and he made a gift of it to the quisling sectarian mayor, who showed his joy with a broad grin. Begin quoted the Psalms and the Torah, but after the cameras had stopped rolling and the flashbulbs had stopped he sank into a daze. His officer in charge of the assault on the castle stated that he had suffered over two hundred casualties—either dead or wounded—including a number of officers. With an honesty that was forced on him, he said, "What we've seen will certainly go down in history. I can't tell you everything. We've seen hell in this castle."

What was in the castle?

Thirty-three men. Seeing the intensity of the attack, the Palestinian commander told his men, "You know, we'll have to fight them to the death here. They'll only get in over our bodies."

The Israeli commander said, "I'll never forget this battle as long as I live."

---

[5]*Ashbal* is the plural of *shibl*, a lion cub. Young Palestinian boys between the ages of 8–14 go to camps especially assigned for *ashbal*, where they are trained in cooperative work, communal action, and physical fitness. The *ashbal* camps compensate for the lack of such extracurricular activities in the refugee camp schools.

Other generals said, "No, this isn't like any other war. All the earlier wars were easy."

The Zionists remained terrified, even after they'd seized Beaufort Castle, and didn't dare go into the tunnels and store rooms for fear of the *fidaain*.

As for 'Ain al-Hilweh, the tin camp with its tumbledown houses and narrow alleys, of its greatness let me speak.

The voice of one of the *ashbal* was heard on the transmitter: "They're at the entrance of the camp a few meters away. The men have all gone to face them. I'm the only one here . . . Just a moment . . ."

The voice stopped, but the transmitter stayed open. The *shibl's* dead, we said, and we feared for 'Ain al-Hilweh, for the *shibl*, for our people.

Suddenly . . . Yes, suddenly the voice came.

"We've destroyed two tanks. They're completely burnt out and the other tanks have fled. Morale's rocketed, it's sky high!"

In the first days of their all-out assault the Israelis reached Tyre and Sidon and surrounded Beaufort Castle. They advanced? Yes. They penetrated? Yes. They surrounded? Yes. Some of the officers on our side failed to hold their positions? That's true. But at Beaufort Castle we saw the glory of the Palestinian fighter; at Sidon, in 'Ain al-Hilweh, we saw the glory of the Palestinian camps; at Rashidiyyeh we saw the glory of our *ashbal*, who fought till their ammunition ran out, then raised the Palestinian flag and proudly advanced. The Israeli officer had saluted them and declared that he understood nothing. That's good; they're not an army set up for parades. They carry, as their burden, the concern each of us has for our culture; because of that they're not bothered about computers, and American tanks can't crush their spirit.

Yes, it's the resurgence of the spirit! How can we possibly compare the enemy's planes, warships, tanks, and rockets with the power of the spirit?

Yes, it's the power of the spirit!

The Zionists had been used to swift, clean wars, followed by the taking of photographs, photographs of easy victories. They'd advanced, surrounded the camps in the South, cut the roads—then moved swiftly on to Beirut.

They Stab Us in the Back

The war stretches from the South of Lebanon to the Fakhani. The Fakhani's our last street. Who will defend it, who'll build the barricades to bar it against the invader, who'll stand fast and carry his life in the palm of his hand?

A week's past now since this war began. Seven days of planes dropping their bombs, of warships hurling their fire, of artillery never before used in any part of the world, burning all before it. God created the world in six days, and on the seventh he rested. That, says the Torah, is why we have the Sabbath. On that Sabbath, the fifth of June, the God of battles wasn't resting! He was counting his guns and calculating his rockets and preparing his planes—all American, all new, specifically sent for the Palestinians and the Lebanese. On the twelfth of June, the Lord who hadn't rested on the fifth was still out of breath.

Our brothers didn't come to our rescue. All is silence in the land of the Arabs. Capitals play the game of wait and see, and I swear in the face of the exalted hell before me that some of them are assisting, assisting in the war and financing it; that some know exactly what is going on; that some have managed to crush people's spirits and destroy their minds, so that they're no longer able to make a move or open their mouths.

Seven days, but only slow movement—so slow—from our friends. My God, is this the way things are? The bitterness in our hearts is beyond description. It's true that we're fighting the battle for our homeland, not a battle on behalf of others; yet this is still the battle of all our peoples, of all our friends. Such slow movement after a week of hell—it is not a pleasant sight.

We've seen the pictures of the Israeli troops in the *Al-Nahar* newspaper, we've seen the receptions, we've seen the Phalangist[6] girl coquettishly presenting a carnation to an Israeli soldier. These are the sects. They feel no identity with the homeland, they have no belief in the nation—and it's the Palestinian who must pay the price. As long as he fights for the nation, he must pay sectarianism the price of his identity. As long as he carries the burden of Palestine, he must pay, with his flesh and his blood, the price for whole ages of decline.

Ahmad, the Lebanese photographer, wanted to use his camera as a

---

[6]Phalangists: are faschist Lebanese factions responsible for the Lebanese civil war which erupted in 1975, fighting first against other Lebanese groups, particularly Muslim groups, then against the Palestinians. They were responsible for the massacres of Tal al-Zaatar in 1976 in which over 15,000 Palestinians and Lebanese died (see in this volume, Liyana Badr's story, "A Land of Rock and Thyme"), and the massacre of Sabra and Shatila, two refugee camps in Beirut in which hundreds of Palestinians were murdered in cold blood including whole families. This took place under the eyes of the Israelis who had occupied Beirut after their invasion of 1982.

witness. The Phalangists told him, "You're a Lebanese from West Beirut. Don't say a word. Don't open your mouth, or else!" They thrust a rifle in his face. He came back stunned.

What did you expect from the Phalangists, Ahmad? From people of the sectarian age who boast of their alliance with the Zionists? What do you expect, Ahmad the Lebanese, Ahmad the Palestinian—Ahmad the Arab?

Candles of Sorrow

Yes, Beirut's sad. Beirut's angry. First it was reproachful, then stunned at what it heard from the Arab radio stations. When it saw the Israelis pass through the mountains, without a fight, its heart was rent.

Beirut heard the gloating statements of Arab officials, who were settling their own accounts at the expense of Palestinian and Lebanese blood. We can take no hope from such people.

Water's scarce and there's little electricity. There's a flourishing trade in candles and gas lanterns and flashlights the size of a pen. At night the thick darkness is made thicker by smoke, and fires blaze in barrels. Fighters roam the streets on foot, or go round in cars, singing in support of the revolution and of Beirut.

In a moment of sorrow, anxiety, and depression, I remembered a girl I'd once loved in Jericho. Why, I wondered, was I remembering this? It must be that at moments of death we seek shelter in love and dreams. She came to me in a moment between sleeping and waking, tender and gentle. There was sorrow in her eyes, and a question.

I was seeking shelter, in love and dreams, from the ugliness of everything that's happening. What does Palestine have except love . . . and dreams?

When I opened my eyes, I saw the candles in the windows round about. I saw candles in every window in Beirut, and I saw Beirut itself as a candle, glowing and flickering—glowing despite all the darkness surrounding it.

The People of Beirut

This is Beirut, of which so many things have been said. This is Beirut, the Lady of the Sea, the Lady of Time—though some Arab visitors here have seen only a city of pleasure where everything's for sale.

This is the Beirut that doesn't live in cabarets, that doesn't belong to the brokers and the pimps and the people who are ready to sell everything.

This is Beirut the beautiful, the Canaanite, the Arab. This is the Beirut of al-Shayyah, of al-Awza'i, of Ras Beirut, the Beirut of al-Basta, of Abu Shāker, of Abi Haydar;[7] the Beirut of honest women and men who paid the price for Arab Lebanon and Palestinian Lebanon.

This is the face that the buyers and sellers haven't known. This is Beirut, home of all who dream of an honorable life. Beirut isn't cabarets, it isn't banks, it isn't a nest of spies, it isn't the domain of sects whose allegiance is to everything hostile to a progressive and unified homeland. Beirut is the noble fighter, standing firm.

This is Umm Ahmad, a woman of Beirut, energetic and courageous. She trades in clothes and goes to Japan to do business. When the bombardment started she wailed and kept on saying she'd go out of her mind with fear. She'd leave the Fakhani, she said, and go to Al-Hamra.[8] Yet she didn't leave.

We sat on the steps behind an enormous barricade of sand; Umm Ahmad was running from the kitchen to the storeroom. She was making tea and coffee and cooking lunch—all to help the fighters living in the building and those, like me, who'd come for a hot meal. She was happy doing what she was doing.

Umm Bshara is Palestinian. She comes from Jerusalem, but she's been living in Beirut for a very long time. Her children are in the United States. She lives alone.

Every morning she greets us with her smile. Her face is the homeland . . . She's a real mother. She beckons to us with dignified grace and we go to her house to eat cheese and olives and drink hot tea.

This splendid woman organized the distribution of bread in our street and helped solve the problem of water. One day her children phoned from the States.

"Leave Beirut," they said, "and go to Cyprus. We'll meet you there and take you to America."

"If you're looking for a mother," she told them, "then go and find someone else. I have my children who need me here. I'm going to stay with them."

---

[7]These are all quarters in West Beirut.

[8]Al-Hamra Street is one of the more elegant streets still operating after the destruction of Beirut through both the civil war and the Israeli invasion.

The vegetable and fruit sellers amaze me, especially the ones with stalls on the pavement in al-Mazra'ah.[9] Falling shells plough up the asphalt and destroy buildings, yet they go on selling. Still more astonishing, they go on sitting there even after they've sold all their produce.

Opposite the Barbir Hospital, behind an enormous barricade of sand, there are two T-34 tanks. One of the people responsible for this important position is a vegetable seller, and he can often be seen leaving his stall to give orders interspersed with improbable Beiruti curses.

The young men and women of the Civil Defense are amazing. They're all volunteers, and wherever you go you can see them in their white masks, braving the fires to save their Lebanese and Palestinian brothers.

This is Beirut—or a part of it. And let the gods of carnage and utter destruction flaunt their might as they will, Beirut will still speak Arabic and dream of Jerusalem and the Sea of Jaffa.

A Last Request

I stood on the balcony, thinking, recalling my wife's face and the faces of my children. I tried to visualize the features of my brothers, who I haven't seen for many years. They live in Amman, and I'm denied entry there.

My father and brothers are in Amman, my wife and children are in Damascus, and I'm in Beirut. This is the state of one Palestinian family.

'Abd al-Hafeez is a fighter. His immediate family is in Galilee. One of his brothers is in London, the other's in West Germany, and some of his sisters are in the Gulf. They couldn't all meet together in any Arab state, so they met in London. They're considered a lucky family because they did manage, finally, to come together; a family unable to meet since the 1948 disaster might well envy them.

The Jews talk a good deal about their suffering over the years and across the ages. The difference between us and them is that they weep a lot and demand a lot from the world. The United States and Europe are very much on their side, even in their advance to destroy Beirut.

We're not asking for the world's pity. We're seeking our own role in life and history. They want to eliminate us, their existence depends on eliminating us from life and history. That existence will remain

---

[9]An area in West Beirut joining al-Fakhani with the once elegant seaside area in which many hotels, restaurants, and cafés flourished before the war.

weak and fragile as long as we're alive. That's why they've come for the kill.

Associations

Beirut was anxious about Naji al-ʿAli.[10] All who love his cartoons—those cartoons that so clearly express oppression and rage—all the offspring of the camps, all the poor of Beirut, the journalists, the writers, the poets, the artists—all these people were wondering fearfully about his fate. Naji lives in Sidon, and the Israelis would love to catch him.

Rumors arose that he'd been killed; then there was a rumor that he was captured. Some rumors said he was missing, others that he'd left Sidon but been killed at Damoun.

Then suddenly—a call came. "Naji's waiting for you."

It was Naji al-ʿAli, Naji, with his pinched, suffering face, his gray hair, the sorrow and anxiety of his eyes. He spoke in his strong Palestinian accent. "They called us out on the loudspeakers, so out we came, everyone between the age of twelve and seventy. That's how I came to go with my eldest son. We stayed on the beach for three days under the terrible sun, we drank salt water, we were hungry, we were dizzy, stunned by it all. We thought it was all over, but the battles carried on round ʿAin al-Hilweh. How I love that camp! I kept going back there, despite the bombardment and the siege. ʿAin al-Hilweh is my camp. I grew up there.

"Afterwards they came to us. They said that the old men and children should go home. A soldier called me. I said, 'I'm a young man. I'm not old, I only look old. My hair's gray—and my face is . . .' 'Go on' he said, 'go home.' I pushed my son in front of me. I was frightened they'd keep him, especially as Palestinian children look older than they really are. He's twelve, but he's not a child any more."

Naji al-ʿAli didn't waste any time, but started drawing cartoons for the war. He surpassed himself drawing ʿAin al-Hilweh.

Afterwards we began meeting together. He would be in the streets—roaming the alleys, thinking, pondering, snapping up impressions, storing them. He's an original artist, who doesn't flaunt the depth of his culture and consciousness and reflection, but lives without pretension.

---

[10]Naji al-ʿAli was a famous Palestinian cartoonist who was assassinated in London in 1987 because of his struggle to expose, through his art, Israeli aggression and intrigue against his own country and people, and the indiscretions and deviation of some of his fellow compatriots. His memory is revered by all loyal Palestinians.

That's why he merits all the anxiety about him and all the love people feel for him.

All the people in my building have left it, except for one paralyzed woman. She's totally paralyzed, her arms and her legs. She can't even speak. Where were her children to take her? They kept her at home. Just imagine, almost all the apartments in the building were hit, everything around this old woman was destroyed—except her own apartment. This is the force of life. When we returned we found her alive, and I went and kissed her white hair and her forehead, and wept. I saw the tears streaming down her age-worn face—and I understood what was going on within her, I understood her spirit and her torment. She was still alive, and everything was exploding, everything was destroyed and collapsing around her.

I'm in my apartment now. So goodbye, apartment. I take back what I said—I've no home anywhere.

These are my books. No, they are just books.

I left my first library in Damascus, in 1965, when a pardon was declared [allowing some previously Palestinian persona non grata to enter Jordan,] and I went back to Jordan with my father.

My second library I left in Jericho, the day it fell in June 1967.

My third library I left in Amman in September 1970.[11] My wife and my father destroyed my books and papers for fear of raids and questioning.

My fourth library I sold in Damascus the day I was hungry there.

This is my fifth library. How many times have I bought the same book, and it was gone before I could read it? How many places have I been in and written the same short story or novel or article?

These are books—my books.

What is a Palestinian to do when he's without a home, without Palestine, without a library, without a place to settle in; when he reads and writes between one massacre and the next, between one departure and the next?

Goodbye, then, home . . . books . . . Beirut.

Farewell

The first ship has left.

It took them and left. Beirut surprised the fighters with its farewell; it surprised the world.

---

[11]This is an allusion to the "Black September" civil war in Jordan in 1970 between Palestinian fighter groups and the Jordanian army.

Beirut is loyalty.

The Palestinians left beneath a shower of rice and ululations, amid the salute of bullets.

This is my cousin Nasr. He's leaving with the heroes of the Badr Brigade.

This is the Palestinian, being dispersed among the Arab lands.

They're dividing up his exile, so that he won't have one exile only. They want him to be many exiles, so that his parts can't meet.

Tomorrow, I've been told, you leave.

So its goodbye, Beirut.

My head's throbbing. It's full of sand and noise and songs and friends, full of the living, the martyred, the books I've read, the novels I haven't written—together with the slap that rang out, on my face and no one else's, simply because I was Palestinian.

Sites of departure are weary of the Palestinians, places of exile are weary of the Palestinian. Countries hostile to him are weary of the Palestinian. Radio stations that have lived off his blood are weary of him; they've filled their programs with songs and commentaries and the announcement of coups—at his expense.

Mothers, wives, children, fathers have been gathering since dawn. The distant cannons are sounding out their farewell.

A Lebanese fighter fired an RPJ rocket into the air. He flung himself onto a military car to embrace the departing fighters, then jumped back. A cry was wrenched from his throat: "Where are you leaving for?"

Everyone who leaves goes back to his homeland, except the Palestinian—he leaves carrying his homeland within him. He can't go back home; he's destined to go on carrying this homeland which brings him only exile, departures, prisons, death—and the noblest, most wonderful role to be found in modern history.

This is the ship. This is the *Solferine* that will take us to Bizerte in Tunisia.

Going to the Sea

Sea, O Sea! It is I, the Palestinian, going to the water . . . the water. "From water have We created every living thing."[12] This sea is ours. Our mothers and grandmothers call it the Sea of Jaffa.

When I was still not one year old, I had a skin infection. "Take him to the sea," said the doctor, and my father and mother took me to the

---

[12] A verse from the Quran.

Sea of Jaffa. They baptized me in its waters, in its salt and its iodine; then, when night fell, they slept on the sand. My mouth became full of sand, and they squeezed an orange into it, into my throat, into my veins. They baptized me with seawater and oranges.

I saw the Palestinian journeying through time, sea, and sand. I saw him, vigilant, fighting with sorceresses; I saw him storming archipelagos, wrestling against monsters with his bare hands—and with a heart that never missed a beat. And . . . I saw you, Beirut, glowing, and I saw beyond your horizon and your sand and our times within you. I saw the shape of the first Palestinian orange. I saw my mother's arms, the sand where she and my father slept beneath the open sky and the stars—in that beautiful time.

I have sailed from the beginning of creation, when there was only water. I have taken ship across archipelagos and gulfs, beneath the naked sky, through the heart of tempests and clamor and madness.

I will sail till eternity. Nothing will defeat me.

My breast swells up with the sand of Beirut, with the orange of Palestine. The sky of Jaffa is in my eyes, and always I see the light, like a vision. And I lay bare my breast, my heart, my spirit, my bastions; and I depart. You, Beirut, are in me, you are the barricades and brave men and *ashbal* and flowers, you are noble women . . . you are the water.

O Beirut!

—translated by May Jayyusi and Christopher Tingley

Muhammad al-As'ad

For his biography, please see under his name in the poetry section.

From Children of Dew

"When the children got thirsty, we used to collect dew with our hands
from the leaves of trees and rub it on their lips. When the roads changed
direction and branched in the darkness among rocks and dense
branches, my father told us to follow him, for he knew the way . . .
Many others had gone astray and fallen into Jewish ambushes lurking
at wells or the bends of obvious roads, but my father chose a different
secret way, rugged and winding amidst trees. That's how we became
separated from the rest of the Imm al-Zinat[1] inhabitants as we walked
towards Dalya[2] in the north." Here my mother stopped to announce
her differences with the women of the family, while my father, who
had already wandered incessantly among the villages, advised us to
leave everyone and choose a road which offered no water but the dew.

My mother said, "We saw corpses lying around the wells, and on
the roads . . ." I always heard the tone of isolation in her voice as if it
had gripped her after everything had happened. She had been awakened
in the middle of the night by the sound of bullets. She looked towards
Imm al-Zinat and saw it become a ball of fire . . . She awakened the
Haj[3] (who had not yet taken the pilgrimage) and made her way toward
town, toward her father, Abu Taleb's, house, in order to find out what
was happening. It was as if the house had called out to her at that
moment and pulled her home. She was surprised to see her brother

[1]A Palestinian village on one of the summits at the southern end of Mount Carmel,
about twenty-seven kilometers from Haifa. It was one of the biggest villages of the Haifa
district, with a large area of its cultivated land planted with olive trees. The village was
attacked by Zionist forces of the Haganah on May 15, 1948. When the civil inhabitants
fled for safety, the Zionists demolished the village so that none of its inhabitants could
return, then chased them towards the city of Jinin. In 1949 the Israelis founded a colony
one kilometer away from the site of the destroyed village.

[2]An Arab village north of Imm al-Zinat inhabited mostly by Palestinian Druzes.

[3]Although a man has not yet been on a pilgrimage to Mecca, he is often propitiously
called the *'haj'* in anticipation.

staring down from the roof of the house, shouting, "What are you doing here? Everyone has left. Go back, go back!"

My uncle stood alone, with his rifle. I have no idea what he was doing there, after the town had been evacuated. I thought maybe he had gone a little mad. Mother said, "He had kept the women and children at home, and announced he would shoot them if the Jews should force entry into the house."

He was obstinate, and hard. It was said about him that the bullets of the British had ripped into his shoulders, yet he forced himself to carry a wounded comrade who needed his help. He saved him from being lost to the battle of Imm al-Daraj,[4] that battle which the big books call the battle of Imm al-Zinat, while Mother calls it the incident of Imm al-Daraj, attributing its failure to the leader, Yusuf Abu Durra.[5] However, when I read now about all this, I find no trace whatsoever of these details, for my uncle is not mentioned, nor are any of the other names. It does not seem these particular people even existed. Neither the rattle in their throats was heard, nor the neighing of their horses, nor any traces of their footsteps ever noticed. History does not bring people alive; it sifts through them, using them until they disappear like passing clouds. My mother was to return, of course, from the evacuated town, and to tumble down the valley and take us with her as we fought off sleepiness in the dark. Father walked ahead of us. She had left my uncle on the roof of his house, his voice reverberating in her ears.

We did not disappear suddenly, like those who vanish in the wilderness as they relate in stories, but found our gradual way to Dalya

[4]Imm al-Daraj is a water spring near Imm al-Zinat where a large battle between Palestinian and Mandatory forces took place during the revolution of 1936 in Palestine.

[5]Yusuf Abu Durra (1900–1939) was one of the military leaders of the Palestinian revolution of 1936–1939. He had earlier joined the revolutionary group of Izziddin al-Qassam and fought with him at the battle of Ahraj Yaʿbud in which al-Qassam fell martyr. Abu Durra was able to escape from the tight siege by the British army and disappeared for some time, only to join the great Palestinian revolution in 1936 led by Shaikh Ahmad ʿAwad, the leader of the Jinin district. His exploits during those years were acknowledged everywhere in Palestine. One of the biggest battles he waged against the British army was the November, 1938 battle of Imm al-Zinat in the area of al-Carmel, in which a handful of Palestinian revolutionaries fought over a thousand British troops who were being helped by thirteen aeroplanes. When the Palestinian revolution was halted in 1939 (due to the start of World War II) Abu Durra went to Damascus then to East Jordan where the Jordanian army seized him. After a short incarceration there he was handed over by General Glubb, the then leader of the Jordanian army, to the British authorities in Palestine. He was sentenced to death and executed on September 30, 1939. His name lives on from generation to generation.

in the north just as the other inhabitants of the burned villages had done, from different directions. They would call to each other from the distance revealing their names and avoiding surprises. Although they knew the ways very well, their knowledge did not save them completely. Suddenly the roads were assailed by ogres and legendary beasts that had been lurking behind the bends, and no direction felt completely familiar or steady under the feet any longer.

A hyena rattles and roars, but when it faces you screaming, sensing your fear, you are transfixed. You feel utterly lost and fog encircles you so you lose all directions. You even seem to lose your hands and feet, and your head is filled with air. Now you move without a will of your own, eyes glued on the hyena, not really seeing him, but feeling him all the time moving and stopping to gaze at you with his yellow eyes. Then he hops in front of you, as if to pave your way, and you walk behind. Is it possible to grow bewitched by machine guns and men shouting *"Kadima,"*[6] by the din of stone hedges in the dark? My father alone kept his sanity that night, leading us to Dalya away from the jeers of hyenas as they lurked in the dark, ready to jump at the faces of lost villagers and lead them to their caves. Perhaps because my father did not know the stories well, or perhaps, as has been related, he had already met the hyena, and been bewitched by him so that the creature had no power to overcome him any more.

For it can happen only once in a lifetime. If you are lucky, the entrance to the hyena's cave would be low. The hyena might slip inside, but your head would knock against the entrance, your blood flow, and you would wake up. You would find yourself standing in a place you did not know, nor how you got there. You would take your rifle and aim it at the hyena now dazed from the situation's sudden change. You would shoot and shoot and the hyena huddle on himself, raving, baring his teeth, while his short back legs contracted and his longer front legs stretched, pressing the dirt with his claws. You'd be awake then, but who knows how long this trip behind the hyena would take? What countries would this bewitched man cross while people watched his trail behind the limping hyena?

I imagine the scene as if it had started that very night, its chapters continuing as the number of watchers increased, year after year. No one would ever approach to throw a stone and wake him up, or stop him, or kill the hyena.

Before we were born we had our hyenas, and this inevitable scene

[6]Kadima is the Hebrew word for "advance."

in which we will be heroes later on. In Dalya, we found that many had reached there before us, and had began discovering how many had been lost on the way. No one knew if hyenas had devoured them, or stolen their senses so they were still running hither and thither, crazily; or if, on the other hand, they had stayed on in villages like my obstinate uncle. The time for crying had not yet arrived; later, tears would be stamped forever on the soul. No elegies yet, for the children needed to eat on that strange day in which villagers cracked out of their nut shells for the first time in their lives, outside familiar salt and water . . . outside familiar shapes of days and outside their own souls. Now something strange happened, which turned the journey of one single night into a thousand years. Mother decided to return home, to bring back food for us. My father and older brother accompanied her on that nocturnal journey. It was the same rugged road, but without the little children who wailed occasionally, begging for water, and ended up licking the dew.

The mountain resounded with the roars of hyenas. They harbored great danger. Shadows assumed shapes which kept changing. Nothing could be heard nearby except the quiet rustling of trees.

There, in the valley's desolation, it seemed that no one had approached our house. Darkness surrounded and submerged it. Only the pigeons flapped awake when my parents entered, and they did something which Mother still remembers: they fluttered onto my parents' shoulders and flapped right in their faces. The fluttering and cooing in the dark continued. It was as if dawn had suddenly arisen, as if nature had started its wakefulness at midnight.

This reversal in the cycle of night and day was to continue for us. No longer did solar time have any dominance. Whether it was night or day, pigeons would flutter their wings, and trees unfurl their green branches. We would stay awake, awake, and my mother would repeat the story whenever she wanted in front of whomever believed or did not believe that pigeons of a house could know their owners better than time.

They, the people, are the masters of time that disappeared because they disappeared. And the same goes for the dew, and the calendars of days; for this was Palestine's dew, and Palestine's winds, and those flowers were Palestine's anemones.

I think of those pigeons that fluttered that night abandoning their old habits for the first time; elated, perhaps, by the return of those who had left them to sudden silence. I think of my brother who lifted the pigeons from his shoulders and went searching for a sack of flour or a jar of olives, of my mother as she grabbed the kitchen utensils, of my father as he peered through the dark looking for something to carry.

I think of our remote house that seemed to fall into the bottom of the valley as I climbed up to the village, our house protected from the hyenas by its remoteness from the paved road and its isolation from the village houses perched higher on the mountain. I follow in my mind's eye my family's quick panting movement—no time to waste as the land trembled under the rattles of hyenas, and the trees behind which ogres hid were struck with silence, and Haifa became a black coal at the bottom of the mountain, while the sea was clothed in darkness. This was the second of seven nights that we had begun to count, the night on which the ogres devoured all the roads, and cut off our way.

My uncle was to come down later. I don't know how he eventually abandoned his stubbornness to accompany his family to Dalya, carrying the rifle. He had, in fact, arrived at the very place where the hyena lurked, where he became a mobile ambush moving from rock to rock and tree to tree, calmly filling his rifle with bullets from two belts of ammunition he wore crossed over his breast. He had ammunition enough to halt a whole herd of enemies infiltrating into the margins of our existence, gripping with claws to the stony hedges, staring at the fire of the villagers, but not daring to approach it yet. They had now infiltrated everywhere, yet Uncle could not see them directly. He thought that the village, empty of enemies only a few hours after its fall; and the wells, abandoned except by corpses; and the calm olive groves, were the best proof that the enemies would not return again. The night had swallowed them, he thought. They did not disperse like locusts, as some stories relate. The larger battle had not yet taken place, when, as legend has it, blood would rise as high as knees, horses would wade in it, and Muslims would avenge themselves against the enemy, who would find no escape. If the enemies hid behind rocks or trees, the hiding places would shout to reveal them. But this would happen at the end of time, and we were still at the beginning.

Uncle went round the house of the Englishman, examining the roads. No one was awake in Haifa. The Hadar[7] alone rose like a phantom

---

[7]This is the name of the Jewish quarter in Haifa during the Mandate. It is built on the slopes of Mount Carmel and overlooks the Arab quarters lower down on the slopes of al-Carmel and in the valley. The author is here referring to a Jewish building in the Hadar from which snipers aimed at the Arab quarters.

with a thousand black holes, but it seemed oblivious to the presence of my uncle as he approached the back wall. He jumped up and his tall figure with belts of ammunition criss-crossed over his chest startled the Englishman.

Uncle told us, "I had known Mr. Gallagher for a long time. When he rubbed his eyes and woke completely, he invited me to enter. I sat down with my rifle in my hands. He asked, 'What has brought you here?' I said, 'I want to know what I should do. The Jews have occupied my village, and here I stand in front of you, totally confounded, unsure of my next move!' "

"The Englishman laughed and said, 'Are you quite mad to come to Haifa when the Jews have occupied it?' "

" 'Tell me what I should do?' " my uncle asked.

"The Englishman paused long. What could he say? Eventually he answered, speaking calmly, 'Listen, Taleb, everything is over now, the big states have sold you. These are things you will not understand just yet, but you must go away!' "

My uncle says, "I went out into the dark and made my way to Dalya."

And I say to him now, as if speaking to a small pupil, "The Englishman was right. But the fault was not yours or Abu Durra's or the rest of the peasants'. Your land was being stolen out from under you. Other people were bargaining with the British and with the Jews."

He does not answer, this man now nearing seventy, with his two torn shoulders that have no whole bones left in them since the bullets hit him in Imm al-Daraj. I feel ashamed at his silence. I knew he still crouches there in his memory, a young man moving about with his rifle and his belts of ammunition. In his eyes I see something no words could define. I have been cruel without knowing it. I have tried to steal his past from him; what he had been in the past. I, who now have warm relations with words, while his relations are still with the dew and the rocks.

—translated by May Jayyusi and Naomi Shihab Nye

Mu'een Bseiso

For his biography, please see under his name in the poetry section.

Palestinian Notebooks

These excerpts are selected from Mu'een Bseiso's book, published in 1978. However, the *Notebooks*, which are eleven in number, were written as diaries at the beginning of the sixties. They describe mainly the author's experiences as a political activist between 1948 and 1963 and the way Egyptian authorities persecuted members of communist and other nationalist parties in Gaza because they embraced different beliefs from those of the Egyptian authorities. The coercive measures taken against citizens in Gaza and against prisoners in the custody of the government are graphically and sensitively portrayed by the author. Bseiso mentions many people known to the Arab readers either as writers or, like Anwar Sadat and Jamal 'Abdel-Nasser, as men in the political sphere. The diaries reflect the way people during that early period looked at political and cultural life, and how the long night of the Palestinians started as soon as the catastrophe of 1948 divided their country and scattered their people.

From Palestinian Notebooks
From the Fourth Notebook

We woke up one day to find that a family had settled under the mulberry tree, near our house that was built on the sand. They were our neighbors, and their home was a tree. My mother gave them all our blankets, keeping only one for us, and with the blankets I made a house for them. She also gave them some pots and plates. She divided all our groceries equally between us and the emigrant family—the Abu Nahl Family—that consisted of two married brothers and their families.

We became one family. A few days before the March Upheaval, Abu

Nahl was assigned to watch me. He had become a policeman in the Bureau of Investigations. What I really want to say is that whenever a person becomes a policeman in the Bureau of Investigations, or of Intelligence, he will do anything. He will drain the milk from his mother's breasts and offer it, like a glass of cognac, to be drunk.

What my mother had expected came to pass. Military honor of the Bureaus of Investigations and Intelligence showed itself in its final shape on the nights of March 8 and 9, 1955. The police raid extended from Rafah to Bit Hanun. It was directed against the homes of the Communists, the Nationalists, and even the Independents in the Gaza Strip. It raided Muslim Nationalists and Communists equally. The police force that raided our house at that time was headed by Abu Nahl.

The police raid took my father by surprise. He asked Amneh to offer coffee to Abu Nahl and the rest of their squad.

Amneh used to work in the house of my grandfather. Then she joined my father's household. It was she who raised me and the rest of my brothers and sisters.

Amneh was from Jabaliya, and I still remember the moment she entered my room, carrying the coffee tray. There were Investigations police everywhere. I was sitting there with my brothers—S.B., S.B., and A.B.—when my mother came in. She smacked the tray with her hand and sent cups of coffee showering down on the heads of the police.

"There'll be no coffee served in my house to those who've come to arrest my children!" she shouted. Then she looked at Abu Nahl, who wanted to hide behind anything so as to avoid her eyes. "You've come to arrest him—Why?" she yelled. "He used to help your children! . . . There was nothing more he could have given you but his own skin to use as a blanket!"

I looked at Abu Nahl, but he was staring abstractedly down at his feet, trying to hide his eyes from me.

Investigations policemen are always staring at their big feet—feet that have grown bigger from always chasing after those who write . . .

They requested that my three brothers and I accompany them to the police station to answer some questions, after which we would be able to return home. I was well aware that some arrests would be made, but I couldn't believe that they would arrest a whole family—four sons belonging to the same mother and father. But arrest us they did, all of us.

The driver of the jeep was a Sudanese soldier. As I got into the vehicle, I told him that we were four brothers. I don't know why I said this. I don't know how, but he seemed to have known it. He put his face between his hands, and drove off, a repressed look in his eyes.

My brothers and I were taken to a stable, where we joined a long line of people who'd been arrested. The place had served as a stable during the British Mandate, but had been transformed now into torture chambers and annexed to the headquarters of the General Administrative Governor of the Gaza Strip.

Many came to watch us through the bars: first came Mustafa Hafez, the Director of the Bureau of Intelligence; then came Saad Hamza, Director of Intelligence . . . They all wanted to glimpse those Palestinians who had had their Palestinian Republic for seven days!

"Four from one family?"

"Let's release one and keep the rest."

They didn't flip a coin, but they released my brother (S.B.) before dawn.

He did not want to leave us but they dragged him out. He went on his way, weeping.

We arrived at the Cairo railway station; it was closed to the public. Only policemen stood on the sidewalks.

. . . We proceeded in groups of seven, wearing prison clothes and with our heads shaved. The cells they had prepared for us were two meters long and three meters wide. Into one of them they pushed seven prisoners, including me. We had to lie piled up on the concrete floor of the cell, one on top of the other.

I wanted to sleep. For seven days you wanted to announce to the world that night was not your enemy!

All you wanted now was one hour of sleep. They locked the prison door, but they would be back at five in the morning.

On that same day, 10 March, 1955, the students of the Jabaliya Elementary School in Gaza where I taught gathered in their playground and refused to enter their classrooms.

"No education without Mu'een!" they declared.

These students would spend the next three days demonstrating. They were like a chair fighting a mill, a bird smacking into a thousand walls; they were like a group of children celebrating their birthday under an electricity pole . . .

A little after dawn I was awakened by Hasan Mushrif, the ward sergeant, shouting, "Wake up, spies!"

They told the other wardens that we were a bunch of spies, sentenced to death, which was why they were beating us more ruthlessly than they had ever beaten a prisoner in Egypt's public prisons. Since we were to die anyway, the question of torture was a simple matter that would find its resolution in two meters of earth.

Our voices rose, "Long live the struggle of the Palestinian people!" This was our battle cry, and it provoked this response: "Beat the backs of the pining Palestinians!"

From the Fifth Notebook

Ismail Shammut[1] used to carry a cookie tray and his school books together; then he'd go sell sweets to the refugee children in the Khan Yunis Camp. A Palestinian painter, selling sweets!

In the Academy of Fine Arts in Rome, Ismail Shammut painted the fire of the Palestinian winter for the trees springing from the chest of Spartacus.

Oh! . . .

The hand of a Palestinian detainee accidentally hits the flayed back of his companion.

In the mosque of Sit Ruqayya, in the Saja'iyya, I used to jump over the backs of the men as they prostrated themselves in prayer. "Bring him to me," the *imam* of the mosque would say, "Let me blow into his ear or mouth. He won't jump over people's backs after that."

And I said No!

It feels as if you are falling to the bottom of a well . . . The Palestinian is killed in his sleep, but the dream always tells him, "You shall wake up . . ."

They used to beat Muhammad al-Najjar on the hand he was unable to use; they would beat him on its fingers.

As birds feed their young with their beaks, so did the fingers of Muhammad al-Najjar feed us all.

I used to go with Abdel Rahman al-Sharqawi[2] to edit *Al-Katib* mag-

---

[1] A famous Palestinian painter who, in his art, has commemorated the plight and struggle of the Palestinians.
[2] A famous Egyptian poet and dramatist.

azine—voice of the Egyptian Peace Movement in the aftermath of the Revolution of July 23, 1952. The general censor was called Anwar al-Sadat. We would leave after he'd reduced *Al-Katib* to a sheet of white cardboard, sprinkled with spots of ink. Blank spaces in newspapers are an old song.

You fall deeper into the well. You hit the water. You wake up.

What have they done to the Palestinian face? They shaved the hair off its head and its eyebrows, and while you stood naked before your companions, they mowed your pubic grass.

The shaving machine that razed the Palestinian head was moving like a plow in the land of Palestine. I did not know those who were crammed into the cell with me, but when we woke up at six o'clock in the morning at the sound of the jailer's key and the feel of his lash, we knew that we could be nothing but Palestinians.

One Palestinian wakes up, and he awakens all the others in his cell.

They used to beat us with whips made of plaited telephone wires. The Palestinian, who did not own a telephone, was being beaten with telephone wire.

They denied us everything: contact with other detainees, writing letters, our daily walks—half an hour in the morning and half an hour in the evening—in the prison courtyard. During their daily walks both the Communists and Muslim Brothers would throw us packs of cigarettes, and wave to us also. Anyone who waves to you while you are in hell is like someone who shakes a palm tree between your hands.

One day Sayyed Qutub[3] stopped in front of my cell door. I asked him to send us some cigarettes. He replied, "Read the Qur'an."

Reading was forbidden for the Palestinian. He was allowed one thing only: to smoke his fingers.

The "Bride" stood firm before us. The Bride was a wooden frame shaped like a woman—a wooden woman, with her arms always open, each having an opening into which a prisoner would insert his hand. The head too was open enough for a person to put his own head in it. After taking off his shirt, every one of us had to marry this "bride."

You would go up to the Bride, and the jailer would insert your arms,

[3]One of the early protagonists of the Muslim Brotherhood movement in Egypt, famous for his fine literary writings on religion and literature.

then your head, into the openings. Holding his long whip, the jailer stepped back and got ready.

Ismail Hemmat used to supervise this wedding operation. He was a hyena with honey-coloured eyes.

"Whip the Palestinian's back!"

The ropes of the whip would wrap themselves around your body. The first lash gave you the sensation of having lost some ribs. It was as though you'd been hit with a prong of fire. One stroke followed another, and at the tenth you felt as though you'd fallen into a pond of ants. There were some seventeen-year-old students with us who were whipped twenty times.

While you were feeling like a tree with a hatchet stuck in its back, the jailer took you down from the Bride. He forced you to wear your prison shirt over your flayed back. The plowing of the Palestinian back was over.

Every twenty-three detainees were placed in a single cell originally designed for one prisoner. We would take turns standing.

While standing we would try to remember things that would help us in this posture. We'd remember the sycamore tree—that peasant of all trees, which procreates more than once during a year. We'd climb it, and when we could not reach its fruit we would shake its branches violently until the fruit fell to the ground.

The following morning we found out that our shirts had stuck to our backs; removing them was like having our skins peeled off. The responsibility of treating our backs fell to the two Communist doctors who were detained with us—Dr. Yusif Idris[4] and another, Dr. Basyuni. When he was alone our jailer, a sergeant, used to mutter to us, "Of all those I've seen marry this wooden "bride," you were the most courageous."

. . . Detainees who ordinarily neglected their birthdays usually remembered them in prison. A prisoner always tries to rejoice. A prisoner's birthday is a focus of celebration for his cell. His mates offer him a full package of cigarettes, while the other cells send such gifts as tea and sugar. While we were in the Egyptian public prison, we celebrated the birthday of Dr. Yusuf Idris. He lived on the second floor.

[4]An Egyptian, Yusuf Idris is considered to be the greatest short story writer in the Arab world. He was also a prominent novelist and dramatist. He died in London in 1991.

He invited me to his party. I went, and took with me my cell's gift: a full package of cigarettes containing twenty virgin cigarettes, each dreaming of a matchstick.

Yusuf Idris smoked them, one virgin after another.

We smoked the whips, and he smoked the virgins.

During the flooding of the Nile, the fishermen wait on the shore to see the river of mud that cuts through the sea, carrying to them the striped mullet fish. Thus Egypt, which bears fish for the Palestinian in Gaza, was made to carry whips to him in its public prison.

They began moving the Muslim Brethren away. One day, Sayyed Qutub left and never returned.

When we arrived at the al-Qanatir al-Khayriyya Prison, all the Egyptian Communists welcomed us. We could hear them from the third and fourth floors, shouting, "Long live the struggle of the Palestinian people!"

We were housed on the second floor. The Palestinian had moved a step upward—from the first to the second floor.

The wind coming from Gaza began blowing the smell of the lily that grew on the Gaza shore our way . . . It began to carry good news for us.

Likewise, the wind coming from Egypt carried news of new victories. In the al-Qanatir al-Khayriyya Prison, the prisoners celebrated President Nasser's decision to break the chain of the arms monopoly. Cairo's mouth was on Prague's arm. Cairo's beauty mark was on Moscow's cheek. In the al-Qanatir al-Khayriyya Prison, Jamal Abdel Nasser raised his arm and announced the nationalization of the Suez Canal. All those who had been given twenty lashes in prison cells for having cheered five minutes for the survival of the Palestinian people were now cheering, from the same cells, for the survival of the Egyptian people.

In each cell it was like a wedding. Now, the detainee was not marrying a wooden "bride," but a woman called "River Nile." That night the cells served tea and offered cigarettes to their jailers. These latter could not understand, at first, why a detainee would cheer his jailer while he was still inside his cell.

In January 1957 there was a big surprise. An Egyptian comrade entered the cell waving a book in his hand. It was a collection of poems I had written in that cell, along with the work of some Egyptian poets— Zaki Murad, Muhammad Khalil Qasem, Mahmoud Tawfiq, and Kamal Abdel Halim. The book was entitled *Egyptian Poems*. It was illustrated by the militant painter Zuhdi and published by Dar al-Fikr. The poems were dedicated to "The Hero of National Liberation, Jamal Abdel Nasser."

This was my second published collection; this time, it was moored, like a ship, in a cell.

During that same period, Salah Jahin[5] had finished writing his collection entitled *A Word of Peace*. It included a poem he'd written about me and the demonstrations of March, 1955. In it, he says:

> Oh Mu'een, voice of victims past,
> Let your words roar out with mine
> And frighten my enemy and thine;
> We shall win at last.

... We announced our hunger strike. It lasted seven days, until a representative from the staff of the General Administrative Governor met with us and asked us to put an end to our hunger strike, promising to have us released gradually and sent back to Gaza ...

During those days, a comrade visited me and told me that Shafiq al-Hut[6] had written my obituary in an article published in the Beirut magazine, *Al-Hawadeth*, in 1956. He had also adapted "The Flood," a poem in my collection *The Battle Book*, to the stage, and presented the play at the American University in Beirut. At the same time, Abdel-Karim al-Karmi (Abu Salma)[7] had written an elegy on me that he broadcast over the Damascus Broadcasting Service.

And just as no patient remains forever in hospital, so also no prisoner remains forever in prison. The first batch of Palestinian detainees was released, and was followed by a second group. We began to feel our turn was drawing near, and that soon we would be travelling on the train home.

---

[5] An Egyptian folk poet, popular in the whole of the Arab world.

[6] A Palestinian journalist who quit journalism to work with the P.L.O.

[7] Among the pre-fifties generation of Palestinian poets, Abu Salma shares the foremost place with Ibrahim Tuqan. He continued writing his fiery and patriotic verse during the diaspora.

We were set free on the first of July, 1957. I realized then that the train was the most beautiful of man's inventions, and that coal was a cake you wanted to cut with a knife and eat with a fork.

I went to the house of my uncle 'Assem. I was carrying a bundle that contained all I owned: a shirt, a toothbrush, and a piece of soap. When I came in they thought I was a door-to-door salesman, but I had nothing to sell. My aunt Wazifa recognized me; she opened her arms, and I fell into them.

I left the door of the room open, opened all the windows, and slept. I woke up the following evening.

For the first time after two years and two months of detention, I slept while hearing the roar of the sea.

Blessed be the sea.

From The Sixth Notebook

Sahba' al-Barbar and I decided to announce our formal engagement. Her mother lived in Cairo, and she asked me to go to her there. But I was restricted from travelling, except as a detainee on a train. Some friends, however, intervened on my behalf with the General Administrative Governor, and the Investigations Bureau granted me a three day pass.

I travelled to Cairo in the company of an Investigations officer—he might almost have been sent as a witness for the wedding. Climbing the stairs behind me to my fiancée's mother's apartment and carrying a large bouquet of red carnations, he looked funny. I had bought them, and he insisted on carrying them. Imagine, an Investigations officer carrying a bouquet of carnations! . . .

We announced our engagement, and I wore a ring. We went to a modest restaurant. The Iraqi comrade, Nouri 'Abdel Razzaq Husain, was our only witness. His presence was a gift of the Iraqi Communist Party.

At that time, Dar al-Fikr published my epic, *A Giant Made of Spikes*. In it I had written:

> Here they come,
> There is no room for compromise.
> Glory to the Resistance in its mission.

The introduction to the epic was written by Dr. 'Abdel 'Azim Anis.[8]

---

[8] A famous Egyptian Marxist writer.

In another collection, *Jordan Crucified*, I wrote: "Crucified, I sing/
To Amman, Nablus, and Irbid."

The introduction to this last *diwan* was written by Abdel Rahman
Shuqir.[9] The income from its sales was set aside for the Jordanian
detainees.

When the United Arab Republic was formed, we were the first to
lead demonstrations in support of the move. We never thought, while
we were filling the streets to show our backing, that soon afterwards
all our forces, whether democratic, nationalist, or communist, would
be put into a tub of liquid acid.

We were like the fisherman who returns home without any fish in
his basket; instead, he fills it with wild lilies from the Gaza shore. Our
consolation was the revolution of July 14 in Iraq.[10] It was the wild lilies'
fragrance that emanated, solitary, in the vipers' nest in which we'd been
placed.

The propaganda campaign against the democratic and communist
forces swept away all positive aspects of life in the Arab world. It moved
like hordes of hyenas. The talks between Anwar al-Sadat[11] and Mahmoud Amin al-'Alem,[12] the representative of the Egyptian Communist
party, had failed. The Party was asked to dissolve itself—since all was
going well in the country. Mahmoud Amin al-'Alem refused—not because all was well, but for the simple reason that no one person had
the right to dissolve a Communist party.

The consequence was, naturally, a raid on the Egyptian Communist
party. Its members were arrested on January 1, 1959.

Cairo secret police began reopening their files on the communist
and democratic forces of the Gaza Strip.

In his resort home on a beach in Gaza sat Kamal Mahdi Hamida,
who had presided over the military tribunal that sentenced Saadi al-

[9]Leader of the Marxists in Amman, Jordan, during the fifties, and weighty opponent
of the government at the time. He was hunted in 1957 and escaped to Damascus.

[10]On July 14, 1958, a major coup d'état took place in Iraq which toppled the government and the Hashemite throne of young King Faisal II, and established a republic.

[11]Bseiso's *Notebooks,* published in 1978, were written between 1959 and 1963 but even
as early as that, this courageous writer openly exposed the roles of many Arab leaders.
Here, Anwar Sadat, the well-known (later) Egyptian president who concluded the peace
treaty with Israel in 1979, is shown to have been engaged in the fifties in coercive measures
against people who differed in belief from him and the Egyptian government.

[12]A prominent Egyptian left wing writer and an influential social and literary critic.

Shawwa[13] to death. Beside him was his dog, as well as a basket of sardines, still alive. Hamida would pick up a fish, which then almost jumped from his hand, and feed it to his dog.

This "shark" wanted to deal with us the way he was dealing with the fish. He wanted to throw us into the mouths of all the fascist forces, especially the most hostile of them—the dogmatic fascists and the scattered remnants of the Muslim Brotherhood.

Blood, iron, and fire were directed against communists and democrats. The Arab nation was required to stand against them. In schools, students were shouting:

> We declare it loud and clear—
> There is no place for Communists here!

Inside the classrooms, some students who had been recruited by the Bureau of Investigations—which had taken advantage of their poverty— were threatening those of their teachers who were communists or nationalists. Nor was this all. Both teachers and students were being called to the offices of the Bureaus of Investigations and Intelligence. Teachers were asked to denounce communism in the press or in the school courtyards before their students.

Also, the Bureau adopted a strange and unprecedented procedure. Suddenly one day the gate of the Salah al-Din Elementary School was broken open by a mob carrying stones and branches of the castor-oil plant. Shouting, "Down with 'Abdel-Kareem Qassem!"[14] they invaded the courtyard of the school.

Some agents of the Bureau of Investigations were among the students. Both the Bureau of Intelligence and the Bureau of Investigations wanted, by any means, to see the demonstrators clash with the students, and to have an excuse to commit a massacre.

I went into my office. Abu Saleem, the porter, closed the door and stood in front of it with some of the teachers. Stones began flying against my office windows . . . Then the demonstrators broke down the door. They stood in the doorway, not knowing what to do next. Taking advantage of their hesitation, which lasted a few seconds, I walked out calmly. They followed me into the courtyard, and one of them lifted me onto his shoulders while another shouted, "Say, 'Down with 'Abdel Kareem Qassem! Down with Communism!' "

---

[13]A dignitary from the Shawwa family in Gaza.

[14]The man who took hold of the Iraqi government after the successful military coup of 1958 in Iraq. He was a Marxist.

Suddenly an Investigation Bureau officer took out his gun and fired a shot over my head. He was certainly under instructions, and the shot was the signal for an attack. But the demonstrators were taken aback by the gun shot. There was an opening in the circle that had formed around me. It was enough to allow me to get away and run as fast as I could. My escape surprised them, as it did the policemen; but they were quick to give chase, throwing stones and shouting, "Stop him!"

I went into the first door I saw. It happened to be that of Dr. Saleh Matar—to this man I owe my life; peace be upon him, wherever he is. For, when the demonstrators began throwing stones at the windows, and hammering with their sticks on the door, he and his wife put all the furniture they could carry behind the door, which was now shaking under the blows of the demonstrators. He sent me up to the second floor and began calling the authorities who delayed for an hour before returning his call. They thought that the demonstrators would then have broken into Dr. Matar's house and killed me. But the demonstrators had been intimidated by the presence of neighbors.

Kamal Husain, Director of the Bureau of Investigations, sent an officer to Dr. Matar's house to escort me to his office. When the officer arrived, the demonstrators disappeared. On arriving at the Director's office, he shouted, "Listen, this time you escaped! The next time, you won't get away! Go home, and don't leave the house at all. I may summon you at any time."

The next day the raiding spread from my school to all the other schools of the Gaza strip. It even reached the girls' schools. Some of the students and teachers at the Al-Zahra Secondary School for girls were incited to pull certain teachers by the hair. They formed a circle around Sahba' al-Barbari, and screamed threats of death against Communists.

Gaza, where the walls of houses rise between the shoulders of olive trees . . . Gaza, the sea shell, where the ships sailing from the various seas used to take refuge . . . Gaza, who used to spread lilies and sweet basil at the feet of its scholars and poets, and revere its writers like the sun . . . was transformed in January, February, and March of 1959 into a stable for knives, and for the guns of the Bureau of Investigations, and the clubs of the Bureau of Intelligence, and the Muslim Brotherhood, and the fascist, as well. They made students spit on their teachers' hands—the same hands that had taught them to write.

It was obligatory to have a special demonstration organized by the Muslim Brotherhood; they roamed the streets of Gaza. One of them went up a minaret, and from its top shouted, "Down with communism!" instead of *"Allahu akbar."* [15]

One black day in April 1959, they carried copies of the Qur'an into the street, shouting: "Your Qur'an is in danger! Down with communism!" But the Qur'an is never in danger, except when *they* carry it—those who consent to enter the defiled offices of the director of the Bureaus of Intelligence and Investigations, Qur'an in hand.

The staff of the Administrative Governor-General of Gaza sent for Mr. Khalil 'Uweidah, the General Inspector for elementary education for the refugees. He was handed a list of the names Relief Agency teachers to be fired if the demonstrations were to be stopped. Khalil 'Uweidah refused. He demanded that the authorities responsible protect the schools, and held the Administrative Governor responsible for maintaining order.

No sooner had Khalil 'Uweidah left, than his name was added to the list of those slated for arrest.

The largest dragnet operation was mounted at midnight on April 23, 1959. On the stroke of twelve they were at our door. My Aunt Wazifa refused to open. From behind the door she shouted, not knowing what she was saying, "Come back in the morning . . ."

But my uncle opened the door. In they rushed, wearing their battle fatigues and their helmets. They carried rifles, while the officer in charge held a revolver.

At this frightening sight, my aunt collapsed. They did not allow me to come to her aid. They closed in around me and ordered me to accompany them. My uncle had collapsed beside my aunt. "Call Dr. Haydar 'Abdel Shafi immediately!" he cried. But one of the soldiers pulled the telephone off the table and threw it on the floor, where it broke into pieces. While I was still standing at the door, my aunt Wazifa died of a heart attack.

In my cell in the military prison of Cairo, this heart took the shape of a seagull in my mind. Every time Hamza al-Basyuni shouted, "Denounce Communism!", the murmur of my aunt's heart—that heart I'd

[15]Arabic for "God is great!"

left behind on the floor—would drown out Hamza al-Basyuni's voice, imploring me, "Don't let them kill me again with another heart attack!"

On April 27, 1959, three days after my arrest, my family—father, mother, brothers, and sisters—were expelled from Kuwait, along with dozens of teachers and employees.

This is how they killed my aunt, expelled my family, and put me and my fiancée in prison.

—translated by Aida Bamia and Thomas G. Ezzy

Mahmoud Darwish

For his biography, please see under his name in the poetry section.

From A Memory for Forgetfulness

The Time: Beirut; the Place: August

Out of one dream comes another: Are you well? Are you alive, I mean?

"How did you know I was sleeping with my head on your knee?"

"Because you woke me when you stirred in my belly. I knew then I was your coffin. Are you alive? Can you hear what I'm saying?"

"Am I often woken from a dream by another dream explaining the dream?"

"Does it happen to you and me? Are you alive?"

"Almost."

"And have the devils touched you with evil?"

"I don't know, but in time there's room for death."

"Don't die completely."

"I'll try not to."

"Don't die at all."

"I'll try not to."

"Tell me, when did it happen? I mean, when did we meet? When did we part?"

"It's been thirteen years now."

"Did we often come together?"

"Twice: once in the rain, and then once more in the rain. The third time we didn't meet. I went away and forgot you. And a little while ago I remembered. I remembered that I'd forgotten you. I was dreaming."

"That's how it happens with me too. I was dreaming. I got your telephone number from a Swedish friend who'd met you in Beirut. Good night! Don't forget not to die. I still want you. And when you come to life again, I want you to call me. How the time flies! Thirteen years. No. It all happened tonight. Good night!"

Three o'clock. A dawn riding on fire. A nightmare coming from the direction of the sea. Roosters made of metal. Smoke. Iron preparing the feast of iron, master of all. And a dawn that flares up in all the senses before it appears. A roaring that chases me from my bed and throws me into this narrow hallway. I want nothing, and I hope for nothing. And I can't direct my limbs in this all-encompassing confusion. No time for caution, and no time for time. If I only knew—if I knew how to organize the crush of this death that constantly pours out. If I knew how to free the screams held back in my body—a body that, in its efforts to save itself amid this ceaseless chaos of shells, no longer feels like mine. "Enough! Enough!" I whisper—to see if I can do something to guide me to myself, to locate the abyss opening out in six directions. I can't surrender to this fate, nor can I resist it. Iron that howls, only to have other iron bark back. The fever of metals is the song of this dawn.

What if this inferno were to pause for five minutes—then let things happen as they will! Just five minutes. I almost say, "Five minutes to make my final preparation, then consider my life or my death." Will five minutes be enough? Yes. Long enough for me to sneak out of this narrow corridor that opens onto the bedroom, and the study, and the bathroom where there's no water; onto the kitchen I've been waiting to leap into for the past hour, without being able to. I haven't been able to get into it at all.

Two hours ago I went to sleep. I put two pieces of cotton in my ears and went to sleep after listening to the last newscast. It didn't announce my death; that means I'm still alive. I checked all my limbs and found them all there. Ten toes below, ten fingers above, two eyes, two ears, a large nose, and a finger in the middle of my body. As for the heart, it can't be seen, and nothing points to its existence except my extraordinary ability to count my limbs and notice a revolver lying on one of the bookcases in the study. An elegant revolver—clean, sparkling, small, and without bullets. The people who gave it to me presented me with a box of bullets that, fearing folly, or a stray outburst of anger, or a stray bullet, I hid I no longer know where. The conclusion is, I'm alive; or, more accurately, I exist.

No one responds to the request sent aloft on the rising smoke. I need five minutes to put this dawn, or my portion of it, on its feet; to get ready to launch into this day born of howling. Is it August? Yes, it's August. The war's turned into a siege. I search the airwaves—on the radio that has become a third hand now—for the hourly news; but I find no one there and no news. So the radio's asleep.

I no longer wonder when the steely howling of the sea will stop. I live on the eighth floor of a building that would tempt any sniper, much less a fleet that's turned the sea into one of the sources of hell. The northern face of the building is glass, which used to give the people living here a pleasant view over the wrinkled roof of the sea. Now this has turned into a naked battlefield. Why did I choose to live here? That's a stupid question! I've lived here for the past ten years without complaining about the scandal of glass.

But how do I reach the kitchen?

I want the aroma of coffee. I want nothing except the aroma of coffee, and all I want from the passing days is the aroma of coffee. The aroma of coffee, so that I can pull myself together, stand on my feet and be transformed from some crawling thing into a human being. The aroma of coffee, so that I can stand my portion of this dawn on its feet. Let us go then, together, this day and I, down into the street in search of another place.

How can I diffuse the aroma of coffee through my cells while shells from the sea swoop down into the sea-facing kitchen to spread the stink of gunpowder and the taste of annihilation? I've begun to measure time by the period between two shells. One second. One second—a time shorter than the interval between breathing in and out, between two beats of a heart. One second isn't long enough for me to stand in front of the butane stove by the glass facade overlooking the sea. One second isn't long enough for me to open the bottle of water or pour the water into the coffee pot. One second isn't long enough to strike a match. But one second is long enough for me to burn.

I turned off the radio. I no longer wondered if the wall of the narrow hallway will really protect me from the rain of rockets. What concerns me is that there is a wall veiling the air that fuses into metal; metal aimed at human flesh, hitting it directly, or scattering into shrapnel, or choking it to death. In such cases a mere dark screen will provide a shield of imagined security. For it is death to see death.

I want the aroma of coffee. I need five minutes. I want a truce for five minutes for the sake of coffee. I have no personal wish except to make a cup of coffee. With this kind of obsession I have defined my aim. All my senses are ready in one call, setting themselves to spring in the direction of the one goal: coffee.

Coffee, for an addict like me, is the key to the day.

And coffee, for one who knows it like me, means making it yourself, not having it brought to you on a tray. For the bearer of the tray is also the bearer of talk, and the first coffee's spoiled by the first words because it's the virgin of the silent morning. Dawn, I mean my dawn, is the antithesis of talk. The aroma of coffee can absorb sounds even if they're made up of nothing more than a gentle "Good morning!" Then the coffee's spoiled.

For coffee is the silence of the morning, early and unhurried. It's the only silence in which you can be alone, in a self-created peace, with yourself and with things around you; together with the water you reach for lazily and in solitude, and pour into a small copper pot with a mysterious shine, yellow shading into brown, before placing it over a low fire. Oh, if only it were a wood fire!

Stand away from the fire a little to observe a street just waking, in search of its bread as it has been ever since the ape learned to leave the trees and walk on its feet. A street borne on vegetable and fruit carts, and on the cries of the sellers, characterized by flabby eulogy of their produce, and by the transformation of their goods into a mere matter of price. Stand back a little and breathe in the cool night air, then return to your low fire (Oh, if only it were a wood fire!) and watch with affection and patience the relation of the two elements: the fire that takes on colors of green and blue, and the water that wrinkles and breathes out tiny white granules that turn into a fine film and then grow. Slowly they expand, then quickly swell into bubbles that become larger and larger and break. Swelling and breaking, they're thirsty, ready to swallow up the spoonfuls of coarse sugar. Then, no sooner do they intermingle, than the bubbles hiss quietly and grow calm—only to take up their cry again for another substance, for the vibrant coffee, that cock bird of aroma and eastern manliness.

The leaden dawn still advances from the direction of the sea, riding over sounds I hadn't known before. The sea's stuffed to the brim with stray shells. The sea's changing its nature as a sea and turning into metal. Does death have all these names? "We'll leave," we said. So why does this red-black-gray rain keep pouring over those who leave as well as those who remain, whether people, trees, or stones? "We'll leave," we said. "By sea?" they asked. "By sea," we answered. So why are they arming the foam and the waves with this heavy gunnery? Is it so that we can hasten our steps towards the sea? But first they must break the siege of the sea. They must open the last road for the thread of our last blood. As long as this is so—and it is so—then we won't leave. And so I'll go ahead and make the coffee.

The neighborhood birds woke at six in the morning. They've carried on the tradition of neutral song ever since they first found themselves, all alone, amid the first glimmering of light. Who are they singing for in the crush of these rockets? They sing to free themselves of a night that's passed. They sing for themselves, not for us. Did we know this before? The birds have opened up their own space in the smoke of the burning city. The arrows of sound dart from side to side, wrapping themselves around the shells and pointing to an earth safe beneath the sky. It's for the killer to kill, the fighter to fight, and the bird to sing. As for me, I've abandoned my quest for metaphor. I've totally halted my search for hidden meaning, because the nature of wars is to debase symbols and to bring human relations, space, time, and the elements back to their raw state, so that we rejoice over water gushing from a broken pipe in the road. Water here comes to us like a miracle.

Who said water has no color or taste or smell? Water does have a color, which reveals itself in the unfolding of thirst. Water has the color of birdsong—the song of the sparrow in particular—the song of birds who, so long as their space is safe, pay no heed to this war that approaches from the sea. And water has the taste of water, and a fragrance which is the scent of the afternoon breeze, blowing from a field where swelling ears of wheat wave in an expanse of strewn light like the flickering points of light left by the wings of a small sparrow flying low over a field. Not everything that flies is a plane. One of the worst words in Arabic perhaps is *ṭā'irah* (plane), which is the feminine form of *ṭā'ir* (bird). The birds persist in their song, asserting their voices in the midst of the naval gunnery's roar. Who said that water has no taste or color or smell, and that the plane's the feminine form of a bird?

Yet all of a sudden the birds are quiet. As the storm of flying metal begins to rage, they've stopped their chattering and their regular soaring in the dawn air. Have they fallen silent because of its steely roar, or because of the unbalanced parallel between name and form? Two wings of iron and silver versus two wings of feather. A nose of steel and electricity against a beak of song. A cargo of rockets alongside a grain of wheat and a straw. The birds have stopped singing and paid heed to the war because their skies are no longer safe.

The sky falls like a cement roof collapsing. The sea's changing into dry land, coming closer. Sky and sea are one substance. The sea and the sky make it hard for me to breathe. I switched on the radio to have news of the sky. I heard nothing. Time had frozen. It sat on me, choking me. The planes passed in between my fingers. They pierced my lungs. . . .

It stopped there, on the other side of the street, the day we released the call against the myth advancing on us from the south. The day human flesh clenched the muscles of its spirit and cried out: "They will not pass, and we will not leave." Flesh joined against metal, triumphing over the odds, and the conquerors were halted by the walls. There will be time to bury the dead. There will be time for arming. And there will be time for time to pass as we would wish. Let the heroism go on; for we are the lords of time.

Then bread sprang from the soil and water gushed from the rock. Their rockets dug wells for us and their language of killing tempted us with the song which proclaimed: "We will not leave." We saw our faces on the screens of others, boiling with the great promise, piercing the siege with signs of a victory that will not be broken. From this moment we shall lose nothing as long as Beirut is here. And as long as we remain here in Beirut, in the midst of this sea and at the gates of this desert, we are here as names for a different homeland, and our very existence brings meanings back to the words. Here there is a tent for wandering meanings, for words gone astray, and for the orphaned light banished from the heart of things.

Who is that woman rising out from my dream?

Did she really speak with me before dawn came, or was I delirious, sleeping and waking at once?

We met only twice. The first time she learned my name, and the second I learned hers. The third time we never met at all. Why then is she calling me now, from a dream in which I was sleeping on her knee? I didn't say to her, that first time, "I love you." And the second time she didn't say to me, "I love you." And we didn't drink coffee together.

The street. Seven o'clock. The horizon is a huge steel egg. Who shall I offer my innocent silence to? The street has become wider. I walk slowly, slowly. I walk so slowly a plane couldn't miss me. The void opens its jaws, but doesn't swallow me. I move aimlessly as if I were seeing these streets for the first time, as if I were walking on them for the last time. A one-sided farewell. I am the one walking in the funeral procession, and the one whose funeral procession it is. Just one cat. If

I could find a cat. No sorrow. No joy. No beginning. No end. No anger. No satisfaction. No memory. No dream. No past. No tomorrow. No sound. No silence. No war. No peace. No life. No death. No "yes." No "no." The waves were wed to the rock mosses on a distant shore, and, straightway, I turned my back on this marriage of a million years. I left at once, but I didn't know where I was. I didn't know who I was. I didn't know my name, or the name of this place. I didn't know if I'd be able to unsheathe one of my ribs to find there a dialogue for this absolute silence. What is my name? Who gave me my name? Who is going to call me Adam?

A building's swallowed up in the depths of the earth. It was whisked away by the hands of the cosmic monster, lying in ambush for a world made by man, on an earth whose only view is of the sun, the moon, and the abyss—whisked away, to push him into a bottomless pit. We realize, on the brink of this pit, that we learned to walk, read, use our hands only to reach an end we forget, so as to go on with our search for a reason for this comedy, to cut the thread connecting the beginning with the end, to imagine that we are an exception to the only truth.

What is the name of this thing?

It's called a vacuum bomb, and it hollows out an immense space beneath the target, depriving it of the base on which it sits. Then the new vacuum sucks the building in and turns it into a buried cemetery, no more and no less. There, below, in the new realm, the old shape is kept, and the inhabitants of the building preserve their previous shapes too, and the various forms of their last movements. There, below, beneath what only a second ago was under them, they're transformed into sculptures of flesh, with not enough life even to say goodbye. The one who was asleep remained sleeping. The one carrying a coffee tray was still carrying it. The one opening a window was still opening it. The one suckling at his mother's breast was still suckling. And the one making love to his wife was still making love to her. But the one who happened to be standing on the roof of the building could shake the dust from his clothes and walk into the street without using the elevator, because the building had become level with the ground! That's why the birds remained alive, perched in their cages on the roof.

Why did they do that? Because the commander in chief was there, and had left a little while before. Had he really left? Our anxious question transformed him from a father to a son. We didn't even have time to pass judgment on the question. What if he was there? Does that justify the massacre of a hundred human beings? Another question occupied us constantly: has he managed to survive his attempted assassination by jet fighter and through the most modern weapons, like the vacuum bomb? Yesterday, he played chess before the American cameras, to push Begin[1] into further madness and deprive him of any justification for political attack—justification that he replaced by invective against Palestinians as human beings: "These Palestinians aren't human. They're animals walking on all fours." He had to strip us of our humanity to justify our killing; for the killing of animals—unless they're dogs—isn't taboo in western law. Begin was reclaiming the history of his madness and crimes, for he thought his soldiers, the hunters of these animals, were out on a hunting picnic. But hundreds of coffins were thrown in his face, raised by thousands shouting, "How much longer?" We aren't human because we didn't let him enter an Arab capital. He couldn't believe human beings could stand against the transformation of the myth into an absolute court for judging all values and all humanity, in all places and at all times. And so he had to change the nature of those resisting him into something nonhuman, into an animal nature, after the myth he believed in had closed off all windows onto the possible question: "Who is the animal?" The ghosts of those he had butchered at Dair Yasin,[2] whom he banished from time and place so that he could set his own presence on that time and place, have pounced on the dreams of his sleep and his wakefulness. Now these ghosts, their flesh, bone and spirit heroically regained, have laid siege to him in Beirut. The ghost who was a victim has come back as a hero. And, between the ghost and the hero, the prophet of lies was besieged by a crippling obsession—an obsession that stopped him seeking help from chapters in the Bible that could, in themselves, have written the history of humanity.

—translated by Ibrahim Muhawi and Christopher Tingley

[1] Please see footnote 2 of Rashad Abu Shawar's excerpt from *O Beirut!*
[2] Please see footnote 3 of Mahmoud Shaheen's story, "The Sacred River."

Subhi Ghosheh *(b. 1926)*

A writer on politics and a well-known patriot, Subhi Ghosheh is a medical doctor by profession. Born in Jerusalem, he studied first at its government schools, then studied medicine at the University of Cairo. He later practiced medicine in Kuwait where he lived for a good number of years and where he distinguished himself by his sober and illuminating ideas about the problems of his country and people and by his political integrity. He has also written constantly about the political and social predicament created by the particular situation of the Palestinians both at home in occupied Palestine and in exile. His book, *Our Sun Will Never Set*, (1988) vol. I, about his early life in Jerusalem and his memories of the customs and lifestyle of that city, was first published in serialized form and quickly gained great popularity among its readers. He is now preparing the second volume.

From Our Sun Will Never Set

One of my friends recently asked me, a tone of blame in his voice, why I had stopped sending cards for various feast days, and why I never seemed to enjoy any of these occasions. I did not deny this, for I have definitely neglected some wonderful traditions since I was forced to leave Jerusalem. I am neither the first nor the last person to experience such loss; many others before and after me have known it. Quite a few centuries ago one medieval poet expressed this in verse:

> Jerusalem, not one cloud ever passed over my head
> without my addressing it, brokenly,
> 'By God, pass over Jerusalem, cloud,
> carry my greetings to its valleys and hills.'
> I've been bitterly separated from you
> my eyes are almost blind from crying
> After you my eyes can only see the world
> as a dismal night of a dark day.[1]

[1] Poetry and other literature on Jerusalem abound in old text books, written mainly when the crusaders occupied the holy city in medieval times.

The feast is not simply one special day or two; it is the sum total of a whole civilization, of the experiences, traditions, and customs of generations that are embodied by an occasion. Each one has deep roots in the history and conscience of every man, that can only be fully sensed within a whole natural, historical, geographical and cultural framework. I compare this to a tree or flower or fruit that will not bloom or ripen or give forth its fragrance except in the right environment and ground within the natural surroundings that have produced millions of similar fruits or flowers . . .

For me and for many others, the feast should be a crystallization of repeated memories and practices. We cannot enjoy them unless we live them in the wholeness of time, in a natural environment, among their true people. With them we revive the memories of childhood and the hopes of old age. We also hope to share the experience of such days with our children and grandchildren.

Feasts began early, in advance of the official days, increasing our joys and excitement, until the day of the small *waqfa*, which is the day before the eve of the feast; then the day of the big *waqfa*, which is the eve of the feast; then the feast day itself. Children used to gather in groups and roam around the streets and quarters singing, "Tomorrow is the feast and we'll celebrate it . . ."

For children, feast preparations took place on many levels. Some families began by buying clothes or sewing new ones for the kids. Two or three days before the feast, fathers used to accompany their sons to the shopping centers to buy them new suits or new pairs of shoes. The beauty of new attire would lose its gleam if bought much earlier. We were not allowed to keep those new clothes near us until the night before the feast. Then we'd put our new shoes near our beds or even under the sheets with us, and drape the new suits nearby to prepare for wearing them the next morning. The same thing happened for the girls. Mothers used to take their daughters to the dressmaker to have new dresses made for them if they couldn't make them at home; in those days most of our women were clever in the arts of sewing and embroidery, as well as cooking and taking care of large families with many children. They did this to perfection, without any outside help.

Despite the limited means of our families during those days, they used to save as much as they could to buy special treats for the feast. Children's clothes were always bought before adults'. However, sometimes even this was difficult. Parents would resort to other means that made children happy and preserved the family's pride at the same time.

An older brother's suit might be repaired to fit a younger son, and become new again. A girl's dress could be transformed into a smaller size. Faded suits could be turned inside out to make a respectable new suit. Only one thing would look different: the upper pocket was on the right instead of the left.

As for shoes, Abu Daud, the cobbler, knew how to apply soles which made shoes practically new again, and how to patch them so their holes would not show. He would polish repaired shoes with great care so they looked as if they were new. Even socks could be skillfully mended on heels and lower parts.

All this used to happen with the knowledge and understanding of the children, who understood their parents' circumstances and accepted them without complaint. No one created family storms by demanding new clothes or toys. Parents would promise to do better for the next feast. But many times they went on patching and repairing for years.

Then there was the lamb of the feast. If a family could afford to buy one, it was butchered early in the morning. Women woke up early with the dawn's *adhan*[2] and began preparing primuses and large pots, as well as the stuffing for the lamb. As for the feast bread, it was made of a special kind of dough with added spices, anise or *qazha*[3] or fennel. It would be baked either on the eve of the feast or in the early morning together with the feast cakes, and *maʿmul*[4] which they used to prepare at night. Families used to agree with the bakers to send them the baker's boy early. He would return with their baked bread first, in exchange for a generous tip. The main feast sweet was baklava, made those days with authentic butter and nuts and almonds and pistachios. It would be ordered long before the feast, but the baklava tray was to arrive only on the morning of the feast day. The two most famous baklava makers in Jerusalem were Abu Talʿat Habb Rumman and Zalatimo, but many others had sweet shops too. Families who could not afford a whole large tray of this sweet would buy baklava or *maʿmul* or cakes by the kilogram from various shops, or from the spreads which were set up in front of Damascus gate all during the feast.

[2]The *adhan* is the call to prayer, made from minarets of mosques five times a day and on feasts and other important occasions.

[3]The *qazha* seeds are tiny black and tasty seeds which are either added to bread or savory cakes, or are made into delicious sweets. They are regarded as very healthy to eat.

[4]*Maʿmul* is a rounded or oval cake made of semolina and stuffed with spicy walnuts.

Most people, whether young or old, wanted to appear at their best the first days of the feast. So the barber shops would be crowded on the eve. We had to wait in line a long time. When I was a little boy I used to have my hair cut at Abu Ramzi's at the Silsila gate. A haircut for children cost two millims[5] on ordinary days, and half a piaster or even a whole piaster during the feast period. Traveling barbers would even set up jerry cans in the streets, particularly at the Jaffa or Damascus gates, where the customer would sit and, they'd cut his hair very quickly or give him a nearly clean shave for two millims or half a piaster.

After the haircut came the bath so each child could welcome the feast with a clean body. We welcomed this so we could wear our new clothes. Most people in those days did not have bath tubs or showers. The water would be heated in a jerry can over the primus and poured on the body from a round vessel or bowl. The skin would be scrubbed with a scratchy loofah and soaped briskly with Nablus soap.[6]

On the eve of the feast we went to sleep hugging our new or renewed shoes and our new suits, dreaming of the feast and the money gifts (*'idiyyeh*) we would receive. Every now and then during the night we would raise our heads to see if our parents had awakened yet. Boys were impatient to accompany the men of the family to the Aqsa mosque for the feast prayer. No sooner would noises and movement begin, than we would rise from our bed and dress quickly, kissing the hands of our parents, then going to our grandparents room and kissing their hands twice, beginning with our grandfather. This was the tradition that everybody, either small or grown-up, faithfully followed. In those days we led lovely domestic lives that were almost uniform all over the country. We made rounds of our aunts and uncles, kissing their hands. During feast days the kissing of hands was always followed by good wishes for many happy returns of the feast, after which we always received the *'idiyyeh*—sometimes a shilling and sometimes ten piasters or two shillings. Then we would wait until our grandfather, father, and uncles had finished their ablutions and walk out with them in a single file headed toward the old city, where the Aqsa mosque is. The road would be crowded with neighbors and peasants who had come walking from their villages for the feast prayer at the Aqsa. One of the loveliest

---

[5]The *millim* was the smallest monetary unit in Palestinian money. Ten *millims* made one piaster, five piasters made one shilling, and one hundred piasters made a Palestinian pound.

[6]Nablus is famous for its wonderful nonfragrant soap made of pure olive oil.

scenes my memory retains is this vision of the affection and warm unity of society in those days. We'd see handshakes and hear congratulations and good wishes passing from person to person whether the people knew one another or not. Congratulations were a holy duty which everyone was committed to offer.

We'd arrive at the large courtyard of the holy mosque to find it crowded with people who had come from all directions. We'd follow Grandfather and Father near to where they performed the feast prayer, while we waited outside the Aqsa. We were then very young, less than seven or eight, and had not yet begun performing daily prayers ourselves.

The sounds of men repeating the sentence, "There's no God but God" and, "God is great" filled us with reverence, awe, and security. When prayers were over, the men would leave the courtyard of the mosque moving towards the graveyards to visit their dead ones and read the *Fatiha*[7] on their souls. I used to hear my father say whenever I accompanied him there, "Listen, son, all of us are destined to this place, to the earth. We visit our dead ones to assert our connections with our roots. No man enters the grave with any possessions; nothing remains for man except his good name and charitable deeds."

Women visited the graveyards in the afternoons. They went there carrying cakes which they distributed. I still do not know the secret of this tradition, which is now obsolete, although the visiting of graveyards is still faithfully carried on. The women often asked a number of the Quran reciters who frequented the place to read a few chapters of the Quran for the souls of their loved ones. Then they would pay them some money. Many of those Quran reciters did not know how to read well, but that did not affect their employment.

After visiting the graveyards the men used to go visit their women relatives. This holy tradition was never flouted; the head of the family would visit all the daughters of the family on these occasions. He began the round by visiting the daughters or sisters of the family who were married to men outside the family. This was meant to let them feel they were still part of their own families and to intimate to the husband and his family that the girl was not rootless but, in fact, had a family who could protect and care for her even though she had moved to her

---

[7]The first chapter of the Quran read on all important occasions such as marriage, betrothal, death, and other momentous occasions.

own home. This felt like a beautiful custom to me, again representing family unity which is one of the bastions of society.

Of course, such visits were accompanied by money gifts to the daughter of the family, and no matter how small the amount, it was always regarded as the girl's own property;[8] she could use it to buy whatever she wanted for herself. I have always respected and kept this tradition, offering money gifts to my married sister and her children whether small or grown-up just as I used to do so with my other sisters when we were still at home in Jerusalem.

And just as we would visit the daughters of our own family, my mother's family came to visit her. We used to await this visit impatiently, for we always got a large *'idiyyeh* from them, in addition to the gifts of mixed nuts, chocolates, and cakes that they always brought.

Everyone convened at the feast breakfast. All the sons of the family and their wives and children came to participate in this meal and afterwards in the games and enjoyment. Great merriment dominated the reunion. When I got married during our Jerusalem days I did not once relinquish this habit.

As far as the children were concerned, the formal rituals of the feast ended with breakfast, and we would be allowed to go out alone to buy sweets or other things. When we were very small we couldn't do this, of course, but had to accompany one of the grown-ups. More often than not, these grown-ups had their own plans, and we would confine ourselves to the courtyards in front of our homes where we played and exchanged some of the delicacies we had acquired during the day.

Our greatest joy on feast days was to spend a day in the old city where we visited members of our families who had remained living there.[9] As soon as we arrived at the old city, we would go to the carnival area, which we called the "swings." These were erected in a large square near the Hutta gate in the vicinity of the courtyard of the holy mosque. They were really old fashioned ferris wheels made up of four little cars

---

[8]In Islam, money owned by a female or given to her at any time by her father, brother, husband, or anyone else, or as compensation for work, is regarded as her own property and is not considered, legally, property to be shared by the husband.

[9]When Jerusalem enlarged, people went out from the old city within the famous walls and built their homes outside, forming the many new quarters of the city such as the Upper Baq'a, the Lower Baq'a, the Qatamoun, Bab al-Zahira, al-Shaikh Jarrah and others, all inhabited, prior to 1948, by Arab families. (The last two quarters are still inhabited by Arab families in the nineties.) Dr. Ghosheh's immediate family were among those who had gone outside the old city to live, prior to 1948.

in which boys and girls sat, enjoying the rising and circling rounds several times. We paid one millim for every ride, which was raised later on to half a piaster. The carnival was always full of boys and girls and vendors shouting about their goods and children screaming and joggling for their turn at the rides.

At the carnival we chose from a varied selection of foods for sale. The most exciting was turnip pickles which the vendor placed in an earthenware dish for us to eat. We loved the salty brine which we used to enjoy sipping without any attention to cleanliness or health. We would dip the bread in it and eat it. We also enjoyed eating lamb fat with ground lamb meat, and the Badran *kubaibeh*[10] and broiled liver which were offered to us with the sentence, "He who cannot pay now can pay next year." We also enjoyed *falafil*[11] and *muhallabiyyeh*[12] and *hareeseh*[13] and sesame or hazel nut confections and *turmus*,[14] and peanuts and ice cream if the feast came in summer.[15]

We used to spend a wonderful time there and did not leave the carnival until all our money was spent, or evening arrived. Then we'd return, broke and exhausted, and begin waiting for the next feast to come.

When we grew up we began visiting the cinema. Some of us would promenade along Jaffa street or in the other Jewish quarters, and others would make trips to the Dead sea or the Qalt valley or 'Ain Fara, or sometimes even to Jaffa and other towns. But I never went to these towns when I was still a student.

After I finished my university education, I continued our family traditions for the first days of the feast. We added trips to Qibya or the Solomon ponds or the Rawda gardens in Jericho with other Palestinian

---

[10]*Kubaibeh* or *kubbeh* is one of the most delicious Palestinian (and Lebanese and Syrian) dishes. It is made of ground meat pounded to perfection and mixed with finely crushed wheat. Spices are added and the whole paste is either made into oval shaped balls stuffed with cooked meat and onions and fried; or spread in two layers similarly stuffed, on larger trays and baked in the oven.

[11]*Falafil* are fried savory balls made of ground soaked chick-peas, cumin, minutely cut onions, and other optional ingredients, fried in oil.

[12]*Muhallabiyyeh* is a pudding made of milk and ground rice or fine starch, and sugar.

[13]*Hareeseh* is another sweet made up of semolina, sugar, and butter, and baked.

[14]Lupines, a kind of bean, yellow in color which are soaked in salty water until they are soft to eat. They are delicious and nourishing.

[15]Muslims observe the lunar time system which means that the dates of religious occasions revolve with the years. Since the lunar year is eleven days less than the solar year, feasts and other religious occasions take place in various seasons in any person's lifetime.

families, until the Destroyer of All Joys and the Separator of People came with the Zionist occupation, and the feasts lost their glamour and merriment. But I never felt we lost our authenticity and attachment to our traditions until I was forced to leave Jerusalem. Even now I still practice a few of those traditions, and yearn to go back to my roots in Jerusalem, so the joys of the feast might once again feel complete.

—translated by Salwa Jabsheh and Naomi Shihab Nye

Yusuf Haykal *(1907–1989)*

Born in Jaffa, Haykal was one of the first men in Palestine to study abroad, obtaining a *doctorat d'état* in law and economics from the University of Paris in 1935 and a Ph.D. in political science from the University of London in 1937. On his return home he occupied several distinguished positions in Palestine, including that of judge in Nablus from 1945 until the Palestine catastrophe in 1948. After 1948, he represented the kingdom of Jordan as ambassador to several countries, spending almost ten years in this capacity in the United States, three years in France, and two in Britain. After his retirement Haykal traveled extensively, living part of the year in Jordan and the other in Washington D.C. He wrote many books of history, politics, travel, and memoirs, among which are: *Palestine Before and After* (1971); *Towards Arab Unity* (1943); *Days of My Youth* (1988); and *The Prime of Life* (1989).

From Days of My Youth
Our Life at Home

Our house was in the northeastern part of Jaffa, east of the railway . . . on a strip of land measuring around twelve *dunums*.[1] The house itself was on the southern half of this land; the other half containing the house of the man who tended the orchard, a stable, a chicken coop, places for the keeping pigeons and rabbits, the well and pool of the orchard, and a raised bower at the height of the pool, with a small fountain in the middle of it. Water from the well poured into this fountain, then flowed in a narrow rivulet to the large pool, irrigating the oranges and other fruit trees with which the land was planted.

. . . Our house was actually made up of two buildings: the first had five rooms with a kitchen, bath, and rest room, and the second had four rooms, also with a kitchen and conveniences. Two rooms stood on each side of a large covered and tiled courtyard, with a little fountain in the middle which was fed from the pool in the orchard.

---

[1] A *dunum* is one thousand square meters.

The two buildings were separated by a large piece of land about twenty-four meters long and twelve meters wide. On the western side of this was a wall joining the buildings and separating the inner part of the land from the outer one. On the eastern side was a row of four rooms, with the well serving the two buildings in the middle, and a bathroom; the doors of all these, and their windows too, opened onto a tiled corridor two meters wide, raised half a meter from the ground and covered with a roof of red brick. On the sides there was a beautiful wooden fence overlooking the inner piece of land, which was in fact a delightful garden with many flowering shrubs. Mother, who loved flowers, took great care of this garden, and she used to send beautiful bouquets to my married sister Asya, to her own mother, and to other relatives and neighbors as well. When I was eventually allowed to go out by myself, I used to carry these bouquets to them.

We occupied the two buildings at once, as if they were the same house. In all, they had thirteen rooms with two kitchens, one bathroom and three rest rooms.

We entered into these two buildings by a large gate at the beginning of the street. In front of the house there was a wide, sandy piece of land, and beyond this the land where the rail tracks were; the barrier between these two was partly wall and partly a simple wooden fence through which we could see the trains pass. In the middle of the land, near the entrance, there was a large mulberry tree which never bore fruit, and so never attracted the flies . . .

Some of us lived in the small building and some in the large one. Father, Mother, my little sister, and I occupied the small one, with Father having one of the two western rooms and the rest of us the other. There was an inner corridor between them. In my father's room there was a large bed of brass, and two armchairs with a little table between them which always had an ashtray and a vase on it. Next to the door was another table about one and a half meters long, where the tea service stood; Father was fond of drinking tea and had a special mixture that he prepared himself from two or three kinds. There was also a brass samovar on the table to boil water in, and white china teacups with gilded edges, and small plates for cakes . . .

My mother's room had a wide bed of brass and a small bed for my sister Dunya; I myself slept next to my mother. The room also had a large sofa and a Persian rug, and there were luxurious curtains on the four windows.

In the dining room there was an oval table which could be pulled out to seat twelve people, with the appropriate number of chairs, and a sideboard. The room had two windows overlooking the small inner garden.

My brother, Muhammad, and my five sisters Shuhrat, Nafisa, Munira, Fatima, and Saʿdiya, occupied the larger building in which two rooms were used as drawing rooms. The maid had her private room next to the kitchen.

I won't describe the furniture of the house at length; suffice it to say that it was all imported from France, and was almost unique among the families of Jaffa in the last quarter of the nineteenth century and the first quarter of the twentieth.

Mother would receive other ladies who were her friends in one of the drawing rooms in the large building; she was very sociable and loved to visit and be visited. This annoyed my father, for he didn't like Mother to visit others too much, and there were often quarrels between them on this account. Mother was very beautiful and had a strong personality, while Father had a hot temper and a strong will.

Mother also received members of our family in the courtyard in front of the large building. It was, in fact, a long porch overlooking the inner garden, with a red brick roof. The maid would lay the carpet there, then put down various kinds of cushions, on which people would sit. Conversation would be warm and my sisters would offer orange or lemon drinks, then coffee and sweets.

I well remember how we used to enjoy the stories of my aunt, Imm Rafiq Mannaʿ, my mother's sister, who was a little younger than my mother herself. Whenever she got up to leave, we'd hold on to her, insisting that she stay a little longer to tell us more stories.

I also had a paternal aunt called Imm Hasan Shihab, who was older than my father and wore a wide white robe called a *sabla*. On her head she wore a long white scarf, leaving her face unveiled. I don't remember any other woman in Jaffa wearing the *sabla*; they all wore the *mulaya*, which was made up of a long black skirt that reached down to the feet and a large black garment covering the head and the upper part of the body, and they wore a transparent black veil over their faces.

This aunt of ours visited us a lot, and her stories were funny because they were so unbelievable. She told us once she wasn't afraid of snakes; she'd approach a snake, she said, and tell it: "You, blessed one, do not move!" and then pick it up by the head. I had a plastic snake about half a meter long which would move slightly when thrown on the floor, just as a live snake does. When I heard what she said, I went to my room, took the plastic snake and stood near the window overlooking the porch where my aunt was sitting. Then I threw the snake at her and up she jumped, like lightning, terrified and screaming, "May God preserve us from the devil!" We all laughed, and I asked her, "Why were you scared of the snake when you said you're not afraid of them?" She gazed at me angrily and reproachfully, then she grew a little calmer. "This snake's an infidel snake," she said, to save her face. "It's not Muslim. It's Muslim snakes I'm not afraid of!"

Mother enjoyed cooking, and was helped in this by our maid and my older sisters. Our main meal was in the evening. My sisters and the maids would lay the table, assigning each member of the family his or her own plate, knife, fork, and spoon. The serving dishes were oval-shaped and were placed in the middle of the table, laden with rice, vegetables, and meat or fish or poultry. When all was ready, Father would come and sit at one end of the table and Mother at the other, while we took our places on each side. After my parents had served themselves we would do the same, and when we finished eating the table was cleared by the maid and my sisters, and fruit was brought in. My father always drank tea after a meal and my mother coffee.

My mother was an expert at making round cakes stuffed with dates, and *ma'mul* which was stuffed with nuts and *ghuraibeh*.[2] I remember her making large quantities of these in Ramadan[3] and before the feasts. My two sisters, Shuhrat and Nafisa, would help her, assisted by the maid. I used to pass by the kitchen and gaze at them as they made all these kinds of cakes that I loved, and I'd often try and snatch some date paste to eat it, but Mother would scold me, ordering me not to touch anything with my hands; then she'd put some date paste for me on a small plate and I'd eat it as I stood there with them. The next day the man who tended the orchard would take the large trays to the oven and return them looking tremendously appetizing. Mother would put some of them on plates for us and we'd eat them hot with great relish. I still love these particular sweets, perhaps because I used to see Mother make them, or perhaps they remind me of the beautiful family life that we had.

Father would take his early evening tea in his room, and he liked us to have tea with him there. My sisters would bring the chairs from the dining room, and we'd all sit around the tea table. Mother sat in one

---

[2]These are delicious shortcakes made of semolina, sugar, and a lot of butter.
[3]The Muslim month of fasting.

armchair and my brother, Muhammad, sat in the other if he happened to be at home at the time.

Father would pour tea from the small china pot in which the tea was brewed to perfection. He'd pour a little into each cup then put each cup under the tap of the samovar and open it for the hot water to pass. My sister Shuhrat would put sugar in the cups, while my sister Nafisa would pass them to us all, beginning with my mother. We used to enjoy drinking it and eating a piece of cake. Father, though, preferred to drink it without taking anything else.

Whenever my sister Fatima entered the room, with her tall and lovely figure, her smooth white complexion, long, dark, soft hair, and her large, black eyes, Father would exclaim, "Welcome, angel!"

Those tea-drinking rituals are still alive in my heart and when I remember them I feel elation and also a wistfulness because they're no more. Is it because of them that I'm so fond of drinking tea, and preparing tea mixtures of all kinds? I still drink tea three times a day: with breakfast, then at eleven o'clock in the morning, and afterwards in the late afternoon; and I still prepare the mixture we drink with my own hands from two fine brands of tea.

The eve of feast days and the feast days themselves were the most wonderful times in our lives. Our parents would buy us new clothes and new shoes, and my sisters Sa'diya and Dunya and I used to lay them near our beds on the eve of the feast to wear in the morning. We'd get up with the dawn on those feast days, but Mother wouldn't allow us to wear them before we'd taken our baths. So we'd hurry to the bath one after the other, then joyfully walk about the house in our new clothes, waiting.

After my father had dressed, we used to go to him and kiss his hand, saying, "Many happy returns of the day, Father." Then he'd kiss us and give each of us a silver *majidi*, which was equal to one fifth of a gold Ottoman pound. Then we'd go to Mother, and kiss her hand saying, "Many happy returns of the day, Mother," and she in turn would kiss us and give each of us another silver *majidi*. The *majidi* bought a great deal in those days.

Then we'd all meet at the breakfast table.

I used to wait impatiently to take two bouquets of flowers, one to my sister Asya, and the other to my maternal grandmother. I'd go to my sister's first, and kiss her hand and that of her husband Sayyid Yusuf Hannoun, and they'd kiss me and give me a silver *majidi* and insist that I eat a piece of cake; but I'd excuse myself, because I'd be in a hurry to go to my grandmother's. I'd go into my grandmother's home, which was on the second floor of the Za'balawi house in al-Manshiya quarter, and I'd kiss her hand and that of my uncle Mustafa Sakkijha and his wife Fatima, daughter of Haj 'Ali Haykal, my father's uncle. They'd all kiss me, and then my grandmother too would give me a *majidi*. I used to love my grandmother very much and loved taking her a bouquet of flowers whenever I could. She never failed to give me a *majidi*.

My grandmother was a gracious, beautiful, dignified woman. She was also rich, and owned many orange groves and *Waqf* possessions[4] that her father had left her, as she was his only child.

On the morning of the first feast day my sister Asya and her husband would visit us and stay for lunch. Their son, Rushdi, who was their first born, lived with us from the time he was one year old.

My father took enormous pleasure in the education of his children. He sent my brother, Muhammad, to the Frère French school in Jaffa, then to the American College, which later became the American University in Beirut; Muhammad was a student there when the First World War broke out. Father also sent his daughters Asya, Shuhrat, Nafisa, Munira, and Fatima to the British school in Jaffa, from which they graduated one at a time, as each was two years older than the next. Girls' education was rare in those days, and many viewed it with suspicion.

We used to play under the mulberry tree in front of the house, sheltering within its shade. The man who tended the orange grove took great pains to keep the land clean and would go over it collecting all the fallen leaves. Often the family would spend the summer evenings under this tree, with mats and cushions laid for my mother, my sisters, and the guests to sit on. The maid would offer coffee to the older people and some nuts of which we children also partook.

There was a broker in Jaffa who specialized in selling animals. He used to visit Father frequently, for Father was fond of animals, and had owned many of them before I came into the world. One day the

---

[4]*Waqf* is an Islamic institution into which property and monies are put in trust either for charity and then regarded as a pious endowment, or for specific members of the family as in family *waqf*. In the latter case a supervisor was appointed to administer the fund for the beneficiary or beneficiaries of the trust. In Haykal's account, his grandmother's father made sure that she got the proceeds of his estate by putting it in this kind of Islamic trust. In the Sunni sect, women do not inherit outright, but have to share their inheritance with male relatives. In the absence of brothers, these may be uncles or cousins, even remote relatives.

broker told father about a brisk young mule, beautiful and strong, with bright, wine-colored hair. Father asked to see this mule, liked the look of it, and bought it. The man who tended the orange grove looked after it, and it became well-known in Jaffa.

After three years the broker came to my father and persuaded him to buy a lovely pedigree colt and sell the mule to someone who wanted to buy it. Father sold the mule, but after three months began to regret his decision, and one night, in a dream, he saw the mule gazing at him and weeping. He got up perturbed from his bed, sent for the broker and asked him about the mule. The broker told him that the original buyer had sold it at a profit and that its new owner had begun to use it to pull carriages with another mule; but because it stepped so quickly, the balance would be lost, and also it would bolt at every sound it heard, so that its new owner wanted to sell it if he could only find a buyer. Father told the broker he was willing to buy it back, and the day the mule returned to us was one of great joy.

—translated by May Jayyusi and Christopher Tingley

Jabra Ibrahim Jabra

For his biography, please see under his name in the poetry section.

From The First Well

On the edge of the Valley of the Camel, a little below the New Road, a huge azarole tree soared upwards, visible from our house on the hill above. The slopes of the valley were covered with olive trees wherever you looked, but this wild azarole prided itself on its height, its spreading branches, and its towering grandeur. No one knew who had planted it; perhaps it had simply burst out from the earth between two big rocks, too long ago for anyone to remember. We always saw it clearly from the road, because its upper branches rose up higher than the road's edge, and it would sway with every breeze as if beckoning to us, deliberately and willfully inviting us. We had only to climb a rock or two and jump on to one of its branches, then carry on up into its dense network of branches and leaves, and fill our pockets with its sweet little yellow fruit.

During the olive-picking season we'd make it our point of entry to the trees in the valley. The croppers, with their sticks and ladders, would pick the olives with a deftness that went back thousands of years, singing merrily as they did so. "'Ala dal'una"[1] was everyone's favorite song; and in autumn the valley would be filled with the sound of it, as men, women, boys, and girls shook the trunks and branches, beat them with their sticks and climbed to the higher, more difficult branches on ladders, making the green olives fall, like pearls, on to the red earth. They'd move from tree to tree, picking up handfuls of fruit to fill their baskets and bags, and their songs and the tunes of the double reed and the flute would move on with them. Whatever the time of day, there was always someone, perhaps visible, perhaps not, sitting alone on a rock somewhere and playing the double reed or flute, pouring out a flood

[1] "'Ala dal'una" and "'Ataba" (see p. 665 below) are two major folk songs sung in the region of Palestine, Jordan, Syria, and Lebanon.

of tunes which echoed through every part of the broad valley like the playing of a gentle breeze.

Here and there a few olives would cling stubbornly to their branches, or lie hidden among the pebbles or between the cracks in the earth that were lined with nettles and various kinds of autumn anemone; and we'd take our school bags (school being closed for a few days, so that the students could take part in the olive harvest) and glean behind the croppers, picking up any stray or stubborn olives they'd missed, however few these might be. These were free to anyone who took them; and when we'd filled our little bags with them, we'd go back to our lonely azarole tree if there was any daylight left, and climb it, singing our own songs, happy with what we'd gathered.

I tried to understand the bedouin words of the song and took pleasure in the uncommon ones among them. I liked to imagine how the "north wind" changed the color of lovers; I saw them, dark, tanned by the sun as it lit up their large, kohl-painted eyes, eyes that glittered and shone, gleaming white and intensely black, while the north wind blew on them and deepened their darkness—and their sweetness:

> 'Ala dal'una, 'ala dal'una,
> The north wind has changed my color.
> I'll write to my sweetheart on blue paper
> And send many greetings to my beloved girl.
> But if, my darling, you're bent on staying apart,
> Talk to me on the telephone.

I tried to imagine the voice of this adored sweetheart as she lisped over a telephone. I'd seen a telephone once at some people's house, but I'd never put the receiver to my ear—and many years later, when I spoke on the phone for the first time, this song and these words were the first thing that came into my mind. I wished the person at the other end had been that beloved girl bent on staying apart from her lover, while I picked olives in the Valley of the Camel and filled my pockets with azaroles; then I could have asked her, "Tell me, please, why *are* you bent on staying apart?"

One day I was coming back from the azarole tree, on my way home with Sulayman. Near the tree a lane turned off from the New Road and went up till it reached the top, by the garages of the Bethlehem buses whose company had recently been established. At that point the lane turned to join Ras Iftays Street as it carried on upwards; our house was on the heights above this lane, which had actually, for many centuries, been the original road to Jerusalem, before the New Road was built and paved in the early 1920s. The New Road led directly to Manger Square, skirting the edge of the valley in a wide arc and missing the old town.

One of the owners of the garages where the lane turned off was a relative of ours called Abu Ilyas. After my father's sciatic nerve disease had forced him to leave his job at the convent hospital, he'd sometimes go to Abu Ilyas to amuse himself and talk to the two or three men who worked there and who were acquaintances of his. He'd watch the car engines being repaired, enchanted by their complexity and movements, and he'd say, "That's the kind of work I always wanted to do!"

One day Abu Ilyas asked my father why he didn't go and work for them; and when my father said he was too old now to learn a new trade, and was too sick in any case, he insisted that my father would simply be allowed to help the workers as best he could. The wages, he said, would be very small—one shilling a day.

My father agreed to this, despite my mother's objections (my brother was in Jerusalem, and didn't know what was happening at home). I argued as strongly as I could, too, because I was afraid my father would do himself an injury with the physical exertion involved. But my father insisted; the work was easy, he said, and it would give him something to do.

It was just a few days after he'd started work at these garages that Sulayman and I were, as I said, going back home up the hill from the hospitable azarole tree, and I saw my father busy carrying a number of tires inside from the sidewalk.

"Let me help you, father," I said.

"No, no," he said. "You go and play with your friend."

"Let me carry the tires with you," I said. "I'll go home afterwards." I turned to my friend. "You go," I said, "I'll follow on later."

Sulayman went off, and I helped my father with what he was doing.

A few meters below us there was a car hoisted up on a jack, ready for a front tire to be put on. One of the workers had already fitted the tire on to the iron rim of the wheel and pumped it up, and he asked my father to carry it to the car.

I volunteered to carry it myself, and, finding that it was heavy, I stood it on its edge. It was pumped up hard, like a football, so I decided I could roll it along instead of carrying it. In fact, I only had to give it a little push and it rolled along easily in front of me.

I ran after it, pushing it once or twice, and it started to roll downhill faster. Then, when I tried to push it sideways toward the car hoisted up on the jack, my hand hardly touched it, and it went on rolling in the direction it had chosen for itself.

I ran quicker behind it, but it outstripped me like a bolting horse, going faster and faster down the road as I still sped after it with all the strength I could muster. I saw it getting further and further ahead of me, while I panted behind, vainly trying to catch it. It looked like a furious animal that had thrown off all restraint. There was a man peacefully riding his donkey up the road, and I was afraid the crazy tire would run into him and throw him and his donkey to the ground, but it crashed into the side of a stone, bounced two or three meters up into the air, and came down on the edge of the New Road. I hoped it would fall flat and finally come to a stop, but instead the cursed tire fell on its inflated rim and bounced again, with increased force, toward the azarole tree. Still I ran and panted on, unable to grasp the meaning of what I saw, and I heard my father shouting at me from a long way off, "Now look what you've done! Look what you've done!"

At the edge of the valley, near this azarole tree, the tire gave one last bounce, then disappeared into the depths.

I sprang to the edge in my turn, and caught sight of the tire still running on, being thrown from one rock to another with tremendous force, as though a genie freed from hell was inside it. I grew frightened. My God, when would it stop? When was this cursed tire ever going to stop?

The crazy tire began to land on one retaining wall after another, then fly off them, bouncing its way on down the terraced slope of the valley, and, by some subtle miracle, it didn't crash into any of the olive trees, as though it knew they'd put an end to its mad flight. Panic gripped me; I felt as though I'd committed some fearful offense, for which there was no redemption.

My father caught up with me, as confused as I was, his eyes fixed on the unjust tire—for I felt that the tire was treating us with injustice by its satanic flight. I was afraid the owners of the garage would insist my father paid for it, and that he wouldn't be able to, and so would have to work for them for nothing because of what his careless son had done.

Suddenly the tire hit an olive tree at the bottom of the valley, and, from our point far off, we saw it fall and vanish. My father moved quicker than I did, leaping from one rock to the next like a leopard.

"You stay where you are," he shouted back at me, "so I don't lose my way. Do you hear me? No, don't come down. Stay where you are!"

In a twinkling my father's youth and mobility came back to him. He took my position as a bearing point for his descent, for it was easy to get lost in that great, deep valley; apparently he'd drawn an imaginary line in his mind, tracing the movement of the tire in its successive jumps from the place where we'd been standing. Still I watched him as he descended the terraces one after the other, looking up toward me from time to time till I could see him no longer. I was in despair, feeling that he could never possibly find the tire.

Then a little while later, although it seemed an eternity to me, he reappeared, and I saw him waving to me from far away in the distance.

He didn't stay to rest even for a moment; I saw him lift up the tire and begin his ascent. I didn't hear anyone singing at that painful hour, nor did I hear the tune of a flute or a double reed. The valley seemed desolate, dreary, and oppressive. My father carried the wretched tire, heavy as it was, climbing from stone to stone, from rock to rock, now appearing, now disappearing again.

At last I saw his head rise up over the edge, near the friendly azarole tree, and he looked amazingly proud. He was panting, and the sweat was running down his face. The tire in his mighty hand was like a brass bottle into which he'd returned the genie to its prison.

As I rushed up to him, he saw that tears were flowing from my eyes and that I was shaking uncontrollably. He patted my head with his free hand. "Stop it, lad!" he said. "Aren't you ashamed of yourself? I'm your father, you know I wouldn't let you down!"

I tried to take the tire from him, and found, to my surprise, that he was still able to laugh. Yes, he could still laugh and joke with me, the culprit who'd been imagining the most terrifying things! "What?" he said. "You're not going to send it flying off again, are you?"

As we made our way back up to the garage, he pushed me gently with his hand. "Off with you, now," he said. "Go home, and no more of this work and this nonsense! Go and study, and sing "ataba'!"

I hesitated, gazing at his eyes and his big black moustaches. His forehead was straight and broad, his cheeks full and shining. He seemed to me like a handsome, towering giant, like the azarole tree I loved. In spite of what I'd done, he'd never lifted his hand to strike me, or raised his voice against me in anger. In those moments he seemed to me like a young man again, radiating strength and vigor despite his exhaustion.

It was the last time. When he came back home in the evening pain returned to crush him in its relentless grip, and, though he was only in his late thirties, youth began to leave him quickly. He no longer sang with his old vitality, and stopped dancing with his friends at weddings. He no longer told so many stories either; and at last, one day, he said, "It's your turn now. You must sing to us, and tell us stories from the books you read, and you must be the ones to shake the earth with your friends when you dance."

—translated by Issa J. Boullata and Christopher Tingley

Khalil al-Sakakini (1887?–1953)

One of the most distinguished men of his generation in the Arab world, al-Sakakini was writer, patriot, educator, and a man of great moral and intellectual integrity. He was born and educated in Jerusalem and, aside from a short sojourn in America, lived in Jerusalem all his life, where he was a center of intellectual life there. He worked in education, becoming one of the two highest inspectors of schools at the Department of Education in the metropolis. A great believer in the value of knowledge and education, he founded such schools in Palestine as Al-Dusturiyyah (Constitutional) School (1909) where he was also headmaster; and Al-Wataniyyah (National) School in Jerusalem (1925). However, his service to education was even more enhanced by the many original books he wrote for use in Palestinian schools, in which he applied modern methods of educating children and having them learn both reading and grammar with ease and joy. He wrote many books ranging from grammar and reading to history, literature, and poetry. His reading books, *The New Method*, in four volumes, were taught all over Palestinian schools and had numerous printings. Among his other books are: *Palestine after the Great [First] World War* (1920); *Readings in Literature and Language* (1925); and *In Memoriam*, a book of poetry and prose on his dead wife (1940). He also published frequently in various Palestinian and Arab periodicals. The diary he had kept all his life was published posthumously by his daughters, Dumya and Hala al-Sakakini, under the title, *Such Am I, O World* (1955). The following excerpts come from this diary.

From Such Am I, O World

Saturday, 17 November 1917

For the past nine days the Ottoman government has been withdrawing from Jerusalem, because the English army's now knocking at the gates. Opinions differ as to what the fate of Jerusalem and Palestine will be. Some say it will become British because the English are the victors. Some say it will become part of Egypt, while others say it will be free. . . . In any case, these are days of momentous historical importance for Palestine. Many generations have passed waiting for them.

It was rumored last night that Hebron had fallen to the British, and that the airplanes circling over Jerusalem yesterday dropped leaflets saying they'll enter Jerusalem tomorrow in a grand ceremony. I also heard last night that the Ottoman government's going to set up a line of defense around Jerusalem, near Mar Elias; and if that should prove correct, Jerusalem will see unprecedented events tomorrow.

Tuesday, 20 November 1917

What have I done in this war? It's true that I dislike war, and disapprove of it regardless of the reason or the result . . . But even if I hate war, should I hate humanity too? If I don't like to carry arms, isn't it still my duty as a human being to tend the wounded? And who is more worthy of help than the Turkish soldiers? When a soldier falls in the field of battle, he's no longer a Turk or an Englishman, but a human, pure and simple; for the dead must be honored, and the wounded must be cared for with kindness, regardless of whether their countries are on the right or wrong side of a war. As long as a soldier's fighting in battle, he represents his nation; but when he falls, or he's wounded or captured, then he represents only himself. A war isn't between individuals but between nations . . .

Sunday, 2 December 1917

. . . I don't know why the Ottoman government wants to banish me from Jerusalem. Do they really think the British might need someone like me, when I'm best fitted for teaching, and ask nothing more than to carry on with my work? Whether the British come or the land stays under Ottoman control, I'll always remain a teacher, and I'll teach only what my conscience dictates. I don't toady to anyone, and I don't serve anyone else's purposes. Besides, I'm not particularly concerned about the coming of the British, because I've decided, if we survive the war, to emigrate to America and put my son in one of its schools. Wherever I find myself, I'll always be a human being, pure and simple. I don't belong to any of the religious or political parties . . . I work simply as an educator, and education doesn't belong to any one country . . . If patriotism means being healthy in body, strong, active, open-minded, with good morals, affable and kind, then I'm patriotic. But if patriotism means the enmity of one sect for another, or of a human being for a brother who doesn't belong to his sect or his country, then I'm not patriotic. . . .

Damascus—Tuesday, 18 December 1917

On Tuesday night (27 November 1917) I went to bed . . . It was dark and very cold. The rumble of artillery round Jerusalem was like the roll of thunder. Suddenly, there was a light knock on the door. When I opened, I found an American Jew standing before me, fearful and seeking refuge. The government had announced that every American between the ages of sixteen and fifty must give himself up within twenty-four hours; anyone who failed to do so would be considered a spy, and anyone who hid an American, whether knowingly or not, would be considered a spy also. Rather than give himself up, this man had fled, and had, perhaps, knocked on many doors without being given refuge before he came to me. I was faced with a dilemma. Either I must receive him against the orders of my government, and so expose myself to its anger and revenge, which would be all the fiercer during its last days when it had lost its dream of power and its sense of pro-portion; or I must turn him away, thereby acting in a manner contrary to the spirit of our Arabic literature, which I've loved passionately since my childhood, and whose revival and invigoration has been the goal of my life. It's a literature that constantly urges us to give refuge and help to those seeking it, to guarantee protection for those who are afraid, and to respond to those crying out. If I accept him, I'm a traitor to my government; and if I refuse him, I'm a traitor to my language. Which of these two should I betray?

These thoughts passed through my mind with the speed of lightning, and in the end I didn't hesitate to receive him. God forbid that I should receive a spy into my house . . . But if a crime had indeed been com-mitted, then it wasn't the crime of spying, but simply of running away. If I didn't consider him a spy, would I be a spy if I took him into my house? Of course, such a consideration didn't remove the danger I'd be in if the government found him hiding in my house, nor would the government consider it a valid excuse . . . I told myself that he wasn't appealing simply to me for refuge, but to my whole people as repre-sented in me. He was appealing to the literature expressed in my lan-guage, before the coming of Islam and after it. He was appealing to that ancient bedouin who sheltered a hyena fleeing from its pursuers and entering his tent. And I should add that he'd bestowed a great honor on me by coming to me for refuge, since he gave me the chance to act in a manner best representing the spirit of our history and culture in giving refuge to the seeker. I hoped it would please my people too, that a stranger had sought refuge with them through me, and that I'd accepted him in their name when his own people had refused him and closed their doors in his face. In short, the man clearly isn't a spy, and didn't seek refuge with Khalil al-Sakakini as one might think, but with the Arab nation as represented in one of its members. I'm not one to relinquish this honorable position, and have too much self-respect to play havoc with the honor and culture of my nation, even if what I've done exposes me to the danger of execution by hanging or firing squad. And if I'm made to suffer, he's not the one who's making me suffer, since nothing would have been easier than to turn him away just as his own people did . . .

I'd begun to believe I was safe, and that no one knew of the man hiding in my house. But at three o'clock on the morning of Tuesday, 4 December 1917, while I was sound asleep, there was a fierce knocking on the outside gate. Who was it knocking? Was it someone else seeking refuge? But this wasn't the knocking of someone looking for shelter. Was it a friend? But this was hardly the time for visiting. The knocking continued. Should I get up and open the gate, or should I let them knock till they got tired and went away? The knocking continued. Who was it knocking? There! Some of them had already climbed the outer wall. Footsteps in the courtyard. The house was surrounded. The rattling of weapons . . . When I opened the door, there was . . . a police officer, and with him an old Jewish woman who'd guided them to the house. "Where's Alter Levine?" he asked, and I showed him to the room where he slept. They woke him up and took him away, and me along with him. I didn't doubt for a moment that this would be the end of us. I said my final goodbyes to my loved ones and went with the police and the soldiers. You can imagine what kind of departure it was!

And who was this old Jewish woman who'd guided them?

When Alter Levine took refuge in my house, he assured me no one knew he'd come to me. We invited him to eat with us at mealtime, but he'd only take some bread, with a few olives, and a cup of tea. One day, while we were occupied with other things, he looked out of the window and, seeing a Jewish man, called him over and asked him to send the old woman so she could bring him some kosher food. She came and went every day, until the police, who'd been on his trail, found her out and asked her where he was hiding. Then, when she denied all knowledge, they beat her mercilessly until she confessed and came with them to guide them. His own people refused him, and then it was they who led the way to his hiding place. Man, why didn't you eat our food, God forgive you? If you thought our food was impure, then we must be impure too, because we eat impure things. So how could you take refuge with us? Oh, religions! Oh, foolish minds, rather! How you've made humanity suffer! How many victims have you claimed?

We stayed at police headquarters for two days, with no one paying any attention to us because the government was in such great turmoil. And perhaps that was fortunate because if they'd had time for us, we would certainly have been tried and executed there and then, as a reprisal against us and to terrorize others . . .

After this they transferred us to the military prison in the Russian Compound, but put us in a special room with eight others, some of whom were shackled with chains . . . We stayed in this prison for two days . . . We stood by the prison window, with the war raging all around and the shells falling everywhere. People were in great confusion, and soldiers were running in all directions. Everyone was afraid . . .

There's no space to describe the prison we were in or the mental and spiritual state of our fellow prisoners . . . We understood from them that the guards would come around midnight to wake up those sentenced to death, then lead them away and execute them. While we were fast asleep, we became aware of movement in the prison. Then the soldiers came in with their weapons in their hands. We got up, consumed with fear, certain they'd come to lead us away to execution. It was a dreadful moment, which I shall never forget as long as I live . . . I was handcuffed and bound to my comrade in adversity, Alter Levine . . .

When we left the prison we were told they were taking us to Damascus; our fears were calmed, and we began to feel there was a ray of hope . . .

We marched along the road to Jericho, which was crowded with Ottoman soldiers retreating with their vehicles and artillery. "If we haven't seen the attackers coming in," we said, "at least we've seen the defenders going out."

We continued our march until we arrived in Jericho, which we found chock-full of retreating soldiers and their officers. The only place they could find to lodge us was a stable on the edge of town, and here we sat on the dirt floor, assaulted immediately by the foul odors of the stable. My greatest concern at that moment was to find someone from Jerusalem and ask him if he could manage to get some food for us; It had been thirty hours since any food or drink had passed my lips. I also wanted to borrow some money in case I needed some before we reached Damascus. But everyone turned his back on us, till I met a gallant former student of mine, Mikhail al-Qazzaz, who got us coffee and food and some money; then, next morning, came again carrying a basket with enough food to last us all for several days.

Before we got to the river Jordan, and while it was still night, a party of bedouin horsemen passed by. Some of our companions began calling out to them to save us, but they just rode on, spurring on their horses as if they hadn't heard us at all.

We continued our march until dark, when we were still a very long way from Salt. Our guards decided we should spend the night in a cave at the foot of a mountain that was used as a shelter by some of the Armenians who worked on the road. We crawled on our bellies till we got deep inside, while the guards slept at the entrance . . . When we got up in the morning, I gathered the Armenian children together and gave them some money in the name of my son Sari . . .

It was a beautiful morning as we walked on toward Salt. One of us, a dark-complexioned fellow from Izmir, began to sing, and the enraptured guards fired their guns in the air as if we were a party of victorious conquerors. Finally we reached Salt, where we learned they'd celebrated the recapture of Jerusalem the day before.

Early on Wednesday morning, before sunrise, we walked on to Amman, and were put in the prison; then, before dawn the next day, we left Amman for the train station.

We'd been walking for four days, with my companion and I carrying the food between us, and my socks had been torn, so that my feet had almost begun to bleed. I took them off and wore my shoes without socks.

When we left Jerusalem, our guards, who were fierce Albanians, had looked on us with disdain, but after just two or three days we became like friends. If all the Ottoman soldiery had been like these men, the Ottoman nation would have been more courageous and powerful, and better respected. They had strong bodies, and their faces bore signs of nobility, courage, and pride . . .

We slept in the train that night, and the morning saw us rolling toward Damascus, which we reached on Friday, 14 December 1917. We said goodbye to our guards as if to brothers . . .

Wednesday, 2 January 1918

If vengeance was the reason for my imprisonment, then I've suffered the unendurable during this time. If prison exists to punish, then my agony and the term of my imprisonment have gone beyond all reasonable punishment. And if there are lessons to be learned in prison, and experiences to benefit from, then thirty days of prison life have been enough to teach me every possible lesson . . .

I long for Jerusalem; yet I would, in any case, have gone out to one of the nearby villages for a week or two when the British entered, so as to avoid seeing the antics of the hypocritical hangers-on who change their color every day . . . Yesterday they flattered the Turkish government, fawned on it and sang its praises. Today, they'll do the same with the British. Sights like these sicken me, and however much I've suffered by being parted from my family, I feel utterly thankful I wasn't there to see such things.

Friday, 1 March 1918

After finishing my day's work I went into town . . . to visit Mr. Levine in prison, and found him despairing of ever being released. I was greatly affected, and resolved to exert my efforts in his behalf.

Friday, 12 April 1918

The Middle Eastern man still holds himself responsible for the honor of his wife and sister and daughter, and so he claims the right of guardianship over all her movements, treating her oppressively and violently. He'd shelter her from the breeze if he could, to affirm his care for her honor and proclaim his lack of confidence in her. In view of this, the debased state of women in the Middle East comes as no surprise; but really it's the man who debases himself by treating her like this. The woman must have her personal honor, for which she herself should be responsible, and she has the total right to be free and not to obliterate herself in her husband, father, or brother. A woman can't be honorable unless she has her personal honor, and she can't protect her honor unless she's responsible for it. Again, she can't make any progress in her thoughts and manners and morals unless she's free. Clearly, this is her natural right, which no one should begrudge her or take away from her.

Saturday, 13 July 1918

The Flight from Damascus

The month of August 1918 had no sooner set in than the Arab revolt against the Ottomans spread, and my honorable friends in Damascus, spurred on by true patriotism and high aspiration, naturally joined it. They left Damascus on the tenth of August, and I had the honor of being with them.

What a contrast between the way I entered Damascus and the way I left it! I came in shackles like a criminal, and left in the company of noble patriots.

I hadn't realised men like these existed in this country. A nation with such men in it will not perish . . .

Sunday, 13 April 1919

. . . At noon . . .

Sultana and I went to the house of General Storrs for lunch.

. . . The conversation moved to the subject of the International Commission which was about to come to Palestine, Syria, and Iraq.

"France," he said, "has claimed she has major interests in Syria and Palestine, using these as grounds to be appointed by the League of Nations as the mandatory power over Syria and Palestine. But Lloyd George said: 'Maybe you do have interests there, but the mandate over Syria and Palestine must, according to the principles set down by President Wilson, be based on the wishes of the local population and not on the interests other states have in them.' Finally, President Wilson suggested sending a committee to discover the wishes of the local population. England agreed, and France had no choice but to follow suit."

"I must say frankly," I answered, "that the consensus in the country is for an American mandate, because the people know it was England who promised Palestine as a national home for the Jews. And besides that, people have seen what the British are doing in the country by way of encouraging the Zionist movement, and believe that if England were to be given the mandate over Syria and Palestine, it would do everything in its power to realize Zionist aspirations . . ."

Sunday, 15 June 1919

The American Mission arrived in Jerusalem on the evening of Friday, 12 June.

Today, before sunrise, the Arab Club (al-Nādī al-ʿArabī) and the Literary Club (al-Muntadā al-Adabī) strung a rope . . . with banners and placards, declaring in large letters: "We demand total independence"; "Syria[1] shall not be divided; we reject Zionism and oppose the immigration of the Jews into our country." . . . But the government immediately protested and the banners were brought down at eleven o'clock in the morning.

Monday, 28 June 1920

Yesterday, I received a letter from Captain Law saying the military governor wished to see me in the morning. When I went to see him, he said, "You know that in our country no one asks about anyone else's religion . . . Whereas here in the Middle East you're concerned with a person's religion before anything else. As far as Herbert Samuel's concerned, we see him as an Englishman and you see him as a Jew. The British Government's chosen him to be the first High Commissioner for Palestine, firstly because he's an able man, and secondly because the Jews would accuse him of fanaticism if he were a Christian. As such, the government's seen fit to appoint a Jew so that they won't be able to accuse him of treating them with contempt and acting against their interests. However, regardless of what Herbert Samuel may be, he'll act only as an Englishman who carries out British, not Jewish, policy . . ."

Thursday, 27 April 1933

. . . The state of the country's going from bad to worse. Every day ships deposit hundreds of Jewish immigrants, and every day another large piece of land gets sold. The people act haphazardly in their attempt to forestall the danger; or rather, they're concerning themselves with other things, or sleeping. They've surrendered to despair . . .

The Jews and the British realize the Arab nation's divided and at odds with itself, that it's poor and ignorant, and they've taken the chance accordingly to put their politics into effect. They're serious in what they're doing, and time only increases their seriousness. And what's laughable and tragic at the same time is that we hold meetings and conferences, and shout and curse, as if shouts and curses were magic tools to relieve sorrow and avert misfortune. In short, we're a nation that's given up the will to live. It's as simple as that.

[1]This is greater Syria, comprising present-day Syria, Lebanon, and Palestine.

Saturday, 28 October 1933

Yesterday and today, Palestine was a battle zone—demonstrations everywhere, attacks on police and train stations. Hundreds killed and wounded. The people are burning with anger. What tomorrow will bring, only God knows.

Anyone following the Palestinian revolts under the British must notice that they're getting steadily bigger. The first was a local one, confined to Jerusalem; the second a little larger, but still restricted to the cities. But the third was much larger, with the whole country taking part in it, whether city-dwellers, villagers, or bedouins. This revolt will certainly not be without its effect on policy. Suffice it to say that it clearly demonstrates the futility of the government's efforts to build a national home for the Jews, reconcile Arabs and Jews, and safeguard the interests of the Arabs. The Jews are panic-stricken, seeing a people armed only with their shoes attacking machine guns and mounted soldiers, bringing the soldiers down from the horses and trampling them. If they can do this with no organization and no weapons in their hands, what would things be like if they were organized and armed, or if the entire Arab world were to take part in coming revolts? . . .

Saturday, 7 October 1933

[to his son, Sari]

If the *Filastin Paper* has reached you, you must have read about the suicide of a rich Jew.

And do you know who that wealthy Jew was? None other than my companion in prison, Mr. Alter Levine, the man who took refuge in our house during the last days of the Ottoman Empire in Jerusalem! I sheltered him, then they sniffed him out, dragged us off to prison together and transferred us to Damascus, in fetters. Poor man! I felt very sorry for him. He was a poet in Hebrew, with a collection or two to his name, and a cultivated man, who spoke French, English, German, and Hebrew well. His library was one of the biggest in Palestine, and he used to read a great deal. Whenever we chanced to meet, he'd incline his head to honor me, because I risked my life and sheltered him in my house after he'd knocked on so many doors among his own people and been turned away. They say he committed suicide for family reasons. If the British had entered Jerusalem a little later, his fate and mine would have been the gallows. This man was saved from being hanged by the Turks, then hanged himself with his own hands. There is no power or strength except in God. He escaped from death, and into death he fell. May God have mercy on his soul!

Thursday, 10 January 1935

[to his son, Sari]

. . . Let me take this occasion to tell you how worrying the state of the country now is. The gates of immigration—legal and illegal—are wide open, and every day the sea deposits thousands of new immigrants. There's a great demand for land in Marj Ibn Amir and in the mountains. Yes, we still remain the majority, and yes, the land is still Arab; the Jews have only bought a small part of it, not more than two million *dunums*. If you were to travel from Jerusalem to Nablus and Jinin, or to a large part of Marj Ibn Amir; or if you were to go from Jerusalem to Hebron, to Rafah, to Khan Yunis, to Gaza, to Majdal, and to Jaffa; or if you travelled east to the River Jordan, up to Lake Tiberias and down to the Dead Sea—all this land is still Arab and you can hardly find any trace of Jews in it. Yet if you assess the future in terms of the past, and if the immigration continues, and if the Arabs continue to sell land and the Jews to buy it, then the future of the country appears— God help us!—very dark. In view of this, we must awake, we must rise up, we must work . . .

Saturday 26 October 1935

Today was the day appointed for the strike, which was effective throughout the length and breadth of the land, with no exceptions . . .

The British government claims that the League of Nations granted it the mandate for Palestine, charging it with establishing a national home for the Jews while safeguarding the civil, political, and religious rights of the inhabitants. Yet its actual emphasis has been on establishing the national home, by whatever means, rightly or wrongly, with a total disregard for the rights of the native inhabitants. What's more, they've cooperated with the Jews in uprooting them, and not a single day passes without some violation of the conditions of the mandate . . .

Saturday, 4 April 1936

My decision to cancel my talks on Radio Palestine, in protest over the Jews' claim that Palestine is the land of Israel, has raised a great clamor

throughout the country, as evidenced by the reaction in local newspapers . . .

As a result of my cancellation, the government was forced to announce that they've forbidden the Jews to refer to Palestine as the "land
of Israel." But will they now reschedule my radio talks? I doubt it.
Anyway, we'll see.

Saturday, 2 May 1936

. . . No doubt you heard the news yesterday. There were demonstrations
in Acre, Haifa, and Jaffa, which the police attempted to suppress by
force. There were many killed and wounded. But the nation's bent on
its strike, and it's spreading further by the day, with more demonstrations and burning down of settlements. If all this comes to nothing,
there are only two options: either the religious *jihad*,[2] or the formation
of armed bands on the Irish model.

Tuesday, 19 May, 1936

The country's now been on strike for a whole month. It's more like a
state of war . . .

Tuesday, 7 July 1936

. . . I'm sending you two issues of the English-language, Jewish-owned
Palestine Post, to keep you informed of our news, even if it is through
the mouth of an enemy. Read and marvel. Read about the fierce battle
that took place in Hebron between a handful of rebels and an army
unit equipped with all the implements of war. When the battle grew
hot and the two groups were almost in hand to hand combat—the
soldiers with bayonets and the rebels with daggers—the commander
ordered the soldiers to withdraw. What a disgrace for the British Army!

Jerusalem—Thursday, 1 January 1948 to Thursday, 8 January 1948

We said goodbye to the old year to the tune of screaming lead—from
big guns and small, and from all kinds of rifles, all of them automatic.
And we welcomed the new year to the same tune. It's as if we're in a
theater of war, the most important sites being the Old City, Shaikh
Jarrah, and Qatamon . . .[3]

---

[2]*Jihad* is a holy war that Muslims are called to wage against enemies of Islam.
[3]Shaikh Jarrah and Qatamon are two quarters in Jerusalem, outside the walls.

The second major event was that some Jews sneaked into Jaffa in disguise; people thought they were a troop of English or Scottish soldiers. They blew up the old police headquarters and many shops close by. Many Arabs were killed under the rubble.

The third major event was that a group of Jews stole into the Qatamon quarter of Jerusalem one cold, dark night, around two o'clock in the morning, when people felt safe in their homes. They blew up the Semiramis Hotel, which collapsed on top of its owners and clients, causing many deaths.

It's not wise, after all this, to feel safe alongside the Jews, or trust to their mercy. We've therefore decided to guard Qatamon ourselves. We held meetings at my house day and night, tried to bring out whatever arms we had, and collected money to buy arms and hire guards. Then we set up barrels of dirt at the entrance to the quarter . . .

Tuesday, 16 March 1948

By God, I don't know how we'll be able to hold out against this Jewish aggression. They're trained, organized, united, and well-armed with the most modern weapons, while we're nothing of the sort. Can't we finally grasp the fact that unity is better than dissension, organization better than chaos, and readiness better than neglect?

We formed a delegation to meet with the Higher Committee . . . We asked for arms, and they said: "We don't have any weapons to give you." Then we asked for guards, and they said; "We can't give you any guards." "What are we to do then?" we asked. "Arm, and defend yourselves on your own," they said . . .

Saturday noon, 30 March 1948

There's been a huge Jewish attack against our quarter, Qatamon, beginning at midnight last night and still going on now. There's been shelling by heavy artillery and shots from all sorts of lighter weapons, with places being blown up on a scale never seen here before. Perhaps Kitchener himself never heard, in any of his battles, the things we heard last night . . .

With the situation as it is, people are naturally thinking about moving to another quarter of the city, or to another city altogether, to be rid of this constant worry and perhaps be safe from the danger facing them day and night. Many, in fact, have already left our quarter for the Old City or for Beit Jala,[4] or even for Amman, Cairo, and other places. Only a very few of the property owners have remained, apart from ourselves . . .

[The following is part of a speech entitled, "No, We Will Not Forget," which al-Sakakini gave at the Orthodox Club in Heliopolis, Cairo, on 11 October 1948, after his exodus from Palestine.]

. . . Goodbye, my precious, valuable, well-chosen books! I say *my books*, meaning that I didn't inherit you from parents or grandparents . . . And I didn't borrow you from other people either; you were brought together by this old man standing in front of you . . . Who would believe that doctors used to borrow medical books from me because they could only be found in my library? . . . No linguistic problem ever arose in one of the government departments without those concerned consulting me, because they knew my library was the most likely place to find a solution to the problem, or because they thought I'd at least know where a solution could be found.

Goodbye, my books! I don't know what became of you after our departure. Have you been looted or burned? Have you been honorably transferred to a public or private library? Or have you been carted over to grocery shops so that your pages could be used for wrapping onions? . . .

Goodbye, my books! . . .

You're too precious for me to be without you. You've been my spiritual food, which I've always hungered for and still hunger for. I used to keep you company night and day, and it was a rare visitor, by day or by night, who didn't find me poring over my books.

—translated by Ibrahim Muhawi and Christopher Tingley

---

[4]A village not far from Jerusalem.

Mai Sayigh

For her biography, please see under her name in the poetry section.

From The Siege
Beirut:
Personal Impressions

Buildings stick to each other, hug each other. It was a city of cement and steel, they said, of shops and banks, of millionaires and their deals, of middlemen, and peddlers of goods and ideas.

It had sea and sun, they said, tourists, hotels, cafés and amusement centers, money-changers, smugglers, and smokers of pot.

Beirut was jam-packed with people, they said, and surging with an ocean of cars. It had theaters, art galleries, poetry readings, and speech-making. It had book exhibitions, publishing houses, a press that was sometimes free and sometimes bought. Some writers were bought and sold off by auction. Political parties sprang up like weeds after the rain. There were weapons everywhere, to defend the political estate, to distinguish the factions, to demonstrate joy or anger or grief in the streets. There was an immeasurable spirit of rebellion.

It's ringed with wretchedness. Houses of tin and mud. Hunger. Poverty. The camps of Palestinian refugees, of defeated nationalities: Arab, non-Arab, Turk, Armenian—brought together, in a journey of want and misery and exile, by the instruments of oppression, and holding the memory of a lost land.

Alleys of mud. Open drains. The stench of filth and vermin. Children grow up on charity, on a diet of bread, salt, and onions: malnutrition and a variety of diseases. The relief agency. Boys selling chewing gum. Begging.

Poor workers flood in from the south and from the mountains, seeking a livelihood in the labor market, but denied social security and the services of the state. Their shoulders it is that have raised the other Beirut. They've built the tower blocks, they've paved the roads. Deprived, racked by hunger, they stand outside the brightly lit hotels and cafés and swimming pools and restaurants. Away from the blaze of elegance and excess, it's their hearts and hands and feet that have borne the strain.

In the south people worked in the tobacco fields. They were skilled at reading the face of the land and the secrets of the meadows. They observed the seasons and the festivals. They toiled for the sake of food for their little ones and for the sake of company profits. They resisted the state and the feudal princes who tried to snatch their livelihood from their mouths. Stubbornly they stood up to successive assaults of the Zionists on their homes and villages. The fishermen became browner and more confident as the sun of each new day shone on them. For they are the ancient friends of waves and rocks.

How well we knew the land, the stones, the lanes, and the orange trees! The heart of downtown Beirut with its narrow streets, its lights, its stalls of vegetables, its trays of sweetmeats, the good nature of its people, recalled for us the narrow streets of Gaza. Beirut brought us together and treated us as Beirutis.

Beirut lies sprawled on the coast and reaches up to the mountains; and the shore and mountain trees are the frontiers of my heart.

Beirut's old quarters fill my mind with their houses and faces. This is a land of children and oleanders, of joy in chains, of households awaiting a new dawn. One community stretches from Tel al-Zaatar to the southern suburbs and Sabra and the Arab University. The poor and the revolutionaries have one religion, one sect, and one banner.

Where shall I start my story? I know it well and I can recall the agony. Time passes as I pause amid the pain and the inspiration. The lie of the land has been shattered. I see bloodshed whenever I gaze on pavement and balcony.

The war took place in the streets, before every window; and the Arab nation from the Atlantic to the Gulf followed the fighting as if reading chapters of a novel or watching a film. It held back its weapons and continued to bow its head to the police, to be constantly beneath the heel of the secret services and those in the seats of power. The Arab homeland is no homeland, it is a port of constant departure, a place of hunger and harassment, of fear for the future, of successive disasters, of surveillance, purges, and prisons. Oil swamped us and devoured our obligations, our honor and our self-respect. Patriotism was now a matter of choice, and treason a point of view. This was the era of the "Pax Americana," designed to make the world safe for rulers and kings with a common interest in the shibboleth of national sovereignty. We were polluting the Arab atmosphere. They were preserving their territories immaculate—ready to admit the enemy.

While their frontiers remain calm, our children fall like burned moths; their toys and shoes and little trifles remain after them, while the whole world's busy forming organizations for the Protection of Animals. They proscribe our blood, and friends and loved ones leave us while posters carrying their pictures remain on the walls, and in our hearts, till the rain and tears wash them away. Their blood falls drop by drop over the Arab cities, but they kindle only the echo of words in the newspapers; while the streets remain imprisoned, and spring remains slain, and the whole Arab nation forgets.

But we go on, counting our wounds, checking our blood group, totting up our soaking bandages and drugs—alone, always alone.

For the Arabs, time stands still. They do nothing about the retreating armies and the feet of the invaders and the endless progression of graves. Victory is postponed "till further notice."

They killed Kamal Junblat[1] . . . They wanted to crush the will of a nation. Beirut was fashioning new streets and landmarks. Quarters were marked by barricades and given the names of the martyrs. But in spite of the war Beirut still celebrated and mourned. Beirut swelled till it took in the whole of Lebanon.

During nights of air raids when buildings collapsed, when power was cut off and we could hear the cries of the wounded, I'd feel lonely and depressed. I saw the brains of my neighbor, the pilot's wife, spattered and scattered at the crossroads. Another neighbour, Hajj Abdu, collapsed on his balcony playing tricktrack with his son. He'd diced with death as if it were all a game.

Here they mutilated the corpses of Zaatar, and here we took in the children and the martyrs.

---

[1]*Kamal Junblat* was a prominent Druze leader, a socialist who was assassinated early in the Lebanese Civil War.

But in spite of the deaths, life went on. The bombing would cease for a while, funerals would take place, and then the streets would fill with people. The bread shop would open, so would the other stores, so would the cinemas. Sellers of milk and licorice would go their rounds. Abu Khalid would sell his sweetmeats in the light of a candle or a gas lamp. The loudspeaker in the mosque would work from a generator. Neighbors would sip coffee on the balconies.

The road to Cola and Sabra was always open. Unless bombs cut the road on Corniche al Mazraʿa, unless snipers dogged your steps or took aim at balconies and passers-by, life revolved around the spirit of the Quʿranic verse: "Nothing will happen to you unless God decreed it."

"We should stay where we are," Laila once said, as the building across the road was engulfed in an explosion, burning the neighbor's clothes and children. They killed her sister, Khaldiya, and her sister's husband in their house . . . A stray bullet killed Lena in her house, near her child's bed. One of Ruwaida's brothers was killed, with his neighbors, at the front door. Another brother's missing.

Beirut made us feel bombardment was a phenomenon of nature, that sniping and the stray bullet were like the weather, and death a human requirement like sleeping, eating, drinking, and moving. Cruel Beirut! How often I grew weary of it, hating it because of the bombs and the deaths of friends.

Cruel Beirut! . . . It's part of me, my lost bastion with its bright, smiling face that refuses to acknowledge death, the face that's a part of all of us. . . . Life flows out of the houses to those passing in the street, sparkles and blazes away. Liveliness brightens the faces of the fighters at night, when vigil's kept till dawn. Everybody knows everybody else. Beirut's a sea of relations, an arena of political and literary ideas in conflict. Coffeehouses are absorbed in supplying coffee and attacking ideas and their holders. You can find everything on the pavement stalls: from fruit and vegetables, clothes, cigarette lighters, cassettes, and songs to news about the Sino-Soviet conflict, or disputes about the row that broke out just yesterday between two local factions, or arguments about whether Fatah's[2] petty bourgeois or upper bour-

---

[2]Fatah is the main wing of the PLO (the Palestine Liberation Organization.

geois. From the outset, ideology permits neither error nor conjecture. History's full of wise sayings and answers. . . .

Everything's subject to analysis. Every statement has to be proved. A rumor goes round and round and round until it ends up where it began. Jokes and quips are the property of all. There are no secrets. Alliances, friends, enemies, and armed camps are well-defined. . . .

Heroes march out from the base camp side by side with men of the intelligence forces who work by barter, blowing up one building in exchange for another, one car for another.

The Jamal ʿAbdul Nasser hall is full of smoke and sweat. The bodyguard of the leadership fills the place, and curses against imperialism, and particularly against America, are common. Differences of opinion as to whether the Soviet Union is at the head or merely in the vanguard of the socialist camp. Banners hang calling for total liberation. Or half of it. Or a quarter of it. Calling for establishing a state on what has remained of Palestine—or hasn't remained of it. The PLO (Palestine Liberation Organization) is the sole representative. Imm ʿAli dances. Press photographers, foreign journalists, and solidarity groups take pictures of her.

The illustrated press, fifty or sixty magazines, papers, and publications: are they all alike in production, pictures and subject matter? Some say, "Yes." Some say, "No." Others are lost between Yes and No. Radios and car horns spread their messages. Posters and wall sheets and graffiti in all colours and scripts. Down with . . . Long live . . . Victory to . . .

On the back page of the newspaper, *Al-Safir*, the Palestinian child continues to turn his back on the world in the daily cartoons of Naji al-ʿAli.[3] Patches grow on the garb of his Arab toiler. As he gets ever thinner, he grows in wisdom and knowledge. Pride thickens the necks of the lords of oil and rule. Their bellies and their cloaks are filled with wind. Meanwhile the Arab nation shrinks and dwindles in the face of open aggression against its possessions and the things it holds sacred.

Beirut is all this and more. And so they burnt it, they destroyed it, they killed its children.

---

[3]Naji al-ʿAli was a famous Palestinian cartoonist who was assassinated in London in 1987 because of his struggle to expose, through his art, Israeli aggression and intrigue against his own country and people, and the indiscretions and deviation of some of his compatriots. His memory is revered by all loyal Palestinians.

The enemy has no respect for anything, from Dair Yasin, Qibya, and Kufr Qasim to Sabra and Shatila.[4] A history heavy with hatred, enmity, and bloodshed.

In the Old Testament, the children of Israel came, primitive nomads from the wilderness, and destroyed the civilization of Canaan under the leadership of their prophet, Joshua, at the behest of their God, Yahwe. They were given a free hand and killed everything in the city of Jericho, "Both man and woman, young and old, and ox, and sheep, and ass, with the edge of the sword."[5] On the seventh day the city was a furnace for the Lord. "Only Rahab the harlot shall live, she and all that are with her in the house."[6]

"And the Lord said unto Joshua, 'fear not, neither be thou dismayed; take all the people of war with thee, and arise, go up to Ai . . . And thou shalt do to Ai and her king as thou didst unto Jericho . . .' And so it was, that all that fell that day, both of men and women, were twelve thousand, even all the men of Ai."[7]

The pine trees cast their shadows on the courtyard of the Children of Resistance Orphanage in Tel al-Zaatar. A green light filters through to the dining room. A sweet fragrance drifts in from the balconies and mingles with the talk about the role of women in the Palestinian revolution, and about the children. We're seated around the lunch table, and it's a quarter to three.

Here's Qasim Aina, the Director of the orphanage, the Egyptian poet Zayn al-Abdin Fuaad, Dr. Fathiya al-Saaudi and Anush, her Algerian friend. Zayn al-Abdin was due to leave the following day for Cairo. Pleased to be going back to Egypt, he's come to say goodbye. Anush wanted to know exactly where I stood on the feminist issue. She belonged to a woman's group preparing research papers on the position of women in the Third World, and was working as a volunteer in the Palestinian revolution.

---

[4]Names of four massacres inflicted upon the Palestinians in recent times, Dair Yasin by Zionist factions, Qibya and Kufr Qasim by the Israeli army and Sabra and Shatila by the Lebanese Phalangists. For more on Dair Yasin and Kufr Qasim, see notes No. 3 and 4 of Mahmoud Shahin's story above, "The Sacred River"; Qibya is a village whose inhabitants were attacked at night in 1952 by Israeli troops who blew the houses on top of its sleeping people; Sabra and Shatila are the two camps where the hideous massacre of the Palestinians took place during the Israeli occupation of Beirut. According to the latest statistics, at least 1700 people were killed in cold blood.

[5]Joshua, Chapter 6, verse 21.

[6]Joshua, Chapter 6, verse 17.

[7]Joshua, Chapter 8, verses 1–2 and 25.

The workers had the day off, so the children were cleaning up and getting the dining room ready. The older ones arranged the distribution of food to their younger brothers and sisters. Then they all went off to play in the front yard.

The planes came from nowhere. The hands of the clock pointed to a quarter to three, and the planes came from nowhere.

There was a noise like a frightful clap of thunder. The sun swooped down. The sky swooped down. The peace was destroyed. Speech and food were all over the place. The specter of death and fire shut out the light of day and created terror and despair.

We rushed to pick up the little ones who couldn't yet walk very well and hurried the older ones down to the shelter. As I hugged a child to my breast, I picked out the words, "I don't want to die! I don't want to!"

"You're not going to die. Death's a long way away."

I see terror in the eyes of the little ones. Two hundred children between the ages of one and seventeen. Time marches slowly, like some fabulous beast threatening destruction to the innocent who aren't aware of what's going on.

The city flows in my veins—its alleys, its old roofs, its trees, my friends and loved ones. As we stagger to the shelter we're drowned in the flames and smoke. . . .

My mind wanders off by chance, as if to grope around the streets and look for people one by one, and ask about my husband, Muhammad; and I wonder, where has death struck? I pull myself together.

"We must get the children away from the walls."

"No. Let them be protected by the walls."

"This is no shelter."

Qasim embraces the children with his hands, his eyes and his heart.

"If only they'd given us time to move the children up to the mountain."

"But the other children in other quarters and camps of the city, where can they go?"

I pick out the voices of Jamila and Butros.

"They're targeting their raids on the Sports Stadium and our area of Bir Hasan."

The two young imps didn't come down to the shelter with us; they'd gone to the upper floors to watch the raids.

These children came to us, having narrowly escaped, as if by the distance between the blade of a knife and the wound it makes, between the head and the body from which it is severed. They've come out from among the pieces of torn flesh and limbs, from the seas of blood. They've plunged into the depths of death and come out to us, frozen pieces of humanity, their faces expressing only terror or apathy.

Jihad was not yet a year old. For a whole year he offered no response to anything. The doctors were sure he was retarded. He was transferred to the Children's Deaf and Dumb Institute . . . Suddenly he came out with complete sentences. Rashida Taha, the Director of the orphanage at that time, shed tears of joy when she told us the story. We celebrated that day. Jihad was born anew.

Ahmad came to us with a swollen belly when he was eighteen months old. He'd been living on grass for a week before people discovered him and brought him to us. A lorry took him to Damour. When the other passengers got down, nobody claimed him. The will to live is stronger than death.

When they drew pictures, they drew pictures of tanks and cannons, black airplanes, houses that had been demolished, men who looked like crows. The black was very black. When they added color, they used deep red. They painted blood on faces and on walls. Wounds were everywhere.

The older ones made up words, to the tune of a popular song:

> We can drink water mixed with blood,
> Tel al-Zaatar, O my beloved,
> They envied me for your defiance.
>   At night, O Zaatar, at night.
> We can eat lentils for all we care,
> We can drink water mixed with blood,
>   At night, O Zaatar, at night.

Then they'd sing:

> What can I say? What has happened to Beirut?
> Beirut groans and weeps. There are no longer houses there.
> The rockets have destroyed the houses. Mama, Children are dying.

It was no shelter.

"If a rocket falls behind us," Fathiya said, "everything will be destroyed."

The shelter was a cellar with windows near the ceiling at ground level. Part of the cellar served as a store. The main room was used as a play area for the children on rainy days.

A rocket fell in the playground outside. The earth was ripped up and the glass of the windows in the building shattered. Pipes burst and water poured into the main room. The air pressure was awful and the walls almost caved in. The air pressed on our chests and deafened us. The turbulence built up with intervals of deceptive tranquillity. Dazed, we were thrown against the walls.

A group of little ones came to me for comfort. The children hung on to us—we're their foster mothers. They clung to our bosoms, our clothes, all around us . . . The planes went away only to return. Between one explosion and another, time would return to normal. Seconds went by; minutes, hours. Little Ahmad asked me, his wide black eyes fighting back tears, "Are you scared?"

"The planes are a long way away."

"But I'm scared . . . Not for myself, but for my brother and sister here."

Two little children were flat against the wall. The girl wasn't yet one year old and her brother was three. He held her with his arms around her. I sat down on the floor and pulled the three of them to me.

Ahmad went on talking. "My mother and father were working in Saudi Arabia. We came back to Tyre. Then there was the air raid and they were killed. I love our home here but I'm scared they'll destroy it. If they do where can I take my little brother and sister?"

"Don't be frightened. I'm not going to leave you."

"You mustn't die as well."

Little Najwa pulls at me.

"It's most important. We mustn't die."

"We're not going to die. The raid's a long way away."

"Where is it? It might be at the camp." We all burst into tears. "I'm worried about Nazmi, my brother. He went to the camp yesterday to visit my grandfather and hasn't come back."

Najwa's a big girl, eight years old. Her grandfather, a man of about eighty, brought her with her brother, Nazmi. We were standing at the gate bidding farewell to the Commander-in-Chief. Najwa crossed the ranks and stood in front of him. "Are you Abu Ammar?" she said. "I love you and I know you from your pictures."

Nazmi, hardly six years old, interrupted her: "Please, brother, take me and my sister; we don't have any parents or home."

The grandfather added, "I wander round offices and commando

bases with them. The young men are generous, and let us eat and sleep with them."

The children didn't stop shouting and crying. There was no letup in the situation of total breakdown. Each of us tried in turn to calm the children's nerves, but terror was a wall of steel that we couldn't pierce. We talked a lot but it didn't help. We shouted, "You can hear the sound of our artillery fighting back." Then we sang a patriotic song, and that stopped the crying.

There was a change of atmosphere in this room packed with terror-stricken children. The rhythm of the song worked like magic. The words were echoed on their lips. Blood returned to faces that had been drained of colour. We were vanquishing primitive fear.

When we finally came out of the sodden shelter, it was seven o'clock in the evening. We realized that we'd absolutely have to move the children to Suq al-Gharb.[8] Nobody knew what tomorrow had in store.

The noise of ambulances is the real noise of death. It's what confirms its presence. The sirens of scores of cars are heard everywhere. Evening turns into a funeral. The city turns its back on festivities. Its aspect has changed. Four hours have altered the city. It now has the appearance of a wounded hero leaving the wrestling arena. Holes, red mounds, burst pipes, and the rubble of buildings block the roads.

We turn off towards the Awza'i road. People are gathering around radio sets, or dashing to bakeries and other shops to get what's needed for the hard times ahead. Everybody's rushing around looking for wounded relations. Muhammad and Nazih are watching the raid from the balcony. Bombs fall and rip up everything that's under ground, churning up the red soil with bits of metal, water, parts of destroyed buildings, and bits of human flesh. It's all burnt and the ashes are tossed sky high and then thrown down again. The city's drowned in flames and smoke. Muhammad looks at me closely. "The war's begun, but it's not like the other wars. They'll open up the main front here."

I don't believe him. I don't want to believe him.

There was a power cut. We had to make provision for the years of war. I took out the gas lamp and cleaned it. In the evening light coming from the kitchen balcony, I discovered that it wasn't working. I lit a candle and stood gazing at the mountain.

[8]Suq al-Gharb is a Lebanese town in the Shouf district of the mountains of Lebanon.

The evening light was a mass of white and blue. Above Beit Meri, Brummana[9], and Bhamdoun[10] it spread a translucent mantle of spring brightness. Through it twinkled the lights overlooking Beirut, announcing the beginning of the night. But it wasn't a night like other nights. There was something different about everything—even the songs that could be heard coming from radios on the balconies of our neighbors.

"We're going to sleep in the hall," I said. "It's safer."

"This is a different kind of war," he commented, "it hasn't been defined yet. Let's go and look for our dead. They don't have any faces or names nowadays." In the candlelight I saw his face consumed with anger. He was breathing with difficulty, as if he were going to burst.

—translated by Peter Clark and Christopher Tingley

[9]Brummana is a Lebanese town in the Matn region of the mountains of Lebanon.
[10]Bhamdoun is a Lebanese town in the Shouf district of the mountains of Lebanon.

Hisham Sharabi *(b. 1927)*

One of Palestine's most distinguished intellectuals, Sharabi was born in Jaffa and studied philosophy, first for a B.A. at the American University in Beirut (1947), then for an M.A. at the University of Chicago (1948). In 1953 he obtained his Ph.D. in the history of culture, also from the University of Chicago. He has worked mainly in university teaching and since 1963 has been full professor at Georgetown University. He has many distinguished books and studies published, in both English and Arabic. His major publications are: *Nationalism and Revolution in the Arab World* (1966) and *Arab Intellectuals in the West: the Formative Phase* 1875–1914 (1970), both in English; and his books in Arabic, *Introduction to the Study of Arab Society* (first edition 1978, further editions 1980, 1981) and *Strategy and Diplomacy of the Arab–Israeli Conflict* (1975). His autobiographical work, *Embers and Ashes (Memoirs of an Arab Intellectual)* (1978), written in Arabic, is a moving and poignant account of the earlier phases of the author's life first in Palestine, then in Lebanon and the United States.

From Embers and Ashes
Memories of Acre

From the time my father enrolled me, at seven years old, as a boarder at the Friends' Boys School in Ramallah to the time I graduated from the American University in Beirut and left for the United States in 1947, I would spend the greater part of every summer holiday at my maternal grandfather's house in Acca, or Acre.

For me, Acre, where I spent probably the happiest days of my childhood and my boyhood, was and remains the loveliest city in the world. It lies on the northern cape of the Gulf of Haifa, and the name Acca, which is an arabicised form of the french St. Jean d'Acre, has been used since the city was occupied by the Crusaders in the eleventh century. Relics of this time are still visible in the Old City, especially in sections of the formidable surrounding wall which stands unchanged to this day; and, indeed, whether viewed from the sea or land (from Napoleon's hill, the artificial elevation built by Napoleon in 1799 to bombard the city), Acre still seems like a Crusader city forgotten by time. The Ottomans encouraged the building of houses outside the wall to enlarge the city, and, at the turn of the century, laid out a spacious public park in the European style, with a bandstand in the middle where martial music and songs were performed every Friday afternoon. The Ottomans also built the railway station opposite the park, by the side of the sea and just outside the East gate, and from here we'd often make the forty-five minute trip to Haifa on the little Turkish train. South of the station is the sandy beach where we used to go swimming on Fridays and Sundays. I've visited many parts of the world since, and I've seen many sandy beaches, but never one to equal the beauty and splendor of the beach at Acre. The sand is pure white, the water of the Gulf clear and blue, the waves calm and broad, breaking gently and smoothly. The beach was always empty; the people of Acre had no taste for swimming, preferring to spend their leisure time sitting on their balconies, or in their porches, or in cafés, or walking out after sunset. So the beach was left to us for our enjoyment, shared only with a few visitors from Haifa and the soldiers who, for one hour in the afternoon, came for their daily swim from the British barracks near the city.

There were two cinemas, one, called the Al-Burj, in the Old City, the other, the Al-Ahli, in the New City. The first of these was simply a large hall built on the city wall, overlooking the bay near the East gate. There we used to see American cowboy or detective films, and, on leaving this make-believe American world, we would suddenly find ourselves back in the Middle Ages, surrounded by Crusader and Islamic ramparts and battlements. Our footsteps would echo in the empty, ancient paths and alleys, and we'd reach home at midnight when everyone was asleep.

My room opened directly onto the sea, and my bed was near the window, so that I slept and woke to the roaring of the waves. In the morning, as they broke on the rocky shore, I could tell whether the sea was stormy or calm and whether it would be good for fishing or swimming.

As my companions, Kamil and Akram, only returned from their jobs in the afternoon, when there was no good fishing, our fishing was done at the weekend. Then we'd wake early and hurry to the shore; fishing till sunrise before eating our breakfast and going to the sandy beach near the railway station to swim and surf till the end of the day. When there was good fishing weather on weekdays, Kamil would go sick from work, and we'd spend hours fishing and going from place to place till noon. Those were, beyond all doubt, the happiest days of my life. Sometimes we'd make a plentiful catch of sea perch or striped mullet; sometimes we'd catch nothing. When the catch was good we'd have a magnificent evening meal of fried fish with parsley and sesame cream salad, fried bread, chickpea dip-salad, and aubergine dip-salad, prepared by Kamil's mother and eaten up on the roof. Then, after dinner, we'd go to the cinema or sit at Habibo's café, drinking soda, playing backgammon, joking, and watching the girls as they walked by, arm-in-arm, laughing, and stealing shy glances at us.

My grandmother (God's blessing on her soul!) loved me very much. She'd never had any sons, so apart from my grandfather I was the only man in her daily life. It would worry her to see me sitting apart every day, reading and writing for hours on end. This, she felt, was unnatural, and she would be especially anxious when I sat alone in the porch, motionless and lost in thought as I gazed out at the sea.

"Why are you sitting alone, dear?" she'd ask me tenderly. "Do you have a headache? Are you feverish?"

Her sole remedy for all illnesses, both physical and psychological, which she imposed on every member of the family, but especially on my grandfather and myself, was a species of camomile, a wild herb that is boiled in water to produce a very bitter drink with the color of tea. My dose was at least three or four cups a day, which I drank reluctantly and only at my grandmother's insistence. She was always waiting for me, and whenever she saw me coming down from the roof, where I had built a little tent to work in, or returning home from anywhere, I'd immediately be confronted with the cup of camomile tea she'd poured for me.

"Drink this, dear," she'd say. "It'll do you good."

"But I'm not ill, grandmother," I'd answer. "I haven't got a stomachache or a headache!"

"Drink a cup to please your grandmother. Just half a cup."

Then I'd tell her that too much camomile tea gave me constipation.

"What nonsense!" she'd say. "Whoever said camomile causes constipation? It does just the opposite. It keeps you regular and protects you against all the different diseases."

If I complained of slack bowels, she'd bring me camomile tea and declare: "There's nothing like camomile tea to stop that!"

In addition to the comprehensive medical protection she gave me with her camomile tea, my grandmother used to give me powerful spiritual protection by means of continual prayers and invocations. She firmly believed I owed her my life on account of these, and that but for her I could never have escaped the dangers of the world outside—a world she knew only from her window or from occasional visits to families who, in her view, were of comparable social status. It hurt her if she saw me fail in my religious obligations, and she'd compensate for this by doubling her own acts of worship for my sake. When I was ten or eleven she made her first and last attempt to reform me directly, sending me to the *shaikh* of the small mosque next to our house to learn the principles of religion. For reasons I never knew, the *shaikh* would arrange our lessons for dawn, and every day I'd wake up at around four o'clock, while it was still dark. I'd throw on my clothes and run to the mosque, where the *shaikh* would be waiting for me, cleaning his teeth with a *miswak*.[1] He made me read from a book whose title I no longer remember, but that treated of acts of worship and religious observations such as ablution, prayer, and fasting. When I'd read the lesson, he'd begin to explain its contents.

My religious studies didn't last long, the reason for this being my rejection of *tayammum*, which is ablution with sand instead of water. We reached this topic one dawn, and as I didn't know what it was and had never heard of it, the *shaikh* began to explain the circumstances in which it should be resorted to.

"This drawing," he said, "illustrates the circumstances in which we ought not to expose our souls to perdition and in which *tayammum* is the appropriate course."

He then pointed to an illustration in the book which showed a shaggy lion standing threateningly in front of a pool of water in the desert.

"This drawing shows the correct way to observe *tayammum*," he said, indicating another illustration, which showed a man standing at some distance from the lion and the pool of water, covering his face with dust as if raising a small sandstorm. The remainder of the class was spent discussing the techniques of *tayammum* and the circumstances in which it was permissible. Thus, for example, if you were traveling in the desert and you found a dishevelled lion standing between you and the ablution water at the time of prayer, you'd know what to do. When I'd told my grandmother about all this—the lion and the dust and the circumstances in which *tayammum* was or was not permissible—she didn't insist that I go back again. She was afraid that if the *shaikh* continued to teach me, I'd lose what faith I still had left.

---

[1]*Miswak* is a twig that separates to form a bushlike head when it is cut. It is used to clean the teeth and has been in use among Arabs since pre-Islamic times.

My grandmother was from a pious, upper-class family. Every Friday she would give alms to the poor following the noon prayer, and she always turned up the radio as high as it would go to listen to the recitation from the Holy Quran, filling the house with the reader's voice and the smoking incense she carried from room to room as she uttered her prayers and invocations. After the Friday sermon dozens of poor people would come and sit in the garden in front of the eastern entrance to the house, next to the kitchen, and there they'd be given food that they'd eat in silence, standing in the sun or sitting on the outer steps. After this my grandmother used to distribute old clothes and money to them, together with a few loaves of bread which she would first 'press' on my head while reciting, three times, the Throne verse[2] from the Holy Quran. For all my grumbling about my grandmother's 'pressing' and murmuring, I accepted these rituals without question. I never felt any anger or embarrassment over the implications of these acts of piety and charity until, many years after my grandmother's death, I began to see life in a different light.

My grandmother was slim, with a fair complexion, reddish hair, and light brown eyes, and she must have been extremely beautiful in her younger days. She had what you might call a strong personality, and my grandfather submitted to her commands, never opposing her in anything, though he was sometimes obstinate about smoking and coffee. My grandmother allowed him to smoke half a cigarette and drink half a cup of coffee at specified times, within the framework of a precise daily program, but he would always try to gain further concessions, such as smoking a whole cigarette or drinking a whole cup of coffee. Their life was calm and happy, especially after they'd moved to their new house when I was eight years old.

My grandmother had always dreamed of owning her own home, and this dream was realised in the 1930s when she'd saved enough money to build a large house. To build it she commissioned a young architect named Emile Bustani, who, after the Second World War, became the biggest building contractor in the Arab world. He made her a thoroughly modern house, although the bathroom's modern equipment didn't function as perfectly as one might have wished.

When my grandparents had to abandon their home in 1948, it was

---

[2]The Throne verse is a verse from Chapter Yasin in the Quran. Regarded as particularly effective, with powers to heal and give support and success, it is memorized by many Muslims and recited when occasions call for divine help.

the bitterest blow they had ever experienced, and the last years of their life in exile were filled with sorrow and despair. My grandmother lost her vitality and joy, while my grandfather lost his sense of bearing altogether and no longer recognized those around him. They went to live in Beirut with my aunts, my mother, and my youngest brother, in a two-roomed house that belonged to a lady distantly related to my grandmother.

My grandfather died in 1950. In his last years he would periodically try to sneak out of the house unnoticed and return to Acre.

"I'm only going home," he'd say when they caught him in the street. "My home's in Acre. Why don't you let me go back home?"

Then he'd take a key from his pocket, and say, "You don't believe me, do you? This is the key to my house."

When they brought him back inside, he'd sit in silence, with tears flowing down onto the beard that my grandmother no longer trimmed for him as she used to do in Acre, and he'd refuse to say anything for a long time afterwards. My grandmother lived on for eight years after his death.

In April 1948 the impossible had happened: the Jews occupied Acre and drove out the remaining inhabitants, except for those who'd taken refuge in the Old City.

My grandfather's family left when the attack began, though Kamil and Akram stayed in Acre till the last moment and didn't leave till the Jewish forces had entered the suburbs. They carried what they could with them and left with their mother and two younger brothers for the nearest town over the Lebanese border.

How did it happen? As I was to learn later, until May morale was still high because a detachment of the Liberation Army, composed of Palestinians, Syrians, and Lebanese, led by Adib al-Shishikli[3] had arrived to defend the city; this encouraged people, and refugees from Haifa began to entertain hopes of returning to their homes. But al-Shishikli and his troops soon withdrew on orders from the leadership, people lost heart and despair set in once more. Food supplies were becoming low and ammunition for the fighters was almost exhausted; bread and ammunition were being sold at exorbitant prices on the black market. Though al-Shishikli promised to send help and reinforcements, nothing came of it. At this time there was a battle between al-Shishikli's forces and the Jewish forces around Safad, and al-Shishikli sent to Acre for

[3]Syrian commander who led the Liberation Army in 1948.

help. The fighters in the city hurried to help him in the vehicles that were left, and when they returned a few days later the wounded were taken to al-Jazzar mosque, where some of them died for lack of drugs, and those unable to escape when the city fell were taken prisoner. Al-Shishikli himself withdrew across the Lebanese border with what remained of his fighters, leaving the whole of Western Galilee at the mercy of the Zionists.

As Kamil told me years later, he, his brother Akram, and their family first took refuge in Rumaysh, a village on the Lebanese side of the border, where they took a small room in an old house at a very expensive rent. Then, when the village became full of refugees, the villagers stopped offering them food and water, and water finally became so scarce that a can of it was sold for two Palestinian pounds. Kamil and Akram decided to return to Acre to see how things were there. They stole over the border and reached the city before sunset; then, finding nobody in the streets, they went straight to my grandfather's house, where a family related to Kamil and Akram was now living. They entered the house in complete darkness, since the electricity had been cut off from the city.

Their relative 'Adil informed them of the situation. "Everyone's fled. The Jews made anyone who was still outside the wall leave Acre or else take refuge in the Old City."

Kamil asked him about the food situation.

"There's no food," he was told. "Everyone's hungry."

"How about you?" Kamil asked. "Will you stay here?"

"Where could we go, with all our small children? We don't have any relatives in Jordan or Syria or Lebanon. We'll stay here."

Kamil and Akram wandered with 'Adil in the nearby street, and all they saw, Kamil said, was cats crying with hunger. Kamil approached one of them, but it arched its back and bared its teeth threateningly. Any return to Acre was clearly impossible.

A few days before Acre fell (I was told this over thirty years later in Washington by an eyewitness who emigrated to the United States) a number of resistance fighters, including Simaan al-Ghafri, occupied the Taggart Building, the British police stronghold outside the city wall. They fought on against the Jewish forces for several days, inflicting severe losses on them, and stopped only when their ammunition ran out. Some of them were killed, while others managed to steal into the Old City and, from there, escape to Lebanon by sea. I read of the fall

Salah Ta'mari *(b. 1942)*

Born in Bethlehem to a poor bedouin family from the ancient Ta'amira tribes, Ta'mari obtained his M.A. in English literature from Cairo University. He joined the Palestine resistance movement early and was the leader responsible for al-Karama refugee camp when it foiled the Israeli attack in March 1968. He has never faltered in the struggle for the liberation of his people and is now a member of the Palestine National Congress. Because of his dedication to the Palestine cause, he has experienced exile and harsh imprisonment, the worst of which was his three and a half months of solitary confinement in an Israeli prison after the fall of Sidon to the invading Israelis in June 1982. In September of the same year he was taken to the notorious Ansar prison in southern Lebanon and released in November 1983 as part of an exchange of prisoners. After joining his family in Jordan and being forced to leave it again in 1986, he came to the United States and established ROOTS, a youth organization that aims at familiarizing the younger generation of Palestinian and other Arab-Americans with their cultural roots.

Ta'mari's remarkable personality, his passion for justice, his unwavering resistance, and his great integrity have inspired many people. In 1970 he married princess Dina Abdel Hamid, the former queen of Jordan, who in 1988 published a book about him, *Duet for Freedom*. John le Carré, who lived as Ta'mari's guest in Sidon for two weeks when undertaking research for *The Little Drummer Girl* (1983), said in his introduction to *Duet* that Ta'mari had introduced him to the Palestinian heart. The Israeli journalists Aron and Amalia Barnea, who interviewed him while he was a prisoner of the Israelis, made him the subject of their best seller, *Mine Enemy* (which appeared in Hebrew in 1986 and in English in 1988), and David K. Shipler devoted a chapter to him in his book *Arab and Jew* (1986). The following selection describing his solitary confinement is part of the diary that he began writing in prison. It will be part of the autobiography he is now preparing for publication by Little, Brown of Boston.

of Acre the day after it occurred, in the *New York Times*, as I sat on a bench one fine day in April 1948, in the Midway in Chicago, watching the children play baseball.

Those who have visited Acre recently say that it's a big city now, extending for several miles beyond the wall. My grandfather's house still stands, and a Jewish family now lives there; a little while ago my friend, Uri Davis, who is an Israeli citizen, sent me a photograph of it. I didn't recognize it at first, because there were no trees around it any longer and the windows fronting on to the street had been blocked up. It appeared to me as things appear in a dream: familiar and yet, at the same time, strange, as though it came from another world. The nearby mosque where I learned my first Quranic lessons is still there too, but the *shaikh* has left it and it's derelict now. Those Palestinian inhabitants who remain are forbidden to live in the New City outside the wall. They're forced to live inside, in the Old City, which the Jews now regard as a "casbah" and which is visited by tourists wishing to buy locally made articles and see "the Arab population of Israel."

—translated by Issa Boullata and Christopher Tingley

Journey into Hades: Diary of a Palestinian in an Israeli Prison

"You can take the bag off," commanded the warden.

The handcuffs fastened tightly around my wrists made it painful to pull off the bag, which fitted closely around my head. It was like surfacing from deep under water. My eagerness to breathe freely and my curiosity to examine my surroundings were stronger than the pain in my wrists, however. For several moments I inhaled air in huge gulps, gasping for more. My vision had blurred so it took my eyes a while to accustom themselves to the light.

There wasn't much to see. The room reminded me of a walk-in closet where brooms and buckets and cleaning supplies are kept in a home. It was tiny, no more than four feet by three feet, and painted red with a high ceiling. A huge black bucket occupied one corner, almost one-fourth of the whole room. Next to it sat a dirty plastic jug, half full of drinking water. The floor was rough and wet.

Even after the heavy door had been closed, I remained standing in the center of the cubicle, waiting for it to open again. I thought I was only there temporarily and would soon be moved to the interrogation room. It was hard to realize this might be my new cell. More anxious than tired, I tried to recline in the driest corner of the cell, leaning my head back against the wall, and facing the door.

I closed my eyes trying to absorb it all. How strangely and rapidly everything shifted in life, instantly altering old conceptions and ideas. The previous cell, where I had spent the last fifteen days, seemed large and luxurious compared to this one. An hour ago it had seemed like the most hideous place in the world. I could barely tolerate it.

Now, in this new place, I couldn't even stretch out my legs. Even a rough mattress would have felt like luxury. Everything seemed far away as childhood dreams. I stared at the ceiling, the walls, the bucket, the jug. There was so little to see.

What did they want from me? I was haunted by that question. I kept remembering things in a kind of hallucinatory swirl. Could it be Abu Dawud[1] and his yellow smile? Everything about him was jaundiced and weird. His smile, his eyes, even the way he shook hands with me before he left the cell, congratulating me for my courage! Had I been

[1] An Israeli prison guard.

too reckless by challenging his opinions and expressing how I felt toward him and the rest of the Israelis?

How could I have behaved any differently? He seemed rude, provocative, false. "How can you bear it here without a fan? So hot and humid—and don't you have asthma?"

I wouldn't answer. His false concern was transparent. It must be him, I kept telling myself. I am here for punishment. My back and neck ached and the chains felt so heavy. I tucked the edge of my trousers between the chains and my ankles to keep the flesh from being scraped, but the skin was already raw.

Those were the same chains that are used to tie up horses. I smiled to realize it. There were so many things to think about and now, even something to smile at.

This new cell was too small for any real movement. In the previous cell I'd begun pulling threads off the blankets and rolling them into beads. I could even exercise by stretching.

It became almost a chant. "Pull the threads! Make beads! Stretch! I must be dreaming . . ."

Time moved more slowly than a tortoise trapped in a swamp of glue. Each second elongated toward the century mark. To speed up time would have been as impossible as spurring a dead horse to make him go. The cell was so well-sealed I didn't even have daylight to give me a clue about time. The bright, constantly lit bulb made it impossible to differentiate between day and night. It also made the bright red walls seem vulgar, slapping their color across my eyes. So red it hurt . . . how could I bear such ugliness?

Since my knowledge of time and place was lost, it could have been noon or dawn, and I could have been in Lebanon or Palestine, it could be north, south, east, west. A feather in the wind, a plucked-up tree with its roots in the air. That's how I felt. Water was my only possession, more precious to me than to a desert traveler, my only link with sanity. It was not that I feared dying of thirst but simply that taking my small sips of water was the only normal act I felt able to perform. The possibility of losing it made me panic.

I breathed with difficulty in that hot, humid cell, as if a stone had been laid on my chest. The bare bulb's reflection made the red walls seem even more garish. I could hardly have shielded my eyes from its glare even if my hands had been free, since the room was so cramped. All I could do was sit opposite the sanitary bucket and rest my head against the corner.

I noticed the brand name on my handcuffs—"Smith and Wesson"—
the same famous Smith and Wesson that manufactures guns and pistols.
"Which is worse," I wondered, "a product that takes away your life or
one that takes away your freedom?" I rubbed the clean, shining metal,
hating the very substance of it. Still I realized it was not the metal's
fault, but the way man had used it that was to blame. As man grows
away from his innocence, I mused, so do his toys.

"Here, in this boxy cell," I pondered, "All I can do is think. I will
think positively. How can I choose an idea that will not lead me toward
despair? How can I start out along an unknown path without fearing
it leads to a dead end? Everything is so difficult! A new idea is like a
road in a jungle, it may lead to dark swamps or to open meadows."

I felt on the brink of exploring a new dimension of myself but didn't
know if I would be up to it.

Pain in my chest, in my eyes . . . aching ankles and wrists. Handcuffs
and chains nibbling at my flesh. I didn't know which part of me hurt
worse as I floated in that ocean of pain. Was it possible that one pain
really canceled out another? My aching limbs almost eased next to the
roaring throb of my mind. It is in the human mind that the most
ferocious hurricanes take place, not in the oceans.

I remembered the mountains of south Lebanon ten years before,
with a group of fighters, in freezing weather.

I had asked someone, "Why does our conception of hell involve
flames, fire, people shrieking in the heat? From now on I'll believe hell
is cold!" I remember smiling and my friends begging me to quit philosophizing about our misery.

In this prison cell, I decided hell wasn't crowded either. Hell was
isolated compartments, solitary confinement. Shrieking multitudes as
images of hell were no more than fanciful metaphors. It was all in the
human mind. My mind was still alert.

This new idea comforted me a bit. My mind was still alert. I was
sleepy, absolutely exhausted, and obsessed with thoughts about the
cruelty of sleeplessness when imposed on a body. In my previous cell
I had been awakened by heavy knocking every time I drifted off.

Now the stench of lysol drifting from the sewers seemed unbearable.
Mostly I worried the odor would trigger an asthmatic crisis in me. My
lack of knowledge concerning time and actual location in which I
dwelled only contributed to my imbalance. I had to invent them. I
had to invent everything.

Anyway, time is the invention of people. We pretend dates and records can be absolute marks. Now I was walking in the desert, bereft of landmarks except for one blazing sun which became compass as well as inferno. I could neither see my tracks in the sand behind me, nor how far ahead was my destination. Was there a destination? I invented it.

The moment the door of the cell had closed, I felt deserted. The rest of the world was on the other side, a united front against me. Then the old giant within me rose to protest: "You are not alone! So many others are with you or struggling for you. Don't give in to abandoned feelings! Don't give in to the present moment! In this instant you make your own history, so do it the best way you can. Think of twenty years from now when you will sit around a table with family and friends telling the story of this moment. Think how proud you will be to have survived when the mention of this moment comes up. Don't complain! The more severe it is, the more glorious it will be. It is paradoxical that, for freedom fighters, the moments of prison are the most heroic of our memories. You may be confined inside four walls right now but don't confine yourself within wrong conceptions. That would only help your enemy to pull you down. Your family is not alone in missing you, and you are not alone in confinement! Thousands are in even worse situations. This is not a cell, this is a womb from which you shall be delivered, stronger, purer! Think of it as a womb!"

Before that brave voice within me could catch his breath to continue, I answered, "Oh, but I hurt! Pain, agony, I don't know what I am, I want to see things, I am sick of walls, I want to sleep, you say it is a womb but I call it a filthy horror!"

The voice responded, "Your eyes are lasers. Fix them on the walls till the rays make them collapse."

I did as I was told. Focusing hard, I sent rays forward, onto one spot, till it started to melt. I made a little hole, which gradually grew larger and larger. I could see the outdoors again, trees, grass, domesticated flowers. My eyes roamed through the sky, alighting on trees.

"See? You can see. So don't complain about the walls."

A plastic dish slid in under the door. It could have been breakfast, lunch, or dinner. Now which day was this again? Each second dragged along as if it bore tons of sand on its back. How long are seconds? How bright is real light?

The sudden sound of laughter pierced me like a flaming arrow. What agony to be reminded of laughter, life, joy! I felt magnified on the screen of that laughter, desperate, like a subhuman degraded to the very bottom. The person who laughed was completely unaware of my existence. The sound repeated; a man and woman, walking together along a nearby path. I was separated from them by a wall that separated joy and misery, life and nihilism. I pressed my forehead on my crossed wrists.

I felt I was standing up in a small boat, facing hundred-foot ocean waves. I didn't know whether I'd fallen asleep or gone into a trance. The more my body was confined, the more my mind rattled fast and wild. I felt weaker and weaker, crushed by despair, pulled to the bottom.

When you drown, when you go deep down, nymphs and fairies lull you into soft restful peace. But it is the end of the struggle. Your whole life illuminates on a screen. It is amazing how years can be summarized in seconds, how they can be so vivid.

Dream: On my way to the bottom, I passed by our old house in Bethlehem. I could see the old cracked wooden door, the thick stone walls, and our neighbor's house standing opposite. My mother leaned against our neighbor's walls, chin resting on one fist. The other fist was placed on her waist in a stance she used to take when I was a child, when she watched me first learning to walk. She looked at me, amazed, and said, "What are you doing to yourself?"

"What do you mean? What are *they* doing to *me*?!"

"What *are* they doing to you?"

"Can't you see?" I rattled my handcuffs and chains.

She said, "You must be imagining things."

"Imagining? These handcuffs and vulgar red walls are hardly imagined!"

"Remember when you had asthma attacks when you were young? You used to cry and tell me you were suffocating and drowning while in fact your head still rested on the pillow. You only imagined you sank. Now you are doing the same."

"Yes, I do remember," I said, and she told me to go to sleep. Her voice was gentle as any caring mother's. I dozed off. The wall felt softer than a pillow.

But I was awakened by pain in my back and neck. I opened my eyes to see my mother still standing there. "Oh Mother, I am not imagining," I cried. "The chains are real, real, real. I want to stretch and move my arms!"

"Even if your arms were free, there's not enough space here to stretch," she said.

My eyes measured the cramped cell and I nodded.

"You're right," I said. And then she vanished, or rather, I went past her to the bottom, traveling more slowly. And at the bottom I saw her again, with the same expression on her face.

"Mother!" I shouted. "Don't talk me out of complaining! It is definitely better and less agonizing not to wear chains! At least without them I would have no pain, no torn flesh!"

But my arguments had no effect. She remained composed as ever. In her firm but gentle voice she asked, "Do you remember Ibrahim Ghannam?"[2]

"Ibrahim Ghannam? What on earth makes you think of him now?"

"Do you remember him?"

"Of course! He's a good artist. I always liked his paintings. So?"

"What else do you know about him?"

"He is paralyzed, confined to a wheelchair."

"He will never be able to use his legs again, yet he is creative, productive. Your confinement is temporary, yet you complain. How is he able to cope with his endless confinement while you can't even bear a temporary one?"

The embarrassment I felt hurt worse than my pain. I lowered my eyes to avoid her gaze. "I'm sorry," I said. I spoke more to myself than to her.

Ibrahim's paintings flew through my mind, waving their titles: "The Wedding"—"The Orange Harvest"—"The Kindergarten"—lulling me with their simple, deep colors.

But the pain in my extremities engulfed me with such extreme sharpness that I cried out once more—"Mother! I cannot tolerate this! No words of yours can comfort me!"

My voice rose until I was yelling. She did not utter another word. Her green eyes darkened with sadness and glittered with tears. They rolled down her cheeks—clear and silent as drops of dew on a rose bush or leaf. It felt like the same deep sadness and the same silent tears she had known when my sister Almaz reached a terminal stage of her illness. Nothing could help keep her alive, not even my mother's love. Almaz died while my mother and I were watching. I kept alternating my gaze between my sister's small face and my mother's. Through my mother's expression, I could tell what was happening with my sister. When she

[2]A Palestinian painter who lived as a refugee in the Shatila refugee camp in Beirut. He died in 1989.

finally bent over her, her tears were faster than her lips to kiss the little innocent face.

"There's nothing I can do for you, Son. I did my best. Auda'tak Lillah,[3] I entrust you to God."

She turned her back and walked away. I jumped up, begging her not to leave. She paid no attention to my screams. She waved farewell, without looking back, and disappeared.

My desperate screams echoed after the calmly composed echo of her words. Then all the echoes faded away and a stillness prevailed as if I were sitting in a huge hollow cave.

At that moment the tip of my toe touched bottom—the muddy bottom of nihilism. Her last words rushed in, penetrating my ears like a bell that shocked me back to awareness.

One million giants stood up in me and began fighting their way to the surface again, with determination, fury, and force. No way to make me give up. I was stronger, I would fight back, I would rise to the challenge.

—translated by the author and Naomi Shihab Nye

[3]*Auda'tak Lillah*: I entrust you to God's protection.

Fadwa Tuqan

For her biography, please see under her name in the poetry section.

From A Mountainous Journey

XXII

I was not in a position to participate actively in the kind of life necessary to a poet. My only world, in that dreadful reality, empty of any meaningful emotion, was the world of books. I lived with the ideas planted in books, isolated from the world of people, my femininity whimpering like a wounded animal in a cage, finding no means of expression.

While I was in this state of psychological siege and exile, Father often came and asked me to write political poetry. He wanted me to fill the empty place Ibrahim had left behind. Whenever a national or political occasion arose, he would come asking me to write something on the subject. A voice from within would rise up in silent protest: How and with what right or logic does father ask me to compose political poetry, when I am shut up inside these walls? I don't sit with the men, I don't listen to their heated discussions, nor do I participate in the turmoil of life on the outside. I'm still not even acquainted with the face of my own country as I was not allowed to travel. With the exception of Jerusalem, which I came to know thanks to Ibrahim taking me in when he worked in Radio Palestine, I was not familiar with any other city beside Nablus.

One of the irrefutable laws of nature is that plants and animals cannot live and thrive without particular environmental conditions. As for me, the home environment in which I grew up was not conducive to the creation of a concern for the outside world and its struggle.

Father was demanding that I write on a subject totally removed from my interests and having no connection with the psychological struggle going on inside me. Feelings of incompetence so inundated me that, when I went to bed, I would give myself over to weeping.

When we arrive at a point where things exceeding our natural capabilities are demanded of us, the resulting shock and the difficulties we encounter often cause us psychological harm. Father thought I was capable of composing on any subject. Despite the fact that I had already planted my feet firmly in poetry, my psychological current was flowing in a direction that differed entirely from that in which Father wanted me to drift along. A poet must be familiar with the life of the world around, before dealing with it in poetry. From where was I to obtain suitable raw material required? Where was I to have the intellectual and psychological environment conducive to writing such poetry? Would I derive it from the newspaper Father brought every day at noon when he came home for lunch? Reading the papers, however important, was not enough to light the flame of political poetry within me. I was completely isolated from life on the outside. This isolation had been imposed upon me; I didn't choose it of my own free will. The outside world was taboo, forbidden to the women of the family, depriving them of any community activities or political concerns. Mother was a member of a women's charitable committee, but that didn't change the picture in any way. She seldom attended their meetings, nor was she permitted to travel to the women's conventions, as other members were. Above all, she was absolutely forbidden to participate in the women's demonstrations. Family tradition would never allow that.

A women's committee had been founded in Nablus in 1921, under the leadership of the late Mariam Hashim (died 1947). This society was, at first, of a charitable nature. Then in 1929 it united with the general Arab Women's Federation, founded in Egypt by the late Huda Sha'rawi. At this time, the Palestine Women's Federation undertook the organization of the Palestinian women's participation in the political struggle in most of the cities and sometimes in the villages. The city women's activities were confined to demonstrations, to sending telegrams of protest, and convening meetings through the women's organizations that the bourgeoisie of that era had created. Being unveiled, the country women had greater and more effective freedom of movement. They were the ones who carried arms and food to the rebels holing up in the mountains.

With this total isolation imposed upon the women of our household, it was not strange that the atmosphere in the female quarters was devoid of any political or community awareness. The house was like a large coop filled with domesticated birds, contented to peck the feed thrown to them, without argument. That was the be-all and end-all of their being. The vocation of those tame birds was confined to hatching the chicks and wasting up the days of their lives between the large brass cooking pots and the firewood burning constantly in the stoves, winter and summer.

As happens in backward societies where a woman's life revolves around trivialities, the female environment in our house did not deviate from this pattern, which prevailed in all families and all homes. Therefore, the family environment offered me nothing; rather, it only increased my burden.

I was struck with a deep hatred for politics. During this particular period, I underwent a severe psychological and intellectual conflict. I was trying to comply with Father's wishes, in order to please him and win his favor, while everything in me was protesting, refusing, and rebelling. Since I was not socially emancipated, how could I wage war with my pen for political, ideological, or national freedom? I still lacked political maturity, just as I had no social dimensions. I possessed nothing but a literary dimension that was itself still deficient.

I knew myself; I was aware that the self could not become complete, except in a community of people. But between me and the community there, outside the walls that confined me, lay the distance of many centuries of the world of the harem . . .

My feelings of incompetence continued to dominate me. The ability to write poetry failed me. I even stopped composing personal poems. Poetical barrenness enveloped this whole difficult period of my life.

My keen awareness of the repression and tension I was under affected both my spiritual and physical being, making me lose more weight. I was scarcely ever without a headache; mental weariness weighed heavily upon every part of my body; at night I was bathed in sweat.

Life no longer held any meaning or relish for me. When I tried to fathom my private anxieties and personal feelings, it was as if something had been broken inside; misery inflated my consciousness of myself and my own existence. I was bleeding from the two-edged blade of that old proverb: "If I am not for myself, who will be for me; if I am for myself, who am I?" My weak links with reality and my need for contact with the outside world remained the source of a psychological conflict which I endured for a long time. Father was the one who had sowed the seeds of this conflict, which haunted me, in other ways as well, during the subsequent stages of my poetical career.

I went on feeling completely alone, that there was no one who felt my misery except myself. It was my being that was being stretched taut, torn apart; the heart that was constricted and crushed was my heart; and the ordeal that was becoming more critical was my ordeal. There was no other being to share all this with me, no other person.

As the misery of repression and subjugation increased, my feelings of individuality and identity also increased. My existence inside the harem wing of the house made me shrink and recoil, so that I was bottled up inside myself. I got to the point where I could do nothing but stare into the reflection of that self shut up inside the cursed bottle. The poetry I published in the papers was the one social activity I could use as a bridge to link me with others, as I crouched within those ancient walls. Thus my feelings of alienation deepened, and my sense of being robbed of my dreams, my desires, and my aspirations began to take the form of a sickness.

It was during this period that I swallowed the whole contents of a bottle of aspirin. The family doctor, Nadeem Salah, saved me from the death that had become my only means of escape from the torment I was in.

I did not bear any strong attachment to my father. My feelings toward him remained neutral: I did not hate him, neither did I love him. He never occupied any space in my heart, except when he was sick, imprisoned, or in exile for political reasons. To me, he was the tent that sheltered us; if we lost him we would be exposed to the storms of life. I was continually in fear of him dying and leaving us to the mercy of others. Thus my emotions seesawed between a sense of need for his presence and a sense of estrangement and lack of any emotional relationship to him. He never manifested any sort of concern or affection for me. Whenever I fell victim to malaria in my childhood, he never came near me or asked how I was. That neglect pained me. Thus Ibrahim, with his overflowing compassion and love for me, replaced the father who never let me feel the warmth of fatherly sentiments. When Ibrahim died and Father was still living, I truly felt like an orphan. When Father passed away I was experiencing a fearful psychological crisis at the time, due to the severe emotional repression that I had endured all those years. I tried to write an elegy for him, but failed. However, I missed him severely later on when the winds of family problems began to blow our way.

I never took sides in any dispute or quarrel; I always stood apart from the disputes, seeing, hearing, and suffering. During this period, I wrote "Life," one of the few poems I composed in a few consecutive hours. In this poem, my true feelings at the loss of my father are revealed; feelings that went very deep.

XXIII

Father died amongst the tumult of the 1948 debacle.

Thousands of refugees, moving eastward in their flight, arrived in Nablus. Houses, mosques, schools, and the caves in Mounts 'Aibal and Jerzim were jam-packed with them.

Many long months passed after this first scandal on Arab soil, before I returned to writing poetry. Behind this silence, a process of preparedness and storing was going on all the time in my depths and I no longer suffered feelings of emptiness and desolation.

Eventually my tongue was loosened. I wrote the patriotic poetry to which Father had so often wished to see me dedicate myself, in order to fill Ibrahim's place. I wrote that poetry quite voluntarily, without any outside coercion.

After Father's death my reaction to politics was no longer wanting. Although it was not too strong it still swayed me at different times, but it lacked the quality of permanence. It would catch fire on certain occasions when things were inflamed, then die down when things were calm; I would flare up when there were general outbursts and cool off when there were lulls. With the status quo of the Palestinian situation, a numbness began creeping over my political sentiments. I entered into life, drinking it in large drafts, touching it and clinging to the fleeting moments, not allowing them to escape me, enjoying it second by second and minute by minute.

In the first half of the fifties, I escaped from the prison of the harem. When the roof fell in on Palestine in 1948, the veil fell off the Nablus woman's face. She had struggled for a long time to free herself from the traditional wrap and the thick black veil.

Before the final lifting of the veil, the Nablus women had succeeded in changing their outer covering, by stages, over a period of thirty years. In the twenties they got rid of the full black flowing skirt, substituting a black or brown coat or one of some other somber color. At the beginning of the forties they got rid of the triangular bolero-like cover that was worn on the head and came down over the shoulders down to the waist, concealing the shape of the upper half of the body, and behind which the woman would fold her hands over her breast, so the men could not see her fingers. In the middle forties the transparent black kerchief became more transparent, revealing the face under it;

and in the middle fifties the black veil was finally lifted, allowing the beauty of their God-given faces to shyly speak for itself.

The evolution of the veil in Nablus was slow compared to Jerusalem, Haifa, and Jaffa. The path our development took was neither easy nor smooth. Nablus remained a bigoted city, clinging to the old traditions in which social changes were not easily carried out. The established molds and patterns remained the prevailing order, despite the many well-educated young men and women. It is strange that this city, whose inhabitants are famous for their dynamism and great enterprise, remained adamantly against anything new touching their traditions. However, the inevitability of development eventually overpowers all resistance. It is life's march, impossible to check or halt.

My hunger for life was relentless. Someone who has squandered many years of her life in the desert of the Empty Quarter cannot turn her back on a green oasis when its doors are opened to her. The child of life emerged now into the life that had given her birth. Being completely sincere, she faced life with a genuine and natural frankness that society, with its stern rules and customs, insists on counterfeiting and covering up with a false mask. This child of life was not selfish; she took and she gave. Giving was her way of life, an inseparable part of her nature. Previously, when she stole out to the wheat fields, she would feel downcast and sad at seeing the gift the wheat had to offer, when she had nothing to offer. A heart filled with love suffocates if it finds no one to love.

The time arrived for this daughter of life to speak and, when a truthful woman speaks, it is life that is speaking.

Our Eastern Arab society suppressed the sentiment of love, just as it continually oppressed the woman. This beautiful human emotion, whose magic hand even touched the hearts of prophets. It was because of this emotion that the noble Prophet Muhammad (God bless him and grant him salvation!) said: "Praise be to God! Praise be to the director of hearts!" the moment he saw Zaynab Bint Jahsh,[1] suddenly appear to him. In our Arab society, this beautiful human emotion is

---

[1]One of the Prophet's wives. She was first married to his adopted son, Zayd. However, the Prophet, on seeing her once in her ordinary house clothes (as opposed to the coverings a Muslim woman would wear in the street) as he went seeking Zayd, was struck with her revealed beauty. Zayd divorced her so the Prophet could marry her. This story, about the Prophet's tenderness toward beauty, is mentioned by Tuqan here in praise of love which is denied to young people in the traditional culture in Palestine.

the victim of the split personality of our society and still carries connotations charged with disgrace and shame.

As far as I'm concerned, love bears a wider concept than the affirmation of a woman's femininity. To me it is the affirmation of my crushed humanity and its very salvation. All my life, I have been drawn to love, driven by a poetic sentiment difficult to explain. Just as birds respond instinctively to the magnetic field in determining the path of their flight, so have I always responded to love. It remained to me the most attractive torch that beckoned me among life's various aspects.

I am not straying far from the truth when I say that, with me, love remained a concept; an absolute world. For me the "other" was the embodiment of that idea, whose horizons I was never able to relinquish. It became an instinct and a natural impulse, forever warm and throbbing in my heart, and I'd plunge into the warm sea of emotion that cleansed my soul of bitterness. This abstract concept had no shore or harbor where I could cast anchor. It was a vast sea where, sometimes, the waves were so high that they became a whirlpool turning me in a circle until I lost all sense of the outside world around me.

Before emerging from the harem, my adolescent emotions were on fire. I was a repressed soul who responded to the first word of love received on the page of a letter. Love by correspondence. I would fall into this sort of imaginary love and wallow in it, while the old walls of the harem lay between me and the actual experience. So that imagination and the exchange of letters were at once the length and breadth of my sphere of action. I hungered for something that did not exist; I was lost, alone, possessing nothing but this fired imagination.

The liberation came at last; I found myself merged with the "other," discovering myself through the compass of reality. My heart has ever been a fresh garden ripe for love. During moments of love a person feels his humanity intensifying. He or she leaves the far distant icy pole to travel to radiant sunshine. The "other" becomes the bridge to a world whose scattered parts have been brought together to become one inseparable whole; a world that, by its sweetness and bitterness, its contradictions and ironic situations, paves the way to mental and spiritual well-being; it is a beautiful, harsh, tender world, just like life itself. And after all is said and done, love is proscribed like life and death, especially upon those with poetic natures. For them there is no escape from it.

There is nothing sweeter than when love touches even trivial things, transforming them into things of beauty and worth: a restaurant bill, a theater ticket, a dried flower, a ballpoint or fountain pen. All these and similar trivial things become rare and priceless when touched by love.

My vivid imagination created a magic halo around the beloved, projecting upon him what he did not have. I would see the faults, but, in my view the faults did not stand in the way of love. Which of us searches for a Christ to love? In my opinion, the exemplary ones make poor lovers. Their idealism makes them review the affair in a manner that strips love of all its great excitement. I have always believed that love is a treasure whose worth we can never estimate until we have exhausted it or lost it in a gamble.

When time—that gigantic force of destruction—has played its role in things and relationships, I do not linger amongst the ruins. I do not remain faithful to the past, after it is over and done with. I do not allow myself to give the past permission to rob the future, for the past is a thief that takes away but does not give. It is not strange for the heart to love more than once. It is unnatural that a person's heart should be bound up in one person all its life. It is normal for more than one relationship to form and for love to recur in the heart. And each time one falls in love, the emotions are just as strong, and just as sincere and fragrant as the previous time. But there has never been a place in my heart for casual love, for frivolous relations and reckless carousing.

Frequently, I find that the past has not only gone in its physical sense, but in its psychological sense also. What is in the past bears a certain value that differs entirely from my present view, causing it to lose its psychological significance. I feel that I am another person with no connection to my former self, no longer acquainted with it except in memory.

The world of my childhood is the only one that has not lost its psychological meaning for me. It is the only world to which I return with the old warmth of heart. With that exception, everything, in my view, submits to the laws of change.

—translated by Olive Kenny

First Translators

Roger Allen

Roger Allen is Professor of Arabic at the University of Pennsylvania and chairman of the Department of Comparative Literature there. He studied Arabic at Oxford University and has been active as editor, translator, anthologist, and scholar of Arabic, specializing in particular in modern Arabic fiction. However, he takes a keen interest in all aspects of Arabic literature and, as consultant and spokesman for PROTA, has helped greatly in the task of selection, evaluation, and promotion of the Project's goals, which aim at the dissemination of Arabic literature in the English-speaking world. His book, *The Arabic Novel, an Historical and Critical Introduction,* was published in 1982 and has been translated into Arabic by Hussa Muneef and published in 1986. Dr. Allen has written widely on contemporary Arabic drama and the short story. Among his many translations are three works by Najib Mahfouz: *God's World* (1973); *Mirrors,* (1977); and *Autumn Quail* (1985). He has translated, with Adnan Haydar, two of Jabra Ibrahim Jabra's novels: *The Ship* (1986), and *Search for Walid Mas'ud* (1978). He has also published his translation of 'Abd al-Rahman Muneef's novel, *Endings* (1988). He selected, translated and annotated material for a large anthology of modern critical writings in Arabic, titled, *Modern Arabic Literature,* (Library of Literary Criticism Series), the reference series by Ungar, New York, 1987. He has contributed numerous articles to many books including two chapters on modern Arabic fiction for Volume IV of *The Cambridge History of Arabic Literature,* forthcoming. Following the award of the Nobel Prize to Najib Mahfouz in 1988, Dr. Allen participated in the activity which resulted from the award, giving numerous appearances all over the United States. He has edited, with Salma Khadra Jayyusi, PROTA's large anthology of Contemporary Arab Theater. He lives in Philadelphia with his wife, Mary, and two children, Timothy and Mary Anna.

Aida Adib Bamia

A Palestinian and an associate professor of Arabic language and literature at the University of Florida at Gainesville, Dr. Bamia obtained a Ph.D. degree in Arabic literature in 1971 from the School of Oriental and African Studies of London University. She is one of the few specialists on North African literature, having written her doctoral thesis on the evolution of the novel and short story in modern Algerian literature. In 1972–1973 she obtained a post-doctoral fellowship at UCLA, through a Ford Foundation grant, where she continued her research on the Algerian short story. She has taught at the University of Utah and at the Universities of Oran, Constantine, and Annaba in Algeria before coming to teach in the United States. She has published *The Evolution of the Algerian Short Story, 1025–1967* (1982) in Arabic, and a translated work from French, *Towards an Algerian University* (1981), also in Arabic. She has also published five monographs on Algerian folklore, the proverbs and the tales as well as customs and traditions, which she studied while teaching at Algerian universities. Dr. Bamia is a member of PROTA's editorial board.

Peter Clark

Peter Clark was born in Sheffield, England, and has two degrees in history. He has been employed by the British Council since 1967 and as British Council representative has worked in Jordan, Lebanon, Sudan, Yemen, Tunisia and, at present, in the United Arab Emirates. This long sojourn in so many countries of the Arab world has given him an intimate knowledge not only of Arabic culture as a whole but also of the various local sub-cultures of the different Arab countries where he has lived and performed his intercultural responsibilities with so much success. He published *Henry Hallam* in the Twayne English Series in 1982. He is also the author of a study on the novelist and translator Marmaduke Pickthall, *Marmaduke Pickthall, British Muslim* (1986), and has translated *Karari, the Sudanese Account of the Battle of Omdurman,* by Ismat Hasan Zulfo (1980), and *Dubai Tales* by Mohammad al-Murr (1991).

Issa Boullata

Born in Jerusalem, Palestine, Issa Boullata graduated with a Ph.D. in Arabic literature from the University of London in 1969. He taught at Hartford Seminary in Connecticut, then joined McGill University, where he is now professor of Arabic literature and language. His publications include *Outline of Romanticism in Modern Arabic Poetry* and *Badr Shakir al-Sayyab: His Life and Poetry,* both in Arabic; *Modern Arabic Poetry,* an anthology in English translation; and as editor, *Critical Perspectives on Modern Arabic Literature.* His latest work is *Trends and Issues in Contemporary Arab Thought* (in English), which is an analysis of contemporary Arab thought, especially in the years following the 1967 June War.

Sharif S. Elmusa

Scholar, poet, and translator, Sharif Elmusa spent his childhood in the Nuawayʿimeh refugee camp near Jericho. He took a degree in engineering from Cairo University before coming to Boston in 1971, where he worked as a civil engineer before taking a Ph.D. in Urban Studies and Planning from M.I.T. in 1986. He then worked as adjunct professor at Georgetown University teaching political economy of development, then moved to the Institute of Palestine Studies in Washington DC, where he did research on more than four hundred Palestinian villages that were depopulated in 1948 and largely destroyed by Israel. The village of his birth was part of this destruction and he is currently co-writing a reference book on this titled *All That Remains.* Currently, Elmusa holds a grant from the Ford Foundation to conduct a study of water as a strategic resource in the Palestinian-Israeli conflict. He has published his poetry in periodicals such as *Poetry East, Painbrush,* and *The Christian Science Monitor,* and his poems were nominated in 1984 for the Pushcart Prize. He has been a PROTA reader, reviewer, and translator and participated widely in the translation of selections, both prose and poetry, for PROTA's various anthologies: *Modern Arabic Poetry, An Anthology* (1987); *Literature of Modern Arabia* (1988); and *Modern Palestinian Literature* (1992). He has also co-edited and contributed to *Grape Leaves: A Century of Arab American Poetry* (1988). His book, *A Harvest of Technology: The Super-Green Revolution in the Jordan Valley* will be published by Georgetown University Press. Elmusa lives with his wife, Judith Tucker, a Middle East historian and their two children, Karmah and Layth, in Washington DC.

Ferial J. Ghazoul

An Iraqi scholar who was educated in the Arab world, Europe, and the United States, Ferial Ghazoul is presently Professor of English and Comparative Literature at the American University in Cairo, and participates widely in Cairo's active literary life. Dr. Ghazoul is the author of many studies published in Arabic, English, and French on literary theory, comparative, medieval, and modern literature. She has published two books to date, *The Arabian Nights: A Structural Analysis* (in English, 1980) and *Sa'di Yusuf* (in Arabic, 1989). She has written in French on the Syrian poet, Adunis, and the Egyptian poet, Muhammad 'Afifi Matar; in English on the Panchatantra, the Brethren of Purity, Ibn Khaldun, Shakespeare, Ungaretti, Sa'di Yusuf, Borges, and John Barth; in Arabic on Vico, Lévi-Strauss, Edward Said, Edward al-Kharrat, M.A. Matar, Sa'di Yusuf, Yusuf Idris, Mahmoud Darwish, Salwa Bakr, Alifa Rifaat, Elias Khouri, and Mahmoud al-Mas'adi. She has translated from Arabic into English, poems of Badr Shakir al-Sayyab, Muhammad 'Afifi Matar, and Anton Shammas; from English into Arabic, Riffaterre and C.S. Pierce; from French into Arabic, Ricoer and Althusser; and from Russian into Arabic, Bakhtin. She was the co-founder of the tri-lingual *Alif: Journal of Comparative Poetics,* published in Cairo, and is currently its editor.

Faris Glubb

Faris Glubb is an Irish poet and historian. He was born in Jerusalem in 1939 and spent most of his early years in Jordan, where his father was Chief of Staff of the Jordanian Army. He was educated in Jordan, Switzerland, and Britain, graduating from London University in Arabic and Islamic Studies. After the 1967 June war, Glubb returned to Jordan where he worked for three years as a teacher in the United Nations Relief and Works Agency (UNRWA) Teachers' Training College at Wadi al-Seer and also produced radio programs for Jordanian Broadcasting. In 1970 he moved to Lebanon, where he lived until 1982 when he left Beirut after the siege of the city by the Israelis. His work has mainly focused on the Palestine problem and he is an enthusiastic speaker about the Palestinian cause. In 1970 he published his first book, *The Palestine Question and International Law,* followed in 1975 by his *Zionism: Is It Racist?* Other books of his are *Zionist Relations with Nazi Germany* (1978) and a book of Palestinian short stories, which he translated into English, *Stars in the Sky of Palestine* (1978). He is now working on another political book, *The Star of David and the Swastika.*

Adnan Haydar

Before taking up his appointment as associate professor at the University of Massachusetts in Amherst, Dr. Haydar taught Arabic language and literature at the American University of Beirut, at the University of California at Berkeley, and, for six years, at the University of Pennsylvania. His training is in critical theory and poetics, and he has written several articles on modern and classical Arabic poetry. With Michael Beard he has published a book of translation and interpretation of the late poet Khalil Hawi's collection, *The Threshing Floor of Hunger,* titled *Naked in Exile.* He has a genuine interest in folk poetry and has prepared a book on the metrics of the Lebanese *zajal.*

Salwa Jabsheh

Salwa Jabsheh studied biology at Beirut University College and continued her studies in London, obtaining the degree of Master of Science in nutrition from King's College, London University and specializing as a dietician at the same university. She is well-acquainted with the culture and dialects of the Gulf countries where she lived for nine years. She is a Palestinian and lives with her husband and two children, Shireen and Omar, in London.

Lena Jayyusi

Born in Amman, Jordan, to Palestinian parents, Lena Jayyusi was educated first in England, where she obtained an M.A. (Econ.) and a Ph.D. in sociology from the University of Manchester, then at Boston University, where she obtained an M.Sc. in film studies. In 1981 she was assistant to the producer on three documentary films about women in the Middle East. Her first book, *Categorization and the Moral Order*, was published by Routledge and Kegan Paul in 1984. She writes and publishes in the areas of language and communication studies (with particular interest in media and textual analysis), cine-semiotics and visual practices, and ethnomethodology. A member of the International Advisory Board of the International Institute of Ethnomethodology, she is now Chair of the Department of Communication Studies at Cedar Crest College. Lena Jayyusi is one of PROTA's readers and reviewers and has translated for four of PROTA's anthologies of modern Arabic literature. Her other PROTA books are *Songs of Life,* a collection of poems by Abu 'l-Qasim al-Shabbi (with Naomi Shihab Nye) (1985); and selections from the poetry of Mahmoud Darwish and Nizar Qabbani. She has also prepared an English language version of the well-known epic folk romance, *Sayf ibn Dhi Yazan* (part translation, part retelling.) Lena Jayyusi also speaks widely on topics related to the Middle East, especially on Palestinian women. She lives with her daughter, Jinan, in Allentown, Pennsylvania.

May Jayyusi

Born in Amman, Jordan to Palestinian parents, May Jayyusi did her undergraduate studies in London where she read philosophy at University College of London University, graduating in 1979. She obtained the degree of a Master of Science in Film Studies from Boston University in 1991 writing her thesis on the Postmodernist film: "A Critical Reading of the Postmodern Problematic, with Particular Reference to Film." Widely read in European thought and literature, she has concentrated on the novel, particularly Balzac. She has worked as production assistant on *Wedding in Galilee,* a film made by the Palestinian film maker Michel Khleifi. She is a PROTA reader, has helped greatly in the process of selection of the poetry and fiction translated by PROTA, and has translated widely for the Project. Aside from the many selections for PROTA's four anthologies: *Modern Arabic Poetry, an Anthology* (1987); *The Literature of Modern Arabia, an Anthology* (1988); *Anthology of Modern Arabic Fiction* (in press); and the present anthology of Palestinian Literature, she has translated three works of fiction: Ghassan Kanafani's *All That's Left to You and Other Stories* (1990); Ibrahim Nasrallah's novel, *Prairies of Fever*, due to appear early in 1992; and Zayd Mutee' Dammaj's novel, *The Hostage*. She has also translated a collection of the poetry of Muhammad al-Maghut, *The Fan of Swords*, (1991). She lives with her husband and two children, Nasser and Ruanne, in Jerusalem.

Salma Khadra Jayyusi

Poet, scholar, critic, and anthologist, Salma Khadra Jayyusi was born in East Jordan of a Palestinian father and a Lebanese mother. She spent her childhood and early youth in Acre and Jerusalem, graduated in Arabic and English literature from the American University of Beirut, and later obtained a Ph.D. in Arabic Literature from the University of London. She has traveled widely and has lived in many places in the Arab world, Europe, and the United States—first as a diplomat's wife, then as professor of Arabic literature. Jayyusi taught at several Arab and American universities before leaving teaching in 1980 to found PROTA (Project of Translation from Arabic Literature), after having realized how misrepresented and ignored abroad Arabic literature and culture were. She has published her poetry and critical writings in many journals and her first collection of poems, *Return from the Dreamy Fountain,* appeared in 1960. In 1977, her two volume critical literary history, *Trends and Movements in Modern Arabic Poetry,* was published by Brill of Leiden and has recently been translated into Arabic. Under PROTA, Jayyusi has so far edited around thirty volumes ranging from single author works to five large anthologies of modern Arabic literature. She has so far published *Modern Arabic Poetry* (New York, Columbia University press, 1987) and *The Literature of Modern Arabia* (London: KPI and Texas University Press, 1988 and 1990, respectively.) Aside from the present anthology, she now has two in press: *Modern Arabic Fiction;* and, with Roger Allen, *Contemporary Arabic Drama.* Jayyusi's latest work is a large volume of essays, *The Legacy of Muslim Spain,* targeted to appear in 1992 to coincide with the five hundredth anniversary of the end of Islamic rule in Spain. Since 1989, she has been working on a new anthology, *Poets of the End of the Century, New Voices in Arabic Poetry*; she is also preparing two collections of her critical articles in Arabic and English.

Lorne M. Kenny

Professor Emeritus at the University of Toronto, Lorne Kenny has taught for many years at the Department of Middle Eastern and Islamic Studies of this University and was its chairman from 1975–1979. One of the most informed specialists on modern Arab and Egyptian history and on modern Islamic thought with a special emphasis on al-Afghani, Muhammad ʿAbdu, and Rashid Rida, he has written and lectured extensively on subjects pertaining to his areas of specialization, including many presentations on Palestinian issues addressed to various groups, organizations, and societies. In 1982, he was chosen to be the first Chairman of Toronto Universities Middle Eastern Group (TU-MEG), which is a group of academics concerned with contemporary Middle Eastern issues on behalf of justice for the Arabs. Professor Kenny has also done many translations for PROTA's various anthologies and has participated with his wife, Olive E. Kenny, on three of PROTA's novels: Muhammad Y. al-Qaʿid's *War in the Land of Egypt* (1986); Hamza Bogary's *Saqifat al-Safa* (1991); and Hanna Mina's *Fragments of Memory*, forthcoming. He has also translated Khaldun Hasan al-Naqib's book *Society, State in the Gulf and the Arab Peninsula* for the center of Arab unity studies in Beirut and done under the aegis of PROTA. At present he is finishing translating Ishaq Musa al-Husaini's *A Chicken's Memoirs*, one of the earliest successful Palestinian novels, and working with Olive Kenny on the translation of selections from Khalil al-Sakakini's Diaries, *Thus Am I, O World*, for PROTA.

Olive E. Kenny

Olive Kenny spent many years in Egypt where she taught English and studied Arabic at the School of Oriental Studies of the American University of Cairo. Her work among students, and her contacts, afforded her a great opportunity to absorb Arabic culture and thought and to understand the Egyptian scene. Mrs. Kenny is the translator of

Najib Mahfouz's novel, *Wedding Songs,* which was published by the American University in Cairo Press in 1984. She is also the first translator of two books of Mahfouz's famous *Trilogy, Palace Walk,* published by the A.U.C. Press in 1989, and *Palace of Desires,* published by Doubleday, New York and the UK, in 1991, both with William M. Hutchins. She has also revised the translation of the third book of the *Trilogy, Al-Sukkariyya,* forthcoming. She has been an active translator with PROTA for many years and has translated many selections of fiction for PRO-TA's three anthologies, *Modern Arabic Poetry* (1987), *The Literature of Modern Arabia* (1988), and the present anthology; she has also translated Walid Ikhlasi's long play, *The Straight Path,* for PROTA's large drama anthology, ed. S.K. Jayyusi and Roger Allen, forthcoming. She has also translated (in participation with Lorne Kenny) three PROTA novels: Muhammad Yusuf al-Qaʻid's *War in the Land of Egypt* (1986); Hamza Bogary's *Saqifat al-Safa,* on life in Mekka before the advent of oil (1991), and Hanna Mina's *Fragments of Memory,* forthcoming—the last two published by the Center of Middle Eastern Studies, University of Texas. She is now working for PROTA with Lorne Kenny on the translation of selections from Khalil al-Sakakini's Diaries, *Thus Am I, O World.*

Ibrahim Muhawi

Ibrahim Muhawi is a Palestinian scholar, writer, and translator. He was born in Ramallah, Palestine, and studied first engineering then English and American literature. He taught in Canada and the United States before coming to Tunisia where he is now Professor of English at the University of Tunis, a post which he has occupied since 1980. He has done many translations of Palestinian poetry, which have been published in various magazines and is co-author/editor of a study and anthology of Palestinian folklore, *Speak Bird, Speak Again* (1988).

Editor's note: The following colleague has helped in checking some of the translations in this anthology:

Amin ʿAbd al-Hafeez

Amin ʿAbd al-Hafeez is a Palestinian former high official of the B.B.C. where he worked for many years, becoming deputy head of the Arabic Service. Previous to his B.B.C. appointment, Mr. ʿAbd al-Hafeez worked for about five years with ARAMCO, the Arab American Oil Company in Saudi Arabia. He works now as counselor at the press office of the Saudi Arabian Embassy in London.

Second Translators

Jack Collom

Born in Chicago, Illinois, Jack Collom now lives and works in Colorado. He received a Master of Arts from the University of Colorado and in 1980 was awarded a Poetry Fellowship from the National Endowment for the Arts. He is author of seven books of poetry, including *The Fox,* United Artists, New York. He has also authored a book on poetry written by children called *Moving Windows,* published by Teachers and Writers Collaborative. A book of ecology poems, *Arguing With Something Plato Said,* has been published by Rocky Ledge Cottage Editions, Colorado. He teaches writing and literature on a free-lance basis in several colleges, including Metro State College, Naropa Institute, and the University of Colorado. He also works a great deal with school children, doing poetry workshops and has published a number of his translations of German poetry in various magazines. He is the father of four children.

Dick Davies

Dick Davies read English at Cambridge University and lived for eight years in Iran. He has published three books of his own poems, *In the Distance, Seeing the World,* and *The Covenant;* with his Iranian wife, Afkham Darbandi, he has translated Farid al-Din al-Attar's *Conference of the Birds* from Persian, published by Penguin Classics in 1984. He is at present literary fellow at the Universities of Durham and Newcastle in England.

Charles Doria

An American poet and translator, Charles Doria did his graduate studies in classics and comparative literature at Harvard and SUNY, Buffalo and has taught at various institutions including Rutgers University. During the eighties, he edited the *Assembling Press* in New York. Aside from many scholarly articles on literature, particularly on the classical period, he has published three books of poetry: *The Game of Europe, Short,* and *Shorter.* His translations include *Origins: Creation Texts from the Ancient Mediterranean; The Tenth Music: Classical Drama in Translation;* Muhammad al-Mahdi al-Majdhoub's long poem, *Birth,* on the birth of the Prophet, which combines mysticism and a realistic depiction of the festivities on that occasion, (1979); and eight poems of Salma Khadra Jayyusi's published in *Women Poets of the Fertile Crescent* (1977).

Thomas G. Ezzy

A citizen of both Canada and the United States, Thomas Ezzy was born to a Lebanese-American father and a French-Canadian mother. He received a B.A. in French and classics from Holy Cross College in Worcester, Massachusetts and an M.A. in English from the University of Toronto. A poet and writer of fiction, he has so far published two volumes of poetry, *Parings* and *Arctic Char in Grecian Waters.* He resides currently in Montreal and teaches English language and literature at Dawson College, where he has taught several courses on fiction from the Arab world. He has a special interest in languages and history and has recently begun research toward a social history of the European novel. He has co-translated for PROTA, with Michael Young as first translator, Bechir Ben Slama's novel *Aisha* (forthcoming). He has also co-translated a wide variety of selections for the following PROTA anthologies: *Modern Arabic Poetry* (1987), *The Literature of Modern Arabia* (1988), *Modern Arabic Fiction* (forthcoming), *Modern Palestinian Literature* (forthcoming), and *Contemporary Arab Theatre* (forthcoming).

Elizabeth Warnock Fernea

Elizabeth Fernea lectures in the Department of English and the Center for Middle Eastern Studies of the University of Texas at Austin. She specializes in cross-cultures such as Middle Eastern and Western cultures, or male/female cultures. With her husband, the anthropologist Robert Fernea, she has lived two years in Iraq, six years in Egypt, and fifteen months in Morocco—sojourns that have afforded her rich first-hand material for her books: *Guests of the Sheikh* (1968); *A View of the Nile* (1970); and *A Street in Marrakech* (1975). Her continued interest in Middle Eastern society, particulary in the life of women, has informed much of her later activity in both writing and film-making. It has resulted in two large anthologies, *Middle Eastern Muslim Women Speak,* which she edited with Basima Q. Bezirgan (1977) and *New Voices: Women in the Muslim Middle East* (1984). Her latest films on Middle Eastern women were a series of three and a half hour films on social change in the Arab world: *A Veiled Revolution* (religious change); *The Price of Change* (economic change); and *Women Under Siege* (political change as seen in the Rashidiyya Palestinian refugee camp in the South of Lebanon.) Elizabeth Fernea has co-translated poems and selections from fiction including Sahar Khalifeh's novel, *Wild Thorns,* which she co-translated with Trevor LeGassick for PROTA (1985).

John Heath-Stubbs

English poet, critic, and translator, John Heath-Stubbs took his first class degree in English from Queen's College, Oxford, in 1942 and lectured at the universities of Alexandria, Michigan, and the College of St. Mark and St. John in London. He now lectures at the University of Oxford. Among his many writings is his long poem, *Artorius,* for which he won the Queen's Gold Medal for poetry in 1972. In 1978, he won the Oscar William-Gean Durwood Award. He has published a number of volumes of criticism, plays, and poetry collections—the last of which is *Naming the Beasts,* 1983. He has also translated *Selected Poems and Prose of Giacomo Leopardi* with Iris Origo, from Italian; and with Peter Avery has translated *Hafiz of Shiraz* and *The Rubaiyat of Omar Khayyam* from Persian. In 1988 Carcanet published his *Collected Poems* and in 1990 his volume of *Selected Poems.* He is now preparing a new volume of his poetry to be published also by Carcanet.

Anselm Hollo

Anselm Hollo, a native of Helsinki, Finland, has lived and worked as a poet, translator, editor, journalist, and teacher in Sweden, Germany, Austria, England, and, since 1967, the United States. He is the recipient of a NEA Fellowship in Poetry (1979) and two translation prizes from the American-Scandinavian Foundation, New York (1980 and 1988). His most recent book of poems is *Outlying Districts: New Poems* (1990). Recent translations include the novel *The Whales in Lake Tanganyika* by Swedish author Lennart Hagerfors (1989) and *Franz Werfel: The Story of a Life* by Austrian biographer Peter Stephan Jungk (1990). Mr. Hollo is on the faculty of the MFA Poetics and Writing Program of The Naropa Institute in Boulder, Colorado.

Ruth Lenox

Ruth Lenox is the daughter of a well-known British educator who founded a school for boys in Safad, then moved it to Haifa. Ms. Lenox was brought up in an Arab atmosphere and learned to speak, read, and write Arabic. She has consecrated most of her life to the welfare of Palestinians and still lives in Nazareth. A graduate of London University, she studied English literature, which explains her interest in translating literary works from Arabic into her own language.

W.S. Merwin

American poet, playwright, and translator, he is the author of several volumes of poetry, including *A Mask for Janus, The Dancing Bears, The Moving Target,* the Pulitzer Prize-winning *The Carrier of Ladders,* and *The Compass Flower.* His many translations include *Spanish Ballads, The Satires of Persius, Products of the Perfected Civilization* (selected writings of Chamfort), *Twenty Love Poems and a Song of Despair* (poems by Pablo Neruda), and *Sanskrit Love Poetry.* He lives in Hawaii.

Christopher Middleton

An English poet and translator, Christopher Middleton's most recent book of new poems is *III Poems* (1983). A book of essays, *The Pursuit of the Kingfisher*, also appeared in 1983, in Manchester and New York. Among his many translations are *Goethe, Selected Poems* (1983); and Gert Hoffman, *The Spectacle at the Tower* (1984). A book of short prose, *Serpentine*, appeared in London, published by Oasis Press. In 1989 he published *Selected Writings* (poems and prose); a paperback edition was published in the same year. His latest work is a translation of about 60 Arab Andalusi poems, which he translated, via Spanish, with Leticia Garza-Falcón, which will first have a special edition by Thomas Taylor in January, 1992, then by David Godine in summer, 1992. Dr. Middleton is professor of German literature and Comparative literature at the University of Texas at Austin.

Naomi Shihab Nye

Naomi Shihab Nye was born in St. Louis in 1952, daughter of Aziz Shihab, Palestinian from Jerusalem, and Miriam Allwardt. She lived in Jerusalem, attending St. Tarkmanchatz Armenian School in the Old City, in 1966 and 1967. In 1988 she was selected by W.S. Merwin to receive the Lavan Award from the Academy of American Poets and was also co-winner of the Charity Randall Prize for Spoken Poetry given through the International Poetry Forum, Pittsburgh. A poet and a translator of poets, she has had three volumes of poetry published. The first, *Different Ways to Pray*, appeared in 1980 and won the Texas Institute of Letters Prize. The second, *Hugging the Jukebox*, was one of the National Poetry Series selected by Josephine Miles, and one of the American Library Association's Notable Books for 1982. The third, *Yellow Glove*, appeared in 1986. She is currently working on a book of stories. As a fine translator of literature, she has translated, with Lena Jayyusi, *Selections from the Songs of Life*, (1986) by Tunisia's famous poet, Abu al-Qasim al-Shabbi, and with May Jayyusi, *The Fan of Swords*, selections from the poetry of Muhammad al-Maghut, in press, both for PROTA. She has also translated many poems and prose selections for four of PROTA'S anthologies. Nye has worked also as a writer-in-residence, has twice traveled to the Middle East and Asia for the Arts American Program of the United States Information Agency, and resides in San Antonio with her husband and son. Her grandmother and many of her relatives continue to live in the occupied West Bank.

Jeremy Reed

A poet and novelist, Jeremy Reed was born in Jersey, the Channel Islands. Amongst his many books of poetry and fiction are *Selected Poems* (1987). He received the Somerset Maugham Award in 1985 for his book, *By the Fisheries* and since then he has published three novels: *The Lipstick Boys, Blue Rock,* and *Red Eclipse.* His book of essays, *Madness the Price of Poetry,* was published in 1989 and a new collection of poetry, *Nineties,* was published by Cape in 1990. Dr. Reed lives in London and devotes his life to writing.

Christopher Tingley

Born in Brighton, England, Christopher Tingley received his education at the universities of London and Leeds. Following initial teaching experience in Germany and Britain, he lectured in the fields of English language and linguistics at the University of Constantine, Algeria; the University of Ghana; the National University of Rwanda; and the University of Ouagadougou, Burkina Faso. In the field of translation, he has collaborated with the author on the translation of the extracts of Arabic poetry in Salma Khadra Jayyusi's two volume work *Trends and Movements in Modern Arabic Poetry* (1977); for PROTA, he has co-translated (with Olive and Lorne Kenny as first translators) Yusuf al-Qaʿid's novel, *War in the Land of Egypt* (1986) and (with various first translators) a number of short stories in Salma Khadra Jayyusi's anthologies, *The Literature of Modern Arabia: An Anthology* (1988), *Modern Arabic Fiction, an Anthology* (forthcoming), and the present anthology. He has also provided comprehensive stylistic and scholarly editing for PROTA's large volume of essays on Muslim Spain entitled *The Legacy of Muslim Spain,* ed. Salma Khadra Jayyusi, forthcoming.

Transliterated List of Arab Authors

Yūsuf ʿAbd al-ʿAzīz
Ibrāhīm al-ʿAbsi
Khālid Abū Khālid
Yūsuf Abū Lawz
Abū Salmā (ʿAbd al-Karīm al-Karmi)
Rashād Abū Shāwar
Zuhair Abū Shāyib
Ṣāliḥ Abū Uṣbaʿ
Ṭāhā Muḥammad ʿAli
Laila ʿAllūsh
Nāji ʿAllūsh
ʿAbd al-Laṭīf ʿAql
Muḥammad al-Asʿad
Ḥanān Mīkhāʾīl ʿAshrāwi
Gharīb ʿAsqalāni
Samīra ʿAzzām
Liyāna Badr
Murīd Barghūthi
Muʿīn Buseiso
Ḥasan al-Buḥairi
Riyāḍ Baydas
Aḥmad Daḥbūr
Maḥmūd Darwīsh
Zaki Darwīsh
Muḥammad al-Dhāhir
Najwā Qaʿwār Faraḥ
Tawfīq Fayyāḍ

Ṣubḥi Ghosheh
Emile Ḥabībi
Walīd al-Halīs
Akram Haniyyeh
Yūsuf Haykal
Sulāfā Ḥijjāwi
Aḥmad Ḥusain
Rāshid Ḥusain
Maḥmūd Saif al-Dīn al-Īrāni
Jabrā Ibrāhīm Jabrā
Līna al-Jayyūsi
Salma al-Khaḍrā' al-Jayyūsi
Sālim Jubrān
Ghassān Kanafāni
Amīna Kazak
Saḥar Khalīfa
'Ali al-Khalīli
Walīd Khāzindār
Rāsim al-Madhūn
'Abd al-Raḥīm Maḥmūd
Ḥaydar Maḥmūd
'Izziddīn al-Manāṣra
Khairi Manṣūr
Zakariyyā Muḥammad
Sharīf al-Mūsā
'Ali Khālid Muṣṭafā
Ṭāhā 'Abd al-Ghani Muṣṭafā
Muḥammad Naffā'
Kamāl Nāṣir
Ibrāhīm Naṣrallah
Naomi Shihāb Nye
Jamāl Qa'wār
Kamāl Qaddūra
Muḥammad al-Qaisi
Samīḥ al-Qāsim
Walīd Rabāḥ
Yaḥyā Rabāḥ
'Abdallah Raḍwān
Hārūn Hāshim Rashīd
Faḍl al-Rīmāwi
Maḥmūd al-Rīmāwi

Ṭāhir Riyāḍ
Laila al-Sā'iḥ
Khalīl al-Sakākīni
Khalīl al-Sawāḥiri
Walīd Sayf
Mai Ṣāyigh
Tawfīq Ṣāyigh
'Umar Shabāna
Māzin Shadīd
Maḥmūd Shāhīn
Sulaimān al-Shaikh
Anṭūn Shammās
Hishām Sharābi
Yūsuf Shrūrū
Maḥmūd Shuqair
Sa'āda Sūdāḥ
Muḥammad 'Ali Ṭāhā
Ṣalāḥ Ta'mari
Khalīl Tūmā
Fadwā Ṭūqān
Ibrāhīm Ṭūqān
Fawwāz Turki
'Abd al-Raḥīm 'Umar
Fārūq Wādi
Yaḥyā Yakhlif
Ghassān Zaqṭān
Tawfīq Zayyād

Glossary

This is a glossary of Arabic words that appear more than once in this volume. Some of them have also been explained in footnotes where special explanation was necessary to clarify meaning.

Abu	Father of, hence Abu Fadl means father of Fadl. Men are usually called by the name of their first-born son.
Adhan:	The Muslim call to prayer.
Dabka:	or "Dabkeh" in Palestinian dialect, is the traditional dance in the Palestinian countryside (and in the Syrian and Lebanese).
Diwan:	A book of poetry. *Diwan* can also mean a reception room for men.
Dunum:	A thousand square meters.
Fidaain:	These are the freedom fighters sworn to fight and redeem their country with their blood. The root of the word is *fada,* "redeemed with his life."
Haj (m.); Hajjeh (f.):	The person who has performed the pilgrimage to Mecca, one of the five holy duties of every Muslim.
Imam:	The man of religion who leads the prayer and is often responsible for the affairs of a mosque.
Imm:	The Palestinian word for *umm,* mother. Women are usually called by the name of their first-born son, particularly in traditional society.
Iqal:	The head band that keeps the *Kaffiyyeh* or *kufiyya* in place.
Kaffiyyeh:	or *kufiyya,* is the large square headgear worn by men and kept on the head by the *iqal.*

Kohl:	Traditional black eyeliner used to line the eyelids all over the Arab world. In English it is known as "pulverized antimony."
Kufiyya:	See *kaffiyyeh*.
Muezzin:	The caller to the Muslim prayer usually from a minaret or another high place.
Mukhtar:	Village mayor.
Oud:	Lute.
Shaikh:	An old man, or the mayor of a village.
Souq:	Market, marketplace.
Ustadh:	A teacher, a university professor, a learned man. It may also simply mean 'Sir' when used in the vocative.
Zaatar (za'tar):	Thyme, a herb that grows profusely on the mountain slopes of Palestine, Syria, and Lebanon and is made into a breakfast dish by pounding the leaves, mixing them with such ingredients as *summaq* (for its sour taste) and roasted sesame seeds, and eating it with olive oil and bread. *Za'tar*, like the orange and the olive, has become a symbol of Palestine, particularly in literature.

Selected Bibliography

ʿAbbas, Ihsan, Fadl al-Naqib and Ilyas Khouri. *Ghassan Kanafani, Insanan wa Adiban wa Munadilan.* Beirut: 1974.

ʿAbd al-Hadi, Faiha', *Waʾd al-Ghad, Dirasa fi Adab Ghassan Kanafani.* Amman: 1987.

Abu Matar, Ahmad. *Al-Riwaya fi 'l-Adab al-Filastini, 1950–1975.* Beirut: 1980.

Abu 'l-Shabab, Wasif. *Shakhsiyyat al-Filastini fi 'l-Shiʿr al-Filastini 'l-Muʿasir.* Beirut: 1981.

Abu Usbaʿ, Salih. *Filastin fi 'l-Riwaya 'l-ʿArabiyya.* Beirut: 1975.

ʿAllush, Saʿid. *ʿUnf al-Mutakhayyal fi Aʿmal Emile Habiby.* Casablanca: 1986.

Aruri, Naseer and Edmund Ghareeb. *Enemy of the Sun, Poetry of Palestinian Resistance.* Washington: 1970.

Al-Asad, Nasir al-Din. *Al-Ittijahat al-Adabiyya 'l-Haditha fi Filstin wa 'l-Urdun.* Cairo: 1957.

———. *Khalil Baydas. Ra'id al-Qissa 'l-ʿArabiyya 'l-Haditha fi Filastin,* Cairo: 1963.

Boullata, Kamal and Mirène Ghossein. *The World of Rashid Hussein.* Detroit: AAUG, 1979.

Boulus, Habeeb. *Al-Qissa 'l-ʿArabiyya 'l-Filastiniyya 'l-Mahalliyya 'l-Qasira.* Nazareth: 1987.

Canova, Giovanni. *La Poesia Della Resistanza Palestinese.* Rome: 1971.

Elmessiri, A.M., ed. and translator. *The Palestinian Wedding, A Bilingual Anthology of Contemporary Palestinian Poetry.* Washington DC: 1982.

Frangieh, Bassam K. *Al-Ightirab fi 'l-Riwaya 'l-Filastiniyya.* Beirut. 1989.

Habiby, Emile. *The Secret Life of Saeed, the Pessoptimist,* translated into English for PROTA by Salma Khadra Jayyusi and Trevor LeGassick. New York: Vantage, 1982; London: ZED Books, 1985.

Al-Hasan, Bilal. *Al-Filastiniyyun fi 'l-Kuwait.* Beirut: 1974.

Jayyusi, Salma Khadra, ed. *Modern Arabic Poetry, An Anthology.* New York: Columbia University Press, 1977.

———. *Modern Arabic Fiction, An Anthology.* New York: Columbia University Press, in press.

Kanafani, Ghassan. *Al-Adab al-Filastini 'l-Muqawim Tahta 'l-Ihltilal.* 1948–1968. Beirut: 1968.

_____. *Adab al-Muqawama fi Filastin al-Muhtalla,* 1948–1966. Beirut, n.d.

_____. *All That's Left to You.* Translated for PROTA by May Jayyusi and Jeremy Reed. Austin, Texas: Center of Middle Eastern Studies, 1990.

Al-Kayyali, ʿAbd al-Rahman. *Al-Shiʿr al-Filastini fi Nakbat Filastin.* Beirut: 1975.

Khalidi, Walid. *Before Their Diaspora, A Photographic History of the Palestinians, 1876–1948.* Washington D.C., 1984.

Khalifeh, Sahar, *Wild Thorns.* Translated for PROTA by Trfevor LeGassick and Elizabeth Fernea. London: 1986.

Khalil, Ibrahim. *Fi 'l-Qissa wa 'l-Riwaya 'l-Filastiniyya.* Amman: 1984.

Khouri, Ilyas. *Zaman al-Ihtilal.* Beirut: 1985.

Mahmoud, Husni. *Emile Habiby wa 'l-Qissa 'l-Qasira.* Zarqa: 1984.

_____. *Shiʿr al-Muqawama 'l-Filastiniyya, Dawruhu wa Waqiʿuhu.* 3 vols. Amman: 1984.

Al-Musawi, Muhsin Jasim. *Al-Mawqif al-Thauri fi 'l-Riwaya 'l-ʿArabiyya 'l-Muʿasira.* Baghdad: 1975.

Mustafa, Khalid ʿAli. *Al-Shiʿr al-Filastini 'l-Hadith.* Baghdad: 1978.

Poetry East. Fourteen Poems by Mahmoud Darwish. Translated for PROTA by Lena Jayyusi with Anselm Hollo, W.S. Merwin, Christopher Middleton, Jeremy Reed, and Anne Waldman. No. 27 (Spring, 1989).

27 Qissa Qasira min al-Qasas al-Filastini fi 'l-Manatiq al-Muhtalla. Beirut: 1977

Salih, Fakhri. *Al-Qissa 'l-Filastiniyya 'l-Qasira fi 'l-Aradi 'l-Muhtalla.* Beirut: 1982.

Wadi, Faruq. *Thalath ʿAlamat fi 'l-Riwaya 'l-Filastiniyya.* 2d ed. Acre: 1985.

Yaghi, ʿAbd al-Rahman. *Al-Adab al-Filastini 'l-Hadith.* Cairo: 1969.

_____. *Dirasat fi Shiʿr al-Ard al-Muhtalla.* Cairo: 1969.

_____. *Al-Juhud al-Riwaʾiyya min Saleem al-Bustani ila Najib Mahfouz.* Beirut: 1972.

_____. *Maʿ Ghassan Kanafani wa Juhudu 'l-Qasasiyya wa 'l-Riwaʾiyya.* Amman: 1983.

_____. *Shiʿr al-Ard al-Muhtalla.* Amman: n.d.

Yaghi, Hashim. *Al-Qissa 'l-Qasira fi Filastin wa 'l-Urdun, 1850–1965.* Cairo: 1966.

Zaytun, Safaʾ, ed. *ʿAsafeer ʿAla Aghsan al-Qalb, Ashʿar Filastiniyya.* Cairo: 1985.